THE LORE OF SCOTLAND

The Lore of Scotland

A guide to Scottish legends

JENNIFER WESTWOOD
AND SOPHIA KINGSHILL

BOOKS

Published by Random House Books 2009

2 4 6 8 10 9 7 5 3 1

First published in Great Britain in 2009 by
Random House Books
Random House, 20 Vauxhall Bridge Road,
London SW1V 2SA

www.rbooks.co.uk

Addresses for companies within The Random House Group Limited can be found at:

www.randomhouse.co.uk/offices.htm

The Random House Group Limited Reg. No. 954009

A CIP catalogue record for this book
is available from the British Library

ISBN 9781905211623

The Random House Group Limited supports The Forest Stewardship
Council (FSC), the leading international forest certification organisation. All our
titles that are printed on Greenpeace approved FSC certified paper carry the FSC logo.
Our paper procurement policy can be found at www.rbooks.co.uk/environment

Mixed Sources
Product group from well-managed
forests and other controlled sources
www.fsc.org Cert no. TT-COC-2139
© 1996 Forest Stewardship Council

Typeset by Palimpsest Book Production Limited, Grangemouth, Stirlingshire

Printed and bound in Great Britain by
Clays Ltd, St Ives plc

To Jennifer Westwood (1940–2008)
and to Peter Kingshill (1922–2008)

CONTENTS

Introduction   ix

List of contributors   xv

ARGYLLSHIRE & ISLANDS   1
The county of Argyllshire and the islands of Arran, Bute, and Lismore

CENTRAL & PERTHSHIRE   48
The counties of Clackmannanshire, Dunbartonshire, Fife,
Kinross-shire, Perthshire, and Stirlingshire

DUMFRIES & GALLOWAY   121
The counties of Dumfriesshire, Kirkcudbrightshire, and Wigtownshire

GLASGOW & AYRSHIRE   170
The counties of Ayrshire, Lanarkshire, and Renfrewshire

LOTHIAN & BORDERS   209
The counties of Berwickshire, East Lothian, Midlothian, Peeblesshire,
Roxburghshire, Selkirkshire, and West Lothian

NORTH EAST   290
The counties of Aberdeenshire, Angus, Banffshire, Kincardineshire,
Moray, and Nairnshire

NORTHERN HIGHLANDS   343
The counties of Caithness and Sutherland

ORKNEY & SHETLAND ISLANDS   379

SOUTHERN HIGHLANDS   418
The counties of Inverness-shire and Ross & Cromarty

WESTERN ISLES   455

Bibliography   507

References   518

Index of Migratory Legends and Tale Types   531

Index   533

Illustrations   555

INTRODUCTION

When my mother Jane was about eight years old, she went to stay in Perthshire with a close friend of the family, Katharine Briggs, in those days not a well-known folklorist, but already a commanding presence. Katharine took her for a walk on the hills one evening, and as the mist and darkness rose around them she recited, in low tones of menace punctuated with expressive wails, the rhyme of 'The Strange Visitor'. The story tells of a woman sitting alone one night and wishing for 'company', which soon comes in the form of a pair of bony feet, followed by a pair of bony shins, knees, and so on until the entire skeleton is present, and when asked what it has come for, shouts 'FOR YOU!' My mother was so frightened that she was ill for a fortnight.

'The Strange Visitor' is a famous tale, printed in Robert Chambers's collection of *Popular Rhymes of Scotland* (1870), and several localised legends have much the same plot, as described for example at KIL-NEUAIR (Argyllshire & Islands) and DORNOCH CATHEDRAL (Northern Highlands). Scottish folklore is full of terror. In tradition the landscape is peopled with evil beings, fairies or trows which kidnap mothers and children, kill livestock, and whisk the unwary on journeys through the air, while Water-horses and Kelpies are always in wait to lure travellers into deep lochs or rivers or to tempt innocent girls

to their doom. Much Scottish legend reflects a hostile though beautiful environment, one in which for centuries survival was a never-ending struggle against harsh land and hungry sea.

To personify the forces of nature is a way of understanding them, and stories which explain the world help to give people (if only in imagination) some control over their surroundings and circumstances. That is the essence of folklore, by definition the 'lore' or body of traditions and knowledge shared by the 'folk' – ordinary people – as distinct from educated opinions passed down by those in authority. Although legends may not have been considered as literally true, they gave structure and guidance, bridging the gap between human beings and the invisible powers around them. It is doubtful how much anyone ever *believed* that still-birth or cot-death were caused by baby-snatching fairies, but, as mentioned at CAERLAVEROCK (Dumfries & Galloway), it is certain that straw crosses or steel pins were widely used as protection against the marauders, just as today we often touch wood without any real conviction that bad luck will be averted.

Other tales embodied entirely practical concerns of a kind shared by parents throughout history, to keep their children away from deep water or dangerous animals and to warn their daughters against taking up with strange men. Where plain advice might have been forgotten, a horrid anecdote of disembowelment by the Waterhorse must surely have stayed in the mind.

While the hardships and perils of day-to-day existence may have suggested the presence of unseen and unfriendly creatures, the landscape of Scotland evokes a mightier shaping force, dramatised in legends of devils hurling rocks from the heights or nature spirits flooding the valleys, as at CRAIL (Central & Perthshire) and LOCH AWE (Argyllshire & Islands). Ancient myth attributes creation to the gods, but the folklore of later ages tends to shift focus from the heavens to intermediate powers, crediting demons, giants, or even certain humans with the ability to move mountains. Holy martyrs are said to have made springs flow from the ground, and not only saints such as Columba but champions like William Wallace are reported to have left the prints of their feet or hands in solid rock, marking the land forever with their presence. Other sites are linked with magicians, scholars and scientists from the Middle Ages to the Enlightenment who were remembered in popular tradition as wizards, and reputed to have diverted rivers or cleaved the hills with the help of their arcane knowledge.

Legend offers a means of interpreting history as well as geography, and Scotland's battle-torn past has substantially inspired its folklore. Invasion, civil war, and discord with England, clan feuds, border raids, and religious persecution have shaped the country's mythology. Towering heroes are remembered at key moments of their destiny, like Robert the Bruce watching the spider at UGADALE (Argyllshire & Islands), and demonized villains such as Robert Grierson, Laird of Lag, are said to have suffered damnation for their part in suppressing seventeenth-century Presbyterian dissent (see IN LEAGUE WITH THE DEVIL, p. 142).

Rumours of men who sold their souls to the Devil could have spread partly because of the earlier witchcraft panic, when it was widely believed that women and men had entered into infernal pacts and become instruments of Satan. This shameful episode, which caused about two thousand needless deaths after the introduction of the Witchcraft Act in 1563, was perhaps influenced in its turn by long-standing acceptance of the malign supernatural powers of the fairies. The connection between black magic and fairies was made in several notorious witch trials, such as that of Bessie Dunlop, whose story is told at RESTALRIG LOCH (Lothian & Borders).

Whatever the harsh realities of the past, in retrospect, after the trauma of the 1745 rebellion and the oppression which followed, some of it appeared idyllic. Although it is quite improbable that either James IV or James V in fact travelled around the realm in disguise, enjoying adventures and dealing out spontaneous justice, the remarkable body of tales dealing with THE GUIDMAN OF BALLANGEICH (p. 98) – their legendary alias – shows how fondly and even intimately the fifteenth- and sixteenth-century kings were regarded, at least in memory.

In the early nineteenth century, nostalgia for a vanished age led to the revival or reinvention of Scottish 'tradition', a strand of folklore whose blend of the authentic and the bogus to this day affects perceptions of the country's history. To take one notable example, many people believe without question that clans were distinguished by their tartans. This was not the case: although regional variations doubtless existed, there were no rules for who wore which pattern. The later claim that each clan had its own exclusive weave, however, made a lot of money for the wool merchants. Fascinating details of this and other manufactured legends are given in Eric Hobsbawm's *The Invention of Tradition* (1983).

Legends are passed on both by word of mouth and by print. An interesting story (whether or not it actually happened) is remembered within a community, and repeated and embroidered until it becomes part of the local colour. Told to outsiders, or written down and read by people far away, it may then come to be told in a new region as part of a new history, its action ascribed to different protagonists and related to different landmarks, but still remaining identifiably the same tale.

In Scotland, the agent of transmission may have been an itinerant tailor, a figure who appears himself in many tales as a cunning outwitter of the fairies or the Devil, or it may have been one of the Traveller storytellers who have done so much to preserve Scottish legend (see TRAVELLER TALES, p. 298). Equally, it may have been one of the many great writers who have valued their country's tales and poetry, and without whose work this book could not have been compiled. A few outstanding names require credit. First and truly foremost is Sir Walter Scott (1771–1832). It is hardly possible to exaggerate his importance to Scottish tradition, not only in the preservation of ballads and lore of the Borders and Lowlands, but as an example to those who a little later undertook similar work in the Highlands. He is often unfairly blamed for the myth-making of the early nineteenth century. Although his extraordinarily popular poetry and novels were without doubt largely responsible for the lustre of all things Scottish at the time, he was guiltless of the distortions which followed. Scott was a dedicated scholar and a talented writer whose eye for detail and sense of drama awaken enthusiasm today as they did in his own time, and over the course of this book's compilation he has become a personal hero to me, as he must be to anyone who loves Scottish literature and legend.

Robert Chambers (1802–71) was another pioneering figure, responsible for the first printed collection of Scottish fairy tales (i.e. tales of magic, understood as fictional, rather than legends about fairies) in the 1841 edition of *Popular Rhymes of Scotland*. He also gathered verses, superstitions, and legends both supernatural and historical, which he relates in a lightly ironic style that remains very readable.

John Francis Campbell of Islay (1821–85) collected Gaelic tales throughout the Western Isles and West Highlands, many of which have been published, but a vast number of which remain in manuscript at the National Library of Scotland. Campbell's insistence on taking down a storyteller's exact words set a standard unsurpassed until the era of sound recording, while his comparative analysis of tales was also far ahead of his time. Apologies now for the many appearances of his full name in this book in order to differentiate him from the next and last on my short roll of honour, the Reverend John Gregorson Campbell (1836–91), whose information on popular belief in the Highlands and Islands was taken entirely from oral sources, and whose books are some of the best guides to what lore was actually current in his day. His writing is, again, vivid and engaging: for a splendid example, see 'The Grey Paw', told at BEAULY (Northern Highlands) – another version of 'The Strange Visitor'.

Many others deserve mention, and anyone who enjoys what they find in this book is urged to take a look at sources listed in the bibliography. There is any amount of fascinating material, and several important works have been reissued by the invaluable Birlinn press of Edinburgh. Not to be omitted is the collective activity of the School of Scottish Studies. Since it was founded as a department of Edinburgh University in 1951, the School's fieldworkers, students and volunteers have recorded stories and songs from all over Scotland. Many are available in published collections, while thousands more are held in the archives, together with material on customs, place-names, language and many other topics. The School continues to gather tales and music throughout the country, preserving a vital part of the national heritage. Visit *www.celtscot.ed.ac.uk* for details of its resources and research, and for courses at the Department of Celtic and Scottish Studies.

Even in the earliest records Scotland was inhabited by many different tribes, and invasions by Celts (a blanket term embracing a number of peoples), by Vikings, and by the English left a country speaking until quite recently three distinct tongues, Scots in the Lowlands, Gaelic in the Highlands and Western Isles, and in Orkney and Shetland a dialect derived from the Scandinavian language Norn. From the eighteenth century onwards, the Scottish diaspora has taken emigrants all over the world whose descendants still embrace a Scottish identity. Such diversity is tackled here by an entirely local approach, identifying legends associated with specific places – which does not mean that they are exclusive to those places. Folklore does travel, sometimes very widely, as shown by famous legends like St Mungo's miracle of the salmon, indelibly associated with GLASGOW (Glasgow & Ayrshire), but deriving from a far older Greek tale of Polycrates, tyrant of Samos. Who knows whether a ring was ever really retrieved from the belly of a fish? It may be unlikely but it's not impossible. With all such tales, the interesting question is not whether it was ever factually 'true', but what led different people, in very different climates

and ages, to adopt the narrative as their own. What in pagan Greece was a cautionary tale, a warning against tempting fate by boasting of good fortune, became in Christian Scotland a celebration of a saint's power to forgive sin.

Like *The Lore of the Land* by Jennifer Westwood and Jacqueline Simpson (Penguin, 2005), this book is arranged by place, alphabetically within regions, both so that readers can easily identify tales associated with a particular area, and to give an idea of the local characteristics of legend. The maps which accompany each region show the approximate position of each place named, and Ordnance Survey coordinates supplied in the References section give precise locations.

This scheme means that excellent stories have had to be omitted if they are unlocalised, and problems can arise even when the scene of events is specified, particularly in the Gaelic-speaking Highlands and Islands and in Shetland and Orkney. Not only do the names of landscape features, houses, and even villages change over time, but collectors have frequently transcribed an anglicised version of the name they heard, which may be quite unrecognisable from today's maps. Masterful detective work by Jutta Schettler and Clare Graydon-James, with the kind assistance of staff at several libraries (named below), have resolved some questions, enabling me for example to identify the elusive 'Lochan-Wan' as LOCHAN UAINE (North East), and even to track down the mermaid's grave at STINKY BAY (Western Isles), but errors have doubtless crept in. They are regretted, and anyone who has better information is cordially invited to supply it. Similar comments apply to the brief passages of Gaelic which appear. Many of these are quoted verbatim from earlier authors, and where necessary I have added a revised version in square brackets, with heartfelt thanks to Margaret McKay of the School of Scottish Studies and her colleague Ian Fraser for their help.

Scotland's county system has changed several times. The current units may suit administrative purposes, but vast tracts of land called 'Highland' or 'Strathclyde' do not serve the present work well. The pre-1973 counties have therefore been divided here into ten regions, giving the old county name after the place-name, and we hope that readers will follow the logic. Modern usage would suggest 'Argyll', for instance, rather than 'Argyllshire', but the latter has been adopted to avoid confusion when, as often, there is a county town with the same name as the county.

The concept of this book was Jennifer Westwood's. Realising that her long fight with cancer was drawing to a close, she invited me to be her collaborator. Her death in May 2008 deprived us all of a huge talent, a treasure of scholarship, and an incomparably generous and gallant spirit, and left me to finish the book alone, an honour and a challenge. Very much of the research and writing is hers, and any deficiencies undoubtedly mine.

Above all others I must thank Brian Chandler, Jennifer's husband, whose moral and practical support has enabled me to finish the book. Brian's sister Nim and Jennifer's son Jonathan have also been towers of strength. Janet Bord has given unstinting help and has provided pictures from the Fortean Picture Library, while Jacqueline Simpson has devoted much precious time to the tale-types, and Marion Bowman has been a source of vital contacts. Other friends of Jennifer's who have leapt to my assistance are Tristan Gray Hulse, Jeremy Harte, Gabrielle Hatfield, Lizanne Henderson, Sandy Hobbs, and Steve Roud, all authors of essays in the book. Nat Edwards, Katie and Jonathan

Fischel, Suzi Hopkins, Jane Kingshill, and Graeme Rosie have been sensitive and generous critics.

Sophie Lazar is a wonderfully sympathetic and encouraging editor. Her keen eye and perceptive comments have greatly improved the text, and Caroline Pretty's inspired copy-editing has ironed out many remaining wrinkles. Emily Rhodes has done an outstanding job as picture researcher, Darren Bennett has designed the maps and map icons with skill and flair, Louise Campbell has given much-needed advice on publicity matters, and Nigel Wilcockson has patiently overseen the process.

Many thanks also to Jenny Booth and Helen Osmani of the Museum of Scotland; Wendy Campbell of the Strathmore Estates Office; Denise Davey of the National Maritime Museum, Cornwall; Milford Georgeson, Thelma Miller and Chris Sleat of Lerwick Library; Morag Hamilton and Douglas Wilson of the Stirling Central Office of Historic Scotland; the Reverend George Hastie of St Cyrus; Jacqueline Hutcheon of VisitScotland; Margaret Job of Stirling Smith Art Gallery and Museum; Sarah Kelly and Jill Reed of Perth Library; Sandra Linklater and Sarah Maclean of Orkney Library and Archives; Ron Livingstone of Aberdeen Library; Alistair McGechan of Inverness-shire Council; Andrea McMillan of Cupar Library; Andrea Massey of the National Library of Scotland; Aileen Rodger of Forfar Library; Joan Sanderson of Duns Library; Steven Timoney of Perth and Kinross Heritage Trust; and the staff of the James Watt Library, Greenock; the Mitchell Library, Glasgow; the Montrose Library; the National Maritime Museum, Greenwich; and St Andrews Library.

SOPHIA KINGSHILL

LIST OF CONTRIBUTORS

JANET BORD worked in publishing for some years, before becoming a writer and also running a picture library specialising in mysteries and strange phenomena. She now concentrates on studies relating to the folklore of the British landscape, her most recent books being *Fairies: Real Encounters with Little People* (1997), *The Traveller's Guide to Fairy Sites* (2004), *Footprints in Stone* (2004), *Cures and Curses: Ritual and Cult at Holy Wells* (2006), and *Holy Wells in Britain: A Guide* (2008). She lives in North Wales.

TRISTAN GRAY HULSE is an historian with an especial interest in British saints' cults and holy wells. He has written many papers in these fields, including 'A Fragment of a Reliquary Casket from Gwytherin, North Wales' (by Nancy Edwards, F.S.A., and Tristan Gray Hulse, *The Antiquaries Journal*, vol. LXXII, 1992, pp. 91–101) and 'A Modern Votive Deposit at a North Welsh Holy Well' (*Folklore*, vol. 106, 1995, pp. 31–42). He is currently closely involved with the development of an archive and museum at Britain's major holy well, St Winefride's Well at Holywell in Flintshire.

JEREMY HARTE is a researcher into the overlap between folklore and the landscape, especially places of encounter with the supernatural. His books include *Explore Fairy Traditions* (2004), *The Green Man* (2001) and *English Holy Wells* (2008). He trained as a museum professional, and is curator of the Bourne Hall Museum in Ewell, near Epsom, Surrey.

DR GABRIELLE HATFIELD is a botanist (BA Cambridge) and folklorist (PhD Edinburgh) and has served on the committee of the Folklore Society. Her work on East Anglian plant remedies won the Michaelis-Jena Ratcliffe Prize for folklore in 1993. For the past twenty years she has researched plant medicines in Scotland and England during the eighteenth, nineteenth and twentieth centuries, work which led to her appointment as an Honorary Research Associate at the Royal Botanic Gardens, Kew. She has taken part in local and national BBC radio programmes and apart from papers in academic journals, her own publications include *Country Remedies: Traditional East Anglian Plant Remedies in the Twentieth Century* (1994), *Memory, Wisdom and Healing: the History of Domestic Plant Medicine* (1999), *An Encyclopedia of Folk Medicine: Old World and New World Traditions* (2003), *Medicinal Plants in Folk Tradition: A British and Irish Ethnobotany*, with David E. Allen (2004), and *Hatfield's Herbal:*

The Forgotten History of British Plants
(2007).

DR LIZANNE HENDERSON is a Lecturer in
History at the University of Glasgow
Dumfries Campus. She is author (with
E. J. Cowan) of *Scottish Fairy Belief:
A History* (2001; 2007) and editor of
*Fantastical Imaginations: The Supernatu-
ral in Scottish History and Culture* (2009).
She has written several articles on such
topics as the Scottish witch-hunts,
charmers, and supernatural beliefs, and is
currently working on Scottish connections with the Transatlantic slave trade
and the Scots in the Caribbean and
Africa. She is a board member of The
Folklore Society (London) and has
lectured on Scottish and cultural history
in Europe, North America and Australia.

SANDY HOBBS was born in Aberdeen in
1937 and is a graduate of Aberdeen
University. He is a Chartered Psychologist and has worked in several Scottish
universities, and is currently Honorary
Senior Research Fellow at the University
of the West of Scotland. He has been a
member of the Folklore Society for over
forty years, and is a founding member
of the International Society for Contemporary Legend Research.

DR LICIA MASONI has a PhD in Scottish
Ethnology, and is a post-doctoral fellow
in the department of Celtic and Scottish
Studies, University of Edinburgh. Her
research interests are in the study of
both past and contemporary uses of folk
narratives.

STEVE ROUD is a retired local studies
librarian from Sussex, and now a free-
lance writer and researcher on folklore
topics. Publications include *A Dictionary
of English Folklore*, jointly with Jacqueline Simpson (2000), *Penguin Guide to
Superstitions of Britain & Ireland* (2003),
The English Year (2006), *London Lore*
(2008), and the online databases *Folk
Song Index* and *Broadside Index*.

JACQUELINE SIMPSON was born in 1930
and studied English Literature and
Medieval Icelandic at Bedford College,
London University. She has been an
active member of the Folklore Society
since the 1960s, having served at various
times as Editor, Secretary and President.
She is particularly interested in local legends, both English and Scandinavian.
Her books include *Icelandic Folktales and
Legends* (1971), *The Folklore of Sussex*
(1973), *The Folklore of the Welsh Border*
(1976), *British Dragons* (1980), *Scandinavian Folktales* (1988), *A Dictionary of
English Folklore*, jointly with Steve Roud
(2000), and *The Folklore of Discworld*
(2008). She is a member of the Ghosts
and Scholars Society and the Dracula
Society. She lives in Sussex.

THE LORE OF SCOTLAND

ARGYLLSHIRE & ISLANDS

*The county of Argyllshire and the islands of Arran,
Bute, and Lismore*

ACHINDUIN, LISMORE

'Gormal Mor', or 'Big Gormal', was a member of the Livingstone family. He lived in Achinduin (Acha-an dùin) at the south-west end of Lismore, facing GARBH SHLIOS in Morven, a wild and craggy hill once clothed in thick and inaccessible woods. Gormal was as strong as five ordinary men, and very proud of his strength. The Devil wished to destroy him, and tempted him with a challenge to fight.

Gormal persuaded his friends to row him over to the lonely shore of rugged Garbh Shlios.

There he begged of them to leave him and return to Lismore, and he bade them farewell, as it might be that he would never see them again; so they went away in their boat, as he had requested, and their eyes followed him as he climbed up the hill and disappeared into the thicket, and in the waning light they thought they saw a huge black bull, terrible and grim, descending the hill to meet him; but they rowed steadily on, for they had promised Gormal to render him no help, whatever they might see or hear to alarm them on his behalf; and as the distance increased, they heard through the thickening night fierce bellowings, and sullen roars, and the tramping of feet, and the breaking of branches far away and beyond the nearer measured plash of their oars in the water of the Linnhe.

The men returned to Achinduin, and spent the night in great dismay and fear for their brave strong friend and kinsman. Next day they crossed the Linnhe, hoping against hope that they might see him waiting for them on the shore, safe from whatever conflict or terror the night had brought him.

But they found only his trampled body lying in the wood on the hillside, and they brought him home with weeping and wailing, and laid him with his kindred dust by the cross of Lismore.

The spot in Morven where Gormal landed was called Camas a' Ghuirm ('Bay of Gormal'), and was a very wild and lonely part of the shore.

Miss Jeanie MacGregor, who related this story to Lord Archibald Campbell in the late nineteenth century, added that it was told to her in a cottage in Lismore, and was held to be perfectly true. A 'practical neighbour' endorsed the facts but disallowed the supernatural element: he said that Gormal was a foolish man, proud of his strength, which pride induced him to enter an unequal conflict, and attributed his death to the wild, fierce cattle which once ranged the hills.

ARGYLLSHIRE & ISLANDS

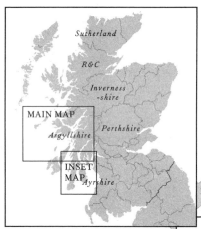

Coll

*Passage
of Tiree*

Tiree

INSET
MAP

Toward
Castle

Point House Cairn

Bute

Kingarth

Deil's Cauldron

Kintyre

Arran

Saddell
Castle

Machrie Moor
Stone Circle

Arran

Gortan

Ugadale

King's
Cave

Giants'
Graves

Largiebaan

Kildalloig

Torrylin
(Torlin)
Cairn

Southend

*Firth
of
Clyde*

Carskiey

	Animal legends
	Battles and escapes
	Clan and family legends
	Death and burial
	Devils and demons
	Dragons and sea-serpents
	Fairies and trows
	Ghosts and omens
	Giants and ogres
	Heroes and villains
	Landmarks and local customs
	Legendary beings
	Murder and robbery
	Pipers and fiddlers
	Prehistoric remains
	Royalty
	Saints and miracles
	Supernatural creatures
	Talismans and magical objects
	Witches and witchcraft

0   10   20   30 MI

0   10   20   30   40   50 KM

Islay

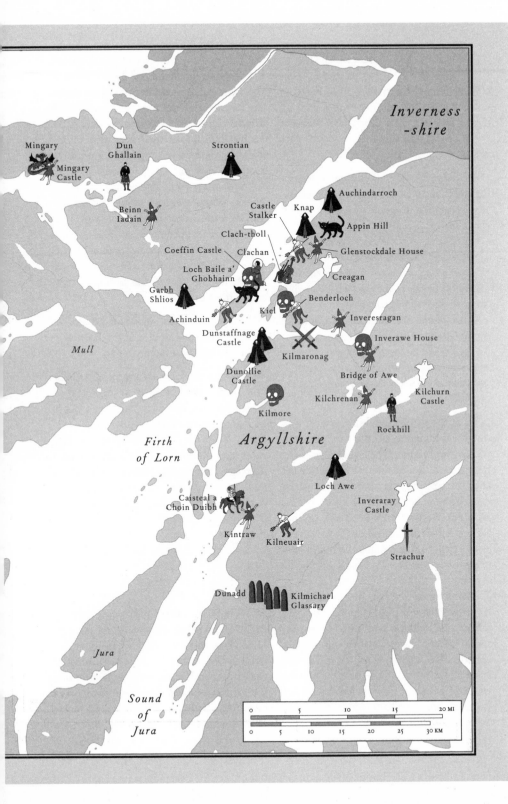

APPIN HILL, ARGYLLSHIRE

K.W. Grant got many of her stories from her grandmother and other relatives. In *Myth, Tradition and Story from Western Argyll* (1925), speaking of seventy years earlier, she observes:

> Those were the days of elemental spirits; of sights and sounds relegated by present-day sceptics to the realm of superstition or imagination. The old people were ency-clopædias of fairy tale, family tradition and historic incident, while the young folk formed a ring of eager listeners at the frequent rehearsals round the fireside on the long winter evenings.
>
> What an ordeal it was on a dark winter night, after having an imagination raised to the highest pitch, to be obliged, when the time came to disperse, to traverse the space of a few yards to the various homes around!

Two of the stories the children were told concerned huntsmen in the wild territory around Appin Hill. One, weary from the chase, came to a hut where an old crone sat at the fireside. She told him that if he was coming in he must tie up his two dogs, and plucked a hair from her head, saying, 'Here's a hair which could hold a five-masted gallant ship against the might of a seven-fold tempest.' The hunter took the hair but secretly bound it round the leg of his chair instead of to the dogs. As he was warming himself, he noticed the old woman swelling and swelling, bigger and bigger. When he remarked on it, she replied, 'My fetheries-and-fitheries are rising at the sight of the kilt.' When he remarked a second time on her continued swelling, she attacked him, shouting, 'Tighten, O hair! Strangle, O hair!' The hair had nothing to strangle except the leg of the chair, and the two hounds

sprang upon the hag. While the dogs held her down, the hunter hewed her to pieces, but when he had finished he observed that the various parts of her body were drawing nearer and ever nearer to each other. He thought it time to leave the hut. As he looked back he saw the pieces of her body sticking themselves together, and so he made speedily off.

Another terrifying tale concerned a little kitten which used to come out of the woods and sit by a huntsman's fire. One day the hunter shot a wild cat, and as it was dying it told the man to say to the kitten, 'I have killed Bladderum.' When he reached his shelter he said to the kitten, 'I have killed Bladderum.'

> 'That was my sister,' replied the kitten. It then swelled and swelled to a monstrous size and killed the hunter.

This is a particularly savage variant of the tale known as 'The King of the Cats', in which one cat learns of another's death and announces that it is now lord of its kind. The story of Bladderum is also related to the theme 'The fairies send a message', where supernatural beings pass news to each other via a human intermediary. A gentler example is told at TAFTS (Orkney & Shetland Islands) concerning the trows.

ARRAN

In *The White Wife* (1865), 'Cuthbert Bede' (Edward Bradley) tells the story of 'The Apparition of Arran'. His informant had heard the tale at the beginning of the nineteenth century from someone who many years before had known the heroine, a little old woman called Marie Nic Junraidh or Mary Henderson. Although tiny, Mary was chockful of courage and very bright. One dark night she had to cross a bridge which had the reputation of being haunted by something dreadful.

But although it was night-time and dark, yet the bold little woman took courage to cross the bridge; and when she came to it, she saw something of an awful appearance standing before her. She would not turn back; so she spake to it, and it spake to her again, and then assumed a human shape, which she readily recognised, and said, 'An tu Fionla [Fionnlagh]?' – 'Art thou Finlay?'

He was a man she had known when he was alive. He said that he had several times appeared to strong men, who had always been too frightened to speak to him. She, however, had stood her ground and spoken. He told her that while he was living he had stolen some plough-irons, and could not rest until they were restored to their owner. She would find them in a certain place, and if she laid them by the wayside, he would be at peace. The ghost predicted how long Mary and her husband would live, and asked her to warn a neighbour to repent of his evil ways. Then he vanished.

Next day, she found the plough-irons and laid them by the wayside. There their original owner found them and picked them up, though it was noticed that he did not live long afterwards. The neighbour who had been given the warning took heed and repented, and both Mary and her husband died at the time foretold. 'After her interview with the spirit, the bridge was not haunted by night, nor was anyone troubled by the apparition.'

John Gregorson Campbell notes that a spirit who had concealed 'cold iron' could not rest while it remained hidden, and illustrates the point with a story set at LOCH MEIG (Southern Highlands).

AUCHINDARROCH, ARGYLLSHIRE

The farmhouse of Auchindarroch (Achadh nan darach, 'Field of Oaks') was haunted by a Glaistig, also known as the Gruagach (maiden) of Glen Duror. John Gregorson Campbell writes in *Superstitions of the Highlands and Islands of Scotland* (1900) that 'She followed the house (not the family), and was alive not many years ago.' Her face was described as being like a grey stone covered with lichens.

This Glaistig looked after the cattle, taking particular care to keep the calves away from the cows at night so that there would be enough milk for the household in the morning. In return, a portion of milk was poured out for her every evening on the Glaistig Stone. Once, when a new tenant neglected to do this, the calves were found in with the cows next morning.

A servant girl, going one dark evening to draw water from a nearby stream, was asked by the other servants if she were not afraid of the Glaistig. She spoke of the spirit with contempt, and on her way to the stream got a slap on the cheek that twisted her head to one side. The next evening, going down to the stream on the same errand, she got a slap on the other cheek that put her head right again. (The same story was told of another Glaistig at Sron-Charmaig, Argyllshire.) Speaking of spirits with disrespect, implying they were not as powerful as people said, or even denying their existence, was always a dangerous thing to do.

In *Folk Tales and Fairy Lore in Gaelic and English* (1910), the Reverend James MacDougall does not name the farmhouse which the Glaistig haunted, but says: 'Two or three hundred years ago she was a dairymaid between Glen Duror and Glen-a-Chulish; and her name and surname, and even the farm where she was reared, are still remembered.' He only tells us, however, that her spirit form was known locally as 'The Maiden'. Tradition said that she was taken away out of childbed by the fairies and changed into a Glaistig, who took shelter in the rocks between the glens.

The explanation of her as the spirit of a dairymaid no doubt evolved to account for her particular fondness for and affinity with cattle, though this is shared by many Glaistigs. MacDougall writes that she was often to be seen in the midst of the herd as if counting them, and before and after markets she would separate the outgoing part of the stock or take possession of the part newly come in. If she happened to have a particular liking for one tenant, she would take extra care of his cattle. She had last been seen about thirty years earlier, i.e. in the second half of the nineteenth century, although Alasdair Alpin MacGregor in *The Peat-Fire Flame* (1937) says hopefully that she 'might still be alive for all we know!'

See also THE MAIDEN OF INVERAWE (p. 24).

BEINN IADAIN, MORVERN, ARGYLLSHIRE

In the Highlands, fairies were known to steal women, usually just after they had given birth so that they could suckle the often-ailing fairy infants. In a case reported by John Gregorson Campbell in *Superstitions of the Highlands and Islands of Scotland* (1900), a man from Loch Sunart lay down for a few minutes' rest by the bed in which lay his wife and new baby. When he awoke, woman and child were gone. They were taken, the woman said afterwards, up to the 'Black Door', a way into Beinn Iadain. On entering the mountain, widely believed to be an abode of the fairies, they found a large company of people.

> A fair-haired boy among them came and warned the woman not to eat any food the fairies might offer, but to hide it in her clothes. He said they had got his own mother to eat this food, and in consequence he could not now get her away. Finding the food offered her was slighted, the head Fairy sent off a party to bring a certain man's cow. They came back saying they could not touch the cow as its right knee was resting on the plant *bruchorcan* (dirk grass). They were sent for another cow, but they came back saying they could not touch it either, as the dairymaid, after milking it, had struck it with the shackle or cow-spancel (*buarach*).

The woman appeared to her husband in a dream, telling him that by going to the Black Door, taking the black silk handkerchief she had worn on her wedding day, with three knots tied in it, he could recover her.

> He tied the knots, took the handkerchief and a friend with him, entered the hill at the Black Door, and recovered his wife and child. The white-headed boy accompanied them for some distance from the Black Door, but returned to the hill, and is still there in all probability.

The protective magic used against the fairies is of great interest. *Bruchorcan*, or dirk grass (a sort of rush also known as stool-bent or *Juncus squarrosus*), was probably dangerous to fairies because of its association with dirks (daggers), for many Highlanders the readiest 'cold iron' to hand. By the same token, the cow-spancel or shackle was probably made of either iron or rowan wood. The knots, much used in witchcraft to trap or inhibit, may simply have frozen any action purposed by the fairies. The warning against eating fairy food, an act which put people in their power, features in numerous fairy abduction stories, testimony to its having been an old and widespread belief.

According to a second story, also recorded by Campbell but of quite different import, another woman was taken to Beinn Iadain and placed in the lap of a gigantic hag who said it was no good trying to escape, as her arms would enfold the woman as close as ivy round a tree, or flesh round the bone. The woman answered that she wished it was an armful of dirt the fairy hag held. In saying this, she used a very coarse word. As such talk is not tolerated among the fairies, the giantess called on others to take the woman away and leave her in the hollow where she had been found, and this was done.

The fairies' daintiness over language reflects the common image of them as a courtly society, forever dancing and feasting. The word the woman used was probably the Gaelic equivalent of 'shit', and perhaps she used it deliberately, knowing that it would offend the hag. It was, however, a risky thing to do.

BENDERLOCH, ARGYLLSHIRE

A shepherd in Benderloch saw a large bundle of ferns rolling down a hillside, apparently by its own motion. Finally it went over a waterfall and disappeared. 'Of course this was Black Donald; what else could it be?'

Black Donald (Dòmhnull Dubh) was a name for the Devil in the Highlands and Islands. If not the Evil One himself, the bundle might well have been one of his minions. Demons were thought in the Middle Ages to be able to assume any shape they chose, even those of inanimate objects, a trait inherited by the hobgoblins (including Shakespeare's Puck) and the shape-shifting bogeys of later centuries. Bogey beasts customarily appearing in animal shapes could also take on inanimate forms: in England, trusses of straw, sheets, woolpacks, and even 'a roll of Irish linen' are all recorded, while in Scotland such manifestations include the Sac Bàn (White Sack) at CREAGAN.

BRIDGE OF AWE, ARGYLLSHIRE

Approaching from the Pass of Brander to the foot of Glen Nant, the A85 crosses the River Awe at Bridge of Awe. John Gregorson Campbell in *Superstitions of the Highlands and Islands of Scotland* (1900) gives the story of a weaver at Bridge of Awe who was left a widower with three or four children. He was an industrious man, who worked all day and then did jobs about his house in the evening.

One moonlit night when he was thatching his house with fern, he heard a rushing sound as of a high wind, and a swarm of little people settled on the roof and the ground like a flock of starlings. He was told he must go with them to Glen Cannel in Mull to fetch a woman. He said he would not go unless he could keep whatever was foraged. The fairies agreed, and off they all flew to Mull.

When they got to Glen Cannel, the weaver was given an arrow, but, while pretending to aim at the woman, he threw it through the window and managed to kill a pet lamb. The lamb immediately came out through the window, but the fairies said that it would not do and that he must throw again. This time he aimed at the woman, and she was taken away by the fairies and a log of alderwood left in her place.

When they got back, the weaver claimed what he had been promised and the fairies had to leave the woman with him, though they vowed that they would never make such a pact again. The woman lived happily with the weaver and they had three children.

Then a beggar passing that way stayed with them the night. All evening he stared so at the wife that the weaver finally asked him why. The beggar said he had once been a farmer in Glen Cannel on Mull, and pretty well-to-do, but his wife had died, since when he had fallen into destitution. He claimed that the weaver's wife was none other than his lost spouse. After some discussion the beggar was given the choice of the wife or the children, took the wife, and once again prospered.

This story, which combines the themes of the fairy flight and the stolen wife, leaves some details unexplained simply because for the original audience they needed no explaining. First, the arrow would be understood to be 'elf-shot', the tiny missiles (in reality Neolithic flint arrowheads) used by fairies to inflict illness or seeming death. The lamb that comes out of the window is not a spirit but the real lamb, and a simulacrum of the animal would have been left behind.

The 'fairy stock', or substituted image, is an old and widespread theme, found in medieval Scandinavia as well as Britain, and is clearly based on analogy ('lifeless as a log'). In this particular story, the substitute lamb would be seen as dead, just as the alderwood log left for the wife was taken for her corpse. However, in many stories, the stock is animated, a deceptive substitute for the person stolen by the fairies, though appearing listless or ill. An exact parallel is the belief that fairies could steal the 'foison' (goodness) out of food while leaving the foodstuff looking the same to the human eye.

CAISTEAL A CHOIN DUIBH, ARGYLLSHIRE

The name of this ancient fort means 'Castle of the Black Dog', referring to a legend in which there was a fight between Fingal's dog Bran and For, a black dog belonging to the Prince of Innse Orc. For was killed and given honourable burial beneath a standing stone. Local tradition supposes this to be the large stone, once standing although no longer upright, a short way north-east of the fort.

FINGAL (p. 10) or Finn is the Irish hero Fionn mac Cumhaill, a great hunter and owner of many hounds, of which the most famous was Bran. He (in some versions she) was a huge dog, with fierce eyes, whose finely made head came as high as Fingal's shoulder. He is said to have had two white sides, a purple-tinged haunch, and bluish feet. Whenever Fingal's followers were hungry, Bran would go into the forest and bring them something to eat. Fingal loved the dog deeply, but one day when they were out hunting Bran began to yelp, warning off the quarry, and Fingal angrily hit him over the head with the leash. Bran's eyes filled with tears as he stared at his master, deeply wounded, then breaking loose he ran to a lake and drowned himself. After that, Fingal's heart nearly broke every time he heard the baying of a hunting hound.

In Scotland several legends of Bran were told, one concerning an enchantment laid on Fingal and the ransom paid for his release to Cormac, the Irish king, who demanded that two of every bird and beast should be made to pass before him. As Otta Swire tells it (1963):

> Bran and the Grey Dog brought a pair of every animal that lived and made them walk round the base of Tom-na-hurich while Cormac sat on top and looked

important. Easy it was for them, great dogs that they were, though mouse preceded cat and rabbit walked with fox; easy it was until they came to a pair of whales. The walking of the whales was a feat worthy of the Great Dogs.

The 'Grey Dog' is Sceolaing, sister of Bran.

CARSKIEY, KINTYRE, ARGYLLSHIRE

Lord Archibald Campbell in *Records of Argyll* (1885) gives an account of the Brownie of Cariskey, now Carskiey, at the southern tip of Kintyre, an estate which had been in the possession of the MacNeill family since 'before the time of the plague'. Buried in the churchyard at Keil was Lieutenant-Colonel Malcolm MacNeill, who had served in Jersey, probably at the end of the eighteenth century.

Down as far as Colonel MacNeill's time, a creature called the brownie was believed in, and the Colonel is said to have been the last of the family she followed; and the following account of the brownie is no old wife's tale, but has been affirmed by many people belonging to the locality. It is, that there was an old creature that attached herself to the Cariskey family called Beag-Bheul, from Ireland, who had previously followed the Montgomery family of that country, and came over with them to Kintyre.

The Brownie accompanied the colonel to battle in Jersey. When a bullet went through the crown of his hat 'he jumped four feet from the ground', and, turning to her, said it was a good thing for him that she was behind him that day.

When any gentry came to Cariskey House to visit the Colonel, if the house was not properly cleaned by the maids, she would come after they would go to bed and pull them out, and make them clean the house. She was very careful of the Colonel and his property; and is said to have told him of a battle that would be fought in Kintyre, and that the magpie would drink human blood off a standing-stone near Campbeltown.

By 1885, Campbell reports, no battle of any note had taken place. The stone had been moved and placed as a bridge over a mill race, and there was hardly a magpie to be seen in Kintyre.

A female Brownie is unusual, just as in England it is rare to find a female hobthrust. The Glaistig, on the other hand, *is* female, though often said to be attached to houses rather than people (*see* THE MAIDEN OF INVERAWE, p. 24). The Carskiey creature, although exhibiting characteristic traits of both Brownie and Glaistig, came originally from Ireland and may be more closely related to the Irish banshee, a warning or protective spirit associated with certain families.

See also BROWNIES (p. 80).

CASTLE STALKER, ARGYLLSHIRE

In *The Lure of the Kelpie* (1937), Helen Drever tells how in Glen Creran an orphan lad met one of the Stewarts of Appin, whose residence was at Castle Stalker. This fine gentleman was reputed by some to be a wizard, although others whispered that he was the Devil himself. The boy tricked from him a volume of spells, the Red Book of Appin, of which he then became the guardian, imparting its wisdom to others until he was an old, old man.

This is a version of a famous tale known to John Gregorson Campbell, who theorises

Fingal

In Ireland, the adventures of Fionn mac Cumhaill (pronounced Finn Mac Cool) have been told for over one and a half thousand years. Between the tenth and fourteenth centuries, his fame spread to Scotland, where he became known as 'Fingal', and tales of him and his band of warriors were passed down the generations throughout the Highlands and Western Isles.

In the earliest sources, Fionn appears as a clearly mythical god-figure. These legends may have become conflated with historical traditions of some great war-leader, and medieval accounts present him as a human though supernaturally gifted fighter, hunter, and seer who lived in the third century CE. Before his conception it was prophesied that he would be a hero. At birth he was in danger of being murdered by his tyrannical grandfather, who feared that the child would take his power, but an old nurse rescued the baby and took him to the wilderness, where he grew to be strong and intelligent. One day he met a one-eyed giant cooking a salmon. Touching the fish, the boy burned his thumb and put it in his mouth, and thereby gained miraculous insight, since this was the magical 'salmon of knowledge'.

His first great victory was over a hostile spirit which came every year to the High King's court at Tara, put everyone to sleep with enchanted music, and then set fire to the building. Fionn killed this marauder, and as a result was put in command of a fighting troop called the Fianna, or in Scottish versions the Fians.

A diffuse series of stories deals with the hunts, battles, and quarrels of Fionn or Fingal and his followers. One principal figure is Diarmaid, who eloped with Fingal's betrothed, Grainne, and another is Fingal's son Oisín or Ossian, said to have survived the rest of the Fians for centuries and to have known St Patrick. In 1760, the poet James Macpherson produced what purported to be a translation of an epic cycle about Fingal and the Fians written by Ossian himself, and although after Macpherson's death it was proved that he had concocted his work from Gaelic fragments supplemented with his own compositions, the historical existence of 'Ossian the bard' remained an article of faith with many enthusiasts for long afterwards.

Animals feature prominently in the legends of Fingal, one story telling how his wife was transformed into a deer, and while in that shape gave birth. Later, Fingal's hounds gave chase to a doe which escaped but left behind a boy who proved to be Fingal's own son Ossian. A similar fate befell Fingal's aunt Uirne, metamorphosed while pregnant into canine form. She was sent to the King of Dublin and his wife, who was also about to bear a child. The queen had a son and Uirne two fine puppies, and Fingal was engaged to protect them from an ogre who had previously kidnapped all the royal couple's children. That night a gigantic hand and arm appeared through the roof. One of Fingal's helpers seized the arm and pulled it clean off, but the giant snatched the baby and pups with his other hand and bore them off to his castle. Fingal and his assistants followed and succeeded in rescuing all the children, and the male pup Bran tore out the giant's entrails with his paw. Bran and the other puppy, Sceolaing, became Fingal's two favourite hounds, and accompanied him in many exploits.

This nineteenth-century illustration shows one of Fingal's followers grappling with an ogre who is attempting to carry off the King of Dublin's son. Fingal's Aunt Uirne, transformed into a dog, fiercely defends her puppies and the baby.

Fingal's death, according to a Perthshire tale, came when he was courting a lady in Glen Dochart and was challenged to leap to an island on Loch Iubhair. He accomplished the feat, but unwisely ventured the same leap backwards, fell, and was beheaded by a warrior of the lady's clan. The more usual tradition, however, is that like King Arthur and some other heroes Fingal never died, but remains sleeping with his warriors in a hill, sometimes identified as TOM-NAHURICH (Southern Highlands) or as Glenorchy in Argyllshire.

The folklorist John Gregorson Campbell spent over thirty years gathering Scottish legends of Fingal and the Fians from oral sources. In his collection, published in 1891, he remarks on the extraordinary popularity of the tales: it had become a common saying, he reports, that 'if the Fians were twenty-four hours without anyone mentioning them they would rise again'.

See also CAISTEAL A CHOIN DUIBH; GIANTS' GRAVES; KING'S CAVE; MACHRIE MOOR STONE CIRCLE (Argyllshire & Islands); TONGUE; UAIGH DHIARMAID (Northern Highlands); DUNDREGGAN; DUN TELVE AND DUN TRODAN; KNOCK-FARRIL VITRIFIED FORT (Southern Highlands); FINGAL'S CAVE (Western Isles).

in *Superstitions of the Highlands and Islands of Scotland* (1900) that the book was in fact a veterinary treatise belonging to the Stewarts of Invernahyle. The family owned a herd of cattle so magnificent that enchantment was believed to be responsible, and the volume was said to be 'so powerful that its owner had to place an iron hoop about his head every time he opened it'. It had been won by an apprentice of Bearachan near Loch Awe, who was invited by a stranger to meet him on a certain night at the Crooked Pool in the Middle Mountain and to write his name in a big red book. The boy was wary, and sixteen ministers, summoned to give their advice, told the lad to attend the rendezvous, draw a circle round himself with a wand, and on no account to step outside it. This the boy did, and when he was handed the book he refused to give it back, although the diabolical stranger resorted to terror tactics, turning first into a grizzled greyhound, then into a roaring bull, and then into a flock of crows sweeping so low and fast that the wind created by their wings would have blown the lad clean out of the circle had he not clung to the heather. The Devil, like the ghost of Hamlet's father, disappeared at cockcrow, leaving the boy with the Red Book.

Campbell's informant assured him that this was 'the only correct account' of the book's origin, although there was a simpler tale of a man who attended a gathering of witches, riding there on an 'entire horse' (i.e. not gelded: a stallion was considered to be 'an animal that no evil power can touch'). Presiding over the meeting was the Devil, who wrote in a red book the names of those assembled. The man asked permission to write his own name, and once he had the book in his hands he made off with it.

John Francis Campbell of Islay heard the legend in the mid nineteenth century from a carter named John, who had had his own experience of the book's magic. When he was a boy, there had been a time when all his family's cattle had been dry of milk, and John's big brother had gone to Appin to consult 'the man of the RED BOOK'. This man had immediately told him that it was a neighbour's wife who had bewitched the cows, and advised him to nail the shoe of a stallion above the door of the byre. This was done, and from that day onwards there was plenty of milk.

John the carter told how the book was gained by an orphan boy who withstood the Devil in much the same way as did the apprentice of Bearachan in J. G. Campbell's narrative. In the carter's tale, the earliest of these accounts, the protective circle was drawn not with a wand but with a sword, which would have been the implement used by a real-life 'cunning man' or conjuror for defence against evil spirits. When the boy was left in possession of the book, he handed it over to his master, Stewart of Appin, and this is how the family came to be keepers of its magic. By the time of Drever's retelling, however, Stewart had himself become the satanic figure from whom the book was won.

CLACHAN, LISMORE

Christianity was brought to Lismore by St Moluag, who founded a monastic community and a church at Clachan, where his body is said to be buried. He is sometimes known as the brother of St Columba, though in real life this was probably only in the spiritual sense. Popular tradition also relates that Columba and Moluag were heading for Lismore together in their boats, competing to reach it first. As they were nearing land, Moluag took up an axe; cutting off the little finger of his left hand, he cast it onto the shore saying, 'In the name of the Holy Godhead of the blessed

Trinity, my flesh and blood are on the land.' The story is similar to a Cheshire legend that two rivals for the Eaton Hall estates by the River Dee agreed that the first claimant to touch the land would own it. One man cut his hand off and threw it ahead of him, thus winning the dispute, and a red hand in the family's coat of arms was explained by this drastic deed.

Columba is said to have been sorry to lose Lismore, which he had intended to make the centre for his missionary endeavours, and went on his way. Before he left, there took place between the two saints what Alexander Carmichael, transmitting this story to Lord Archibald Campbell, calls 'a friendly altercation', but which actually sounds more like a duel between rival magicians. Carmichael translates their dialogue, in which Columba spitefully wishes the island ill and Moluag counters his efforts by turning the curse:

Columba: The edge of its (Lismore's) rock be upwards.
Moluag: Be its venom under.
Columba: Alder be their fuel
Moluag: May it kindle like the candle!

The curse and counter-blessing are explained by the islanders' conviction that, though the limestone rocks of Lismore are sharp, their edges never injured man nor beast, and that though the alder generally makes poor firewood, on the island it burns very well – a statement endorsed by Lord Archibald in a footnote: 'This is a fact.'

Another tale showing St Columba in a rather equivocal light is told at REILIG OGHRAIN (Western Isles).

CLACH-THOLL, ARGYLLSHIRE

At Clach-tholl, says K. W. Grant in 1925, was the entrance to a tunnel leading beneath the sea, into which a daring piper strode while playing the bagpipes. He had vowed to go on playing to let his friends waiting at the entrance know from the music what befell him. Presently the tune changed. To the waiting group above ground it said:

'Woe, woe is me! Would my two hands were three!
Two hands for the pipes and a third for the claymore!'

Then the pipes wailed:

''Tis the hound of the sea, the green hound of the sea
Hath undone me.'

Silence followed. Later the piper's dog came howling from the cave, not a hair on its body, and the piper himself never returned.

What happened to him is clear from the hairless dog. In similar stories found the length and breadth of Britain, the dog comes out, sometimes days later, with all his hair singed off and a smell of brimstone hanging round him – in other words, he has met a demon or the Devil in person. The implication is that the tunnel leads (like many pits and pools) to hell. It might be supposed that the 'green hound of the sea' is a figurative expression for a flooded tunnel, and that the piper has been washed away and drowned, but comparison with similar stories set at TROTTERNISH (Western Isles) and GICHT CASTLE (North East) suggests strongly that he has encountered an infernal power.

COEFFIN CASTLE, LISMORE

Norsemen dominated the Western Isles and the Isle of Man for over 200 years, until the Scots broke their power at the battle of Largs in 1263. A tale of their final days in Lismore was supplied to Lord Archibald Campbell by Alexander Carmichael, himself the author of the *Carmina Gadelica* (1900), a collection of incantations and folklore mainly from the Hebrides. His story is set on the north-west of the island at Coeffin Castle, today a total ruin, though at the end of the nine-teenth century parts of the walls stood firm and seemed as if they would last for ages yet to come.

Carmichael knew the place as Caisteal Chaifean ('the Castle of Caifean'), and he reports that this Caifean was the son of a king of Lochlann, the old Scottish name for Scandinavia. Prince Caifean had a sister Beothail, who was good, beautiful, and adored by all, but died of a broken heart when her lover was killed far away in the wars. Near the old castle of Caifean is a level escarpment divided into two parts, called the Greater and the Lesser Eirebal. When the sea was higher, they must have formed two islands, flat and grass-covered on top, and they were used as burial places; here, on the very edge of the south end, was Beothail's grave, a great boulder in the face of the escarpment preventing her body from falling down the rock.

The spirit of the princess could not rest: 'Beothail cried in her grave, and called on her brother to come and carry her home, and place her beside her fair-haired lover, whom she loved so well.' Her lament was translated by Carmichael:

My heart is grinding behind the stone,
Down to dust, down to dust.
While he of the fair and clustering locks
(Man of my love, man of my love),
Lies in quiet, and I not near him,
Far from the tower, far from the tower.

The grief of his daughter reached the King of Lochlann, and he sent a ship to bring her body home. Her bones were washed in the holy well of St Moluag at Clachan and then carried home to be buried beside her lover and among her kindred. But still Beothail could not lie easy, for the joint of one little toe was missing, and so the ship was sent back and the toe joint found in the well in which she had been washed. This was taken to Lochlann and buried with the rest of her remains, and finally Beothail was at peace.

Carmichael adds:

When a boy, I often stood in Beothail's grave on the Greater Eirebal . . . The place had all the appearance of an empty grave. Within the last few years the large stone which formed one side of the grave on the edge of the rock has fallen down, and lies at the foot of the rock.

He says, 'I see no reason to question the substantial accuracy of the body of Beothail having been disinterred and taken to Lochlann,' but there is a similar story told at TOBERMORY (Western Isles) and KIEL of a Spanish princess, also said to have been unable to rest when a single tiny joint, in her case a finger, was missing from her body.

CREAGAN, LOCH CRERAN, ARGYLLSHIRE

Creagan, on the north shore of Loch Creran, was once possessed of a singular spirit known as the Sac Bàn, 'White Sack'. Preserved in Gaelic in the manuscript notes of John Francis Campbell of Islay and published with a translation by John McKay in 1940 was a brief but horrific description of its activities: 'The White Sack used to roll itself round (*lit.* before) men's feet, bringing them down; then getting on top of them, it used to flatten them out and murder them.'

In the *Transactions of the Gaelic Society of Inverness* (1897) appeared a tale of a servant girl whose sweetheart's mother was jealous of her. The woman sent her one evening to buy drink at the Creagan Change House, past the Hollow of the White Sack. On her way the girl found the White Sack's *luman*, a coarse covering or garment of sackcloth. Knowing that the spirit was powerless without his garment, the girl gave it to the landlady at the Change House and asked her to keep it long enough to give the girl time to get home. No sooner had the girl left, however, than the White Sack started banging on the door of the inn so fiercely that the terrified woman of the house gave back his *luman*, and he then gave chase to the girl. Her lover saw her coming with the White Sack close behind, and stood in the doorway to catch her. He managed to drag her away from the spirit, but the White Sack caught hold of her plaid or shawl and she died of fright. The young man's mother, who had sent the girl into danger, was now sorry and never had a quiet conscience thereafter. (A slight inconsistency in this tale is the ferocity of the White Sack's assault on the door of the inn when without his *luman* he was supposed to be powerless.)

It seems that the White Sack was also known further south. In *Galloway Gossip* (1901), Robert de Bruce Trotter mentions a death omen called 'the Seckyban', otherwise Sacbaun or Sedgeband, which rolled along ahead of people. When it stopped outside a house, a sudden death would occur there.

DEIL'S CAULDRON, BUTE

James King Hewison, minister of Rothesay in the late nineteenth century, took a great interest in the antiquities of the island, including what he calls the 'mysterious stone circus, adjacent to St Blaan's Church in the southern extremity of Bute' which was popularly known as 'the Deil's (Devil's) Cauldron'.

He describes the structure as a massive circular wall of huge unhewn blocks of stone with a narrow entrance, and surmises that its real purpose was as a robber-proof safe. The legend which must be connected with the name 'Deil's Cauldron' he does not explain, but he gives another name and tradition associated with the stone circle:

> The natives of Bute, in continuing to call it 'The Dreamin' Tree Ruin,' preserve both its Celtic name and the memory of an ancient superstition. The 'Dreamin' Tree' is no other than the Celtic words *Druim-en-tre* [*Druimean-tré*], the little ridge-dwelling; while the custom itself is clearly a survival of tree-worship.

Within living memory, says Hewison, there grew within the circle an ash or fir tree which pairs of lovers would climb together. They would then pick the leaves and eat them, believing that this would give them prophetic dreams revealing their future spouses.

DUN GHALLAIN, ARGYLLSHIRE

On the north shore of Loch Sunart, south of Salen and between Camus Inas and Laga, is the Iron Age stronghold of Dun Ghallain, the setting for the romantic tale of the 'Swan of Salen'.

The succinct narrative in the undated *Exploring Sunart, Arnamurchan, Moidart and Morar*, in the West Highland series, tells how a local chieftain fell in love with a beautiful but low-born maiden. His mother, opposing the match, caused the girl to be transformed by magic into a swan, which the chief, when out hunting, shot and killed. He was horror-struck to see the swan at the moment of its death resume the form of his beloved. Overcome with grief, he fell on his own sword, and the lovers are said still to lie together beneath the ruined walls of Dun Ghallain.

The story is retold in 'medieval' vein by Judy Hamilton in *Scottish Myths and Legends* (2003). Here the mother engages a witch to transform the girl, the hero uses a bow to shoot the swan, and the fort is not mentioned. We still know where events take place, for the bodies of maiden and man sink under the water, seeing which the other swans desert Loch Sunart for ever.

More romanticised yet is 'The Swans on the Loch', in George Macpherson's *Highland Myths and Legends* (first published 2001). The action is cast into the vaguely Ossianic past ('for so were men before the mists of false religion hid them from the gods'), and the hero and heroine are, unusually for local legend, given names: Aoidh, greatest of all the hunters, and Ealasaid, daughter of Morgei the 'enchantress' (a word with more glamorous connotations than 'witch'). It is this 'enchantress' who turns her own daughter into a swan, and after the hunter has shot her with an arrow through the breast she switches roles and offers him relief by transforming him into the same likeness.

This version is totally detached from location. The girl is buried in an unnamed knoll above a loch 'now known' (because of the tragedy) 'as the Dhu loch' – this should be 'Dubh loch', the dark loch, which could be one of many. Glossed over is the somewhat distasteful detail that Morgei must have dug her up, as she later takes both bodies to a nameless hill overlooking the sea and buries them

beneath an equally anonymous stone cairn. 'But their spirits flew off together to be forever in Tir-nan-og.'

The mythologising evident in this retelling has in effect turned it into fairy tale – accepted, except perhaps by children, as fiction – rather than legend, a story told as true. By distancing the action in time and detaching it in space, the teller has made its impact less immediate – no longer 'here on this very spot', no longer the story that marks this place, for locals and strangers alike, as special. The danger of this is obvious: when there is no longer a visual mnemonic, something that prompts the telling over and over, the story often dies.

Far more 'real' is a personal experience of Otta Swire's narrated in her *Highlands and their Legends* (1963). She writes that swans rarely visit the loch at Fasnacloich in Argyllshire, but are said always to appear there before the death of a 'Stewart of Fasnacloich', despite the fact that the Stewarts sold the property a good while ago.

Once when I was staying at Fasnacloich with other guests, a visitor came in from shooting, very apologetic, because, he explained, he did not know his hostess did not like swans to be shot and, seeing a bevy of wild swans on the loch, he had fired before the keeper could stop him. His hostess replied that it was only on account of a local superstition that she protected swans; it did not really matter. 'Swans,' she added, 'are very rarely seen on the loch. These are the first for many years.' In the middle of dinner a telegram was brought to her. It was to say that 'Stewart of Fasnacloich' had died that day and they were bringing his body to the family graveyard for burial.

Swire adds that the dead swan could not be used for food but was discreetly buried.

DUNADD, ARGYLLSHIRE

A little to the north of KILMICHAEL GLAS-SARY, a craggy rock with twin peaks rises from Crinan Moss, topped by ancient and complex fortifications. Twentieth-century accounts of the site vary as to topography (they are unable to agree even on the orientation of the two summits, much less the layout of the defences), but consistently state that this was the Dark Age capital of the kingdom of Dàl Riata or Dalriada, founded by Scots who emigrated here from Northern Ireland around the end of the fifth century. A cup-mark and footprint cut into a slab of rock are often mentioned as having formed part of the ceremonial inauguration of the Dalriadic kings. Just how fragile – and comparatively recent – these assertions are is shown by archaeology and recorded history.

No local tradition concerning Dunadd seems to antedate a lecture given by the Celtic historian William Forbes Skene at Potalloch in 1850. It was this lecture and his later publications that apparently fixed the identification of Dunadd as the capital of Dàl Riata in local and antiquarian records, since when it has been repeated as fact.

F. W. L. Thomas in 1879 first proposed that this was the inauguration site of Dàl Riata's kings, and by now fantasy has entered the picture. Thomas reports a story that at some unspecified but distant date when Ossian, son of FINGAL (p. 10), lived at Dunadd and was hunting along Lochfyneside, a stag his dogs had brought to bay suddenly turned and charged him. Ossian fled, and coming to the hill above Kilmichael village leapt from there to the top of Rudal hill, and thence to the top of Dunadd. Landing there, he fell on his knees and put his hands out to stop himself toppling backwards. 'The mark of a right foot is still pointed out on Rudal hill, and that of the left

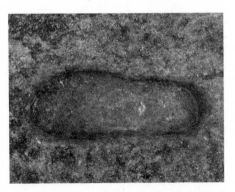

Many rock-cut footprints can be found in Scotland and Ireland. This one at Dunadd is claimed to mark the spot where Ossian, son of the legendary warrior Fingal, landed when he fled from a charging stag.

is quite visible on Dunadd, with impressions of the knee and fingers.'

The left footprint and knee-mark were the famous rock-cut footprint and cup-mark, known by 1878. It has been suggested that the supposed finger-marks were an Ogam inscription also found here, though Thomas may not have known of this marking, the first description of which was published in 1965. A second footprint was not described until 1976; nor was a rather jolly graffito showing a figure wearing a crown or hat and smoking a pipe, hailed by its accompanying inscription as 'King Fergus' (the founder of Dalriada was traditionally said to be Fergus Mor mac Eira, Fergus the Great of Ireland). This addition is thought to have been made after 1904, being immediately behind a (much older) delicately incised carving of a boar, revealed in excavations of that date. In 1928 a box was placed to shield the carvings from further vandalism and weathering, and in 1978 the entire surface of the slab except for the rock basin was protected under artificial stone.

Successive excavations have shown that the hill was certainly an important and strategic site, occupied if only intermittently for a very, *very* long time. Objects found include a Neolithic stone ball, a fragment of a Bronze Age food vessel, small bits of Germanic and Roman glass, a garnet in a gold setting (probably sixth- or seventh-century Anglo-Saxon work), and a stone disc with the inscription I(N)NOMINE, 'in the name of (the Lord)', seemingly from the eighth century, which, together with a small piece of orpiment, used in the illumination of manuscripts, suggests that some of the inhabitants were Christian, perhaps monks.

The inaugural use of the famous Dunadd footprint is by contrast only scantily supported. Rock-cut footprints survive in several places in Scotland and Ireland, and there were probably once many more. Sometimes they occur in pairs, as at St Columba's Stone near Londonderry, which the chiefs of the O'Dohertys used at their inauguration. The new king or chieftain placed his foot or feet in such footprints, which perhaps symbolised their predecessors in whose footsteps they were to follow. But as Janet Bord has shown in *Footprints in Stone* (2004), there are more reasons than one for delineating footprints, and they are found in many cultures widely separated in space and time.

Nor was such an inaugural use remembered in the oral history of the region. Thomas says that local people rather laughed at the idea, since they had always considered the marks to be the mould for an axe-head. A more fanciful tradition held that Dunadd was the abode of fairies. Possibly a modern development of this, as Janet Bord speaks of it as in the present, is that the footmark itself is attributed to supernatural beings and known as 'the Fairy's Footmark'.

This is a site not to be missed: the rock carvings alone are worth the climb, not to mention the impressive remains of defences and the view. Though from pictures the hills look dauntingly steep, they are not as

difficult as those of many hill-forts – it is possible to get up and as importantly down with a leg in a cast, as proved by one of the writers of this book.

DUNOLLIE CASTLE, ARGYLLSHIRE

On top of a rocky ridge on the road to Ganavan, just to the north-west of Oban, is Dunollie Castle, a tower house probably built mostly in the fifteenth century. The castle, now ruined, was formerly the seat of the MacDougalls, and was commonly reported to have a Glaistig in permanent residence. John Gregorson Campbell writes in *Superstitions of the Highlands and Islands of Scotland* (1900) that at dusk she could sometimes be seen making her way to the house, where she would make herself useful overnight by sweeping the floors and washing the clothes. She was, however, moody, and was said to put dust in the family's meals, although she never did so to her special favourite, the fool attached to the castle.

Like the traditional Brownie, this Glaistig seems to have been a busy worker and mainly helpful about the house. That she did not herself live in the castle is indicated by the fact that she would sometimes be seen arriving in the evening for her night-time stint, and maybe she also took care of the cattle, like the Glaistig of AUCHINDARROCH.

See also BREACACHA (Western Isles); THE MAIDEN OF INVERAWE (p. 24).

DUNSTAFFNAGE CASTLE, ARGYLLSHIRE

'According to vulgar tradition this castle was founded by Edwin, a Pictish monarch, contemporary with Julius Caesar.' Though perhaps not as old as Francis Grose in his

Antiquities of Scotland (1789–91) would have it, Dunstaffnage was indeed once the seat of Scottish princes, and their stone of inauguration was kept here until Kenneth II transferred it to SCONE PALACE (Central & Perthshire), from where its journey can be traced to EDINBURGH CASTLE (Lothian & Borders).

The fifth-century capital was not the massive-walled castle we see now, which dates from the middle of the thirteenth century. It was captured from the Mac-Dougalls by Robert the Bruce in 1309, and later passed to the Campbells of Argyll-shire. In 1746 it became the prison of Flora Macdonald after she had helped Bonnie Prince Charlie to escape.

In popular tradition the castle was the home of a Glaistig, referred to by John Gregorson Campbell in *Superstitions of the Highlands and Islands of Scotland* (1900) as the Siannag or Elle-maid of Dunstaffnage. 'Elle-maid' signifies elf-maid, but this was no ethereal creature: a stranger who stayed overnight at the castle had his bedclothes pulled off twice by the Glaistig, and heard her walking through the room and in the adjoining passages all night. 'Her footsteps were heavy like those of a man.' She would break into cries of joy or sorrow whenever a happy or unfortunate event was about to befall the inmates of the castle, a premonitory function similar to that associated with the Irish banshee, commonly said to wail in warning of approaching death. Links between Argyllshire and Ireland go back to before 500 CE, when the Scotti of Antrim arrived to found the kingdom of Dalriada: like the Brownie of CARSKIEY, the Dunstaffnage Glaistig may derive some of her character from Irish legend.

The Glaistig is said to have watched over the Campbells until 1810, when the castle was gutted by fire. She was not the only spirit associated with them. In *Records of Argyll* (1885), Lord Archibald Campbell reports:

> There is said to be a small old man in Truish, with a grey plaid and Lowland bonnet, called the Bodach Glas (old grey man), who appears on the death of any of the Dunstaffnage family (or on the death of the head of the family – all do not agree on this point).

This Lowlander, while living, had taken part in a raid with one of the 'Dunstaffnage family' (meaning the Campbells of Dunstaffnage). Being pursued, the Lowlander had wished to leave the loot and run, whereupon Dunstaffnage called him a coward and stabbed him. Dying, the man told Dunstaffnage that he too would die that day, and that he (the Bodach Glas) would appear and exult over the death of the rest of the family for ever. The pursuers overtook Dunstaffnage, who was killed, and the Bodach Glas duly continued to appear, even putting in a turn as Sir Walter Scott's 'Gray Man' in *Waverley* (1814).

Given their experience with the Glaistig and the Bodach Glas, the Campbells should have been well able to spot the supernatural in all its manifestations. Lord Archibald also gives a story taken from the Gaelic concerning MacAonghais an Dùin, 'MacAngus of the Fort', the patronymic of the Dunstaffnage Campbells. Mac-Angus and his manservant were once crossing the moor between Lochawe and Glenfaochan when they overtook an old woman drawing a heather rope after her. The servant commented what strange work it was, and MacAngus told him that, little though he might suppose it, the woman was drawing after her in that rope all the milk in Glenfaochan.

> Having said this, he drew his sword and cut the rope, and they were all nearly drowned in milk. The old woman was a witch from Lochaweside, and was in

Glenfaochan extracting the substance from the milk.

The rope of heather is a variation on the common tradition of the 'hair tether', described at DELORAINE (Lothian & Borders).

See also THE MAIDEN OF INVERAWE (p. 24).

GARBH SHLIOS, ARGYLLSHIRE

In her collection of Argyllshire folklore published in 1925, K. W. Grant gives the story of Big Shalvach McKelvie (Sealbhach Mòr) who farmed at Frackersaig in Lismore, and one day crossed to Garbh Shlios on the opposite shore of Loch Linnhe to collect timber. Other boats had come on the same errand, but had set out on their return journey before he was ready. He was just about to embark when a sudden storm came sweeping in from the east, and at that moment a wretched-looking old hag came down to the water's edge.

She asked if McKelvie would take her across the loch, and he said he would, if she did not think it too rough. If he did not think so, she replied, neither did she. He therefore helped her into the boat and pushed off in the teeth of the storm, plying his oars as hard as he was able.

The tempest rose to a hurricane, and the crone told him to pass her an oar. Shalvach, a big strong man, said that even he was struggling, so it was unlikely she would do better, but when she insisted he handed her one of the oars. As it turned out, he had underestimated this old woman.

'Keep her going, McKelvie!' cried she, turning the boat full round by the strength of her rowing.

'Go at it, brave lass!' answered Shalvach, correcting their direction.

'Go ahead, McKelvie!' cried the crone, again turning the boat.

'Go ahead, brave lass!' he replied, once more setting them right.

'Off she rides; who can curb her!' shouted the old woman, as they swept full speed past all the boats that had set out before them.

On reaching the shore, the two mighty rowers leaped out of the boat and had her drawn up beyond the tidemark before any other boats arrived. Shalvach invited the old woman to spend the night at his house but she refused. Before leaving, she forbade him to take note of where she went. But, curious about her, he turned round in time to see her plunge into the sea and start breasting the waves on her way back to Morvern. 'It was then that he understood that he had been helped by a glastig – a woman-demon.'

The amazing strength of the glastig (more often written 'Glaistig') is accounted for by John Gregorson Campbell, who in *Superstitions of the Highlands and Islands of Scotland* (1900) writes of the species:

Her strength was very great, much greater than that of any Fairy, and one yell of hers was sufficient to waken the echoes of distant hills. Strong men are said to have mastered her, but ordinarily people were afraid of meeting her. She might do them a mischief and leave them a token, by which they would have cause to remember the encounter.

Big Shalvach, however, braver and stronger than most, seems to have got off his encounter with the Glaistig scot-free.

See also THE MAIDEN OF INVERAWE (p. 24).

GIANTS' GRAVES, ARRAN

Two neighbouring chambered cairns on Whiting Bay on Arran are known as the Giants' Graves (although some sources record only one Giant's Grave). It is possible that the giant or giants concerned have something to do with the tradition mentioned by the well-known traveller and author Martin Martin in about 1695:

> The Name of this Isle is by some derived from *Arran*, which in the *Irish* Language signifies Bread: Others think it comes more probably from *Arjn*, or *Arfyn*, which in their Language is as much, as the Place of the Giant *Fin-Ma-Couls* Slaughter or Execution . . . the received Tradition of the great Giant *Fin-Ma-Cowls* Military Valour, which he exercised upon the Ancient Natives here, seems to favour this Conjecture; this they say is evident from the many Stones set up in divers Places of the Isle, as Monuments upon the Graves of Persons of Note that were kill'd in Battle.

The Giant 'Fin-Ma-Coul' or 'Fin-Ma-Cowl' is Fionn mac Cumhaill, perhaps historically an early Irish war-leader, although he is remembered as a god-like figure and his followers, known as the Fianna, are celebrated as heroes. Between the tenth and fourteenth centuries his legend became widely known in Scotland, but here he was called FINGAL (p. 10).

Fionn and the Fianna are often described as having superhuman strength and dimensions, being up to 500 times as big as men of today. As King Arthur was pictured in tradition as huge enough to sit in ARTHUR'S SEAT (Lothian & Borders), so Fingal was said to be of a size to occupy FINGAL'S CAVE (Western Isles) and to sit there in Fingal's Chair. Again like Arthur, who was said to sleep beneath Arthur's Seat, so in one version of the legend of TOMNAHURICH (Southern Highlands) the giant warriors asleep inside it are said to be 'Fin and his warrior band'.

GLENSTOCKDALE HOUSE, ARGYLLSHIRE

In her 1925 collection of traditions and stories from western Argyllshire, K. W. Grant records:

> The threshold of Glenstockdale House, once the dower-house of Stewart ladies, was supposed to be made from a block of wood, which had been left in a bed there to simulate a young mother whom the fairies had carried off.

This is just one of the 'fairy stock' traditions found in both Britain and Scandinavia, in which a wooden image or even a plain wooden log is left in a bed as a simulacrum of a stolen woman, often a new mother whom the fairies have taken to nourish their own dwindling race.

Grant goes on to give two very different views of fairies held by local people, the first a strikingly 'realistic' account given by an old lady, identified as 'Mrs M.', of a little woman about the size of a four-year-old child who came one summer's evening to the farmhouse where Mrs M. was staying. Food was offered to this tiny woman, and a seat by the chimney corner.

> She accepted the food, putting part of it aside into her apron. On seeing that the skin of a dead lamb was about to be thrown into the ashpit, she begged for it, saying, 'This will do for our little people.' She rolled it up and bestowed it also in her small apron. When the family retired to rest, the fairy was left sitting at the fireside, but she was gone before they got up in the morning.

Enquiries were made in the district, but nobody had seen the little woman except the family at the farm. The description could be of a human caller, a Traveller perhaps, who was taken to be a fairy because of her very small stature.

The next 'sighting' recounted by Grant is much more conventional, and quite possibly tinged with fairy lore from books:

Mrs S.'s description was altogether different. She had been crossing a wide moor far up among the hills. Suddenly there floated in front of her a slender figure in a gauzy, greeny, rainbow-tinted dress. This figure glided over the tops of the heathery hillocks and rushy, moss-covered tussocks of the wet moorland, keeping within sight in advance of her a great part of the way. Then, as suddenly as she had come into view, she disappeared. Mrs S. had not the least doubt but she had seen a fairy.

The fairy's gliding across the boggy ground makes her sound like the treacherous Will o' the Wisp, the name given to gleams of light caused by burning marsh gas and characterised as an imp which led travellers astray. Here, however, since Mrs S. reached home safely, there is an implication that she was guided across the dangerous terrain by some kind of guardian spirit.

GORTAN, LORN, ARGYLLSHIRE

John Gregorson Campbell in *Superstitions of the Highlands and Islands of Scotland* (1900) tells of a curious event that befell a cooper when he was digging in a drain at 'Gortan du', probably Gortan on the Moor of Rannoch:

One evening, having left the spade standing in the drain, he was startled by something striking it with a loud knock. He found the noise was made by the blow of a smooth, polished, flint-like stone. He put this in his pocket and took it home.

A few days later he showed the stone to 'Calum Clever', whose flight with the

fairies is described at INVERESRAGAN. Calum declared that it had been thrown by himself at the instigation of the fairies, who had wanted to take the cooper to make a barrel for them; by implication, Calum had missed his aim on purpose. This was reportedly done by others whom the elves ordered to shoot their fellow mortals, as at BRIDGE OF AWE. Campbell adds that the fairies could not throw their stones themselves, but had to compel a human being to do so for them.

Campbell identifies the stone as a fairy arrow, which he describes as a triangular piece of flint 'bearing the appearance of an arrow head'. He surmises, correctly, that it was originally part of the armoury of the people of the Stone Age. Throughout Britain, small, delicate Neolithic flint arrowheads were regarded as fairy arrows or elf-stones and believed to be the cause of disease – in Anglo-Saxon times, they seem to have been regarded as the source of rheumatism in humans and also of livestock diseases, particularly the bloat got by horses and cattle from overeating greenstuffs in the spring. In a 1607 Scottish witchcraft trial, Bartie Paterson confessed to using a charm against elf-shot:

I charge thee for arrowschot
For doorschot, for wombschot,
For liverschote, for lungschote,
For hertschote – all the maist:
In the name of the Father, the Sone, and Haly Ghaist.

Illnesses known as 'elf-shot' in cattle could be cured by dipping the elf-stone in water and giving that to the afflicted beasts to drink, and the title Campbell gives this story, 'Struck by the Fairy Arrow Spade', suggests that there may have been some overlap with the idea of the fairy spade, a smooth and slippery black stone shaped like the sole of a shoe, which was put in water given to sick people and cattle.

INVERARAY CASTLE, ARGYLLSHIRE

H. W. Hill, who paid several visits to Inverary (now usually spelt Inveraray) in the early twentieth century, was a friend of Charles Lindley, Viscount Halifax, and contributed some stories to *Lord Halifax's Ghost Book* (1936). In August 1914 he was having tea in the castle library when he heard a loud noise, as if a shelf of books had been thrown to the ground. He looked up but said nothing, as nobody else seemed to have noticed anything. Later the Duke of Argyll's sister Lady Elspeth told him that she was not surprised he had heard a noise, because when she had gone into the library before tea she had seen 'the old man' there:

> This was the ghost of the Harper, who was hanged at Inverary by Montrose's men when they came up the glen in pursuit of the great Marquis of Argyll. The Harper always appears in the Campbell tartan and is a harmless little old thing.

Hill thought the story strange, as the present castle was only built in 1750 and on a different site from the previous building. He surmised that the old man appeared where the tree grew on which he was hanged. When he suggested to Lady Elspeth that as a bishop was currently staying in the castle this would be an opportune time to lay the Harper to rest, she would not hear of it. 'He was, she said, a friend and in some sense a guardian; he was quite happy and never did anyone any harm.'

After that, Hill often heard the Harper. When he was staying at Inveraray towards the end of October 1922, the duke was unwell and declared himself unable to attend the Marquis of Breadalbane's funeral. That evening, Lady Elspeth and

Ian Campbell, a lad of nineteen who was the duke's second heir, were sitting in the library when they heard the noise as of books being thrown about in the adjoining turret, and after a few minutes the doors opened. 'Nothing could be seen, but something had entered and was slowly and deliberately scuffling about the room.' They ran upstairs to tell the duke, who said the 'old man' must have appeared on account of the death. Seemingly this was the Harper's way of expressing his annoyance that the duke, the chief of the clan, had not attended the funeral of his vassal.

INVERAWE HOUSE, LOCH ETIVE, ARGYLLSHIRE

> This is the tale of the man
>   Who heard a word in the night
> In the land of heathery hills,
>   In the days of the feud and the fight.
> By the sides of the rainy sea,
>   Where never a stranger came,
> On the awful lips of the dead,
>   He heard the outlandish name.
> It sang in his sleeping ears,
>   It hummed in his waking head:
> The name – Ticonderoga,
>   The utterance of the dead.

Thus Robert Louis Stevenson in 1887 announced his retelling in verse of one of the most celebrated ghost stories of the nineteenth century. Told over and over again, the different versions varying in detail, it is the extraordinary tale of a death warning at Inverawe House, given here as told by Miss Isabel Smith to Lord Archibald Campbell and printed in 1885.

In the fields one day, Campbell of Inverawe was approached by a ragged, dishevelled man named MacNiven, who begged for his protection. Inverawe led the man to a secret cave in the side of Ben Cruachan,

The Maiden of Inverawe

Some Glaistigs performed domestic tasks around the house or castle, but many preferred the outdoor life, helping to care for the sheep or cattle, and guiding the herds with strident yells.

A resident spirit of Inverawe House in Argyllshire was known as the 'Maiden of Inverawe'. At least until the end of the nineteenth century she was apparently to be heard rustling about in the rooms, and at night she would upset pails of water and move the chairs. Such a being was generically known as a Glaistig (pronounced 'glashtig'). According to John Gregorson Campbell, who included several reports of these creatures in his *Superstitions of the Highlands and Islands of Scotland* (1900), Glaistigs were originally mortal women who had been put under enchantment and given a fairy nature: the Maiden of Inverawe, for example, was said to be the spirit of a former mistress of the establishment who had proved unfaithful to her husband and been buried alive.

Glaistigs were reported to haunt pastures and households throughout Argyllshire and the Western Isles. Some would undertake domestic tasks when the rest of the household was asleep. Like helpful BROWNIES (p. 80) they would sweep the floor and arrange the furniture, but they were not reliable servants. If anything happened to upset them they would disturb the bedclothes, put dust in the food, and in general behave rather like poltergeists or mischievous demons. Other Glaistigs took a particular interest in cattle, horses, and sheep, and their strident voices could sometimes be heard yelling on the hills to guide the herds. They liked to drink milk, and if they did not find their expected portion poured into a hollow stone they could become spiteful: farmers who neglected the evening offering might find a dead cow in the pasture next morning.

Those who saw Glaistigs described them as thin little grey women with long yellow hair, often dressed in green. Although small they were stronger than most men, and the story was told of how a Glaistig helped Big Shalvach McKelvie row through a storm from GARBH SHLIOS (Argyllshire & Islands).

One remained at Mearnaid Castle on the Kingairloch coast long after the building was a ruin, and echoed a distinct reply when anyone called to her 'Are you in, maiden?' Another, at Strathglass, once took a fancy to a neighbouring shepherd, and made herself a nuisance by shifting his clothes, stealing his cheese, and pulling his blankets off at night, giggling 'hee, hee, hee' as she did so. Some young men came one evening to hear the mysterious noises she made, but nothing happened until they were about to leave, when a pot was suddenly lifted from the floor by invisible hands, and clods of earth were thrown at the visitors. Although troublesome, this Glaistig never did any real damage, and on the whole, writes Campbell, 'of all the beings, with which fear or fancy has peopled the unseen world, the Glaistig and her near relation the Brownie are among the most harmless.'

Not all authorities agree on this. Writing in 1900, the folklore collector Alexander Carmichael describes her nature as vicious, and a Gaelic dictionary of 1925 defines a Glaistig as 'half-human, half-beast; a gorgon'. In *The Supernatural Highlands* (1976), Francis Thompson remarks that the Glaistig seems to have changed over the years:

> From the lovable creature of tradition, she degenerated into a kind of female ruffian . . . Instead of offering her help around the sheilings [pastures], she threw stones at humans and caused no end of bother.

Perhaps, Thompson comments, it is the character of the Highlands that changed, rather than the Glaistig. Deprived of many of her ancestral castles and her pastoral way of life, she may have felt dispossessed and embittered.

In their day, however, Glaistigs were powerful beings. They could bestow skill on their favourites, giving them the choice between 'ingenuity without advantage' or 'advantage without ingenuity'. People who chose the first proved clever workmen but never prospered; those who made the second choice turned out stupid fellows who made fortunes. On Iona, a still more equivocal present was given to a woman by the name of Livingstone who was sitting alone eating her dinner one tempestuous day when a Glaistig came to take shelter in her house. Being very wet, the Glaistig dried herself in front of the fire but carelessly set light to her clothes, and 'she left as her parting gift, that no fire can be kindled at dinner-time by a woman of the name of Livingstone'.

See also AUCHINDARROCH; DUNOLLIE CASTLE; DUNSTAFFNAGE CASTLE; KNAP; STRONTIAN (Argyllshire & Islands); LOCHABER (Southern Highlands); ARDNADROCHAID; BREACACHA (Western Isles).

and promised to return later with food and clothes for him.

On his way home, he met a man who said to him, 'If MacNiven comes later to ask you for a safe-conduct, do not give it to him; he has slain your foster-brother.' Inverawe was now in a quandary: he had been greatly attached to his foster-brother, but his code of honour demanded that he shield the murderer as he had promised, and this he determined to do.

Reading in bed that night, he saw a shadow fall on his book. Looking up, he saw the form of his foster-brother, pale and bloodstained. The apparition begged him to give up MacNiven, but Inverawe said that he could not. 'I have warned you once,' said the ghost, and vanished.

Next day Inverawe took supplies to the fugitive, and that night the figure appeared to him again. 'I have warned you twice.' Inverawe then told MacNiven that he should find another hiding place, but still he did not betray the man. For the third night the figure of his foster-brother visited him; he said in threatening tones, 'We shall meet again at Ticonderoga.' The name meant nothing to Inverawe, but when he found that MacNiven had vanished from the cave he told his family everything that had happened. There was much speculation about 'Ticonderoga' and its whereabouts, and the word became a kind of family joke.

A couple of years later, Inverawe and his son were sent with their regiment, the 42nd, to fight the French in America. Camped one night near a fortified town, the officers were swapping stories. When it came to Inverawe's turn, he related his vision. A little later he asked the colonel what fort they were to storm next day. The colonel replied – somewhat shortly – that it was St Louis.

Next day the assault failed, and both Campbells fell. The son was dead, the father dying. The colonel asked if he wished any message sent home to Scotland:

> Slowly Inverawe opened his eyes, and recognising the Colonel, he said in accents of deep reproach – 'You have deceived me, Gordon! I have seen it again, and this is Ticonderoga.'

Father and son were buried together, and the colonel, who it was said kept a record in his commonplace book of the story, later raised a monument to them on the spot.

Events at Ticonderoga had not gone unwitnessed in Scotland. At the time the attack was taking place, the two Misses Campbell of 'Ederlin' (Ederline on Loch Awe) were out walking, and saw an extraordinary vision in the sky. They recognised it as a siege, and could tell the different regiments by their colours and identify many of the men including the Campbells, father and son, whom they saw cut down. Afterwards they told their friends what they had seen, and noted the names of the fallen. A physician and his servant who were walking round the castle also witnessed the phenomenon, and supported the testimony of the Misses Campbell. Weeks later, their statements were corroborated by published details of the siege.

One reason why the story attracted so much attention in the nineteenth century, apart from the exotic and hypnotic name of the destined place, may have been the promise made by the ghost, with its echo of *Julius Caesar*, Act IV:

> *Brutus*: Then I shall see thee again?
> *Ghost*: Ay, at Philippi.
> *Brutus*: Why, I will see thee at Philippi, then.

But the story also spoke for itself, and such a dramatic tale of a man haunted by the impossibility of choosing between his two duties as a Highlander – hospitality and protection to those who asked for it, and blood-vengeance for murdered kin – inevitably went the rounds, picking up variations and additions in its course.

As a matter of history, the action of the story takes place during the Seven Years' War (1756–63). In an attempt to drive the French out of Canada, a British attack was launched in 1758 up the Hudson Valley by way of the Great Lakes. On 8 July 1758, the attempt on Ticonderoga failed. The next year, however, Quebec, Fort Niagara, and Ticonderoga were taken, and in 1760 Montreal fell, leaving Canada under British control.

In fact, neither father nor son died directly. The son, who had had his arm broken in the battle, reached Scotland alive and died in Glasgow when his wound festered. Inverawe himself also had an injured arm and was sent to Fort Edward, where he died after an amputation. He was buried in the family lot of his relatives the Gilchrists, but in 1871 the body was moved to the new Union Cemetery between Fort Edward and Hudson Falls (formerly Sandy Hill), where his gravestone was photographed, its inscription outlined in chalk for clarity, for Frederick Richards's *The Black Watch at Ticonderoga* (1912). It is still there today, the oldest headstone in Washington County.

See also THE MAIDEN OF INVERAWE (p. 24).

INVERESRAGAN, ARGYLLSHIRE

From many parts of Britain come traditions of 'flight with the fairies', when people are transported great distances in a very short time. In the Highlands and Islands they are said to travel with the *sluagh*, a word which means 'army' or 'people', implying that they are caught up in a flying host.

John Gregorson Campbell, reporting instances of this in his *Superstitions of the Highlands and Islands of Scotland* (1900), includes one set at DALNACARDOCH (Central & Perthshire), and another remembered from when a Dr McLaurin lived at Inveresragan (he gives the name as Invererragan) near Connel Ferry in Benderloch. He was often visited by a man known as 'Calum Clever' from his musical skill and speed in travelling, both gifts of the fairies. The doctor sent Calum to Fort William with a letter, telling him to procure the assistance of 'his own people' and be back with an immediate answer. Calum asked as much time as one game of shinty would take, and was back in the evening before the game was finished. 'He never could have travelled the distance without Fairy aid.'

This was in the late eighteenth century. The survival of belief in fairies (if only of the twee sort) in the twentieth century is attested by James Lees-Milne, who in his diary for Tuesday, 21 September 1943 describes a conversation with the Duke of Argyll:

> At tea the Duke talked of fairies, in whom he implicitly believes, as do all the people here. He described them as the spirits of a race of men who ages ago lived in earth mounds, which are what they frequent. They are usually little green things that peer at you from behind trees, as squirrels do, and disappear into the earth. The duke has visited numerous fairy haunts in Argyll. So has his sister, Lady Elspeth [Campbell], who at dinner one night announced with solemnity, 'The fairies are out in their sieves tonght.' 'Crossing over to Ireland, no doubt,' her brother replied. 'We are not good enough for them in Scotland. Why! last year at Tipperary there were so many of them that they caused a traffic block.'

Witches, rather than fairies, were commonly said to travel across water in sieves, as they did for instance at DELNABO (North East) and at NORTH BERWICK (Lothian & Borders).

KIEL, MORVERN, ARGYLLSHIRE

It was believed in the Highlands as elsewhere that the last person buried in a graveyard had to keep watch over it until the next funeral came. This was called *Faire Chlaidh*, 'the graveyard watch'.

Unusually, it is a living person who keeps watch in a story told by John Gregorson Campbell in *Superstitions of the Highlands and Islands of Scotland* (1900). In Morvern there once stood a church dedicated to St Columba, Kilcolmkill, contracted to Kiel. Even by the mid nineteenth century only traces remained of the building, but the burial-ground adjoining it was still used by a few families, and was said to be the resting place of a Spanish princess who had died when the ship *Florida* was blown up in Mull in the late sixteenth century. Two young men of the area had promised each other that, whoever died first, the other would watch the churchyard for him. The surviving friend, when keeping the promised watch, shared the sight of the dead one, and was able to see both the material world and spirits.

Each night he saw the ghosts leaving the churchyard and returning before morning. He observed that one of the ghosts was always behind the rest when returning. He spoke to it, and ascertained it to be the ghost of the Spanish Princess. Her body had been removed to Spain, but one of her little fingers had been left behind, and she had come back to where it was.

What is particularly interesting about this tale is that it seems to combine the notion of the graveyard watch with that of 'watch-ing in the church porch', a practice recorded in England in the seventeenth century, when those keeping watch were believed to be able to see the 'fetches' or wraiths of those who would die in the coming twelve-month. There is also an echo here of accounts of friends who make a pact that the first to die will appear to the other, usually to prove that there is an afterlife. As in other of Campbell's 'superstitions' taken from oral tradition, some reading in antiquarian and literary sources may have influenced the report. The story of the Spanish princess had been widely repeated, printed, and embroidered upon, as described at TOBERMORY (Western Isles).

See also COEFFIN CASTLE, LISMORE.

KILCHRENAN, LOCH AWE, ARGYLLSHIRE

A child was taken by the fairies from Killichrenan, now Kilchrenan, on Loch Awe, to the fairy dwelling in Nant Wood. Its father got it back by drawing a furrow round the fairy hillock with a plough. 'He had not gone far when he heard a cry behind him, and looking back found his child lying in the furrow.'

Drawing the furrow was twofold magic. A circle was traditional protection against supernatural spirits, as used for instance at CASTLE STALKER to guard a boy from the Devil, while the 'cold iron' of the ploughshare was always powerful against fairies and witches. John Gregorson Campbell, who recorded the story in *Superstitions of the Highlands and Islands of Scotland* (1900), learned this in childhood: 'The writer remembers well that, when a schoolboy, great confidence was put in a knife, of which he was the envied possessor, and in a nail, which another boy had, to protect us from a Fairy.' The fairy was said to appear at a spot near Campbell's road to school in

Appin, at 'the Hawthorn Bush between Black Nose and the Pass of the Dead'.

Such folk wisdom was not always attended to. Campbell gives another tale of a wife taken in childbed by the fairies. She appeared to her husband in his sleep and told him that by drawing a furrow three times round a certain hillock sunwise (*deiseil*), he could get her back. Unfortunately, he decided to consult his neighbours and in the end they agreed that it was better not to heed dreams. Consequently he did not draw the furrow and she did not return.

KILCHURN CASTLE, ARGYLLSHIRE

At the north-east end of Loch Awe, on a rocky outcrop almost surrounded by the water, stand the impressive ruins of Kilchurn (pronounced 'Kilhoorn') Castle. The tower house, with its massive defensive walls and barrack ranges, was struck by lightning in the 1760s and never restored.

The original building was founded in the fifteenth century by Sir Colin Campbell of Glenorchy, a Crusader. While in Palestine, according to a legend reported by Lord Archibald Campbell in 1885, Sir Colin had a strange dream which he could not interpret: consulting a monk, he was advised to return home immediately, as only his presence could avert a trouble about to descend on his family. He made all speed for Scotland – and as well that he did, for in his absence Baron MacCorquodale had persuaded Sir Colin's wife, Lady Margaret, that her husband had perished. She and MacCorquodale were about to be married, but on the wedding day itself Sir Colin arrived at the castle disguised as a beggar.

This 1895 print from *The Magazine of Art* shows Kilchurn Castle, founded in the fifteenth century by the crusader Sir Colin Campbell. Warned in a dream, he returned from Palestine just in time to stop his wife marrying another man.

When questioned as to what he wanted, he replied, 'To have my hunger satisfied and my thirst quenched.' He ate of the food, but refused to drink except from the hands of the lady of the house; and on her handing him a cup, he drank the contents, and returned it again to her with the ring she knew so well, which he had dropped into it.

The legend embodies the old and ever-popular theme of the 'homecoming husband' who arrives in the nick of time to prevent his wife marrying another – a story as old as Homer, who tells it of Odysseus and Penelope. In England, it was told of Sir Francis Drake, whose signal to his wife was a cannonball fired clean across the globe from the Antipodes. Here it is coupled with the motif of 'recognition by means of a ring', often attached to crusading knights. The requisite for both motifs is that the hero should be away on a journey lasting some years, like Odysseus' voyage, the Crusades, and Drake's circumnavigation of the world.

KILDALLOIG, KINTYRE, ARGYLLSHIRE

In 1885, Lord Archibald Campbell related a tradition concerning the estate of Kildalloig. A small conical hill on the property had a circle round the top, once upon a time the lair of a huge serpent which devoured sheep and cattle in immense quantities.

> At last a deliverer arose. A man engaged to fight the serpent on condition that a barn, which stood where the ship-building yard now is, should be placed at his disposal. The barn was at once given him. Causing a quantity of hay to be placed in it, he rode off to do battle with the serpent. On

arriving at the mound he found the serpent asleep. Riding up to it, he dealt it a tremendous blow with his sword. Although terribly wounded the beast followed hard after him. On coming to the shore, he plunged his horse into the sea and swam across the loch. By the time he reached the other side the beast was close on his heels. Riding into the barn by one door, he rapidly rode out at the other, shutting it immediately behind him. Round he rode to the one which the dragon had entered by, and had the satisfaction of seeing the serpent's tail disappearing into the barn, and they had the monster fast. They then set fire to the barn, and burned the dragon to death.

The loch mentioned is Campbeltown Loch, and the conical hill in question might be the circular Kildalloig Dun on the hillside overlooking the entrance to the loch on the south. The other possible candidate is Kildalloig Fort, its ramparts built round an oval, flat-topped hillock west-south-west of Kildalloig. In either case the tradition evidently arose as an explanation of the circle, as in the comparable story set at LINTON (Lothian & Borders).

KILMARONAG, ARGYLLSHIRE

A Tiree man told Lord Archibald Campbell about the last feudal battle in this part of the Highlands, fought on a field near Kilmaronag between the MacDougalls and the Campbells.

When both sides were assembled, went the tradition, their chiefs walked a little south of the battlefield to arrange an armistice. The place where they held their consultation was still known in the 1880s as Cnocan na Comhairle ('Council Hill'). Before going, they commanded their men not to budge unless they saw them raise their swords, but unfortunately as they were talking a snake crept from under a bush and they took up their weapons to kill it. Seeing them do so, their followers thought they had been given the signal and began the attack.

Finally only two men were left, both named John. John Campbell killed John MacDougall, and so the Campbells were the victors of the battle.

Lord Archibald goes on to tell a story of the 'restless dead'. An Irishwoman died at Kilmaronag and her spirit was often heard singing a dirge, expressing her longing to lie at Derry. At length an Irishman travelled that way who heard what the ghost said. He opened the grave, gathered the bones, and did as she wished, and after that the voice was never heard again at Kilmaronag.

Another spirit that could not rest until her bones were returned to her native land was the Spanish princess killed at TOBERMORY (Western Isles) and said to have been buried at KIEL.

KILMICHAEL GLASSARY, ARGYLLSHIRE

The parish of Kilmichael Glassary is packed with ancient monuments – cairns and standing stones, as well as the fort of DUNADD, and KILNEUAIR CHURCH. Many have stories to go with them, of which one of the oddest and most resonant is that attached to the Scodaig stone.

The rock bears natural cup-marks, probably as a result of its volcanic origins, but one of these has been 'improved' to enhance the tradition attached to it, which is that it carries hoofprints left by the horse of 'Scota, daughter of Pharaoh'. This Scota was the second wife of Míl Easpaíne, a fictional ancestor of the Irish people, whose name was invented by historians based on the Latin *miles Hispaniae*, 'soldier of Spain'. The idea of this Spanish ancestor seems to have grown from the supposed derivation of 'Hibernia' (the Latin name for Ireland) from Iberia.

The imaginary Míl and his equally imaginary forebears and descendants are described in the Irish *Lebor Gabála*, or 'Book of Invasions', composed in early medieval times and received as history by poets and scholars down to the nineteenth century. The Irish are said to have come from Scythia, and after many years living in Egypt and around the Caspian Sea, settled in Spain. Míl is reported as having married a princess in Scythia and later, after her death, travelling to Egypt where he took Scota as his second wife. Tradition credits him with thirty-two sons, twenty-four born of affairs in Spain before his departure for Scythia, two by his Scythian wife, and six by Scota. These conquered Ireland, and are the Milesians of Irish mythology.

This pseudo-history sheds no light on how and when Scota (whose name is simply the Latin word for an Irishwoman) came to be riding in Kilmichael Glassary, but the local story says that she landed here, mounted her horse, and leaped to land, leaving the hoofprints behind her.

KILMORE, NEAR OBAN, ARGYLLSHIRE

A man living near Oban, on his way home from Loch Awe, crossed the hills above Kilmore, where he was joined by three strangers. When he spoke to them, they gave no answer. Notwithstanding this, on arriving at a small public house by the roadside, he asked them in for a drink, but they said they had business to attend to. They warned him, however, not to leave the inn that night. They then turned off the high road onto a private track leading to a local gentleman's house.

The night was unusually stormy, and the Oban man stayed at the public house as he had been instructed. When he got up in the morning, he heard that the gentleman to whose house the three strangers had gone had died the previous evening, at just about the time they would have arrived. No one in the neighbourhood had seen them.

John Gregorson Campbell, telling this story in *Superstitions of the Highlands and Islands of Scotland* (1900), gives it as an example of 'coming for the dying', citing also the three demonic ravens who came for the soul of MICHAEL SCOT, THE WIZARD OF BALWEARIE (p. 62), and the twelve ravens who carried off a wicked robber in LOCH CON (Central & Perthshire).

KILNEUAIR, KILMICHAEL GLASSARY, ARGYLLSHIRE

About a mile east of the head of Loch Awe, in the parish of KILMICHAEL GLAS-SARY, is Kilneuair with its ruined church. Inside the church on the south wall, to the left of an earlier door, is a mark said to be the handprint of the Devil, who in the form of a decaying corpse once emerged from a grave to terrorise a tailor.

The story is the same, with minor variations, as the one told of SADDELL CASTLE. While in that story the Devil comes in the form of a giant, in most other versions it is a corpse or skeleton that appears, as in the famous tale of 'The Grey Paw' set at BEAULY (Southern Highlands). At DORNOCH CATHEDRAL (Northern Highlands), the tailor is sitting cross-legged in front of the altar when a skull comes rolling towards him which gradually builds into a whole skeleton, then gives chase and leaves its bony fingerprints on the doorpost.

The story of the tailor's encounter is a narrative version of 'The Strange Visitor', a cumulative tale in Robert Chambers's *Popular Rhymes* (1870 edition) which begins:

A wife was sitting at her reel [spinning wheel] ae night;
And aye she sat, and aye she reeled, and aye she wished for company.

In come a pair of 'braid braid soles' (broad broad feet) which sit down at her fireside. Still the wife sits, and still she spins, and still she wishes for company. Next come the 'sma' sma' legs', and so on up the body until finally a great big head sits down on the sma' sma' neck. Now the wife can talk to the 'visitor':

'What way hae ye sic braid braid feet?' quo' the wife.
'Muckle ganging, muckle ganging.'
[Much walking, much walking.]

Whenever she enquires about the broad bits of the body, the gruff reply is that their size is due to praying, sitting, carrying a broom, and so forth. When she asks about the small bits, the answer is a weird mourning wail. Finally she reaches the top and asks her final questions:

'What way hae ye sic a muckle muckle head?'
'Muckle wit, muckle wit.'
'What do you come for?'
'FOR YOU!'

Chambers comments, 'The figure is meant for that of Death.' He lists the rhyme among his 'Fireside Nursery Stories', and it is of course comparable to that other children's horror story 'The Golden Arm', given by Joseph Jacobs in *English Fairy Tales* (1894), in which a man digs up his dead wife to cut off her golden arm and then is visited by her ghost:

'What hast thou done with thy golden
   arm?'
'THOU HAST IT!'

Both 'The Strange Visitor' and 'The
Golden Arm' are designed to be spoken
aloud by the scarily flickering half-light of
a fire, which is why Chambers adds stage
directions for how the strange visitor's
replies to the wife should be recited, in
order to focus the children's attention and
arouse their vague apprehensions: 'Thus
wrought up, the concluding words come
upon them with such effect as generally to
cause a scream of alarm.' Hear this in
action in the film *Troop Beverly Hills*
(1989), in which the refrain 'Give me back
my Golden Arm!' of American versions is
rendered in hollow tones by a 'Wilderness
Girl' telling the story.

KINGARTH, BUTE

The seventeenth-century Kingarth session
records provide some fascinating details of
charms and spells used by supposed
witches. James King Hewison in 1893 gave
a description of how to discover criminals
by koskinomancy – divination using a
sieve. One blade of a pair of scissors was
driven into the wooden rim of the sieve,
which would then be allowed to dangle and
turn while a charm was spoken. Directions
for the procedure are given, writes Hewison, in 'The Universal Fortune-Teller':

Stick the points of the shears in the wood
of the sieve; let two persons support it,
balanced upright with their two fingers;
then read a certain chapter in the Bible
and ask S. Peter and S. Paul if A or B is
the thief, naming all the persons you suspect. On naming the real thief, the sieve
will suddenly turn about.

Questions could also be asked about love
affairs or other matters. On 24 April 1649

a woman was 'delated' (informed against)
on suspicion of using the spell, but it was
decided that her husband was the guilty
party.

Hewison goes on to mention a much
later instance of 'belief in necromancy' as
having occurred in Rothesay in 1857.

A child was pining away, without any
discoverable cause, when an Irish woman
informed the child's mother that it was a
case of the 'evil eye,' or bewitching. She
was permitted to use the following
charm, which she declared to be unfail-
ing: To place some water in a basin along
with some salt. A needle was to be
dropped into the mixture. If the needle
stood up on end the 'evil eye' would
cease its baleful influence, and the child
would recover. The charm wrought: the
needle stood erect; the boy immediately
recovered, and is still alive.

KING'S CAVE,
BLACKWATERFOOT, ARRAN

Robert the Bruce is said to have hidden in
the King's Cave on Arran between
Machrie Bay and Drumadoon Point. This
is one of several places at which the well-
known story of 'Bruce and the Spider' has
been set, another being UGADALE; at
Blackwaterfoot, a chair cut out of the solid
rock to the west of the entrance has been
pointed out as being where Bruce sat while
he received his object lesson, leading to the
partial destruction of the seat by souvenir
hunters.

A different tradition was recorded in 1772
by Thomas Pennant, who refers to the cave
as 'Fingal's Cave' – not to be confused with
the one on Staffa. He writes that FINGAL (p.
10) is said to have stayed on Arran for the
sake of hunting, and that around the cave
'are various very rude figures, cut on the

Robert the Bruce, shown here in an eighteenth-century engraving, is sometimes said to have been hiding in the King's Cave on Arran when he observed a spider spinning its web and learned his life-changing lesson about perseverance.

stone, of men, of animals, and of a *clymore* or two-handed sword: but whether these were the amusements of the *Fingallian* age, or of after-times, is not easy to be ascertained; for caves were the retreats of pirates as well as heroes'.

James Robertson in 1768 likewise observed 'figures of deer, hounds in chase, men of extraordinary stature with bows, swords, and durks', but by the beginning of the twentieth century these carvings had disappeared.

The cave has, as a matter of fact, been used for various communal purposes. During the eighteenth century, meetings of the Kilmorie Kirk Session were frequently held in the cave, and J. A. Balfour, writing in 1910, adds that 'men still living in Shisken tell how they received a large portion of their education within the cave; it was the school of the district for a considerable number of years.'

KINTRAW, ARGYLLSHIRE

Near the village of Kintraw is the hill of Gorlach. This may be what is called the Fairies' Hill in a story recounted by Lord Archibald Campbell in 1889:

Many years ago, the wife of the farmer at Kintraw fell ill and died, leaving two or three young children. The Sunday after the funeral the farmer and his servants went to church, leaving the children at home in charge of the eldest, a girl of about ten years of age. On the farmer's return the children told him their mother had been to see them, and had combed their hair and dressed them.

The children were told that this could not be true, but persisted in their statement and were punished for lying. The next Sunday, however, they said that the same thing had happened. The father now told his children that if their mother visited them again they were to ask her why she came. Next Sunday the eldest daughter put the question to her mother, who said that she had been carried off by the 'Good People' and could only get away for an hour or two on Sundays. If her coffin was opened, she added, it would be found to contain only a withered leaf.

The farmer, much perplexed, went to the minister for advice, who scoffed at the idea of any supernatural connection with the children's story, ridiculed the existence of the 'Good People', and would not allow the coffin to be opened. The matter was therefore allowed to rest. But, some little time after, the minister, who had gone to Lochgilphead for the day, was found lying dead near the Fairies' Hill, a victim, many people thought, to the indignation of the Fairy world he had laughed at.

The legend of a dead mother revisiting her childen is found in several countries. In a similar tale set at FEARN (Southern Highlands), the additional motif of a wicked stepmother gives a stronger reason for the spirit's return. Punishment for mocking the supernatural is also a theme that is widespread, as at AUCHINDARROCH. The unintentional moral for modern readers of this particular version might be always to believe your children, or conversely not to believe the minister.

KNAP, ARGYLLSHIRE

Opposite Shuna Island in Appin is the Cnap (meaning 'the Lump'), a name retained in the nineteenth century in Tigh a' Chnaip ('the House of the Lump'), the Gaelic name of the Balachulish hotel on the road to Glencoe, 'well-known to tourists'. The ownership of Knap by the MacMillans was attested by oral charter:

M 'Millans right to Knap
While waves strike rock.

A chief of the MacMillans, says John Gregorson Campbell in *Superstitions of the Highlands and Islands of Scotland* (1900), was once caught by a Glaistig who came up behind him and held him so tight he could not struggle, much less escape. She asked him if he had ever been in greater straits. He said, he had, and she asked when that had been. He said, 'Between plenty and penury,' upon which she let go her hold.

He said, 'I give my word I will not be weighed on the same scales again,' and stabbing her with his dirk killed her.

The story makes the point that a quick-witted reply, or the correct answer to a riddle, could free a captive from the fairies or other supernatural powers. It also demonstrates a belief that the Glaistig, though supernatural, could die.

See also THE MAIDEN OF INVERAWE (p. 24).

LARGIEBAAN, MULL OF KINTYRE, ARGYLLSHIRE

Writing in 1885, Lord Archibald Campbell records the legend of a large rock near the Largiebaan caves, said to have been the residence of a giant couple. A little way to the north, at Aonan More, lived another giant who fell in love with the wife at Largiebaan, and tried to persuade her to elope with him while her husband was absent on a fishing expedition.

He used all the flattery he could command; but that which seemed to have the most weight with her was his assuring her that she would get 'shell-fish in plenty upon the bonny shores of the Aonan.' So intent was he in pressing his suit that he took no heed of time. Happening to look seaward, what was his astonishment to see the enraged husband returning, and almost within a (giant's) bowshot of him, at the top of his speed! Off set the enamoured swain; but just when going over the hill, an arrow – sent after him by the jealous husband – overtook him, piercing him to the heart.

Giants are often associated with rocky, mountainous terrain, as for example at BENNACHIE (North East), where several landscape features are associated with the battles of two titanic figures.

LOCH AWE, ARGYLLSHIRE

In *Myths, Tradition and Story from Western Argyll* (1925), K. W. Grant tells the origin legend of Loch Awe. The familiar tale of 'The Overflowing Well', found in all Celtic-speaking lands, is here attributed to the negligence of the Cailleach (pronounced 'kaliach'), said to have been the guardian of a spring on top of Ben Cruachan.

She was charged with the duty of covering it with a slab of stone every evening at sundown, and of removing the lid at daybreak. But one evening, being aweary after driving her goats across Connel, she fell asleep by the side of the well.

The fountain overflowed, and a stream went rushing down the mountainside. As the flood broke open an outlet through the Pass of Brander, the roaring of the waters awoke the Cailleach, but her efforts to stem the torrent were in vain. It flowed into the plain, drowning all that stood in its path. Thus was formed Loch Awe.

The Cailleach was filled with such horror over the result of her lapse that she turned into stone and sits for ever among the rocky ruins at the Pass of Brander, overlooking the loch. This is the origin of Creag na Caillich, 'Old Wife's Rock', at the head of Loch Etive.

Though others mention the tradition before her, Grant's account is more minutely localised. A similar tale was told to account for Loch Eck in Cowal, where the Cailleach was also said to have been turned to stone, and a comparable legend is associated with LOCH KATRINE (Central & Perthshire).

Of greater interest to cryptozoologists is a brief account in John Gregorson Campbell's *Superstitions of the Highlands and Islands of Scotland* (1900) of the Big Beast of Loch Awe, an animal with twelve legs which was to be heard breaking the ice in winter. 'Some say it was like a horse, others, like a large eel,' writes Campbell: he must mean something along the lines of an enormous centipede. Also said to haunt Loch Awe, as well as other lakes, was the Water-bull. John MacCulloch wrote in 1819 that of the 'imaginary specimens of natural history' found in the Highlands, 'the water-bull seems as yet to maintain his ground with some obstinacy; and, like other goblins, is not in want of positive ocular testimony in proof of his existence.'

He is occasionally angled for with a sheep made fast to a cable secured round an oak, but as yet no tackle has been found sufficiently strong to hold him.

He adds in a footnote that on one of his excursions he met a farmer watching for one of these creatures, while his two sons were poking around with dung forks in the deep holes where the beast was supposed to be lying. The farmer himself was armed with a musket loaded with six-pences, 'as it was reputed that he is vulnerable by silver shot only'. Why the farmer should have wanted to shoot the animal is not explained: the Water-bull is usually represented as harmless and indeed benign. Perhaps there was some confusion with the twelve-legged monster mentioned by Campbell, or with dangerous KELPIES AND WATER-HORSES (p. 364).

See also GUARDIAN OF THE WILD (p. 352).

Many stories were told in Scotland of witches who could turn themselves into hares. If such an animal was injured by a huntsman, the witch would later be found to bear the wound on her own body.

LOCH BAILE A' GHOBHAINN, LISMORE

A young man was out shooting on Lismore and when he was near Loch Baile a' Ghobhainn (Balnagown Loch) he started a hare and fired at it. The hare gave an unearthly scream, and then for the first time it crossed his mind that there *were* no hares on Lismore. Terrified by the thought, he threw his gun down and fled. Next day he returned for the gun, and heard that a woman of the neighbourhood reputed to be a witch was laid up with a broken leg. From time to time after that, this woman or something that looked like her would meet him and give him a thrashing. 'This preyed on his mind, and he never came to any good. He proved brooding, idle, and useless.'

This story, recorded by John Gregorson Campbell in *Witchcraft and Second Sight in the Highlands and Islands* (1902), is a good localised example of the international tale in which a witch is wounded in animal form but bears the marks on her

human body. James King Hewison, minister of Bute, wrote in 1895:

The belief that a witch could assume the form of a hare was so tenaciously held by one wise laird of Ambrisbeg, that he would on no account molest the timid rodents. A worthy Buteman still tells that his father used to recount how, when herding, he saw a hare stand up and suck a cow; and although he hounded the collie upon the thief, the dog would not give chase to what even the dog realised to have been a witch. It is also said that one of the doctors of Rothesay, in the past generation, was called upon to extract a crooked silver sixpence from the body of an old woman who, in the shape of a hare, had received this charmed shot by a dead marksman.

Stories of witches as hares go back to at least the eighteenth century, and a comparable tale is set at MAXTON (Lothian & Borders). The hare's generally uncanny reputation may owe something to its size and speed – it is larger and faster than the more approachable rabbit – and the spring phenomenon of male hares fighting has led to the proverbial phrase 'mad as a March hare'.

MACHRIE MOOR STONE CIRCLE, ARRAN

The island of Arran is one of the richest archaeological and historical sites in Britain. When Martin Martin visited the island in about 1695, he was much impressed by the extraordinary landscape of Machrie Moor, and made it his business to investigate the supposed history of the site:

> In the *Moor* on the *East-side Druin-cruey*, there is a Circle of Stones, the Area is about thirty Paces; there is a Stone of same shape and kind about forty Paces to the *West* of the Circle, the Natives say that this Circle was made by the Giant *Fin-Mac-Cowl*, and that to the single Stone *Bran-Fins-Mac-Cowls* Hunting-dog was usually tied . . . There is a Circle of Big-stones a little to the *South* of *Druin Cruey*, the Area of which is about twelve Paces; there is a broad thin Stone in the middle of this Circle, supported by three lesser Stones, the Ancient Inhabitants are reported to have burnt their Sacrifices on the broad Stone, in time of Heathenism.

Fionn mac Cumhaill, or FINGAL (p. 10), is associated with many giant-sized monuments and objects in Scotland, including the GIANTS' GRAVES, also on Arran. His dog Bran is also remembered at various sites, such as CAISTEAL A CHOIN DUIBH. He was a fairy dog, and parti-coloured:

> Bran had yellow feet,
> Its two sides black and belly white;
> Green was the back of the hunting
>   hound,
> Its two pointed ears blood-red.

The green coat was characteristic of fairy dogs. Bran had a venomous spur on his foot with which he killed any living creature he struck, and when he ran at speed he appeared to be three dogs intercepting the deer at three passes – a story which is echoed as a joke in the 'tall tales' of raconteurs such as Bilzy Young of DUNBLANE (Central & Perthshire).

MINGARY, ARGYLLSHIRE

Mrs Lilian Lowe of Harborne, Birmingham, wrote to Tim Dinsdale, author of *The Leviathans*, of a sea monster she, her husband, and her cousin had sighted off the west coast of Scotland on 21 June 1965. They were standing on the end of Mingary Pier, near Kilchoan, looking out over the sea, which was glassy and calm. Her husband was looking through binoculars (specified as Taylor Hobson ex-army x6) at the ruins of MINGARY CASTLE.

> I saw what I thought to be a seal appear above the water, about 100 yards offshore. Then, another hump appeared directly behind it and a few feet away. As it moved I came to the conclusion that the two humps belonged to one object. I said, 'What's that?' My husband immediately sighted the creature but was silent. He said afterwards he was too amazed to speak.

He could see a huge shape about forty feet long in the water and at first thought it was a submarine. Then he noticed what seemed to be legs or flippers paddling at the side of the body and creating turbulence under the water, though Mrs Lowe and her cousin could only see the two humps moving steadily along. They appeared to be solid, dark, and shiny, the texture of the skin like hide. She was anxious to see through the binoculars, but just as she got it in view the creature submerged. Her husband, who had excellent eyesight and had seen basking sharks off Cornwall, said he had never seen anything like it in his life.

In the opinion of Graham McEwan, who categorised alleged 'sea serpents' into different types, this seemed to be one of the long-necked sort with a fat-covered body, humps of which may show above water. *See also* THE LOCH NESS MONSTER (p. 442).

MINGARY CASTLE, ARGYLLSHIRE

Mingary Castle, perched dramatically on a rock stack on the shore just south-east of Kilchoan, is visible from afar and by the same token commands wide views over Mull and Morvern. Begun in the thirteenth century and modified off and on until the eighteenth, it has had a colourful history of attack, defence, and siege.

Attached to it was one version of the story of Luran, a tale widely distributed and evidently popular in the West Highlands, told here by John Gregorson Campbell (who spells the name 'Mingarry' but means the castle in Ardnamurchan, not the settlement in South Uist).

Luran was a butler boy who entered a fairy dwelling one night and found the company feasting and making merry within. A shining cup was produced and passed round the table; whoever held it could name whatever liquor they wished for, and would find the cup full of the same drink.

Whenever a dainty appeared on the table, Luran was asked, 'Did you ever see the like of that in Mingarry Castle?' At last, the butler boy wished the cup to be full of water, and throwing its contents on the lights, and extinguishing them, ran away with it in his hand. The Fairies gave chase.

Some one among them called out to Luran to make for the shore. He reached the friendly shelter, and made his way below high-water mark to the castle, which he entered by a stair leading to the sea. The cup remained long in Mingarry Castle, but was at last lost in a boat that sank at Mail Point (*Rutha Mhàil*) [*Rubha a' Mhàil*].

This 'stair' may serve to date the story: the castle has no good anchorage nearby and the sea-gate in its south wall is thought to have been added in the late sixteenth century.

Similar tales of the theft of a fairy cup were told at DUNVEGAN CASTLE and RAASAY (both Western Isles) among other places. Here the 'some one' who calls out to Luran with good advice may be another mortal, stolen by the fairies; like the fair-haired boy at BEINN IADAIN, such people often help other humans who find themselves in a fairy mound.

In a Lochaber tale involving 'Luran', he is not a boy but a dog, and there is no enchanted cup. A farmer who owned land above Brackletter had a white cow which was stolen by the fairies, and to add insult to injury they brought it back every night to the farm to feed on his corn. He set his hound Luran in pursuit of them, but they threw bread behind them, which the dog stopped to devour. The fairies were heard saying among themselves, 'Swift would be Luran if it were not for the hardness of his bread.' In the late nineteenth century, the field where this happened was still known as the Field of the White Cow.

As Campbell rightly observes, there is a 'want of uniformity' in popular tales of this kind.

POINT HOUSE CAIRN, BUTE

Point House Cairn, in North Bute, is a large cairn that was mostly destroyed between 1841 and 1858. At its centre was a stone cist, opened by Malcolm Mackinnon of Kames Castle Lodge, and afterwards built into the wall of the castle gate. James King Hewison, writing in 1893, gives the legend as told to him by Mackinnon:

> The cairn covered the remains of a great hero. He was wont to wear a belt of gold, which, being charmed, protected him on the field of battle. One day, however, as he rode a-hunting accompanied by his sister, the maid, coveting the golden talisman, prevailed upon him to lend it to her. While thus unprotected he was killed – whether by enemies or mischance the attenuated tradition does not clearly indicate; and this cairn marked the warrior's grave.

Who the 'great hero' was is an open question. An 1848 source names Spens, a young laird of Wester Kames, but Hewison comments that 'this is not in keeping with the age of the cists found in the cairn'; his theory is that the cairn held the remains of Aidan, King of Alban (r. 574–606). Rulicheddan, the farm where the cairn (or what is left of it) stands, was referred to in the eighteenth century as 'Realigeadhain', which Hewison translates as, roughly, 'relics of Aidan'.

Other charmed objects, held to protect the life of the owner or wearer, feature in Scottish legend: examples traditionally obtained through pacts with the Devil are Claverhouse's coat, described at DUNDEE (North East), and General Dalyell's boots, said to have been preserved at LINGO HOUSE (Central & Perthshire). Hewison's 'attenuated tradition' does not mention whether the magic belt was an infernal or a fairy gift.

RANNOCH MOOR, ARGYLLSHIRE/PERTHSHIRE

See CENTRAL & PERTHSHIRE.

ROCKHILL, LOCH AWESIDE, ARGYLLSHIRE

An account of a hereditary apparition was passed on to Lord Archibald Campbell in the late nineteenth century by Miss Isabel Smith. Her grandfather Dugald Campbell was having a new house built at Achlian, and while it was being constructed he stayed for a while at Rockhill, near Port Sonachan, Loch Aweside. This house belonged to another Mr Campbell whose mother was of the MacDougalls, 'treacherous friends and implacable foes' of the Campbells from the time of Robert the Bruce.

> Whilst occupying this house of Rockhill, and during hay-harvest, as my grandmother, Mrs Campbell, and another lady – a Miss Lindsay . . . were busy washing up the breakfast dishes in the dining-room . . . they were startled by a noise coming from the chimney. They looked to see its cause, when to their surprise they beheld two huge bloodhounds rise as if from the hearthstone, stretch themselves, and trot out at the window – then closed. They were so astonished by the occurrence, that they were for a little silenced. Miss Lindsay found expression first, saying –
> '*Sin coin Mhicdhùghaill is bi'dh feòil 'g a reubadh*' – i.e., 'These are Macdougall's dogs, and flesh will be torn.'
> The MacDougall's bloodhounds were the terror of the land for many centuries.

Mrs Campbell and Miss Lindsay agreed to tell as few people as possible what they had seen, but they did tell Miss Smith's other grandfather, Patrick Smith of Croft. He was a truthful man of great integrity, and also a believer in dreams and forewarnings, of which there were many in his family. He regarded the ladies' vision as such a forewarning, and often told Dugald Campbell of Achlian and his wife to steer well clear of anything in which Campbell of Rockhill had even a distant hand. Campbell of Achlian used to laugh at this advice, but lived to wish it had been taken.

Some years after he had left Rockhill, Campbell of Achlian, who was a Justice of the Peace, became caught up in a dispute as to the boundaries between the Rockhill property and land belonging to the Duke of Argyll. As Achlian had surveyed these lands some years previously, he was called in to arbitrate. Going over the lands once more and taking his earlier chart with him, he saw at once that Rockhill was claiming huge advantages. He therefore pronounced in favour of Argyll, an offence that was never forgiven.

Campbell of Achlian rented his farmland from Colonel Campbell of Monzie, and in the last year of his lease, following an agricultural depression, he fell behind with his rent. Unfortunately Monzie's factor (estate manager) was Campbell of Rockhill, who immediately foreclosed and served Achlian with notice to quit. All Achlian's property had to be sold, and Rockhill had so arranged things that he was able to buy most of it at bargain prices. The sale was ruinous to Achlian.

Campbell of Monzie had been absent on the continent and knew nothing of what had been going on. When he found out that his friend Dugald Campbell had been forced to leave he was furious. Rockhill was denounced and thrown out of the house, and eventually another Campbell was put in possession of the property, in an effort at 'repairing the wrongs that could not be righted'.

SADDELL CASTLE, KINTYRE, ARGYLLSHIRE

Saddell Castle was built in the early sixteenth century for the Bishop of Argyll. In one of the pillars of its gate are indentations which Kintyre tradition claims are the finger-and thumbprints of the Devil.

The story goes that the Laird of Saddell mischievously wagered a village tailor to spend a night in the graveyard of the ruined mid twelfth-century Abbey of Saddell, which was thought to be haunted. The tailor accepted the challenge, and they agreed that he would take with him enough cloth to make a pair of trousers in the course of the night.

Off he went and sat cross-legged tailor-fashion on a tomb. Suddenly the earth began to rumble and a slab lying on the ground nearby started to heave. Then an enormous head appeared, and the tailor heard a voice saying, 'Do you see this great head of mine?' 'Ay, ay, I'm seeing it,' said the wee tailor, 'but I'm too busy making my breeks.'

Then an enormous pair of shoulders appeared and the voice enquired, 'Do you see these great shoulders of mine?' And the wee tailor said, 'Ay, ay!' but went on stitching.

The earth rumbled again and a great body appeared, and the voice asked, 'Do you see this great body of mine?' 'Ay, ay, I'm seeing it,' said the wee tailor, 'but I must get finished with my breeks.'

Then a great leg and foot appeared and stamped on the slab so hard that the whole graveyard quaked. 'Do you see this great foot of mine?' asked the voice. 'Ay, ay, I do that,' replied the wee tailor, 'but my breeks are finished, though the stitches may be ower long.'

Tucking the trousers under his arm and the thimble in his pocket, he cut off the thread and quickly took to his heels. The Devil – for it was he – followed in hot pursuit. Down the glen ran the tailor, towards Saddell Castle, the Devil gaining on him every step. The tailor just managed to reach the castle gate and close it fast behind him. In his frustrated rage, the Devil smote one of the pillars supporting the gate, 'and the imprint of his fingers and thumb may be seen there to this day,' says Alasdair Alpin MacGregor, telling this story in 1937.

It is told in several other places in Scotland: one is the church at Fincharn, also on Loch Awe, and another is the old chapel of KILNEUAIR.

SOUTHEND, KEIL POINT, KINTYRE, ARGYLLSHIRE

Under an overhanging rock, close by on the roadside, is St Columba's Well, and on the top of a hillock, overlooking the west end of the burial ground there is a flat rock bearing on its top the impress of two feet, made, it seems, by those of the saint whilst he stood marking out and hallowing the spot on which his chapel should rest.

This account is quoted by James MacKinlay in 1893. St Columba's landing place in Scotland is traditionally held to have been near Southend village at Keil Point.

St Columba or Colm Cille was born in the sixth century in Donegal, Northern Ireland. He was of royal blood, but instead of claiming a throne he founded monasteries in Ireland, and at the age of forty sailed across the Irish Sea to promulgate his faith in Scotland, where his first choice of residence is sometimes said to have been CLACHAN on Lismore. His pre-eminence in the history of the early Christian Church in Scotland is due not only to his personal achievement and obvious charisma, but also to the biography, written a century after his death, by Adomnan, abbot of Iona. Stories of the saint are widespread, and several landscape features bear his name both here and in Ireland.

See also SAINTS OF SCOTLAND (p. 490); SCOTLAND'S HOLY AND HEALING WELLS (p. 44).

STRACHUR, ARGYLLSHIRE

Peter Campbell was born in Inveraray in 1839. In 1882, he repeated to Lord Archibald Campbell some old tales he remembered hearing from his aunt Agnes, including one about the Duke of Argyll – either the first or the second duke, said Peter, although from the context of Queen Anne's death it should have been the third, who inherited the title in 1743. The duke was in London, and was due to be presented with a fine embroidered coat by some courtiers, but though they pretended friendship, they were jealous of his favoured position at court and ordered the coat to be stuffed with poison. A tailor named MacKonochie from Strachur worked in the tailor's shop where the coat was being made, and warned the duke of the plot. When the master-tailor arrived to fit the coat, the duke asked him to try it on first, so he could see how well it looked. The tailor demurred, saying, 'I can't do that, as that would be taking the honour from my Lord Duke.'

'But,' said the Duke, drawing a sabre, 'I insist on you trying it on.'

Much against his will, the master-tailor was eventually forced to agree. The apartment they were in was well heated, helping the poison to act quickly, and after having the coat on for a short while the man dropped down dead. As a reward for his loyalty the duke gave MacKonochie money to buy up a lot of black cloth: Queen Anne was then on her deathbed, and when she died (1744) there was such a rush for mourning clothes that MacKonochie could name his own price. He later returned to Scotland, his fortune made.

Also included in Archibald Campbell's *Records of Argyll* (1885) is a quite different story involving a duke of Argyll and a coat, this one told by George Clarke, a gamekeeper at Rosneath.

It is said that the morning John Roy (second Duke) left Inverary for the wars in Flanders, he was met at Boshang by an old man named Sinclair, who presented the Duke with a small round stone taken out of the head of a white otter that the sea had cast ashore, and which bore a charm. The man said, 'If you will accept this from me, you will live to come back to your own country again.' The Duke accepted; and the story has it that after a hard-fought battle his Grace would unbutton his coat and give himself a shake, when the bullets would fly off him as snow-flakes fly off a person when shaking themselves. This was a much credited tale, and believed in by persons the writer knew.

Possession of a bulletproof coat was also attributed to 'Bluidy Clavers' of DUNDEE (North East), a tradition which may have influenced Clarke's tale.

STRONTIAN, ARGYLLSHIRE

A story located at Strontian concerns a Glaistig that came after dark and worked in the smithy there. As John Gregorson Campbell tells it in *Superstitions of the Highlands and Islands of Scotland* (1900):

The smith was very much annoyed at the noises in the smithy at night, and at finding in the morning tools mislaid and the smithy in confusion. He resolved to stay up and find out the cause. He stood in the dark, behind the door, with the hammer on his shoulder ready to strike whatever should enter. The Glaistig came to the door, accompanied by her bantling, or *Isein* (*i.e.* a young chicken). The chicken thought he heard a noise, and said, 'Something moving, little woman.' 'Hold your tongue, wretch,' she said, 'it is only the mice.' At this point the smith struck the old one on the head with his hammer, and caught hold of the little one. On this, the *Isein* reproached his mother by saying, 'Your old grey pate has got a punching; see now if it be the mice.' Before the smith let his captive go, the Glaistig left a parting gift – that the son should succeed the father as smith in the place till the third generation. This proved to be the case, and the last was the smith in Strontian some forty years ago.

The Glaistig's 'young one' goes by different names (*isein*; *gòthan*, 'perky little fellow'; or *méilleachan*, 'a bleater', i.e. a lamb). It is never said, however, that the Glaistig has a mate, so how she comes to have offspring remains a mystery.

See also THE MAIDEN OF INVERAWE (p. 24).

TORRYLIN (TORLIN) CAIRN, ARRAN

Torrylin, or Torlin, Cairn is a long chambered cairn at the mouth of Kilmorie Water, on the east bank of the stream. The tomb was plundered before 1860, and the robber is said to have taken home the largest of the human skulls he found. As soon as he entered his house its walls were struck as if by a tornado.

Again and again the avenging blast swept over his dwelling, though not a sigh of the gentlest breeze was heard in the neighbouring wood. The affrighted victim hastened to re-bury the bones in their desecrated grave, but day and night shadowy phantoms continued to haunt his

Scotland's Holy and Healing Wells

Near Munlochy in the Black Isle, Ross and Cromarty, is St Boniface's Well, long reputed to possess healing powers. Pilgrims seeking a cure would leave as an offering a 'cloutie' (rag) torn from their clothes, hanging the scrap on a tree or bush nearby. Nobody would remove the rags, since it was believed that anyone who interfered with them would take on the ill health they represented. To this day the well is festooned with hundreds of pieces of cloth, so many in fact that the area has become rather an eyesore.

Few modern visitors hope for a miraculous cure, but the site is still visited as a wishing well. The ritual is to spill a few drops of well-water three times on the ground, tie a rag on a tree, make the sign of the cross, and then drink some of the water.

Rags, ribbons, handkerchiefs, and so forth were and still are often left by springs and wells as votive offerings (gifts signifying a vow). Today, indeed, the practice is becoming more common: clouties are found at wells where they were never seen even twenty years ago, signifying the renewed popularity of pilgrimage to sacred sites. At ST FILLAN'S POOL (Central & Perthshire) in the eighteenth century, not only human garments but halters and ropes were deposited, by those who wanted their sick animals cured. Here the process for healing involved complete immersion, a practice impossible at St Boniface's Well, which consists only of a pipe from which the water flows into a small stone basin. Some 'holy wells' are not strictly speaking wells at all, but surface springs, ponds, or even water that has collected in a tree stump or a hollow stone.

Many saints are remembered at springs and pools, and several are said to have supernaturally created the wells which bear their names. One of these is St Medan or Medana, an Irish princess who developed a Christian community on the Rhinns of Galloway in the early medieval period. A former suitor is said to have followed Medan, but she escaped across Luce Bay on a stone which miraculously became a boat. Her besotted lover, however, pursued her, saying he could not live without her beautiful eyes, whereupon she plucked them out and threw them at his feet. On the spot a spring began to flow in which the saint washed her face, and her sight was restored. The spring later became known as Chincough or Kingcost Well, and its water was reputed to cure whooping cough (rather than eye afflictions, as one might expect); it can still be visited, although it is hidden among the rocks and is difficult to find.

ST CATHERINE'S WELL, Edinburgh (Lothian & Borders) contains minerals which may help to heal skin complaints, and other water sources known

Holy wells and springs can be found throughout Scotland, even on the most remote islands. Many are reputed to possess healing powers.

as chalybeate springs are impregnated with iron salts. In the eighteenth century, some were developed as commercial spas where the sick would both bathe in and drink of the waters. One of these, the Doo Wells at Innerleithen, originally had no sacred associations but later became known as St Ronan's Well after Sir Walter Scott's novel of that name was published in 1823.

Although most of Scotland's holy wells are linked to saints, especially local Celtic ones, there are other sites with fairy lore attached to them, like Tamlane's Well at CARTERHAUGH (Lothian & Borders), associated with the ballad of 'Young Tamlane' in which a youth is held captive by the Fairy Queen. A tale reported by the folklorist Anne Ross has more macabre overtones: in the 1970s she was taken to Tobar a Chinn, 'the Well of the Head', in a place she identifies only as 'an isolated township in Wester Ross' where some 200 years earlier a local woman had committed suicide and been buried on the moor (traditionally, suicides were not laid in consecrated earth). After a time, 'her skull appeared miraculously lying on the surface of the ground', and was then placed in a stone container like a small coffin by a well a little higher up the hill. From then onwards epileptics were cured by drinking the well-water out of the skull itself, a ritual still sometimes practised, according to Ross, in the late twentieth century.

See also SOUTHEND (Argyllshire & Islands); CARFIN LOURDES GROTTO (Glasgow & Ayrshire); ST TRIDUANA'S WELL; WHITEKIRK (Lothian & Borders); ST TREDWELL'S LOCH (Orkney & Shetland Islands).

mind and track his steps, and a few months after the commission of his rash deed, whilst riding along the high road towards Lag, he was thrown from his horse over a steep embankment, and dashed against the rocks of the stream beneath.

To this account, written in 1861, John MacArthur adds that the tradition was then well known in Arran, 'and has tended to deepen the feelings of superstitious dread with which these monuments are generally regarded'.

TOWARD CASTLE, INVERCHAOLIN, BUTE

When the Lamonts of Cowal lived in their stronghold of Toward Castle, young Lamont and a companion were hunting one day in the Forest of Etive. In the valley called Greyfir Shoulder they met the son and heir of MacGregor of Glen Strae, accompanied by one or two followers, and the men continued hunting together.

As dusk fell, they went to the Kingshouse Inn for the night and a quarrel arose which ended with Lamont stabbing MacGregor and fleeing into the night. Eventually he found a house with a light in the window, and with MacGregor's men hard on his heels he asked there for protection, which was granted. Little did he know that this was the house of MacGregor of Glen Strae; nor did MacGregor have any idea that he had given shelter to his own son's slayer, until young MacGregor's followers arrived.

Despite the lamentations of his wife and family, and the protests of his son's men, MacGregor was true to his word. Lamont stayed safely in his house for a time, until one morning MacGregor in person conducted him across the hills to Loch Fyne and provided a boat for Lamont to row himself over the loch to Toward Castle and safety.

Some years later, the MacGregors were ousted by the Campbells, and MacGregor himself, now an old man, was driven into Cowal and forced to ask for refuge at Toward Castle. By now he had forgiven young Lamont for killing his son, while Lamont was glad to repay the man who had earlier spared his life. So it was that, in time, MacGregor breathed his last at Toward Castle and was buried by the chapel of Toward-ann Uilt, far from the tomb of his forebears.

This story is told by Alasdair Alpin MacGregor in *The Peat-Fire Flame* (1937) as an outstanding example of the operation of the old Highland code of hospitality and safe refuge given to any who sought it. In the tale told of INVERAWE, the conflict was more tragically played out between this obligation and that demanding vengeance for the blood of kindred.

UGADALE, KINTYRE, ARGYLLSHIRE

The story most people know about Robert the Bruce is the legend of 'Bruce and the Spider'. This tells of how, fleeing from the English after the Scottish defeat at the battle of Falkirk (1298), Bruce found shelter in a cave. As he sat gloomily considering his future – or lack of it – his eye was caught by a spider at the entrance to the cave trying to spin its web from the ceiling to the wall. Each time the first strand was placed across the cave mouth it became detached from its anchorage on the roof. But the spider did not give up. It set to work a second time, then a third, a fourth, a fifth. At the sixth attempt, the strand held and the spider could finish its web. Bruce had learned his lesson well:

'Try, try and try again.' Instead of abandoning his ambitions, he took up the struggle once more and in 1314 finally defeated the English at the battle of Bannockburn.

Several different places have laid claim to this story. They include Inverurie in Aberdeenshire, the KING'S CAVE on Arran, and Uamh an Righ ('Cave of the King') at Craigruie near Balquhidder, as well as a cave on Rathlin Island in Ireland where Bruce took refuge in 1306, not long after he had been crowned King of Scotland.

Be that as it may, according to an Argyllshire tradition given by N. M. Kelly Robertson to Lord Archibald Campbell in the late nineteenth century, Bruce landed at Portrigh near the Aird of Carradale and from there made his way down to Ugadale, where he came in the evening to the house of a family called MacKay. Without telling them who he was, he asked for lodgings, which were granted to him. Then, sitting down by the fire, he asked, 'Did you hear about the travelling guest that goes about?'

'What is he?' asked Mrs MacKay.

The king replied, 'That poor fellow they call Robert the Bruce.'

In great indignation, Mrs MacKay took up the tongs, exclaiming, 'Thou impudent rascal!' Her husband and second son, she said, were with the Bruce, and if he wished it, he would have her other son too. (The disguised king's impudence must lie in his disrespectful reference to 'that poor fellow'.)

He was taken to the barn and put to bed, and before he rose in the morning the spider climbed the baulks on the barn-roof six times, which was the same number of times Robert was unsuccessful in battles, and at last succeeded. This is a token from heaven, thought the King to himself, and I will attempt it another time.

In the morning, MacKay's son accompanied the king across country. When they came to the top of the hill at Arnickile, Bruce (who must have revealed his true identity by this time) asked the boy to look around, and however far he could see, he and his family would be granted that extent of land if the Scots won the next battle. The boy replied that he wished only for the family's own farm and the one they had passed on Arnickile hill. When the battle of Bannockburn was gained, MacKay got a charter to the lands the boy had named.

'Portrigh' was supposedly named after Bruce's landing here, the name interpreted as 'the king's port'. Portree on Skye is similarly said to be so called from a visit of James V in 1540, but the name is explained by modern etymologists as 'harbour (*port*) of the slope (*ruigheadh*)'.

As for the priority of Ugadale over any other site for the tale of 'Bruce and the Spider', Campbell observes that as Bruce's fortunes were at their lowest ebb when he landed in Argyllshire, 'the above legend has strong probabilities in its favour.'

CENTRAL & PERTHSHIRE

The counties of Clackmannanshire, Dunbartonshire, Fife,
Kinross-shire, Perthshire, and Stirlingshire

ABERFOYLE, PERTHSHIRE

See THE MINISTER AND THE FAIRIES
(p. 112).

ALDIE, KINROSS-SHIRE

Before the Reformation, there lived in the
village of Aldie an old woman known as
'Muckle Meg', or the Witch of Aldie. No
one knew where she came from, or what her
origins were, but she was what was known
as a 'skilly body' (someone credited with
healing powers). She could work cures on
horses, cows and sheep, and even people.
Though regarded on account of this as
'unchancy', her fame spread far and wide
and young people would come to her cottage to hear their fortunes, good or bad. She
knew the virtues of herbs and owned a
'Tade's Stane' (toad-stone) about the size
of a pigeon's egg, supposedly removed from
the head of a toad and capable of healing
venomous bites and sores. Though its surface was normally smooth, she would put it
in boiling water, when it would become
rough as sandstone, before applying it to the
diseased part.

Meg's cottage stood apart from the rest of
the village. About half a mile away, on the
summit of a mound, stood a huge ash tree,
hollow in the centre and full of holes. This
tree was seen at night lit up by flames, as if
fire had been kindled within it. No one
would go near it after dark and everyone
feared it. Finally a deputation of women
went to consult Muckle Meg but she was
evasive in her answers. When they threatened to punish her if she did not answer, she
replied, 'Ye dauna for your vera lives lay a
single finger-neb upon me, for I'll gang
ower to room [Rome] in a jiffey and get
protection frae the laird.' They wondered at
this, for Meg was poor and could not afford
the voyage. Their wonder grew to terror
when they asked how she could get there
and she replied, 'O, just gi'e me the half o'
an egg shell, and I'll be there by some time
the morn.' Stopping to hear no more, the
women rushed from the house and the news
sped through the village till everyone was
saying, 'Meg *maun* be a witch!'

Toad-stones, supposedly removed from toads'
heads, were reputed to have magical properties and
healing powers, and were among the amulets cherished by witches such as 'Muckle Meg' of Aldie.

Towards evening of that day, her cottage was surrounded but she was not to be found. Months passed and there was no sign of her. Then at the year's end she returned with a paper signed (says tradition) by the laird, which put a stop to people harassing her. But she had not been back many weeks when she died and was buried. It was said that she did not lie long, for a 'big touzie [rough, hairy] man wi' horns and a long tail gaed to the kirkyard, houkit her up, and vanished in a blench o' fire'.

When Muckle Meg said she would go to Rome to get protection from 'the laird', she may have meant the Pope rather than the local landowner: there are, perhaps, confused memories here of traditions concerning the flying visit to the Vatican made by MICHAEL SCOT, THE WIZARD OF BALWEARIE (p. 62). Meg was, however, also said to have accompanied the Laird of Aldie on an expedition to the Holy Land, and used her powers to prevent the fulfilment of his vow to climb Mount Sinai. It was reported that the laird, on awakening one morning, found written on his arm:

'The Laird of Aldie you may be,
But the top of Mount Sinai you'll never see.'

And he never did, though he returned safe and sound to his native land.

BALCARRES, FIFE

Earl Colin of Balcarres was the chief political agent in Scotland for James VII and II, King of Scotland and England, and a friend of John Graham of Claverhouse, Viscount Dundee, commander of the Jacobite forces. At dawn on 28 July 1689, the earl awoke and saw the curtains of his bed drawn back. There by his bedside stood 'Bonnie Dundee', with his long curled locks and his glittering breastplate. Colin was dumbfounded to see him there, since as far as he knew the viscount was many miles away.

Claverhouse gazed sorrowfully at the earl for some time, his face pale and stern, then turned towards the fireplace and leaned for a time on the chimney piece. Then, with a last look at Earl Colin, he passed out through the door without either of them speaking a word.

Earl Colin had no suspicion at the time that the uncanny was involved and was only astonished at his friend's presence and behaviour. Leaping from his bed, he called repeatedly on him to return, but received no answer. In that moment, he heard later, the viscount had been killed at the battle of Killiecrankie by a silver bullet that pierced his right spule-blade (shoulder blade).

The reason why Claverhouse merited a *silver* bullet is that, like some other military leaders of the time, he was reputed to be IN LEAGUE WITH THE DEVIL (p. 142). That has little if anything to do with the appearance of his wraith. There are many stories of people being seen at the moment of their death by distant loved ones, as for instance at THURSO (Northern Highlands).

See also DUNDEE (North East).

BALCOMIE CASTLE, FIFE

Balcomie Castle was said to be haunted by the ghost of a boy starved to death 500 years or so ago. According to James Wilkie, who dates these events around the time of the battle of Flodden in 1513, the Laird of Balcomie had in his service a lad who loved music and incessantly blew the ancient equivalent of a penny tin whistle at the top of his lungs. Early on a dark winter morning, the boy was

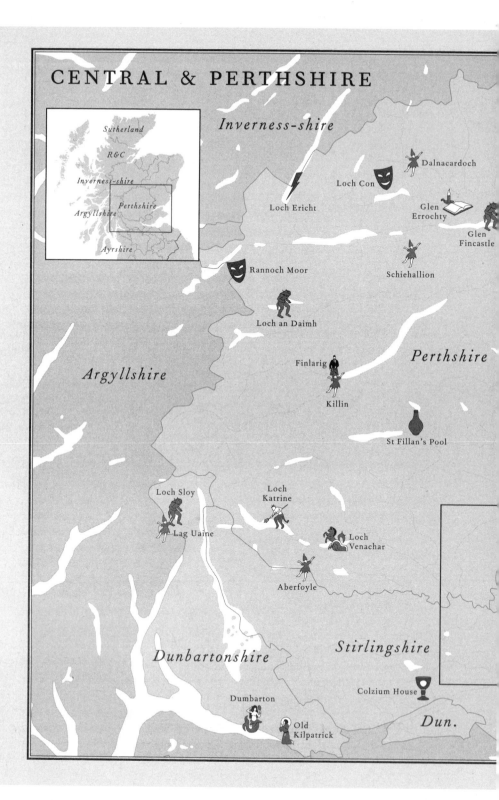

CENTRAL & PERTHSHIRE

Inverness-shire

Sutherland

R & C

Inverness-shire

Perthshire

Argyllshire

Ayrshire

Dalnacardoch

Loch Con

Loch Ericht

Glen
Errochty

Glen
Fincastle

Rannoch Moor

Schiehallion

Loch an Daimh

Perthshire

Finlarig

Argyllshire

Killin

St Fillan's Pool

Loch
Katrine

Loch Sloy

Loch
Venachar

Lag Uaine

Aberfoyle

Dunbartonshire

Stirlingshire

Colzium House

Dumbarton

Old
Kilpatrick

Dun.

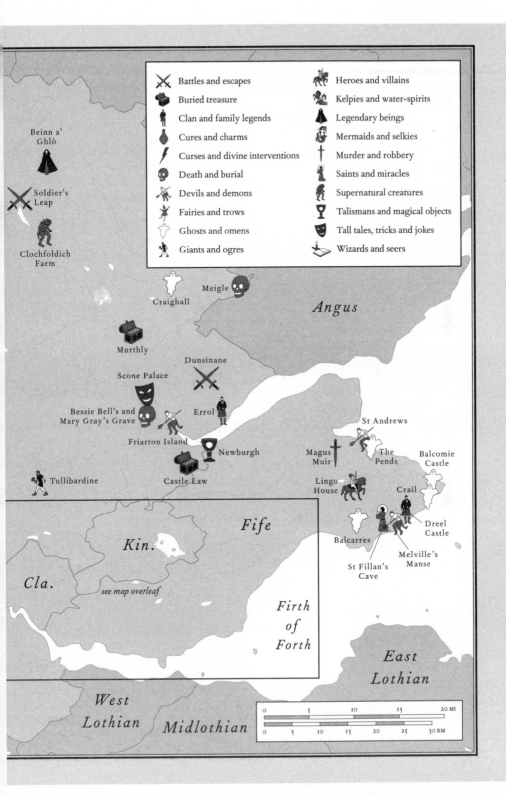

Battles and escapes
Buried treasure
Clan and family legends
Cures and charms
Curses and divine interventions
Death and burial
Devils and demons
Fairies and trows
Ghosts and omens
Giants and ogres

Heroes and villains
Kelpies and water-spirits
Legendary beings
Mermaids and selkies
Murder and robbery
Saints and miracles
Supernatural creatures
Talismans and magical objects
Tall tales, tricks and jokes
Wizards and seers

Beinn a' Ghlò

Soldier's Leap

Clochfoldich Farm

Meigle

Craighall

Angus

Murthly

Dunsinane

Scone Palace

Bessie Bell's and Mary Gray's Grave

Errol

Friarton Island

Newburgh

St Andrews

Magus Muir

The Pends

Balcomie Castle

Tullibardine

Castle Law

Lingo House

Crail

Dreel Castle

Balcarres

Melville's Manse

Fife

St Fillan's Cave

Kin.

Cla.

see map overleaf

Firth of Forth

East Lothian

West Lothian

Midlothian

0   5   10   15   20 MI

0   5   10   15   20   25   30 KM

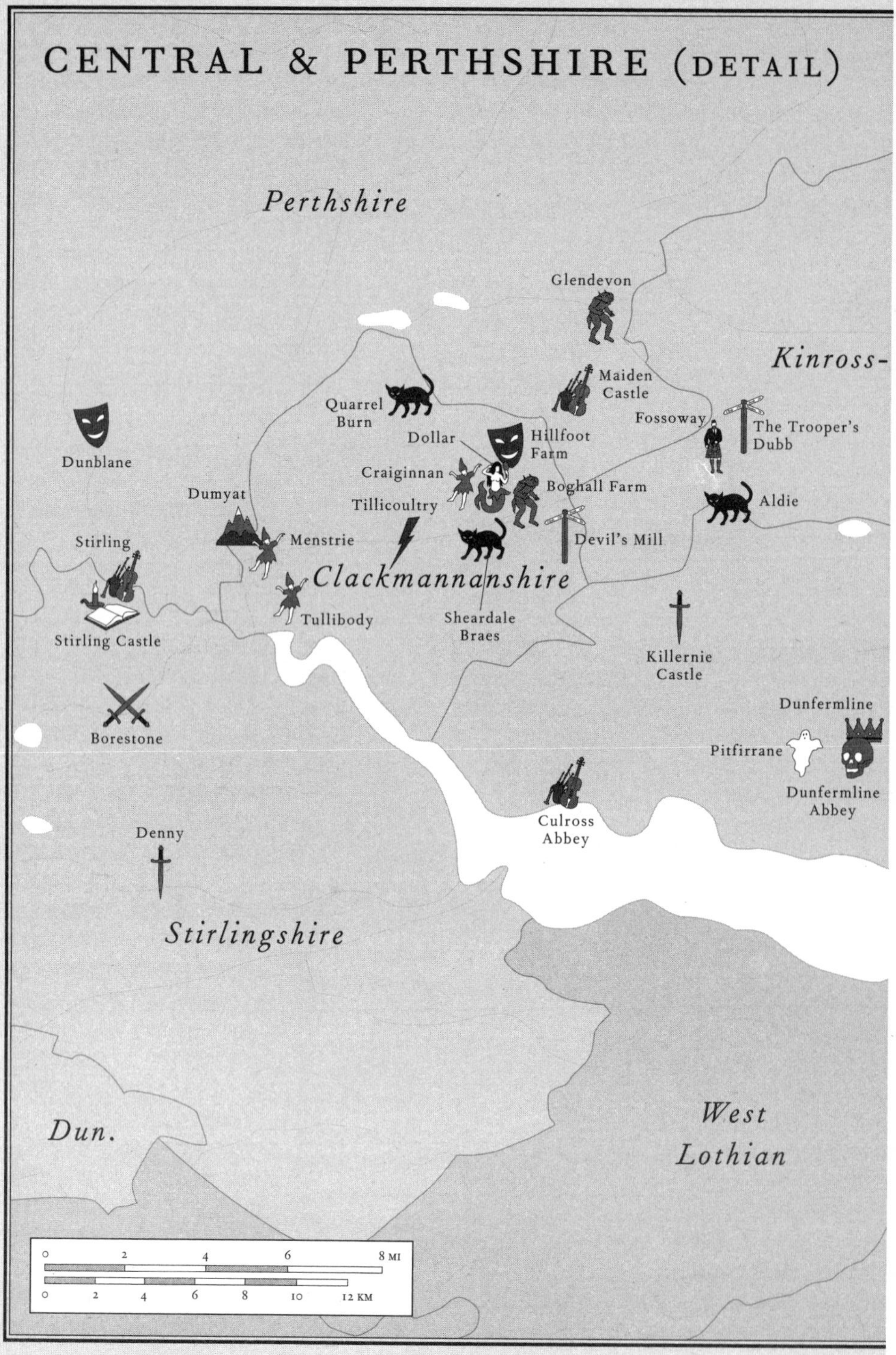

CENTRAL & PERTHSHIRE (DETAIL)

Perthshire

Glendevon

Kinross-

Maiden Castle

Fossoway

The Trooper's Dubb

Quarrel Burn

Dollar

Hillfoot Farm

Dunblane

Craiginnan

Boghall Farm

Aldie

Dumyat

Tillicoultry

Menstrie

Devil's Mill

Stirling

Clackmannanshire

Sheardale Braes

Stirling Castle

Tullibody

Killernie Castle

Dunfermline

Borestone

Pitfirrane

Dunfermline Abbey

Culross Abbey

Denny

Stirlingshire

Dun.

West Lothian

0   2   4   6   8 MI

0   2   4   6   8   10   12 KM

Norrie's Law

Falkland

Lundin Links
Standing Stones

Milnathort

Orwell

Wester Durie

shire

Loch
Leven

Leven

Kinneston

Methil

Fife

Easter
Wemyss

Buckhaven

Wemyss
Castle

Cardenden

Kirkcaldy

Balwearie
Castle

Powguild

Kinghorn

Firth
of
Forth

Midlothian

⚔	Battles and escapes
🧰	Buried treasure
👤	Clan and family legends
⚡	Curses and divine interventions
💀	Death and burial
✦	Fairies and trows
👻	Ghosts and omens
🏛	Landmarks and local customs
⛰	Landscape legends
🧜	Mermaids and selkies
†	Murder and robbery
⚑	Phrase- and place-name legends
🎻	Pipers and fiddlers
⫿⫿⫿	Prehistoric remains
👑	Royalty
🦁	Supernatural creatures
🎭	Tall tales, tricks and jokes
🐈	Witches and witchcraft
📜	Wizards and seers

heedlessly playing his whistle while pacing the corridor in which his master slept. The laird, who had been drinking the night before and wanted to be left in peace to sleep, rushed from his room, seized the boy, bore him down to a dungeon under the keep, locked him in, and then went back to bed. When he awoke next morning, thanks to his previous excesses he had quite forgotten the incident, and set off with his retainers from the castle. Several days passed before his return. When he came back and heard that the boy was missing, he was horror-struck, as he had only meant to shut him down there for an hour or two. Hastening down to the dungeon he found his worst fears confirmed – the boy lay dead.

> The story runs that through the passages and up and down the stairs he trod so long ago, a boyish form has been seen to flit by those who through the centuries have had eyes to see, and that on winter nights when the stars burn sharp and clear and the moon is on the wane he wanders beyond the confines of the castle.

Chairs in the castle were said sometimes to move of their own accord and candles to burn blue. At such times wild bursts of unearthly music would be heard beyond the castle walls, and there were tales of a spectral boy seen sitting on the Tower of Balcomie with a whistle at his lips.

Candles burning blue traditionally signalled the presence of the supernatural, as mentioned also in the legend of BLACKETT TOWER (Dumfries & Galloway). An early seventeenth-century verse records the belief:

> When candles burne but blue and dim,
> Old folkes will say, Here's fairy Grim.

Another man said to have been starved to death, at SPEDLIN'S TOWER (Dumfries

& Galloway), became a far more unruly ghost than the victim of Balcomie.

BALWEARIE CASTLE, FIFE

Many a strange tale was once told of Balwearie Castle, overlooking the valley of the Tiel, not least that it was the birthplace of MICHAEL SCOT, THE WIZARD OF BALWEARIE (p. 62). It was Scot who by his magic spells made the road up to the tower, and when his demons demanded more work he set them to weaving ropes of wet sand on the shore beyond Linktoun, said to be still visible when the tide ebbed low. Balwearie was a place to be shunned after dark, and it was a bold man who dared to enter there at midnight.

'Ye Legend of Ye Lady of Balweirie', said to date from the sixteenth century, was published in the Fife *Advertiser* in about 1850. A note explains that at the time of the Reformation Scott of Balwearie had disposed of lands formerly belonging to the Church, and that the legend recorded in the ballad probably related to that sale.

The ballad itself tells how a monk, banished from Balwearie, came one stormy night to the castle and in the presence of its lady pronounced anathema upon house and family.

> 'My curse be now upon yis hous
> And on yat bairnie near ye –
> Lane [deserted] be your bow'rs an' bare
>   ye tow'rs
> O' ye castel o' Balweirie. . . .
> Wha spoils ye kirk sall spoilet be,
> Grim vengeance doon sall bear ye;
> Ye name o' Scott sall be forgot
> In ye castel o' Balweirie.'

The wind was howling as he left, and he died on that rough night near the castle. But his curse remained, and came all too true. The lady's 'bairnie', the only son and

Balwearie Castle, birthplace of the notorious wizard Sir Michael Scot, was later cursed by a monk who had been banished from the land during the Reformation.

heir, soon dwindled and died, and she was left lamenting:

> 'How can I be but dull ye day –
> How can I be but drearie?
> I ance was glad, but now I'm sad
> In ye Castel o' Balwearie.'

Some confusion appears to exist between this castle and that of KILLERNIE. It may be that the ballad of 'Lamkin', a far more macabre tale than that of the dispossessed monk, is set at Balwearie.

BEINN A' GHLÒ, BLAIR ATHOLL, PERTHSHIRE

In *Superstitions of the Highlands and Islands of Scotland* (1900), John Gregorson Campbell tells a story of two huntsmen who were out on the high mountain of Beinn a' Ghlò, north-east of Blair Atholl. A heavy snowstorm came on and they lost

their way, wandering until they came to a hut where they decided to take shelter. When they entered, there was an old woman such as they had never seen before:

> Her two arms were bare, of great length, and grizzled and sallow to look at. She neither asked them to come in nor go out, and being much in need of shelter, they went in and sat at the fire. There was a look in her eye that might 'terrify a coward,' and she hummed a surly song, the words of which were unintelligible to them.

Despite her forbidding aspect, they asked the old woman for food and she laid a fresh salmon-trout before them, saying, 'Little you thought I would give you your dinner to-day.' She added that she could do more, and that it was she who had covered the mountain with mist to make them come to her home. They stayed there all night, and she was very kind and hospitable towards them. When it came time for them to leave, she told them that she was 'the wife of Ben-y-Ghloe'.

Afterwards, they could not say whether she was human or not. She sounds rather like the Cailleach, a guardian of the wild animals of the mountains who could be friendly or dangerous according to circumstance, and who was encountered at BEINN A' BHRIC (Southern Highlands) among other places, but she might have been one of the fairies, who in the late nineteenth century were still said to haunt Beinn a' Ghlò.

See also GUARDIAN OF THE WILD (p. 352).

BESSIE BELL'S AND MARY GRAY'S GRAVE, NEAR PERTH

The gravestone of Bessie Bell and Mary Gray is still to be seen near Burn Brae on the banks of the River Almond, inscribed with the words:

They lived – they loved – they died.

According to tradition, the girls were good friends, both loved by one young man of Perth who ultimately caused their deaths. No jealous murder was involved, as one might suppose: it was a case of a fatal infection. In 1666, Bessie, daughter of the Laird of Kinnaird, was visiting Mary at her father's house of Lynedoch, at the time when the great plague broke out. To avoid the disease, the two built themselves a shelter with a roof of green rushes, 'in a very retired and romantic spot called the Burnbraes', where they were supplied with food by their admirer. Alas, from him they caught the plague and both died, being buried, for fear of contagion, not in the churchyard but in a lonely place by the river. As Black's *Picturesque Tourist of Scotland* concludes the story:

Some tasteful person, in modern times, has fastened a sort of bower over their double graves, and there 'violets blue and daisies pied' will for ever blow over the remains of unfortunate beauty.

A ballad was composed on the tragic theme:

O Bessie Bell and Mary Gray,
    They war twa bonnie lasses,
They biggit [built] a bower on yon burn side,
        And theekit [thatched] it ower
            wi' rashes.
They theekit it ower wi' rashes green,
        They theekit it ower wi' heather;
But the pest came frae the burrows-town,
        And slew them baith thegither.

BOGHALL FARM, NEAR DOLLAR, CLACKMANNANSHIRE

The Brownie was very like a man in shape. His entire body was covered with brown hairs, hence his name. He slept all day and worked all night, when the whole farmhouse was hushed in slumber. Although possessed of great strength he was harmless, and had more of a forgiving than a revengeful turn of mind. His food was sowans (oats steeped in water) and sweet milk, while his bed consisted of straw made up in some cosy corner of the barn. To the farm of Boghall, near Dollar, Brownie rendered essential services; but it happened one very severe winter, when the snow lay deep upon the ground, and the frost was so intense as to freeze every running stream and well, that the woman of the house, afraid that her friendly Brownie would die, laid down some warm blankets on his heap of straw. Seeing this, he immediately left the place, saying:

To leave my old haunts, oh! my heart it is
    sair,
But the wife gae me blankets – she'll see
    me nae mair;
I've worked in her barn, frae evening till
    day,
My curse on the blankets that drove me
    away.
All the boon that I asked were my
    sowans and strae,
But success to Bogha' although
    Brownie's away.

Although he wished well to his former home, Boghall was never the same again. 'At the present day, it is little better than a wilderness,' ends this account of the Boghall Brownie printed in the *Scottish Journal of Topography* in 1848.

See also BROWNIES (p. 80).

BORESTONE, STIRLINGSHIRE

On a hill not far from St Ninians, a large granite stone was once to be seen sunk in the earth, pierced by a round hole about four inches (10 cm) in diameter. Comparatively recent tradition states that Bruce's flag was fixed here before the battle of Bannockburn in 1314, at which Scottish independence was won: reports of the rock's significant function do not appear to pre-date the early eighteenth century, and are probably untrue. Up to the mid nineteenth century, the landmark was charmingly known as the Bored Rock. Later sources, perhaps to avoid the inevitable misunderstanding, call it the Bore Stone, then contract the name to Borestone. In 1870 the Dumbarton and Stirling Oddfellows erected a flagstaff near the monument, and in 1960 the stone, which had by then been broken into several pieces, was built into a pedestal, but by 1967 the fragments, according to an Ordnance Survey report, had been stolen.

The *New Statistical Account of Scotland* (1845) mentions a stone not far from Sauchieburn House 'in which it is said that the standard was fixed', but here the standard is that of James III, and the occasion is the battle of Sauchieburn (1488). The writer evidently knows of the earlier legend, since he writes that the place 'is little more than a mile from the Bored Stone', but he draws no conclusion from the curious coincidence of *two* pierced stones, relics of two significant battles, existing in such a small area. It is almost certain that the same rock must be meant.

The later conflict arose when the barons of Scotland, dissatisfied with the king's rule, rose in rebellion and drew James's eldest son into their party. In the battle of Sauchieburn James's party was defeated, but even before the fate of the day was decided, the king had fled alone from the field and made towards the Forth in the hope of escaping by ship. James 'was never very distinguished for courage', remarks Robert Chambers in *The Picture of Scotland* (1827).

At the Bannock Burn, about a mile eastward from the battle-ground, a woman was taking water from the river in a pitcher. Frightened at the sight of an armed man riding towards her, she threw the pitcher aside, startling the king's horse, which reared and threw its rider. The king fell, badly hurt.

The accident had happened near a mill, to which the king was carried and where he was treated kindly by the miller and his wife. When he recovered consciousness, fearing death, he expressed a wish for a priest, and being asked for his name, replied, 'I was your king this morning.'

The miller's wife ran outside where, seeing some men passing, she called for a confessor to the king. 'I am a priest,' said one of them, but he lied. Being taken to James, whom he found lying in a corner of the mill covered with a coarse cloth, he knelt and asked if the king thought he might recover with medical help. James replied that he thought he might, upon which the man stabbed him to the heart. The murderer's name was never discovered, but it was supposed that he was one of the malcontent barons.

> The place where this atrocity was committed, is well known in the neighbourhood by the name of Beaton's Mill, and said to be so called from the person who then possessed it. The author of this work had the curiosity to visit it, and to inquire into the traditionary account of the circumstance above related, as preserved by the people of the place, which he was surprised to find tally in every particular with the historical narrative. He was even shown the particular corner in which the king was slain.

Even a sophisticated and usually cynical commentator like Chambers, it seems, can sometimes be convinced by this sort of 'evidence'.

BUCKHAVEN, FIFE

According to Black's *Picturesque Tourist of Scotland* (1845), Buckhaven was then 'a curious antique fishing village, inhabited by a most extraordinary race, supposed to be the descendants of the crew of a vessel from the Netherlands, which was wrecked near this place'.

The folklorist John Ewart Simpkins repeated the same tradition in 1914, and quoted Dr Harry Spens, a former minister of Wemyss, as saying in a letter dated 20 August 1778 that, as far as he had been able to ascertain, the original inhabitants of Buckhaven came from the Netherlands some time in the late sixteenth century. Their vessel had been stranded on the

shore, and the Laird of Wemyss gave them permission to settle there. They gradually acquired the Scots tongue and adopted local dress, 'and for these threescore years past, they have had the character of a sober and sensible, an industrious and honest set of people'. Their only odd custom was that brides 'of good condition and character' would wear at their wedding a certain richly ornamented girdle or belt, which was then put away and given to the next bride considered worthy of it.

In Spens's time, the village consisted of about 140 families, 60 of which were fisherfolk. He adds that the fishermen generally married young, and that all of them married fishermen's daughters from the same village. Other authors likewise comment on this refusal to marry outside their own society, and on the villagers' stand-offishness towards incomers.

Whatever their origin, the inhabitants of Buckhaven were considered by other Fife dwellers to be not so well educated or well mannered as the people of, say, the university town of St Andrews, and there was a standing joke about the 'College of Buckhyne'. James Wilkie says in *Bygone Fife* (1931) that he recollected it being said of any lad who was particularly backward and uncouth that 'he's surely been brought up at the College o' Buckhyne', and in the early nineteenth century there was even a satirical pamphlet published on the subject, *The Ancient History of Bucky-harbour*, giving an account of the 'college'. This, according to the Reverend J. W. Taylor writing in 1868, was a two-storey house with a gateway of whale bones:

> This house for many years, was held the chief, if not the only school in Buckhaven . . . It came seventy or eighty years ago, into the possession of a sailor, who engaged in smuggling. The smuggled goods were concealed on the premises; and the gin, which was a principal article,

often gave rise to drunken brawls. In one of these the sailor's wife, whose name was Maillie, met with her death. Thereafter, her ghost haunted the spot. It became a dreaded place; and instead of passing it in the dark, many, both old and young, within the last thirty years, preferred giving it a wide offing, by going down along the sands.

Nor was Maillie's ghost the only supernatural peril in Buckhaven. The town was also said to be haunted by a Will-o'-the-Wisp, as was nearby WESTER DURIE.

CARDENDEN, FIFE

In *Rebus's Scotland* (2005), the writer Ian Rankin describes his return in August 2004 to cut the ribbon on 'Ian Rankin Court', part of a new housing development sited where in his Cardenden childhood a builder's yard had stood:

> I was shown around the development. Some of the gardens backed on to a trickling stream. It ran through the Den, an area of overgrown wilderness we had all been taken to on primary school outings. Denend Primary sat just the other side of the railway bridge.

This 'wilderness' was well known in Victorian times. Here was supposedly buried a pot of gold which could only be found at full moon by two brothers, one of whom was destined to die at the other's hand, as prophesied by Thomas the Rhymer of EARLSTON (Lothian & Borders).

A recluse called Anthony Rodney once inhabited a cave in the Den. 'He was so swift of foot that he could run down a hare in the open plain,' wrote John Ewart Simpkins in 1914. Rodney would put his pot on the fire and return from Kirkcaldy with the ingredients for his dinner before the water had boiled, and

was therefore known as Anthony Speedyfoot or Lightfoot. The ability to travel far and fast is often attributed to wizards or fairies, who may sometimes help mortals to do likewise, as they did for 'Calum Clever' at INVERESRAGAN (Argyllshire & Islands).

CASTLE LAW, NEAR ABERNETHY, PERTHSHIRE

On the flank of Castle Law, a hill about a mile south-west of Abernethy, is a ruined but still imposing fort. Occupying a strategic position overlooking the rivers Earn and Tay to the north and Abernethy Glen to the south-east, it was defended by a great stone wall, now collapsed into rubble, and had its own water supply, from a rock-cut cistern inside the fort on its south side.

On the top of the hill are three small round lochs: legend says that in one of them is hidden a golden cradle in which the Pictish king's children used to be rocked, and that somewhere between here and Cairnavain in the Ochil Hills an immense treasure is buried, enough to make rich every man, woman, and child in Scotland. By local tradition, writes the Reverend Andrew Small in 1823, at some distant time in the past a set of golden keys was found in a small stream, which were supposed to have belonged to Cairnavain.

A rhyme recording that belief was printed in 1845 in the *New Statistical Account of Scotland*:

> In the Dryburn well, beneath a stane,
> You'll find the key of Cairn-a-vain,
> That will mak' a' Scotland rich ane by ane.

The age of this particular verse is uncertain, but similar predictions of treasure couched in rhyme are found throughout the British Isles, some of them dating to the sixteenth century.

The contributor notes that 'Cairn-a-vain', to the north of Orwell parish, had in former times been a huge collection of stones but by then was much reduced in size due to excavation of the site. The workmen who had removed the stones had eagerly expected to find some treasure, but all they actually discovered was a rough stone coffin in the centre of the cairn containing an urn full of bones and charcoal.

The tradition of the 'Pictish king' probably arises from observation or antiquarian knowledge of ancient remains in the neighbourhood. Abernethy appears to have been a place of some importance in the Dark Ages: early carved stones in the vicinity include a seventh-century Pictish symbol stone now set against the wall of the eleventh-century round tower beside the churchyard gate off Main Street.

As is often the case with buried treasure, there were rumours of a menacing guardian. In 1861, Alexander Laing noted a belief that if you ran three times round the loch muttering a spell 'the words of which, however, are too modern to be genuine' (so he doesn't give them), 'a hand will arise from a golden cradle and pull you in.' He adds, 'well do I recollect of having in my schoolboy days, an undefined feeling of terror in approaching too near its dreaded waters.'

CLOCHFOLDICH FARM, NEAR PITLOCHRY, PERTHSHIRE

Altmor Burn near Clochfoldich was haunted by a Brownie who could be heard paddling and splashing about in it until everyone at Clochfoldich Farm had gone to bed. Then he would go up to the house with wet feet and clear away all the dirty dishes, though he would throw everything that had already been cleaned on the floor. Milk was left out for him and he would leave some kind of gift in return. It was counted unlucky actually to meet him, and the nearby road between Pitlochry and Dunkeld was avoided at night.

Unlike many other Brownies, he was not laid by the gift of clothes, but by a nickname. A man returning from the market one dark night heard him splashing about in the burn and cried out, 'Well, Puddlefoot, how is it with you the night?' 'Oh!' cried the Brownie, 'I've gotten a name! 'Tis Puddlefoot they call me!' And with that he vanished, never to haunt the place again.

In her *Personnel of Fairyland* (1953), the folklorist Katharine Briggs calls this a tale 'lately current in Perthshire', and in *The Vanishing People* (1978) she says, 'It is a traditional story of the road between Pitlochry and Dunkeld' – as she gives no printed source, the tale is probably one she heard herself while living in Perthshire.

The dismissal of the Brownie by naming him relates to a traditional belief in the power of personal names over fairies, as in the folk tale of 'Rumpelstiltskin' and the Suffolk fairy tale 'Tom Tit Tot', a belief extended to include a ghost at WHITTINGEHAME (Lothian & Borders). A parallel idea is that it is dangerous to call fairies by their generic names. Just as the Greeks cautiously referred to the vengeful Furies as the Eumenides, or 'Kindly Ones', so, according to a Scottish rhyme current in the early nineteenth century:

Gin ye ca' me imp or elf,
I rede ye look weel to yourself;
Gin ye ca' me fairy,
I'll work ye muckle tarrie;
Gin guid neibour ye ca' me,
Then guid neibour I will be;
But gin ye ca' me seelie wicht
I'll be your freend baith day and nicht.

[If you call me imp or elf,
I counsel you to take good care;
If you call me fairy,
I'll cause you great vexation;
If good neighbour you call me,
Then good neighbour I will be;
But if you call me blessed spirit
I'll be your friend both day and night.]

COLZIUM HOUSE, STIRLINGSHIRE

Chambers's *Book of Days* (1864) relates that the widow of Graham Claverhouse – 'Bonnie Dundee' – was courted by the Honourable William Livingstone, later Viscount Kilsyth. At Colzium House he gave her a ring on which were engraved the words 'Yours only and for ever', but she lost it in the garden, and this was taken as a bad omen for the marriage that followed. Misfortune ensued: living in Holland, she and her only child were killed in the collapse of a house. Almost exactly a hundred years later, the lost ring was unearthed in the garden at Colzium, and in the mid nineteenth century was still preserved in the house.

There is nothing impossible or even particularly unlikely in this story, but lost and recovered rings feature in many traditional legends, including that of St Mungo at GLASGOW (Glasgow & Ayrshire).

CRAIGHALL, PERTHSHIRE

In the *Gentleman's Magazine* in 1731 appeared a vivid account of the ghost of David Sutor, who was remembered in the area to have enlisted as a soldier and gone abroad around thirty-five years earlier, at the turn of the century. Over the years 1728 to 1730 his spirit appeared demanding the burial of some bones: a 'restless

ghost' often wants his own remains buried, but in this case the bones were those of a murder victim.

The narrative, 'given by a Gentleman of unexceptionable Honour and Veracity', according to the magazine, tells of one William Sutor, a farmer in Middlemause near Craighall. The relationship between man and ghost is not precisely specified, but it seems likely that William was a nephew of the dead David.

In December 1728, William was in the fields with his servants when they heard an 'uncommon skreeking and noise'. They thought they saw a dark-grey dog, and as it was a dark night concluded that it was really a fox, though none of the hounds would approach it. About a month later, in the same place and at about the same time of night, the grey dog or fox was seen again and in passing struck William's thigh, so that he felt the pain all night. After that nothing seems to have happened until December 1729, when the thing passed William at some distance, but still in the same area of his fields. The following June it made yet another appearance, and by now William was convinced that this was no ordinary animal.

On the last *Monday* of Nov. 1730, about sky-setting, as he was coming from *Drumlochy*, this officious visiter passed him as formerly, and in passing, he distinctly heard it speak these words, *Within eight or ten days do or die*; and instantly disappear'd, leaving him not a little perplex'd.

Next morning, William told his brother James everything that had happened. At about ten o'clock that night, the two brothers and a servant visited 'the remarkable spot'. No sooner had they arrived there than the strange being appeared again to William, who pointed to it, but neither James nor the servant could see anything.

Michael Scot, the Wizard of Balwearie

Tradition holds that Michael Scot or Scott was born in about 1175 at BAL-WEARIE CASTLE (Central & Perthshire) and later lived at AIKWOOD TOWER (Lothian & Borders). It is known that he spent much of his life abroad: in around 1217 he was at Toledo, translating scientific works from Arabic, and he later served the Holy Roman Emperor Frederick II at Palermo as court physician, philosopher, and astrologer.

Scot was one of the greatest European scholars of his time. Although he condemned magic in his writings, he had read widely in esoteric texts, and his interest in astrology and Arab learning gave him the reputation of being a wizard within a generation of his death. In the early fourteenth century, Dante wrote in the *Divine Comedy* of 'Michael Scott, who verily / Knew every trick of the art magical', placing him in the company of witches and pagan prophets in hell. When Dante sees the sorcerer, he is one of those whose face (in Dorothy Sayers' translation) is 'turned towards his own backside', as punishment for having looked into the future.

Later folklore recounts Scot's magical exploits. He was said to have at his command a number of imps – sometimes named as 'Prig, Prim, and Pricker' – who among their achievements divided in three the EILDON HILLS (Lothian & Borders). In England, the great Roman highway Watling Street was sometimes known as 'Mitchell Scott's Causeway', having supposedly been built in one night by the Devil and 'Mitchell', and other engineering feats are attributed to the wizard at BIGGAR (Glasgow & Ayrshire) and CRIFFEL (Dumfries & Galloway).

On one occasion the magician wanted to visit Rome in a hurry, to learn the date of Shrovetide from the Pope. Scot rejected three fairy horses that could travel respectively as fast as the wind, faster than the wind, and as fast as 'the black blast of March', and took the fourth horse, which was 'as swift as the thought of a maiden between her two lovers'. The story is similar to one told of the equally famous magic practitioner Dr Faustus, who called up one spirit as swift as an arrow, another as swift as the wind, and a third as swift as the thought of man or 'as the transition from good to evil'. In Scot's case, despite his speed the Pope said he was too late – until Scot observed that the Pope was wearing a woman's shoe (having been interrupted in an illicit encounter). The Pope thereupon gave him the information he wanted.

Some said that Scot finished his days in Cumberland, where Wolsty Castle was rumoured to have been built especially to safeguard his secret works. In 1629, a visitor to nearby Burgh-under-Bowness was shown what was purportedly one of Sir Michael's books, which nobody had ever dared to read. Other places, however, laid claim to Scot's library and his body, including GLENLUCE ABBEY (Dumfries & Galloway) and MELROSE ABBEY

The wizard Michael Scot in his tomb, as shown in an illustration to the 1854 edition of Sir Walter Scott's narrative poem 'The Lay of the Last Minstrel' (1805).

(Lothian & Borders). He died in around 1230, and Sir Walter Scott writes that he fell 'a victim to female art':

> His wife, or concubine, elicited from him the secret that his art could ward off any danger except the poisonous qualities of broth, made of the flesh of a *breme* [mad] sow. Such a mess she accordingly administered to the wizard, who died in consequence of eating it; surviving, however, long enough to put to death his treacherous confidant.

A variant account in the nineteenth-century *Denham Tracts* is that having been poisoned with the sow's flesh, Scot knew that the only remedy was drinking some of the water in which it had been cooked. His wife had thrown out the liquid, but he found enough for the cure remaining in the hollow made by a cow's foot, and punished his spouse by causing two roasted eggs to be put under her armpits, so that she was 'burnt to death, the heat reaching to her heart'.

Another legend, reported by John Gregorson Campbell in *Superstitions of the Highlands and Islands of Scotland* (1900), is that when on his deathbed Michael told his friends to place his body on a hillock, where three ravens and three doves would fly towards it. If the ravens were first his corpse should be burned; otherwise it should receive Christian burial. The ravens were in such a hurry that they overshot the mark. 'So the devil, who had long been preparing a bed for Michael, was disappointed.'

See also DUMBARTON; KINGHORN (Central & Perthshire); TOMNAHURICH (Southern Highlands).

The following Saturday, when William was at his sheepfold, it approached him and said, 'Come to the spot of ground within half an hour.' William obeyed, taking with him a stick with which he drew a circle around himself. This was an approved technique for protection from evil spirits, similarly employed by a woman at ORSAY (Western Isles) when menaced by the Water-horse.

> He had scarce encircled himself with a line of circumvallation, when his trouble-some familiar came up to him, he ask'd it, *In the name of God, who are you?* It answer'd, *I am David Sutor, George Sutor's Brother: I killed a Man, more than 35 years ago, at a bush by East the road as you go into the Isle.* He said to it, *David Sutor was a Man, and you appear as a Dog.* It answer'd, *I killed him with a Dog, and am made to speak out of the mouth of a Dog: and I tell you to go bury these Bones.*

The news of this strange encounter soon spread. The minister of Blair went with about forty men to the 'said Isle', not described more precisely in the *Gentleman's Magazine*. They dug in several places but could find no bones. Then on 23 December at about midnight, when William was in bed, it came to his door and said, 'Come away: you will find the bones at the side of the wither'd Bush, and there are but 8 left.' It told him that he would find the mark of a cross on the ground to show the place.

Next day, William and James followed these instructions and found the bush and the cross. The two men began to dig, watched by a crowd of fascinated bystanders, and had not got far down before they found the eight bones the spirit had described. These were then wrapped in clean linen and put in a coffin, and buried that evening in Blair churchyard. The whole affair had by then become notorious, and the burial was accomplished with an audience of around a hundred people. After this the ghost seems to have rested in peace.

CRAIGINNAN, CLACKMANNANSHIRE

There was once a farm at Craiginnan, but by the mid nineteenth century it was a ruin. The meadows around it, however, were still famous for the quantity of hay they produced, and the land had once flourished under the management of a farmer called David Wright. After the grass was cut, Wright's men had always left the spreading and stacking to the fairies, who came from Blackford, Gleneagles, Buckleburn, and elsewhere, and assembled on the summit of the Saddle Hill before beginning work. Their labour was always paid at sheep-shearing time with a few of the best fleeces, and this mutually beneficial relationship continued happily until David Wright died, leaving the farm to his son.

Young Wright had been told to keep on good terms with the fairies, but he was a mean and greedy man. Grudging the fleeces his father had handed over, he had his own servants dry the hay and pile it up, but next morning they found the whole harvest scattered again. This happened night after night, and in revenge on what he called the 'greengoons', young Wright ploughed up the fairy rings and fairy knolls.

From then on, nothing went well with the farm. One day a dairymaid was washing the butter in the well as she always did before sending it to market, when a small hand appeared and snatched it down into the water, and she heard a voice say:

> 'Your butter's awa'
> To feast our band
> In the fairy ha'.'

Wright's animals sickened and died, and finally Wright himself, returning from market, was lost after dark in the pass of Glenqueich. Wandering about, he sank at last into a 'well-eye', or bog, in which he died.

This cautionary tale, printed in the *Scottish Journal of Topography* in 1848, does not spell out whether Wright was led into the marsh by the fairies, but that is quite likely. Will-o'-the-Wisps and malicious spirits were well known to misguide travellers; their tricks often proved fatal, as they did at WESTER DURIE.

CRAIL, FIFE

A tradition lingered in the East Neuk of Fife in the late nineteenth century that the dark complexion of some inhabitants of Crail derived from shipwrecked seamen of the Armada too poor or too disabled to return home. 'It is difficult to test this persistent rumour, which has perhaps nothing but a pair of black eyes or the bright red dyes of a bonnet or a shawl to support it,' says Aeneas Mackay, writing in 1896, 'but when we are told that the Gosmans of Anstruther are descendants of Gomez, the Spanish admiral, or Guzman, a Spanish grandee, incredulity becomes at least pardonable.' There was a similar tradition concerning the origin of the people of BUCKHAVEN.

In 1858, John Jack told the story of one of Crail's ghosts, who kept a dairy when alive, and when she was dead could find no rest. She continually haunted the neighbourhood where she had lived and worked, 'chasing home the night-wanderer, pale and trembling'. The minister was applied to and accepted the horrid task of speaking to the ghost, who in a spectral voice explained the reason she walked:

'The watered milk, and the light pund stane
They gar me wander here my lane.'

(In other words, the watered milk and the short weight she had given her customers were the reason she walked there alone.) Her confession in itself was enough to release her, for she then vanished for ever. Fraudulent milk-sellers came back as ghosts with similar rhymes in various parts of Britain and the Continent.

The Blue Stone of Crail, also known as the Devil's Stone, is a boulder which lies not far from the churchyard gate, and according to a local writer was once kissed by any resident leaving the town in pledge of their return. Legend has it that the Devil, bearing some special grudge against the church at Crail, took his stand on the Isle of May and hurled the rock, which in its flight split in two. The smaller part, bearing the mark of the Devil's thumb, stayed on course and fell just short of the church, while the larger bit flew east and landed on Balcomie Sands. That the Devil was given to throwing rocks is a widespread tradition; he was, however, a notoriously bad marksman.

CULROSS ABBEY, FIFE

According to a local legend recorded by John Simpkins in 1914, an underground passage runs beneath the medieval abbey of Culross. In this a man is seated in a golden chair, ready to give treasures to any who manage to find him.

The story is told of a blind piper and his dog who entered the vaults at the head of the Newgate, and was heard playing his pipes on his subterraneous march as far as the West Kirk, three quarters of a mile distant. But the gnomes or subterranean demons got hold of him, and he never again emerged to the upper air. His dog managed to effect his escape, but the faithful animal of course could tell no tales.

The legend is a variant of one found the length and breadth of Britain: by a natural progression of thought, any cave or underground tunnel whose end was not known was assumed to lead to hell or to be haunted by the Devil. In England the lost musician is usually a fiddler, but in Scotland he is almost always a piper. Perhaps the most famous disappearance of this kind was that of the great MacCrimmon, said to have occurred at TROTTERNISH (Western Isles).

Another supernatural tradition attached to the abbey was that witches were formerly imprisoned in the steeple. James Wilkie in 1931 notes that 'there can be seen on the turret stair leading to the room on the first floor . . . the mark of a foot said to have been made by one of them.' A similar legend was recorded by the Reverend James Hall in his

Travels in Scotland (1807), who writes that on Culross common was a large stone bearing a human footprint, and that 'even yet it is believed that a witch, who happened to light here, from riding through the air on a broom stick, imprinted this mark with her foot.'

Possibly such rumours of witches' doings sprang from a report which had appeared earlier, in George Sinclair's much-quoted tract *Satans Invisible World Discovered* (1685). According to this, a certain beldame called Creich was held in the steeple at Culross by Alexander Colvil, the Justice Depute. He called on her to deny on oath that she was a witch, but, when she lifted up her hand and swore, her arm became so stiff she could not lower it again. The Justice Depute, however, fell on his knees and beseeched God to have

Legend has it that a subterranean passage runs beneath the medieval abbey at Culross, where a man sits in a golden chair. He will, it is said, bestow treasure on anyone who finds him, but those who go to seek him are never seen again.

mercy on her. His prayer was duly heard and, although it is not explicitly stated, readers are left to infer that she was forgiven.

DALNACARDOCH, PERTHSHIRE

In *Superstitions of the Highlands and Islands of Scotland* (1900), John Gregorson Campbell gives an interesting brief example of 'flight with the fairies', the theme of a number of English and Scottish tales concerning a man carried long distances by elves, or in the Highlands specifically by the *sluagh*, the wind-borne fairy troop. In some accounts, he is returned to his starting point, in others left in a strange place, bewildered as to how he got there.

Campbell's story concerns Red Donald of the Fairies, a name which came from the man having seen the elves as a boy. When he grew up he became a cowherd, and while taking care of his cattle above Dalnacardoch one evening he was taken by the fairies to his father's house in Rannoch, a distance of about twelve miles.

> In the morning he was found sitting
> at the fireside, and as the door was
> barred, he must have been let in by the
> chimney.

Such traditions have their antecedents in medieval and later traditions in which no clear distinction is made between fairies and petty demons. MICHAEL SCOT, THE WIZARD OF BALWEARIE (p. 62), made a magical journey to ask a question of the Pope in Rome with the help of a spirit conjured up by his occult powers, while at INVERESRAGAN (Argyllshire & Islands) a very similar trip was made by 'Calum Clever' and attributed to his friendship with the fairies.

DENNY, STIRLINGSHIRE

A young student was told a horror story in 1975 by an elderly man from Stirling. An escaped lunatic was hiding in a house 'up the old Denny back-road'; he was highly dangerous, having killed his own mother with an axe. A man came to look at the house, which was for sale, and the lunatic attacked him with a spade, decapitating him. He then took the head and went to the car where the man's wife (known personally to the man who told the story, he claimed) was waiting. 'It was dark by now,' explains the narrator, 'so he knocked on the window and showed her the man's head, and he laughed (because he was mad),' but at that point, luckily for the wife, the police arrived.

Probably many readers have heard a similar story: one of the present writers was told something almost identical at school in the 1970s. It is a variant of a modern or 'urban' legend known as 'The Boyfriend's Death' of which the most usual Scottish versions, according to David Buchan, writing in 1984, involve a courting couple whose car won't start, or runs out of petrol; the boy goes in search of some, telling his girlfriend on no account to get out of the car until he comes back. She waits obediently, despite hearing a strange continuous knocking sound from above. At last the lights of a police car shine on her, and an officer shouts that she is to run towards him. She is not to look back, but of course she does so. Her boyfriend's body is hanging from a tree above the car, his head striking it; or a madman has severed the head and is knocking it against the roof. A related myth, 'The Hook', involves a luckier pair, both of whom escape with their lives thanks to the maniac's false hand getting wrenched off by their car.

The man who told the Denny story to the student said that it had happened only three or four years earlier, and that he personally knew the wife of the murdered man. Urban myths are sometimes known as FOAF tales from their frequent references to a Friend of a Friend or similar second-hand claims to truth.

DEVIL'S MILL, CLACKMANNANSHIRE

West of the village of Fossoway, the River Devon runs through a deep channel. A peculiar noise produced here by the water rebounding from the rocks is said to resemble the clacking of a mill – a sound more familiar in earlier centuries than now, but the name 'Devil's Mill' has stuck; devilish, explains Robert Chambers in 1827, 'because it pays no regard to Sunday, but works every day alike'. A little further on is the 'Rumbling Bridge', again named for the echoes produced by the stream brawling below. The view from the bridge down into the rift is dizzying. Both landmarks feature in a local proverb, recorded in 1896:

> If the deil's mill has ceased to grind, and
> the Rumbling Brig rumbles no more,
> there will be sorrow in the Vale of Devon.

Not far away is the Caldron Linn. Here the river enters a deep gully, where the action of the current against the rocks has worked out a rounded cavity in which the foam is so boisterous that the water appears to boil. From the 'cauldron' the water finds its way through a hole beneath the surface into a lower cavity, in which again it swirls round and round, and from there into a third, from which it flies in a sheer fall of about forty-four feet (13.4 m). Above the Caldron Linn the banks are not far apart, and there is a projecting rock

between them. In around 1810 a Mr Harrower, out seeing the sights, was reckless enough to jump across, but caught one of his spurs and fell. He was at once swept over the waterfall into the first of the 'cauldrons'. Here he managed to get himself upright and support himself on a bed of sand while his companion ran for a rope. The nearest farm was some way away, and by the time the friend got back Mr Harrower had sunk perceptibly into the sand. The rope turned out to be too short, and the friend had to run back again for a longer one. This time when he returned he made a noose with it and threw it over Harrower's head, where it twisted round his neck. The man was now in danger of both strangling and drowning, but managed to hold it with his hands and after about half an hour in the water was finally pulled free.

The story makes an instructive contrast to legends of 'heroic leaps' like those at the BRIDGE OF POTARCH (North East) and SOLDIER'S LEAP, where someone is said to have jumped to safety across a chasm.

DOLLAR, CLACKMANNANSHIRE

Describing Dollar, Black's *Picturesque Tourist of Scotland* (1844) declares with a flourish:

> In the neighbourhood is the remarkable ruin of Castle Campbell, occupying a wild and romantic situation on the top of a high and almost insulated rock. The only access to the castle is by an isthmus connecting the mount with the hill behind. The mount on which it is situated is nearly encompassed on all sides by thick bosky woods, and mountain rivulets descending on either side, unite at the base. Immediately behind rises a vast amphitheatre of wooded hills.

In the *Scottish Journal of Topography* (1848), a flowery tale is told of the castle in the days when it was held by Ranald, a chief of the McCallums who had one much-loved son named Edwin. On the boy's twenty-first birthday, a splendid feast was held, and after a good deal of food had been eaten and wine had been drunk, talk turned to the 'Maiden Well' a little to the north of the castle in the pass of Glenqueich:

> The well was the haunt of a genii or spirit, who, when invoked, rose from it in a thin vapour, which, on dispersing, a lady of the most ravishing beauty was revealed to view. Many an attempt was made to carry her off, but they invariably proved abortive.

Edwin, however, now declared that he would capture the spirit or die in the attempt. The final outcome of the adventure is given in verse, telling how Edwin twice invokes the spirit without result; the third time, she appears in all her loveliness, but with a wild and piercing eye:

A chill crept Edwin's bosom through,
    He grasp'd his trusty brand;
But something on his shoulder laid
    Withheld his manly hand.

Again he tried – his strength was gone –
    A lifeless corpse he fell;
And with the victor spirit sunk
    Down in the crystal well.

Not much can be said for the literary quality of the poem, but the story, for all its romantic trappings, is at heart a legend of a fatal freshwater mermaid. Many such stories were told, partly to keep children away from dangerous deep water, although in Scotland such warning tales are more likely to involve malicious KELPIES AND WATER-HORSES (p. 364).

DREEL CASTLE, ANSTRUTHER EASTER, FIFE

Only fragments now remain of Dreel Castle, said to have been the ancestral seat of the Anstruthers. The family's founder, or at least an early representative, Sir William Anster, or Anstruther, had interests in the herring fishery and was familiarly known as 'Fisher Willie'.

The laird of neighbouring land with the curious name of 'Third-part', presumably commemorating an ancient division of a larger estate into three, invited Anstruther to dinner, but meant, once he had Sir William beneath his roof, to kill him. It so happened that a beggar took shelter at Third-part the night before the intended murder, overheard the laird plotting with his servants, and immediately went to warn Sir William.

Sending a message to excuse himself from his dinner engagement, the Laird of Anster asked the Laird of Third-part to come to Dreel instead. Third-part duly arrived, 'accompanied by a retinue which seemed to betoken an intention of making up by open violence for his disappointment', but was forestalled: as he was climbing the narrow spiral stair of Dreel Castle, Fisher Willie cut him down by a blow from his poleaxe.

The question now arose of how to win pardon for his deed. Having mortgaged a good deal of his property in order to buy suitable clothes for court, Sir William went to the king – we are not told which king – and declared that he had come with the whole lands of Anster on his back, to ask permission to continue to wear them. He confessed to having slain Third-part, but as the motive was clearly self-defence he was forgiven, and the family of Anstruther granted a coat of arms with a poleaxe for their crest.

Fisher Willie's coat was said to have

been preserved for centuries at Ely House, the later residence of the Anstruthers:

> It is described by people who have seen it, as having been a most voluminous garment, with cuffs turned up almost to the shoulder, and so stiff with lace as to be almost able to stand on its own.

Unfortunately, says Robert Chambers, in the early nineteenth century 'it was cut down into shreds by a capricious lady, and destroyed.'

DUMBARTON, DUNBARTONSHIRE

A story with far-reaching consequences is told of a Dumbarton merchant who was shipwrecked on a desert island. All the crew having drowned except himself, he wandered about until he found a cave by the shore, and took up residence in it. He was found there by a mermaid:

> She had a fondness towards the stranger, and they afterwards lived together in that cave. The mermaid every day went to her own element, or the sea, and brought provisions.

There the merchant lived for a whole year, until one day when his mermaid wife was not at home he hailed a passing ship which sent a boat ashore to him. He told them how he had been living all this while, and how the mermaid brought him not only food and wine but gold, silver, and jewels, so much treasure in fact that he did not know what to do with it. The captain and he plotted that in a year and a day from that time the ship would return, and in the meantime he should ask the mermaid to gather all the booty she possibly could.

This seventeenth-century engraving shows a mermaid, a popular figure in Scottish folklore. At Dumbarton, a tale is told of a mermaid who fell in love with a merchant only to be heartlessly abandoned. Some say she was the mother of the renowned wizard Michael Scot.

They cam at the time appointed, and the mermaid being out, they made quick dispatch to get all the stores on board before she cam, which done, they sailed away, and when she cam home she found the cave desolated and herrid [despoiled].

The betrayed mermaid swam quickly after the ship and overtook it. She then demanded her husband back, and her belongings too.

The Skipper cast off a bundle (to the mermaid) of books, and hecht [promised] her to get her husband after she counted them. Which she did and requested her love, and the skipper gave her another bundle, again and again, till they reached Gourock and Lawrence Bay.

The disloyal merchant, once he was on dry land, refused point blank to go with the mermaid again:

But this mermaid told him that he must meet her at the cave whre they spent sae monie happie days, a year and a day hence, and she committed her bairn (or mongrel half fish and man) which she bore to the merchant, to its father.

She told him he was to take good care of it and make sure it had a good education, since he had so much money which really belonged to her. She gave him besides a book which he was not to let the child see until it was able to read perfectly. After that, she said, from the instructions in the book, the 'miraculous bairn' would be able to do whatever he liked, 'such as to order the foul Thief do onie thing when he pleased', i.e. to command the Devil. The merchant did as he was told, and in time the child came into his inheritance of the magical book.

The mermaid's bairn took up his abode in the auld castle of Ardrossan. He went under the name of Michael Scott.

Thomas Davidson, quoting this story in *Rowan Tree and Red Thread* (1949), leaves it at that, but he must expect his readers to know that Michael Scot or Scott was a famous magician. He was a historical character, born around 1175; his parentage is unknown, but is not usually reported to have been other than human, while his home is generally said to have been at BALWEARIE CASTLE. It seems likely that the sorcerer's name was added as a dramatic final twist to a pre-existing story, which has authentic traditional elements such as the skipper's delaying strategy of repeatedly giving the mermaid bundles of books to count – a ploy reminiscent of tactics used by Sir Michael Scot himself to distract his busy imps.

See MICHAEL SCOT, THE WIZARD OF BALWEARIE (p. 62).

DUMYAT, CLACKMANNANSHIRE

'A day spent in Glendevon will be sufficient to satisfy the most inordinate appetite for romantic natural scenery,' writes Robert Chambers in 1827, adding a pleasant domestic legend of Dumyat (which he spells Demyat), the most southerly of the Ochil Hills, which forms the west side of the mouth of Glendevon.

The proprietor of the estate upon which it is situated, when travelling abroad, happened to meet an English gentleman who had recently been in Scotland, and who talked loudly of the romantic beauties of that country. In particular, he spoke with rapture of the view which he had obtained from the top of a hill called Demyat. The Scottish gentleman heard with astonishment, that he possessed upon his own property in Scotland, a view superior to any he had come so far in search of; and he lost no time in returning home to ascend Demyat.

Travelling in pursuit of something which turns out to have been at home all the time is a widespread theme in literature and legend, from Maeterlinck's tale of the Bluebird of Happiness to the famous story of the Pedlar of Swaffham (a Scottish version of which is told of DUNDONALD CASTLE, Glasgow & Ayrshire). Converting the quest into a search for the picturesque is a conceit worthy of Henry James.

DUNBLANE, PERTHSHIRE

Bilzy Young, who died in about 1800, was renowned in Dunblane as being able to tell the greatest lie of any man present. John Monteath, writing in 1835, describes him as a 'chattering, unsettled, work-little, dingy, and gill-drinking' weaver, never short of a story in return for a drink.

An Englishman once boasted that he could out-lie Bilzy, and described an enormous cabbage, grown in Yorkshire, 'under the shade of which the whole British army might have found shelter'. Bilzy promptly said that he could now guess the use of the immense copper saucepan made at Carron, so wide that when it was being made the men working at one side couldn't hear those striking on the other side, and so deep that when a hammer was dropped from the top it took an hour to fall to the bottom. The Englishman admitted defeat, saying that 'your copper shall boil my cabbage.'

Another Bilzy exploit, as related by himself, was that in order to catch two hares he had fixed his knife so as to kill one, and set his dog on to the other, but having miscalculated the position of the knife, saw the hares run one to each side of it while the dog, running straight, cut himself 'exactly in two *perpendicularly*'. The two halves of the dog then turned right and left and proceeded to catch both hares. This is a classic example of a 'Münchhausen tale', a genre named after an eighteenth-century German baron celebrated for his tall stories. One anecdote told how the original Münchhausen used a cherry stone to shoot a stag which was later found with a cherry tree growing out of its forehead, and another, notably similar to the surprising achievement of Bilzy's dog, was of a horse which was cut in half but then sewn back together, none the worse for its dissection. The whole point of such narratives was their complete impossibility.

DUNFERMLINE, FIFE

A traditional story from Dunfermline concerns the infancy of Charles I. One night, Charles's father King James was woken by a loud scream from the boy's nurse, and when he asked her what was the matter she told him she had seen something like an old man come into the room and throw his cloak over the prince's cradle. The apparition had then pulled the cloak and cradle towards him as if he wanted to steal the baby. 'I'm feared it was the thing that's no canny,' she said, meaning the Devil.

King James replied, not very sympathetically, that he wished the old man had really taken the whimpering brat away. If the child ever became king, he exclaimed, no good would come of his reign: 'the de'il has cussen [cast] his cloak ower him already.' The last words thereafter became a byword in Dunfermline for an unlucky child.

According to Robert Chambers, the story accurately portrays the character of King James VI of Scotland and I of England, who not only believed in the Devil and witchcraft, as his authorship of *Daemonologie* (1597) attests, but by English court standards was somewhat rough in his manners. What is certain is that it reflects a historical truth about Charles I, who was sickly from infancy and no doubt given to crying in the cradle.

The witches who plotted against the life of James himself were centred around NORTH BERWICK (Lothian & Borders), but Dunfermline too had traditions of witches, or people regarded as such, beliefs which continued into the nineteenth century. In 1886, Alexander Stewart wrote of 'Auld Bessie Bittem', who was deemed unsafe to meddle with. One day she appeared by the loom of a weaver identified only as 'Johnnie K.' and asked him to come and dig her potatoes. Johnnie's wife Kirsty shouted from the kitchen that he would do nothing of the kind: he had quite enough to do at home. Johnnie tried to persuade his wife, but she was adamant, and in the end Bessie toddled off, followed by her equally suspect black cat, with the parting words that Johnnie might find himself none the richer for refusing to help.

Johnnie had scarcely set to work than out flew his shuttle and fell to the floor. He went to pick it up and started off again, but with the same result. In an attempt to break the spell he took his shuttle to the kitchen and drew it three times through the smoke of the fire, repeating dolefully that he had known how it would be. 'O Kirsty!' he said, 'Ye micht hae mair sense than contrar' that auld witch Bessie Bittem.'

A similar story is told as a first-hand memory at CRAIGDARROCH (Dumfries & Galloway).

DUNFERMLINE ABBEY

In the churchyard of Dunfermline Abbey there stood until 1784, when it was blown down by a tempest, a thorn tree of vast size and great apparent age. The tree, reported Robert Chambers in 1827, was said by tradition to mark a notable grave:

that of the mother of WILLIAM WALLACE (p. 204).

How that lady came to die here, is not known; but the tradition that this was her burying-place is positive and general. It is added, that on burying his mother here, the Scottish patriot desired to erect a monument to her memory, but had not time, being obliged to remove his quarters, either in pursuit of, or flight from his English enemies. As a *next best*, he planted this thorn, which continued to commemorate the event till its destruction, time and cause above-mentioned; when it was replaced by a stem from the old tree.

By 1827, the new tree had already reached a considerable size.

Also believed to be buried here are St Margaret and her husband Malcolm III, and inside the church is the tomb of Robert the Bruce. A more mysterious

A drawing by Sir Noël Paton (1821–1901) shows St Margaret expounding the scriptures to her husband, Malcolm III. The king and queen are believed to be buried at Dunfermline Abbey.

burial was discovered in about 1750 when workmen taking down part of the old walls found a human body which at first appeared to be perfectly preserved:

It was the figure of a lady splendidly attired, and standing upright. On making the discovery, the men called to their master, who was standing at no great distance; he instantly ran to the place; but, so rapid was the process of decomposition, that, when he came, there was nothing to be seen but a heap of dust. This, however, on account of the great proportion of gold in the clothes, absolutely shone, as he expressed it, like so much gold dust.

Was this a nun who had broken her vows of chastity and been bricked up alive? This historically suspect explanation was often trotted out when skeletons were found upright in walls, a not uncommon mode of burial. In this case, however, since Dunfermline was not a nunnery, Chambers concludes that the lady must have been someone of high birth 'who had been thus buried by way of distinction'.

DUNSINANE, PERTHSHIRE

See MACBETH (p. 318).

EASTER WEMYSS, FIFE

The Wemyss Caves, in the sandstone cliffs of East Wemyss, are strung out like beads along the shore. Now listed as ancient monuments, their evident links with the Picts have excited the interest of antiquarians and archaeologists since the 1860s: their walls are embellished with incised drawings of animals, humans, and symbols. In the Court Cave, the smaller entrance cave shows what may be a stag, together with a figure waving a spear, and the larger cavern within is decorated with a double-disc and what is sometimes called a 'sceptre', which may have given the cave its name.

There is, however, another possible derivation in a story reported by James Wilkie in 1931. According to this, James IV was wandering incognito about the country when he fell in with a band of gypsies, and went with them to their headquarters in the cave. After much merrymaking and drinking a fight broke out between the gypsies. James tried to make peace, but they would have none of it; at last he threw off his homespun disguise and revealed his true identity. At once the tumult ceased: all the gypsies and poor folk of Fife held the king in great affection and respect, and the gang drank his health and escorted him on his way.

A similar story is given in Black's *Picturesque Tourist of Scotland* in 1845, set in the 'King's Cave' (which may be another name for the Court Cave) where James IV took shelter one night.

He found it already occupied by a band of robbers, but having gone too far to retreat, he was under the necessity of joining the company. After some time, supper having been served up, two of the gang approached him with a plate on which lay two daggers – a signal that he was to be put to death. He instantly snatched a weapon in each hand, laid the two robbers prostrate at his feet, and rushed through the rest toward the mouth of the cave. Having fortunately succeeded in making his escape, he returned next day with a sufficient force, and captured the whole band.

Many more or less apocryphal tales are told of the incognito travels of James IV

and James V, including those set at MIL-
NATHORT and COCKBURN'S CASTLE (Lothian & Borders).

See also THE GUIDMAN OF BALLANGEICH
(p. 98).

ERROL, PERTHSHIRE

The noble origins of the Hay family, formerly earls of Errol, are said to date from
the Danish invasion of Scotland in 980.
The Scots were on the verge of defeat at
Luncastry when a countryman called Hay
and his two sons rallied them, and armed
with no more than farm tools fought off
the Danes. After the battle, the old peasant was taken to King Kenneth, who at
Scone granted him as much land as a hawk
let off at Kinnall should fly over before it
settled. The hawk alighted at the Hawk's
Stane, or Falcon Stone, in the parish of St
Madae, or St Madoes, and all the country
between became the property of the Hays.
Milton wanted to write a drama based on
this legend, and Shakespeare used it in
Cymbeline.

Another tradition of the Hays is reported
by John Hay Allan, a member of the
family, writing in 1822:

. . . it appears by an ancient MS and the
tradition of a few old people in
Perthshire, that the badge of the Hays was
the mistletoe. There was formerly in the
neighbourhood of Errol, and not far from
the Falcon stone, a vast oak of an
unknown age, and upon which grew a
profusion of the plant: many charms and
legends were considered to be connected
with the tree, and the duration of the
family of Hay was said to be united with
its existence.

Thomas the Rhymer of EARLSTON (Lothian & Borders) is credited with a prophecy
on the subject:

While the mistletoe bats on Errol's aik
  [clings to Errol's oak]
And that aik stands fast,
The Hays shall flourish and their good
  grey hawk
Shall nocht flinch before the blast.

But when the root of the aik decays,
And the mistletoe dwines [dwindles] on
  its withered breast,
The grass shall grow on Errol's hearthstone,
And the corbie roup [raven croak] in the
  falcon's nest.

The two most unlucky deeds which could
be done by one of the name of Hay were
to kill a white falcon and to cut down a
limb from the oak of Errol. Allan continues:

When the old tree was destroyed I could
never learn. The estate has been some
time sold out of the family of Hay and, of
course, it is said that the fatal oak was cut
down a short time before.

While the tree still stood, a sprig of
mistletoe cut from it on Hallowe'en with a
new dirk, by one who walked thrice round
the tree sunwise, was a certain charm
against witchcraft and 'glamour' (magical
illusion). Mistletoe has been held to be a
sacred and powerful plant in many traditions: the Greeks and Italians counted it as
an emblem of the sun. Fastened to a cradle
it would guard a child from theft by the
fairies, and it was also believed to protect
warriors in battle.

FALKLAND, FIFE

The palace of Falkland was built by James
IV and greatly embellished by James V,
who so loved it that after his army's defeat
at Solway Moss he returned to die in the
palace. Charles II was imprisoned here for

ten days but was luckier than Robert, Duke of Rothesay, said to have been starved to death in the dungeons of the older medieval castle of Falkland.

Rothesay was the son of Robert III (r. 1390–1406), a weak king who governed only in name, leaving the management of the country to his brother the Duke of Albany. Rothesay presenting a challenge to Albany's authority, the wicked uncle is alleged to have taken his nephew captive, as recounted by Robert Chambers in 1827:

There is a tradition in Falkland, that he was for a long time supported by two women, the wives of tradesmen in the town, one of whom purveyed bread to him through a chink in the wall of his dungeon, while the other conveyed the milk of her breast to his mouth by means of an oaten reed. Being at length discovered, his supplies were cut off, and he perished of hunger.

There seems no good reason why the woman should have given the prince her own milk rather than cow's milk (which would surely have been easier to get down the straw), but the image of a woman feeding a starving man from her breast is a deeply moving one, used perhaps to greatest effect in John Steinbeck's *Grapes of Wrath* (1939).

A happier piece of royal history or tradition, also reported by Chambers, is that James VI (r. 1567–1625), walking one day in the garden at Falkland, happened to see one of his courtiers, Alexander Ruthven, lying fast asleep wearing a ribbon which the king recognised immediately as one he had given quite recently to his wife.

Overwhelmed with jealousy and rage, he immediately made off to tax his queen with the infidelity which some historians assert he had but too much reason for suspecting. Before he could see her, however, a ready-witted attendant of the queen's,

who had witnessed his surprise, and guessed the occasion, went up to the person of the incautious gallant, and, stripping the ribbon from his neck, took it to her mistress. She had scarcely time to tell her majesty that she might soon have occasion for it, when the king came in and demanded to see his late love-token.

Thanks to her attendant's quick wits, the queen was able calmly to produce the ribbon, upon which the king was reassured and observed only that '*Like* was an ill mark,' meaning that one should not be deceived by appearances.

Except that it involves a ribbon rather than a ring, this is a secular version of the story told of St Kentigern (St Mungo of GLASGOW, Glasgow & Ayrshire), and can be assumed to be legend (or ill-natured gossip, perhaps) rather than fact.

FINLARIG, PERTHSHIRE

A story translated from a manuscript source and included in Lord Archibald Campbell's *Records of Argyll* (1885) tells that the local court was once at Killin. When the gentlemen came to court they had to stable their horses at the inn, where there was a shortage of space.

Campbell of Glenurchy (Glenorchy) said one day to MacNab of Kinell, who owned most of the land thereabouts, 'I wish you would sell me a bit of land at Finlarig, that I might have a place where to tie my horse when I come to the Court of Killin.'

MacNab asked how much land the knight had in mind. 'Were I to get the length and breadth of a thong,' Campbell replied, 'that would suffice.'

It seemed to MacNab that so much would be but a small bit, and he named the price for which he would sell such a bit of land;

and the knight took MacNab at his word. He got a hide as large as could be found in the country. He got a good shoemaker, and made him begin at the border of the hide and cut it in one thong about the thickness of a latchet [shoelace]. He went to Finlarig, got MacNab himself to be present, and he measured the length of the thong in one direction, across which he measured its length again. So he got a large piece of land for a small price. This was the commencement of the Campbells getting into the land of MacNab; but by little and little they got the whole thereof.

Though this sounds like oral history, the theme of the 'ox-hide measurement' is an ancient one, going back to traditions of the founding of Carthage, and is found in several places in Britain. Tonge in Kent, Tong in Shropshire, and the Kyle of Tongue in Caithness are all said to have got their names from having been encircled with a strip of hide or a thong, although in fact the derivation is from Old Norse *tunga*, 'a strip of land'.

FOSSOWAY, KINROSS-SHIRE

According to David Beveridge, writing in 1888, a stretch of moorland interspersed with hillocks and scrub was known to the people round Fossoway as 'the Monk's Grove'. This, he says, is a corruption of 'the Monk's Grave', the name given to 'a locality now obliterated and forgotten, but connected with a curious legend'.

A chieftain of the Murrays had committed sacrilege by setting fire to a church in which an enemy clan had taken refuge. As a penance, he was made to hand over the lands of Pethwer, or Pitfar, and some other land to the monks of Culross Abbey. Later, a dispute arose with the abbey as to the boundary of the lands they held. A

meeting of the two parties was held, at which one of the Culross clerics said under oath that he was at that moment standing on soil belonging to Culross Abbey. One of the Murrays, infuriated by the seeming perjury, struck the monk down and killed him; it was then found that he had filled his shoes with earth from Culross. The cheating monk was buried where he fell and his grave was long shown as a memorial.

FRIARTON ISLAND, PERTHSHIRE

On the Tay about a mile below Perth is Friarton Island (also known as Moncreiffe Island) and near it in the river is the Friarton Hole. A very large church bell was once being brought to the town, and when unloaded at this place fell into the water. Some years afterwards, according to an early nineteenth-century account, a diver undertook to recover it, but came up without success, and in breathless terror, 'declaring that he had found the devil and his dam making their porridge in it'.

This is a sceptic's joke version of older tales in which church bells, dropped into lakes or rivers, are about to be retrieved when one of the divers incautiously invokes the Devil, upon which the bell sinks and is never seen again.

GLEN ERROCHTY, PERTHSHIRE

Alasdair Challum was 'a poor harmless person' who went about the country in the late nineteenth century paying for his food and shelter by making divinations. For these he used a small four-sided spinning top which John Gregorson Campbell calls a *dòduman* or teetotum. On one occasion, a widow asked him where her late husband was now:

> Alasdair spun round his teetotum and, examining it attentively, said, 'He is a baggage horse to the Fairies in Slevach Cairn, with a twisted willow withe in his mouth.'

Slevach Cairn, a mound at the head of Glen Errochty, was said to be famous as a fairy haunt. It may be the same as what is now listed as 'Sithean' or 'fairy dwelling' in the parish of Blair Atholl.

Alasdair Challum used also to say that the men of nowadays were very small compared to their ancestors, and by means of his spinning top predicted that they would go on getting smaller and smaller, until at last it would take six of them to pull a wisp of hay. This is, of course, the converse of what has happened since the Middle Ages, but Alasdair's thoughts on the subject may have been swayed by the belief that the great heroes of the past, including FINGAL (p. 10) and King Arthur, were much bigger than people today. There is a quite opposite belief that the ancient Picts in particular were very small, so small that in the declining years of the race they gave rise to legends of the fairies: *see* PICTS, PECHS, AND PIXIES (p. 430).

GLEN FINCASTLE,
PERTHSHIRE

In the archives of the School of Scottish Studies is a tale of a Perthshire Brownie, told by Andrew Stewart and recorded by Hamish Henderson in the 1950s. There was once a mill at Glen Fincastle near Tummel Bridge, begins Andrew, which was never worked at night because it was supposed to be haunted. A girl who was to be married next day needed to make food for her wedding, so she went to ask the miller to grind

more flour, even though it was after dark. The miller would not go in himself, but gave her leave to do so if she dared. She lit a fire, put water on to boil, and began to grind the meal. At midnight the door opened and in came 'a wee hairy man'.

'What are you doing here?' said the girl. 'What are you doing yourself, and what is your name?' said the Broonie.

The girl replied that she was '*Mise mi fein*' – 'me myself'. Broonie kept grinning and edging closer, until she got frightened and threw a dipper full of boiling water over him. He gave an awful yell and went for her, but she threw another dipperful over him and he went out of the door yelling.

In the wood was Maggie Moloch, Broonie's wife. Broonie was dying and Maggie said to him, 'Who did this to you?' 'Mise mi fein [me myself],' he cried. 'If it had been any mortal man,' said Maggie, 'I would have taken revenge on him, but since it's you yourself I can do nothing.'

The girl finished her grinding, had her wedding, and moved to Speyside. One night all the women were sitting together spinning and telling stories, and when it came to her turn she told them of her adventure at Fincastle Mill.

When she had finished, a voice outside the door said, 'Aye, was it you killed my man? Ye'll no kill another.' It was Maggie Moloch, and she picked up a stool and threw it at the girl and killed her.

After that, Maggie Moloch changed her living quarters again and went to live near a farm, where the servants put out milk and bannocks for her, and she did good work about the farm and about the house. But times were hard and the farmer thought he had more than enough servants so paid some of them off. Maggie said, 'If they're paying off the servants, I suppose I must be paid off too.' After that she did no more work, but played awful tricks about the house, spilling the milk, breaking the crockery, and ruining everything. The farmer's wife said, 'We'll have no luck until we get all the servants back, every one of them.' Some of them were married and far away by this time, so the farmer had to pay double wages to get them back, but eventually they all returned, Maggie Moloch came too, and things went well again.

Female Brownies are unusual, but Maggie Moloch is a figure with quite a wide circle of operations. In the seventeenth century, John Aubrey mentioned a family spirit of the Grants of Strathspey called Meg Mullack, and Sir Walter Scott, quoting from a manuscript history of Moray, records that the family of Tullochgorm had an 'ancestral being' called May Moulach, 'a female figure, whose left hand and arm were covered by hair'. It is interesting to find her still going strong in twentieth-century Perthshire.

See also LOCH SLOY; ORSAY (Western Isles).

GLENDEVON,
CLACKMANNANSHIRE

Thomas Keightley's *Fairy Mythology* (1850) gives a story set in Glendevon of a farmer who left out some clothes one night for his resident Brownie, who was then heard to depart, saying:

Gie Brownie coat, gie Brownie sark,
Ye'se get nae mair o' Brownie's wark!

A variant given by Keightley suggests that it is the forthright manner in which the offer is made that gives offence:

A good woman had just made a web of linsey-woolsey [a woollen cloth], and, prompted by her good nature, had manufactured from it a snug mantle and hood for her little Brownie. Not content with laying the gift in one of his favourite

spots, she indiscreetly called to tell him it was there. This was too direct, and Brownie quitted the place, crying,

A new mantle and a new hood;
Poor Brownie! ye'll ne'er do mair gude!

This implies that Brownie would have accepted the clothes if she had not been so tactless about it, but in most such tales the gift of clothing is unwelcome in itself.
See also BROWNIES (p. 80).

HILLFOOT FARM, DOLLAR,
CLACKMANNANSHIRE

Not far from Hillfoot Farm in Dollar there was once a large stone 'of peculiar formation, in every way like a cradle', of which a tradition is reported in the *Scottish Journal of Topography* (1848):

It is currently believed by the superstitious in the vicinity, that the stone, every Hallowe'en night, is raised from its place, and suspended in the air by some unseen agency, while 'Old Sandy,' snugly seated upon it, is swung backwards and forwards by his adherents, the witches, until daylight warns them to decamp.

'Old Sandy' is the Devil, often referred to by such nicknames to avoid mentioning him directly, and the stone was known as the 'Deil's Cradle'.

The writer goes on to tell of a 'curious affair' that occurred when a young man had been drinking on Hallowe'en, and had bet his companions that he would visit the stone. Having made his journey through the dark woods, he sat down on the rock and kept his spirits up with the help of a bottle he had brought along, until at last he fell asleep. Now his friends, who had quietly followed him, had their chance. Rushing out, they seized the man by head and feet, carried him to the stream, and

Brownies

A characteristic story of Brownies appears in Thomas Keightley's *Fairy Mythology* (1850). In Strathspey, two such beings were attached to the Tullochgorm family, for whom they performed tasks around the house and farmyard until one of them was rewarded for his labours with a gift of clothes. Immediately he downed tools, announcing that now he had a coat and hood he would never work again.

Variations on this tale are reported in many places throughout northern Europe. The idea of a household spirit or guardian is a very old one, perhaps derived from the Roman *lares*, sometimes said to be the spirits of departed ancestors watching over their descendants. In medieval Europe, stories of supernatural beings who gave a hand with the housework were often linked with warnings that it was a mistake to give them clothing in return. In the fourteenth century, the preacher John of Bromyard mentioned a demon who was offered garments in payment for his toil and at once declared that he would do no more. The same motif is repeated again and again in reference to Scottish Brownies and their relatives such as the English hob or hobgoblin, the breed to which Shakespeare's Puck belongs. *The Mad Pranks and Merry Jests of Robin Goodfellow*, an Elizabethan chapbook used by Shakespeare as a source for his character, tells of a maid who left out a waistcoat in gratitude for the imp's help. Her present was greeted with a contemptuous 'Ho! ho! ho!' and she received no further assistance.

As to *why* it is a bad idea to offer such incentives, the jury is out. Explanations range from the practical – in the Elizabethan source cited above, Robin Goodfellow wanted food, not a fancy waistcoat – to the sartorial, as at DOLPHINTON (Glasgow & Ayrshire) where the Brownie had his heart set on something smarter or more comfortable than a coarse shirt. The folklore collector George Henderson said in 1856 that 'Brownies were commissioned by God to relieve mankind under the drudgery of original sin, hence they were forbidden to accept of wages or bribes,' but Brownies were not usually considered to be creatures of God. On the contrary, some, like the helpful Brownie of DALSWINTON (Dumfries & Galloway), were cast out by interfering priests, while others took off if they saw someone reading a Bible, as reported at COPINSAY (Orkney & Shetland Islands). None of the theories is entirely satisfactory. That neither clothes nor blankets should ever be given can be seen particularly clearly in the story of BOGHALL FARM (Central & Perthshire), where the Brownie is obviously sorry to go but is in some way forced to leave by the gift, against everyone's wishes. No rationalisation can quite make sense of the phenomenon: certain features of legend have to be accepted as things that simply *are*.

Apart from this recurrent theme, other characteristics of the Brownie are fairly consistent. It is usually male, and very rarely harmful, although an exception was Maggie Moloch of GLEN FINCASTLE (Central & Perthshire), female and fatal when provoked to vengeance by the death of her husband. Much more typical was the 'Broonie' described by the Traveller and storyteller Betsy Whyte in 1978, with its iron teeth and protruding eyes, and 'covered in brown hair like a coconut'. Because of its hideous appearance it was feared by all the neighbourhood

Scottish Brownies and English hobgoblins like Shakespeare's Puck were said to be helpful creatures, but would immediately stop work if anyone gave them clothes to wear.

except a young miller named Jack and his wife Katie, who used to leave milk and oatmeal for it to eat, and it helped the couple around the mill. When Katie was about to bear a child, Jack's jealous mother cast a spell to delay the birth, in the hope that the girl would die. After she had lain in agony for many days, the clever Broonie advised Jack to tell his mother that Katie had been delivered of a son. When he did so, the old woman started cursing and naming the charms she had put on Katie: witch-knots in her hair, pillows stuffed with raven's feathers, and a black kitten that was a demonic beast. Jack was too upset to do anything useful, and so it was the Broonie who loosened Katie's hair, threw out the pillows, and strangled the cat. Then Katie bore a beautiful baby boy, and the Broonie stayed on about the place until the wicked witch died. After that it disappeared, but the young couple lived happily ever after.

See also CARSKIEY (Argyllshire & Islands); CLOCHFOLDICH FARM; GLEN-DEVON (Central & Perthshire); BODESBECK FARM (Dumfries & Galloway); CRANSHAWS FARM (Lothian & Borders); NOLTLAND CASTLE (Orkney & Shetland Islands); BAUGH; BERNERAY (Western Isles).

repeatedly dipped him in the cold water, to the accompaniment of hideous yells. The drunkard, convinced that devils and witches were tormenting him, cried for mercy so loudly and piteously that the jokers relented and set him on his feet, at which he immediately ran off as fast as he could, vowing to touch no more liquor and never on any account to visit the Deil's Cradle again.

Stories of practical jokes such as this one do not always have so happy an outcome. Sometimes those on the receiving end go mad, and in the famous case of 'Downie's slaughter' at ABERDEEN UNIVERSITY (North East) the victim reportedly died.

KILLERNIE CASTLE, FIFE

According to the *Statistical Account of Scotland* (1791–9), the estate on which Killernie Castle stands (or stood, since it is now ruined) 'is said to have belonged formerly to one Scot of Balneiry'. By this is meant MICHAEL SCOT, THE WIZARD OF BALWEARIE (p. 62), and David Beveridge, writing in 1888, remarks that 'Killernie Castle used to be known also as the Castle of Balwearie.' There seems something wrong with this, since BALWEARIE CASTLE is a separate building some way away, and surely it would have led to confusion for even a great magician such as Scot to have two residences with exactly the same name.

However that may be, by Beveridge's time only two towers remained of Killernie, of which the southern tower was said to be the more recent, and to date from 1592:

A strange legend is recorded of this part of the building regarding Lady Scott having commissioned a mason to erect it

for her as a summer-house. She refused to pay the stipulated cost, and the disappointed artist revenged himself by murdering her and her child. He was punished for the crime by being shut up in the tower, where he starved to death, having previously been reduced to feed on his own flesh.

This is the grim tale of 'Lamkin', best known as a ballad, a form of which was once current in the parish. The song survives in numerous versions, most of them fragmentary, twenty-six of which are printed in Francis Child's collection of 1857–9. The Northumbrian 'Long Lonkin', communicated to Bishop Percy in 1775, is probably the oldest, but less complete than surviving Scottish transcriptions. According to one of these, printed in *Jamieson's Popular Ballads* (1806):

It's Lamkin was a mason good
as ever built wi' stane;
He built Lord Wearie's castle,
but payment got he nane.

'O pay me, Lord Wearie,
come, pay me my fee:'
'I canna pay you, Lamkin,
for I maun gang oer the sea.'

Although Lamkin vows that he will give Lord Wearie cause to be sorry if he is not paid, the lord tells his lady to keep Lamkin out of the castle and then sails away. A treacherous 'nourice' (nurse), however, lets the mason in at a little window and, when he asks where everyone is, reveals that the men are in the fields, the women washing at the well, and the lady up in her bower sewing. She herself has charge of the baby, and Lamkin takes a sharp knife and stabs the child. In one of the most chilling moments of balladry, Lamkin then rocks the baby while the nurse sings, until the blood flows from every hole of the cradle:

Then Lamkin he rocked,
     and the fause nourice sang,
Till fra ilke bore o the cradle
     the red blood out sprang.

The lady calls down to ask why her baby son cries so, and the nurse lures her down to an encounter with Lamkin, who asks:

'O sall I kill her, nourice,
     or sall I lat her be?'

receiving the casually vindictive answer:

'O kill her, kill her, Lamkin,
     for she neer was good to me.'

The deed is done, but three months later, when Lord Wearie returns and sees the bloodstains of his wife and child on the floor, retribution follows. Lamkin is condemned to die (unspecified how), and the nurse is burned at the stake.

On both sides of the Border, the villain of the ballad was used as a nursery terror – an imaginary character used to frighten the young into good behaviour. Until at least 1891, Northumbrian children were told to be home before dark or Lonkin would get them, while in Scotland the ironic name 'Lamkin' ('Little Lamb') belies the horror evoked by this childhood bogey.

The name 'Wearie' occurring in the text suggests that BALWEARIE is the castle referred to, but in any case it is most unlikely that events there or at Killernie gave rise to the ballad. The song probably came first, the events then becoming localised at various old houses, and family names slotted in to fit the characters.

See also BORDER BALLADS (p. 224).

woman making porridge. The dish boiled so fiercely that a spark from the porridge flew and struck him in the eye. He saw the fairies ever after with that eye.

Sadly that is not the end of the story as told by John Gregorson Campbell, minister of Tiree, in *Superstitions of the Highlands and Islands of Scotland* (1900). One day, at the St Fillan market at Killin, the man saw a great number of fairies riding about the market on white horses. Meeting one whom he recognised, he commented on how many of the fairies were there. The fairy asked in return which eye he saw him with, and, on being told, put it out. This is standard fairy procedure with humans who gain the ability to see them, usually by using 'fairy ointment', meant only for the eyes of fairy children.

The idea of a fairy making porridge may seem out of character to modern readers, used to the whimsical portrayal of fairies derived largely from children's books. However, fairies in Highland belief were thought to pursue the same occupations as mankind. They were said to practise all kinds of trades and handicrafts and to possess cattle, dogs, and weapons; they needed food, clothes, and sleep, and sometimes drank liquor. Like human beings, they were not immortal, but liable to disease and could be killed. Campbell writes that people entering fairy dwellings found the inmates engaged in weaving, making weapons, dancing, or sitting round a fire in the middle of the floor (as a Perthshire informant put it) 'like tinkers'.

KILLIN, PERTHSHIRE

Near Killin, in Perthshire, a man entered a Fairy Knowe and found inside a

KINGHORN, FIFE

A 'grim old story' lingered in the nineteenth century of John Scrimgeour, minister of Kinghorn in the sixteenth century, whose wife fell into a trance and was believed dead. When she was laid in the tomb the sexton tried to wrench the rings from her cold fingers; the assault awakened her, and she arose. The robber fled in terror, and the dead-alive wife walked home in her shroud and appeared in her astonished husband's study. They say she never smiled again. 'The lady restored to life' is an international theme, and the same story was told in 1858 of the minister's wife of Crail, whose husband mistook her for a ghost on her return home. Of her, too, it was said that after this experience 'a smile was never observed on her countenance'.

Another local legend tells how King Alexander III came to his death. One version says that the king was returning on horseback at night to Glammis Tower, his castle above Kinghorn. His horse shied and threw him over a high and sheer cliff

Some claim that the death of Alexander III (r. 1249–86) at Kinghorn was foretold by Thomas the Rhymer, the famous poet and seer; others that it was prophesied by the notorious wizard Michael Scot.

along the summit of which the path led. He fell, and died hitting his head on a rock thereafter 'known as the King's Stone'.

According to a second story, the king was passionately fond of hunting and rode a high-spirited horse. Thomas the Rhymer of EARLSTON (Lothian & Borders) told the king that the horse would be his death, and one day on the Kinghorn road an archer shot an arrow which glanced off a tree, struck the horse, and killed it. 'And how can your prophecy come true?' asked the king. Some months later, the king was riding that way on another horse, which shied at the bones of the first horse still lying there and threw the king, who was killed in this way.

Yet a third version records that it was MICHAEL SCOT, THE WIZARD OF BALWEARIE (p. 62) who prophesied that the king's favourite charger would cause his death. Hearing this, Alexander, in a fit of passion, killed it on the spot. A year later, as he rode another horse the same way, it shied on seeing the bones, throwing the king and fulfilling the prophecy. Attempts to avoid a predicted death are always futile, as shown for instance in the story of CONON HOUSE (Southern Highlands).

KINNESTON, KINROSS-SHIRE

A traditional anecdote of Kinneston recorded by David Beath in 1902 explains a local saying:

A neighbouring laird in the estate of Kinneston . . . on one occasion called out to one of his young lads, who was passing somewhat smartly, 'Whaur noo, Jock?' 'Od, maister, I'm gaun to my supper; it's sax o'clock isn't [it]?' 'Maybe it is, Jock,' says the laird, 'but what hae ye been daein' the day?' 'O,' says Jock, 'I was helpin' Tam Broon.' 'Just so,' says the

laird, 'but what was Tam Broon daein'?'
'Weel,' says Jock, . . . 'he was daein'
naething.'

Beath says that, down to his own day, it was proverbial in the district to say of anyone skiving off work that he had been 'helpin' Tam Broon'.

KIRKCALDY, FIFE

In his 1914 book on the folklore of Fife, John Ewart Simpkins quotes an old couplet apropos of Kirkcaldy's traditional nickname of the 'Lang Toun':

> Some say the deil's dead
> And buried in Kirkcaldy.

He reports that the buried Devil kept complaining that his toes were cold, so house after house was added to the long length of Kirkcaldy to make his feet warm and keep him quiet. The nineteenth-century antiquary Robert Chambers more prosaically derives the epithet from the fact that the original town was extended westward over the Links or Downs, the additional part being called the 'Link Town', gradually corrupted to 'Lang Town'.

LAG UAINE, DUNBARTONSHIRE

North-west of Arrochar, between Beinn Ime and Ben Vane, runs the Allt Coire Grogain, a tributary of the Inveruglas Water. Near the head of the valley is a pool in a hollow known as Lag Uaine, 'Green Hollow', where the fairies of the Lennox Hills are said to have had a secret dye factory. 'Far removed from the interferences of men, they were able to keep to themselves the secret processes whereby they dyed such articles as were sent to them from time to time,' writes Alasdair

Alpin MacGregor, telling this story in *The Peat-Fire Flame* (1937). He does not explain who sent these articles to be dyed, but obviously the cloth would be turned green, the fairy colour.

The people of Loch Lomond and Loch Fyneside were inquisitive about the fairies' work, and made many attempts to spy on them. One day, a fairy on Beinn Ime gave warning that a great number of men were making their way up the mountain from Butterbridge in Glen Kinglas, and having no time to hide their apparatus, the fairies emptied their dye into the pool. 'And this explains how, to this day, the waters of this pool in the Green Hollow among the mountains have such a wonderful green colour.'

LEVEN, FIFE

The trade of an antiquarian can be a perilous one. Entering the burial-ground of Leven, Robert Chambers saw to his astonishment a notice overhanging the road with the laconic and fearfully emphatic inscription: *Take notice, – any person entering this church-yard will be shot.* 'The reader,' he says, 'will have no difficulty in referring this formidable advertisement to its proper cause, – the alarm which everywhere prevails regarding resurrection-men.' He was writing in 1827, the very year in which Burke took up lodgings with Hare off the GRASSMARKET in Edinburgh (Lothian & Borders) and moved bodysnatching into a new dimension.

'The fear of nocturnal attempts upon the tombs of their friends may be said to have succeeded, in the minds of the common people, the old superstitions regarding ghosts and fairies,' Chambers continues, adding that this is so particularly in remote rural areas, where strangers are automatically considered as having their eye on the graves. While researching his book *The Picture of Scotland* he visited the churchyard at Torphichen in West Lothian to look at the remains of the Preceptory of the Knights of St John:

> While engaged in a drawing, I was accosted by an old woman with a very civil observation upon the fineness of the day. I heartily agreed with her, that the day was very fine. She then hinted the supposition that I was a stranger in this country-side. I confessed the fact.

Had he friends there? she asked. He replied that he had not. She said the people did not like to see folk coming about the churchyards that had no business with them. She asked what he had come there for.

> Before I could answer this question, another old lady came up, and, apparently resolved to treat me with less delicacy, cried with a loud screeching voice, 'Faith, billy, ye needna think for to come here to play your pranks . . .'

The first speaker was inclined to believe that Chambers had simply come to see the old kirk, but the second would have none of it: he was fonder of kirkyards than of kirks, she was sure. A third old lady was appalled to notice that Chambers had his legs astride over a grave, as if already making sure of a corpse.

> 'Oh, the blackguard!' Other old women were now gathering around me, alike alive to the horror of my supposed character, not knowing how soon it might be their fate to come under my hands . . . Suffice it to say that I had at last to make a precipitate retreat from Torphichen.

Grave robbery is perhaps the nearest real-life equivalent to vampirism, rumours of which provoked mob behaviour in early twentieth-century Glasgow in the case of THE VAMPIRE WITH IRON TEETH (p. 186).

See also TRAVELLER TALES (p. 298).

LINGO HOUSE,
PITTENWEEM, FIFE

In the house of Lingo which had once belonged to the priory of Pittenweem there hung, 'till recently' said James Wilkie in 1931, a portrait of General Dalyell, bald and bearded, and under it the general's huge riding boots:

> Legends yet linger concerning these boots. On nights when the moon shone in fitful gleams as the clouds scudded over the sky, or when the stars of winter alone burned in the heavens, they would disappear from their accustomed place. Out on the moors that of old comprised the Boar's Chase flew a ghostly steed, the boots striking spurred heels into its flanks and the feet of a bearded phantom filling them. It was the shade of the fierce old cavalier in wild pursuit of invisible Whigs as in the days when word was brought in of an unlawful gathering in some remote hollow, and the General buckled on the broadsword ever by his chair and leaped on his ready-bridled horse calling on his men to follow.

There is no obvious reason why the general's boots should have been at Lingo when he lived at THE BINNS (Lothian & Borders), but the legend of Dalyell was widespread in lowland Scotland. He was, as Wilkie remarks, one of those who 'peopled the inferno of the Whigs', his fellow-demons including John Graham of Claverhouse and Robert Grierson of Lag. All three were said to have been IN LEAGUE WITH THE DEVIL (p. 142) on account of their persecution of Covenanters, the religious rebels who struggled against the established Church in the seventeenth century. Many Covenanters were poor people whose diet included a good deal of sour milk or whey, called *whigg* in Scots, and they thus became known as Whiggamores or 'sour milk men'. This was soon abbreviated to 'Whigs', a word which was then applied generally to those supporting a Protestant succession to the throne, and later still to the Liberal party as opposed to the Conservatives or Tories.

LOCH AN DAIMH, PERTHSHIRE

The old winding road from Rannoch to Aberfeldy skirts Schiehallion, a mountain once home to hundreds of wild goats, the last of which was said to have been shot by a Canadian soldier stationed at Dall during the Second World War. The road is sometimes called 'the Goat Track', a name possibly given by the Canadians, though according to another version it commemorates the Gabhar, half-man, half-goat, which once terrorised the environs of a stream running into Loch an Daimh. Any traveller who forded the stream by night would be followed by the creature, suddenly looming out of the darkness. Because of this, no one dared go near the place after nightfall, but one man who came to visit relatives at Kilichonan cannot have been warned. He never arrived, and a fortnight later a woman of Rannoch suggested looking around the loch above Crossmount, as she had 'seen' something there among the rushes. She was known to have SECOND SIGHT (p. 474), and sure enough the man's body was found cruelly mangled by the Gabhar.

A relation of the dead man, Cailein Suil Dubh ('Colin Black-eyes'), came from Lochaber to catch the Gabhar. Late one evening he set off, and called at a house near the ford to ask if he was in the right place. The weaver who lived there showed

concern for his safety, asking how he could defend himself if attacked. Colin answered that he had his gun, his sword, and 'the cat behind the hip', by which he meant his *sgian dubh*, or dirk. The phrase mystified the weaver, who sent Colin on his way.

As the light was fading the creature appeared and prepared to spring at Colin. It looked like a goat walking on its hind legs, but with the claws of a cat, the fangs of a dog, and an otherwise human face. Colin fired his gun, but the trigger failed; he tried to draw his sword, but it stuck in the scabbard. The monster knocked him to the ground and went for his throat, but Colin managed to pull out 'the cat behind the hip', and thrust the blade into the Gabhar's side and chest. Shrieking with pain, it vanished into the night.

Bruised and bleeding, Colin made his way back to the weaver's house, where he found its owner lying in bed. Pulling back the covers, Colin saw that the man had been wounded in his chest and side. Colin pulled out his dirk again, and the weaver leaped up and ran. Colin caught up with him on top of a cliff, where the Gabhar resumed his demon shape, but Colin stabbed him to the heart, cut off his head, and threw it far into the loch.

Today a road and a culvert have replaced the track and the ford, but as you pass between the cliff and the loch it is said that you can still see a headless goat turned to stone on the clifftop.

The story of Colin and the weaver is an unusual variant of an international story known as 'The witch that was hurt', other versions of which are told at MAXTON and YARROWFOOT (both Lothian & Borders). Here the theme of the wound inflicted on the wer-animal showing up on the witch's own body has been conflated with the theme of the demonic guardian of the ford.

LOCH CON, LOWER RANNOCH, PERTHSHIRE

Loch Con is linked by the River Con with the larger Loch Errochty to the south. Near here a robber once made an underground house for his wife so that he could swear he had no wife above ground, a prevarication to suggest that he had no wife living. Thinking that his oath was good, he then felt free to marry again, but his evasion did not help him. At his death, twelve ravens were waiting to carry off his soul, like the three demonic ravens sent to claim MICHAEL SCOT, THE WIZARD OF BALWEARIE (p. 62). In the magician's case the ravens were baulked of their prey, but the robber was less fortunate.

LOCH ERICHT, PERTHSHIRE

A local legend relates the creation of Loch Ericht, one of a long line of traditions, reaching back at least as far as the story of Atlantis, concerning a city drowned for its sins. Not far from Rannoch, goes the story, lay the town of Feodail, amid rich and fertile fields watered by the River Ericht. Not content with their luck, however, the people of Feodail would often descend on Rannoch and steal the cattle, doing this so often that eventually the people of Rannoch found themselves in great need. The wise elders of the district, however, told them that the wickedness of Feodail would surely be punished.

And so it came to pass. One night, Rannoch people felt the ground tremble beneath their feet and then an eruption in the valley of the Ericht released great spouts of water from underground. Men and beasts alike disappeared into the torrent, and where Feodail had been, the morning light revealed the great expanse of Loch Ericht.

Now on a clear day, so the story goes, if you look down into its waters, you may perhaps see the village of Feodail – its church tower, its thatched roofs, its gardens, and its fields. And when the wind gets up and stirs the surface into choppy waves, you may hear the church bell ringing a warning to the wicked: 'Remember Feodail.'

Perthshire seems to have been prone to this sort of thing, though in the similar tale of LOCH KATRINE a demon rather than a divine punishment was said to have been at work.

LOCH KATRINE, PERTHSHIRE

According to John Barbour, writing in 1886, a clergyman enquiring after 'Celtic traditions' around Glen Gyle was told the story of the lake's origins by 'an old highland crone'. In ancient times, she said, the valley now filled by Loch Katrine was dotted about with the dwellings of a wise and virtuous people. They were shepherds and foresters who gave offence to none, except to a demon who lived in a cave on Ben Venue. He often wished to work them some harm, but was for a long time foiled. Finally, however, he succeeded all too well.

There was a sacred spring in the side of Ben Venue which the villagers guarded jealously for their use. A girl by the name of Katrine was charged with watching over it at night. One evening, however, the demon came to her in the shape of a handsome young man bearing a bowl of mountain berries, which he persuaded her to eat. She did so, and because he had treated them with some drug, she soon fell into a deep slumber. He meanwhile let out all the sluices of the well so that the water poured

This peaceful photograph of Loch Katrine belies the tradition that it was created by a malicious demon.

down into the valley. Because by now it was night and all the villagers were asleep, most of them were drowned. 'On the evening of the next day, when the girl came to the well, she saw the disaster that had befallen because of her want of vigilance and in despair threw herself into the lake, which ever since has borne her name.'

The 'crone' said that ever since then the valley had remained flooded, and she pointed out near the banks of the loch what she said were the remnants of buildings. She said that the demon still had a cave by the loch, known as the Cave of the Goblin or the Den of the Ghost, 'and that at nightfall he was often heard to utter yells of malicious joy, which some of the natives mistook for the screams of the eagle'.

Barbour notes that the tradition bears a strong resemblance to one concerning the origin of LOCH AWE (Argyllshire & Islands). It is indeed an international legend, 'The Overflowing Well', traditionally told in Celtic-speaking areas of the creation of lakes and the drowning of cities and villages.

LOCH LEVEN, KINROSS-SHIRE

A number of local traditions are attached to Loch Leven. A 'popular saying' recorded by David Beveridge in 1888 connected its name with the number eleven, the loch being eleven miles round, surrounded by eleven hills and the lands of eleven lairds, fed or drained by eleven streams, and containing eleven islands and eleven kinds of fish, and Mary, Queen of Scots, having resided for eleven months in the castle that stands on one of the islands. The name 'Leven', however, has nothing to do with the Scots words *eleevin, alevin*, or other forms meaning the number eleven: it is probably derived from the Gaelic *leamhan*, related to the Latin *lemo*, *limo*, meaning 'an elm', making Loch Leven a cognate of Lac Leman in Switzerland.

By modern medical standards, perhaps the most curious traditional belief concerning the loch was that eels from its waters cured deafness – they are said to have been sent to London for this purpose. The *Statistical Account of Scotland* for 1791–99 does not mention this practice, but comments on the remarkable quantity of eels in the River Leven:

> In the month of September they begin to go down from the loch in great numbers to the sea, but only during the night. When this season arrives, the fishers place their nets in the river, which they draw every two hours during the night, and frequently find them full. As the bulk of the people have an aversion to them as food, from their serpentine appearance, this fishing turns to little account in the view of profit.

It seems, therefore, that some quick-witted local entrepreneurs may have promoted as medicine what they could not sell as food.

LOCH SLOY, DUNBARTONSHIRE

A man passing through Strath *Duuisg*, near Loch Sloy, at the head of Loch Lomond, on a keen frosty night, heard an Urisk on one side of the glen calling out, 'Frost, frost, frost' (*reoth, reoth, reoth*).

This was answered by another Urisk calling from the other side of the glen, 'Kick-frost, kick-frost, kick-frost' (*ceige-reoth*, etc.). The man, on hearing this, said, 'Whether I wait or not for frost, I will never while I live wait for kick-frost'; and he ran at his utmost speed till he was out of the glen.

This obscurely threatening little story comes from John Gregorson Campbell's *Superstitions of the Highlands and Islands of Scotland* (1900), and illustrates the Urisk's liking for lonely mountains. The creature would most often be seen in the evening as a large grey form sitting on top of a rock and watching those who might come by. It was, says Campbell, 'a large lubberly supernatural, of solitary habits and harmless character', and might even guide benighted travellers, although it sometimes gave them a beating, and the Loch Sloy man evidently fears something of this nature.

Although most often referred to as 'he', there were both male and female Urisks. The race is said by some to have sprung from the union of fairies and mortals, and may be identified with the Brownie. Campbell raises the objection that they live in remote localities rather than in or near houses; in this the Urisk resembles the hobs and hobthrusts of north-eastern England, many of whom seem to have preferred solitude.

Highland stories told of the Urisk coming down for warmth to the farmhouses in the wintertime, and then being put to work grinding or threshing. In Strathglass, Inverness-shire, a farmer wished to domesticate his Urisk and so gelded it: 'The weather at the time being frosty, it made a considerable outcry for some time after.'

Another nasty trick played on the harmless Urisk was told by Thomas Keightley in *The Fairy Mythology* (1850). A miller noticed that his mill was being operated mysteriously at night-time when there was nothing to grind. Annoyed and worried about possible damage to his machinery, he set a man to watch and see who the intruder was, but as the watchman had made up a good fire of peats, the warmth lulled him to sleep. When around midnight he awoke, he saw sitting opposite him a rough, shaggy being. Boldly he asked its name and it answered, 'Urisk.' On being asked what his own name was, he said, 'Myself.' After this exchange, the Urisk fell fast asleep by the fire and the man tipped a panful of hot ashes into his lap, setting his shaggy fur alight. Screaming, the Urisk ran to the door, and several of his kind outside were heard yelling, 'What's the matter with you?' 'Oh, he set me on fire!' cried the Urisk. 'Who did?' 'Myself!' 'Then put it out yourself,' they replied.

This relates to an international folktale found in ancient Greece in the 'Noman' story of Odysseus and the giant Polyphemus, and also involves the general belief that it was hazardous to give one's true name to fairies and other supernatural beings. Scottish versions of the tale are set at GLEN FINCASTLE and ORSAY (Western Isles), and another story involving the Urisk is told at GLEN MALLIE (Southern Highlands).

LOCH VENACHAR, PERTHSHIRE

On 16 July 1800, John Leyden was travelling near Loch Venachar. He writes:

Our guide informed us that the people of the vale had been a good deal alarmed by the appearance of that unaccountable being the water-horse (*Each Uisge*) during the spring, which had not been seen there since the catastrophe of

Corlevrann, *the wood of woe*, when he carried into the loch fifteen children who had broken Pace Sunday. I made enquiries concerning the habits of the animal, and was only able to learn that its colour was brown, that it could speak, and that its motion agitated the lake with prodigious waves, and that it only emerged in the hottest midday to be on the bank.

Many similar stories were told of KELPIES AND WATER-HORSES (p. 364), partly to warn children to keep away from dangerous rivers and pools. There is often a moral element to such tales: here, for instance, the victims have 'broken Pace Sunday'; in other words, they have indulged in worldly pleasures at Easter.

That the Water-horse could carry as many as fifteen riders implies that he could magically lengthen his back. This was a common attribute of such evil creatures, although the ability was also ascribed to Bayard, the famous horse of French romance that carried the hero Renaud of Montauban and the Four Sons of Aymon.

LUNDIN LINKS STANDING STONES, FIFE

At a little distance westward from Largo, in the middle of a park on the north side of the road, is the celebrated curiosity called 'the Standing Stanes o' Lundie.' Three tall straight sharp stones, resembling whales jaws more than any thing else, rear themselves at the distance of a few yards from each other, and, though several yards high, are supposed to pierce the ground to the same depth. According to the common people, they are monuments to the memory of three Danish generals slain here in battle; but it is more probable they are of Roman origin, it being the site of a Roman town.

Many theories have been proposed concerning the standing stones at Lundin Links. One claims that they are of Roman origin, another that they are monuments to Danish chieftains vanquished by Macbeth. Neither is true, since the stones date from the second millennium BCE.

This is how Robert Chambers described the stones in 1827, and Black's *Picturesque Tourist* of 1844 agrees cautiously that they 'are supposed to be of Roman origin', but is right not to be too definite, since the stones are now thought to date from the second millennium BCE. They may have had some funerary significance, as 'ancient sepulchres' are said to have been in the vicinity; these may have been cremation deposits such as have been found near other standing stones, for example the Orwell standing stones at the north end of Loch Leven.

Another theory current in the 1840s was that the stones were 'Druidical' remains, but the most interesting tradition is that of the 'Danish generals' referred to briefly by Chambers; what he does not say is that these chieftains were supposed to have been defeated by Banquo and MACBETH (p. 318).

MAGUS MUIR, FIFE

At Holy Trinity Kirk, St Andrews, is a marble monument to the memory of Archbishop Sharp with a statue of the archbishop in kneeling posture, his countenance 'that of a thin, cunning-looking old man, with a cocked nose'. A delineation in bas-relief of his murder shows his assassins in the costume of the time – flat blue bonnets, long cravats, wideskirted coats, and boots. He reclines on the ground, and while one is leaning forward to shoot him with a pistol, another is standing behind and fetching a dreadful back-stroke at his head.

The crime was part of the backlash that followed Charles II's restoration of episcopacy to the Church of Scotland. James Sharp, formerly minister of Crail, had been appointed Archbishop of St Andrews, and had been involved in the government reprisals following the Pentland Rising of 1666, when dissenters had marched on Edinburgh. The rebellion had been brutally repressed, and Sharp was therefore a target for the Covenanters, as the dissidents called themselves. In May 1679, a band of fanatics pursued the archbishop's coach along the road across Magus Muir.

> Being all mounted on the ordinary little horses then used by Scottish gentlemen, they found that the carriage was gaining upon them, when Hackstoun of Rathillet, who happened to have a blood-mare, ordered his servant to mount, and if possible, cut the traces of the vehicle, so as to stop it. The man overtook the carriage and having with his sword cut the traces on one side, caused it immediately to diverge from the road towards the left hand, and eventually to stop.

The archbishop was then pulled from his carriage and hacked to death. 'It is a shocking fact that these inhuman enthusiasts did not leave their butchered victim till they observed the contents of his stomach projected upon the ground,' observes Robert Chambers in *The Picture of Scotland* (1827).

It was, however, later remarked that hardly any of the murderers came to a peaceful end. One strange story was told to Chambers by 'the grandson of a person who witnessed it': in the 1730s, an aged man, forlorn and wretched-looking, asked for lodging at a small inn at Portsburgh, Edinburgh. He seemed to have had a long and painful journey, and was supposed to have come from the west. During the night his dreadful groans alarmed the people of the house, who ran to his bedside. A light was brought, and it was plain from his glazed eyes, his clenched jaw, and the convulsions that wracked his body, that he was on the point of death.

> In a little time, collecting the remnants of his strength, he raised his right hand above his head, and exclaimed in a broken but terrific voice, 'There's the hand that slaughtered Bishop Sharpe. Is there ony blude on't, think ye?' Having uttered this, he expired. The body was buried amidst the strangers in the Greyfriars churchyard.

See also IN LEAGUE WITH THE DEVIL (p. 142).

MAIDEN CASTLE, NEAR GLENDEVON, PERTHSHIRE

Near Dollar in the Ochil Hills is the village of Glendevon. At the top of the glen through which runs the Queich is a low round hill known as Maiden Castle, and traditionally believed to be a fairy hill.

Here is set the story of 'The Piper of Glendevon', told by Sir John Rhys in his *Celtic Folk-Lore* (1901). He had it from the Reverend Andrew Clark, who had heard it from the late sexton of Dollar. The sexton, who had died about twelve years previously, aged seventy, had learned the tale from his father.

> A piper, carrying his pipes, was coming from Glendevon to Dollar in the grey of evening. He crossed the Garchel (a little stream running into the Queich burn), and looked at the 'Maiden Castle,' and saw only the grey hillside and heard only the wind soughing through the bent. He had got beyond it when he heard a burst of lively music: he turned round, and instead

of the dark knoll saw a great castle, with lights blazing from the windows, and heard the noise of dancing issuing from the open door.

The piper incautiously went back, just as a procession of fairies came from the mound. He was caught and taken into a great hall ablaze with lights, full of people dancing. He had to pipe for them for a day or two, but became anxious because he knew his family would be wondering what had happened to him. The fairies promised to let him go if he played a particular tune to their satisfaction. He played his very best, the dance was fast and furious, and at the end he was greeted with loud applause.

> On his release he found himself alone, in the grey of the evening, beside the dark hillock, and no sound was heard save the purr of the burn and the soughing of the wind through the bent. Instead of completing his journey to Dollar, he walked hastily back to Glendevon to relieve his folk's anxiety.

Entering his father's house, he found not a single face he knew. When he protested that he had been gone only a day or two, a grey old man was roused from a doze beside the fire, and told how when he was only a boy he had heard from his father that a piper had gone away to Dollar on a quiet evening, and had never been seen nor heard of since, nor any trace of him found. The piper had been in the 'castle' for a hundred years.

Katharine Briggs assigns this story to an international tale type known as 'The seven sleepers'. However, the Piper of Glendevon and the fairies are anything *but* asleep inside the mound, unlike the Seven Sleepers of Ephesus, King Arthur in British legends, or Thomas the Rhymer or FINGAL (p. 10) in Scottish ones. The story, which has several Welsh parallels, is a local combination of the themes of the fairy hill

entered by a mortal, and the supernatural lapse of time in fairyland.

MEIGLE, PERTHSHIRE

In Meigle Museum is a remarkable collection of Pictish carved stones dating from the transitional or Early Christian period, that is from around the eighth century. The dominant stone is an upright cross-slab with a depiction of Daniel in the Lions' Den, a motif used from the second century onwards to symbolise the delivery of the faithful from the power of evil; on this stone are also representations of equestrian figures, angels, hounds, a centaur, and a dragon. Another exhibit, a recumbent gravestone, shows coiled serpents, sea-horses, a four-legged beast with a human head (perhaps a manticore) pursuing a naked Pict who looks apprehensively over his shoulder, and a pair of animals devouring or disgorging a man's body: one holds his leg in its mouth, while the severed head appears above.

It is not at all surprising that legends were woven around these stones where they originally lay in Meigle churchyard. The early sixteenth-century chronicles of Hector Boece, translated by John Bellenden in 1531, give the story that 'Guanora', Queen of Britain and wife of King Arthur, is buried here, adding that any woman who walks on her grave will be barren, 'and quhether this be of verite or nocht', he vouches for the fact that 'euery woman, except nunnys, aborris to stampe on that sepulture.'

The tale is repeated by Robert Chambers in 1827, although he acknowledges that this is only one of many burial places assigned in popular tradition to Guanora, Vanora, or Guinevere (the name Guendolen is also mentioned in a story told at POWSAIL BURN (Lothian & Borders), where she is said to be the wife of Merlin). Chambers is particularly interested in the human body being eaten by what he identifies as dogs, and mentions a story that 'Queen Vanora', after the defeat of her lover (unnamed here), took up her abode in a fort on top of the hill of Banna near Meigle. Soon afterwards, hunting in the forest, she was attacked and torn to pieces by dogs, which ate every part of her 'except the right hand that had committed so many iniquities'.

It seems strange, Chambers comments, that the monument is so elaborate if nothing is buried there except a hand. He must, however, be well aware that the tale is one that goes back to Old Testament times: 'The dogs shall eat Jezebel by the wall of Jezreel . . . And they went to bury her: but they found no more of her than the skull, and the feet, and the palms of her hands.'

MELVILLE'S MANSE,
ANSTRUTHER EASTER, FIFE

Melville's Manse in Anstruther Easter was once the home of the Reverend Edward Thomson, 'the Curat of Anstruther', who was apparently claimed by the Devil on a dark Saturday night, 19 December 1685.

He had been married for about twelve years and had six children, but his wife had recently died, leaving him 'very sad and heavy', and he had resorted to drink. Robert Louis Stevenson, telling his story, puts him on the verge of delirium tremens. However that may have been, he was returning from a visit to a friend beyond the Dreel Burn, accompanied by a maidservant with a lantern, when as they set foot on the bridge a monstrous bat-like shape bore down on them, passed them by, and vanished into the darkness.

The maid, perhaps because she had heard strange talk about the 'Curat', did not

doubt that the shape was the Devil come to claim his own. The minister seemed to think so too, for he fell to his knees and prayed for deliverance, then stumbled onwards with the terrified maid. On reaching the manse, he took the lantern from her hand and his look was so despairing that with a horrifed scream she fled through the darkness home to her parents. The minister entered his manse and was not seen alive again. Next morning when he was called, his room was empty, and in the early dawn they found his body in Dreel Burn.

James Wilkie, recounting this story in *Bygone Fife* (1931), attempts to identify Thomson as the licentiate of ST ANDREWS, but the two traditions are a poor fit unless the minister is thought carelessly to have sold his soul *twice*.

MENSTRIE,
CLACKMANNANSHIRE

Black's *Picturesque Tourist of Scotland* (1844) gives a vivid description of the hills near DUMYAT:

In its neighbourhood is Bencleuch, which shoots up into a tall rocky point called Craigleith, remarkable in ancient times for the production of falcons. In a hollow near this the snow often lies far into the summer. The people give it the picturesque name of Lady Alva's Web.

Alva village lies at the bottom of the hill, and 'Lady Alva' was the title given to the lady of the manor, supposed to have been fond of bleaching linen (a 'web' is a piece of cloth). The author goes on to quote a 'fairy rhyme', without further explanation:

Oh, Alva woods are bonnie,
    Tillicoultry hills are fair,
But when I think o' the bonnie braes o'
    Menstrie,
        It mak's my heart aye sair.

The verse is taken from a story quoted in the *Scottish Journal of Topography* (1848) about a Menstrie miller whose wife was stolen by the fairies, and who heard her every morning singing that mournful little song. Fortunately one day he happened to stand on one foot, 'as the hens do in rainy weather'; this broke the spell and he found his wife beside him. Robert Chambers, telling the same tale twenty years earlier, merely mentions the miller's 'magical posture' without saying what it was.

It might have been the same fairies who sometime in the mid eighteenth century met a man known as the 'Black Laird of Dunblane' late one night in Menstrie Glen and took him merrymaking with them. They were riding bundles of straw, but the Black Laird needed something more substantial and took an old plough-beam. With a cry of 'Brechin to the Bridal' they all seemed to be mounted on white horses which took them flying through the air to Brechin, where they took part in a banquet, unseen by the mortal guests. Then calling out, 'Cruinan to the Dance,' they flew on to Cruinan. At last the Black Laird, overcome with admiration, exclaimed, 'Weel dune, Watson's auld plough-beam!' and immediately found himself alone in Menstrie Glen.

In such magical journeys with fairies and witches, the extra traveller is more likely to find himself stranded in the distant place where he has been taken, and is often the scapegoat for the pilfering of his supernatural companions, as happened for instance at KINTAIL (Southern Highlands). The Black Laird, however, as his nickname hints, was not quite the innocent mortal of similar tales. He was in fact no laird but a travelling tailor, men of which profession were often said to be in closer communication than others with the fairies. He also practised herbal medicine, and had even seen and spoken with the

Devil. He never told the details of this interview, except that the fiend had 'tried to terrify the Laird from using his herbs in removing witch-spells', but as he continued his cures it must be assumed that he got the better of the encounter.

METHIL, FIFE

In the early seventeenth century, David, Earl of Wemyss, built himself a house at Methil in the shape of a ship. It was a long building with two rows of windows like the portholes on a double-decker vessel, and with a nearly flat roof, arched slightly in the centre like the deck of a man-o'-war. A new pointed roof of tiles was later added.

A phantom was reported to haunt the ship-house, of whom an account was given by Henry Farnie in around 1860:

> The ghost in question was once a wood merchant or carpenter, and contracted to supply the wood work of the double-decker. Somehow or another, his little account was not paid, and in despair (having to meet a bill very likely), he drowned himself in Methill harbour. And this would have been bad enough – but he was vindictive, and concluded to haunt the place which he had fitted up at his unrequited pains. Taking, therefore, upon himself, by common consent, the somewhat unaccountable name of Thrummy-cap, he proceeded to disturb, and still disturbs, the midnight equanimity of the crew of Earl David's double-decker.

Farnie adds that he tried to get some more information from an old fisherman who lived in the house, but the man said he did not remember Thrummy-cap – which, says the narrator, was likely to be true, as the carpenter had drowned himself about a century and a half earlier.

A 'thrummy cap' is a hat made of frayed

cloth, and the name 'Thrummy Cap' was used as a euphemism for the Devil, probably in reference to the traditional image of Satan as having shaggy hair. Robert Burns's cousin John Burness wrote a poem, well known in the nineteenth century (though apparently unfamiliar to Farnie), in which 'Thrummy Cap' is the name given not to the ghost, but to the man who encounters him: *see* FIDDES CASTLE (North East).

MILNATHORT, KINROSS-SHIRE

In 1823, the Reverend Andrew Small told a story of the 'Gudeman of Ballengeich', the pseudonym used in this case by James V, although some other tales of the Gudeman relate to James IV. The king happened to be taken prisoner by three tinkers or gypsies and had to travel with them for several days so that his nobles lost all trace of him. He was forced not only to lead the tinkers' ass, but to help it by carrying part of its load, and two of the men treated him with great harshness, although the third was gentler.

At last, while the tinkers were getting drunk at the east end of Milnathort, just north of Kinross, having left him on the green with the ass, he managed to write a note on a slip of paper and gave it to a boy together with half a crown, asking him to run to Falkland with it and so let his courtiers know what had happened to him and where he then was.

It did not take the nobles long to cover the distance and rescue the king. He spared the life of the kinder-hearted tinker, but had the other two hanged a little southwest of the village, at a spot thereafter known as the Gallow Hill. James also then made it a law that whenever three male gypsies were found together, two should be hanged but the third set free.

Another story is told at EASTER WEMYSS of gypsies and King James – James IV, in that instance. *See also* THE GUIDMAN OF BALLANGEICH (p. 98).

MURTHLY, PERTHSHIRE

Near Murthly, north of Perth, there is a standing stone of which the tradition is that a man brave enough to move it would find a chest with a black dog sitting on it, guarding it. It is said that a schoolmaster's sons once shifted the stone with gunpowder but were terrified by the dog and so put the stone back again. Katharine Briggs gives this 'on the authority of the Rev. Routledge Bell, who had it from one of his parishioners'.

The stone to which the tradition refers is probably Murthly Castle Standing Stone, Little Dunkeld. It is unusual to find a dog among supernatural treasure-guardians, which are far more often birds, including eagles, and black cocks or hens, although the fairy tale 'The Tinderbox' features three guardian dogs, each progressively larger until the third has 'eyes as big as mill-wheels'. The colour black is generally the sign of a diabolic presence, but in England phantom Black Dogs could sometimes perform a protective function to travellers on lonely roads.

NEWBURGH, FIFE

Near Newburgh once stood Macduff's Cross, a 'rude upright stone'. The common legend, recorded by Robert Chambers in 1827, was that Malcolm Canmore endowed Macduff, thane of Fife, with three privileges, in recognition of his help in deposing Macbeth. First, he and his heirs should have the honour of placing the crown on the king's head at any coronation; secondly, whenever the royal standard was displayed

The Guidman of Ballangeich

Legend has it that James V (1513–42) would often travel through his realm in disguise, righting wrongs and punishing evil-doers.

Two successive kings of Scotland, James IV and James V, are said to have been in the habit of travelling about their realm incognito, and many tales were told of their adventures while in disguise. It must be supposed that all are apocryphal, since such reports date from long after their actual reigns, 1488–1513 and 1513–42 respectively.

According to these legends the king travelled under the title 'the Laird o' Ballangeich', and an ancient gateway at the back of STIRLING CASTLE (Central & Perthshire) through which he made his private excursions was known as 'the Laird of Ballangeich's entry'. Other chroniclers report the king's alias as the 'Gudeman' or 'Guidman' of Ballangeich, giving him lower status – the 'goodman' of a farm was its owner or tenant, ranking below the local laird. Robert Chambers, writing in 1827, explains that *ballangeich* means 'the windy pass', and was the name of a farm near Stirling Castle and of a narrow road which led there. A street in Stirling is still called Ballangeich Road.

A characteristic anecdote tells how the King visited Anstruther in Fife disguised as a strolling piper. When he came to the Dreel Burn, which then had no bridge and could only be forded, he hesitated, wondering how to cross without wetting his feet. A buxom gaberlunzie (beggar woman) came marching along, and when he explained his predicament she picked the king up and carried him bodily to the other side. He rewarded the woman by handing her his purse, but we are not told whether he revealed his true identity. He could have done so safely: we are told in the story of EASTER WEMYSS (Central & Perthshire) that all the poor folk of Fife loved and respected the king.

On another occasion, when the court was feasting in Stirling, James V sent for some venison from the neighbouring hills. The deer were killed and put on horseback to go to Stirling. Unluckily, they had to pass the castle gates of Arnpryor in Kippen, where a chief of the Buchanans was enter- taining guests who were rather hungry, although they had had plenty to drink. Seeing so much food passing the very door, Buchanan seized it despite protests that it belonged to King James, replying that James might be king in Scotland but he, Buchanan, was king in Kippen. When James heard what had happened, he rode to Arnpryor where he was told that the laird was at dinner and could not be disturbed. James instructed the porter to tell his master that the Goodman of Ballangeich had come to feast with the King of Kippen. When Buchanan heard these words, he knew at once that James had come in person. He hastened to kneel and ask forgiveness, which was granted, and James entered the castle to enjoy his own venison. Buchanan of Arnpryor was ever afterwards called the King of Kippen. The 'Guidman' was not always so merciful: at COCKBURN'S CASTLE (Loth- ian & Borders), a robber who refused to come out and speak to his anony- mous visitor was hanged for his defiance.

'The king in disguise' is an international theme, attached to monarchs such as Alfred the Great (when he burned the cakes), Robert the Bruce at UGADALE (Argyllshire & Islands), and Hārūn al-Rashīd, the eighth-century caliph of Baghdad whose exploits are related in the *Thousand Nights and One Night*, also known as the *Arabian Nights*. These Persian tales became known in Europe in the early eighteenth century, and may have influenced the stories told of the Scottish kings. It is not surprising to find such leg- ends associated with James IV, an energetic, able, and cultured ruler whose reign was long and relatively peaceful, but his son is a less obvious candi- date for fame or affection. James V succeeded to the throne at less than two years old and died at the age of thirty-one. During his period of power he was inclined to be mean and authoritarian, and was moreover a staunch upholder of Catholicism, making his later heroic reputation in the Pres- byterian Lowlands rather unexpected. He is, however, represented in pop- ular folklore as a 'poor man's king', friend to the lowly and oppressed, and many of the tales identify him, rather than his father, as the 'Guidman'. Probably by the time these traditions achieved common currency, they enshrined a romantically vague image of days before the 1603 Union when the king of Scotland was close to his people.

See also MILNATHORT (Central & Perthshire); CRAMOND BRIDGE (Lothian & Borders).

in battle, they should lead the vanguard of the army; 'and, lastly, that any person related to him within the ninth degree of kindred, having committed homicide without premeditation, should, upon flying to this obelisk and paying a certain fine, obtain remission of his crime'. The cross was said to retain its sacred character almost until the Reformation, when it was demolished as a relic of popery; anyone who is interested, says Chambers, 'may still see the block of stone in which it was fixed, together with many tumuli, or mounds, said to contain the bodies of such refugees as, having failed to prove their consanguinity to Macduff, were sacrificed on the spot by their enraged pursuers'. The block or pedestal can still be seen, in a field between the roads leading to Easter Lumbennie and Auchtermuchty.

The privilege was invoked successfully at least once, if we believe the horror story of John Melville's death at GLENBERVIE (North East), when the laird of Arbuthnott claimed immunity on this account.

See also MARTIN'S STONE (North East); MACBETH (p. 318).

NORRIE'S LAW, FIFE

People living in the neighbourhood of Largo Law once supposed that a rich mine of gold was under or near the mountain which had never been properly searched for. So convinced were they of its reality that whenever they saw a sheep's wool tinged with yellow, they thought the colour came from the sheep having lain above the gold. John Ewart Simpkins records the similar belief that the teeth of sheep feeding on the Eildon Hills in Roxburghshire became yellow from the gold hidden beneath, and the same was popularly held true of Dunideen Hill, Aberdeenshire, a legend

recorded in the sixteenth century by Hector Boece.

A tradition mentioned by Robert Chambers in his *Popular Rhymes of Scotland* (1826) is that a ghost once appeared on Largo Law who was supposed to know the secret of the mine. It had to be spoken to before it would answer questions, so the problem arose of who dared do it. At length a shepherd, inspired by the thought of the gold, took courage and asked the ghost why it revisited the same spot. The ghost told him to meet it there on a particular night at eight o'clock, when, it said:

'If Auchindownie cock disna craw,
And Balmain horn disna blaw,
I'll tell ye where the gowd mine is in
    Largo Law.'

The shepherd took all the care he could, for not a cock 'old, or young, or middle aged' was left alive at the farm of Auchindownie, and at Balmain the cowherd, Tammie Norrie, was told not to blow his horn to signal the housing of the cattle — but either ignored or forgot his instructions, for he blew a loud blast on his horn at eight o'clock as usual. The ghost, which had appeared ready to share the secret, disappeared, exclaiming:

'Woe to the man that blew the horn,
For out of the spot he shall ne'er be
    borne.'

Tammie was duly struck dead on the spot and it being found impossible to move his body, a cairn of stones was raised over it, which, grown into a grass-covered hillock, is called Norrie's Law. It can still be found, via the track to Bonnyton from the New Gilston road, a short way south-west from Norrieslaw Cottage.

In the *Book of Days* (1864), Chambers gives a different story attached to the Law. He writes that 'the popular tradition respecting this spot, has ever been that a great warrior, the leader of a mighty army, was buried there, clad in the silver armour he wore in his lifetime,' and records that in about 1819 a man from Largo digging at Norrie's Law (either for sand or 'induced by the ancient tradition') found a cist or stone coffin containing a hoard of silver. He kept the find secret, but it was observed that the cairn had been broken into, and the man was noticed to have money to spend. It turned out that he had unearthed and sold a considerable amount of pure silver, some to a silversmith, who melted it down. He had not, however, taken everything there was: the mound was excavated again and further silver relics were found, including the remains of a silver sword-handle, a shield, and a suit of scale armour. Today, what remains of the hoard is in the Museum of Scotland, Edinburgh.

This shield is part of the ancient treasure trove discovered at Norrie's Law in the early nineteenth century. For many years before the find, so it is said, rumours circulated of a warrior buried there in silver armour – these reports, however, were probably added with hindsight.

Chambers claims that the finding of the mailcoat was indisputable evidence of 'the very long perseverance which may characterize popular tradition': only by tradition, 'and that from a very distant period', could the local people have known that the person interred at Norrie's Law was buried with silver armour. However, as this story was not included in the earlier *Popular Rhymes,* and there is no other evidence that it existed before the mound was searched, it is reasonable to assume that it is a post-excavation tradition, invented to explain the find.

Age-old or comparatively recent, the warrior legend attached to the Law lived on in local custom, combined almost inextricably with the earlier tradition. In 1931, James Wilkie recorded a dialect account from the *People's Journal* in 1908 of a game that children would play facing Norrie's Law. It is well known, he says, that a 'wee, wee goblin' sits at the foot of the hill and guards the silver hoard that was hidden in the deep lair of 'the Warrior-Chieftain, Tam o' Norrie', slain in battle. One girl would recite as follows:

'I'll tell ye a story
Aboot Tam o' Norrie
If ye dinna speak in the middle o't –
Will ye no?'

Those who knew the game would just shake their heads, but finally someone would be goaded into speech. She was then 'out' and the rest of the girls would chant:

'The spell is broken, ye hae spoken,
Ye'll never hear the story o' lang Tam o' Norrie!'

Wilkie notes that the name 'Norrie' or 'Norie' always rhymed with 'story'. Some supposed it to be the name of a great chief who with his men fell in a conflict and whose resting place had otherwise been forgotten; others that it reflected some incident of the Viking period and that the name is a corruption of 'Norroway's Law', 'Norroway' being the early Scots spelling of 'Norway'.

The story ignores the fact that before he arrived in Ireland Patrick had been a fairly ordinary and not particularly religious youth – but perhaps the Devil saw what was to come.

See also SAINTS OF SCOTLAND (p. 490).

OLD KILPATRICK, DUNBARTONSHIRE

'Kil' as an element in Scottish place-names comes from the Gaelic *cill*, meaning a church or a hermit's or monk's cell. The holy man in question here is St Patrick, patron saint of Ireland, sometimes said to have been born in Old Kilpatrick. *Butler's Lives of the Saints* remains neutral, saying that 'Whether his birthplace . . . was near Dumbarton on the Clyde, or in Cumberland to the south of Hadrian's Wall, or at the mouth of the Severn or elsewhere is of no great moment,' and adding that 'We cannot be far wrong in supposing that he was born about 389, and that about 403 he with many others was carried off by raiders to become a slave among the still pagan inhabitants of Ireland.'

Local tradition gives a more colourful reason for Patrick's departure. According to the account given by Jack House in 1960, Satan so beset the saint that he was forced to leave his home town and flee to Ireland:

When the devil saw the holy man escaping, he wrenched a rock from Dumbuck Hill and threw it at him. Fortunately it missed St Patrick and today it's known as Dumbarton Rock. The Clyde Navigation Trust don't quite agree with this story. They think the De'il threw the stone all right, but it wasn't Dumbarton Rock. They have a stone of their own right in the middle of the river . . . It's plainly marked 'St Patrick's Stone Light,' because they have a guiding light on top of it.

ORWELL, KINROSS-SHIRE

Only the foundations of the old church of Orwell now survive, on the north bank of Loch Leven. From here comes an account of a magical practice normally attributed to witches – the ability to stop various agricultural activities in their tracks. Horses and carts commonly feature in such stories, but this was a case of stopping a plough.

The *Scots Magazine* for September 1756 records a case brought in that month against Peter Pairny, the servant of a minister at Orwell. Pairny's master was leader of the seceding congregation, i.e. those who opted out of the established Church of Scotland: possibly the accusation reflected religious opposition to the nonconformist minister. Whether the charge was deliberate slander or arose from genuine belief, Pairny was said to have used 'pranks somewhat like inchantments', pretending to stop, or make unfit for working, a wheel-plough, by touching its beam with a rod and bidding the plough stop until he loosed it.

The session agreed to declare the man 'under scandal', and he was ordered to appear and receive a public reprimand. 'This sentence was intimated from his pulpit by Mr Mair on Sunday Sept. 12.; and the man appeared, and was rebuked.'

Twenty years earlier, he might not have got off so lightly: witchcraft was decriminalised in 1736, and the last execution of a witch took place only nine years before that, at LOTH (Northern Highlands).

THE PENDS,
ST ANDREWS, FIFE

Writing in 1893, Andrew Lang tells 'the curious tale of Sharpe's double, or wraith', which he sets at New Inns, the house in which Archbishop James Sharp resided while at St Andrews. Sometime in early 1667, the archbishop was in Edinburgh examining prisoners taken during the Pentland Rising, an insurrection of Covenanters against the government and the Anglican Church. Needing a paper which was in his cabinet in the New Inns, he sent a runner to look for it who left Edinburgh at ten and reached St Andrews at four in the afternoon, having made good speed. Robert Wodrow's account, dating from 1707 though not printed until 1842, gives the details:

When he opened the closet door and looked in, he saw the Bishop sitting at a table near the window as if he had been reading and writing, with his black gown and tippet, [and] his broad hat, just as he had left him at Edinburgh, which did surprize the fellow at first, though he was not much terrified; for being of a hardie frolick temper . . . he spake to him myrrily thus, 'Ho! my Lord! Well ridden, indeed! I am sure I left yow at Edinburgh at ten o'cloak, and yet yow are here before me! I wonder that I saw yow not pass by me!'

The archbishop looked over his shoulder with a sour and frowning countenance, but said nothing. The man ran downstairs and called the steward, and they both saw the archbishop standing at the top of the stairs, looking angry. Returning to Sharp's study in a short while, the servant found the room empty, took the paper he had been sent to find, and returned to Edinburgh.

The next day he told Sharp the story, and was told to keep quiet about it. Either,

therefore, he disobeyed, or Wodrow made up the tale. The latter is likely, since Wodrow was a Presbyterian writer eager to discredit the archbishop, and suggested in his account that Sharp was in league with the Devil.

New Inns was demolished in 1803, and St Leonard's and St Catherine's School now occupies part of its former site on the Pends. Current tradition reports that the ghost of Archbishop Sharp is still sometimes seen in the area, although the archbishop's murder took place at MAGUS MUIR.

PITFIRRANE, FIFE

Frae the auld elm tree,
    On the tap o' the knowe [the top
        of the mound],
A seed shall fa' aff,
    Whilk a tree shall grow;
And a craddle it shall mak',
    To rock the wee bairn
Wha'll conjure the ghaist
    That haunts Pitfairen.

This verse appears in an 1848 article in the *Scottish Journal* which goes on to relate that 200 or 300 years earlier the villagers of 'Pitfairen' were much disturbed by a ghost that appeared every night in its shroud, as if newly risen from its grave, and circled an old elm tree while repeating the words. At last a new elm did spring near the old one; when it had grown large, it was cut down and lay for a long time in the carpenter's yard, until one day he had an order to make a cradle.

'Putting implicit confidence in the veracity of the prophecy, and thinking the fulfilment of it at hand, he, unknown to any one, made the cradle from the identical elm tree.' His faith was justified, since the child rocked in the cradle grew up a wise and pious lad, and went to study for the

Church. The carpenter, by now an old man, then told the boy the story.

The young cleric, arming himself with book and candle, went after dark to the haunted spot. The dead soul confessed a murder committed during its life, and told the boy to dig to the roots of the old elm tree, where he would find the bones of the victim. This was done, the bones were given proper burial in a nearby church-yard, and the ghost was never seen again.

Embellished though this story is, the legend it embodies is the widespread one of a person predestined to lay a spirit. The verse spoken by the phantom is like the song of 'The Cauld Lad o' Hilton', one of northern England's most famous haunts:

'Wae's me, Wae's me,
The Acorn is not yet
Fallen from the Tree
That's to grow the wood
That's to make the cradle
That's to rock the bairn
That's to grow to a Man
That's to *lay* me!'

Like the Cauld Lad, the ghost of Pitfairen was probably glad to be freed.

'Pitfairen', said in the 1848 article to be on the south bank of the river Devon, is not an entirely satisfactory match for Pit-firrane church, a little way south-west of Dunfermline, but perhaps the author did not trouble to identify the place too precisely. He describes the village as consisting of 'a few miserable houses', and is evidently more interested in the story than in the exact location.

POWGUILD, LOCH GELLY, FIFE

A white horse was once said to haunt the old house of Powguild, beside the burn that flows from Loch Gelly into Ore Water. The name of the house comes from the Gaelic *poll geal*, 'the white pool', Loch Gelly is 'the white loch', and the white horse may have been a water sprite, although there are no reports of it luring anyone in to drown, as did KELPIES AND WATER-HORSES (p. 364).

Dr David Rorie, writing in 1903, reports:

The garden of the same house has another and a smaller ghost – a mole or 'moudie-wort.' An old woman who lived there, and was a great lover of her garden, vowed on her death-bed that she would return to her garden and live there in the shape of a moudie-wort.

As to the strength of local belief in this ghost, 'Certain it is,' says Rorie, 'that some of the later dwellers in the house have hesitated to interfere with stray moles conducting digging operations there.'

The 'moudie-wort', or as it is more often spelt in regional English 'mouldieworp', a descriptive name meaning 'dirt-thrower', may not be the most dramatic ghost in Scotland, but it is one of the smallest.

QUARREL BURN, CLACKMANNANSHIRE

Towards the end of the eighteenth century, according to an article in the *Scottish Journal of Topography*, Quarrel Burn was a famous rendezvous of the witches of Dollar. Meeting in the evening, they would mount their broomsticks and ride through the air to a spot called 'Lochy Faulds' at the foot of Gloomhill – by this is presumably meant the hill on which stands Castle Campbell, known until the late fifteenth century as Castle Gloume.

Beneath an oak tree was a circle of brown earth on which nothing would grow. Some people said it marked the site of a fire, others that a 'black deed' had been committed there, but a third explanation involved a farmer who had spoken disrespectfully of the witches, and whom they had decided to punish. They carried him to Lochy Faulds 'to stand his trial before the tribunal over which his Black Majesty presided in person', and ordered him to prove that he had not been guilty of slandering them. The farmer declared, 'May a round ring encompass me, and may grass never grow upon it any more, if I am not innocent of the crime laid to my charge.' The circle appeared at once.

RANNOCH MOOR, PERTHSHIRE

A story of 'a laird near Rannoch Moor' was recorded in 1987 as told by Betsy Whyte, a Traveller and a splendid story-teller, who had heard it from her mother.

Now this laird . . . dabbled a wee bit in the Black Art, in mesmerism. But he never used it for any wickedness, only for playin tricks on some o' his friends.

One year at the annual ceilidh he decreed that every guest should take a turn at telling a story, singing a song, or demon-strating another feat of skill or strength, with a prize of a golden guinea for each event.

The laird's cattleman, Sandy, was a simple, shy fellow, and kept quiet through it all. When it came to the competition for telling the biggest lie, the laird said this was Sandy's last chance: he must either join in or leave. But Sandy could think of no lie to tell, and so instead he was ordered to go and clean the laird's boat.

Sad to miss the rest of the party, Sandy went down to the boat and began to bail it out, but as soon as he stepped on board it sped away with him across the water. For a while Sandy sat dazed, and when he came round he saw that he was wearing green satin slippers, silk stockings, and a taffeta dress. 'He felt hissel all up: he was

dumbfoonded before – but he was a thou-sand times mair dumbfoonded then!' Looking at his reflection in the water, he saw that he had become a beautiful woman.

When he arrived at the other shore a young man came along and asked where the lovely lady had come from and what her name was, but she – 'because he was a she now' – didn't want to say she was Sandy the cattleman, so she said she couldn't remember. The young man thought she must have bumped her head and lost her memory, and took her back to his mother's house to recover. Time went by, and she said no more about where she had come from, but after a while she and the young man fell in love, got married, and had two children.

One day they were out for a walk and went down to the water, where they hadn't been for a long time, and she saw the boat she'd arrived in. It was mossy and water-logged, and she stepped in to clean it, but as soon as she did so, the boat started off across to the other shore. She begged it to take her back, and started to cry, covering her face with her hands . . . and when she looked at herself again, 'there on her feet was this old tackety boots and this auld mole-skinned trousers and them aa cov-ered with coo's shearn [all covered with cow's dung]', and then she felt the stubble on her chin. She howled and screamed, 'No, no, no, I want back tae ma man and ma bairns' – but it was no use: she was Sandy the cattleman again.

When the boat reached the land, Sandy ran up towards the farm and passed a barn where there was a ceilidh going on. The laird called out to him, and persuaded him to stop crying and tell them what had hap-pened.

And Sandy had really only been away for twenty minutes! Because the laird had mesmerised him, and the event was still goin on – to see who could tell the biggest lie in fact. So the laird turned roond and he said, 'Well, Sandy, that is definitely the biggest lie we've heard the nicht! You've won the golden guinea!'

See also TRAVELLER TALES (p. 298).

ST ANDREWS, FIFE

Along the east coast of Scotland many landscape features are associated with the Danes. A tall vertical rock near St Andrews was known until at least 1803 as the 'Danis Wark' (the work or building of the Danes). A note to the 1803 edition of Sir Robert Sibbald's *History of Fife* comments that 'the martial deeds, and the rapine and destruction of the Danes has magnified them into giants, who in a night could perform the labour of years, and by the exertions of their brawny arms, could move rocks that have stood fixed from the Creation.' Similar things were said elsewhere of the Fianna, the legendary followers of FINGAL (p. 10).

At St Andrews, the Danes were not the only figures whose reputations were distorted by popular report. John Knox, the leader of the Scottish Reformation, lived here in around 1570, and when he left it was rumoured and generally believed that he had been expelled from the town for raising the Devil. In the late nineteenth century, a university lecturer had an uncanny experience: he had spent Sunday evening at a friend's house and set out to go home at about one in the morning, but only about fifteen minutes later was once more on the doorstep, with a strange tale to tell.

He had reached a point opposite St Katharine's School in North Street without encountering anyone, when he was startled to see coming towards him a man

with a stern and commanding countenance. He was garbed in a Geneva gown, and the ministerial bands worn with it peeped out beneath a long dark beard beginning to be seamed with grey. Behind him at the distance of a few paces marched a halberdier clad in partial armour – breastplate and steel cap. The strange visitants passed without sound of footfall, each fixing the bewildered lecturer with their eyes. Those of the minister chilled him to the marrow, so awful was their cold and penetrating power.

The lecturer instantly recognized the face and form, seen in portraits . . . and in descriptions still more vivid. With a shudder he recognized he had met – John Knox.

The folklorist Andrew Lang (1844–1912) lived in St Andrews at the time, and he was greatly interested in the story. At first he found the man-at-arms a puzzling feature, but he later found a statement in records of the Reformation years that Knox went about accompanied for his protection by one of the City Guard.

Another notable story, set in the latter half of the seventeenth century, was that of 'the licentiate of St Andrews'. A student hoping to be admitted to the Presbytery had been given a text to study, but could make nothing of it (his university career had been far from brilliant). Wandering alone 'in a remote place' he was overtaken by a stranger 'in habite like a Minister', who asked why he seemed so gloomy. The student told his problem, whereupon the gentleman produced from his pocket a sermon on the very text, asking in return only a written promise of service, should it ever be required. The student agreed and, having no ink with him, signed the document in his own blood.

The student's discourse was received with admiration and wonder by the Presbytery – all but the celebrated Robert

Around 1570 the coastal town of St Andrews was home to the leader of the Scottish Reformation, John Knox (1505–72). When he left it was generally believed he had been expelled for raising the Devil, and his ghost was later said to haunt the streets.

Blair, minister of the Kirk of Holy Trinity, who asked the student privately:

> 'Did yow not get the whole of this discourse written and ready to your hand from one who pretended to be a Minister? . . . did not yow give him a written promise subscribed with your blood?'

These points confirmed, the Reverend Mr Blair revealed to the student with whom he had made a compact: 'It was the Divell!'

The student was overcome with terror, but the Presbytery resolved to save him if they could. Next day they took him to one of the loneliest churches in the district, where each in turn wrestled for the student's soul in prayer, the last being Mr Blair, during whose fervent supplications a fierce storm began raging, making the kirk tremble to its foundations. Wild demonic laughter and shrieks of rage mingled with the blast. Then there dropped from the roof in their midst the student's covenant signed in blood. The storm immediately

calmed and all was still. Mr Blair had triumphed and the powers of darkness were vanquished.

This rousing tale was recorded by the historian Robert Wodrow in his *Analecta, or Materials for a History of Remarkable Providences* (1701–31), and a similar thing is said to have happened to a minister in France. 'The Devil's contract' is a well-known theme, associated for example with Sir Robert Gordon of THE ROUND SQUARE (North East).

St Fillan's Cave, Pittenweem, Fife

St Fillan was a seventh-century monk, usually said to have come from Ireland, although there are claims that he was born in Fife. At birth he was held to have 'appeared something like a monster', and in another account to have been 'born with a stone in his mouth'. He was at once thrown into a lake where he was ministered to by angels for a year or more, and then taken out and baptised.

He later became a monk, and lived a hermit's life at Pittenweem in a cave which was rededicated for worship in 1935 and may still be visited, entering through a gateway in the cliff-face on one side of Cove Wynd.

Many miracles were told of the saint. When he became abbot, Fillan or Faelanus is said to have constructed a private cell in which to worship. One night a servant came to tell him that supper was ready, and, peeping through a crack, saw the saint writing in the dark with his right hand by the light shining from his left. Fillan was angry at having been spied upon, and a tame crane that lived at the monastery pecked out the servant's eye (although it is not said that this was by the saint's request). Being then moved by compassion, however, St Fillan restored the eye.

After his death, said to have taken place somewhere round Lochearn, there was a dispute about where he should be buried, Killin and Strathfillan both making a claim. 'Behold a marvel!' writes James MacKinlay in 1893. 'When they could not agreee, they found that instead of one coffin there were two, and so each party was satisfied.' The same tale was reported of St Baldred, who lived on the BASS ROCK (Lothian & Borders), only more so: Baldred's corpse was said to have been multiplied by three.

St Fillan's reputation was enhanced by the tale that he took a posthumous part in the battle of Bannockburn in 1314. The sixteenth-century chronicler Hector Boece tells the story in Latin, translated in 1531 by John Bellenden, relating how the night before the battle Robert the Bruce was weary and anxious and prayed to God and St Fillan (Phillane, here). Robert believed

that he had with him the saint's arm, enclosed in a silver case, but without his knowledge a priest had removed the arm before they set off, having feared for the safety of the holy relic on the battlefield. As Robert prayed, the case suddenly opened, without anyone having touched it.

The preist,	[The priest,
astonyst be this	astonished by this
wounder, went to	wonder, went to
the altare quhare	the altar where
the cais laye, and	the case lay, and
quhen he fand the	when he found the
arme in the samyn,	arm in the same,
he cryitt, 'Here is	he cried, 'Here is
ane grete mirakill!'	a great miracle!']

The king spent the rest of the night in prayer, rejoicing in the extraordinary event, which he rightly took to be a presage of his success.

See also SAINTS OF SCOTLAND (p. 490).

ST FILLAN'S POOL, PERTHSHIRE

Until at least the middle of the nineteenth century a treatment for madness was practised involving a deep pool or linn in the River Fillan in which, according to Black's *Picturesque Tourist of Scotland* (1844), 'a considerable number of lunatics are annually immersed, and then bound hand and foot, and laid all night in the churchyard of St Fillans in the expectation of effecting a cure'.

Further details of the treatment are given by James MacKinlay in 1893. According to his account, it was not only the insane but also the sick and injured who were treated.

The time selected was usually the first day of the quarter, and the immersion took place after sunset. The patients, with a rope tied round their waist, were thrown from the bank into the river. This was usually done thrice. According to previous instructions, they picked up nine stones from the bottom of the stream. After their dip they walked three times round three cairns in the immediate neighbourhood, and at each turn added a stone to the cairn.

MacKinlay cites an unnamed English antiquary who visited in 1798 and reported that as well as the stones, the patients would add a piece of clothing from whichever part of their body was afflicted. They could also, if their cattle were sick, bring some of the beast's food and make it into a paste with the water, to administer when they got home; in that case they had to throw the animal's rope or halter on the cairn. 'Consequently the cairns are covered with old halters, gloves, shoes, bonnets, nightcaps, rags of all sorts, kilts, petticoats, garters, and smocks.'

The patient was then led to the ruins of St Fillan's Chapel, where they were tied to a wooden framework on a stone with a hollow in it large enough to hold a man. They were covered with hay and left there all night, with St Fillan's bell on their head. From all this it seems clear that only one patient could be treated at a time (there being only one bell and presumably one suitable stone).

The bell was said always to lie loose on a tombstone in the churchyard, ready to be employed in the ceremony, and popularly believed to return automatically to its resting place after use, ringing all the way. 'In 1798,' MacKinlay reports disapprovingly, 'this belief was put to a severe test, for in that year the English antiquary, already quoted, removed the relic.'

St Fillan's bell, renowned for its curative powers, was stolen in 1798 but later returned.

'In order,' he says, 'to ascertain the truth or falsehold [*sic*] of the ridiculous story of St Fillan's bell, I carried it off with me, and meant to convey it, if possible, to England. An old woman, who observed what I was about, asked me what I wanted with the bell, and I told her that I had an unfortunate relation at home out of his mind, and that I wanted to have him cured. "Oh, but," says she, "you must bring him here to be cured, or it will be of no use." Upon which I told her he was too ill to be moved, and off I galloped with the bell back to Tyndrum Inn.'

The bell was taken to England, but about seventy years later was sent back and is now in the Museum of Scotland in Edinburgh.

As a cure for insanity, the procedure described might sound unhelpful if not downright harmful, but this was by no means the only place where it was practised. At certain Cornish wells, Janet Bord reports, an even more violent method was favoured, known as 'bowssening' or 'boussening'. The patient would be set with their back to the pool and then hit violently on the chest so as to throw them backwards into the water, where a strong man would toss them about until they had, by losing their strength, also 'somewhat forgot' their insanity. If a cure did not result, the process was repeated again and again as long as there remained in the patient 'hope of life or recovery'. In the nineteenth century a man attempted a similar cure for his mad wife at STROMNESS (Orkney & Shetland Islands), but without success.

St Fillan's Pool is said to have been rendered powerless when a farmer immersed in it his mad bull. A variant version taken down from oral narrative in 1972 refers to a well said to be in Kintail, Wester Ross, which became useless when a tinker-woman washed her clothes in it: 'as soon as she misused it in that way the spring lost all its powers'.

See also SCOTLAND'S HOLY AND HEALING WELLS (p. 44).

SCHIEHALLION, PERTHSHIRE

Two friends who were hunchbacks lived on opposite sides of Schiehallion, one at Braes of Foss on the east side, the other near Tempar on the west. Every Sunday one would visit the other, turn and turn about.

One fine summer evening, the Braes of Foss hunchback set out to visit his friend. As the weather was fine, he went a long way round, and it was near to midnight as he drew near to a little low cave by a burn below a knoll, where he heard voices and the patter of tiny feet. Continuing more carefully, he saw fairies dancing above the knoll. Over and over

again they were singing the same thing: 'Saturday, Sunday'.

Entranced by their singing, the man had a burning desire to join in, and finally he burst in at the end with: 'Monday, Tuesday'. The hunchback had a fine voice, and the fairies danced round and round in delight, singing the whole phrase: 'Saturday, Sunday, Monday, Tuesday.'

At last, some of them approached the man. One said to another, 'What do you wish for him who gives such lovely new words for our song?'

'We ask that his hump will fall off, so that he will stand straight as a rush.'

'We wish him also the best of health,' said another fairy.

'And that he has plenty to the end of his days,' said a third.

Taking his farewell of the fairies, the man went on his way, light of heart and light of step now he was upright as a soldier. His friend hardly recognised him when he arrived.

He explained how he had met the fairies and added to their song. 'I'll do the same,' said the hunchback of Tempar, and immediately hurried off. When he reached the knoll, he heard the fairies singing, 'Saturday, Sunday, Monday, Tuesday,' and he immediately added in a loud, harsh, unpleasant voice: 'Wednesday, Thursday'.

As soon as the fairies heard him, they stopped dancing and dragged him to the ground, jumping on him and pinching him. Angry fairies came forward, saying, 'What shall we do to the man who spoils our song?'

'Make his hump two,' said one.

'Let him be the ugliest man alive,' said a second.

'And may he grow bigger and bigger to his death-day,' said a third.

The man made his way painfully home, hardly able to walk, partly because of the two humps he now carried, but mostly because of all the while getting bigger and bigger. When he got back to his own house, the first hunchback, who had been waiting for him, scarcely knew him, he was so big and ugly, and disfigured now by *two* humps. All too soon he had grown too big to get into his house, so had to sleep outside summer and winter alike, and it took seventeen blankets to cover him. This went on as the fairies had promised to the day he died, by which time he was so big that it took twenty-coffins to hold him.

This story was told in 1989 by A. D. Cunningham, former expeditions master at Rannoch School, who used to take pupils walking and exploring the countryside in the course of their participation in the Duke of Edinburgh's Award. He locates the story quite precisely, naming the burn as the Allt Mór and the cave as Uamh Tom a' Mhor-fhir, both of which can be found on large-scale Ordnance Survey maps. The cave is quite hard to spot as it is small and its entrance is low, but with the small ferns growing inside it is very atmospheric.

One thing Cunningham does not comment on is how the events of the story could take place largely at night, the second hunchback's journey being after midnight. Notwithstanding the long twilight of northern summers, the terrain they had to cross to get to the cave is not easy even by broad daylight. Unless the surrounding groundcover has greatly changed since the supposed time of the story, the first hunchback's route would have taken him through twisted, woody, foot-high stems of heather, inhabited by adders, and made treacherous in places by fissures in the underlying wet peat. Nor is it clear how 'the patter of tiny feet' could be heard here, whether on the rough,

rocky outcrop above the cave, or on vegetation around it.

According to John Gregorson Campbell, in *Superstitions of the Highlands and Islands of Scotland* (1900), Schiehallion had the reputation of being inhabited by fairies, but the story itself is not restricted to this mountain. The tale is widespread in Ireland and Scotland and is even known in Japan, where a boil on the cheek replaces the hunch back. Cunningham's rendition loses the point that the second man's usual mistake is to take the song on to *Friday*, an unlucky day which the fairies do not like to hear named. In some versions it is Sunday that they object to, being non-Christian, but here it seems to be simply the Templar hunchback's unpleasant voice that grates on their ears. Many fairies are sensitive to music, like the Loireag that haunted BEINN MHOR on South Uist (Western Isles).

SCONE PALACE, PERTHSHIRE

Scone Palace is possibly best known as having once housed the Stone of Destiny, now at EDINBURGH CASTLE (Lothian & Borders). It is also the setting for a traditional tale recorded in Gaelic in 1967 as told by Angus Henderson, a retired blacksmith and crofter from Mull, who heard it from his father, also a blacksmith. A Scottish priest had so offended the king – 'one of the Jameses', says the storyteller – that he was to be executed, unless he could answer three questions the king would put to him at his palace in Scone. The priest's brother, a simple man known as 'the fool', volunteered to go in his place, and putting on his brother's habit he set off for the court.

The king was wearing his robes and sitting on his throne, and first he asked where the centre of the world was.

The Minister and the Fairies

Our knowledge of fairy belief in seventeenth-century Scotland would be much poorer had not Robert Kirk, minister of Balquhidder and then of Aberfoyle, pursued his interests in the *sluagh sith*, the people of peace. *The Secret Common-Wealth of Elves, Fauns and Fairies* (1691) is a rare insight into tradition drawn from a range of oral informants, local history, and personal experience. Born in Aberfoyle in 1644, Kirk was his father's seventh son and was thus assumed to have the power of SECOND SIGHT (p. 474). He studied theology, and was an accomplished Gaelic scholar. He was also the first person writing in English or Scots to use the expression 'fairy tale'.

It might seem odd to find a man of the church arguing for the existence of fairies, but Kirk was not unique. At around the same time, other scholars in Scotland and England strove against the rise of atheism and materialism. For men like George Sinclair, Martin Martin, and Joseph Glanvill, incredulity about the supernatural world equated with doubt in the existence of God. Kirk maintained that fairy belief was not inconsistent with Christianity, and his intention in recording 'evidence' of fairies was in part to uphold belief in angels, the Devil, and the Holy Spirit.

Kirk believed the fairies to be a species awaiting scientific analysis like the many animals, birds, and insects then being discovered:

> Every age hath some secret left for its discoverie, and who knows, but this intercourse betwixt the two kinds of rational inhabitants of the same Earth may be not only believed shortly, but as freely entertained, and as well known, as now the art of navigation, printing, gunning, riding on saddles with stirrups, and the discoveries of the microscopes, which were sometimes as great a wonder, and as hard to be believed.

Fairies resembled humans, but their 'light changeable bodies' could be best seen in twilight, and usually only by 'men of the second sight'. Kirk's conviction that only seers were able to perceive the fairy folk had never before been suggested, nor his view that men alone were gifted with this faculty, 'females being but seldom so qualified'. These observations were not consistent with those of other commentators. Plenty of women, and men without 'the sight', claimed to have encountered fairies. It may be that Kirk was reporting ideas then current in Perthshire but not necessarily representative of the rest of Scotland.

Fairies, in Kirk's view, had an ambiguous relationship with Christianity. They would vanish on hearing the name of God or Jesus, and had 'nothing of the Bible', but were still subject to God's command. They were trapped in a state of limbo, a condition which troubled them 'as uncertain what at the last revolution [Judgement Day] will become of them'.

A fairy might appear as a Doppelgänger, also known as a 'double-man',

This seventeenth-century engraving shows fairies dancing. Much of what we know about fairy beliefs in Scotland at that time comes from the writings of Robert Kirk, a Protestant minister.

'reflex-man', or 'co-walker', a kind of mirror-image or wraith, and second-sighted people told Kirk they often saw fairies attending funerals. Places identified as fairy hills were also popularly believed to house the souls of human ancestors, a notion which spawned the idea that fairies were the guardians of the dead.

In Scottish tradition it was thought unwise to reveal knowledge of the fairy folk. Legends surrounding Kirk's death suggest that by telling their secrets he was thought to have incurred their wrath. On 14 May 1692, he collapsed while walking on Doon Hill behind his manse, and was subsequently buried in Kirkton graveyard, Aberfoyle. Some time later, the deceased appeared with a message for his cousin, Graham of Duchray. Kirk explained that he was not dead, but was held hostage in fairyland. When he appeared again, Graham was to throw a dagger above the apparition, thus releasing him. Kirk did indeed reappear, but his cousin was so startled that he forgot to throw the dagger. The spectre vanished and 'it is firmly believed . . . that he is, at this day, in Fairyland.'

Kirk's writing is an unrivalled source of the fairy belief traditions of Reformation Scotland. Perhaps the finest tribute to his work comes from the nineteenth-century historian and poet Andrew Lang:

> He heard, he saw, he knew too well
> The secrets of your fairy clan;
> You stole him from the haunted dell,
> Who never more was seen of man,
> Now far from heaven, and safe from hell,
> Unknown of earth, he wanders free.
> Would that he might return and tell
> Of his mysterious company!

The fool struck the floor and said it was right there. As the world is round, its centre can be anywhere, so the king accepted the reply.

The next question was what the king was worth in money, and the fool answered that he could be worth no more than thirty pieces of silver, because the best man ever born was sold for that. The king had to acknowledge this too.

'The third one – if you can answer this, you're really damned good,' said the king, and asked if the man knew anything the king was thinking at that moment and was entirely wrong about.

The fool said he did: 'You think you're talking to the priest, and you're talking to the fool, his brother.' And the king said that if he was a fool his brother must be very bright indeed and deserved to go free, so he sent the fool home.

This is a version of a widely known tale, whose last question is more often the simpler 'What am I thinking?'

SHEARDALE BRAES,
CLACKMANNANSHIRE

On the summit of Sheardale Braes, in a small cottage, once lived a man named Patie McNicol, a small man who always wore a blue coat, a plush waistcoat and knee breeches, and a tam-o'-shanter bonnet with a red top. It was rumoured that he was in league with the witches, since he never did any work but always seemed to have plenty of money. He would never read a Bible, nor even allow a religious book in his house. The minister, Mr Couples, visited Patie to try to convert him, and apparently succeeded: Patie accepted the gift of a Bible, and started coming regularly to kirk, even though he had to walk three miles to get there.

The sequel, however, was less happy.

Walking one evening, Patie heard the sound of sighing around his head; suddenly he felt himself lifted from the ground and carried through the air with terrible speed. Next morning he was found half-dead of cold and hunger among the highest of the Ochils, and never recovered from his dreadful experience, but dwindled like melting snow until he died.

Next came the turn of the minister. Noises and loud screams began to be heard in all the corners of his house, although when he went to look what was the matter he could see nothing. On one occasion the disturbance was so bad that Mr Couples had to leave his house wearing nothing but his shirt, and was chased down to the next cottage by a huge black boar, and the next Sunday, as he was going to the kirk, 'things like planks o' wood' lurched around in front of him a great part of the way. His faith in God, however, was strong enough to allow him to withstand these demonstrations, and the Devil was overcome.

The teller of this story, printed in 1848, explains Patie's ordeal and the minister's troubles as the work of 'the witches of Dollar', but being lifted into the air and carried long distances was most commonly thought to be the work of the *sluagh*, or fairy host, a phenomenon reported for instance at PEAT LAW (Lothian & Borders). The experiences of Mr Couples are comparable to those reported of other ministers at the hands of witches or ghosts – at PEASTON (Lothian & Borders), Isabel Heriot or something in her shape was said to have thrown stones at the minister who had given her the sack – but in a less witch-aware climate the black boar might have been thought of as a bogey beast, a spirit in its own right rather than something conjured by sorcery. Such beings were also thought to appear as inanimate objects like the bundle of ferns at BENDERLOCH, the White Sack at CREA-GAN (both Argyllshire & Islands), or, as here, planks of wood.

SOLDIER'S LEAP, KILLIECRANKIE, PERTHSHIRE

The battle of Killiecrankie was fought on 27 July 1689, when Highland troops loyal to James II defeated those of William III under General Mackay, though the Jacobite leader John Graham of Claverhouse ('Bonnie Dundee') was killed in the conflict, his wraith appearing at the moment of his death to Earl Colin of BALCARRES. A memorial of the battle still pointed out to visitors is 'The Soldier's Leap' between two vertiginous rocks either side of the River Garry:

A Lowland sentry, who had been stationed at the head of the Pass of Killiecrankie, first knew the result of the battle by seeing a party of Highlanders rushing down upon him. He ran before them and when they were overtaking him, and had actually wounded him on the shoulder, he leapt across the River Garry where the gorge is narrowest and so escaped, for they dared not leap after him. The place is called 'The Soldier's Leap,' and every visitor to the pass has a look at it. The soldier lived many years afterwards and was employed by General Wade who began to make roads in the Highlands thirty-five years later. The soldier often told his story and showed the wound he received in the moment of the leap.

This account dates from 1925, and the story is still sometimes recounted as history, although fabulous jumps across impossible distances feature in many folk tales of Europe and America, making it likely that the Killiecrankie story is legend rather than fact.

STIRLING

Never was Prince more taken up with an army as our King was, especially with the Scotch Highlanders, whom he tearmed the flour [flower] of his forces.

The monarch in question was the young Charles II, at this point king in Scotland though not in England, having been crowned at Scone in January 1651. A little later in the year he was camped at Stirling, where 'it was pretty in a morning' to see him reviewing the regiments on parade.

He saw no less then 80 pipers in a croud bareheaded, and John M'gyurmen in the middle, covered. He asked What society that was? It was told his Majesty: Sir, yow are our King, and yonder old man in the midle is the Prince of Pipers. He cald him by name, and comeing to the King, kneeling, his Majesty reacht him his hand to kiss.

The 'Prince of Pipers' then instantly extemporised a tune, 'I Got a Kiss of the King's Hand', which was greatly admired by all.
'John M'gyurmen' was John MacCrimmon. This report, from James Fraser's seventeenth-century *Chronicles of the Frasers*, is one of the few contemporary written accounts to feature a member of the famous MacCrimmon family, whose piping school on Skye is discussed at BORERAIG (Western Isles). The song mentioned is elsewhere said to have been composed by 'a Macmillan from Glendessary and piper to Lochiel, on seeing his chief kiss Charles Edward's hand at a levee held in the palace of his ancestors by that Prince a day or two after the victory at Gladsmuir'. Two quite different pipers and two royal Charleses separated by nearly a hundred years add up to an

example of the problems in dating and assigning even a very well-known tune from the pipe repertoire.

The significance of the old man being the only one 'covered', i.e. wearing a hat or bonnet, is that he was as royal among the pipers as the king himself among other men: everyone was expected to take off their hat in the presence of the monarch. A story set at CRAMOND BRIDGE (Lothian & Borders) turns on this very point.

STIRLING CASTLE

About 1503, writes Robert Chambers in *The Picture of Scotland* (1827), an Italian alchemist who came to Scotland persuaded James IV that he was on the verge of success in his attempts to discover the secret of the philosopher's stone, by which all other metals could be turned to gold. The king was convinced enough to make him abbot of Tungland, but his hopes were disappointed:

That the abbot had believed in his own impostures, appears from his having provided himself with wings and attempted to fly from the battlements of Stirling Castle. He fell, of course, and broke a thigh-bone. The way in which he accounted for his want of success is highly curious. 'The wings,' he said, 'were partly composed of the feathers of dung-hill fowls, and were, by sympathy attracted to their native dunghill; whereas, had they consisted entirely of eagles feathers, they would, for the same reason, have been attracted towards the heavens.'

This was a true alchemist's explanation, since alchemical theory held that materials of a similar nature were drawn together.

The abbot had of course good precedent for his attempt in the Greek tale of Daedalus. The craftsman used wax to make wings for himself and his son Icarus, who foolishly flew so high that the sun melted the wax, causing him to fall to earth.

See also THE GUIDMAN OF BALLANGEICH (p. 98).

A sixteenth-century alchemist tried to fly from the walls of Stirling Castle, but fell and broke his leg. He blamed his failure on the feathers used to construct his wings.

TILLICOULTRY, CLACKMANNANSHIRE

In 1827, Robert Chambers gave a tongue-in-cheek account of 'a curious and amusing old legend' told him by a friend, concerning a large stone in the churchyard at Tillicoultry. He writes that in the parish, 'as in all other places under the sun', there once lived a wicked laird. The laird happened to quarrel with a priest about the payment of certain church dues, and the debate became so heated that the laird forgot himself and knocked down the holy father.

Of course, a man who had been guilty of such an outrage could not live long; he died, therefore, and was buried. But, as he had not been afflicted by any supernatural torment upon his death-bed; as he had neither drawn air into his lungs and breathed it out blue flame, nor had supplies of water carried to him by relays of servants to cool feet which set the floor on fire, and made cold water splutter and boil as it dashed upon them; more than all, as he had died unshriven, and without having expiated his offence by a consolatory legacy of lands to the church; something yet remained to be done to manifest the indignation of heaven at his impious act. He was buried as dead men wont to be . . . But mark his punishment! The hand, – the sacrilegious hand, – was found, on the morning after the funeral, projecting about the grave, clenched as in the act of giving a blow.

The people dug up the corpse and put the arm back, but to no avail: every time, 'up came the clenched fist'. Eventually it was decided to roll a huge stone on top of the grave, and that did the trick. 'It need scarcely be suggested,' continues Chambers, that if anybody had watched by night, 'they would probably have beheld a detachment of devils, who had wickedly assumed the dress of monks, come and undo the work of sepulture, leaving the hand exposed.'

Chambers's mockery of popular beliefs (his list of divine punishments that might have been incurred but were not, and his suggestion that the monks manufactured the phenomenon) is fairly representative of the patronising tone adopted by nineteenth-century writers retelling what they saw as 'rustic' tales for a middle-class and mainly urban audience.

He adds in a footnote:

It is customary in Scotland, when a child happens to strike, or, as the phrase is, to *lift its hand* to a parent, to say, 'weel, weel, ma man, your hand'll wag abune the grave for that.'

William Gibson, retelling the story in 1883, says the admonishment was used 'when any one had given a blow', and mentions that in his time the big stone was still pointed out in Tillicoultry old churchyard, behind the mansion house.

THE TROOPER'S DUBB, KINROSS-SHIRE

One of the King Jameses (tradition does not say which) was travelling from Stirling to Falkland and called, while passing, on the Laird of Tullibole. The royal party was so large that there was not room for everyone in the house, so temporary sheds were erected for some of the guests. One of these was a trooper equally famous for bravery on the battlefield and for alcoholic capacity, who issued a general drinking challenge to the laird's men. This was accepted by a man named Keltie, equally well known as a drinker, and the two champions began their duel, which lasted for the next two days. As the sun rose on the second morning, the king's soldier, overcome, fell to the ground.

Keltie then took one final draught to prove that he had won. This gave rise to a custom of the Lairds of Tullibole, at the end of a dinner or other entertainment, of ordering a parting cup known as 'Keltie's Mends' to be drained by each guest as he left. An accompanying verse commands:

'Tis 'Keltie's Mends' – drink aff your
    drap
Before you daur to move a stap.

To go back to the original Keltie, he, like the trooper, soon dropped from his seat after his last drink, and when he woke he found that his companion was not asleep, but dead. He was buried on the spot, near a small pool still known as 'The Trooper's Dubb', believed in the nineteenth century to be haunted by his ghost. Some people said they had heard the ghost hiccuping like a drunk man, and calling for another cup of liquor.

The tale probably stems from an attempt to explain an old phrase, 'turn kelty', to turn a cup over after draining it, 'kelt' or 'kilt' meaning to turn upside down. To 'give someone kelty' means to force alcohol on someone who has tried to avoid it, or figuratively to give someone a double dose of punishment. One could of course say that the phrase evolved from the story, but it is far more likely to have happened the other way about.

TULLIBARDINE, PERTHSHIRE

Tullibardine, near Auchterarden in Perthshire, is now the site of a well-known distillery. However, it was once a much wilder place – though even then associated with whisky.

About three centuries ago, wrote John Barbour in 1886, the lands of Tullibardine were owned by a young and beautiful woman, who was fond of walking in the forests along the banks of the rivers from Dunkeld to Blair in Athole. However, the woods were then inhabited by a gigantic wild man and she promised her hand in marriage and a grant of land to any unmarried man who could either kill or enchain him.

Though several attempts were made, all failed until a handsome young yeoman came on the scene. The yeoman observed that at a certain hour every day the wild man would come to drink from a stone basin which caught the water of a cool spring in a dense grove of oaks within the forest. The yeoman one day diverted the stream, and filled the basin with a mixture of honey and something like whisky, plus a little water. Climbing up a tree, he lay hidden to watch what would happen.

The wild man came to the spring at his usual hour and lay face down to drink. Lured on by the delicious mixture, he drained the basin of every drop. The drink soon took effect: he fell sound asleep, and the yeoman was able to fetter him. The beautiful heiress of Tullibardine gave him her hand and her lands as promised. (Some people thought she had wanted him to win so that she could without disgrace marry a handsome young man so far below her in wealth and rank.)

Tradition says that, from that day on, the mixture of honey, spirits, and water that he made was known as 'Atholl Brose', and that the fettering of the wild man inspired the armorial bearings of the Dukes of Atholl. Barbour supports this theory:

Indeed, the figure of a naked man standing in fetters, and the very peculiar and appropriate motto, 'Furth, and fill the fetters,' can leave little doubt as to the correctness of this Highland tradition.

The young champion, beloved by this mightier mistress, did indeed go 'forth and fill the fetters.'

Needless to say, this is naive. Many coats of arms, like many titles to land, have been justified centuries after they were granted by ancestral legends of great deeds.

Nevertheless, the tradition is pleasant, and so is Atholl Brose. According to F. Marian McNeill in *The Scots Kitchen* (1929):

Put a pound of dripped honey into basin and add sufficient cold water to dissolve it (about a teacupful). Stir with a *silver* spoon, and when the water and honey are well mixed, add gradually one and a half pints of whisky . . . Stir briskly till a froth begins to rise. Bottle and keep tightly corked.

She notes that, unlike the yeoman's brew, it was originally made with oatmeal and indeed, for those not given to the bottle, there is a blander dessert version made by mixing soaked oatmeal with heather honey, whisky, and cream.

TULLIBODY, CLACKMANNANSHIRE

From the *Edinburgh Topographical, Traditional and Antiquarian Magazine* for September to December 1848 comes the story of 'The Drunken Sautman of Tullibody'. A sautman is a travelling seller of salt, and perhaps it was the salt that made him so thirsty. His wife was continually scolding him for his misconduct, but nothing she said had any effect.

Seeing she could na be happy wi' him, she prayed that the fairies might tak' her awa'. The fairies took hold of her in a twinklin', and up the lum [chimney] they flew singin' –

'Deedle linkum dodie, We're aff wi' drucken Davie's wife, The *Sautman* o' Tullibody.'

They carried her off to their fairy palace at Cauldhame, where she lived like a queen, but in the end she grew homesick and asked to go back to her husband.

This was granted, and as she left the fairies, one of them presented her wi' a sma' stick, saying, 'as lang as ye keep this, your gudeman will drink nae mair.' The charm was successful. Davie becam' a sober man, and the gudewife never forgot the kindness o' the fairies.

This compact little story turns the theme of the fairies as abductors of women on its head, as here the goodwife is carried off at her own request and not, as in the story of Sandy Harg's wife at NEW ABBEY (Dumfries & Galloway), involuntarily.

WEMYSS CASTLE, FIFE

Wemyss Castle was haunted by a spectre known as 'Green Jean'. In her *Memories and Miscellanies* (1904), the Countess of Munster recounts the experiences of her niece and her sister Lady Millicent Wemyss, and vouches for the truth of the story. One Christmas a theatrical performance had been arranged at the castle for the guests' entertainment. A stage had been set up in the dining room, with a curtain in front of it. Lady Millicent's daughter and a friend were alone in the room when they heard a rustling sound.

It seemed to proceed from the stage, but the curtains were undisturbed. Then as they gazed the hangings were gently drawn aside, and through the aperture glided a pallid form, clad all in green, carrying what seemed to them an Egyptian lamp . . .

The figure took no notice of the startled onlookers; but holding the lamp well in front as if to give her light on her way, passed slowly before them to the door of the empty apartment, her long green robe 'swishing' as she went. She opened it and passed through. It closed noiselessly behind her.

The room the green figure had entered was a butler's pantry, with only one door: but when Miss Wemyss and her friend looked inside, it was empty.

Soon afterwards, Lady Millicent herself saw a tall lady in green coming towards her. Though the house was full of guests, she did not recognise this one and was certain it was a stranger. The lady took no notice of her, but continued steadily, and she guessed that this was 'Green Jean'. She waited until the apparition joined her, then turned and accompanied it. When she tried to speak she found herself tongue-tied as in a dream, and could only walk beside the spectre until suddenly she found herself alone.

The countess's narration of these encounters is in the best tradition of the Victorian and Edwardian literary ghost story. Katharine Briggs comments in a note, 'This is an incomplete story, because we hear neither of the ghost's origin nor her end,' but this is precisely what makes it convincing, literary treatment notwithstanding, as an account of an actual experience.

WESTER DURIE, FIFE

After dark, mysterious lights were sometimes seen moving around the farmyard at Wester Durie, and were known to the local people as 'the Waster Durie Can'les'. James Wilkie, noting this in 1931 as having been the case 'a century ago', records the similar tradition in Angus of the 'Can'les of Kilry', said to have caused the death of at least one traveller by leading him into a deep pool.

The strange 'candles' in both places may belong to the old and widespread tradition of the *ignis fatuus* ('foolish fire'), the spontaneous combustion of marsh gas, conceived of as a spirit bearing some form of light. In Britain he was often known as Will o' the Wisp and thought of as a sprite more mischievous than malicious, carrying a burning wisp of tarred straw. His other common name of Jack o' Lantern, however, indicates a more substantial covered light. In marshy and coastal districts he could be a true nightly terror: such a being was the Norfolk 'Lantern Man', neither small nor sprightly but full-size, physically aggressive, and extremely dangerous.

DUMFRIES & GALLOWAY

The counties of Dumfriesshire,
Kirkcudbrightshire, and Wigtownshire

ANNANDALE, DUMFRIESSHIRE

Adam Bell was a landowner of Annandale. He was handsome and athletic, the best horseman and marksman in the county, and he used to boast of his skill with a broadsword. In the autumn of 1745, he set out for a long visit to Edinburgh. A few days later, his housekeeper was surprised to see him come back, dressed as he had been when he left home. When she greeted him, and asked if he wanted food or drink, he did not answer. A few minutes later, he left the house again, walked slowly towards the River Kinnel, and disappeared into the woods.

A search was made, but no trace of Bell could be found. It was generally thought that the housekeeper must have seen an apparition, and that some ill had befallen her master. Finally a relative took over management of the estate, and enquiries were abandoned.

At about the same time that the housekeeper saw her vision, a farmer named McMillan was staying near Holyroodhouse, in Edinburgh:

During the night he felt so ill and restless that he got up, and went out, in bright moonlight, into St Anthony's garden, at the back of the house. As he stood in the shadow of the wall, a tall man in a drab overcoat came in, and walked impatiently up and down the garden, all the time consulting his watch. Soon another man, shorter and stouter than the first, entered, and came up, and after the briefest exchange of words, they fell to fighting.

The tall man seemed to have the advantage, until a cloud overshadowed the moon, and made them pause. When they were again on guard, at the first exchange of thrusts the tall man's foot slipped, and he fell forward, and was instantly run through the body by his antagonist who, after satisfying himself that the other was dead, quietly wiped his blade, and withdrew.

McMillan decided to say nothing of what he had seen in case suspicion fell on himself. However, next morning, when the news was made public that a murder had taken place outside the house, he went to view the dead body, but nothing was found on it by which it could be identified.

Sixteen years later he heard the story of Mr Bell's mysterious disappearance, and became certain that it was his death he had witnessed. The identity of the murderer remained unknown, and no further light was ever shed on the mystery, which was reported by James Hogg in 1820.

The appearance of a person's wraith at the time of their death is a phenomenon frequently described, as at THURSO (Northern Highlands). *See also* SECOND SIGHT (p. 474).

DUMFRIES & GALLOWAY

✕	Battles and escapes	🐚	Mermaids and selkies
👤	Clan and family legends	✝	Murder and robbery
⚡	Curses and divine interventions	🎻	Pipers and fiddlers
💀	Death and burial	👑	Royalty
🐉	Dragons and sea-serpents	🧎	Saints and miracles
💃	Fairies and trows	🐻	Supernatural creatures
👻	Ghosts and omens	🎭	Tall tales, tricks and jokes
🐎	Heroes and villains	🏺	Wells and springs
⛰	Landscape legends	🐈	Witches and witchcraft
🔔	Legendary beings	📖	Wizards and seers

Ayrshire

Mote Hill

Murder Hole

Kirkcud

Wigtownshire

Galdenoch
Castle

Glenluce
Abbey

Martyrs'
Tomb

Cardoness
Castle

Gatehouse
of Fleet

Kirkwaugh

Dunskey
Castle

Claunch

Borgue

*Luce
Bay*

Dowalton
Loch

High Ardwell

Myrton
Castle

Auchabrick
House

Portencorkie Bay

Kirkmaiden-
in-Rhinns

St Ninian's
Cave

Burrow Head Forts

Auchneight

St Medan's
Chapel and Cave

Lanarkshire

Peebs.

Selkirkshire

Roxb.

Bail Hill

Crawick

Auchengruith

Sanquhar

Ericstane
Hill

Moffat

Bodesbeck
Farm

Drumlanrig
Castle

Tynron
Doon

Closeburn
Castle

Spedlin's
Tower

Annandale

Glencairn

Dalswinton

Dumfriesshire

Craigdarroch

Cowhill
Tower

Dryfesdale

Gilnockie Tower

Routin' Bridge

Knockhill
House

Ecclefechan

brightshire

New Abbey

Blackett Tower

Sweetheart
Abbey

Caerlaverock

Dalbeattie
Burn

Criffel

Whinnieliggate

Palnackie

Borron
Point

Collin
Farm

Buckland
Glen

Rerrick
Parish

Solway
Firth

R&C

Inverness-shire

Perthshire

Argyllshire

Ayrshire

0   5   10   15   20 MI

0   5   10   15   20   25   30 KM

AUCHABRICK HOUSE, KIRKMAIDEN, WIGTOWNSHIRE

The ghost of Auchabrick House at Kirk-maiden is sometimes said to be that of a young man with boots and spurs, astride the grey horse which caused his death in a riding accident. A more poignant story, however, is told by James Maxwell Wood, writing in 1911. According to this, a daughter of the house was betrothed to a young gentleman whose fortune was not equal to his rank. Those were the days of privateering, and to amass some means he found himself a berth on a hitherto suc-cessful ship. While abroad, he sent his betrothed a silk dress, and a large sum of money. However, her unscrupulous brother intercepted the package, sold the dress, and spent the gold. Worried at receiving no response, the lover wrote time and again, but always the brother intervened and she never got the letters.

Then disaster struck the ship, and the young man never returned to hear the truth from his beloved. His ghost, how-ever, came back to haunt the place. No lock could keep him out, and his pen would be heard scratching away as he wrote and rewrote the stolen letters. Var-ious measures were taken to quiet him. At one time a Bible was placed behind a door through which he seemed to pass, but this resulted in terrifying noises and the shak-ing of the house as if by a storm. 'It was also believed that the semblance of the ship on which the wanderer pursued his calling as a privateer was at times seen to sail along a field above the house.'

A ghost ship moving above a field is not unique: in Cornwall, both Porthcurno and Gwennap Head were believed to be vis-ited by spectral vessels that sailed over dry land.

AUCHENGRUITH, DUMFRIESSHIRE

Auchengruith, near Sanquhar, is probably the 'Auchencreath' described by R. H. Cromek in 1810 as the scene of a 'fairy borrowing'. He writes:

A woman of Auchencreath, in Nithsdale, was one day sifting meal warm from the mill: a little, cleanly-arrayed, beautiful woman came to her, holding out a bason of antique workmanship, requesting her courteously to fill it with her new meal. Her demand was cheerfully complied with. In a week the comely little dame returned with the borrowed meal. She breathed over it, setting it down bason and all, saying aloud, 'be never toom [empty].' The gude-wife lived to a goodly age, without ever seeing the bottom of her blessed bason.

This is the equivalent of the magic purse, never without money in it, in European folk tales. Cromek says that the Scottish peasantry thought it 'Unco sonsie' (uncom-monly lucky, propitious) to be on friendly terms with the fairies, and 'uncanny' to refuse their requests.

Versions of this story have been recorded in Canada, probably taken there by Scottish immigrants. A similar tale of fairy gratitude is told at BEDRULE (Lothian & Borders), and a more dramatic example at CULZEAN CASTLE (Glasgow & Ayr-shire).

AUCHNEIGHT, WIGTOWNSHIRE

A herd and his wife lived in a little cottage at Auchneight in the parish of Kirk-maiden. They were in the service of Sir

Godfrey MacCulloch, and on the very day that the herd's wife gave birth to a son, he received an urgent summons to go to Cardoness Castle, where his master lived.

He had much to attend to before leaving his wife and newborn child alone, and it was getting late at night before he set out. He made his way northward along the western shore of Luce Bay towards the Loup of Grennan, a place with an uncanny reputation. It was the last day of October, Hallowe'en, the date when the supernatural is at its most active.

It was very dark, but as he drew near the Loup, he saw a faint glimmer of light from the direction of the sea. As it drew nearer and nearer, it gradually resolved itself into a coach lit with blue lamps and drawn by six horses, bowling swiftly towards him. As it passed, he saw that it was crowded with elfin figures, and guarded by galloping horsemen. His alarm grew no less when he noticed a blue torch, a sure portent of death, burning at the side of the track where the coach and its outriders had passed.

Meanwhile, his young wife, alone with her child in the cottage, was startled to hear, around midnight, the tramping of horses, jingling of bridles, and lumbering of wheels, accompanied by a buzz of voices. Suddenly the door of the cottage flew open as if by its own accord and an eerie light lit up the whole kitchen. A throng of tiny people dressed in green surrounded her bed, continually chattering. One taller and more finely clad than the rest waved his hand for silence and said to the terrified woman, 'This is Hallowe'en. We have come for your child, and him we must have.' 'Oh, God forbid!' she shrieked, and at once there was darkness and silence 'as of the grave'.

In her abject terror she fainted, but when she came to herself she ventured to get out of her bed and light a lamp. To her joy, the baby was still sleeping soundly, and nothing seemed to have been disturbed.

On the same night, the tenant at nearby Barncorkrie, looking out of his door at midnight, had been astonished to see a group of diminutive horsemen riding post-haste through the meadows a bowshot away.

The implication of the blue light in this story, reinforced by the 'silence of the grave', is that changelings – children snatched by the fairies – would be joining the ranks of the dead, often seen in company with the fairies inside their hills. The fairies vanished, as ghosts are also apt to do, at the mention of the Lord's name.

The Mull of Galloway seems to have been an especial haunt of fairies. This account is one of several given by James Maxwell Wood in 1911, and Sir Godfrey MacCulloch himself had an encounter at MYRTON CASTLE, although he must have been a later Sir Godfrey than the one mentioned here, since Cardoness Castle was then in the possession of the Gordons.

BAIL HILL, DUMFRIESSHIRE

A lane running north-west into the hills from Crawick passes close by Bail or Bale Hill, north-east of Kirkconnel. It was traditionally said to be a haunt of the fairies, who would assemble on May Day, to celebrate the start of summer, at the Braes of Polveoch, sited at the west end of the Bank Wood between Kirkconnel and Sanquhar. Groups of them would come from Kello Water, Glen Aylmer, and Glen Wharty, and when they had all gathered together they rode over the knowes towards Bail Hill. It was said that a beautiful doorway would open on the southward slope of the hill through which they would enter two at a time, the turf closing over the doorway behind the last pair in.

BLACKETT TOWER, KIRKPATRICK-FLEMING, DUMFRIESSHIRE

Blackett Tower was a Border fortress, the home of the Bell family. According to local legend, its ruined tower was inhabited by a ghost known as 'Old Red-Cap' or 'Bloody Bell'.

William Scott Irving, who tells the story in his poem 'Fair Helen' (1814), says that at the stroke of midnight, in the light of the low, red eastern moon, the phantom takes its stand on the wall with a bloody dagger in its hand, and its shrieking borne on the wind terrifies the benighted peasant:

Such are the tales at Lyke-wake drear,
When the unholy hour of night draws
        near,
When the ban-dog howls, and the lights
        burn blue,
And the phantom fleets before the view;
When 'Red-Cap' wakes his eldritch cry,
And the winds of the wold come
        moaning by.

Doggerel this may be, but it contains some genuine folk beliefs – the 'unholy hour of night' is of course midnight, when the powers of darkness are strongest; dogs howling at night were thought of as ominous, often a sign of approaching death; while lights burning blue were widely regarded as the sure sign of a supernatural presence, as mentioned at BALCOMIE CASTLE (Central & Perthshire). A 'Lyke-wake' is a vigil kept over a corpse, an effective time for telling ghost stories.

This 'Red-Cap' is one of a family of murderous Border spirits, another of whom served Lord Soulis at HERMITAGE CASTLE (Lothian & Borders).

BODESBECK FARM, NEAR MOFFAT, DUMFRIESSHIRE

The Brownies of southern Scotland, like the hobs and hobthrushes of England, were obliging farm and household drudges, but very quick to take offence. In his *Remains of Nithsdale and Galloway Song* (1810), R. H. Cromek writes that 'Liethin Hall' in Moffatdale was the hereditary home of a notable Brownie. As he was once told by an old woman in confidence, the Brownie had lived there for 300 years. He appeared only once to each new head of the household, 'and, indeed, seldom shewed more than his hand to anyone'. On the death of a master he was fond of, he would be heard to lament, and would eat nothing for days.

His final manifestation was to a new heir of the property who arrived from abroad.

The faithful Brownie shewed himself and proffered homage. The spruce Laird was offended to see such a famine-faced, wrinkled domestic, and ordered him meat and drink, with a new suit of clean livery. The Brownie departed, repeating loud and frequently these ruin-boding lines –

Ca', cuttie, ca'!
A' the luck o' Liethin Ha'
Gangs wi' me to Bodsbeck Ha'.

Liethin Ha' was, in a few years, in ruins, and 'Bonnie Bodsbeck' flourished under the luck-bringing patronage of the Brownie.

'Cuttie' here means 'short' or 'stumpy'; the word could be used as an endearment or an insulting term, usually for a child or a woman. That the Brownie refers to himself by this name indicates his small stature.

In a version supplied to Robert Chambers only a few years later, in 1826, the offended Brownie decamps in the opposite direction, having at first been attached to Bodesbeck or Bodsbeck and made it the most prosperous farm in all Moffatdale. The farmer decided to give him better food as a reward, but the Brownie, like others of his kind, resented the thought of 'wages'. He gave his services freely, and by way of return helped himself to whatever food he fancied. He invariably took the humblest, and not very much of that. So when the farmer left out a bowl of bread-and-milk for him, the Brownie immediately took offence and left the farmhouse for Leithinhall, as Chambers spells it.

The heir to 'Liethin Hall' wants his Brownie to look smarter, whereas the farmer at Bodesbeck is simply grateful, but otherwise this is the same story, and, whether he is given food or clothes, both gifts are traditional. The 'wonted delicacies' mentioned by Cromek undoubtedly refer to the same humble diet that Chambers describes. The important thing to remember about Brownies if you wanted to keep them was that they liked to be independent, eat what they wanted, and wear what they wanted, not what someone else deemed fit for them.

Possibly the two versions of the story were concurrent. However, in Cromek's time, Bodesbeck still flourished while Liethin Hall was long gone, providing a better context for the theme of the luck that goes with the Brownie. And indeed the Brownie was associated with Bodesbeck somewhat earlier. In most later stories of Brownies and their like, the dismissal by the gift of clothes, money, or unasked-for food is accidental, an unfortunate act of kindness which becomes a matter of regret for the farm or household. However, the same conjuration could be used deliberately to get rid of a Brownie you did not want. In 1802, Sir Walter Scott gave a sadder version of the tale in which this useful farm and household spirit is dismissed in the name of religion:

> The last Brownie, known in Ettrick Forest, resided in Bodsbeck, a wild and solitary spot near the head of Moffat Water, where he exercised his functions undisturbed, till the scrupulous devotion of an old lady induced her to hire him away, as it was termed, by placing in his haunt a porringer of milk and a piece of money. After receiving this hint to depart, he was heard the whole night to howl and cry, 'Farewell to bonny Bodsbeck!' which he was compelled to abandon forever.

See also BROWNIES (p. 80).

BORGUE, KIRKCUDBRIGHTSHIRE

One of the stories told to the folklore collector John Francis Campbell at Kirkcudbright in 1865 was about a boy called Johnny Williamson. The boy's father had been drowned, and Johnny was brought up at Borgue by his mother and grandfather, an old man by the name of Sproat.

The boy would disappear for days at a time and no one knew where he went. Though he never spoke of it to anyone, it was understood that he had been taken by the fairies. On one occasion all the people of the neighbourhood were gathered together stacking peats:

> At this time the boy had been away for ten days, and they were all wondering where he could be, when lo and behold, the boy is sitting in the midst of them. 'Johnny,' said one of the company, who were all seated in a ring, eating their dinner, 'where did ye come from?' 'I came with our folks,' said the boy (meaning the fairies). 'Your folks; who are they?'

'Do you see yon barrow of peats a coup-ing [falling] into yon hole? There's where I came from.'

An old man by the name of Brown, the ancestor of a family still living at Borgue in the mid nineteenth century, advised the boy's grandfather to send him to the Catholic priest, who would give him something to frighten away the fairies. Sproat did so, and when the boy returned he was wearing a cross hung round his neck by a bit of black ribbon.

When the Protestant minister heard about this, both the grandfather and old Brown were excommunicated: the Kirk 'believed in fairies, but not in anything a Papist priest could do'. However, after that, the boy did not disappear any more. Some of the oldest villagers alive when Campbell heard this story still remembered Johnny as an old man. 'The whole affair is recorded in the books of the kirk-session of Borgue, and can be seen any day.'

The narrator puts his finger on the dichotomy in the thinking of the early Kirk: 'They believed in fairies, but not in any-thing a Papist priest could do.' Yet in sto-ries of exorcism priests are often consulted, sometimes even by the Protestant ministers themselves, as at GLENLUCE ABBEY. That is not to say that the Kirk was impotent: min-isters such as Robert Blair at Holy Trinity, ST ANDREWS (Central & Perthshire), were renowned for their power over the super-natural. The angle of such tales depends largely on who is telling them.

BORRON POINT, DUMFRIESSHIRE

The Solway Firth has long been said to be haunted by phantom ships. Of the numer-ous stories about them, one of the earliest was recorded in 1822 by Allan Cunningham.

One fine evening, Cunningham went aboard a boat belonging to Richard Faul-der, of Allanbay, Cumberland, and they allowed a gentle wind from the east to drift them towards the Scottish coast. There they saw an old man walking down to the shore carrying a fishing net, accompanied by a girl with a small harpoon.

'This is old Mark Macmoran, the mariner, with his grand-daughter Barbara,' said Richard Faulder, in a whisper that had something of fear in it; 'he knows every creek, and cavern, and quicksand, in Solway . . . and he has seen, too, the Haunted Ships in full sail; and, if all tales be true, has sailed in them himself; – he's an awful person.'

Nonetheless they went to talk to him. Cunningham saw the old man's eyes linger on the black and decayed hulls of two ves-sels half-immersed in the quicksand. The tide came in and hid them, and then while they watched in horror a young fisherman approached in his boat and was swept under. Faulder and Cunningham tried to come to his rescue, but in attempting to swim to them he was drowned. When they returned to the shore, old Mark told them that any man was doomed the minute he touched the Haunted Ship.

The wrecks, said the old man, were those of Danish pirate vessels. One evening many years before, men working in the fields by moonlight had seen two ships heading for the dangerous quicksands. On the foremost, nothing was to be seen but a shadow flitting from bow to stern, seem-ingly trimming the sails and steering, but the decks of the second were thronged with men from whom came the sound of merriment and singing. Though the reapers shouted to warn them, no notice was taken, except that a large and half-starved dog sitting on the prow answered with a loud and mournful howl.

The older men watching said, 'We have seen the fiend sailing in a bottomless ship.' Four youths, however, set off hoping to profit from the disaster. A boat, rowed by a 'shadowy pilot', was sent from the ships to pick them up:

> They leaped in with a laugh, and with a laugh were they welcomed on deck; wine-cups were given to each, and as they raised them to their lips the vessels melted away beneath their feet, 'and one loud shriek, mingled with laughter still louder, was heard over land and water for many miles.'

In the morning, the crowd that came to the beach saw the two wrecks with masts and tackle gone.

The narrative is a little confusing: the physical remains suggest that both ships were real, but in that case how did the decks disappear from beneath the feet of the callous youths? If, on the other hand, the vessels were spectres, perhaps playing out an earlier episode when a demon led the pirates astray in punishment for their crimes, why did the wreckage only appear after this phantasmal event? Cunningham leaves this question unresolved, but adds the popular belief that if you stood on Borron Point on a certain night in the year, you would see those ships sailing up the Solway, hear laughter and singing, and see the ghostly oarsman collect the four whose memorial stone stood in the kirkyard 'with a sinking ship and a shoreless sea cut upon it'.

BUCKLAND GLEN, KIRKCUDBRIGHTSHIRE

In the early twentieth century, according to James Maxwell Wood, belief lingered in a headless lady haunting Buckland Glen. One night, a Monkland farmer was riding his small Highland pony Maggie home from Kirkcudbright, accompanied by one of his farmboys on foot. It was around midnight when they reached the part of Buckland Glen where a small bridge crosses the Buckland Burn. They had no sooner crossed the bridge than the pony reared and swerved, almost throwing the farmer from the saddle. He could not think what ailed the horse until the boy whispered and pointed.

> The old man looked, and muttering to himself whispered, 'Aye, it's there, laddie! It's a' true what hes been mony a time telt! That's the ghost o' the headless leddy wha was murdered in the glen in the aul' wicked times. We'll no gang by, but gang doon the lane and slip hame by Gilroanie.'

They made their way through the woods fringing the Buckland Burn as it runs down to Manxman's Lake, and got home with no more trouble than keeping the nervous pony in hand. A week later, it was learned that two men had lain in wait – for robbery or worse – at a lonely spot on the Bombie road a little beyond Buckland Bridge. They had heard that the farmer had been in Kirkcudbright to draw money, and had the Buckland ghost not made them go roundabout, there might have been another murder in Buckland Glen. The ghost was evidently a warning spirit, trying to prevent a repetition of her own fate.

There was – and still is – a widely held belief that animals are more sensitive than human beings to the presence of the supernatural. In this story, Maggie's horse sense served the farmer well.

Galloway Smugglers

During the eighteenth century, smuggling was by far the most lucrative occupation in Galloway. The coast is perfect free-trader territory: it is laced with caves, some inaccessible except from the sea, others approachable on foot but only with great difficulty. A visitor in the late nineteenth century, quoted in James Maxwell Wood's *Smuggling in the Solway* (1908), had to scramble on all fours up a cliff to reach a hidden crevice:

> After squeezing yourself through the narrow entrance for a few yards, you come to the edge of a precipice. You must get down on your hands and knees, turn your back to the cave, hang on with your fingers to the ledge of the precipice, let yourself down all your length, and . . . allow yourself to drop into darkness. You land about twelve or thirteen feet down.

Within, the cavern was spacious and contained a large rack to hold bottles. 'The use to which the cave has been put – a smuggling cellar – is thus disclosed.' A crack near the ceiling led to a second chamber, even more secure than the first. The place described is known as 'Dirk Hatteraick's Cave', after the free-trading captain in Walter Scott's *Guy Mannering* (1815).

Liquor hidden in such recesses was run in by sailing boats. One of the most famous was the *Black Prince*, said to be named in honour of the Devil. Its skipper, Captain Yawkins, was reported to have given his soul for the safety of his vessel, and like the fairies at CARTERHAUGH (Lothian & Borders) to have paid a 'teind' to hell, one tenth of his crew supposedly perishing on every voyage. Yawkins was once ambushed in Kirkcudbright Bay by two revenue cutters (charmingly named the 'Dwarf' and the 'Pigmy'), but sailed so skilfully that he slipped between the two of them 'like an eel through the neck of a bottle', and impertinently threw his hat on one deck and his wig on the other as he passed.

Yawkins was almost certainly bringing goods from the Isle of Man, which was exempt from many British import duties. In 1670 some Liverpudlians had set up a trading post there, offering such good terms that they acquired many cargoes intended for Bristol or London, and in 1725 the trade received a powerful boost when extra taxes were imposed on malt, making ale far more expensive than before and leading to hugely increased consumption of wine and spirits. Tobacco, tea, lace, and salt were also heavily taxed; all could be brought from the Continent or the Americas to the Isle of Man and then illegally shipped on to Scotland, and all found a ready market in Edinburgh and other towns. Smuggling reached its high point in the 1770s, when the American War of Independence was being fought and

In the eighteenth century smuggled goods were often hidden in the remote coastal caves of Galloway.

the government raised duties still further to pay for it, but began to decline when William Pitt the Younger greatly reduced taxes in 1806, and by 1830 only a trickle remained of what had once been a flood of contraband.

In its heyday, smuggling had involved almost the whole population of the area, from old women who received a few bottles of brandy in return for use of a horse, to gang leaders like Billy Marshall, chief of the Galloway Travellers. Marshall was a figure of legend, renowned not only for daring but for generosity. In *The Tinkler-Gypsies* (1907), Andrew McCormick writes that 'there is scarcely a farm-house in Galloway where, after the lapse of 113 years since Billy Marshall's death, stories of his kindness are not still related. These might be recorded by the hundred.'

A story told by Billy's grandson, 'Black Matthew Marshall', and relayed by William Chambers in 1821, tells how the Marshalls stored their goods in a cavern high on Cairnmuir. One night two Highland pipers, strangers to the area, took shelter there, but were then alarmed by the voices of approaching men. They struck up on their instruments:

> At this very unexpected and terrific reception, – the yelling of the bag-pipes, issuing from the bowels of the earth, just at the moment the gypsies entered the cave, – Billy Marshall with all his band precipitately fled in the greatest consternation, and from that night never again would go near their favourite haunt, believing that the blasts they had heard proceeded from the devil or some of his infernal agents.

The pipers were able to leave in the morning, taking with them some brandy and tobacco.

BURROW HEAD FORTS, WHITHORN, WIGTOWNSHIRE

In his *Remains of Nithsdale and Galloway Song* (1810), R. H. Cromek gives the atmospheric little tale of the 'The Fairy Farewell', saying that it happened 'about twenty years ago', and was well remembered:

> The sun was setting on a fine summer's evening, and the peasantry were returning from labour, when, on the side of a green hill, appeared a procession of thousands of apparently little boys, habited in mantles of green, freckled with light. One, taller than the rest, ran before them, and seemed to enter the hill, and again appeared at its summit. This was repeated three times, and all vanished. The peasantry, who beheld it, called it, 'The Fareweel o' the Fairies to the Burrow hill!'

From Chaucer's time onwards, the fairies are said to have departed or to be a people in eclipse, like the elves in J. R. R. Tolkien's *Lord of the Rings* (1954–5). Cromek gives another account of the last of the fairies, attached to the Ward Law, Dumfriesshire, while Hugh Miller records what was said to be their final departure from Scotland at the Burn of Eathie, Cromarty, and a twentieth-century tale of 'the last of the trows', the fairies of the Shetland and Orkney Islands, is recorded at BURNSIDE on the island of Yell.

Although Cromek does not say where 'the Burrow hill' was, it might have been either of the two prehistoric forts on Burrow Head, at the west end of Wigtown Bay. Such ancient hill-forts as well as natural hills were habitually identified as fairy dwellings in Scottish and Irish tradition.

CAERLAVEROCK, DUMFRIESSHIRE

Now known mainly for its castle, Caerlaverock was once a haunt of fairies. Writing in 1810, R. H. Cromek tells the atmospheric story of a fairy changeling:

> A beautiful child, of Caerlaveroc, in Nithsdale, on the second day of its birth, and before its baptism, was changed, none knew how, for an antiquated elf of hideous aspect. It kept the family awake with its nightly yells; biting the mother's breasts, and would neither be cradled or nursed.

One day the mother had to be away from home. She left the infant in charge of a servant girl, who sat grumbling that she couldn't get on with her household tasks. The baby then spoke, telling her that he would do her work if she would loosen the band that kept him in the cradle. When she did as he asked, he leaped up, and all the jobs around the house were completed with amazing rapidity.

'What'll we do wi' the wee diel?' wondered the mother when she heard what had happened, but the servant girl knew what to do. At midnight they covered the chimney top and barred every opening into the house. They blew up the embers until they were glowing hot, and the maid, undressing the infant, tossed it in the fire.

> It uttered the wildest and most piercing yells, and, in a moment, the Fairies were heard moaning at every wonted avenue, and rattling at the window boards, at the chimney head, and at the door. 'In the name o' God bring back the bairn,' cried the lass. The window flew up; the earthly child was laid unharmed on the mother's lap, while its grisly substitute flew up the chimney with a loud laugh.

The fairies were known to be given to taking beautiful and healthy babies. Families once took the precaution, when a pretty child was born, to consecrate it to God and pray for its protection. Other safeguards were Bibles, crosses made of straw, and steel pins stuck in the pillow, although Cromek adds that such measures could provoke a spiteful revenge:

When the mother's vigilance hinders the Fairies from carrying her child away, or changing it, the touch of Fairy hands and their unearthly breath make it wither away in every limb and lineament, like a blighted ear of corn.

Tales of the elves' propensity to steal children remained current into the twentieth century. The Traveller and storyteller Duncan Williamson, writing in 1985, reports that the legend of fairy changelings was still common among Travellers in his childhood. 'My mother used to stick a needle in the wean's bonnet at night-time – the fairies can't take the wean as long as something made of steel is fastened to its clothes.' He gives a story told by his grandmother in about 1935 concerning a farmer and his wife whose lovely child was left on a hillock – evidently a fairy mound – and afterwards would not stop crying. A couple of weeks later, the baby was left for a day with the postman (in older stories it might have been a visiting tailor, the point being that the person has travelled and gained experience). As soon as it was alone with Postie, the baby started talking, got up, opened a bottle of whisky, and played jigs on a straw pipe. The postman could not fail to realise that there was something unusual about this child, and when its parents returned he told them it was a 'Taen-Awa' – a changeling, their own child having been 'taken away'. He advised the mother to throw it off a cliff, and when she did so it looked up and shook its fist:

'Ye finally found the answer, but,' it said, 'many's the night when I lay in yir bosom and cuddled ye, I cuid have done terrible things to you – *curse* upon you! And curse upon your old postman!' Like that – he was gone.

It is most unlikely that any such horrendous experiments as dropping a baby off a cliff or throwing it into the fire were ever carried out in practice, but they were widely recommended in folklore, perhaps included partly for their shock value. As John Gregorson Campbell remarks in *Superstitions of the Highlands and Islands of Scotland* (1900), 'There can be no doubt these modes of treatment would rid a house of any disagreeable visitor, at least of the human race.' A more humane method of detection was by means of eggshells, as at KILCHOMAN (Western Isles).

See also DUNDREGGAN (Southern Highlands).

CARDONESS CASTLE, ANWOTH, KIRKCUDBRIGHTSHIRE

'Cardoness' is said to be derived from *caer-donais*, meaning the castle of ill luck or evil. The name is explained in one traditional account by the fact that three successive lairds beggared themselves building the castle without being able to finish it. A fourth managed to complete the walls but was reduced to such poverty that he had to roof them with heather, which he picked himself on Glenquicken Moor and carried on his back to the castle. Though he managed to get the heather up, he was no thatcher, and every time it rained the roof leaked like a sieve.

In *Hereditary Sheriffs of Galloway* (1893),

Sir Andrew Agnew gives an alternative and more dramatic tale of a Border laird who built the castle from the proceeds of violence and robbery. His wife had presented him with nine daughters one after the other, each one less welcome than the last. After a long interval, she was again pregnant, and just before her lying-in, he burst into her room and told her roughly that, unless she gave him a son, he would drown her and all her daughters in the Black Loch. As he was thought fully capable of carrying out his threat, the whole countryside rejoiced when she produced a boy.

It was midwinter, and to celebrate the birth the laird ordered a feast to be held on the frozen loch. On a Sunday of sunshine everyone assembled on the ice, and the lady and her new baby were brought out.

> The glass went merrily round, fun was at its highest, when suddenly the ice collapsed; wife, son, and the whole bevy of daughters save one, who was ill and had been left at home, sank fathom deep in the dark waters, the devil claiming the wicked laird as his own.

When she grew up, the surviving daughter and sole heiress married a MacCulloch, taking with her into that family the house and lands.

Whatever may be the truth about the laird, it is a fiction that the castle came to the MacCullochs by marriage, since it was probably built by Alexander Mac-Culloch, a close associate of James IV, in the late fifteenth century. It had passed out of the family's hands by the time the last of the MacCullochs, Sir Godfrey of MYRTON CASTLE, either came to a sticky end or had a miraculous escape, depending on whether one believes history or fairy tale.

CLAUNCH, SORBIE, WIGTOWNSHIRE

An old tradition of a ghostly carriage drawn by two horses was attached to the farm of Claunch, or Clunch, in the parish of Sorbie. Though the origin of the apparition was unknown, an account of its appearance was given in James Maxwell Wood's *Witchcraft and Superstitions in the South-western District of Scotland* (1911) as supplied by James F. Cannon of Edinburgh, who deemed it an authentic description.

The man who said he had seen it was a blacksmith who had been working at the farm. It was a fine moonlit night by the time he gathered up his tools and set out to walk home to Whithorn. The farmer who had employed him went with him as far as the farmyard entrance, and as they were crossing the courtyard they saw what seemed to be a pair of spectral horses galloping by, drawing after them a spectral carriage. In another moment they had disappeared.

When the smith asked what in the name of wonder it had been, the farmer said it was more than he could tell; he had seen it before, though not often. He warned the smith not to mention what he had seen: 'nae guid'll come o' talkin' aboot it.'

In England, phantom coaches commonly carry the spectres of the 'wicked gentry' on their haunts, but this is a far less frequent phenomenon in Scotland, with its historically quite different social structure. More ominous are those nameless vehicles thought to presage a death when they were heard drawing up outside a house, which seem to be descendants of the medieval hell-cart going its rounds collecting souls: an example was reported at ST BOSWELLS (Lothian & Borders). There are also instances of fairies riding in coaches, as for instance at AUCHNEIGHT.

Closeburn Castle, Dumfriesshire

The loch surrounding the fourteenth-century tower house of Closeburn Castle is the scene of one of Britain's many death omens appearing in the form of a bird (in many cases a white one). Family tradition said that a swan always appeared on the loch whenever one of the Kirkpatricks of Closeburn was about to die.

According to one account, there were initially two swans, and their appearance was considered fortunate, since twice their visits coincided with the recovery of one of the family from serious illness. Every summer for 150 years they came, until the twelve-year-old heir, Robert Kirkpatrick, saw Shakepeare's *Merchant of Venice*. Taken with the lines 'he makes a swan-like end, / Fading in music', and wishing to test the truth of the old wives' tale that swan-song was only heard at the death of the bird, he killed one with his crossbow. Then he took fright at what he had done, buried the bird, and said nothing. Next year there appeared on the loch a lone swan with a blood-red stain on its breast, and in under a week the head of the family died. From then onwards, this swan always appeared as a harbinger of death.

Craufurd Tait Ramage, in 1876, added that the last recorded appearance of the swan cast a gloom over the marriage of Sir Thomas Kirkpatrick, the first baronet, who was marrying for the third time. On the day of the wedding, his son Roger saw the fatal bird on the loch. Overwhelmed with melancholy, he went back to the castle where his father, seeing his despondent appearance, teased him by suggesting that he was sad because of his new stepmother. 'Perhaps ere long you may also be sorrowful,' the young man

A swan's appearance on the loch around Closeburn Castle was said to foretell a death in the Kirkpatrick family.

responded, and he died suddenly that same night.

Francis Grose does not mention the swans when writing about the castle in 1789, although his histories often include local tales to 'enliven the dullness of antiquarian disquisition'. Neither does the story appear in the fourth edition of Black's *Picturesque Tourist of Scotland* in 1845, but it was up and running by the time John Bernard Burke compiled his *Family Romances* (1853), giving a rough date for the inception of the legend.

See also IN LEAGUE WITH THE DEVIL (p. 142).

Collin Farm, Rerrick, Kirkcudbrightshire

In an article on poltergeists in the *Encyclopaedia Britannica* (1911), Andrew Lang mentions a pamphlet with the lengthily descriptive title *A True Relation of an Apparition, Expressions, and Actings of a Spirit, which infested the House of Andrew*

Mackie, in Ring-Croft of Stocking, in the Paroch of Rerrick, in the Stewartry of Kirkcudbright, in Scotland, 1695. The author is Alexander Telfair, minister of Rerrick, who according to Lang showed 'unusual regard for securing signed evidence', and took care to record what those concerned 'particularly saw, heard, and felt'; indeed, some of the manifestations he experienced himself.

The trouble began in February 1695, and included the releasing of tethered animals, the setting of fires, and showers of stones inside and outside the house. At Mackie's request, Telfair called at the house on the hill above Collin Farm, but saw nothing, though he was hit by a few pebbles.

Things became more violent in mid March. The stones were bigger, and were thrown particularly on the Sabbath and when the family was at prayer. The minister visited again, and was struck several times on the sides and shoulders.

> That night as I was once at prayer, leaning on a bedside, I felt something pressing up my arme; I casting my eyes thither, perceived a little white hand and arm, from the elbow down, but presently it evanished.

Apart from this, all that was ever seen was an apparition of a boy of about fourteen, in grey clothes and with a bonnet on his head. Like the little hand and arm, this phantom soon disappeared, but the violence became worse: not only the family but neighbours calling at the house were beaten and stoned.

On 5 April, Andrew Mackie's wife felt a slab by the door wobble. When the stone was lifted, there was revealed a scrap of bloodstained paper wrapped round seven small bones and some flesh, and a few days later Mackie found a letter written with blood. It contained a short, obscure, and semi-literate message, the burden of which was that Scotland should repent and take warning, and that 'this man' (Mackie, presumably) would be troubled for twenty-three days.

The phantom had always been vociferous, emitting whistles and groans and crying 'Take that till you get another' when it threw a missile, but towards the end of April it became more directly communicative, announcing that it had a commission from God to take everyone in the house to hell, and that if the country did not repent it would return with a hundred worse than itself and would trouble every family in the land. Then it urged, 'Praise me and I will whistle to you; worship me and I will trouble you no more.'

On 27 April, it set fire to the house seven times, and the next day, being the Sabbath, it kept starting fires from sunrise to sunset. In the evening it pulled the gable end down, and hoisted a huge log in the air above the children, crying, 'If I had a commission I would brain them.' On 29 April the fire-raising continued, and Andrew Mackie, understandably, was said to be 'weary quenching it'.

On 30 April the landlord, Charles Macklelane of Collin, was praying when 'he observed a black thing in the corner of the barne, and it did increase, as if it would fill the whole house.' No form could be discerned within the cloud, but it threw barley chaff and mud in the faces of the watchers, and several people felt themselves gripped by the arms or round the waist so hard that they could feel the bruises for days afterwards. The next day a small sheep-house was burned to the ground, but this was the last damage caused: the gory letter found by Mackie had been almost accurate in its forecast of another twenty-three days' disturbance. After 1 May, the spirit ceased to trouble the house.

No explanation was ever found for the

phenomena. A theory advanced at the time, that the Mackies had been involved in witchcraft, was dismissed by Telfair. Modern commentators generally associate poltergeist activity with the presence of children around the age of puberty, but Telfair's account gives little hint that this may have been so at Ringcroft. The entity's declaration that it held a commission from God was in line with medieval demonology, according to which demons, and indeed Satan himself, were active in the world by God's permission, acting as his agents. Otherwise, the cynical might say that the stone-throwing, arson, and interference with livestock, and more especially the written message and hidden bones, sound suspiciously like human activity, possibly by family members, or by someone who wanted the Mackies out of the house.

COWHILL TOWER, DUMFRIESSHIRE

The remains of Cowhill Tower stand on the banks of the River Nith above Dumfries. Writing in 1810, R. H. Cromek spells the name 'Cowehill', and describes the building as beautifully situated amid groves of oak and other trees. It was said to have been the home of William Maxwell, the bridegroom in the ballad 'The Mermaid of Galloway'; Cromek heard the verses from Jean Walker, a young Galloway woman who remembered several traditional songs.

Every night of the new moon for over ten years, the ballad begins, the mermaid had been seen sitting on the green bank and combing her yellow hair. Like the sirens of classical mythology, she had a seductive and fatal voice: though the very birds in the trees were charmed by her singing, whoever listened or went to her never wakened again in this life. One summer her song was heard by the heir of Cowehill, and although he was about to be married he became determined to find the singer.

His page had dreamed of his master kissing a pair of lips that dripped blood, and warned William:

'Kiss nae the singer's lips, master,
Kiss nae the singer's chin;
Touch nae her hand,' quo' the little footpage,
If skaithless hame ye'd win.'

Nonetheless, William sought out the mermaid and tried to persuade her to come back with him to 'bonnie Cowehill'. Although the mermaid herself reminded him of his young bride waiting at home, he asked the mermaid for a love token. Round his head she tied a lock of her hair so tight that it caused him burning pain, and he begged her to loosen it. Then he laid his head among the water lilies, and while he slept she worked her magic:

She weaved owre his brow the white lilie,
Wi' witch-knots mae than nine;
'Gif ye were seven times bride-groom owre,
This night ye shall be mine.'

Roused by her taunting mentions of his bride preparing for her splendid wedding, William looked up 'faintlie, slowlie' and tried too late to free himself from the witching bands. She took his green mantle, silken cap, and bridal ring and threw them in the sea, then, folding him in her arms, she plunged below the waves.

The bride, meanwhile, waited in vain for William's coming and finally lay down to sleep, putting the bride cake under her head and feet. About midnight, her silver bell rang and there came a cold touch on breast and on cheek:

'O cauld is thy hand, my dear Willie,
O cauld, cauld is thy cheek;
An' wring thae locks o' yellow hair,
Fra which the cauld draps dreep.'

'O seek anither bridegroom, Marie,
On thae bosom-faulds to sleep;
My bride is the yellow water lilie,
Its leaves my brydal sheet!'

Marie's placing of bride cake under her pillow is a reference to the custom continued in Britain into the twentieth century and perhaps today of girls placing a piece of someone's wedding cake under their pillows to dream of their own future husbands (in Shetland sometimes called 'dreaming bread'). The ballad leaves it uncertain, therefore, whether what she sees is the ghost of Willie returned from his watery grave or her magically invoked dream.

See also DALBEATTIE BURN.

CRAIGDARROCH, DUMFRIESSHIRE

A 'memorate' is the term used by folklorists for a story told from first-hand experience. One included in David Buchan's *Scottish Tradition* (1984) and taken from an article first printed in 1890–1 is the story of a witch of Craigdarroch.

The narrator, a young girl at the time of the events, tells how 'Auld Jean', whose mother and grandmother before her were both witches, came in one morning to ask the girl to come and stack her hay. The girl was very reluctant, because she wanted to go to the fair at Moniaive. Her mother supported her, saying she was too young to help with the hay, but after Jean had gone away looking ill-pleased, she said, 'She's an ill body, and ye should maybe hae gaen.' The girl laughed and thought no more about it.

Well, next morning, believe me or no as ye like, I couldna lift my heid, an' I had gaen tae my bed as weel as I ever felt in my life. My mither said 'Oo, lassie, I think she has bewitched ye;' an' tae tell the truth, I thocht sae mysel', for I never felt the same aither afore or since. I was doost ill wi' a queerness, but for the life o' me couldna tell what was wrang. Next day I was a' richt again, but by that time, of coorse, I had missed the fair.

Although set out as personal memory, the story is very similar to another told in the late nineteenth century at DUNFERMLINE (Central & Perthshire), and obviously represents the behaviour expected of a local witch.

CRAWICK, DUMFRIESSHIRE

William Wilson, in his *Folk Lore and Genealogies of Uppermost Nithsdale* (1904), says that the village of Crawick Mill, just north of Sanquhar, was well known for its gatherings of witches:

Their doings and ongoings have been talked of far and near, and many a tale is told of revels at the 'Witches' Stairs' – a huge rock among the picturesque linns of Crawick, where, in company of other kindred spirits gathered from all parts of the country, they planned their deeds of evil, and cast their cantrips to the hurt of those that had come under their displeasure.

Sometimes a farmer's best cow would lose its milk; sometimes a mare would lose her foal. Once the minister's churn was bewitched so that no butter would come, however hard the dairymaid churned:

The manse at Sanquhar at that time was situated close to the river on the site now occupied by the farm-house of Blackaddie, and the good man told the servant girl to carry the churn to the other side of the Nith, thinking that the crossing of a running stream would break the spell. But it was to no purpose; neither was the rowan tree branch that was fixed in the byre, nor the horse-shoe nailed behind the door.

The minister was at a loss, but his wife knew what to do. She made up a roll of butter from a previous churning and sent it with a pitcher of milk to the beldam at Crawick Mill, who was thought to have cast the spell. The gift was received with thanks and there was no more trouble with the churn.

The Crawick miller at that time was Robert Stitt, an honest and respected man. He refused to give meal to one of the witches, and she told him that he would be sorry before many days had passed. On a dark night about a week later, the miller missed his footing by the river and was drowned.

One morning, a young man met one of the witches and 'some words passed between them' (he probably said something disrespectful). The witch said to him, 'Ye're gaun briskly awa', my lad, but ye'll come ridin' home the nicht.' Sure enough, he got his leg broken and was brought home in a cart.

An old woman named Nannie was said to have been the last of the witches living on the banks of the Crawick. She knew her reputation and rather encouraged it, for it brought her many gifts as a form of insurance against her spells.

See also WITCH-HUNTS (p. 270).

CRIFFEL, KIRKCUDBRIGHTSHIRE

According to tradition, the great eminence of Criffel, south of New Abbey, had a supernatural origin. The celebrated MICHAEL SCOT, THE WIZARD OF BALWEARIE (p. 62), was obliged to keep the Devil constantly busy, and one of the tasks the magician gave the Fiend was to build a causeway over the Solway Firth. While the Devil was carrying rocks from Cumberland to Scotland, the string of his creel (basket) broke as he flew over the River Nith. The heap of rocks that fell out formed a mountain, which was ever after called 'Criffel', supposedly from 'Creel Fell'.

The Devil was often held responsible for rocky formations, more usually as the result of his leather apron-strings breaking. One wonders, however, if Criffel's link with him was also inspired by historical fact. According to the law of the Marches, bale-fires had to be kept in readiness to give warning against English invasion. In Galloway, Criffel is the most considerable of the heights used for this purpose. Rising from near sea level and dominating the plain, it is easily visible on both sides of the Solway Firth. When an alarm was given at night, the peak may well have looked from afar like one of Satan's burning mountains.

DALBEATTIE BURN, KIRKCUDBRIGHTSHIRE

R. H. Cromek had much to say of the Mermaid of Galloway, of whom he wrote in 1810 that she had talked to 'many of the good old folks' and given them advice on household matters and recipes for making healing ointments. A young man whose sweetheart was dying was reproved by the mermaid in song:

'Wad ye let the bonny May die i' yere hand,
An' the mugwort flowering i' the land?'

He plucked and pressed the mugwort and gave the juice to his beloved, who duly recovered. Her complaint might have been consumption (pulmonary tuberculosis), like the girl at the FIRTH OF CLYDE (Glasgow & Ayrshire), but is perhaps more likely to have been one of those diseases 'peculiar to women' for which mugwort (*Artemisia vulgaris*) was particularly recommended as a cure.

Tradition said that the Mermaid of Galloway was so beautiful that no man could behold her face without falling ardently in love with her. She had long golden hair and was always represented letting down her locks with one hand and combing them with the other.

Such sirens could be deadly, and not only to their lovers. Cromek writes that a favourite residence of the mermaid was a deep and beautiful pool formed in the mouth of Dalbeattie Burn by the eddy of Orr (or Urr) Water. In the light of the new moon, she would seat herself here on a rock, comb her hair, and deliver her 'healing oracles'. A devout woman of the neighbourhood, however, became greatly troubled at the presence of this 'heathenish visitant' sitting in the stream on the smooth block of granite:

The good woman, in a frenzy of religious zeal, with her Bible in her hand, had the temerity to tumble this ancient chair into the bottom of the pool. The next morning her only child was found dead in its cradle, and a voice from the pool was often heard at day-close, by the distracted mother:

'Ye may look i' yere toom [empty]
   cradle,
And I'll look to my stane;
And meikle we'll think, and meikle
   we'll look,
But words we'll ne'er hae nane!'

All the noxious weeds and filth that could be collected, were thrown into the pool until the stream was polluted, and the Mermaid departed, leaving a curse of barrenness on the house, which all the neighbours for several miles around, are ready to certify has been faithfully fulfilled.

In this tale of misplaced religious zealotry, the mermaid's parting words seem tinged with regret at a barrier erected by a jealous Church, and the storyteller's sympathies appear to be entirely with the water nymph. A more sinister mermaid is said to have visited the banks of the River Nith near COWHILL TOWER.

DALSWINTON, DUMFRIESSHIRE

'In the olden times' the daughter of Maxwell, Laird of Dalswinton, was the most beautiful woman in all Nithsdale. She was involved in a clandestine love affair in which she was helped by the Brownie of the household, who used to convey her from her bedchamber in a high tower to a trysting place in the woods, and back again, so swiftly and silently 'that neither bird, dog, nor servant awoke'. When she married, he undressed her for her bridal night so assiduously that her handmaiden was left with nothing to do, and dared not so much as lay a hand on her mistress's garments in case this provoked Brownie's resentment.

When Brownie's beloved lady was in childbirth, a serving lad was ordered to fetch a 'cannie wife' (midwife) from the other side of the River Nith but was reluctant to go on such a stormy December night. Brownie therefore wrapped himself in his lady's cloak and, though the Nith was running high, his horse, 'impelled by supernatural spur and whip, passed it like an arrow'. Putting the midwife up on the saddle behind him, Brownie rode back through the deep water and she was amazed to see that although the waves were washing round her, the horse's fetlocks were dry. 'Ride nae by the auld pool,' she said, 'lest we should meet wi' Brownie,' to which he replied with hidden meaning, 'Fear nae, dame, ye've met a' the Brownies ye will meet.' Setting her down at the hall gate, he hurried to the stable, where he found the servant only just pulling on his boots, and gave him such a beating as he would not forget.

This was round about the time of the Reformation, and a priest 'more zealous than wise', persuaded the laird to have this 'Imp of Heathenism' baptised. The priest hid himself in the barn and when Brownie duly came, appearing 'like a little, wrinkled, ancient man', and began his nightly labour, the priest sprang out of hiding and dashed the baptismal water in Brownie's face while solemnly reciting the christening rite. 'The poor Brownie set up a frightful and agonizing yell, and instantly vanished, never to return.'

More often BROWNIES (p. 80) are dismissed accidentally by an ill-considered gift of food or clothes. This cruel banishment of possibly the most faithful member of the laird's household was recorded by R. H. Cromek in 1810.

DOWALTON LOCH, WIGTOWNSHIRE

There was a tradition in Wigtownshire that Dowalton Loch contained in its depths an old village. One might have assumed that this was just another 'sunken city' story of a town or village drowned for its sins, like that told of LOCH ERICHT (Central & Perthshire). However, in 1862, the loch was drained for some reason unconnected with the story, and the report was verified: remains of an ancient settlement were found, which had presumably been covered centuries before, when the water level rose.

The folklorist David MacRitchie, recording this in 1891, comments on this and similar stories: 'Folk-lore, as a popular

inheritance, is perishing fast; but there is, I believe, much veritable history yet to be gleaned from it.'

DRUMLANRIG CASTLE, DUMFRIESSHIRE

Drumlanrig Castle in Nithsdale, built in the late seventeenth century, was the seat of William, Duke of Queensberry, appointed High Commissioner to James II of England in 1685. He was a much-hated man, responsible for atrocities against the Scottish Covenanters, and folk justice (or political propaganda) made him pay for this after death.

A story recorded by John Howie in 1796 tells of a ship sailing 'upon the coast of Naples or Sicily, near one of the burning mountains'. The sailors 'espied a coach and six all in black, going towards the mount with great velocity; when it came past them, they were so near that they could perceive the dimensions and features of one that sat in it'.

One of the sailors recognised the man as Queensberry, and a voice was heard to echo from the mountain, commanding, 'Open to the Duke of Drumlanrig.' This happened at the day and hour when the duke died.

Charles Kirkpatrick Sharpe, repeating a version of this story in his introduction to Robert Law's *Memorialls* (1818), identifies the 'burning mountain' as Vesuvius, although it could equally well have been Etna: Howie's location of the tale near 'Naples or Sicily' leaves the question open. Both volcanoes were often thought of in the Middle Ages as mouths of hell, and it was said that the screams of the damned could be heard amid the grinding and roaring that emanated from their craters. The same was said of Hekla in Iceland, from whose mouth ghosts were said to

In League with the Devil

Thomas Dalyell, a seventeenth-century general who persecuted Covenanters with great zeal and who was said to have made a pact with Satan.

The religious disputes of the late seventeenth century were attended with bloodshed and brutality. In 1638 the National Covenant, a Presbyterian manifesto, had been signed at GREY-FRIARS KIRK in Edinburgh (Lothian & Borders) in protest against measures passed by Charles I imposing changes in church services and empowering the bishops. Conflict between factions within the Scottish Church continued during the Civil War and Interregnum, and after the Restoration of 1660 the government of Charles II took a hard line with the self-styled Covenanters, who held out for a single, uniform religious establishment, free of state or episcopal interference. The dissidents met for worship in the open air or in private houses, and their illicit gatherings, known as conventicles, were targets for their opponents, who hunted them down with military force, killing and imprisoning hundreds and carrying out scores of executions, including those commemorated at the MARTYRS' TOMB (Dumfries & Galloway).

The victims, narrow-minded fanatics for the most part, were perhaps not intrinsically attractive, but minorities on the losing end of a struggle are generally perceived as heroic, and conversely leaders of the government troops became demonised in the popular imagination. Notable persecutors included 'Bluidy Clavers' of DUNDEE (North East) and General Dalyell of THE BINNS (Lothian & Borders), both reputed to have sold their souls to the Devil, and the Duke of Queensberry, whose unholy bargain was supposedly consummated when he was taken from DRUMLANRIG CASTLE (Dumfries & Galloway) to burn in an Italian volcano.

Robert Grierson, Laird of Lag or Lagg, was another brutal instigator of repression. Writing in 1842, the poet David Vedder shudders at his memory:

> In the execution of his commission he was savage and blood-thirsty beyond all his coadjutors . . . the Laird of Lag stood without one redeeming quality.

John Bell of Whiteside, an old man captured by the laird in 1685 and about to be executed, begged for a moment to pray. 'What a devil have you been doing so many years in these hills – have you not prayed enough?' Lag taunted, and shot him out of hand. When troops raided the Hallidays of Mayfield, who had taken no active part in resistance but had merely sheltered some of the rebels, their house was plundered, five men were put to death, and the corpses were left unburied by Lag's orders.

On his deathbed the laird reportedly wished to bathe his feet in cold water, but the moment they were immersed, they made it boil with an infernal heat. After his death, the horses stuck fast while taking his coffin to the graveyard. Sir Thomas Kirkpatrick of CLOSEBURN CASTLE (Dumfries & Galloway) swore that he would drive the hearse though the Devil himself were inside, and harnessed his own team, which galloped to Dunscore churchyard and then fell dead. The horses' difficulties might have been entirely physical – Lag was apparently so stout that his house had to be partly demolished to allow the removal of his corpse – but accompanying the cortège was a raven 'of preternatural blackness and malignity of aspect', probably a demon like those sent to fetch MICHAEL SCOT, THE WIZARD OF BALWEARIE (p. 62).

Long after his death, Lag remained notorious. According to the *Scottish Gallovidian Encyclopedia* (1824), 'to this day, the horrid word *hell*, is ever coupled with his name; the country people say sometimes, when enforcing a fact, "that they are as sure such and such is the case, as they are of the laird o' Lagg's being in hell".' Alexander Fergusson, who devoted a book to Grierson's legend in 1886, writes that throughout south-west Scotland 'there is no name that has attained such an evil notoriety'. In Fergusson's youth it had been customary around Hallowe'en for one of the household to dress up as a monstrous beast meant to represent the laird, to 'follow the evil instincts of its bad original' by playing vicious tricks, to 'smell out Covenanters under the sideboard and other likely places', and to end the performance by pouncing on one of the children.

A popular legend held that at the time of the laird's death a storm-tossed craft in the Solway was passed by another vessel rushing into the teeth of the wind. By a gleam of moonlight the crew saw that it was not a ship but a coach drawn by six jet-black horses. The skipper plucked up courage and hailed it: 'Where bound? and where from?' Back came the answer, 'To tryst with Lag! Dumfries! from – Hell!'

See also ECCLEFECHAN (Dumfries & Galloway).

emerge to warn passers-by of the sufferings that might await them.

See also IN LEAGUE WITH THE DEVIL (p. 142).

DRYFESDALE, DUMFRIESSHIRE

Dryfesdale takes its name from Dryfe Water, a little tributary which rises on the south side of Loch Fell and runs south to join the River Annan. Though small, the Dryfe, being fed by several mountain springs, was always subject to sudden spates. Whereas at times one could cross it dry-shod, at others it was a raging torrent sweeping all before it. For many years it had made such inroads on the parish churchyard on one of its banks that the parishioners abandoned the church and shifted their place of worship to Lockerby. So many coffins in the more exposed part of the churchyard had been carried away that there arose a local saying that a Dryfesdale man had once buried one wife and married another on the same day. Robert Chambers, in *The Picture of Scotland* (1827), elaborates on this tradition:

The truth was, that the man, in taking his second wife to church, met his first spouse coming down the water, and was obliged to take her back and re-inter her, before proceeding to the more lightsome affair of the bridal.

DUNSKEY CASTLE, PORTPATRICK, WIGTOWNSHIRE

The ruins of Dunskey Castle stand on the shore at Portpatrick. Here in the fourteenth century lived Walter de Curry, a 'sea-rover' (i.e. not far from being a pirate) with a violent and quarrelsome nature. Furious at the outspokenness of an Irish piper whom he had captured and forced to serve as his minstrel and jester, he condemned him to a slow death by starvation in his dungeons.

Tradition has it that the piper found his way into a secret underground passage leading from the castle to a cave on the shore, but was unable to find any exit, and died a miserable death.

Along this passage the troubled ghost of the piper was long reputed to march, backwards and forwards, playing the weirdest of pipe music, and so indicating, as was firmly believed, to the awe-stricken listeners above, the line of direction of the secret underground passage.

James Maxwell Wood, telling this story in 1911, adds in a footnote that, curiously enough, a few years previously, men working on the Portpatrick water and drainage scheme came accidentally on a 'large cavernous space' exactly where the sound of the phantom pipes was supposedly heard. The unromantic would conclude from this that the sound had natural causes.

However, the story itself is a variation on a theme popular throughout Britain, that of the piper or fiddler who explores a subterranean passage, playing his music as he goes, so that people above ground can trace its course by the sound. In the usual form of the tale, the music abruptly stops and he is never seen again, though sometimes his little dog emerges days later with all his hair burned off and smelling of brimstone – in other words, he and his master have encountered the Devil. Many similar tales are told in Scotland, particularly in the Western Isles, where a famous example is set at TROTTERNISH.

ECCLEFECHAN, DUMFRIESSHIRE

Ecclefechan was the birthplace of Thomas Carlyle (1795–1881), and a little to the north is the mansion of Orchard. It was here, according to Carlyle, that his father's schoolmaster, 'old John Orr', once laid a ghost. Carlyle writes that this took place in some house or room at Orchard. 'He entered the haunted place, was closeted in it for some time, speaking and praying. The ghost was really and truly laid, for no one heard more of it.'

Orr was remembered by Carlyle as 'religious and enthusiastic, though in practice irregular with drink'. He may have been responsible for an anonymous 'pasquil' (a skit or libel) on the death of Robert Grierson of Lag in 1733. The pasquil, which was printed in at least ten editions, purports to be an elegy for Grierson written by 'The *Prince of Darkness*' in 'Lamentation for and Commendation of his trusty and well-beloved Friend', and is a pungent satire on Lag, General Dalyell of THE BINNS (Lothian & Borders), 'Bluidy Clavers' of DUNDEE (North East), and others reported to be IN LEAGUE WITH THE DEVIL (p. 142). It includes a memorable description of Dalyell:

> Wringing the bluid frae aff his hands,
> And scourin' them in brumstane.

Carlyle said that he had 'authentically ascertained' Orr to be the author.

ERICSTANE HILL, DUMFRIESSHIRE

A steep hill near the River Annan is named as Ericstane Hill on modern maps, but in the nineteenth century it was known as Errickstanebrae. A road runs above the

The historian Thomas Carlyle (1795–1881) was born in Ecclefechan. As a child he heard tales of 'old John Orr' laying a ghost nearby, and wrote that the procedure was effective, since the spirit was never heard of again.

slope at a great height above the valley, and the site is evocatively described by Sir Walter Scott in *Redgauntlet* (1824):

> . . . it looks as if four hills were laying their heads together, to shut out daylight from the dark hollow space between them. A d—d deep, black, blackguard-looking abyss of a hole it is, and goes straight down from the road side, as perpendicular as it can do to be a heathery brae.

The context is a daring exploit, used in the novel and based on a real event, when the Duke of Cumberland's troops were conducting prisoners along this road to Carlisle in 1745. One of the men, passing the precipitous slope, threw himself from his horse and rolled headlong down to the stream at the bottom. Many shots were fired after the fugitive, but the soldiers did not dare to follow him, and he escaped. Stories of extraordinary leaps across chasms are many, but this tale of a plunge to freedom is more unusual. Scott adds in a note, 'The Author has seen in his youth the gentleman to whom the adventure actually happened. The distance of time makes some indistinctness of recollection, but it is believed the real name was MacEwen or MacMillan.' Such claims to truth are of course made of more-or-less legendary events, but it seems that this tale was based on fact.

GALDENOCH CASTLE, WIGTOWNSHIRE

Galdenoch Castle stands near the sea in the Rhinns of Galloway. Once the seat of the Agnews of Galdenoch, it passed out of their ownership and became a farm-house when the family fell on evil days. The most interesting thing about it, says C. H. Dick, was the racketing spirit or pol-tergeist who had made life untenable there: by 1916 it was in use only as a cattle-shed, being said to be too haunted for human occupation.

The story of the haunt was told in 1893 by Sir Andrew Agnew of nearby Lochnaw. In the seventeenth century a young man of the Agnew family, a Covenanter, stopped at a house to ask for shelter after a battle in which his side had been defeated. The householder had Royalist leanings: he fed young Agnew and let him stay the night, but in the morning barred his way to the door, saying he doubted whether he had fought on the right side. Fearing captivity, the lad drew his pistol and killed the man. Rushing out to the stables, he saddled his horse and made his way home.

Having arrived safely back at Galdenoch he went to bed, but hardly were the lights out before strange sounds were heard. These seemed to be made by the ghost of the murdered man, who proceeded to make life unsupportable in the house. Night after night the disturbances continued, and even after the Agnew family had gone, the ghost went on annoying the tenants.

One night they were playing a game in which a burning stick was passed from hand to hand to the chant 'About wi' that! About wi' that! Keep alive the priest-cat!' When the stick eventually got too hot to hold, the flame was put out and a forfeit set. (This is reported from other sources as being a traditional Galloway pastime.) One of the family, seeing the fire glowing red, remarked that it wouldn't be easy to take a coal just then. Scarcely had he spoken when a burning peat vanished as if by magic. A few moments later there came a cry of 'Fire', and the farmstead was found to be ablaze. The same burning peat was identified in the thatch of the barn and no one doubted that this was the work of the ghost.

Then, as the tenant's mother was sitting one morning at her spinning wheel, she was suddenly whisked up and away by some invisible force and dumped in the water of the Mill-Isle burn. Before she passed out, she heard a muttering: 'I'll dip thee, I'll draw thee.' At dinner-time she was missed and every corner of the building was searched, while the children ran around crying, 'Where's granny?' At length a voice informed them, 'I've washed granny in the burn, and laid her on the dyke to dry!' They all ran down to the burn and there sure enough was the old lady, lying naked on the dyke, half-dead with cold and fright.

Several ministers tried to lay the ghost, but to no avail. One, who had a high repu-tation as an exorcist, was annoyed at his defeat and declared he would never return. When the gate of the yard had closed behind him, a voice was heard begging him to come back and promising to tell him something he had not heard before. Out of curiosity, he did come back, only to hear the mocking cry, 'Ha! Ha! I hae gotten the minister to tell a lee!'

After many years of disturbance, a confident and loud-voiced young man named Marshall was ordained to the parish of Kirkcolm. He offered to take on the Galdenoch ghost, and a large number of people assembled to help him. Hanging up his hat, Marshall gave out a psalm, and led off with the singing:

> The ghost sang, too; the company endeavoured to drown his voice, but failed; the fiend sang long and loud, and all had ceased but the minister, whose voice rose to a louder and louder pitch as he kept up the strains alone until the 'witching hour.' He called upon the wearied congregation to join once more. A burst of psalmody was the response; and 'Bangor,' loud if not melodious, resounded through the castle-walls. Again all ceased exhausted, but Marshall undauntedly held on. Faint gleams of light streaked the eastern horizon, when an unearthly voice, husky and weak, whined, 'Roar awa', Marshall, I can roar nae mair!' Marshall still continued, determined to make assurance doubly sure; but the ghost kept his word and was never heard again.

GATEHOUSE OF FLEET, KIRKCUDBRIGHTSHIRE

In his *Popular Tales of the West Highlands*, the folklorist John Francis Campbell of Islay (1821–85) prints a story contained in a letter dated February 1859. The writer relates what he had heard the night before from one Johnny Nicholson, giving Nicholson's own words:

> 'You have been often at the Gatehouse,' said he, 'well, you'll mind a flat piece of land near Enrick farm; well, that was once a large loch; long way down from there is still the ruin of a mill which at that time was fed from this loch.'

One night around Hallowe'en, two young ploughmen went to a smithy to get their ploughs repaired. In passing the mill on their way home, they heard music and dancing and fiddling, singing and laughing and talking, so one of the lads went in to see what was going on. The other waited outside for hours, but his companion never came out again, so he went home 'assured that the brownies had got hold of him'.

> 'About the same time the following year, the same lad went again to the smiddy on the same errand, and this time he took another lad with him, but had the precaution to put the Bible in his pocket. Well, in passing the mill the second time, he heard the same sounds of music and dancing. This time, having the Bible in his hand, he ventured to look in, when who should he see but his companion whom he had left standing there that day twelvemonths. He handed him the Bible, and the moment he did so, the music and dancing ceased, the lights went out, and all was darkness; but it is not said what his companion had seen, or had been doing all that time.'

No doubt, as in other tales of people who are caught in fairyland, he had no idea of how much time had passed, and thought he had been there only for the duration of the dance. The Bible's ability to counteract spells and illusions by its holy presence is a recurring theme in fairy lore, as is the mill, in Scotland and the North of England often said to be the resort of fairies.

GILNOCKIE TOWER,
CANONBIE, DUMFRIESSHIRE

Until the Union of the Crowns in 1603, armed conflict was virtually a way of life along the Scottish–English border. Quite apart from warfare between the two nations, cattle-rustling and feuding were endemic. It was probably the proceeds from ransoms and the theft of cattle and sheep that paid for the building of the many small tower houses that had appeared in the region by the end of the sixteenth century, occupied by local lairds either as refuges from such exploits or as bases for them.

Of the forty or more fortified houses thought to have existed in Eskdale and Ewesdale alone, only one survives more or less intact, though roofless by the time of Sir Walter Scott's *Minstrelsy of the Scottish Border* (1802–3). Gilnockie or Hollows Tower was built in the mid sixteenth century and is now a listed building. It was traditionally a residence of the Armstrongs, who appear to have owned a great part of Liddesdale and the Debatable Lands. They played England and Scotland off against each other, appealing to each in turn for protection, at the same time raiding both.

Longest remembered in oral tradition was Johnnie Armstrong. He is said to have lived at Gilnockie and terrorised the Borders as far south as Newcastle, extorting blackmail or protection money for many miles around. This went on until about 1529, when James V launched an expedition to put a stop to lawlessness in the area, taking the precaution of imprisoning the great Border chieftains who were protecting the raiders. He marched through Ettrick Forest and Ewesdale at the head of an army 10,000 strong, and by some error of judgement, or perhaps acting on treach-

erous advice, Johnnie presented himself to the king, tricked out in all his finery at the head of thirty-six horsemen, hoping to win favour. But he had misjudged his man. According to the Scottish historian Robert Lindsay of Pitscottie (*c.* 1500–65), James, looking on him sternly, said to his attendants, 'What wants that knave that a king should have?' and ordered immediate execution for him and his followers. Johnnie offered the services of himself and his retinue, but to no avail.

> At length he, seeing no hope of favour, said very proudly, 'It is folly to seek grace at a graceless face; but, had I known this, I should have lived upon the Borders in despite of King Harry [Henry VIII of England] and you both; for I know King Harry would down-weigh my best horse with gold, to know that I were condemned to die this day.'

There is no record of a trial and it is to be supposed that Johnny's end was, as tradition avers, summary execution. Sir Walter Scott writes:

> Johnie [*sic*], with all his retinue, was accordingly hanged upon growing trees, at a place called Carlenrig Chapel, about ten miles above Hawick, on the highroad to Langholm. The country-people believe that, to manifest the injustice of the execution, the trees withered away. Armstrong and his followers were buried in a deserted churchyard, where their graves are still shown.

The widespread theme of 'barren ground' at the sites of murder and injustice, where trees wither and no grass grows, is a symbolic way of expressing in local tradition a hatred of tyranny that in real life dared not be spoken. It is interesting in this context to note the alternative tradition of James V as a heroic figure in his own right (*see* THE GUIDMAN OF BALLANGEICH, p. 98),

A nineteenth-century artist's impression of the bandit Johnnie Armstrong riding with his troops past Gilnockie Tower.

and perhaps relevant to remember that in 1529 the king was only eighteen years old.

Also part of the language of dissent is the popular ballad which survives in two versions, one (evidently adapted to an English audience) which transfers Johnnie's home to Westmorland, and 'Johnie Armstrang', said by Allan Ramsay in 1724 to have been 'copied from a Gentleman's Mouth of the Name of *Armstrang*, who is the 6th Generation from this *John*'. This tells a story which corresponds in several details to Pitscottie's account, not published until 1728, and both may derive from an older ballad now lost. Whatever ordinary Borderers thought of Johnnie in his lifetime, here he is both hero and victim. The action begins when the king 'wrytes a luving Letter, With his ain Hand' to lure Johnnie to a rendezvous, evidently already determined to put an end to him. When they meet, Johnnie tries to conciliate him with promises of service and gifts in exchange for the lives of himself and his men, but James cries over and over:

Away, away, thou Traytor Strang,
Out of my Sicht thou mayst sune be,
I grantit nevir a Traytors Lyfe,
And now Ill [I'll] not begin with thee.

When Johnnie finally realises that there is no moving him, he says bitterly and in more or less in the same words as Pitscottie:

To seik het Water beneath cauld Yce,
Surely it is a great Folie;
I haif asked Grace at a graceless Face,
But there is nane for my Men and me.

The balladeer is in no doubt about the injustice of James V's verdict, and the song ends on a stridently nationalist note:

John murdred was at Carlinrigg,
And all his galant Companie;
But Scotlands Heart was never sae wae,
To see sae mony brave Men die.

Because they savd their Country deir
Frae Englishmen; nane were sae bauld,
Quhyle Johnie livd on the Border-syde,
Nane of them durst cum neir his Hald.

See also BORDER BALLADS (p. 224).

GLENCAIRN, MONIAIVE, DUMFRIESSHIRE

A particularly eerie omen of death in Scotland and elsewhere in Britain was the appearance of the 'deid lichte' or death light. John Corrie, writing in 1890, gives a detailed instance of its being seen in Glencairn. Peggy D—, going to lock her door one night, saw a light go past, carried, she supposed, by a neighbour. There was nothing unusual in this, but what was odd was that the light passed right through the stone dyke near the foot of the garden as if nothing had been there. Moreover, though the ground below the house was very uneven, the light never vanished from sight for a moment. Rooted to the spot, Peggy watched it go down through the fields, then along the road to the churchyard. There it passed through the locked gate and was lost to sight in the graveyard. 'A week later, Peggy D—'s daughter was carried a corpse to the same churchyard.'

GLENLUCE ABBEY, OLD LUCE, WIGTOWNSHIRE

In its heyday, Glenluce Abbey must have been an impressive sight. Set in the river plain of the Water of Luce, it had the remote and tranquil setting and the austerity originally associated with the Cistercian order.

The great medieval magician Michael Scot is said to have been buried here with his books of magic. James Maxwell Wood reports a tale current in 1911 of a man who daringly disinterred the skeleton of the wizard and found it confronting him in a sitting position, a sight which drove him stark mad, and John MacTaggart writes in 1824 that one of the abbey vaults contains 'the famous library of Michael Scott, the Warlock'. Apart from the generic books of the black art and necromancy, the titles he mentions appear to be spoofs: at least, none appears in the catalogue of the British Library.

> Here are thousands of old *witch songs* and incantations, books of the *Black Art* and *Necromancy, Philosophy of the Devil, Satan's Almanacks*, the *Fire Spangs* of *Faustus*, the Soothsayer's *Creed*, the *Witch Chronicle*, and the *Black Cluds wyme laid open*, with many more valuable volumes.

While he was in Glenluce, Scot was credited with keeping the witches out of mischief as elsewhere he controlled demons or fairies, setting them to thresh chaff or to spin ropes of sand, fragments of which, it was said, were still visible at low tide in the early twentieth century close to Ringdoo Point near the mouth of the Luce.

Glenluce has rivals as the wizard's sepulchre and library, in Cumberland and at MELROSE ABBEY (Lothian & Borders). One of the most interesting aspects of the Glenluce traditions, however, is entirely local: here they have been transferred, at least in part, to Tam Campbell, a feckless Highland piper. He, too, set a demon to weaving ropes of sand in Luce Bay, and like the magician he rid the district of the plague, though he required help to do so. Scot is said single-handedly to have imprisoned the disease in a casket and locked it away in the abbey vaults. Tam, on the other hand, took the bag holding the plague demon to the Presbyterian minister, who could not exorcise it alone and therefore accompanied Tam to Glenluce Abbey, where the abbot and his monks

prayed the evil spirit to death. This united effort might seem curious, but the tale is not the only example of a Catholic priest being brought in by a Protestant to dismiss a demon or lay a ghost: another can be found at BORGUE, though there the Kirk deeply disapproved of its members' recourse to the Papists.

See also MICHAEL SCOT, THE WIZARD OF BALWEARIE (p. 62).

HIGH ARDWELL, WIGTOWNSHIRE

James Maxwell Wood wrote in 1911 that in the early nineteenth century a carrier used to bring letters and supplies from Portpatrick to High Ardwell. More than once his horse was stopped or his cart made to break down by a woman in white. Once, the horse was so incapable of moving the cart that the carter had to unhitch the animal and ride it home, only to discover the White Lady perched up behind him.

As time went on, the White Lady appeared more and more often, at last evincing a desire to embrace him. She told him that listening even once to her murmurs of love would free him of her future attentions. After much hesitation, the carter agreed that, on a certain night, she should come to the back window of his cottage: he said this to keep some barrier between them.

The White Lady duly came, but the carter had laid his plans and only part-opened the window. She bent down to what was seemingly his face, and, with a quick, savage thrust of her own face towards it, bit it in half. In fact it was a horse skull that the carter had been holding towards her, and, unexpectedly thwarted, the White Lady slunk away, muttering, 'Hard, hard, are the banes and gristle of your face!'

This White Lady is a particularly savage one. Others in Britain and Western Europe are often comparatively harmless ghosts (traditionally clothed in white shrouds), haunters of bridges and fords, or, as 'castle-maidens', guardians of treasure. In the case of the celebrated White Lady of the Hohenzollerns and imitations thereof, they are hereditary spirits attached to particular families.

KIRKMAIDEN-IN-RHINNS, WIGTOWNSHIRE

See SCOTLAND'S HOLY AND HEALING WELLS (p. 44).

KIRKWAUGH, WIGTOWNSHIRE

On the farm of Kirkwaugh, near Bladnoch, there once occurred a horrid mob murder, described by Gordon Fraser in *Wigtown and Whithorn: Historical and Descriptive Sketches* (1877).

> Tradition has it that an enterprising packman lived in or near Wigtown long ago. He had a consignment of cloth on board a vessel which put into a local port. The ship was plague-stricken, and the people in the district, fearing that the infection might spread by means of the packman and his cloth, caught both the merchant and his wares, and taking them to Kirkwaugh digged a deep grave, in which they were deposited – the pack-man alive.

A small mound near the farmhouse door was thought to mark the place, and in Fraser's time was still known as 'The Packman's Grave'. People would take a long way round rather than approach the spot, where it was said that knocks were heard and lights seen. It might also have

been feared that the plague lingered there, as was said of the Bass of INVERURIE (North East).

KNOCKHILL HOUSE, HODDOM, DUMFRIESSHIRE

Hoddom or Hoddam, in a loop of the River Annan just south of Ecclefechan, is best known for the ruins of Hoddom Castle, the fifteenth-century stronghold of the Maxwells, but here too is the classic eighteenth-century mansion of Knockhill House, the scene of a tragic event said to have given rise to a haunting.

According to an account which appeared on 14 March 1902, a young man named Bell had been surreptitiously visiting his sweetheart at Knockhill (she was probably one of the maids there). Leaving through a basement window, Bell was heard by the butler, who shot and killed him. The butler was tried but acquitted, and Knockhill was afterwards so haunted that the servants would not stay there.

Finally the owner, a Mr Scott, asked the Reverend Mr W. Wallace Duncan, at that time assisting the parish minister, Mr Yorstoun, to sleep in the house. It is said that from then on the ghost disappeared from Knockhill.

MARTYRS' TOMB, WIGTOWN, WIGTOWNSHIRE

In the churchyard on the east side of Wigtown, below the main central square, railings surround a group of tombstones dating from 1685, with inscriptions added later to commemorate the Wigtown Martyrs. These were Covenanters, so called because of their adherence to the National Covenant of 1638, the Scottish protest against 'popery'. In the 1670s and 1680s it

The open-air meetings of Scottish Covenanters, who rejected all forms of 'popery', were forbidden by the government of Charles II (1660–85), but were nonetheless attended by crowds of worshippers.

was in the south-west of Scotland that most resistance was offered to Charles II's reintroduction of the bishops: open-air gatherings or conventicles, led by dissident ministers, were attended by hundreds, even thousands.

Government reprisals were savage, led by men such as Sir Robert Grierson of Lag, General Tom Dalyell, and Graham of Claverhouse, all said by popular tradition to be IN LEAGUE WITH THE DEVIL (p. 142). Eighty or more summary executions took place in 1684–5, the most notorious of which were those of two women at Wigtown.

Eighteen-year-old Margaret Wilson and her sister Agnes, not yet thirteen, were imprisoned when they would not join a toast to the king. In the same prison was Margaret McLauchlan or Lachlan, a country-woman of 'singular piety and devotion' and 'more than ordinary knowledge', who refused either to renounce Presbyterianism

or to refrain from helping others persecuted for their beliefs. She was sixty-three at the time of her arrest, but despite her age, she had been allowed neither fire nor a bed in her cell.

All three were tried before Grierson of Lag and some others. The women were condemned to be tied to stakes 'fixed within the Flood-mark in the Water of Blednoch near Wigtoun, where the Sea flows at high water, there to be drowned'. Agnes was released on bail, but sentence was carried out on the two Margarets, at least according to Robert Wodrow writing in 1721–2. In the nineteenth century his statement was challenged, but in 1893 Sir Andrew Agnew recorded that an elder in the parish, told that a question had been raised as to whether the women had really been executed, said, 'Weel, weel, they that doots the droonin' o' the women, wad maybe doot the deein' o' the Lord Jesus Christ.'

Local tradition supports Wodrow. The Martyrs' Monument stands on Windy Hill, and the Covenanters' Monument is thought to mark the site of the drowning, though the waters no longer cover the spot. Popular opinion had little doubt, either, what happened to those who ill-used the martyrs. According to one anecdote, when the women were tied to their stakes, a town constable pressed their heads down in the sea with his halberd and cried, 'Tak' another drink o't, my hearties!' Hardly had he returned home when he was assailed by an unnatural thirst, which nothing could assuage. From then on, he was obliged to carry a pitcher on his back at all times, and whenever he came to a stream he would kneel and lap like a dog. People said his eternal torment had begun.

The best-known story about the martyrs is the tradition of the 'Cleppie Bells'. A constable by the name of Bell was asked after the execution how the women had behaved when the water closed over them. 'Oo,' he said with a laugh, 'they just clepped roun' the stobs like partons, and prayed.' A 'parton' is a crab, and 'clepped' is a word with more than one meaning: here it conveys the crab-like sideways motion of the women trying to creep their way round the stakes (stobs) to where they could breathe, but it also means 'webbed', as in having fingers or toes joined together like a crab's claws. Soon after Bell's callous gibe, his wife gave birth to a child, on delivering whom the midwife cried in horror, 'The bairn is clepped!', meaning its fingers were joined. When other children were born to the pair each was found to be 'clepped', and people saw this as a judgement of Providence. Old sins cast long shadows, and Agnew writes, 'We have been gravely assured that within the memory of man a female descendant of the bad constable, on giving birth to a child, was horrified by the exclamation, "The bairn is clepped!"'

MOFFAT, DUMFRIESSHIRE

See SUICIDAL ARTISTS AND ARCHITECTS (p. 156).

MOTE HILL, DALRY, KIRKCUDBRIGHTSHIRE

According to a story collected by Andrew Lang from oral tradition in Kirkcudbrightshire and published in *The Academy* in 1885, a terrible serpent once used to lie twined around Mote Hill. When the lord of Galloway offered a reward for slaying the monster, the blacksmith of Dalry made himself a suit of armour fitted with retractable spikes. Letting himself be swallowed by the serpent, he made the hidden spikes shoot out, and, rolling about inside it, tore it apart. By the time he had forced his way out of the carcass, the terrible monster was dead – and so mangled that for three days the Water of Ken ran red.

Spiked armour is a feature of several British dragon-slayings, and in Lang's original account the serpent haunted a barrow just as treasure-guarding Germanic dragons are supposed to do. Later Lang emended his story, and identified the serpent's haunt with the present Mote Hill, site of a Norman motte.

MURDER HOLE, LOCH NELDRICKEN, KIRKCUDBRIGHTSHIRE

A well-known Galloway tale is that of the Murder Hole, published in *Blackwood's Magazine* in February 1829. One dark night, a young pedlar was making his way up a lonely mountain road. He saw a light ahead, and recognised the cottage of Widow Mackillop and her two sons. When he had called there with some other travellers a few months before they had been made welcome, and indeed the widow had urged him to stay longer, but he had wanted company on the road and had left with the rest.

Now he knocked at the door, but it was not opened, so he went to the window and looked in. He saw the old woman sprinkling sand on the floor, while her two villainous-looking sons were pushing something large into a sea chest. A bloody butcher's knife lay on the table. Wondering if they had been poaching, he tapped on the glass.

The door was at once flung open and he was hustled inside. He asked for shelter, mentioning that he had stayed at the cottage before. 'Who's with you?' asked one son, a black-haired ruffian, and he said he was alone.

The widow, a stocky woman with ropes of grey hair, said he was welcome, and gave him supper. The second son, a red-bearded fellow, then showed him a room, which was disordered: a table and chair lay on the floor, the bed curtains had been torn down, and the bolt of the door was splintered. Pushing a chair under the handle to secure it, the lad lay down to sleep.

He was woken by a commotion in the next room, and was horrified to see blood oozing in beneath the door. Peering through a crack, he saw the two sons stooping over a dead goat, the black-haired son holding the knife. 'I wish all throats were cut that easy,' said he. The other nodded towards the pedlar's door. 'I'll give it him when we're ready,' said the black-haired son. The red-haired one asked why not directly to the 'Murder Hole', and the other replied that they would see.

Terror-stricken, the boy ran to the window, but while he was squeezing through it he kicked over a ewer. The sons heard the noise, ran in, and found him gone; one called for the bloodhound to be loosed, while the other told his mother to fetch the knife. The pedlar heard them and their words added desperation to his flight. He was barefoot and the ground hurt his feet, and after about a mile he fell onto some sharp rocks and cut himself. The blood he left behind was found moments later by the bloodhound, which then believed it had done its work and gave up the chase. The pedlar was thus able to get to the nearest village.

When he told his story, the neighbourhood was quickly roused. Many people had disappeared out on the moors, and now it seemed plain what had happened to them. The men set out for the cottage in a crowd, and eventually the widow and her sons confessed to over fifty murders, having sunk all the bodies in a deep pool. The body of their last victim was found in the sea chest. The three were summarily hanged on rough gibbets, and not far from the cottage was found the 'Murder Hole', a dark moorland pool, long and narrow, and seemingly bottomless.

These events are said to have happened around the end of the sixteenth century. The whereabouts of the cottage and the Murder Hole are disputed: the version which became famous was that given by Samuel Crockett in his 1894 novel *The Raiders*, setting the cottage south-east of Loch Enoch in the wilds below the Merrick, and the Murder Hole at the west end of Loch Neldricken. The Reverend C. H. Dick described that 'hole' in 1916 as a circular pool of deep water surrounded by sedges growing in the shallows, and comments:

Suicidal Artists and Architects

It is widely believed in Glasgow that the architect responsible for designing the city's Kelvingrove Art Gallery and Museum committed suicide when he discovered that it had been erected the wrong way round. Anyone who doubts the truth of this tragedy is shown the back of the building, which is at least as ornate as the front. This 'evidence', however, is misleading. The gallery's opening was planned to coincide with a major international exhibition in 1901, temporary structures for which were put up in Kelvingrove Park behind the gallery. Visitors to the building could approach from the street or from the park, and the gallery was therefore intended to look equally impressive from both sides. Another inconvenient fact which undermines the legend is that the two designers of the building, Sir J. W. Simpson and Milner Allen, both lived for many years after the gallery opened, and both died from natural causes.

This striking anecdote is by no means unique, but a variation on a standard story. The essential plot is identifiably the same in different places, with individual features varying from location to location. For example, the architect of Aberdeen's Marischal College, built at around the same time as the Kelvingrove Gallery, is fabled to have killed himself in remorse for public controversy caused by his elaborately decorative design. A more circumstantially detailed account relates to Fort George, east of Inverness, constructed in the mid eighteenth century by the British government as a deterrent to rebellion in the Highlands. The fort was supposedly planned to be invisible from the sea, but it is said that when it was completed the builder rowed out into the Moray Firth, where he discovered that a single chimney could be seen. He thereupon drew out a pistol and shot himself. Again, neither the designer William Skinner nor the architect John Adam in fact committed suicide.

Sculptors, too, feature as the subjects of these tales. Two pieces of statuary on public display in Glasgow are supposed to have literally fatal flaws. The statue of Sir Walter Scott in George Square has a plaid over the right shoulder (rather than the left, which would have been the correct way to wear it). Whatever the reasons for this mistake, it did not in reality lead to the artist's death. Neither did Baron Marochetti, as reported, commit suicide when he noticed that he had forgotten to include the spurs on his equestrian statue of the Duke of Wellington. Examination of the piece shows clearly that spurs were originally in place, but were broken off in a later act of vandalism.

A particularly interesting story is told about an estate in Murdostoun, north Lanarkshire, where the pillars at the gateway are embellished with stone lions, open-mouthed but without tongues. Again, it is said that this omission caused the artist such despair that he took his own life. Exactly the same

The creator of the splendid Moffat Ram, William Brodie, is said to have killed himself in remorse for having omitted its ears.

'error', however, traditionally led to the death of a British engineer responsible for a bridge across the Danube in Budapest, opened in 1842, and this is only one case out of many which could be mentioned to show that this type of story is not restricted to Scotland but is truly international.

The popularity of such tales may be partly due to the fact that they are handy bits of what might be called 'tourist lore'. A suicide may make an otherwise unremarkable object rather fascinating, or in other cases may provide a suitably dramatic background to a spectacular landmark. The town of Moffat in Dumfriesshire, for instance, boasts a nineteenth-century memorial known as the 'Famous Moffat Ram'. It is unusual for a piece of public statuary to show an animal rather than a human being, and a visitor's curiosity is naturally aroused by the sight of this magnificent beast with its impressive curly horns, perched on top of a rocky mound above the Colvin Fountain. The reason it is there, to commemorate the place of sheep in the local economy, is perhaps felt to be insufficiently exciting, and a more sensational titbit is the supposed suicide of its sculptor, William Brodie, in penance for a dreadful error. Just as others have shamefully displayed lions with no tongues, Brodie sculpted a ram with 'nae lugs' (ears).

That it could be used for the purpose to which the name points is difficult to believe. The crime would almost certainly be fatal for the perpetrator as well as for the victim. If you try to wade towards The Murder Hole you begin to sink almost immediately in the peaty bottom, and I doubt if it is possible to reach it without a boat.

Crockett was, however, a very popular writer in his day, and his setting has gained wide acceptance. Similarly, his relocation of the story of SAWNEY BEAN THE CANNIBAL (p. 200) from Galloway to Ayrshire has achieved the status of genuine tradition. Origins of a legend are not infrequently found in literature, as can be seen by the many Shakespeare-related tales of Macbeth, such as those associated with FORRES and GLAMIS CASTLE (both North East).

MYRTON CASTLE, MONREITH PARK, MOCHRUM, WIGTOWNSHIRE

In the parish of Mochrum, overlooking the White Loch, are the ruins of Myrton. Castle. The sixteenth-century tower house, raised on top of a twelfth-century motte, was built for the MacCullochs. Their line came to an end with Sir Godfrey MacCulloch, executed in March 1697.

The estates had been mismanaged before Sir Godfrey's day and were heavily encumbered. CARDONESS CASTLE had passed into the hands of the Gordons early in the century, and there was a feud between the two families. On 2 October 1690, MacCulloch went to Bush o' Bield, Gordon's house, 'with the intent of murdering him', according to William and Robert Chambers's *Domestic Annals of Scotland* (1861). The moment Gordon appeared at the door, Sir Godfrey shot him through the thigh, and the victim died five or six hours later. When he learned that the shot had been fatal, Sir Godfrey made his escape and went abroad.

After six years he ventured to return to Scotland, and visited a church in Edinburgh where a man from Galloway recognised him and shouted, 'Shut the doors – there's a murderer in the house!' Sir Godfrey was arrested, tried, and condemned. A broadside ballad of 1697 states that he was beheaded; the Reverend C. H. Dick, writing in 1916, says that Sir Godfrey was 'the last criminal to be executed by means of The Maiden', an instrument which can still be seen in the Museum of Scotland.

Sir Walter Scott, writing in 1802, knew a different end to the story, which he begins some years before the crisis with an account of how Sir Godfrey was riding one day near his own home when he was suddenly accosted by a little old man, dressed in green, mounted upon a white palfrey. The old man said that he lived beneath Sir Godfrey's castle, and complained of a drain or sewer which emptied itself directly into his best room.

Sir Godfrey Macculloch was a good deal startled at this extraordinary complaint; but, guessing the nature of the being he had to deal with, he assured the old man, with great courtesy, that the direction of the drain should be altered; and caused it to be done accordingly. Many years afterwards, Sir Godfrey had the misfortune to kill, in a fray, a gentleman of the neighbourhood. He was apprehended, tried, and condemned. The scaffold, upon which his head was to be struck off, was erected on the Castle-hill of Edinburgh; but hardly had he reached the fatal spot, when the old man, upon his white palfrey, passed through the crowd with the rapidity of lightning. Sir Godfrey, at his command, sprang on behind him; the 'good neighbour' spurred his horse down the steep bank, and neither he nor the criminal were ever seen again.

Sir Andrew Agnew told a version of this story in 1893 in which the fairy man was called the 'king of the brownies'. Agnew added that after the old man had ridden off with MacCulloch, a figure was still to be seen in the hangman's cart, 'wondrous like Sir Godfrey', and so it was generally believed that he had indeed perished:

A few only knew better, but these cared little to speak about the matter. At rare intervals, however, one of the initiated would impart the story to a friend, and tell how a head had rolled upon the ground, leaving a bleeding trunk upon the scaffold; then adding in a confidential whisper, 'It was no' him ava [at all]; it was just a kin' o' glamour.'

The implication is that a 'fairy stock' or image was substituted for Sir Godfrey, and it was this and not the real man which had been executed. The story of the miraculous escape may possibly have originated in the fact that the execution was put off from 5 to 25 March at Sir Godfrey's request, to allow him time to prepare spiritually for his death.

NEW ABBEY, KIRKCUDBRIGHTSHIRE

Alexander or Sandy Harg from New Abbey had courted and married a pretty girl whom the fairies had long tried to lure away from the human world. A few nights after their marriage, he was standing with his fishing net not far from two old vessels stranded on the rocks. These were thought to be the occasional haunts of fairies crossing the mouth of the River Nith.

In one of these wrecks a loud noise was heard as of carpenters at work; a hollow voice cried from the other – 'Ho, what'rye doing!' 'I'm making a wyfe to Sandy Harg!' replied a voice, in no mortal accent. The husband, astonished and terrified, throws down his net, hastens home, shuts up every avenue of entrance, and folds his young spouse in his arms.

At midnight, there came a gentle rap at the door, which was repeated three times. The young wife started to get up, but he held her still and silent. A footstep was heard moving off and immediately the cattle started bellowing, while the horses neighed and pranced and snorted as if surrounded by flames. The husband held his wife fast:

She speaks, cries, entreats, struggles: he will not move, speak, nor quit her. The noise and tumult increases, but with the morning's coming it dies away. The husband leaps up with the dawn, and hurries out to view his premises. A piece of moss oak, fashioned to the shape and size of his wife, meets his eye, reared against his garden dyke, and he burns this devilish effigy.

This tale was told by R. H. Cromek in 1810. Traditional wisdom said that silence was to be observed when dealing with the fairies, for speaking would put one in their power. Holding tightly on to the person they are trying to entice away, or who must be won back from them, is an old theme, illustrated by the traditional ballad of 'Tamlane' at CARTERHAUGH (Lothian & Borders).

Other tales involving the 'fairy stock' are told at NEW DEER (North East) and BRIDGE OF AWE (Argyllshire & Islands), and a very similar case involving the trows is set at WALLS (Orkney Islands & Shetland). A benevolent use of such an image by the fairies is mentioned at MYRTON CASTLE.

PALNACKIE,
KIRKCUDBRIGHTSHIRE

In his *Tales of Galloway* (1979), Alan Temperley includes a story which he calls 'The Simple Giant'. It is a version of a tale found in many countries and known as 'The brave tailor', since that is the usual profession of its hero, but this gently humorous retelling features a farmhand, and is localised in the village of Palnackie, south of Dalbeattie.

One day, long overdue after a stormy passage, the *Sark* came into the estuary near the village. The captain was holding the hand of a boy about three years old, with a simple-minded expression, who had been found floating alone on the rough sea in a rowing boat with the name 'John A. Boe' painted on the side.

Some said that the boy should be thrown back in the waves to prevent the sea taking some of the villagers instead. Ignoring this advice, the captain and his wife adopted the boy, giving him the same name as the boat in which he had been found: John A. Boe. The years passed and John grew — and grew. Before long he was as big and strong as a powerful man, but the schoolmaster despaired of him, being unable to teach him anything but the rudiments of the three Rs.

When the boy was twelve, the captain was drowned at sea and his wife died soon after. People wondered what was to happen to the huge boy, and seeing that he was both strong and eager to please, a grasping farmer from nearby Boreland offered to employ him for odd jobs. For seven years John A. Boe laboured with a will for the farmer, though he received not a farthing in wages. In this time he grew to seven feet tall and was stronger than a carthorse. His wits became no sharper, however, and the children mocked him.

One summer day, he came upon a gang of boys stoning a black cat belonging to an old woman rumoured to be a witch. John picked up the cat and took it back to the old woman. As he was the first person in a long while to show her any kindness, she offered him as a reward anything he wanted, and John managed to stammer that he wished to perform a great deed of valour so that people would no longer despise him. Giving him an open pot of heather honey, she told him to carry it past the gallows along the road to Auchencairn when the sun was high.

Next day, a little before noon, John set off. He passed the vacant gibbet and continued past a bog where the flies hung in swarms; they were soon buzzing around his head and the mouth of the honey pot. John flailed at the flies with his bonnet and saw that the honey was covered with their corpses. He began to pick them out, counting them as he went, but he kept losing track of the total. At last a rhyme came into his head by which he could remember the number. He said it over and over, then he thought he would write it down. Getting a stub of charcoal out of his pocket, he wrote in clumsy letters on the side of the honey pot:

> Here am I, great John A. Boe,
> Who killed a hundred at a blow.

Then, worn out with all that thinking, he lay down on the grass and fell asleep.

A while later, a troop of young men came along on their way to repel English reivers encamped by the Solway Moss. Seeing the gigantic boy by the roadside, the captain called a halt, and when they managed to decipher the rhyme on the honey pot they knew they had found a new recruit. Waking John up, they put him on a great Clydesdale horse and led him along the road. On the way, they stole a sheet and on it painted the rhyme in huge letters. This they carried aloft.

John was bewildered by all this and did not want to go. When they came to the gibbet, he flung his arms round it and the whole thing snapped off at the base. On they went, with John still carrying the gibbet.

When they came face to face with the English raiders, the captain ordered John to tell them who he was. John opened his mouth and roared:

'Here am I, great John A. Boe,
Who killed a hundred at a blow.'

One of the labourers pricked the Clydesdale's rump with his dagger, and the horse galloped away with John on its back still clutching his gibbet. Aghast at this monstrous apparition, the English fled.

On the homeward march, the men put John at the head of the troop. Though he did not understand what was happening, John felt very proud, and when he got back to Palnackie, the townspeople, too, made much of him: the schoolmaster now said he had always predicted a great future for the lad and the farmer at Boreland said how carefully he had trained him, while those who had wanted to throw him back in the sea now claimed they had often said he brought them luck.

When he went to see the old woman who had given him the pot of honey, all she said was: 'Get the name of an early riser, and you may bide in your bed all day,' and although John had no idea what this meant, he found the rest of his life easy and pleasant.

PORTENCORKRIE BAY, WIGTOWNSHIRE

One of the legends recorded by James Maxwell Wood in 1911 is the tale of the 'Barncorkrie Fairy' and her kindness. An old woman was walking one day along a path by the Bishop's Castle near Portencorkrie Bay. She was tired and sad, as she was very poor, and her son and his new wife refused to help her. Sitting down, she wept, and as her eyes were cast down, she noticed lying on the ground at her feet a round stone pierced through by a hole. Absent-mindedly she picked it up and, as she did so, thought she heard whispering. When she looked round, there was no one there, which frightened her somewhat, and putting the stone in her pocket she hurried home.

That same evening, as she was lighting her lamp, the doors of the cottage opened, seemingly of their own accord, and looking down she saw a little old woman dressed in green, who smiled at her and asked her how she did. Now our old woman was proud, and said she was doing fine, but the little woman remarked with a laugh, 'Not much comfort an' a toom [empty] meal-barrel in the hoose.' They chatted amicably for a while, and the fairy gradually teased out of the woman the tale of her woes. As the fairy left, she said that if the woman still had the queer little stone she had found that day, she should tie a little bit of grey worsted thread through the hole and lay it on the meal ark (flour chest): 'It'll maybes be a help.'

Next night, at the Portencorkrie croft where the old woman's son Godfrey lived with his wife, the couple were startled to find a little woman perched on a stool by the kitchen fire. 'What want ye here?' cried Godfrey, and his wife shouted, 'Tak' yer gait, we want nae beggars here.' The fairy gave them a steady look with her piercing grey eyes and said, in a small but penetrating voice, 'The poor folk! Much they get at your hands! But thy old mother shall never want; she shall live at your cost. Her meal-ark will always be full, and yours shall supply it.'

And this is what happened. Though

Godfrey and his wife now tried to make amends, the old woman turned a cold shoulder to their advances.

RERRICK PARISH, KIRKCUDBRIGHTSHIRE

A report was given to the Dumfries and Galloway Natural History and Antiquarian Society in 1896–7 which describes the laying of a 'stone fire' in a Rerrick farmhouse 'within living memory'. The informant says:

> It was at one time a common custom for a farmer who was evicted, or who was leaving his farm under a sense of grievance, to fill up the fireplace in every room with broken bottles and small stones and to lay on his successor a curse which should never be lifted until these fires burned. When the stone fire had been laid and the curse said, the doors were locked and the tenant made his way out by the window, the curse alighting on the first person who entered thereafter. It was a custom also in such cases to sow a part of the farm with sand and to curse the succeeding tenant until the sand should grow. This form of cursing was carried out in the parish perhaps seventy years ago, and tradition said that the incoming tenant did not thrive . . .

In the writer's opinion, this was 'probably due more to the ill-will of his neighbours than to the curse of his predecessor'. The same might be said of the ghost or poltergeist at COLLIN FARM in the same parish.

ROUTIN' BRIDGE, IRONGRAY, DUMFRIESSHIRE

Flowing northwards through Irongray, north-west of Dumfries, is the Old Cluden Water, or Routin' Burn, 'routing'

meaning turbulence or noise. Just before it joins the River Cairn, it drops in a fine cascade between crags spanned by the Routin' Bridge, famous for the beauty of its setting with the waterfall on one side and on the other a deep, dark pool.

This is the dramatic background of a tradition recorded by John Barbour in 1886 concerning a 'poor widow woman' burned for witchcraft in the seventeenth century:

> She lived alone, and was frequently seen, on a summer's eve, sitting upon a jagged rock, which overhung the Routing-burn; or gathering sticks, late in a November evening, among the rowan-tree roots . . . She had also, sometimes, lying in her window, a black-letter Bible, whose boards were covered with the skin of a fumart [pole-cat], and which had two very grotesque clasps of brass to close it with when she chose. Her lips were sometimes seen to be moving when she went to church, and she was observed to predict shower or sunshine at certain periods, which predictions often came to be realised.

Barbour assures us that she was a harmless creature. Her habits, however, were evidently enough to set tongues wagging: young women would occasionally call on her to buy the stockings she made, and if they happened to come out of the smoky cottage with bleary eyes, people said the 'witch' had been telling their fortunes and given them ill tidings. More particularly, if the widow was spinning her thread on a crag by the stream, 'she was sure to be then holding converse with Satan'.

The Bishop of Galloway was repeatedly urged to take action. Finally, for fear of having it reported to the king that he was refusing to punish witches, he had the widow brought to him. She was roughly handled, and several middle-aged and elderly neighbours testified to her wickedness: they said that the black-letter Bible was a book of the Black Art by means of which she consulted the Devil, that at certain times she went widdershins round the well, and that she muttered curses in the kirk. They accused her of working tricks of 'glamour' (magical illusions) among crags and hollows along the Routin' Burn, especially by moonlight, and everyone agreed that she was turning young women's heads by telling their fortunes.

The judge sentenced the widow to be drowned in the Routin' Burn, but the crowd insisted on a crueller punishment. 'The poor woman was enclosed in a barrel, fire was set to it, and it was rolled, in a blaze, into the waters of the Cluden.'

See also WITCH-HUNTS (p. 270).

ST MEDAN'S CHAPEL AND CAVE, WIGTOWNSHIRE

See SCOTLAND'S HOLY AND HEALING WELLS (p. 44).

ST NINIAN'S CAVE, GLASSERTON PARISH, WHITHORN, WIGTOWNSHIRE

There is perhaps no finer example in Scotland of the longevity of some traditions than the story of St Ninian's Cave. The walk to visit the cave begins in Kidsdale, south-west of Whithorn, and leads down Physgill Glen, then along the stony beach to a south-facing cleft in a rocky headland, not much different in appearance from other parts of this coast. According to ancient report, however, this was the hermitage of St Ninian.

Ninian, or Nynia, was a bishop at around the beginning of the fifth century. He built a white stone church, Ad Candida Casa, which probably stood at Whithorn, but was said to prefer the cave for his meditations and prayers, or as an eighth-century poem puts it, he 'studied heavenly wisdom with a devoted mind in a cave of horrible blackness'.

Despite what was claimed by tradition about religious occupation of the cleft, there was no evidence of it before 1871 when archaeologists began investigating.

This study for a stained-glass window, *c.*1925, shows St Ninian, a fifth-century bishop who was said to meditate in a cave near Whithorn. In 1871 it was claimed that the site of his hermitage had been rediscovered, and later excavations revealed thousand-year-old religious symbols carved there.

After several hundred tons of earth and fallen rock had been cleared from the cave, there came to light on its walls or on detached stones eighteen incised crosses, most of them probably cut by pilgrims in the eighth or ninth century to commemorate their visits. Excavations between 1883 and 1886 also discovered among the debris loose stones bearing similar crosses, two pillar stones, and a headstone carved with interlace ornament and part of a runic inscription.

Sir Herbert Maxwell, addressing the Royal Archaeological Institute in around 1890, thought this enough evidence to show 'that the tradition had had sufficient vitality to survive the fourteen centuries and a half which had intervened since its occupation by St Ninian'. This is perhaps going too far: that the cave had been used, and that it had been used by St Ninian, are different things. However, the crosses and headstone confirm that veneration in the cave goes back to at least the eighth century.

See also SAINTS OF SCOTLAND (p. 490).

SANQUHAR, DUMFRIESSHIRE

In 1733 or thereabouts Abraham Crichton, a respected local man, became provost of Sanquhar and inherited the mansion of Carco, but he later fell on evil days and in 1741 was made bankrupt. In 1746 he died, and Robert Simpson's *History of Sanquhar* (1865) gives an account of what happened next:

From his reputed wealth, the good people of Sanquhar were convinced that, before his death, he must have somewhere secreted his money, and acted a fraudulent part. On this account it was supposed that he could not rest in his grave, and hence the belief of his frequent appearances in the sombre churchyard, to the affrightment of all and sundry who passed near the

burying-ground in the evening dusk. The veritable apparition of this worthy was firmly credited by the populace, who were kept in a state of perpetual alarm. Many a maid, with her milk-pail on her head, dashed the whole to the ground when the ghost showed himself at the kirkyard wall, and ran home screaming with affright, and finally fell on the floor in a faint.

The ghost was said to assail anyone who came near his resting place, and the haunting became a topic of discussion throughout the south-west of Scotland.

Finally it was decided that something must be done to allay the general alarm. It was believed that a ghost could be laid by repeating certain sacred charms, and that the person to do this was a minister of the gospel. The minister fixed on was the elderly Reverend Mr Hunter of Penpont. During the night he went to the churchyard and next day announced that he had laid Abraham's ghost, and that in future no one need fear passing the churchyard as the ghost would not trouble anyone ever again. 'Mr Hunter's statement was implicitly believed, and nothing supernatural has since been seen within the ancient burying-ground of Sanquhar.'

When Mr Hunter was asked what he had said or done to the ghost, he replied, 'No one shall ever know that.' However, to reassure the public mind, Abraham's flat gravestone was fixed securely with a strong band of iron or sturdy chain, in order to keep him in his narrow grave and prevent his return. Whether Mr Hunter was a good exorcist or a good psychologist is left to the reader to decide.

SPEDLIN'S TOWER, LOCHMABEN, DUMFRIESSHIRE

Spedlin's Tower, to the north of Lochmaben on the west bank of the River

Spedlin's Tower was famously haunted by the ghost of a prisoner who starved to death in the dungeon. At night it was rumoured to cry, 'Let me out, let me out; I'm dying of hunger!'

Annan, is a ruined Border tower house that once belonged to the Jardines of Applegarth. In *The Antiquities of Scotland* (1789–91), Francis Grose calls it Spedlin's or Spedling's Castle. Two sides were overgrown with ivy, giving it, he says, 'a very gloomy and solemn appearance, favourable to the ideas of witches, hobgoblins, and apparitions'. He writes that the building 'is chiefly famous for being haunted by a Bogle, or Ghost', the story of which was told him by a woman who lived there and seemed convinced of its truth. Her tale was that in the time of Sir Alexander Jardine, during the reign of Charles II, a person named Porteus who lived in Applegarth was arrested on suspicion of having set fire to a mill, and was confined in the dungeon or 'pit' at Spedlin's Tower.

The Lord being suddenly called to Edinburgh on some pressing and unexpected business, in his hurry forgot to leave the key of the pit, which he always held in his own custody. Before he discovered his mistake, and could send back the key, which he did the moment he found it out, the man was starved to death, having first, through the extremity of hunger, gnawed off one of his hands.

From that time the castle was terribly haunted, until a chaplain of the family managed to confine the ghost to the dungeon, which it could not leave so long as a large Bible employed in the exorcism remained in the castle. It was said that the chaplain died soon afterwards.

The Ghost, however, kept quietly within the bounds of his prison till a long time after, when the Bible, which was used by the whole family, required a new binding: for which purpose it was sent to

Edinburgh. The Ghost, taking advantage of its absence, was extremely boisterous in the pit, seeming as if it would break through the iron door, and making a noise like that of a large bird fluttering its wings. The Bible being returned, and the pit filled up, every thing has since remained perfectly quiet. But the good woman declared, that should it again be taken off the premises, no consideration whatsoever would induce her to remain there a single night.

According to Charles Kirkpatrick Sharpe in his 1818 edition of Law's *Memorialls*, after the ghost had been confined to the pit 'he continued to scream of a night, – "Let me out, let me out; I'm dying of hunger!"' He would flutter like a bird against the door of the vault, and strip twigs of their bark if they were thrust through the key-hole, a trick also played by the bogey Redcap of HERMITAGE CASTLE (Lothian & Borders).

The black-letter Bible used by the chaplain was placed in a stone niche, which, says Sharpe, 'still remains in the wall by the stair-case'. Robert Chambers, who called the tale 'one of the best-accredited and most curious ghost-stories perhaps ever printed', added in 1827:

> But the charm seems to be now broken, or the ghost must have become either quiet or disregarded; for the Bible is at present kept in the house of Jardine-Hall. It is of Barker's printing, dated 1634, and, besides being well bound, is carefully covered with rough calf-skin.

The Bible is said by Charles Beard in his *Lucks and Talismans* (1934) to have been still kept at Jardine Hall in the 1930s, preserved in a brass-bound box made of beams from Spedlin's Tower.

Another story of a starved spectre is told at BALCOMIE CASTLE (Central & Perthshire).

SWEETHEART ABBEY, NEW ABBEY, KIRKCUDBRIGHTSHIRE

Devorguilla was the daughter of Alan, Lord of Galloway, and after his death in 1234 she ruled Galloway together with her husband John Balliol. The couple co-founded Balliol College, Oxford, and their son, another John Balliol, was King of Scotland from 1292 to 1296.

In 1275, Devorguilla founded the last Cistercian monastery in Scotland. Nothing now remains of the abbey but the red sandstone ruins of the church, which attest to the scale and grandeur of the original buildings. According to the medieval chronicle of Andrew Winton, prior of Lochlevin, when Balliol died Devorguilla had his heart taken out and embalmed. She placed it in an ivory box bound with enamelled silver, and enclosed it within the walls of the new abbey church near the high altar. Other accounts, however, say that she kept the box by her and for the next twenty years never sat down to meals without it. She left a request for it to be buried on her breast; on her death in 1290 her instructions were carried out, and from that day onwards her 'New Abbey', where she and her husband's heart lay in one grave, was known as Dulce Core, or Sweetheart Abbey.

It seems to be a matter of historical record that when Devorguilla herself was buried at Sweetheart Abbey the heart was taken from its place in the church and reburied in her tomb, making the tradition that she carried the casket about with her untrue. An effigy of her holding the heart casket, however, presides over her reconstructed tomb, which can be seen in the south transept chapel.

Though it was the opinion of the nineteenth-century folklorist G. L. Gomme that Devorguilla's arrangements were 'certainly a relic of the still older custom of sacrificing human victims by building them into the wall, in order to secure the safety of the building', we need not look so far for precedent. Heart burial was once commonplace among the great of the land: those whose hearts were interred separately from their bodies in the thirteenth century include William de Kilkenny, Bishop of Ely, who died in Spain and was buried there, his heart being taken to Ely; Eleanor of Castile, wife of Edward I, whose body was buried in Westminster Abbey, her heart in the church of the Black Friars, London; and Ranulph, third Earl of Chester, whose body was interred at Chester, but his heart in the Abbey of Dieulacres. Robert the Bruce wanted his own heart to be taken to the Holy Land, but in the end it was interred at MELROSE ABBEY (Lothian & Borders).

Several hearts have been discovered accidentally in churches, some named in inscriptions, some not. In 1773, such a heart was unearthed in the foundations of St Cuthbert's kirk, Edinburgh. It had been embalmed with spices, then enclosed in a heart-shaped leaden box. Other churches seem to have adopted or invented traditions of heart burials, quite possibly inspired by the romantic story of Devorguilla.

TYNRON DOON, NITHSDALE, DUMFRIESSHIRE

Tynron Doon is a steep-sided spur of Auchengibbert Hill, between Thornhill and Moniaive. On its summit stands an Iron Age hill-fort dating from the first millennium BCE. Conspicuous in the landscape for miles around, and commanding a correspondingly extensive view, its natural defensive capabilities were strengthened by a stone wall and by a series of scarped ramparts of earth and rock that look, from the air at least, for all the world like the steps leading to some giant's castle. This magnificent site continued to be used off and on, through the Dark Ages down to the early modern period, when towards the end of the sixteenth century an L-plan tower house was built at the north-western corner.

Like other dramatic landscape features and ancient sites, it might be expected to boast legends. Here, however, the tale is not of giants or the age of heroes, but of the more recent past, connected with the ruined tower house. In 1911, James Maxwell Wood wrote:

> Round Tynron Doon there linger memories of a spectre in the form of a headless horseman restlessly riding a black horse. The local tradition is, that the ghost was that of a young gentleman of the family of M'Milligan of Dalgarnock, who had gone to offer his addresses to the daughter of the Laird of Tynron Castle. His presence was objected to, however, by one of the young lady's brothers. Hot words followed, and in high wrath the suitor rode off; but mistaking his way he galloped over the steepest part of the hill and broke his neck, and so, with curses and words of evil on his very lips, his spirit was not allowed to pass untroubled to the realms beyond.

It might seem odd that the ghost is headless when all he did was break his neck, but headlessness is a traditional ghostly characteristic, an indication of the uncanny rather than a reflection of what happened in life.

WHINNIELIGGATE, KIRKCUDBRIGHTSHIRE

From the many accounts of so-called 'witches' it is clear that some old women were neither real practitioners of magic nor mentally deranged, but deliberately fostered their reputation in order to survive in days before pensions. One such was Jean, an old woman who lived near Whinnieliggate, on a lonely part of the road between Kirkcudbright and Dumfries (the modern B727 from Kirkcudbright to Dalbeattie). Her neighbours feared her so greatly that they kept her meal chest full, and gave her food, clothes, and everything she needed. In *Witchcraft and Superstitious Record in the Southwestern District of Scotland* (1911), James Maxwell Wood gives an account based on a minute description of her and her house left by an old man named John:

He told how she was of small spare build, wizened of figure and face, squinted outward with one eye, the eyes themselves being small, but of a peculiar whitish green colour, her nose hooked and drooping over very ugly teeth. She swathed her straggling grey locks in a black napkin or handkerchief, wore grey drugget, and a saffron-tinted shawl with spots of black and green darned into the semblance of frogs, toads, spiders, and jackdaws, with a coiled adder or snake roughly sewn round the border. Her shoes or bauchles were home-made from the untanned hides of black Galloway calves, skins not difficult for her to get.

Her thatched cottage was as quaint as herself. A huge bed of orpine (stonecrop) flourished over one side, at each end grew luxuriant broom bushes, and next to the house was a barberry shrub densely covered with fruit in season. The small windows at the front of the cottage were draped with a row of hair ropes, from which were suspended the whitened skulls of hares, ravens, rooks, and crows.

The interior was also garnished with dried kale-stocks, leg and arm bones, no doubt picked up in the churchyard, all arranged

in the form of a star, and over her bedhead hung a roughly drawn circle of the signs of the zodiac. She was often to be seen wandering about the fields in moonlight nights with a gnarled old blackthorn stick with a ram's horn head, and was altogether regarded as uncanny.

As doubtless she chose to be: this is as fine an example of set-dressing as one could wish for. Though she could not help the hook nose and squint characteristic of the storybook witch, nor the rotten teeth, nor the whitish green eyes – possibly the effect of cataracts – she evidently made the most of other conventional aspects of witches. The frogs, toads, spiders, jackdaws and serpents decorating her clothes, the bones arranged in the form of a star, the signs of the zodiac – all these things confirmed her neighbours' ideas of what witches looked like and got up to.

Meanwhile, the orpine (*Sedum telephium*) and the barberry bush were putting out mixed messages: the stalks of orpine, which John Aubrey (1626–97) calls 'Midsommer-men' and says were used for love divination, were more prosaically also hung up as a fly repellent. The bark of the barberry (*Berberis vulgaris*) was widely used to treat jaundice, but as Maxwell Wood notes, barberries make good preserves: was she brewing folk remedies (like many accused witches) or simply making jam? This, rather than weird rites, could explain the skulls of the creatures draped over her windows – like gamekeepers even today she may have hung up the dead evidence as a warning to predators to keep off the fruit.

Naturally, a person so thoroughly playing a part attracted the standard stories. Old John, who described her, told of two occasions when he was worsted by her. One day he and a farmer's son had set out for Kirkcudbright with two heavily laden wagonloads of hay. The farmer jokingly called after them to take care with Jean: 'Dinna ye stop aboot her door or say ocht tae her, tae offend her.' John was sceptical about witches and scoffed at the very idea that she could give any trouble. As they passed her house, she came out and began plying them with questions: where had they come from, where were they going, whose hay and horses were they, and so on. The lad recklessly asked her 'what deil business it was of hers', and on they went through the woods by the Brocklock Burn until suddenly a hare ran back and forth across the road, scaring the horses so much that they backed both carts over into the wood. John and the boy had to walk into town, where they told the story of Jean's malevolence. Given their encounter with the old woman, it would not have

occurred to them to think of the hare as an ordinary animal zigzagging in front of a moving vehicle as hares and rabbits often do. No, this was a witch-hare, Jean in animal guise, like the witches in all the stories.

Some years later, John had another brush with Jean, again involving the traditional influence of a witch over horses. He was taking a cartload of potatoes to Kirkcudbright and refused to give her two or three for seed. As a result, the horses backed the cart right into the harbour and were only with difficulty rescued from drowning. One wonders from this second incident if John's tales of Jean were simply cover-stories to excuse his incompetence as a driver.

See also WITCH-HUNTS (p. 270).

GLASGOW & AYRSHIRE

The counties of Ayrshire, Lanarkshire,
and Renfrewshire

ALLOWAY, AYRSHIRE

Alloway, the birthplace of Robert Burns (1759–96), is the setting for one of his most famous poems, 'Tam o' Shanter' (1791), in which a tipsy young man spies on a coven of witches at the kirk. Pursued by their 'hellish legion', headed by the pretty but vicious Nannie, he reaches the River Doon just in time to escape the witches, who as tradition dictates cannot cross running water.

Phrases from Burns's verse have entered popular culture. The hero's name has become that of his hat (a 'guid blue bonnet'

in the poem), and the famous ship *Cutty Sark* was named after Nannie's revealing shift, applauded by Tam with the exclamation 'Weel done, Cutty-sark!' when it gives him a glimpse of her charms. The site of his river-crossing, not named in the poem, can be no other than Brig o' Doon, a medieval bridge south of Alloway, and this too has become famous, its name adapted to that of the fictional village that appears only once each century, in Lerner and Loewe's 1947 musical *Brigadoon.*

Burns drew inspiration from existing local legend. Francis Grose wrote in 1791 that Alloway kirk was notorious as a place

In Robert Burns's 'Tam o' Shanter' (1791) the hero sees the witches' revels, and is pursued by a comely young witch wearing a 'cutty sark' (short shirt) who tears off his horse's tail, as shown in this 1896 illustration of the poem.

where witches and warlocks would dance 'to the pipes of the muckle-horned Deel'. That Satan should have piped for the revellers was an idea with a long history: the Greek god Pan, a prototype of the goat-legged devil, is traditionally shown playing a flute with seven reeds. Seventeenth-century Scottish belief named the bagpipes as the Fiend's favourite instrument. In 1679, witches burned at Bo'ness were accused of meeting near Kinneil, 'where they all danced, and the Devil acted as piper', and William Barton's wife of DALMENY (Lothian & Borders) confessed to having danced with the Devil 'in the likeness of a rough brown dog, playing on a pair of pipes'. Another story of the Devil as bagpiper is told at GLASGOW.

BIGGAR, LANARKSHIRE

Robert Chambers, in his *Picture of Scotland* (1827), tells what was probably even then an old joke: 'London, says the Clydesdale peasant, is a big town, but there is one in Scotland that is Biggar.'

To the east of the town, there was once a tract of marshy ground running from the brink of the Clyde towards the vale of the Tweed, of which Chambers records a legend 'strenuously asserted by the common people' that the magician Michael Scot attempted to divert the Clyde through this morass and send it into the channel of the Tweed:

Michael's attempt to change the course of the Clyde, was rendered unsuccessful by a circumstance which has not come to our knowledge. But it is well known at Carnwath and Libbertoun, what prevented his imps from building a bridge over the water near Covington. He had set an extraordinary number of devils to this meritorious and public-spirited work; and they were all busy carrying stones from

the Yelpin Craigs, a place about four miles north from the river, beyond Carnwath, for the purpose of immediately afterwards proceeding to the architectural part of their duty, when the joyful intelligence was communicated to them, that their master had suddenly died.

Finding themselves relieved from duty, the imps threw down the stones they were carrying, which in Chambers's day could still be seen in a line between the Yelpin Craigs and the river near Covington, though one or two local farmers had cleared them from their fields at considerable expense.

The stones are from three to thirty hundred weight, and the line may be an acre or two in breadth – a thing worthy of attention even as a natural phenomenon.

This was one of the wizard's many attempts to occupy his assistants or familiars, sometimes identified as three imps called Prig, Prim, and Pricker. In other accounts there is a larger gang of anonymous sprites, but however many there were, they were an intolerable nuisance to Scot unless he kept them constantly at work.

As to Scot's death, news of which forestalled the building of the bridge at Covington, there are several conflicting accounts: *see* MICHAEL SCOT, THE WIZARD OF BALWEARIE (p. 62).

CARFIN LOURDES GROTTO, LANARKSHIRE

The most popular of Scottish holy wells is also the most recently established. Its foundation by Father (later Monsignor) Taylor was inspired by a visit he made in about 1920 to the original Lourdes in France, and by the example of the Oostacker Grotto in Belgium, where a miraculous cure had been reported. This account comes from the Carfin website:

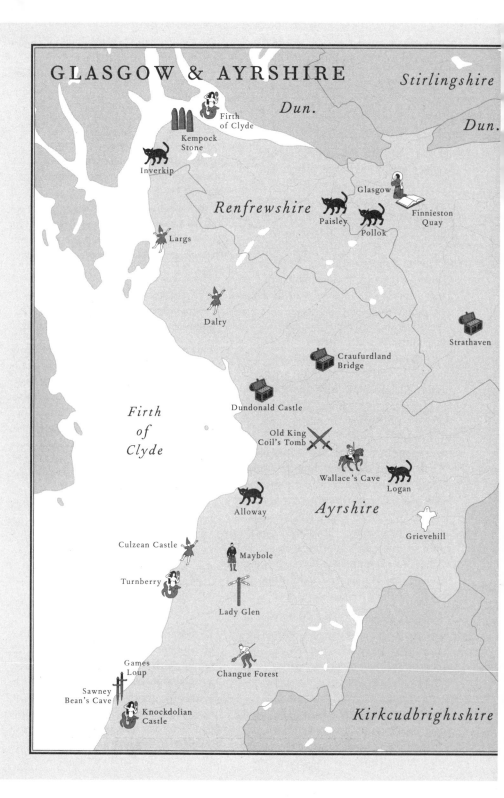

GLASGOW & AYRSHIRE

Stirlingshire

Dun.

Dun.

Firth
of Clyde

Kempock
Stone

Inverkip

Renfrewshire

Glasgow

Paisley

Pollok

Finnieston
Quay

Largs

Dalry

Strathaven

Craufurdland
Bridge

*Firth
of
Clyde*

Dundonald Castle

Old King
Coil's Tomb

Wallace's Cave

Logan

Alloway

Ayrshire

Grievehill

Culzean Castle

Maybole

Turnberry

Lady Glen

Games
Loup

Changue Forest

Sawney
Bean's Cave

Knockdolian
Castle

Kirkcudbrightshire

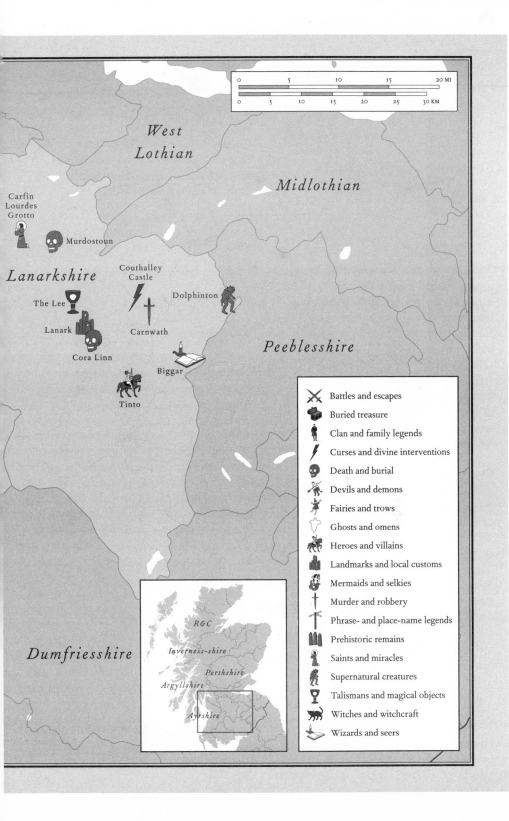

West
Lothian

Midlothian

Carfin
Lourdes
Grotto

Murdostoun

Lanarkshire

Couthalley
Castle

Dolphinton

The Lee

Lanark

Carnwath

Peeblesshire

Cora Linn

Biggar

Tinto

Dumfriesshire

R&C

Inverness-shire

Perthshire

Argyllshire

Ayrshire

⚔ Battles and escapes

Buried treasure

Clan and family legends

⚡ Curses and divine interventions

💀 Death and burial

Devils and demons

Fairies and trows

Ghosts and omens

Heroes and villains

Landmarks and local customs

Mermaids and selkies

† Murder and robbery

Phrase- and place-name legends

Prehistoric remains

Saints and miracles

Supernatural creatures

Talismans and magical objects

Witches and witchcraft

Wizards and seers

On April 7 1875, a man by the name of Peter de Rudder visited the shrine seeking the intercession of the Madonna – seven years earlier he had severely fractured his leg which would not heal and hung like that of a rag doll's. Doctors had advised him that amputation was the only medical treatment that could be carried out . . . while he was in the Grotto, his leg was immediately healed. A full inch of new bone had grown. That very day Peter literally danced with joy and the next day he walked six miles.

Carfin at that time was a village peopled almost exclusively by Catholics, mainly miners from Ireland with a few Lithuanians. An area of waste ground was selected for the grotto, and work was carried out mainly by volunteers, who had time on their hands due to the 1921 miners' strike. Later research discovered a well dedicated to the Virgin Mary just beyond the borders of the site, and a railway cutting revealed bones thought to be those of the monks who had built the well.

The opening of the 'Scottish Lourdes' in 1922 was attended by over 2,000 pilgrims, and since then the site has flourished, attracting around 35,000 visitors in 2005. Over the years many shrines have been added to the site, to saints including St Margaret of Scotland and St Patrick, the latter looking down on a Mass Rock donated in 1934 by an Irish Protestant landowner. In 1989 a chapel was opened, originally to be called 'Star of the Sea', but renamed 'Maid of the Seas' in tribute to the aircraft that crashed during the Lockerbie disaster of 21 December 1988.

The original and central shrine is the Carfin Grotto of Our Lady of Lourdes, with a statue representing the vision of the Virgin Mary seen by St Bernadette in France in 1858. Janet Bord, who visited Carfin in 2006, reports that two taps are incorporated nearby, giving water which has been blessed by contact with water from the original Lourdes, and that plastic bottles are available in which the water can be taken home by the pilgrims who crowd the site in summer:

> The water source performs the same function as a traditional holy well, in that it supplies water impregnated with the numinous aura of the saint.

No actual miracles are reported to have occurred at Carfin, but many people obviously feel supported and uplifted by visiting the shrine.

See also SCOTLAND'S HOLY AND HEALING WELLS (p. 44).

CARNWATH, LANARKSHIRE

There once lived at Carnwath an old man called Thomson who made a little money making and selling straw baskets. One night in around 1770, as he was going to bed, he was called to the door by two men who stabbed him to the heart and immediately made off. Thomson's family found the old man only a couple of minutes later, but he was dead and the murderers had disappeared without trace.

Thomson's son was utterly determined to find his father's killers. According to Robert Chambers's account, written in 1827:

> Alone and on foot, he wandered over all Scotland and most of England, besides a portion of the Continent, making ceaseless and anxious inquiries for the objects of his search, and mixing in every sort of low society, not even excepting that of highway robbers and pickpockets, in the hope of obtaining at least some information respecting them. At last he came home spent and disappointed and settled in his native village, where, however, his mind continued to ponder incessantly

In the seventeenth century the ancient standing stones on Machrie Moor (Argyllshire & Islands) were believed to have been set in place by the legendary warrior Fingal. It was also said that the circle was once used for pagan sacrifices.

The site of Loch Awe (Argyllshire & Islands), seen here in an aerial shot, was said to have been a fertile plain until a spring on top of Ben Cruachan overflowed and filled the valley. The accident was ascribed to the carelessness of the Cailleach, a giantess who frequented the wilds of Scotland and was credited with many creative and destructive acts.

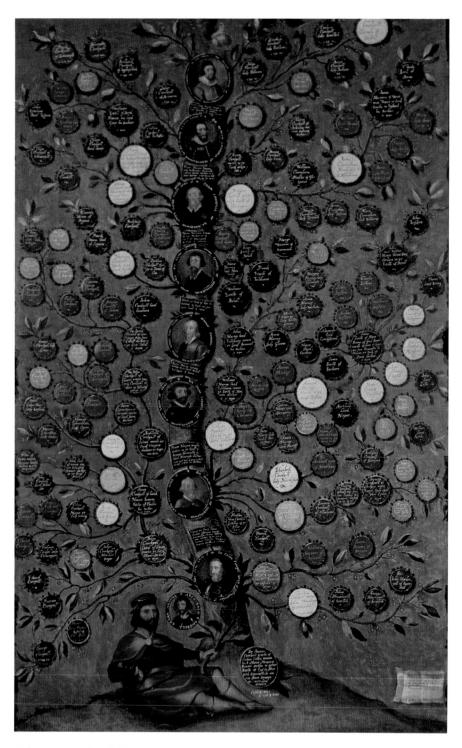

The Campbells of Glenorchy trace their lineage far back, as shown by this family tree dating from 1635. A legend tells that long ago they persuaded the MacNabs to sell them a little land at Finlarig (Central & Perthshire), and by a ruse eventually dispossessed the other clan.

At the Martyrs' Tomb in Wigtown (Dumfries & Galloway) lie the bodies of two women executed in 1685, who are also commemorated here at the Martyrs' Monument. They were Covenanters, religious enthusiasts persecuted by the government, and Constable Bell, who mocked the dying victims, is said to have suffered a curse for his brutality.

The tomb of Robert the Bruce can be seen in Dunfermline Abbey (Central & Perthshire). Others said to lie here are St Margaret, Malcolm Canmore, and William Wallace's mother, while one lady, for reasons unknown, was buried upright in the wall.

This sketch by J.M.W. Turner (1775–1851) illustrates Walter Scott's *Minstrelsy of the Scottish Border* (1802–3). It shows Gilnockie Tower (Dumfries & Galloway), home of the robber Johnnie Armstrong whose death is celebrated in a popular ballad included in Scott's collection.

This ornate lamp post, which stands near Glasgow Cathedral (Glasgow & Ayrshire), features symbols associated with St Mungo's miracles. He was said to have caught a salmon which had swallowed the queen's ring, and also to have restored a bird to life and set a branch of a tree alight with the power of his prayers. The bell which hangs beside the fish represents St Mungo's Bell, made in the fifteenth century in honour of the saint.

A cavern near Culzean Castle (Glasgow & Ayrshire) was famed as a haunt of the fairies. A laird of Culzean behaved generously to a fairy boy and later, when imprisoned abroad and condemned to death, was set free by the sprite in gratitude.

No contemporary portraits survive of Sir William Wallace (*c.* 1270–1305), but this nineteenth-century picture shows a suitably powerful and masculine image. Wallace gained a heroic reputation from his resistance to the English, and legends soon gathered around his name. He was said to have left the print of his thumb in solid rock on top of the hill of Tinto (Glasgow & Ayrshire), shortly before he defeated the enemy in battle.

This illumination from a fourteenth-century psalter shows a mermaid holding her traditional comb and mirror. Near Knockdolian Castle (Glasgow & Ayrshire), a mermaid used to sit for hours on a particular stone in the river, singing and combing her long yellow hair, until the lady of the castle had the stone destroyed. The mermaid cursed the lady's family, which soon died out.

Edinburgh Castle (Lothian & Borders) is now home to the Stone of Scone, also known as the Stone of Destiny. The relic was the subject of a fateful prophecy, and has been the object of several thefts.

The Bass Rock (Lothian & Borders), a notable landmark north-east of Berwick, is shown here in a watercolour by John Sell Cotman (1782–1842). The small island is reported to have been the home of St Baldred, whose body, when he died, was miraculously multiplied so that three churches could have the honour of housing his remains.

This dramatic picture by John Opie (1761–1807) shows the murder of David Rizzio at Holyroodhouse (Lothian & Borders), with Mary, Queen of Scots, stretching out her hand in vain to prevent the crime. The first blow was struck by George Douglas, and the figure glaring in the background must be Mary's husband Lord Darnley.

upon the painful and exciting subject that had so long occupied it. One night, after he had retired to rest, his waking ears were met by a low mysterious voice that seemed to come to him, through the silence, from another world, and whispered the words 'Arise and search.'

Next day he went on impulse to Edinburgh, where he heard that two gypsies were to be hanged the following morning. He had made a point on his travels of visiting all criminals under sentence of death, in case they could give him information about his father's murder, and did so again; this time he was on the right track. The two men confessed that out of jealousy over his father's straw-weaving, which had interfered with their own trade, they had killed the old man. Satisfied in the knowledge that the culprits were to suffer execution, Thomson returned home and settled down as the schoolmaster of Walston.

CHANGUE FOREST, CARRICK, AYRSHIRE

Changue Forest, now a state forest within Glentrool Forest Park, lies just south of the River Stinchar, and a couple of miles east of Barr. William Robertson, writing in 1889, states lyrically that for 'rugged Highland beauty' the district has no match in Ayrshire. In his time people still remembered the 'good old days' when the Fair of Kirkdamdie was held in Barr and drew country people from far and near to barter and sport and fight:

There was abundant store of liquor; there were spae wives and fortune tellers; there were ballad singers and wandering minstrels; farmers and their wives, farm servants, male and female – all gathered on the one spot, full of the common intent.

The early morning was the time for trade in sheep, wool, and stores. After the serious business was done, pipers and fiddlers would begin playing and young people would dance to the music. Later still, after some drinking had been done, fights would take place and be eagerly watched.

One man who came to the fair was known and feared for courage and strength. This was the Laird of Changue, a brewer and smuggler of whisky, 'as bold and desperate as he was notorious':

He cared for neither man nor devil. Amid the quiet of the hills he distilled his liquor, and then he set forth by hidden paths and the most unfrequented routes to dispose of it. He was a good customer at his own still, and wherever he went he was hail-fellow-well-met with those with whom he trafficked.

His prowess in the fights at Kirkdamdie fair, no doubt fuelled by his own liquor, was something to remember and to talk about.

It was said of the laird that he had sold his soul to the Devil in return for wealth and success. After that, he was always fortunate in his smuggling, and never got caught by the excisemen; none of his speculations failed, and he bought more and more land and houses to add to his property. Though he spent money fast, he made it faster, and became very wealthy. As the years went by, he almost forgot his contract with Satan: he had never come to claim his price, so perhaps he never would.

But the Devil had not forgotten: when he thought the laird had had a long enough spell of life and prosperity, he duly appeared in a lonely spot and told him his time had come. Unafraid, the laird drew his sharp-bladed sword and challenged him to combat, first using its point to draw a circle round the spot where they stood. The Devil tried to drive him out of the ring, for once outside, the laird would be within his power. If he himself was driven out, however, he would have to take himself off to hell without his prize.

The pair of them fought long and hard, the Devil resorting to all his armaments, first his cloven hooves, then his tail with its deadly sting at the tip, then his horns. One by one his weapons were destroyed or stripped away from him, but neither he nor the Laird of Changue would give in. Finally, Satan spread his two great wings and with fire pouring from his mouth flew at the man. But with one powerful sweep the laird's sharp sword came down exactly on the joint where the Devil's wings joined his shoulders. Roaring with pain, he sprang at the laird, but in one huge final effort Changue hit him so hard in the mouth that he knocked him clean out of the circle. The Devil had at last had enough and fled the scene, leaving the laird victorious. How things went with him after that, tradition does not say, though, says Robertson, it can be taken for granted that the Devil never returned.

CORA LINN, LANARKSHIRE

The ruins of a fifteenth-century fortress, anciently a seat of the Bannatyne family, can be seen perched above the Cora Linn or Corehouse Fall (marked on modern maps as Falls of Clyde), a spectacular cascade a little upstream of New Lanark in the Clyde Valley. 'Linn' means 'pool', and 'Cora' is said to have been a daughter of Malcolm II (r. 1005–34). The princess's tragic history is related in the nineteenth-century *History of Lanark*:

While hunting in the forest, she had accidentally detached herself from her attendants, and in her search for them, discovering a youth wandering in that lone place; fear seized her, and she urged

her palfrey to its utmost speed . . . Her flight, however, was much impeded by the thickness of the woods; and the youth, who, struck at her amazing beauty, and with dread for her impending fate, had followed after her, gained ground, exclaiming 'stop, O stop'; but reached the brink only in time, to behold her now unrestrainable steed bound over the precipice, into the dreadful cataract, and the boiling waters bury her beneath their dashing foam.

The etymology is a fiction: 'Cora' comes from *currach*, 'marshy area', so the name is merely descriptive.

COUTHALLEY CASTLE, LANARKSHIRE

Couthalley or Cowdaily Castle near Carnwath was once the residence of the Somerville family, reports Robert Chambers in *Popular Rhymes of Scotland* (1826). The first Somerville is said to have come from France, and dispossessed the former proprietor of Cowdaily, 'some of whose vassals he subjected to his authority, though, it appears, without succeeding in attaching them very faithfully to his interests,' Chambers comments.

A good deal of the building had been demolished in Somerville's attack, and the new lord decided that since there was so much construction work to do in any case, he might as well relocate the castle to a better position.

But against this design he found circumstances in strong opposition. As the country people say, 'what of the wall he got built during the day was regularly *dung down* at night.'

Somerville suspected his watchmen's good faith, and therefore undertook guard duty in person. This had no effect in saving his building, for who should come to demolish it but the Devil himself, with four or five attendant demons. These fell to 'like men cutting rice', and undid all the work of the day, chanting the while a rhyme:

'Tween the Rae-hill and Loriburnshaw,
There ye'll find Cowdaily wa',   [wall]
And the foundations laid on Ern.   [Iron]

Somerville bowed to superior force and rebuilt the castle on its original foundations, 'which were of iron', says Chambers. The same architecture was reported of the church at ST VIGEANS (North East), which was said to be supported beneath by iron bars: iron was traditionally used as protection against the supernatural.

Chambers supposes that some of the vassals of the former Lord of Cowdaily impersonated evil spirits in order to frighten the French watchmen, while any Scots whom Somerville had pressed into his service 'considered the whole transaction as a piece of good sport, and connived at it out of secret enmity to their new master'. This is an overly rational explanation of a widely told story in which buildings are moved, or prevented from being moved, by devils, fairies, or even angels, as at RUABHAL (Western Isles).

CRAUFURDLAND BRIDGE, NEAR KILMARNOCK, AYRSHIRE

In his *Popular Rhymes of Scotland*, first published in 1826, Robert Chambers gives a story of a treasure with, like so many other treasures, a supernatural guardian. The popular belief, he writes, is that for many ages past a pot of gold has lain hidden at the bottom of a pool beneath a waterfall below Craufurdland Bridge, about three miles from Kilmarnock.

Many attempts have been made to recover this treasure, but something always occurred to prevent a successful issue. The last was early in the last century, by the Laird of Craufurdland himself, at the head of a party of his domestics, who first dammed up the water, then emptied the pool of its contents, and had just heard their instruments clink on the kettle, when a brownie called out of a bush:

'Pow, pow!
Craufurdland tower's a' in a low!'
[on fire]

Whereupon the laird left the scene, followed by his servants, and ran home to save what he could.

They found that there was no fire at the house. When they returned to their treasure-hunt, they found the water cascading once more over the falls. Now convinced that a power beyond the human was opposed to his researches, the laird gave up the attempt.

Whether this tradition was based on fact or was 'a mere fiction of the peasants' brain', says Chambers, was impossible to tell, but it was a well-authenticated fact that a later attempt to find the treasure had been brought to a halt in circumstances roughly similar. At about the beginning of the nineteenth century, one of the tenants of the estate, then a boy, went with a friend one summer evening at midnight to try to find the pot of gold. They had made a dam and baled out the water, and were about to start digging for the kettle, when they heard a voice high overhead calling out in distress for someone to help right a cartload of hay which had overturned. They stopped what they were doing and ran up the road, where they found that such an accident had indeed taken place. After helping right the cart, they returned to the stream, only to find their dam gone and the stream pouring into the pool as usual.

This convinced them, as it had the laird in the previous story, that all attempts to find the treasure would be in vain.

CULZEAN CASTLE, MAYBOLE, AYRSHIRE

Culzean Castle, perched on a cliff over-hanging the sea on the coast of Carrick, had its beginnings in a late medieval tower house called the House of the Cove, the principal seat of the Kennedys. In the eighteenth century, under the ninth and tenth Earls of Cassillis, this was trans-formed into one of Scotland's finest coun-try houses by the architect Robert Adam.

The owners of Culzean (pronounced 'Culain') were known as the Lairds o' Co', because of the 'co's' or caves beneath it. According to Black's *Picturesque Tourist of Scotland* (1844) there are six caves, but Francis Grose in *The Antiquities of Scot-land* (1789–91) says three, and both are partly right, since the three main caves consist of interconnecting caverns. These were, Grose adds, 'well known for the leg-endary tales related of them'. At least one of these was known to Robert Burns, who opens 'Halloween' (1785) with:

Upon that night, when fairies light
        On Cassilis Downans dance,
Or owre the lays [fields], in splendid
    blaze,
        On sprightly coursers prance;
Or for Colean the rout is ta'en,
        Beneath the moon's pale beams;
There, up the Cove, to stray an' rove
        Amang the rocks and streams
            To sport that night . . .

He explains in his notes that 'Cassilis Downans' is the name given to 'Certain little, romantic, rocky, green hills, in the neighbourhood of the ancient seat of the Earls of Cassilis' and that the 'Cove' is 'A

Robert Burns (1759–96) is widely regarded as the national poet of Scotland. He wrote about many aspects of the country's folklore, including the supernatural traditions connected with Culzean Castle in his poem 'Halloween'.

noted cavern near Colean house, called the Cove of Colean: which, as well as Cassilis Downans, is famed in country story for being a favourite haunt of fairies.'

Robert Chambers, in *Popular Rhymes of Scotland* (1826), gives a story about these fairies which he says had appeared 'some years ago' in the Liverpool periodical *Kaleidoscope*:

One morning, a very little boy, carrying a small wooden can, addressed the laird near the castle gate, begging for a little ale for his mother, who was sick: the laird directed him to go to the butler and get his can filled; so away he went as ordered. The butler had a barrel of ale on tap, but about half full, out of which he proceeded to fill the boy's can; but, to his extreme surprise, he emptied the cask, and still the little can was not nearly full.

The lad insisted on his rights: a full can he had been promised, and a full can he meant to have. The butler was unwilling to broach another barrel, but the laird ordered him to fill the boy's can if it took all the ale in the cellar. Another cask was accordingly opened, but hardly had a drop been drawn from it when the can was full, and the little boy departed with expressions of gratitude.

Some years later at the wars in Flanders (Chambers does not specify dates, but may mean the Dutch wars against the Spanish in the mid sixteenth century), the laird was taken prisoner and condemned to die. His dungeon was strongly barricaded, but the night before his execution was due to take place the doors suddenly flew open. There stood the little boy, the same who had begged ale for his mother. He addressed the prisoner, saying:

'Laird o' Co',
Rise an' go.'

This was 'a summons', says Chambers, 'too welcome to require repetition'. The little boy led the laird from the prison, took him on his small shoulders, and flew off with him, soon setting him down at his own gate on the very spot where they had first met. Before he vanished, the boy said to the laird:

'Ae guid turn deserves anither –
Tak' ye that for bein' sae kind to my auld
    mither.'

The magical vessel, the flight with the fairies, and the reward for kindness are found in a number of other tales, but the outcome – rescue from death – is more unusual. The closest parallel is the story told by Sir Walter Scott in 1802 of Sir Godfrey MacCulloch of MYRTON CASTLE (Dumfries & Galloway).

DALRY, CUNNINGHAME, AYRSHIRE

Dalry in Cunninghame, later an industrial town, was once a haunt of the supernatural.

It was possessed of an 'elf house', a cave overlooking Caaf Water, its main entrance poised above the stream some forty feet (12 m) below. Inside it was long and narrow, with a heavy, massive roof held up on rocky pillars. Here lived the fairies. In later times, Covenanters fleeing persecution took refuge there.

More to be feared than the fairies were the witches and warlocks, of which the parish had more than its share. They were said to roam the countryside nightly in company with Satan, and a man called William Mackie had an encounter with them on the Ward Farm, later writing down his experience as a warning to others. As William Robertson in *Historical Tales and Legends of Ayrshire* (1889) tells it:

He was late out that night, and proceeding homewards. Suddenly the sound of the bagpipes filled the air, and then he heard sung by a multitude of voices, to the tune of 'O'er the hills and far awa',' one of those doggerel ditties so much affected by the witches of the age. Then, round him came hundreds of men and women, all in white, short dresses, and carrying wands in their hands. They hemmed him about. He rushed hither and thither to break from the infernal ring. The sweat poured from him with fear, and the very hair on his head stood up; and it was only after the most desperate exertions that he effected his escape. When he did, however, by the blessing of God, emerge from the legion of the unclean, they disappeared as if by magic.

Many of those he saw in the crowd were already known to him as neighbours, and one was an elder of the kirk which he attended.

Robert Burns talks of witches assembling at the church in ALLOWAY in 'Tam o' Shanter' (1791), and John Barbour in

Unique Traditions (1886) records a similar gathering in St John's Town of Dalry, Kirkcudbrightshire.

DOLPHINTON, LANARKSHIRE

The *New Statistical Account of Scotland* (1845) gives the story of a Brownie at Fortalice of Dolphinton, anciently the manor of Dolfine, elder brother of the first Earl of Dunbar. The Brownie, like most of his kind, worked at night threshing the corn, and in gratitude was given some clothes which were left at the scene of his nocturnal labours. Offended by the gift, he left the place for ever, uttering the words:

Sin' ye've gien me a harden ramp,
Nae mair of your corn I will tramp.

A 'harden ramp' is a shirt made of very coarse linen or hemp. His rhyme is reminiscent of one quoted by Reginald Scot in 1665:

Since thou layest me, hempen, hampen,
Here I'll no longer tread nor stampen.

Here too a coarse shirt made of hemp seems to have been given, and the implication is that these Brownies resented the cheap, unpleasant, uncomfortable material rather than the clothes or reward as such. This is explicit in one story of a Lincolnshire Brownie, who complained when the farmer gave him a hempen shirt, and said:

Had you given me linen gear,
I would have served you many a year.

On the whole, however, it was a bad idea to give any clothes or presents at all unless you actually wanted to get rid of your Brownie, as was the case in one version of the story of BODESBECK FARM (Dumfries & Galloway).

See also BROWNIES (p. 80).

DUNDONALD CASTLE, KYLE, AYRSHIRE

An Ayrshire tradition recorded by Robert Chambers in his *Popular Rhymes of Scotland*, first published in 1826, concerns Dundonald Castle, historically the seat of King Robert II, who died there in 1390. According to an Ayrshire popular rhyme:

Donald Din
Built his house without a pin.

Chambers explains this with the legend of the castle's origin:

According to tradition, it was built by a hero named Donald Din, or Din Donald, and constructed entirely of stone, without the use of wood – a supposition countenanced by the appearance of the building, which consists of three distinct stories, arched over with strong stone-work, the roof of one forming the floor of another.

Donald, the builder, was originally a poor man, but had the faculty of dreaming lucky dreams. One night he dreamed three times that if he went to London Bridge he would become a wealthy man. Trusting the dream, he made the journey to London, where he fell into conversation with another man who happened to be looking over the parapet of the bridge. After a while, Donald confided in this stranger the secret of why he had come to London Bridge.

The stranger told him that he had made a very foolish errand, for he himself had once had a similar vision, which directed him to go to a certain spot in Ayrshire, in Scotland, where he would find a vast treasure, and, for his part, he had never once thought of obeying the injunction. From his description of the spot, the sly Scotsman at once perceived that the treasure in question must be concealed in no other place than his own humble *kail-yard* at home, to which he immediately repaired, in full expectation of finding it. Nor was he disappointed; for, after destroying many good and promising cabbages, and completely cracking credit with his wife, who esteemed him mad, he found a large potful of gold coin, with the proceeds of which he built a stout castle for himself, and became the founder of a flourishing family.

'The treasure at home' is an international tale, known from Denmark to Sicily. It was probably introduced to Europe via oriental collections of tales such as *The Thousand and One Nights*. The earliest known example in Britain is the Norfolk legend of 'The Pedlar of Swaffham', recorded in the seventeenth century by Sir William Dugdale in 1652 and by the Yorkshire diariest Abraham de la Pryme in 1699, and widely circulated in the eighteenth and nineteenth centuries as a chapbook and a children's book. Versions are localised in many places in Scotland: James Hogg includes one in his *Winter Evening Tales* (1820), where he makes the destination Kelso Bridge, but all the other tales refer to London Bridge.

Why should London Bridge be such a lodestone for dreamers and visionaries? It was a wonder in its day, and indeed remains so. Today's bridge, opened by Elizabeth II in March 1973, is the fifth bridge to cross the Thames at or near this point. The first, a little way downstream of the present site, was probably built in the year of the Roman invasion in 43 CE, and its potential as a trading post was recognised from the beginning. Its successors were lined with shops and other buildings, and it passed into folklore as a symbol of wealth — as in the nursery rhyme 'London Bridge is Broken Down', possibly in existence by the reign of Charles II, and seemingly the last vestige of a game or dance mentioned by the Scot-

tish author Sir Thomas Urquhart in his translation of Rabelais' *Gargantua* (1653). As the song says, gravel and stone will wash away, iron and steel will bend and bow, but build it up with silver and gold and it will endure. The 'broken bridge' game is known in many countries, and sometimes particular bridges are mentioned, always important ones. In Britain for many centuries the bridge most vital to civic and national prosperity was London Bridge, its symbolic value translated into strict monetary terms when the nineteenth-century bridge designed by John Rennie was sold in 1969 for a million pounds. It is now in Arizona.

While stories of buried treasure are told all over the country, only in London, as everyone knew, were the streets paved with gold. In legend this fabulous bridge became a path to success: Din Donald was not the only man from afar to find his heart's desire there.

FINNIESTON QUAY, GLASGOW

George Macpherson's *Highland Myths and Legends* (2001) tells a story of 'Iain Dhu', who was apparently well known in many places not only as a 'roving sailor' but as having some magic power as well.

Having been ashore for some time and run short of money, Iain went down to Finnieston Quay in Glasgow to see if he could get a job. Lying ready to sail was a ship he knew, and it turned out to be short-handed. Before Iain could board, however, the captain recognised him and instructed the mate, 'Don't take that man on, he only causes bother with the crew.'

'Is that the way of it?' responded Iain. 'I tell you now this ship will never sail without me aboard her.'

The mate, however, obeyed the captain's commands to cast off but to his and the crew's surprise and horror as fast as they cast off the hawsers they ran themselves back out through the hawse holes and lashed themselves to the bollards on the pier.

After several attempts to cast off, the captain finally gave in and let Iain sign on for the voyage. As soon as he stepped aboard, the hawsers untied themselves from the bollards, and all was as it should be. 'It is claimed that this happening is recorded on the ship's log and can be seen in the Lloyds register of ships,' concludes Macpherson, who is a compelling story-teller but sadly deficient in references: as he never tells what the ship's name was, there is no way of verifying the story.

FIRTH OF CLYDE, RENFREWSHIRE

Once when a girl who lived at Port Glasgow died of consumption, her funeral procession was halted by a mermaid in the Firth of Clyde, who appeared from the waves and cried:

> If they wad drink nettles in March,
>   And eat muggans in May,
> Sae mony braw maidens
>   Wadna gang to the clay.

Nettle tea was a country remedy for consumption, as was 'muggans' or mugwort, mentioned also in the song of the Mermaid of Galloway whose favourite haunt was DALBEATTIE BURN (Dumfries & Galloway).

Mugwort, muggins, and muggans are all country names for *Artemisia vulgaris*, a member of the daisy family which grows in waste places all over Britain. It was believed to ease period pains, and perhaps the idea that it stemmed blood-flow led to its use in cases of tuberculosis where blood was coughed up. As its Latin name implies, the plant was associated with Artemis or Diana, virgin goddess of the moon who also had power over lunar cycles, hence menstruation, and childbirth. She was sometimes represented in half-fish form, and considered to care for lakes and rivers, lending particular interest to the fact that it is a mermaid who recommends the use of mugwort in these Scottish stories.

GAMES LOUP, CARRICK, AYRSHIRE

On the road from Ballantrae to Girvan, just past SAWNEY BEAN'S CAVE (p. 203), a precipitous cliff overhangs the sea, and is said to be the scene of the crimes of a Scottish Bluebeard. As the Reverend C. H. Dick tells the story in *Highways and Byways in Galloway and Carrick* (1916):

> A laird of Carleton amassed wealth by marrying heiresses and then throwing them over this precipice into the sea. He was about to add one more to the series of his matrimonial iniquities by drowning a lady called May Collean or Culzean when he came by a violent end. According to the ballad, however, he had not married the lady, but had merely abducted her and was going to content himself with robbing her of her personal belongings.

The ballad referred to is 'May Colven', which tells us that the girl is her father's only heir. 'False Sir John' comes wooing her, so persistently that she agrees to run away with him:

> He went down to her father's bower,
>   Where all the steeds did stand,
> And he's taken one of the best steeds
>   That was in her father's land.

> He's got on and she's got on,
>   And fast as they could flee,
> Until they come to a lonesome part,
>   A rock by the side of the sea.

'Loup off the steed,' says false Sir John,
  'Your bridal bed you see;
For I have drowned seven young ladies,
  The eight one you shall be.'

But in *this* lady he has met his match. He
bids her take off her embroidered shoes
and her silk gown, whereupon she asks
him to turn his back, 'For it never became
a gentleman / A naked woman to see.'
Foolishly he does so (apparently it does
not occur to him that, as he will see her
naked when he turns to kill her, this is a
trick) and she throws him into the sea.
Though he begs her to save him from
drowning, her response is icy:

  'No help, no help, O false Sir John,
    No help, nor pity thee;
  Tho seven king's-daughters you have
    drownd,
    But the eight shall not be me.'

'May Colven' is a variant of 'Lady Isabel
and the Elf Knight', itself a version of a
ballad known in both the south and the
north of Europe, and better preserved in
Scandinavia, Germany, and the Netherlands than in Britain. Whereas false Sir
John is a mortal though wicked man, the
Elf Knight is a supernatural seducer: his
Dutch incarnation, Heer Halewijn (a forebear of Harlequin) sang a magical song
which made all who heard it long to be
with him. A king's daughter asked her
father if she might go to Halewijn: 'No,'
he replied, 'those who go that way never
come back.' So too said her mother and
sister, but her brother's answer was that
she might do as she pleased as long as she
kept her honour. She put on gorgeous
clothes, took the best horse from the
stable, and rode with Halewijn until they
came to a gallows on which hung many
women. Offered the choice between the
rope and the sword, she chose the sword,
only asking him to take off his coat, for a
maiden's blood would spurt out strongly,

and it would be a pity to spoil his finery.
Seizing her chance – and the sword – she
struck off his head, which still spoke,
asking her to blow his horn and to rub
salve on his neck. She refused to do a
murderer's bidding, and took the head by
the hair. Having washed the head in a
spring she rode home, meeting Halewijn's
mother as she went and telling her that her
son was gone hunting and would never be
seen again. Coming to her father's gate,
she blew the horn 'like any man', and the
family held a feast with the head on the
table.

As to how the Scottish ballad came to be
localised at Games Loup, the Reverend Mr
Dick gives no clue, but the cliff is a highly
dramatic and appropriate setting.

GLASGOW

The site of Glasgow Cathedral is supposed to have been a seat of religion since
the beginning of the sixth century, when
St Mungo settled as a hermit on the spot.

This medieval seal of the bishops of Glasgow
shows St Mungo with a ring and a fish, symbols of
his most famous miracle, which was to retrieve a
ring from the belly of a salmon and thus save the
queen's reputation.

'Mungo', derived from Brythonic *my-nghu* ('dear one'), is how he is usually known in Scotland, although his baptismal name is given as Kentigern or Cyndeyrn, meaning 'royal prince'. The earliest accounts of his life, dating from the eleventh century, contain many legendary themes, and even if he was a real person, the tales attached to his name have given him mythic status. One story associates him with Lailoken, the 'Wild Merlin' of Lowland tradition, said to be buried at POWSAIL BURN (Lothian & Borders).

Perhaps the most famous of Mungo's miracles is that of the ring and the fish, retold in Robert Chambers's *Book of Days* from the account in the *Acta Sanctorum* (1643):

A queen, having formed an improper attachment to a handsome soldier, put upon his finger a precious ring which her own lord had conferred upon her. The king, made aware of the fact, but dissembling his anger, took an opportunity, in hunting, while the soldier lay asleep beside the Clyde, to snatch off the ring, and throw it into the river. Then returning home along with the soldier, he demanded of the queen the ring he had given her.

The queen urgently requested her ring back from the soldier, who of course did not have it. In terror she then consulted St Mungo, 'who knew of the affair before being informed of it'. The saint went fishing, caught a salmon in whose stomach the missing ring was found, and returned the jewel to the queen.

She joyfully went with it to the king, who, thinking he had wronged her, swore he would be revenged upon her accusers; but she, affecting a forgiving temper, besought him to pardon them as she had done. At the same time, she confessed her error to Kentigern, and solemnly vowed to be more careful of her conduct in future.

The tale is not unique: a similar miracle is attributed to St Egwin of Evesham Abbey in Worcestershire. A later and more down-to-earth version, involving no saintly or other supernatural influence, is told of James VI at FALKLAND (Central & Perthshire), and ultimately the theme can be traced back to the *Histories* of Herodotus (fifth century BCE), in which Polycrates, ruler of Samos, was said to have thrown a precious ring into the sea in order to protect himself against Nemesis, always in wait for those who were too successful. Fate, however, could not be evaded, and a short while later the tyrant was presented at dinner with a fish which proved to have swallowed the ring. His alliance with Egypt was broken off as a consequence, the pharaoh believing that such luck could in the end lead only to disaster.

Another legend reported by Robert Chambers in 1827 as having been long current in Glasgow is that 'upwards of a hundred years ago' a citizen reported that passing through the cathedral graveyard at midnight he had seen one of his neighbours, recently deceased and buried, rise from his tomb and dance a jig with the Devil, who played on the bagpipes a tune called 'Whistle o'er the lave o't' (Whistle over the rest of it).

The civic dignitaries and ministers were so sincerely scandalised at this intelligence, that they sent the town-drummer through the streets next morning, to forbid any one to whistle, sing, or play, the infernal tune in question.

The Devil was said elsewhere to be an expert on the pipes, stories of his prowess being related at ALLOWAY among other places. George Sinclair in 1685 wrote:

As the Devil is originally the Author of Charms, and Spells, so is he the Author of several baudy Songs, which are sung. A reverend Minister told me, that one who was the Devils Piper, a wizzard confest to him, that at a Ball of dancing, the Foul Spirit taught him a Baudy Song to sing and play, as it were this night, and ere two days past all the Lads and Lasses of the town were lilting it throw the street. It were abomination to rehearse it.

See also SAINTS OF SCOTLAND (p. 490); SUICIDAL ARTISTS AND ARCHITECTS (p. 156).

GRIEVEHILL, NR NEW CUMNOCK, AYRSHIRE

In *Folk Lore and Genealogies of Uppermost Nithsdale* (1904), William Wilson passes on an anecdote concerning a wraith (a simulacrum of a living person) seen the day before his death by an Ayrshire miner.

When a Dr Simpson was the minister at the North United Presbyterian Church, Sanquhar, one of the most regular members of his congregation was Joseph Black, who lived at Grievehill, near New Cumnock. His seat in church was seldom empty, though this entailed a walk of close on twenty miles. As he generally attended both morning and evening services, his journey home was nearly always in the dark.

The last time he was to hear Dr Simpson, he had attended the evening service, then set out for home. When he had passed the farm of Gateside and was drawing near the 'Brunt Houses', near Wellstrand, he became aware of a figure resembling a man walking beside him. He had not noticed him approach, nor heard his footsteps, and the figure moved slowly along with a strange gliding motion.

At first Black thought it must be his own shadow, but saw it could not be, as the figure was between himself and the moon. Though alarmed, he had sufficient presence of mind to note that it looked like him in every detail, down to the bonnet and plaid. It continued to accompany him as far as the Bank Wood, when it disappeared as mysteriously as it came, without ever speaking.

When he reached home, Joseph told his wife what he had seen. They then had supper and went to bed, but had not been there long when they were suddenly waked by a crash as if part of the house had fallen down. They sprang out of bed and searched the place, which was quickly done as the house had only one room, but found nothing to account for the noise.

They went back to bed, but had not got to sleep before another crash came, which this time sounded as if all the crockery on the china shelf had been dashed to the floor. Getting up again and striking a light, they were more astounded than ever to find everything still in place.

It did not seem worthwhile trying to sleep any more, so they had some breakfast and after prayers Joseph went to the mine. He had just got to his place and begun work when he was buried by a sudden fall from the roof. When he was dug out it was discovered that his back was broken, and he died soon after. His widow often spoke of her husband's having walked with his wraith and of the mysterious noises on the eve of his death.

See also SECOND SIGHT (p. 470).

INVERKIP, RENFREWSHIRE

In 1662 a trial took place at Inverkip of witches from Gourock and Greenock, one of them a teenage girl called Mary Lamont. Charles Kirkpatrick Sharpe calls her confession an 'extraordinary document . . . well worthy of preservation', and prints it in his 'Prefatory Notice' to Robert Law's *Memorialls* (1818).

The Vampire with Iron Teeth

On the evening of 23 September 1954, Constable Alex Deeprose was called to an incident at the Southern Necropolis, a graveyard in the Gorbals district of Glasgow. Previously there had been some vandalism at the cemetery and the constable was expecting something similar, but he was amazed at the scale of what he found. Hundreds of children, aged from around five to twelve years old, had assembled, many carrying primitive weapons, to hunt for a 'vampire with iron teeth' which had killed and eaten 'two wee boys'. The first newspaper account, in the *Bulletin* of 24 September 1954, quoted Deeprose's comments on the situation:

> 'When I appeared I felt like the Pied Piper of Hamelin. All shapes and sizes of children streaming after me, all talking at once and telling me of the "vampire" with iron teeth. This I could handle, but when grown-ups approached me and asked earnestly "Is there anything in this vampire story?" it made me think.'

The children dispersed as darkness fell, but the following evening a similar crowd assembled, and local press reports were taken up and repeated around the world. One reason for the widespread interest is that the occurrence was interpreted by commentators at the time as evidence of the harmful influence of American 'horror comics'. No specific example was brought to light, however, of any comic featuring a vampire with iron teeth. While the concept of a 'vampire' may well have arisen from reading or from the cinema, a broader consideration of this 'hunt' suggests that it had deeper roots.

Did the notion of 'iron teeth' have some other origin? In the Old Testament we find a 'beast, terrible and dreadful and exceedingly strong; and it had great iron teeth' (Daniel 7:7), and there is evidence that Glasgow children were familiar with the idea long before they read horror comics. Early in the nineteenth century, children living near Glasgow Green referred to a local woman as 'Jenny with the iron teeth'. It is possible that they did so because their parents had scared them with rumours like those in a Scottish dialect poem by Alexander Anderson, published in the 1870s and appearing in later anthologies for schools, which bore the title 'Jenny wi the airn teeth'. It is written as if by a mother who is trying to get her child to go to sleep and threatens that, if he does not, 'Jenny wi the airn teeth' will come, sink her teeth into his 'plump wee sides' and take him to her den. Anderson was probably drawing on folk traditions of terrifying figures used by parents to control their offspring. This is not confined to Scotland.

Glasgow's Southern Necropolis, overlooked by tower blocks, was the site of an extraordinary 'vampire hunt' in 1954.

In Shropshire and the Lake District, Jenny or Jinny Greenteeth was a bogey invoked by adults in the late nineteenth and early twentieth centuries to keep the young away from potentially dangerous places. She was said to haunt certain stretches of water, waiting to pull little children beneath the surface and eat them with her sharp green teeth.

Very close to where the vampire hunt later took place, children had assembled in the 1930s to search for 'Spring-Heeled Jack', a mysterious figure whose special boots supposedly enabled him to leap on his victims and then make his escape. Rumours of this ogre had begun in England in the early nineteenth century, and his legend remained in the popular imagination throughout Britain until well into the twentieth century, appearing in plays and weekly 'penny dreadfuls'. Elsewhere in Glasgow, a banshee and a White Lady were similarly searched for by groups of children. Unlike the vampire hunt, these incidents appear not to have been recorded at the time, but were recalled to adults' memories by mention of the events in 1954. An appeal in the early 1980s for witnesses of the vampire hunt brought many responses mentioning the earlier experiences, though only two recalling those of 1954. One correspondent remembered older children laughing at the younger ones for taking the vampire story seriously, while another had travelled about a mile to reach the cemetery, only to find the gates shut.

Reports of a malign presence might be frightening, but they would also arouse curiosity. In overcrowded areas like the Gorbals where young people spent a good deal of their leisure time in the street, company would give children courage to seek out a terror rather than flee from it. Monster-hunting may be a largely overlooked aspect of Scottish childhood.

One passage involves milking cows with a hair tether, as described at DELORAINE (Lothian & Borders). Mary also tells how she and other witches danced to the Devil's music; for once he was not playing the bagpipes, but sang to them. She delivered herself to the Devil by putting one hand on the top of her head, the other to the sole of her foot, and giving to him all between the two. After that he gave her a new name, Clowts, and told her to call him Serpent when she wished to speak to him. He pinched her very painfully on her right side but then healed the place by stroking it, and this was her witch-mark. Such marks were seen by witch-finders as proof of Satanic allegiance, as at INVERNESS (Southern Highlands).

On one occasion she and some other witches met with the Devil in the likeness of a brown dog:

> The end of their meitting [meeting] was to raise stormie weather to hinder boats from the killing fishing; and shee confessed that shee, Kettie Scot, and Margrat Holm, cam to Allan Orr's house in the likeness of kats, and followed his wif into the chalmer [chamber], where they took a herring owt of a barrell, and having taken a byt off it, they left it behind them; the qlk [which] herring the said Allan his wif did eat, and yairefter [thereafter] taking heavy disease, died.

The last item in her statement concerns the KEMPOCK STONE, which she and some other witches intended to cast into the sea 'thereby to destroy boats and shipes'. This plan, however, was evidently not carried out.

All the details Mary reports are well attested by other accounts and trial documents. Her confession is a classic account of witchcraft practices and beliefs of the time.

See also WITCH-HUNTS (p. 270).

KEMPOCK STONE, INVERKIP, RENFREWSHIRE

Overlooking Kempock Point, on the Firth of Clyde, is the Kempock Stone, a grey mica-schist monolith as tall as a man, presumed to have been erected in prehistoric times for a ritual or funerary purpose. In the nineteenth century, local antiquaries with lurid imaginations proposed that it was once a pagan altar at which the Druids worshipped, and that 'it was wont to gleam, more than two thousand years ago, in the light of the Baal-fire, with the blood of human sacrifices flowing round its base.'

However little truth there is in this ahistorical idea, the stone was for centuries an object of reverence. It is vaguely human in shape, resembling a bent old crone, and was often known as Granny Kempock or Kempoch, in line with the custom of addressing elderly witches and wise women as 'Granny' (similarly, a statue-menhir in Guernsey is known as La Gran'mère du Chimquière). Marriages in the district were not regarded as lucky unless the married pair passed round the monument and thus received Granny Kempoch's blessing, and the stone was also credited with great powers over wind and wave. Earth from around its base used as ballast was thought to protect a ship from evil, and according to the Reverend David Macrae, writing in 1880, 'sailors and fishermen were wont to take a basketful of sand from the shore and walk seven times round Granny Kempoch, chanting a weird song, to insure for themselves a safe and prosperous voyage.' A coven of witches once planned to assault the stone, as reported in the confession of Mary Lamont at INVERKIP.

Many standing stones are reported to move at midnight, and Granny Kempoch was rumoured to turn round three times as the hour struck. Other local legends variously had it that a monk used to sell his blessings to ships on this spot, and that a witch who for years lived beside the stone sold favourable winds to sailors. The practice was widely known: Bessie Miller and Mammie Scott were both reported to have traded with sailors for fair winds in STROMNESS (Orkney & Shetland Islands), and fishermen are said to have poured water on the Weeping Stone at FLADDA-CHUAIN (Western Isles) for the same purpose.

As belief in the stone's magic faded, some people became less reverential. On Hogmanay night, the Gourock lads would go and dress Granny Kempoch in a shawl, cap, and apron, ready for New Year's morning. Nonetheless the well-known landmark was fondly regarded, visible to ships sailing up or down the Firth of Forth, and a paddle-steamer was named after her in 1940.

KNOCKDOLIAN CASTLE, COLMONELL, AYRSHIRE

Robert Chambers writes in his *Popular Rhymes of Scotland* (1826):

> The old house of Knockdolion stood near the water of Girvan, with a black stone at the end of it. A mermaid used to come from the water at night, and taking her seat upon this stone, would sing for hours, at the same time combing her long yellow hair. The lady of Knockdolion found that this serenade was an annoyance to her baby, and she thought proper to attempt getting quit of it, by causing the stone to be broken by her servants. The mermaid, coming next night, and finding her favourite seat gone, sang thus:

> 'Ye may think on your cradle – I'll think on my stane;

> And there'll never be an heir to Knock-dolion again.'

> Soon after, the cradle was found overturned, and the baby dead under it. It is added that the family soon after became extinct.

Although Chambers speaks of 'Knockdolion' as being near Girvan Water, he is a river too far north, and is speaking of Knockdolian Castle, now a listed ancient monument, on the River Stinchar, which flows out at Ballantrae.

A similar legend of a mermaid's curse is told by R. H. Cromek in *Remains of Nithsdale and Galloway Song* (1810) concerning DALBEATTIE BURN (Dumfries & Galloway). Such apparently simple little tales are freighted with meaning, which through successive retellings can grow and deepen. While the story is at bottom a warning against destroying supernatural haunts, Chambers, writing in an age of non-belief among the educated, clearly heard it as one against human intolerance. As he says, 'One can see a moral in such a tale – the selfishness of the lady calling for some punishment.' If the lady of Knockdolian in question was as high-handed with her servants as with the mermaid, they may have told the story with some relish against her.

LADY GLEN, NR KILKERRAN, AYRSHIRE

Described by John Barbour in the 1880s as 'precipitous and wildly wooded on both sides', the Lady Glen near Kilkerran, through which flows the Lady Burn, had two different traditional explanations of its name.

One said that a young lady of the house of Kilkerran had fallen in love with a man whom her friends and family wished her not to marry. Instead, they pressed the suit of another man she did not like. As she could not have the one she loved, she decided to remain unmarried. It was said that she used to wander the banks of the little stream, whence its name of Lady Burn. She had a solitary walk and an arbour in the glen into which the brook flowed, and this became known locally as the Lady, or Lady's, Glen. The melancholy girl later fell into a consumption and died, partly of a broken heart.

The second tradition deals with the persecution of the Covenanters, rebels against the established Church who were severely dealt with in the late seventeenth century by men like 'Bluidy Clavers' of DUNDEE (North East) and General Thomas Dalyell of THE BINNS (Lothian & Borders). An elderly woman of the house of Kilkerran is said to have pitied the outlaws and hidden some of them in the glen, where she secretly brought food to them, and it was from this lady's frequent visits to the place that it got its name of Lady Glen. A man named Stevenson, said to have been one of those whom the lady protected, later lived for some years in the parish of Dailly, and was well known in the area.

As Barbour remarks, either or both of the traditions may be true, and both could have contributed to the name of the place. Certainly Presbyterians were hunted down in this area by Sir Archibald Kennedy of Culzean, 'the Claverhouse of this county', and in a churchyard not far from Kilkerran repose many of the murdered Covenanters.

LANARK

On 1 March each year the 'Whuppity Scoorie' children's race is still run. Some associate the tradition with a medieval religious ceremony, when penitent sinners would be whipped three times around the church and afterwards washed – 'scoored' – to cleanse them of their misdeeds, while others suggest a connection with the murder of William Wallace's wife by the English sheriff Heselrig, and yet a third (somewhat far-fetched) theory relates the ritual to ancient Greek history, when an attack on Pausanias by the Lydians was repulsed by Greeks bearing whips.

Whatever its distant origins, by the nineteenth century it still involved running three times round the church, but the next stage had developed into a free-for-all between the boys from Lanark and New Lanark, or between the boys and the officers of the law. By the twentieth century, 'some careful policing' had resulted in a more civilised ritual, according to Richard Stenlake writing in 1990.

Another annual ceremony is Lanimer Day, originally Landmarch Day, held on the Thursday between 6 and 12 June, when the people of Lanark walk round its boundaries. The original purpose was to inspect the boundary stones and make sure none of them had been moved over the year. The moving of landmarks is a very ancient crime indeed, mentioned in the Old Testament: 'Cursed be he that removeth his neighbour's landmark' (Deuteronomy 27:17).

LARGS, AYRSHIRE

Largs looks across the bay towards the island of Great Cumbrae. Now a town and holiday resort, it was once a village frequented by fairies. Near it, says the Reverend John Gregorson Campbell in *Superstitions of the Highlands and Islands of Scotland* (1900), the 'people' had several dwellings:

> Knock Hill was full of *elves*, and the site of the old Tron Tree, now the centre of

the village, was a favourite haunt. A sow, belonging to a man who cut down the Tron Tree, was found dead in the byre next morning.

The reprisal for interfering with a fairy site might be less savage, more of a shaming. One man at least got a dose of fairy flight, a phenomenon reported at many places, including PEAT LAW (Lothian & Borders):

A man cut a slip from an ash-tree growing near a Fairy dwelling. On his way home in the evening he stumbled and fell. He heard the Fairies give a laugh at his mishap. Through the night he was hoisted away, and could tell nothing of what happened till in the morning he found himself in the byre, astride on a cow, and holding on by its horns.

Sometimes the fairies admitted living people to their company. They took a local man one night to a pump near the Haylee Toll, where he danced with them till dawn. As in medieval tradition, the dead too might be seen among them: the gathering at the pump included a headless man.

The fairies were also given to entering human homes:

They often came to people's houses at night, and were heard washing their children. If they found no water in the house, they washed them in *kit*, or sowen water . . . They one night dropped a child's cap, a very pretty article in a weaver's house, to which they had come to get the child washed. They, however, took it away the following night.

Sowen or sowan water is the water in which oats were steeped and fermented, or in which the husks or siftings were boiled to produce a kind of porridge. The same tale is told of the trows at DUNROSSNESS (Orkney & Shetland Islands).

On one occasion, a band of four fairies who had entered a house was heard going over the bedclothes, two women laughing together first, two men coming behind and wondering aloud if the women were far ahead of them.

These Largs fairies could be helpful: 'A present of shoes and stockings made them give great assistance at out-door work.' (This, of course, is quite the reverse of what would happen if you gave clothes to those other household and farmyard drudges, the Scottish Brownie or the English hob: such gifts would infallibly make them leave your service.)

While, like Brownies, the fairies seem to have given an honest day's work and more when so minded, they were also thieves. On market days at Largs, they would go about in the crowd here and there filching a little of the wool or yarn set out for sale.

As easily offended as a Brownie, fairies were more like witches when it came to taking revenge for a slight, as the man who cut down the Tron Tree discovered, and another unwary mortal too. A hawker, carrying a basket of crockery, was met near the Noddle Burn by a fairy woman who asked for a bowl she pointed out in his basket. He refused to give it to her, and, when nearing the village he came to the top of a brae, his basket fell and all his crocks ran on edge right down to the foot. None of them was broken, except the one he had refused the fairy. 'The same day, however, the hawker found a treasure that made up for his loss. That, said the person from whom the story was heard, was the custom of the fairies; they never took anything without making up for it in some other way.'

This sounds like wishful thinking: indignant fairies were usually just plain spiteful, whether out of doors or inside people's houses: 'They were fond of spinning and weaving, and, if chid or thwarted, cut the weaver's webs at night.'

Campbell notes that these are 'genuine popular tales' that he heard at Largs 'from a servant girl, a native of the place'. As he says, they are similar to traditions in the Highlands and the north of Ireland.

THE LEE, LANARKSHIRE

The Lee, on the north bank of the Clyde a little way below Lanark, is alternatively known as Lee House, Lee Castle, or Lee Place. It is the home of the Lee Penny, the legend of which features in Sir Walter Scott's *The Talisman* (1825). In his introduction, Scott quotes an extract from the seventeenth-century 'Books of the Assemblie holden at Glasgow', in which it is said that one Gavin Hamilton of Raploch had made a complaint against Sir James Lockhart of Lee for his superstitious use of a stone set in silver for the curing of diseased cattle:

> The Assemblie having inquirit of the manner of using thereof, and particularly understood . . . that the custom is only to cast the stone in some water, and give the deceasit Cattle thereof to drink, and that the same is done without using any words, such as Charmers and Sorcereirs use in thair unlawfull practices; and considering that in nature thair are many things seen to work strange effects, whereof no human wit can give a reason, it having pleast God to give to stones and herbs a speciall vertue for healing of many informities in man and beast, advises the Brethren to surcease thair process, as therein they perceive no ground of Offence, and admonishes the said Laird of Lee, in using the said stone, to take heid that it be usit hereafter with the least scandle that possibly maybe.

Sir Simon Lockhart was one of the Scottish knights who accompanied James the Good and Lord Douglas on their expedition to the Holy Land with the heart of Robert the Bruce in 1330. In Palestine, Lockhart was said to have taken prisoner a rich emir whose old mother came to the Christian camp to pay his ransom. As well as the sum fixed she had in her purse a silver coin in the centre of which was fixed a red stone. This fell out of her purse, and she made haste to retrieve it, whereupon Lockhart demanded it in addition to the money. She agreed, and explained how it should be used: water in which it was dipped would cure all manner of ills. Lockhart then brought it back to Scotland and left it to his heirs, to whom it became known as the Lee Penny.

This history, in so far as it relates to the Penny, cannot be true if (as stated by some) the coin in which the red stone is mounted is a groat from the London Mint dating from the reign of Edward IV in the late fifteenth century. Another source identifies it as a shilling of Edward I (r. 1272–1307), in which case it is just conceivable, though unlikely, that it could have found its way to Palestine in time to be retrieved by Lockhart.

The Penny was not counted as a Luck – in other words, no harm was supposed to befall the family should it be lost – but its reputation was great. As can be seen from the passage quoted by Scott, it was excepted from the Church of Scotland's prohibition against charms in general, and during the reign of Charles I (1625–49) it was apparently lent to the citizens of Newcastle to protect them against the plague, a vast sum being pledged for its return – £1,000 according to some accounts, rising to £6,000 in others.

One cure is reported to have been that of Lady Baird of Saughtownhall near Edinburgh, who drank daily of the Penny's water and also bathed in it, and was thus relieved of symptoms of rabies. At the beginning of the nineteenth century a

This 1833 frontispiece to Sir Walter Scott's *The Talisman*, a romance of the Crusades, shows a climactic episode when a false knight's treachery is revealed to Richard the Lionheart. The novel employs the legend of the 'Lee Penny', a magic coin said to cure many ills.

Northumberland farmer took four small barrelsful of the water home with him, and at around the same time a Yorkshireman requisitioned a quantity to cure his cattle, which had been bitten by a mad dog. Use for animals apparently did nothing to reduce the Penny's power, whereas the water of ST FILLAN'S POOL (Central & Perthshire) lost its effect when a man bathed his mad bull in it.

LOGAN, KYLE, AYRSHIRE

A story sent to James Maxwell Wood by Andrew Donaldson of Ardwell, Stranraer, and printed in Wood's *Witchcraft and Superstitious Record in the South-western District of Scotland* (1922), is a good example of how witches were supposed to prey on the neighbourhood:

> At a farm-house in the vicinity of Logan an old woman, a reputed witch, was in the habit of receiving the greater part of her sustenance from the farmer and his wife. The farmer began to get tired of this sorning, and one day took his courage in both hands and turned the witch at the gate. The old woman of course was sorely displeased, and told him that he would soon have plenty of 'beef,' and in the course of a day or two many of his cattle had taken the muir-ill. Next time the old woman wanted to go to the house she was not hindered. She got her usual supply, and thereafter not another beast took the disease.

Wood defines 'sorning' as 'exacting free board and lodging', and the 'muir-ill' as 'a disease especially affecting black cattle'. Such stories of blackmail abound, and it may be that, in real life, poor old women with no means of support got a living by pretending to have the 'evil eye'. On the other hand, like the woman of DALKEITH

(Lothian & Borders) whose story was reported by Sir Walter Scott, the 'witch' of Logan may have sincerely believed in her own powers.

MAYBOLE, AYRSHIRE

A tower house at the foot of Maybole High Street is said to have been the prison of the errant wife in one of the finest traditional Scottish ballads, 'The Gypsie Laddie'. This tells the story of a lady who runs away with a gypsy, in the earliest known version named as 'Johny Faa':

> The gypsies came to our good lord's gate,
>   And wow but they sang sweetly;
> They sang sae sweet and sae very compleat,
>   That down came the fair lady.
>
> And she came tripping down the stair,
>   And a' her maids before her;
> As soon as they saw her well-far'd face,
>   They coost [cast] the glamer [glamour] o'er her.
>
> Gae tak frae me this gay mantile,
>   And bring to me a plaidie,
> For if kith and kin and a' had sworn,
>   I'll follow the gypsie laddie.

When the lord came home that night and asked for his wife, her maids and others of the household were bursting with the news that she was 'away with the gypsy laddie'. Giving orders for his black steed to be saddled, he swore he would neither eat nor sleep until he had found her. The pursuit and what happened thereafter is not related blow by blow, but in dialogue between the lord and his lady, he asking her to come home, she meeting him with refusal. However, ultimate tragedy is indicated in the final verse, implicitly spoken by Johny and his gypsy companions:

And we were fifteen well-made men,
   Altho' we were nae bonny;
And we were a' put down for ane,
   A fair young wanton lady.

The ballad seems to have been first printed in the tenth edition of Allan Ramsay's *Tea-Table Miscellany* (1740), from which these verses come.

Attempts have been made to identify the people in the story. Johnny or Johnnie Faa was a well-known name among gypsies, short for 'Egyptians' as they were once known. In 1540, a certain Johnnë Faw's right and title as Lord and Earl of Little Egypt was recognised by James V, though in the next year the 'Egyptians' were ordered to quit the realm in thirty days on pain of death. They were formally expelled from Scotland in 1609, and in 1611 Johnnë or Willie Faa was caught and sentenced to be hanged along with three other gypsies of the name of Faa. Other hangings of gypsies known as Johnnë or Johnnie Faa 'for contemptuous repairing to the country and abiding therein' are reported in 1616 and 1624, and the ballad scholar F. J. Child surmises that the ballad may have come into being not long after these executions. 'Whether this were so or not, Johnny Faa acquired popular fame, and became a personage to whom any adventure might plausibly be imputed.'

As to the lady in the story, she is not identified in the earliest ballad. However, towards the end of the eighteenth century, Ayrshire people were saying that she was the wife of the Earl of Cassilis. In a version written down from recitation in Nithsdale in 1814, the gypsies come to 'my lord Cassilis' yett [gate]', and when he catches up with her, he says:

'O wilt thou go home, my hinny and my
   heart,
   O wilt thou go home, my dearie?

And I'll close thee in a close room,
   Where no man shall come near
   thee.'

Not surprisingly, her answer is no, as before, and the fifteen gypsies, 'Black, but very bonny', lose their lives. The contributor of this version to the *Scots Magazine* fixes the date of the affair as 1643, the earl in question being John Kennedy, sixth Earl of Cassilis, a staunch Presbyterian, known in family traditions as 'the grave and solemn Earl'. He was sent to Westminster to represent the Solemn League and Covenant at an Assembly of Divines, and it was while he was away that his lady allegedly succumbed. She was Lady Jean Hamilton, third daughter of Thomas, Earl of Haddington. However, as far as is shown by historical records, including the *Historie of the Kennedyis* (early seventeenth century), this lady bore three children to her husband and never lost his affections, much less deserted him. Moreover, she died in 1642, a year before her supposed elopement. John Barbour, in *Unique Traditions* (1886), tries to get round this problem by making 'the wee amorous Countess' the much younger wife of Sir Alexander Kennedy.

It has been argued that the earl and countess got into the story by an accident of transmission, someone hearing the 'castle gate' of some versions as 'Cassilis' gate', given that, according to William Robertson, the local pronunciation of Cassilis is 'castles'. However, in *Ayrshire* (1908), Robertson notes:

In 1630 he [John, the sixth Earl] craved advice from the Council as to how to deal with certain gipsies in his capacity of bailie of Carrick; and it may have been that his association with the tradition of Johnny Faa and the Earl of Cassillis's Lady may have arisen from this incident, and from his subsequent dealing with the wanderers.

Notwithstanding this conflicting evidence, believers had 'proof' that the story was true (the 'you can see it there still' principle). According to the 1814 version, the vengeful earl indeed enclosed his wife in a room when he caught her. Robertson writes:

There stands at the foot of the High Street of Maybole a square peel of the old-fashioned type – strong-walled, built by men who meant that their handiwork should bear the brunt of war and of weather . . . and thither the Countess was conveyed. Here she was confined till the day of her death.

As a perpetual reminder of her infidelity, carved round the windows of her room were stone heads to keep fresh in her memory the fate of the gypsies. In this dreary place, she passed her time sewing a tapestry 'still in existence'; some said it lay mouldering in a chest at Culzean.

The 'square peel' is Maybole Castle, the Kennedys' town house, in which there is still a 'Countess's Room', where she is supposed to have been shut away. Presumably she was thought to be safer from future admirers there than at the Kennedys' country seat, Cassillis House, where the story begins and from which she was brought to Maybole.

A 'glamour' is defined by Sir Walter Scott in his notes to *The Lay of the Last Minstrel* (1805) as 'the magic power of imposing on the eyesight of the spectators, so that the appearance of an object shall be totally different from the reality'. He cites the transformation of Sir Michael Scot of AIKWOOD TOWER (Lothian & Borders) by the witch of Falsehope as 'a genuine operation of glamour', and adds, 'To a similar charm the ballad of Johnny Fa' imputes the fascination of the lovely Countess, who eloped with that gipsy leader.' A charm of some sort, of course, takes the responsibility for her actions away from the countess, who by implication is magically seduced into infatuation, not merely with someone below her in rank, but with the lowest of the low, a common gypsy. However, the earliest ballad is unclear on this point, for the lady herself accounts for her desertion as being the result of 'what passed yestreen', though we are not told what this was, whether her first sight of Johnny or some marital difference.

As to the lady's 'well-found face', meaning her beauty, R. H. Cromek in his *Remains of Galloway and Nithsdale Song* (1810) writes, 'There is a tradition extant, that Lord Cassilis' lady, who eloped with Johnnie Faa, the gypsie laddie, had so delicate and pure a skin, that the red wine could be seen through it while she was drinking.'

See also KIRK YETHOLM (Lothian & Borders).

MURDOSTOUN, LANARKSHIRE

See SUICIDAL ARTISTS AND ARCHITECTS (p. 156).

OLD KING COIL'S TOMB, TARBOLTON, AYRSHIRE

Speaking of Coylton, on the Water of Coyle, the *Statistical Account of Scotland* for 1798 says, 'There is a tradition, though it is believed, very ill-founded', that the village derives its name from a King Coilus who was killed in battle in the neighbourhood and buried in the church here. Fergus Loch, to the west of the church, 'is supposed by some to take its name from King Fergus, who defeated Coel King of the Britons in the adjacent field'.

According to others, however, the battle

was fought in the parish of Tarbolton, and they pointed to slabs of stone covering a burial mound known as 'King Coil's tomb' in the grounds of Coilsfield House. The tomb is probably the cairn marked near Coilsfield Mains on modern maps.

The site was investigated in May 1837 by the minister of the parish, the Reverend David Ritchie, whose report went into the *New Statistical Account* in 1845. The excavators unearthed a circular flagstone covering another, smaller stone which itself covered the mouth of an urn filled with white-coloured burned bones. Other urns were found nearby, and though no coins, armour, weapons or other implements were discovered, Ritchie notes, 'An old man remembers that his father, then a tenant on the Coilsfield estate, turned up pieces of ancient armour and fragments of bones when ploughing the "Dead-Men's-Holm."'

Though not mentioned by Daniel Defoe himself in the first edition of his *Tour Through . . . Britain* (1727), the seventh edition of 1769 'with very great Additions, Improvements, and Corrections' records that:

A . . . Trumpet resembling a crooked Horn, which has a very shrill Sound, was dug up in the Field of Battle, and is still kept in the Laird of *Caprington*'s House, called *Coilfield*, and made Use of to call his Servants and Workmen together.

In Ritchie's day, this horn was still preserved at Caprington Castle: 'It corresponds exactly with the description given of it, and it retains its shrill sound.' However, the family had no tradition as to when or where the trumpet was found.

William Robertson, who describes what he calls Old King Coil's Tomb in *Historical Tales and Legends of Ayrshire* (1889), unhesitatingly accepted the urns as supporting evidence of the 'uninterrupted tradition'

and statements of historians that Coil was buried here, and drew the same conclusions from place-names. Finding a 'Bloody Burn' and opposite its mouth a 'Dead-men's-holm', he writes, 'we are inclined to think that these names are not entirely the result of chance-work.' It seems to him a fair conclusion that at one time the stream ran red with blood, and that beneath the water meadow were buried those who fell in conflict.

Not 'chance-work', perhaps, but this is not the same as saying, as Robertson seems to have hoped, that the names have been handed down in oral tradition since the days of Coil. This was a battle-scarred area: the evidence could have been of any battle, not necessarily in the remote past. It is also possible that the names got attached to the places *because* of the legend.

At its simplest, this legend says that an ancient king called Coil met his defeat and death at the hands of the Picts and Scots somewhere in this locality, whence the place-names Coylton, Coilsford, Water of Coyle, and indeed the district-name of Kyle. The legend of Coil goes back at least as far as 1527, when Hector Boece (Boethius) published his Latin *History of the Scots*, which became highly popular for its exciting blend of fact and a great deal of colourful fiction. According to Boece, the Scots were descendants of a pharaoh's daughter called Scota. They first settled in Ireland, and later along the west coast of Scotland from Ayrshire to Argyllshire. Not long after that, ships bearing Picts arrived there from Scythia, and the Scots allowed these incomers to settle along their borders. They also gave them Scottish wives with the proviso that they should always select their kings from the female line.

At that time, says Boece, the south of Britain was ruled by 'the belleall [treacherous] British' (he equated the British with the English, and could say no good of them, but he is speaking of the ancient British kingdom of Strathclyde):

Ane king thai had wes callit Coilus
Doggit and dour, mad and malicious . . .

This Coilus or Coil stirred up trouble between the Scots and the Picts, and the Scots were forced to send to Ireland for more troops. These duly came, but when their leader, King Fergus, learned that Coil was the root cause of the disturbances, he created a new alliance with the Picts against him.

King Coil, operating out of his capital of York, set out with a great army for modern Ayrshire and Galloway, and on arrival camped overnight before the Scots' fortress, meaning to attack at dawn. However, alerted to his presence by scouts, King Fergus led a night raid on the encampment and took the British by surprise. They were utterly routed, some fleeing to safety, others, not knowing the terrain, hunted down or swallowed by the bogs:

Among these last was Coil himself: abandoned by his bodyguards, he was sucked under and smothered, leaving his name of Coil (now somewhat altered to 'Kyle') to the place as a perpetual memorial for posterity.

Boece's tale of Coilus is far from being history: to start with, he places events around 330 BCE, *before* the Scots arrived in Britain, where they did not settle until about 400 CE. On the other hand, it seems to contain some fact: the Scots really did come from Ireland, and in about 420 there really was a British king called, near enough, Coil. Early Welsh poems, prob-ably composed around the turn of the sixth and seventh centuries, speak of the 'sons of Coel', that is, the descendants of Coel, suggesting that this

man was remembered as a great king or leader. Welsh genealogies trace thirteen royal lines, no fewer than eight going back to Coel Hen Guotepauc, which can be translated as 'Old Cole the Splendid'.

It is a curious fact that several of the earliest versions of the nursery rhyme 'Old King Cole', known from the eighteenth century, seem to be Scottish. Contributed by Robert Burns to the *Scots Musical Museum* (1787–1803) is this one:

Our auld King Coul was a jolly auld
  soul
And a jolly auld soul was he
Our auld King Coul fill'd a jolly brown
  bowl
And he ca'd for his fiddlers three:
Fidell-didell, fidell-didell, quo' the
  fiddlers three;
There's no a lass in a' Scotland
Like our sweet Marjorie.

Burns does not say where he got these lyrics, but it could have been Kyle, where he spent much of his life.

PAISLEY, RENFREWSHIRE

Accounts of witches and witch-trials are often given from sources which believe wholeheartedly in the truth and wickedness of what they report. It is worth quoting from a later account, in this case that of Charles Kirkpatrick Sharpe in his 1818 introduction to Robert Law's *Memorialls*. Sharpe writes that in 1697 a number of persons were tried and condemned for bewitching one Christian Shaw, a girl of about eleven:

To sum up a long story in a few words, the young girl, who seems to have been antient in wickedness, having had a quarrel with one of the maid-servants,

Was the success of Paisley as a weaving town in the nineteenth century thanks to a former witch?

pretended to be bewitched by her, and forthwith began, according to the common practice in such cases, to vomit all manner of trash; to be blind and deaf on occasion; to fall into convulsions, and to talk a world of nonsense, which the hearers received as the quintessence of afflicted piety. By degrees, a great many persons were implicated in the guilt of the maid-servant, and no less than twenty were condemned, of whom five suffered death on the Gallo Green of Paisley; and one man, John Reid, strangled himself in prison, or, as the report went, was strangled by the devil.

This is a radical precis of the 'Narrative of the sufferings and relief of a young girl' printed in *A History of the Witches of Renfrewshire* (1809). Lengthy and harrowing though the 'Narrative' is, essentially it differs little from other accounts of late seventeenth-century witchcraft cases. There was, however, an unexpected sequel, recorded by the writer of a 1909 *History of Paisley*:

> After her youthful hysteria and vagaries, which it is to be hoped she remembered with penitential sorrow, [Christian] grew up into a sensible, or, at any rate, a skilful and industrious woman.

She became an expert at spinning and bleaching linen thread, and some of her yarn was bought by lacemakers in Bath. Encouraged by the sale, she imported a thread-mill from Holland, and with her mother and sister built up a successful business. The textile trade already existed in Paisley, as demonstrated in 'Tam o' Shanter' (1791), where Robert Burns describes the pretty witch's scanty garment as 'a cutty sark o' Paisley harn [hemp]', but Christian's activities helped to make it central to the town's economy. At the beginning of the nineteenth century, the Paisley weavers began to produce shawls in imitation of Persian

Sawney Bean the Cannibal

At some time in our remote past, it is said, Sawney Bean and his wife took up residence in a cave in the south-west of Scotland. They had children and grandchildren, and the whole family lived for many years by robbing, killing, and eating travellers. Eventually one of their intended victims escaped and led the authorities to their cave, where not only stolen goods and money were found but also, more horrifyingly, 'arms, legs, thighs, hands and feet of men, women and children . . . hung up in rows like dry'd beef'. Other human parts had been pickled. The culprits were seized, taken to Edinburgh, and executed without trial.

Near Bennane Head in South Ayrshire there is a place known as 'Sawney Bean's Cave', which has led some people to treat the story as a local legend. Although it is certainly legendary, in that no one has ever produced evidence that Sawney really existed, it cannot be said to be local in origin. The first person to associate Sawney Bean with that cave was the author Samuel Crockett, who made him a minor character in his novel *The Grey Man*, published in 1896. Prior to that, all versions of the story had Sawney living not in Ayrshire but further south, in Galloway. The linking of the cave and the cannibal originated as a literary device, but has gained popular acceptance and thus, to an extent, become traditional.

In fact we cannot regard the tale of Sawney Bean as having originated in either Galloway or Ayrshire. All the earliest evidence of the story's circulation is to be found in England. The first example appears to be a sensational book of 1734, *Lives and Actions of the most Famous Highwaymen, Murderers, Street-Robbers etc*. The name of the writer, 'Captain Charles Johnson', is almost certainly a pseudonym, and it has been suggested that the real author was Daniel Defoe. Inspiration for the account of Sawney may have come from a few poorly substantiated stories about cannibalism in remote parts of Scotland, such as those contained in the sixteenth-century chronicles of Lindsay of Pitscottie and Raphael Holinshed. The latter mentions 'a Scotish man' who during a famine in 1341 'spared not to steale children, and to kill women, on whose flesh he fed, as if he had been a woolfe', while Pitscottie's account, set in 1460 and located near ARBROATH (North East), gives prominence to the cannibal's wife and particularly one of his young daughters, depicted as inheriting a fiendish lust for human flesh.

In the eighteenth century, English chapbooks appeared giving reports of the cannibal. One pamphlet set the scene in Devon and called the protagonist 'John

Gregg', but most examples were located in Scotland and referred to 'Sawney Bean'. The name 'Sawney' is a dialect form of 'Alexander'. More significantly, it was used in the Scots language to refer to the Devil ('auld Sawnie'), and was a derogatory term in England for a Scotsman. One could therefore see the story as a piece of scaremongering anti-Scottish propaganda.

Several plays about Sawney Bean were performed in London in the early nineteenth century, but we cannot find an example of a Scot telling the story in any medium until 1843, when it was included by John Nicholson in his *Historical and Traditional Tales, in prose and verse, connected with the South of Scotland*. His version is very similar to the various

This early engraving shows the infamous Sawney Bean outside the cave where he and his family are said to have feasted on human flesh.

English texts and contains no local details, while its dating of the story to the time of James I of Scotland is probably accidental. Earlier accounts refer to 'the reign of Queen Elizabeth whilst James I governed Scotland', obviously meaning James VI of Scotland, so Nicholson's description of the Scottish king as James I seems to have been an oversight. Like Pitscottie, Nicholson emphasised the savagery of the female cannibals. Having cut the throat of a passing woman, they 'fell to sucking her blood with as great a gust as if it had been wine'.

Despite the English origins of the story, Sawney Bean now seems to be widely accepted by Scots as one of their own. He forms a definite part of local colour in Ayrshire, and is often mentioned not only in tourist guides but in works devoted to other subjects. David Steele, discussing Turnberry golf course in 1994, commented that 'perhaps the legendary cannibal Sawney Bean and his incestuous brood may have strayed this far north in search of a tasty passer-by.'

designs, and thus the paisley pattern came into being.

See also WITCH-HUNTS (p. 270).

POLLOK, GLASGOW, LANARKSHIRE

Now a residential suburb south-west of Glasgow city centre, in the seventeenth century Pollok was the setting of a notorious witch-trial. Sir George Maxwell, knighted by Charles II, was 'a person eminent for piety, learning, and other good qualifications', whose bewitching was reported in 1677 in court documents, and in 1684 by his son John in a communication to George Sinclair, Professor of Philosophy at Glasgow. John's letter begins:

> Sir, – I send you herewith the true account my father caused me write from his own mouth, which is the surest relations I can give either of his own trouble or what concerns Janet Douglas first discoverer of these pictures.

On 14 October 1676, Sir George had been suddenly taken ill, and remained in pain for seven weeks. A newcomer to Pollok was a young dumb girl, Janet Douglas, who had become friendly with Sir George's daughters, and she made them understand that his affliction was caused by one Janet Mathie, who had created a wax image of Sir George and stuck it with pins, apparently because Sir George had punished her son for breaking into his orchard. On searching Mathie's house, sure enough, the effigy was found. The woman protested that 'it was the deed of the dumb girl', but was nonetheless searched for 'insensible marks' of which many were found: this was the procedure adopted by witch-finders like 'Paterson the Pricker' at INVERNESS (Southern Highlands).

Sir George, meanwhile, had become first a little better and then much worse. On 7 January 1677, Janet Douglas wrote down that Mathie's eldest son, John Stewart, had made a new effigy, this time of clay, which was to be found hidden in his bed. Thus it was discovered to be, and John was arrested. So too was his little sister, fourteen-year-old Annabil Stewart, who next day confessed to being present when the mommet was made in the presence of 'the black gentleman' (i.e. the Devil) together with three other women, Bessie Weir, Margerey Craig, and Margaret Jackson.

From here the accusations and confessions multiplied, and a third image was found, this time under Janet Mathie's bolster in the Paisley prison. A trial was held, at which Annabil, John, and Margaret Jackson confessed, while Janet Mathie and the other two maintained their innocence. All were found guilty and condemned to be burned, except Annabil 'in regard of her nonage' (youth):

> In the meantime, both she and her brother John did seriously exhort their mother to confession; and with tears, did Annabil put her in mind of the many meetings she had with the devil in her own house; and that a summer's day would not be sufficient to relate what she had seen pass between the devil and her; but nothing could prevail with her obdured and hardened heart.

'It is to be noted,' adds Sir John Maxwell, 'that the dumb girl Janet Douglas 'doth now speak, not very distinctly, yet so as she may be understood; and is a person that most wonderfully discovers things past, and doth also understand the Latin tongue, which she never learned'.

Douglas's previous history, as revealed by herself, was one of abuse; her subsequent career, as documented by others, one of notoriety. She was at length herself imprisoned for witchcraft, scourged, and deported.

See also WITCH-HUNTS (p. 270).

SAWNEY BEAN'S CAVE, AYRSHIRE

See SAWNEY BEAN THE CANNIBAL (p. 200).

STRATHAVEN, LANARKSHIRE

In *Popular Rhymes of Scotland* (1826), Robert Chambers tells the story of a poor man of Strathaven who dreamed three times in succession that there was treasure concealed at a particular spot near Carrenduff, in the neighbourhood of the village. In reliance on his dream he went to the place and began to dig.

After working for some time, he came to what he thought was the lid of a pot, and was just about to lift it when he heard a noise overhead and looked up.

> At a little distance from the scene of his excavations, he perceived a bright blue flame issuing from a rock; which flame addressed him in a rhyme, the express words of which we have been unable to retrieve from oblivion, but of which the sense was, that the treasure was not to be found there, but somewhere on the other side of the hill.

The man obediently took up his pick and shovel and began operations again at the site pointed out by the 'poetical flame'. Here he dug for a long while but found nothing, and eventually went back to the place where he had started. Here, however, he found the hole filled in, the ground smoothed over, and all looking as if it had never been touched.

> Struck with wonder and fear, he resolved to give up the pursuit; and the conse-

quence was, that, ever since, the place has been regarded by the common people as a *fearsome spot*.

The tale starts like that of DUNDONALD CASTLE, but unfortunately for the treasure seeker a supernatural guardian is involved. The 'blue flame' is an interesting apparition: although green is the usual fairy colour, blue is more significant when fire is involved. Candles that burned blue were traditionally said to show the presence of spirits, and the Noggle of FOULA (Orkney & Shetland Islands) was wont to disappear in a blue blaze.

TINTO, LANARKSHIRE

On Tintock-tap there is a mist,
And in that mist there is a kist [chest],
And in the kist there is a caup [cup],
And in the caup there is a drap [drop];
Tak up the caup, drink aff the drap,
And set the caup on Tintock-tap.

This tongue-twister is explained by Robert Chambers in *Popular Rhymes of Scotland* (1826) as possibly relating to the large stone on the top of Tintock or Tinto which is remarkable 'for having a hole in its upper side, said to have been formed by the grasp of Sir William Wallace's thumb, on the evening previous to his defeating the English at Boghall, in the neighbourhood'. The hole, he says, is generally full of water on account of the prevailing drizzle or mist which often envelops the hill, but he comments that if this is indeed what is meant by the chest and cup mentioned, the verse must be intended as a mockery of human strength, 'for it is certainly impossible to lift the stone and drink off the contents of the hollow'. *See also* WILLIAM WALLACE (p. 204).

In his *Picture of Scotland* (1827), Chambers tells another tradition of Tinto,

William Wallace

In the late thirteenth century, William Wallace stood as a champion of Scottish independence from domination by England. In 1291, at the age of about twenty, he killed the son of an English official, and was outlawed after a second brawl. He fled to the forests and began a guerrilla campaign, leading hit-and-run raids against the foreign oppressors. One story from around this period relates that he was captured and thought to have died in prison. His body was thrown on a dung-heap, but his old nurse, coming to bury him, found that he was still alive; he recovered under her care and resumed the fight. Heselrig, sheriff of Lanarkshire, plotted to seize him, and in the raid Wallace's wife or sweetheart was killed. It is said that in revenge Wallace and his men slaughtered Heselrig and his son, and over 200 of the English.

In 1297 he scored a military triumph at Stirling and was knighted, probably by Robert the Bruce, but in 1298 the battle of Falkirk was a disaster for the Scots, and Wallace went back into hiding. Finally, in 1305, he was betrayed by one of his men, captured, and executed in London.

A verse biography of Wallace was written in the late fifteenth century by a somewhat mysterious figure known as 'Blind Harry', who claims as his authority a memoir by Wallace's contemporary John Blair – the earlier account, however, has been lost, if it ever existed. Harry includes several adventures clearly based on folklore rather than fact, for instance when Wallace's men were fleeing from their enemies and one of his followers named Faudon tired more quickly than the rest. In a 1785 version by William Hamilton:

Wallace was loath to leave him on the way
Left to approaching foes he'd fall a prey,
Urg'd him t'exert his strength, with words of love,
But all in vain, no further would he move:
The Chief enrag'd, his sword with fury drew,
And at one stroke the lagging traitor slew;
Backward, a lifeless, headless lump he lay . . .

Later, when Wallace's men were at supper, they heard a horn and went in pairs to investigate the cause. None returned, and at last Wallace was alone. He went to the gate, where to his amazement:

The frightful Faudon stood before his eyes,
Holding his bloody head in his right hand!

The phantom threw its head at Wallace, who picked it up by the hair, threw it back, and ran off. Turning, he saw Faudon standing on top of the tower he had left, which seemed to be on fire.

As described by Harry the episode has a certain rather brutal humour, a quality which spices much of the narrative, for instance when Wallace is said to have introduced himself to the captain of Lochmaben as a barber expert in cutting and shaving, before dispatching the man with his sword, or when the gigantic warrior improbably passed himself off as a girl to avoid capture. Wallace is reported as having been over six and a half foot in height, and his adversary Edward I of England is also remembered as unusually tall, making the two men's warfare a contest of giants.

The heroic patriot Sir William Wallace is remembered as a giant in stature and achievements.

Many places throughout southern Scotland are associated with Wallace's real or fictional deeds. Several sites are claimed as WALLACE'S CAVE (Glasgow & Ayrshire), where he hid from the English and mustered his troops, and the hero's mother is said to be buried at DUNFERMLINE ABBEY (Central & Perthshire). More obviously mythical is the tale reported by Robert Chambers in 1827 that Wallace left his thumb-mark on a stone on top of TINTO (Glasgow & Ayrshire). His reputation remains bright to this day, having received a new polish from the film *Braveheart* (1995). Introducing his eighteenth-century rewrite of Blind Harry's verses, Hamilton remarks that bravery is the most admired of virtues:

> It shines in none of the Heroes of Antiquity, with a truer Lustre, than in
> Sir William Wallace; and none of them have deserved better of their
> Country, than he has done.

explaining the name of the hill as meaning 'hill of fire'. He supposes it to have been used in ancient times either as an observatory or as a place of worship, and explains the cairn on its summit as having been raised by order of the priests of a now-vanished religious house, St John's kirk, who enjoined their parishioners to atone for 'offences of the flesh' by carrying loads of stones to the top of the hill.

He writes further of the ruins on the eastern ridge of the hill of 'an ancient place of strength called Fat-lips Castle', said to have been built by the Laird of Symington in order to pursue his feud with the Laird of Lamington, his purpose being to observe the actions of his enemy, whose house was not far distant in the meadow below:

> He is reported to have said that the laird of Lamington would not be able so much as to water his horses in the Clyde, or even to appear out of doors for much simpler purposes, without being overlooked and watched by him the laird of Symington. This disagreeable system of surveillance, which the unfortunate Lamington could not openly resent, induced him at length to leave his house, and build for himself a tower called Windygates behind the hills, where Symington durst not approach him.

The 'much simpler purposes' referred to presumably mean that Lamington could not even relieve himself without being watched. Chambers adds in a note that there is 'a similar ruin' also known as Fatlips Castle on the top of Minto Crags, Roxburghshire. As to the origin of the name, his guess is that it has to do with an old custom among sightseers and picnickers visiting the top of Minto, 'that every gentleman, by indefeasible privilege, kisses one of the ladies on entering the ruin'.

An entirely different legend of Tinto is recorded by the anonymous author of the nineteenth-century *History of Lanark*:

> The aspect of Tinto is, of a yellowish tinge, which, no doubt gave rise to the fabulous opinion, among the ancient and illiterate peasantry, that it was the repository of mines of gold; – nay, so stupidly credulous were they, within the last fifty years, as to affirm that the sheep which browsed upon the mountain's brow, in a dewy morning, had their teeth dyed with the exhalation of the golden ore.

The same thing was said of sheep which fed on the Eildon Hills in Roxburghshire, and near NORRIE'S LAW (Central & Perthshire) it was the sheep's wool that was supposed to turn yellow from the gold in the ground.

TURNBERRY, CARRICK, AYRSHIRE

Just north of Turnberry on a headland of Turnberry Bay stands a lighthouse, and adjoining that the fragmentary remains of Turnberry Castle. Near here, one fine evening of summer, just as the sun was setting, a Carrick fisherman was sitting on the cliffs looking out over the bay towards Arran. Tradition names him only as William, but records that he lived in the village of Maidens, between Turnberry and Culzean. As he sat, he heard a sweet song like none he had heard before. It came from the sea and he was spellbound:

O, it is happy and blest to be here.
It is lovely on earth in greenwood
    bowers
To wander at eve 'mong the dewy
    flowers;
But sweeter and happier far to be
In the coral groves of the crystal sea.

It was the voice of a mermaid and he could not resist it. His boat lay rocking gently on the sea below, and into it he jumped, cast off, and rowed towards the direction of the sound, but could not come up with the singer. Still the song continued, and drew him further and further out to sea. The sun dropped down behind Arran, and in its place rose the silver moon and the stars. Still he rowed on.

He did not see that, to the west, beyond the sea-girt Ailsa Craig, the clouds were gathering blackly, nor did he care that the wind was rising. Shipping his mast and spreading his sail, he sailed onwards faster and faster, and though he saw the seabirds heading landwards, a sign that bad weather was at hand, he could think of nothing but finding the mermaid. As the storm rose, she sang louder and louder above the whistling wind.

A sudden squall hit William's boat and roused him to the danger, but by now it was too late, and the raging sea took him. He never saw Maidens or the shore of Carrick again. For years afterwards, the fishermen along the coast taught their sons to beware of the mermaid's song and not give in to its dangerous seductions.

This sad little tale, from William Robertson's *Historical Tales and Legends of Ayrshire* (1889), is built upon traditional lore concerning the mermaid going back to the irresistible but deadly songs of the sirens in classical literature. The words sung by this Carrick mermaid are taken from *Ballads Founded on Ayrshire Traditions* (1850).

WALLACE'S CAVE, LANARKSHIRE

More than one 'Wallace's Cave' can be found in Lanarkshire. In *Bygone Lanark* (1990), Richard Stenlake writes that 'Legend has William Wallace fleeing from the English soldiers over both the Clyde at Cora Linn and the Mouse at Cartland Crags. Both sites have caves which might have been suitable as hiding places.'

The nineteenth-century *History of Lanark*, however, doubts both of these. Of the one in Cartlane by the Mouse or Mouss, the anonymous author says that here will be pointed out 'a puny hole, which the peasantry have dignified with the name of "Wallace Cave"':

This, it is quite evident, if it ever was used by the Patriot, could only have afforded a temporary refuge during the night; possessing no accommodation for his gigantic form.

Of the landmark near CORA LINN it is equally dismissive:

Before leaving the brink of the river the stranger will be shewn a cave of large dimensions, hewn out of the solid rock. This excavation has already received the appellation of 'Wallace's Cave', but, it is a modern formation, done by the hands of a person, who lately resided at New Lanark. Another century will confirm it as having been one of the 'Warrior's' retreats.

That forecast has been borne out, judging by a postcard reproduced in Stenlake's book, with the title 'reliable series' and captioned 'Wallace's Cave', showing an impressive but probably man-made structure. A more convincing candidate is in the neighbourhood of another waterfall on the Clyde, Dundaff Linn (*dundubh* meaning 'black hill' or 'the black leap'), where 'a small recess in the rocks' is pointed out 'which tradition dignifies with the name of "Wallace's Chair"'. This, the writer says, 'is not at all improbable; as during the period of the hero's career, this wild would afford him a hiding place, not indeed so dreadfully unapproachable as Cartlane; but, no less secure'.

Wallace's name is commemorated in many landmarks, both man-made and natural. His reputation as a giant of history (of giant stature too, as in the reference to his 'gigantic form' above) is symbolised by the massive Wallace Monument on Abbey Craig, north-east of Stirling, and has been reinvigorated by the Hollywood take on his life and exploits in *Braveheart* (1995). As Philip Crowl comments in *The Intelligent Traveller's Guide to Historic Scotland* (1986), his vision of national self-determination was such 'as medieval Europe would not see again until Joan of Arc appeared before Orleans'.

See also WILLIAM WALLACE (p. 204).

LOTHIAN & BORDERS

The counties of Berwickshire, East Lothian, Midlothian, Peeblesshire, Roxburghshire, Selkirkshire, and West Lothian

ABBOTSFORD, ROXBURGHSHIRE

On 30 April 1818, while the novelist Sir Walter Scott was building his new house at Abbotsford and living in an older, adjoining part, he wrote to Daniel Terry in London:

> The night before last we were awakened by a violent noise, like drawing heavy boards along the new part of the house. I fancied something had fallen, and thought no more about it. This was about *two* in the morning. Last night, at the same witching hour, the very same noise occurred. Mrs Scott, as you know, is rather timbersome [nervous]; so up got I . . . But nothing was out of order, neither can I discover what occasioned the disturbance.

On the morning that Terry received the letter, William Erskine was breakfasting with him and discussing the sudden death of George Bullock, who had been commissioned to furnish the new rooms at Abbotsford, and to whom the Scott family had become attached. It had occurred on the same night and, as far as they could ascertain, at the very hour when Scott was disturbed from his sleep. When Scott heard of Bullock's death, he wrote to Terry, 'Were you not struck with the fantastical coincidence . . . ? I protest to you, the noise

resembled half a dozen men hard at work, putting up boards and furniture; and nothing can be more certain than that there was nobody on the premises at the time.'

Scott was deeply interested in the paranormal, as attested by his novels and his *Letters on Demonology and Witchcraft* (1830). His attitude wavered between conviction and doubt, but at times he believed that he himself had had encounters with the supernatural. Several years before the occurrence at Abbotsford, Scott was riding home after sunset when he saw a figure in dusky brown garments about a quarter of a mile away. When he rode up to it, it vanished. When he rode past, and looked back, there it was behind him. He started back towards it, but, as he wrote later, 'whether it were from love of home, or a participation in my dislike of this very stupid ghost . . . Finella did her best to run away, and would by no means agree to any further process of investigation.' The mare's refusal to return would in itself have seemed disturbing, as horses were considered to possess SECOND SIGHT (p. 474), a belief recorded by Martin Martin in *A Description of the Western Isles of Scotland* (1703): 'That Horses see it is likewise plain, from their violent and sudden starting when the Rider or Seer in Company with him sees a Vision of any kind.' Not surprisingly, Scott was

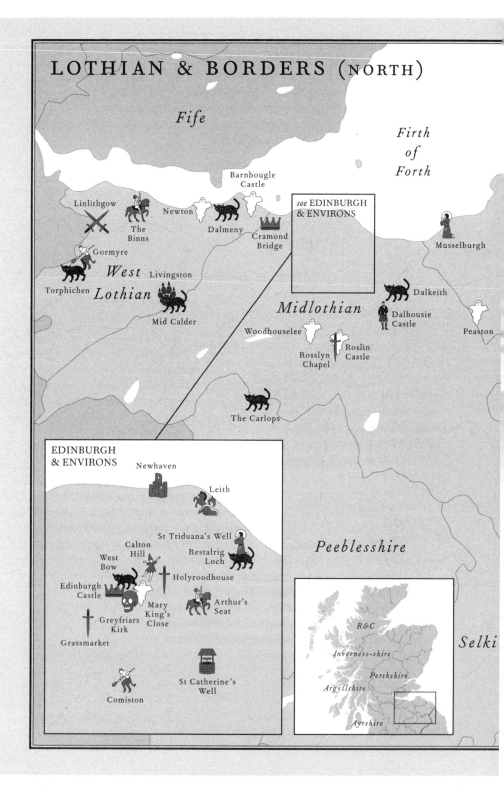

LOTHIAN & BORDERS (NORTH)

Fife

Firth of Forth

Barnbougle Castle

Linlithgow

Newton

The Binns

Dalmeny

Cramond Bridge

see EDINBURGH & ENVIRONS

Musselburgh

Gormyre

West

Livingston

Torphichen

Lothian

Mid Calder

Dalkeith

Dalhousie Castle

Midlothian

Woodhouselee

Rosslyn Chapel

Roslin Castle

Peaston

The Carlops

EDINBURGH & ENVIRONS

Newhaven

Leith

St Triduana's Well

Calton Hill

West Bow

Restalrig Loch

Edinburgh Castle

Holyroodhouse

Greyfriars Kirk

Mary King's Close

Arthur's Seat

Grassmarket

St Catherine's Well

Comiston

Peeblesshire

R&C

Inverness-shire

Perthshire

Argyllshire

Selki

Ayrshire

Bass Rock

North Berwick   Whitekirk

Athelstaneford   Traprain
                  Law

Loth Stone   Whittingehame

East Lothian

Samuelston

North
Sea

Fast Castle

Cranshaws
Farm   Edin's
              Hall Broch   Eyemouth

Soutra Mains   Mittenfu'
                Stanes
                        Longformacus
                                      Langton
                                      House

                  Berwickshire

                  Greenlaw Moor

Allanbank

Bowland

rkshire

Roxb.

0   5   10   15 MI
0   5   10   15   20   25 KM

🐾	Animal legends	🐉	Kelpies and water-spirits
⚔️	Battles and escapes	🏛️	Landmarks and local customs
🧍	Clan and family legends	⛰️	Landscape legends
⚡	Curses and divine interventions	†	Murder and robbery
💀	Death and burial	🪨	Prehistoric remains
👹	Devils and demons	👑	Royalty
🧚	Fairies and trows	🧎	Saints and miracles
👻	Ghosts and omens	👺	Supernatural creatures
🧟	Giants and ogres	🪣	Wells and springs
🐎	Heroes and villains	🐈‍⬛	Witches and witchcraft

LOTHIAN & BORDERS (SOUTH)

Peeblesshire

Peebles

Powsail Burn

Drumelzier

Minch Moor

Peat Law

Yarrowford

Carterhaugh

Aikwood Tower

Cockburn's Castle

Selkirkshire

Deloraine

Dumfriesshire

	Clan and family legends
	Curses and divine interventions
	Death and burial
	Devils and demons
	Dragons and sea-serpents
	Fairies and trows
	Ghosts and omens
	Heroes and villains
	Kelpies and water-spirits
	Murder and robbery
	Saints and miracles
	Witches and witchcraft
	Wizards and seers

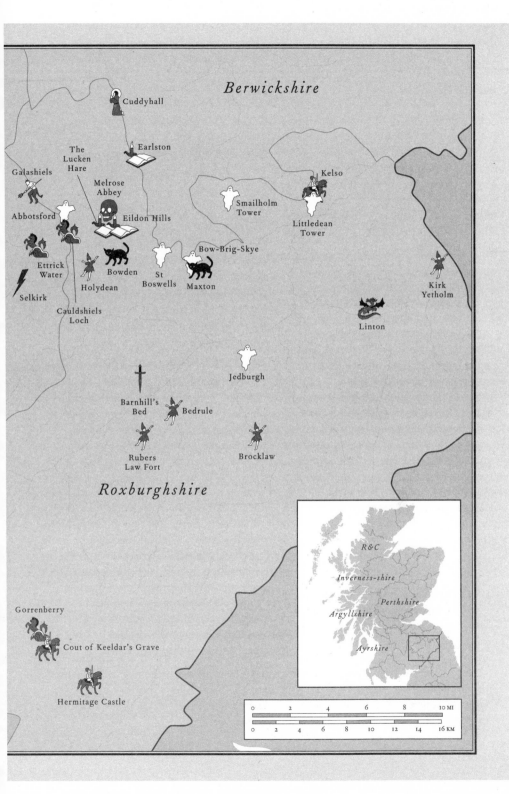

Berwickshire

Cuddyhall

Earlston

The Lucken Hare

Galashiels

Melrose Abbey

Kelso

Abbotsford

Eildon Hills

Smailholm Tower

Littledean Tower

Ettrick Water

Bowden

Bow-Brig-Skye

Selkirk

Holydean

St Boswells

Maxton

Kirk Yetholm

Cauldshiels Loch

Linton

Jedburgh

Barnhill's Bed

Bedrule

Rubers Law Fort

Brocklaw

Roxburghshire

Gorrenberry

Cout of Keeldar's Grave

Hermitage Castle

R & C

Inverness-shire

Perthshire

Argyllshire

Ayrshire

0	2	4	6	8	10 MI

0	2	4	6	8	10	12	14	16 KM

unnerved, feeling 'half inclined to think that this apparition was a warning of evil to come, or indication . . . of misfortune that had already occurred'.

However, he records no unpleasant outcome either of this or of a later experience concerning his wife, Charlotte Carpenter. On 12 September 1826, following her death, he thought he heard her calling him, and on 11 October, before setting out for London, he wrote in his journal, 'My wife's figure seems to stand before me, and her voice is in my ears – "S—, do not go." It half frightens me.'

AIKWOOD TOWER, SELKIRKSHIRE

Aikwood or Oakwood Tower is said to have been the home of MICHAEL SCOT, THE WIZARD OF BALWEARIE (p. 62). In *Minstrelsy of the Scottish Border* (1802), Sir Walter Scott tells how when Sir Michael was living at Aikwood he heard of the fame of the Witch of Falsehope, on the other side of the River Ettrick, and went to call upon her. The woman denied any knowledge of magic, but while he was talking to her he put his wand down on the table, and she suddenly snatched it up and hit him with it.

> Feeling the force of the charm, he rushed out of the house, but, as it had conferred on him the external appearance of a hare, his servant, who waited without, halloo'd upon the discomfited wizard his own greyhounds, and pursued him so close, that, in order to obtain a moment's breathing to reverse the charm, Michael, after a very fatiguing course, was fain to take refuge in his own *jawhole* [sewer].

Having recovered his own form, Michael meditated revenge. Going to the hill above Falsehope, he sent his servant down to ask for a bit of bread. As he expected, this was ungraciously refused, and the servant placed a bit of paper above the witch's door bearing 'many cabalistical words', together with a rhyme:

> Maister Michael Scott's man
> Sought meat, and gat nane.

Immediately the woman began to dance round the fire, repeating the rhyme, and was unable to continue her morning's work, which was baking bread for the reapers. Her husband sent the reapers one after another to see what had delayed their food, but as each one entered the house they too were caught by the spell and began to dance and sing.

> At length the old man himself went to the house; but as his wife's frolic with Mr Michael, whom he had seen on the hill, made him a little cautious, he contented himself with looking in at the window, and saw the reapers at their involuntary exercise, dragging his wife, now completely exhausted, sometimes round, and sometimes through the fire, which was, as usual, in the midst of the house. Instead of entering, he saddled a horse, and rode up the hill, to humble himself before Michael, and beg a cessation of the spell; which the good-natured warlock immediately granted, directing him to enter the house backwards, and, with his left hand, take the spell from above the door; which accordingly ended the supernatural dance.

Aikwood Tower (which was restored in 1992) was indeed originally built for the Scot or Scott family, but not until 1535, around 300 years after the time of the real Sir Michael.

ALLANBANK, EDROM,
BERWICKSHIRE

Mrs Crowe, in her *Night-Side of Nature* (1848), gives an account of a ghost whose 'persevering annoyances' at the mansion of Allanbank near Edrom were so widely rumoured and firmly credited that they had sometimes hindered the letting of the place. The ghost was known as 'Pearlin Jean' from the great quantity of the sort of lace known as 'pearlin' she always appeared in. Her presence may have deterred new tenants but it seems not to have worried resident servants: a housekeeper called Bettie Norrie, who lived for many years at Allanbank, said she and others had frequently encountered Jean, but were so used to hearing her that they were no longer alarmed by her noises.

Mrs Crowe was given her account of Pearlin Jean by the antiquary Charles Kirkpatrick Sharpe (1781–1851), who wrote, 'Pearlin Jean was the most remarkable ghost in Scotland and my terror when a child.' He was told of her by his old nurse, Jenny Blackadder, who had been a servant at Allanbank, and often heard her rustling in silks along the passage and up and down the stairs. Jenny had never seen the phantom, but her husband had.

According to Sharpe, she was a French woman whom the first Baronet of Allenbank, Sir Robert Stuart (then plain Mr Stuart), met in Paris as a young man during his Grand Tour. Some said that she was a nun. Either Stuart in time became faithless or he was suddenly recalled to Scotland by his parents. Either way, he had got into his carriage at the door of the hotel when she unexpectedly appeared and stepped onto the fore-wheel of the coach in order to speak to him. However, he cruelly ordered the postillion to drive on, with the result that she fell and was killed by one of the wheels running over her head.

On a dusky autumn evening when Mr Stuart drove under the arched gateway of Allanbank, he saw Pearlin Jean sitting on the top of it, her head and shoulders bloody. After this, the house was haunted for many years, doors loudly shutting and opening at midnight, and the rustle of silks and patter of high-heeled shoes heard in the passages and bedrooms.

That tireless Victorian visitor Augustus Hare heard another version of the story when staying at Ford Castle. On 10 November 1874, he noted in his journal:

Last night Mr Fyler told his famous story of 'the nun.' It is briefly this: –

A son of Sir J. Stuart of Allanbank, on the Blackadder, where Lady Boswell lives now, was in Rome, where he fell in love with a novice in one of the convents. When his father heard of it, he was furious, and summoned him home. Young Stuart told the nun he must leave Rome, and she implored him to marry her first; but he would do nothing of the kind, and, as he left, she flung herself under his carriage; the wheels went over her, and she was killed. The first thing the faithless lover saw on his return to Scotland was the nun, who met him in the bridal attire she was to have worn, and she has often appeared since, and has become known in the neighbourhood as 'Pearlin Jean.' On one occasion seven ministers were called in to lay her, but with no effect.

The abandoned girl's death by suicide rather than accident is a romantic twist, and, although genteel ghosts clad in silks are fairly commonplace in British tradition, the story is made more poignant, and the quantity of 'pearlin' worn by the ghost explained, by the fact that the wistful victim reappears in the clothes she would have worn as a bride.

Arthur's Seat, Edinburgh

The dominating mass of rock which towers, lion-shaped, beside the city has been known by various names, including 'Dead Men's Rock' (Creag nan Marbh) and more simply 'The Crag', but for several hundred years it has been 'Arthur's Seat'. The eighteenth-century historian William Maitland suggested that this might be a corruption of the Gaelic Aird na Saigheid, 'Height of Arrows'; another theory was that 'Arthur' should really be 'Ard Thor', *ard* meaning 'high', and Thor being the Norse god of thunder. It is simpler to believe the obvious, that 'Arthur' refers to King Arthur, and 'Seat' means that he was thought to have sat there. Like other mythic heroes Arthur was sometimes imagined as a giant, and his throne in proportion – another example is FINGAL (p. 10), who has a somewhat less enor-mous 'chair' in Staffa near FINGAL'S CAVE (Western Isles).

Whatever the reasons for the name, stories of Arthur have become attached to the site, under which he is sometimes said to be asleep and waiting for the call which will restore him to life when he is needed by his country. The 'sleeping hero' is an international theme, with Scottish traditions of Fingal at TOMNAHURICH (Southern Highlands) and of Thomas the Rhymer in several places, including Tomnahurich again and THE LUCKEN HARE. Although less pervasive than in Wales or south-west England, Arthurian legend is by no means unknown in Scotland: Merlin is reported to be buried at the POWSAIL BURN, and Guinevere at MEIGLE (Central & Perthshire).

One odd circumstance connected with Arthur's Seat emerged in 1836, when some schoolboys were looking for rabbit burrows on the north-east slope. They found a

A nineteenth-century engraving of Arthur's Seat, the majestic rock which dominates the scenery near Edinburgh. It is said that King Arthur sleeps beneath it and that one day, when Britain needs him most, he may rise again.

shallow cave in one of the rocks, protected by three pieces of slate, behind which were seventeen tiny coffins, none more than four inches (10 cm) long. The boys threw the little coffins about, losing some and damaging others in the process, but they later told their discovery to their teacher, who happened to be a member of the local archaeological society. Eight coffins were retrieved and examined, and found to contain tiny wooden figures carefully carved and dressed. From the condition of the wood, it seemed that the oldest coffin had been placed in the cave many years before, but at least one very recently indeed.

No final conclusion has been reached about the matter, although witchcraft has been mentioned, and so has the idea that the images may commemorate people who have died abroad or at sea. The eight coffins are preserved at the Museum of Scotland.

ATHELSTANEFORD,
EAST LOTHIAN

The chronicles of Hector Boece (1465–1536), translated in 1531 by John Bellenden, tell us that the Picts were the 'special' people of St Andrew, a belief which arose after the eighth century when St Rule or Regulus was said to have brought the relics of the Apostle to Scotland. Around 815 CE an army led by the Northumbrian king Athelstane met a Pictish force under King Hungus, and in the night before the battle St Andrew appeared to the Pictish king, telling him to be of good comfort, for next day he would have a glorious victory over the English. When Hungus awoke, he found his people staring into the sky, where a shining cross appeared, 'nocht unlyke the samyn croce that the Apostill deit on' (not unlike the same cross that the Apostle died on). What is meant

by this is a 'saltire' or X-shaped cross. St Andrew was said to have been crucified diagonally: the saltire cross is thus the symbol of his martyrdom, and is also known as the St Andrew's cross.

Hungus told the troops of his vision, and at dawn the trumpets sounded with a cry to St Andrew. The Picts fell on their enemies and put them to flight; King Athelstane died at the first charge, his defeat commemorated in the name of the battle site.

After the victory, King Hungus vowed always to use St Andrew's cross as his people's banner in time of battle, a custom maintained by the Scots even after the Picts were no more. A white saltire cross on a blue ground is Scotland's national flag, and one flies at all times over a memorial in Athelstaneford parish churchyard to commemorate the event.

BARNBOUGLE CASTLE,
WEST LOTHIAN

Barnbougle Castle was originally a keep of the Moubray family, Norman knights who came to Britain with William the Conqueror. When one of these knights, Sir Roger, set out to fight in the Crusades, his hound was so upset at his leaving that Sir Roger took him along too, and the faithful animal accompanied him in all his battles. One night, back in Scotland, the sound of a bugle and the baying of a dog were heard, at what was discovered to be the same moment at which Sir Roger met his death, his companion still beside him.

Peter Underwood, reporting this story in his *Gazetteer of Scottish Ghosts* (1982), adds, 'Still, on dark nights a mournful and dismal wailing noise is sometimes heard that local people think is the wail of Sir Roger's hound.'

BARNHILL'S BED, MINTO, ROXBURGHSHIRE

Black's *Picturesque Tourist of Scotland* of 1844 describes Minto crags as 'a romantic assemblage of cliffs' near Minto House on the banks of the Teviot:

> A small platform on a projecting crag, commanding a most beautiful prospect, is termed Barnhill's Bed. This Barnhill is said to have been a robber or outlaw. There are remains of a strong tower beneath the rocks, where he is supposed to have dwelt, and from which he derived his name.

Sir Walter Scott mentions this tradition in *The Lay of the Last Minstrel* (1805):

> On Minto-crags the moonbeams glint,
> Where Barnhill hew'd his bed of flint;
> Who flung his outlaw'd limbs to rest,
> Where falcons hang their giddy nest,
> Mid cliffs, from whence his eagle eye
> For many a league his prey could spy;
> Cliffs, doubling, on their echoes borne,
> The terrors of the robber's horn . . .

There are many traditions of brigands in this part of the country. In the sixteenth and seventeenth centuries, Scots and English preyed upon each other across the border, stealing cattle, taking hostages, and extorting blackmail, their depredations kept barely in check by the wardens of the Marches. Some of these men, violent and greedy though they were, were seen or at least remembered as folk heroes: Johnnie Armstrong of GILNOCKIE TOWER (Dumfries & Galloway) is one example.

BASS ROCK, EAST LOTHIAN

This small, steep island lies off the coast to the north-east of Berwick. 335 million years ago, basalt lava plugged the mouth of a volcano; the surrounding rock having worn away over the aeons, what is left is the plug. This geology makes the Bass kin to other features of the Lothian landscape, notably ARTHUR'S SEAT.

The hermit St Baldred (also known as Balthere or Baudron) once made his home on the Rock, crossing to the mainland, so the legend goes, on another, smaller rock known as St Baudron's Boat, which can be seen in the mouth of Auldhame Bay. The story of his anchorite's existence on the rock is told by the eighth-century chronicler Alcuin, and legends of the saint's conversions and miracles include the famous multiplication of his corpse. A contest having arisen between the three churches of Auldhame, Tyninghame, and Linton as to which should receive the saint's remains, and the quarrel having become violent, the disputants were that night overcome with sleep. On awaking, they found three bodies exactly alike, one of which was buried in each church. A similar tradition is related of St Fillan at ST FILLAN'S CAVE (Central & Perthshire).

The remains of a chapel built on the site of the saint's cell can still be seen on the Bass, and the ruins of a twelfth-century church dedicated to St Baldred at Tyninghame. Several other local landmarks bear his name, including St Baldred's Cradle at Whitberry, near the mouth of the Tyne, and St Baldred's Well at East Linton.

See also SAINTS OF SCOTLAND (p. 490).

BEDRULE, ROXBURGHSHIRE

A tale of fairy gratitude is told in *Folk-Lore and Legends: Scotland* (1889) concerning the farmhouse of Bedrule, south-west of Jedburgh. About the beginning of harvest, as there was no bread for the farm workers, what little barley was ripe was cut down and turned into flour. Mrs Buckham, the farmer's wife, rose early next morning to bake the bread and while she was busy at this a little old woman dressed in green came in and very courteously asked for the loan of a cup of meal. Guessing from her stature and the colour of her garments that she was a fairy, Mrs Buckham judged it wise to grant her request, though there was scarcely a cupful to spare. A short time later, the little old woman returned with an equal amount of meal, which Mrs Buckham put in the meal chest. From that cupful alone, she was able to bake as much bread as served her family and the reapers throughout harvest, and even when harvest was over, the chest was not empty.

The Binns, West Lothian

At the Binns lived General Tam Dalyell, famous historically for his persecution of the Covenanters, and in legend as one who outwitted the Devil. His real-life exploits were remarkable enough. On the execution of Charles I the general's grief was expressed in a refusal to cut his hair or beard, which grew to reach his waist. Under Charles II he was the scourge of the dissenters, who met in defiance of the government to hear their preachers at outdoor 'conventicles'. Lookouts used to be posted by the rebels to guard their open-air meetings from surprise by the dragoons: on spotting the redcoats, the sentry would imitate the call of the curlew or peewit, upon which the worshippers would at once disperse. It is said that Dalyell's response was to introduce camouflage into the British army. When he raised a new regiment at the Binns in 1681, he ordered the uniforms to be made of grey Flanders cloth instead of the traditional scarlet, and thus were created the Royal Scots Greys.

Like some other notable characters of the period, Dalyell was said to be IN LEAGUE WITH THE DEVIL (p. 142). His folk reputation credited him with a pair of enchanted boots which rendered him impervious to shot, as recorded by Sir Walter Scott in *Minstrelsy of the Scottish Border* (1802–3):

> During the battle of Pentland Hills, Paton of Meadowhead conceived he saw the balls hop harmlessly down from General Dalziel's boots, and, to counteract the spell, loaded his pistol with a piece of silver coin. But Dalziel, having his eye on him, drew back behind his servant, who was shot dead.

On one occasion the Devil was said to have thrown a heavy marble table at the general, but missed, breaking a window and sending the table into a pond. In the early twentieth century, soldiers of the Scots Greys visiting the house happened to water their horses at a pool in the garden. The summer that year being very dry, the water level was unusually low, and something was visible below the surface which proved to be a marble table top. This was hailed as a remarkable confirmation of the story, said to have been current before the discovery was made, though it is not hard to imagine that someone might have investigated the pond earlier and noticed so bulky an object. It is claimed in some sources that a Kelpie makes its home in the waters, and if that is a genuine tradition it would indicate that people had felt there was something unchancy about the pool. This feature, however, seems to appear only in fairly modern accounts, and may be no more than embroidery by writers who would like every Scottish pool to contain a water-spirit.

As might be expected, Dalyell's ghost has been seen on occasion galloping home across a ruined bridge over the Errack

Burn, riding a grey charger; this may be at least partly because some people have mistakenly believed that the name 'Scots Greys' referred to the soldiers' mounts rather than to their uniforms. Other ghosts reputed to haunt the Binns include a spirit at the Black Lodge which frightened the horses in Victorian times, and a Brownie or Pecht said to gather wood on the hillside for the giant kitchen oven at the Binns, where Bluidy Dalyell was wont to roast his prisoners. More reliably to be seen are the peacocks, of which it is said that as long as they live at the Binns there will be Dalyells in residence.

BOW-BRIG-SYKE, MAXTON, ROXBURGHSHIRE

A little way east of Maxton near Bow-Brig-Syke, a bridge across a small rivulet, lay the 'Three-corner field', a long, triangular piece of ground in which, for nearly a century, it was averred that the forms of two ladies dressed in white might be seen pacing up and down. Night after night, the people of Maxton would come out to watch them, and, when word got about, curiosity brought others from a distance. The ladies were always seen at dusk, walking arm-in-arm over precisely the same spot of ground until the morning light.

Thomas Wilkie, who collected stories for Sir Walter Scott in the nineteenth century, adds that about twelve years before he recorded this tale, workmen took up the large flat stones on which foot travellers crossed the burn, and found beneath them the skeletons of two women lying side by side. After this discovery, the Bow-Brig ladies were never seen again. Mr Wilkie received this account from a gentleman who examined the skeletons, believed to be those of two sisters of a former laird of Littledean:

Their brother was said to have killed them in a fit of passion, because they interfered to protect from ill usage a young lady whom he had met at Bow-brig-syke. He placed their bodies upon the bridge, and lowered the flat stones upon them to prevent discovery.

Some years later, the murderer met his own end near the same spot. While riding with his dogs, he fell over the brae opposite the bridge and was found lying dead by the Tweedside. Tradition identified this laird as Harry Gilles, another tale of whom is told at MAXTON.

The fact that the bodies were laid under heavy stones in the burn suggests that, unless the murder story is true, the two skeletons might have been those of suspected witches. Traditionally neither these nor ghosts could cross running water.

BOWDEN, ROXBURGHSHIRE

Among the Border traditions collected for Sir Walter Scott by Thomas Wilkie, a young medical student living at Bowden, was the story concerning a man named Ronaldson, who had lived in the village and was said to have had frequent encounters with the local witches:

One morning at sunrise, while he was tying his garter with one foot against a low dyke, he was startled at feeling something like a rope of straw passed between his legs, and himself borne swiftly away upon it to a small brook at the foot of the southernmost hill of Eildon. Hearing a hoarse smothered laugh, he perceived he was in the power of witches or sprites; and when he came to a ford called the Brig-o'-Stanes, feeling his foot touch a large stone, he exclaimed, 'I' the name of the Lord, ye'se get me no farther!' At that moment the rope broke, the air rang as

with the laughter of a thousand voices;
and as he kept his footing on the stone, he
heard a muttered cry, 'Ah, we've lost the
coof!'

A 'coof' is a fool. What with the whisking
away and the laughter, this sounds less like
witches than fairies, who were certainly
thought to inhabit the EILDON HILLS, and
were often said to carry people long distances with the 'fairy host' or *sluagh*, tales
of which were told at DUNDREGGAN (Southern Highlands) among many other places.

BOWLAND, VALE OF GALE, MIDLOTHIAN

Peter Underwood cites Sir Walter Scott as
his authority for a tale of a strange dream,
and although no further references are
given, it is just the sort of story which
would have intrigued Scott, particularly
since it involved a lawsuit: Scott himself
practised as a lawyer. A Bowland man
named Rutherford was being sued for
money which he was convinced his late
father had acquired legally, but he could
find no evidence, and was about to set out
for the trial in Edinburgh when his father
appeared to him in a dream, and told him
that the relevant papers were with a retired
attorney at Inveresk. As the lawyer was
old and might have forgotten the matter,
Mr Rutherford senior mentioned that
when he had paid his account there had
been difficulty finding change, and the
two of them had used up the balance
drinking at an inn. Rutherford junior
called at Inveresk, located the lawyer, and
managed to recall the circumstances to his
mind. The papers were found, and the son
was able to win his case.

A not dissimilar story is related by
Alexander Mackenzie in 1877 of Sir
George Mackenzie of Rosehaugh, Lord
Advocate for Scotland in the reign of
Charles II (1660–85). While staying in
Edinburgh he was accustomed to stroll in
Leith Walk, 'then almost a solitary place',
every day before dinner. One day he was
accosted there by a grey-haired old gentleman who told him that in a fortnight's time
an important case was to be heard in
London. An impostor was claiming an
estate from the real heir, who was unable
to produce his title to the property. 'It is
necessary,' the gentleman informed Sir
George, 'that you be there on the day
mentioned; and in one of the attics of the
mansion-house on the estate, there is an old
oak chest with two bottoms; between these
you will find the necessary titles, written
on parchment.' He then disappeared.

Sir George ignored his strange informant, who, however, met him again on the
two days following. The third time, Sir
George obeyed his instructions and set out
for London on horseback, arriving on the
morning before the case was due. At the
house described by the old man, he met
the true heir and a celebrated London barrister, who was by no means gracious to
his Scottish colleague. In the drawing
room of the house, Sir George saw a portrait exactly resembling the man he had
met in Leith Walk, and asked who was the
subject: it was the heir's great-great-
grandfather.

Searching the attics, Sir George saw an
old trunk and was told it contained nothing, but he kicked it heartily. 'The kick
sent the bottom out of the trunk, with a
quantity of chaff, among which the original titles to the property were discovered.'

Next day, judgement was pronounced
in favour of the true claimant, and Sir
George said in the hearing of the English
lawyer, 'You see now what a Scotchman
has done, and I must tell you that I wish
a countryman anything but a London
barrister.'

BROCKLAW, JED WATER, ROXBURGHSHIRE

Robbie Oliver was a shepherd who lived at Southdean in Jedwater (or, as modern maps spell it, Jed Water) and died in about 1830. In *Scottish Fairy and Folk Tales*, first published in 1896, Sir George Douglas quotes Robbie's account of 'the verra last fairy that was seen hereaway'.

When Robbie's father Peter was a young man, he lived at Hyndlee and was a shepherd on the Brocklaw. In those days it was the custom to milk the ewes, and one evening Peter was herding the Brocklaw sheep to be milked by two girls, with a lot of joking going on between the three of them. Just as it was beginning to get dark, Peter looked up and saw a little creature all clad in green, with long hair as yellow as gold hanging round its shoulders, heading straight for him, whimpering a little and giving a queer unearthly cry, 'Hae ye seen Hewie Milburn? Oh, hae ye seen Hewie Milburn?'

Instead of answering the little person, Peter jumped clear over the gate of the fold to be near the girls, saying, 'Bless us, what's that?' Bessie Elliott, a free-spoken Liddesdale girl, laughed and said teasingly that a wife had come for him, at which, so he said until his dying day, he was so afraid 'that the hairs o' his head stuid up like the birsies of a hurcheon' (the bristles of a hedgehog).

The creature was no bigger than a little girl of three years old, but as well built as any grown woman, and its face was as beautiful as could be, though there was something unearthly in its eyes that made them hard to look at and impossible to describe.

It did not harm them, but kept lingering about the fold, now and then repeating its cry, 'Hae ye seen Hewie Milburn?' They came to the conclusion that it had lost its companion.

When Peter and the girls left the sheepfold, it followed them back to Hyndlee, where they offered it ewe's milk porridge, but it would not take anything. Then at last a ne'er-do-well fellow made as if to grip it with a pair of red-hot tongs. Looking offended, it made off down the side of the burn, its cry more eerie and woeful than ever, and disappeared into a clump of sedge.

Whether the fairy's lost companion was its friend, or husband, or child, is unstated: perhaps Hewie Milburn, whoever he was, had joined in a general 'flitting' of the fairies from Jedwater, as is described for other counties in the British Isles, and left this desolate little person all alone.

CALTON HILL, EDINBURGH

Captain George Burton reported a tale of fairies to Richard Bovet in the late seventeenth century. Burton had been told by a woman about the 'Fairy Boy of Leith' who was said to act as drummer to the elves under Calton Hill:

> She had given me so strange an account of him, that I desired her I might see him the first opportunity, which she promised; and not long after, passing that way, she told me there was the fairy boy.

By 'smooth words, and a piece of money', Burton persuaded the boy to come into the house with him, where he asked him questions on astrology which the boy answered with precocious knowledge. He was, Burton thought, not more than ten or eleven years old.

> He seemed to make a motion like drumming upon the table with his fingers, upon which I asked him, Whether he could beat

a drum? To which he replied, Yes, sir, as well as any man in Scotland; for every Thursday night I beat all points to a sort of people that used to meet under yonder hill (pointing to the great hill between Edenborough and Leith).

The boy said he got under the hill through a pair of invisible gates, and once inside he would eat and drink with the fairies, and sometimes travel at extraordinary speed overseas. He did not say what they did abroad, but similar stories, such as that of DUFFUS CASTLE (North East), suggest that the party might have continued their revels in the cellars of the King of France or Holland. The boy also read Burton's fortune, predicting two handsome wives for him, and enraged a local woman by saying that she would have two bastards before she was married; we are not told whether either prophecy came true.

The fairies were often said to employ human musicians, as they did at MAIDEN CASTLE (Central & Perthshire), although the piper there was trapped in the fairy mound for a hundred years. Despite being known as the 'Fairy Boy', it is clear that the boy himself was a mortal, although he has more than a suspicion of the other-worldly about him, since he has free passage between the human and fairy realms: by the seventeenth century the distinction between fairies and witches was not always clear, and in her commentary Katharine Briggs notes that a suggestion runs through the story that witches as well as fairies meet under the hill, a belief reported in some Scottish witch-trials.

THE CARLOPS, NEWHALL, PEEBLESSHIRE

South-west of Edinburgh, near Newhall on the banks of the North Esk, is a land-mark consisting of two tall rocks known as 'the Carlops'. This is said to be a con-traction of 'Carline's Loups', in conse-quence of a witch or 'carline' having on many nights been observed to leap from one rock to the other.

At this spot, according to Black's *Pictur-esque Tourist of Scotland* (1844), 'near an old withered solitary oak tree', is the site of Mause's Cottage in Allan Ramsay's pastoral *The Gentle Shepherd* (1725). Although in the play the old woman Mause turns out to be no sorceress, there is a striking description of her supposed practices:

She can o'ercast the Night, and cloud the Moon,
And mak the Deils obedient to her Crune.
At Midnight Hours, o'er the Kirk-yards she raves,
And howks unchristen'd We'ans out of their Graves;
Boils up their Livers in a Warlock's Pow [skull],
Rins withershins about the Hemlock Low [fire];
And seven Times does her Prayers back-ward pray . . .

These are all classic black magic tricks that would have been familiar to Ramsay and his audience. Although the days of fren-zied persecution had passed, the last Scot-tish execution of a 'witch', Janet Horne of LOTH (Northern Highlands), took place in 1727.

CARTERHAUGH, SELKIRKSHIRE

The ballad of Tamlane is set in Carter-haugh Wood, where the enchanted knight is said to have met his sweetheart Janet. A spring known as Tamlane's Well can still be seen beside a lane at Carterhaugh Farm, but of the wood itself nothing remained

Border Ballads

The events of 'The Douglas Tragedy' are traditionally said to have occurred near the farm of Blackhouse in Selkirkshire. The ballad tells how Margaret Douglas elopes with Lord William, and when her father and seven brothers catch up with the couple, Lord William fights and kills the lot, although Margaret pleads with him to hold his hand. 'True lovers I can get many a ane [one],' she says, 'But a father I can never get mair.' That night both lovers die, William of his wounds and Margaret of grief.

The song is a localized version of the widely-distributed 'Fair Margaret and Sweet William', which commonly concludes that from the grave of Margaret grew a rose and from William's a briar, which 'grew till they joined in a true lover's knot' and then died together. In 'The Douglas Tragedy' too a rose and briar grow from the graves and entwine, but what follows is both more savage and more comic:

> But by chance that way the Black Douglas rade,
>> And wow but he was rude and rough!
> For he pull'd up the bonnie, bonnie brier,
>> And flang it in St. Marie's Loch.

The original 'Black Douglas' was the fourteenth-century Archibald, third Earl of Douglas. His descendants were known as the 'Black Douglases', and the vandal of the ballad may be any later head of that branch of the clan, to which Margaret must have belonged.

Hundreds of such songs were once in popular circulation, passed from mouth to mouth and changing as they went. The earliest sizeable collection of lyrics dates from about 1650, an anonymous manuscript volume discovered by Bishop Percy in the house of one Humphrey Pitts, where the maids were using it to light fires. Percy's published volume, *Reliques of Ancient English Poetry* (1765), inspired Sir Walter Scott, whose *Minstrelsy of the Scottish Border* (1802–3) is the most important text after Percy's. Not everyone appreciated his efforts. One old lady (mother of the author James Hogg) accused Scott, 'There was never ane o' my songs prentit [printed] till ye prentit them yoursel', and ye hae spoilt them a'togither. They were made for singin' an' no for readin', but ye hae broken the charm now, an' they'll never be sung mair.'

She overstated the case: ballads do not cease to be sung once they have been transcribed, but it is true that once there is a 'canonical' text, there is a tendency to see all further renditions as variations on that. The process is inevitable as a society becomes literate, and without the collectors far more songs would have been lost for ever.

Scott's work did much to shape the body of later tradition. Most of the songs he gathered came from his home territory of the Borders, and thus the 'Border Ballads' came to be identified as a specific group. For centuries the territory was ravaged by feuds, raids, and conflict between England and Scotland, and the background of constant violence is no doubt what gives the songs their characteristic flavour, sceptical, unsentimental, and bloody. It is illuminating, for example, to compare the English ballad 'The Three Ravens' with the

The author and historian Sir Walter Scott (1771–1832) loved his country's songs and legends, and preserved many ballads which might otherwise have been lost for ever.

well-known Scottish variant 'The Twa Corbies'. In the former, three ravens describe a knight who lies dead. They would like to breakfast upon his corpse, but it is protected by his hounds and his hawks, and later buried by his faithful mistress who then dies herself. In the latter, by contrast, the knight's hound and hawk have gone hunting, and, the ravens declare with relish, 'His lady's ta'en another mate / So we may mak our dinner sweet.'

It is suggested that Scott may have tinkered with the lyrics he heard, but this can be seen as legitimate: he has imposed his personality no more than any new performer might have done. In any case, one could hardly improve on this perfect piece of cynical tragedy with its haunting final verse:

Mony a one for him makes mane,
But nane sall ken where he is gane:
O'er his white banes, when they are bare,
The wind sall blow for evermair.

See also KILLERNIE CASTLE (Central & Perthshire); GILNOCKIE TOWER (Dumfries & Galloway); CARTERHAUGH; COCKBURN'S CASTLE; EILDON HILLS (Lothian & Borders).

by the mid nineteenth century. Black's *Picturesque Tourist of Scotland* of 1844 contains a melancholy note:

> The whole of this tract of country was, not many centuries ago, covered with wood, and its popular designation still is 'the Forest.' A native of Selkirk, who died about eighty years ago at an advanced age, used to tell that he had seen a person older than himself who said he had in his time walked from that town of Ettrick, a distance of eighteen miles, and never once all the way escaped from the shadow of the trees. Of this primeval forest no vestige is now to be seen.

The 'Tale of the Young Tamlane' is an old ballad, mentioned in the *Complaynt of Scotland* (1550) and printed in many versions. Tamlane has been captured by the fairies, who are shortly due to pay their seven-year 'teind' to hell, and Tamlane fears that he will be chosen. A 'teind' is a tithe, the word usually used for the tenth part of a parish's produce paid to the church, and here meaning a tax of souls. In order to redeem her lover Janet has to hold him fast, and pay no attention to the changes he will undergo:

> 'They'll turn me in your arms, Janet,
>   An adder and an ask [eel];
> They'll turn me in your arms, Janet,
>   A bale [fire] that burns fast.
>
> 'They'll turn me in your arms, Janet,
>   A red-hot gad o' airn [bar of iron];
> But haud me fast, let me not pass,
>   For I'll do you no harm.'

Janet is true to her trust, and wins Tamlane from fairyland.

> 'They'll shape me in your arms, Janet,
>   A dove, but and a swan;
> And last, they'll shape me in your arms,
>   A mother-naked man:

> Cast your green mantle over me —
>   I'll be myself again.'

The theme of a lover's transformation is very widespread, going back to ancient Greek legend and appearing in folk tales all over the world. The story of John and Mary Nelson in ABERDEEN (North East) has clear parallels to the tale of Tamlane. *See also* BORDER BALLADS (p. 224).

CAULDSHIELS LOCH, NR ABBOTSFORD, ROXBURGHSHIRE

In 1817, Washington Irving, author of 'The Legend of Sleepy Hollow' and 'Rip Van Winkle', stayed with Sir Walter Scott at Abbotsford for a few days. One of the places Sir Walter took his American visitor to see was Cauldshiels Loch, and Irving recorded that the most interesting circumstance connected with the loch, according to Scott, was that it was haunted by 'a bogle in the shape of a water bull, which lived in the deep parts, and now and then came forth upon dry land':

> This story had been current in the vicinity from time immemorial. There was a man living who declared he had seen the bull, and he was believed by many of his simple neighbours. 'I don't choose to contradict the tale,' said Scott; 'for I am willing to have my lake stocked with any fish, flesh, or fowl, that my neighbours think proper to put into it; and these old wives' fables are a kind of property in Scotland, that belong to the estates and go with the soil.'

Scott's attitude towards the supernatural was not entirely consistent, the romantic and sceptical sides of his nature often at war with each other, but he regarded folklore as an integral part of the landscape. As Robert Louis Stevenson remarked, 'To a man like Scott, the different appearances of nature seemed each to contain its own legend ready made . . . in such or such a place, only such or such events ought with propriety to happen.'

COCKBURN'S CASTLE, VALE OF MEGGET, SELKIRKSHIRE

Today only ruins remain of Cockburn's Castle, once known as Henderland Castle. The more modern name must be in memory of the Border robber named Cockburn who once lived there, and was executed by James V. The story goes that when the king and his party arrived, the reiver was at dinner with his family. A message was sent in, requesting him to come out and 'speak to a gentleman'. The reply was that the laird was at dinner and could not come out. A second more pressing invitation met with a more surly reply, and when a third message was sent, Cockburn cried in a rage that he would not come out even for 'the Laird of Ballengeich himself' – meaning the king, who used that name as an alias. The royal messenger then issued the order for Cockburn to come out to the Laird of Ballengeich. 'On hearing these terrible words, the knife and fork dropped from his hands; he went out like a condemned criminal, and was immediately hung up over his own gate.'

Meanwhile his wife jumped out at a back window. According to the account given in Black's *Picturesque Tourist of Scotland* (1844):

A mountain torrent called Henderland Burn, rushes impetuously from the hills through a rocky chasm, named the Dowglen, and passes near the site of the tower. To the recesses of this glen, the wife of Cockburn is said to have retreated, during the execution of her husband, and a place called the Lady's Seat, is still shown, where she is said to have striven to drown, amid the roar of the foaming cataract, the tumultuous noise which announced the close of his existence.

A ballad, 'The Lament of the Border Widow', was said to relate to this pathetic story, and is transcribed in Sir Walter Scott's *Minstrelsy of the Scottish Border* (1802–3):

My love he built me a bonny bower,
And clad it a' wi' lilye flour;
A brawer [finer] bower ye ne'er did see,
Than my true love he built for me.

There came a man, by middle day,
He spied his sport, and went away;
And brought the King that very night,
Who brake my bower, and slew my
    knight.

T. F. Henderson notes that the poem is 'much more refined and faultless than that of the rude Border balladists', who moreover would neither have transformed the Border chief into a knight, nor described his bare stone peel as a bower clad with blossom: Scott may have touched up the verse, or added bits from other ballads. Henderson also points out that the tradition referred to had no foundation in fact, since Cockburn of Henderland was tried and beheaded in Edinburgh. Probably the story of the immediate and brutal hanging was prompted by the treatment said to have been meted out to Johnnie Armstrong of GILNOCKIE TOWER (Dumfries & Galloway) on James's expedition to the Borders in 1529.

See also BORDER BALLADS (p. 224); THE GUIDMAN OF BALLANGEICH (p. 98).

COMISTON, MIDLOTHIAN

The road to the south of Edinburgh, wrote Robert Louis Stevenson in 1879, 'is dear to the superstitious'. Here a carter one night beheld a lady in white, 'with the most beautiful, clear shoes upon her feet'. We are told no more about this white lady and her lovely shoes, which sound like crystal slippers; many of the spirits known as White Ladies have no story to account for their appearances, although some, like the famous White Lady of the Hohen-zollerns in Germany, gave warnings of death to come.

Near Comiston was a roadside inn 'not so long ago haunted by the devil in person', says Stevenson:

Satan led the inhabitants a pitiful exis-tence. He shook the four corners of the building with lamentable outcries, beat at the doors and windows, overthrew crock-ery in the dead hours of the morning, and danced unholy dances on the roof. Every kind of spiritual disinfectant was put in requisition; chosen ministers were sum-moned out of Edinburgh and prayed by the hour; pious neighbours sat up all night making a noise of psalmody; but Satan minded them no more than the wind about the hill-tops.

It was only after years of persecution, apparently, that he left the inn alone.

COUT OF KEELDAR'S GRAVE, ROXBURGHSHIRE

The most powerful adversary of the hor-rendous Lord Soulis of HERMITAGE CASTLE was said to be the Chief of Keel-dar in Northumberland. Attacking the evil lord's castle, Keeldar was beaten back across the river, stumbled, and fell in, upon which his enemies held him down with their lances until he drowned. The eddy in which he perished was still known as Cout (Chief) of Keeldar's Pool in John Leyden's day, and his gigantic grave was

pointed out in the burial-ground of a ruined chapel, although Leyden wrote in 1858 that by then 'the swelling turf, near nine feet long, which was supposed to indicate his gigantic stature' was hardly distinguishable.

Keeldar's memory was honoured as that of the foe of Soulis, and Leyden wrote an imitation ballad in which Lord Soulis's familiar spirit appears:

The third blast that young Keeldar blew,
  Still stood the limber fern;
And a Wee Man, of swarthy hue,
  Up started by a cairn.

His russet weeds were brown as heath,
  That clothes the upland fell;
And the hair of his head was frizzly red,
  As the purple heather-bell.

Note the colour of this creature's hair, which strongly suggests that he is the same 'Redcap' who attends Soulis in other tra-ditions. Leyden refers to him as 'the Brown Man of the Muirs [Moors]' and describes him as 'a Fairy of the most malignant order':

Walsingham mentions a story of an unfortunate youth, whose brains were extracted from his skull, during his sleep, by this malicious being. Owing to this operation, he remained insane many years, till the Virgin Mary courteously restored his brains to their station.

CRAMOND BRIDGE, MIDLOTHIAN

When James V (r. 1513–42) travelled in disguise, he used a name known only to some of his principal nobility and atten-dants. He was called THE GUIDMAN OF BALLANGEICH (p. 98), 'guidman' or 'goodman' meaning owner or tenant, and Ballangeich being a farm near Stirling

Castle, and under that humble designation he would travel around to see for himself the state of his country and his people.

On such a journey, according to a tale included by Katharine Briggs in her *Dictionary of British Folk-Tales* (1970–1), James once got involved in a fight with some vagrants near the Bridge of Cramond. Getting onto the bridge, which was high and narrow, he managed to defend himself with his sword, but was hard pressed since it was four or five to one. A poor man who was threshing corn nearby came to the king's assistance, and with his flail managed to put the attackers to flight, afterwards producing water and a towel for James to wash off the stains of battle.

James asked the man's name, and whether he had any particular wish; his rescuer replied that he was John Howieson of the farm of Braehead, near Cramond, which belonged to the King of Scotland, and he wished he owned the farm himself. James for his part introduced himself as the Goodman of Ballangeich, and said he worked at the royal palace and could show John round if he liked.

A few days later when John arrived and asked for the Goodman of Ballangeich, James came to meet him wearing his disguise as before, including a bonnet, and asked if John wished to see the king. John replied that he would indeed, but wondered how he would know the monarch in a room full of nobles. The king alone, James replied, would be wearing a hat; everyone else would be 'uncovered'.

They walked into a great crowded hall. John looked around for the king, and said he couldn't see him. 'I told you that you should know him by his wearing his hat,' James reminded him. 'Then,' said John, 'it must be either you or me, for all but us two are bareheaded.'

When the penny finally dropped, John was rewarded with his farm at Braehead, on condition that he and his successors were always ready to present a basin of water for the king to wash his hands whenever his Majesty came to Holyrood Palace or passed the Bridge of Cramond. Briggs quotes Sir Walter Scott's report that in 1822, when George IV came to Scotland, John's descendant, who still owned Braehead, attended the king to perform his time-honoured function.

Tales of a king who travels incognito among his subjects are common, and the episode of the 'uncovered' courtiers is also told in France. More tales of James V and James IV, of whom there are similar legends, are set at EASTER WEMYSS and MILNATHORT (both Central & Perthshire).

Cranshaws Farm, Berwickshire

BROWNIES (p. 80) were helpful creatures if you treated them right, but they were touchy. They liked to wear their own clothes (if any) and would leave if you gave them a new suit, but they were apt to take umbrage, too, if they thought their services were taken for granted. In his *Popular Rhymes, Sayings, and Proverbs of the County of Berwick* (1856), George Henderson quotes one such story from an unspecified work by Robert Chambers. An industrious Brownie worked at Cranshaws Farm, reaping and threshing the corn, until one evening he overheard someone say 'that he had not *mowed* it very well, that is, not piled it up neatly at the end of the barn'. This was not to be forgiven: all night the Brownie was busy undoing his own work, carrying the corn out of the barn and throwing it over the Raven Craig, a precipice some way from the farm. As he did so he expressed his rage in verse:

'Its no weel mow'd! Its no weel
     mow'd!—
Then its ne'er be mow'd by me again,
I'll scatter it owre the RAVEN STANE,
And they'll hae some wark ere it's
     mow'd again!'

Chambers comments that 'the people of the farm had almost the trouble of a second harvest in gathering it up again', and they must have regretted their ingratitude.

Another Brownie said to have left his house under a cloud was the helper at BODESBECK FARM (Dumfries & Galloway).

CUDDYHALL, BLAINSLIE, ROXBURGHSHIRE

Speaking of 'Cuddie's Ha'' in 1888, *Chambers's Journal* comments, 'It is only a humble cottage by the wayside, and yet it must be one of the oldest seats of human habitation in the country.' This opinion appears to be based not on any architectural evidence or written record, but on the tradition embodied in its name that it was where St Cuthbert lived 'when, as a boy, he herded sheep on the green hills by the banks of the Leader'.

The likelihood of a shepherd's cot surviving since St Cuthbert's time, the seventh century, is exceedingly small, and so is the idea that oral tradition would carry his memory without a break for 1,300 years or so. For all that, local traditions linking particular places with famous people are popular and enduring.

See also SAINTS OF SCOTLAND (p. 490).

DALHOUSIE CASTLE, MIDLOTHIAN

In 1721, the poet Allan Ramsay described the Edgewell Tree in a note to one of his poems:

An Oak Tree which grows on the Side of a fine Spring, nigh the Castle of *Dalhousie*, very much observed by the Country People, who give out, that before any of the Family died, a Branch fell from the *Edge-well* Tree. The old Tree some few Years ago, fell altogether, but another sprung from the same Root, which is now tall and flourishing, and *lang be't sae*.

Similar prophetic trees are found in other parts of Britain, and the fortunes of the Thanes of Cawdor were said to depend on the tree which grew actually inside CAWDOR CASTLE (North East).

DALKEITH, MIDLOTHIAN

In 1830, Sir Walter Scott, as fascinated by stories of contemporary superstition as by historical legend, recorded an instance of which 'the whole circumstances are well known to me'. An old woman living alone subsisted mostly by raising chickens, at which she had been so successful that her envious neighbours raised the rumour that she had some 'unlawful' method of increasing her profits – i.e. that she was a witch. One year, however, shortly after 1800, there was a dearth of grain approaching famine, and the old woman, finding herself very short of chickenfeed, though not of money, went to a farmer to implore him to sell her some oats and name his own price. He refused, since his grain was all measured out and ready to go to market. The old woman lost her temper at this, scolded the farmer, and wished evil to his property.

The farmer's carts then set off for Dalkeith, but as they crossed the ford near the farmhouse a wheel came off, spilling five or six sacks of grain into the water.

> The good farmer hardly knew what to think of this; there were the two circumstances deemed of old essential and sufficient to the crime of witchcraft – *damnum minatum et malum secutum.*

In other words, the woman had cursed him and evil had followed. The man consulted the sheriff of the county, who happened to be a friend of his, and who assured him that the laws against witchcraft were no longer in operation. The farmer accordingly agreed to look at the whole thing as an accident, but the old woman herself, Scott continues, was less ready to be convinced when the sheriff, quite kindly, warned her to be careful:

> He reminded her that if she used her tongue with so much licence, she must expose herself to suspicions, and that should coincidences happen to irritate her neighbours, she might suffer harm at a time when there was no one to protect her. He therefore requested her to be more cautious in her language for her own sake, professing, at the same time, his belief that her words and intentions were perfectly harmless and that he had no apprehension of being hurt by her, let her wish her worst to him. She was rather more angry than pleased at the well-meaning sheriff's scepticism. 'I would be laith to wish ony ill either to you or yours, sir,' she said; 'for I kenna how it is, but something aye comes after my words when I am ill-guided and speak ower fast.'

In short, Scott says, she was obstinate in claiming occult powers, and her attitude might easily in earlier times have led her to the stake.

See also WITCH-HUNTS (p. 270).

DALMENY, MIDLOTHIAN

In the 1650s, a man named William Barton was tried for witchcraft. In his confession, reported by George Sinclair in 1685, Barton said that if he had twenty sons, he would advise them to shun 'the lust of uncleanness', for it was the love of women that had brought about his downfall. One day, he said, he was going from his own house in Kirkliston to Queensferry, and while passing through the Dalmeny Muir (Moor) he overtook a beautiful young lady. When he approached her, she avoided him, and when he insisted she became angry.

> Said I, since we are both going one way, be pleased to accept of a convey. At last, after much entreaty she grew better natured, and at length we came to that Familiarity, that she suffered me to embrace her, and to do that which Christian ears ought not to hear of. At this time I parted with her very joyful.

His joy did not last long:

> The next night, she appeared to him in that same very place, and after that which should not be named, he became sensible, that it was the Devil. Here he renounced his Baptism, and gave up himself to her service, and she called him her beloved, and gave him this new name of *John Baptist*, and received the *Mark*.

This was the 'witch's mark' which was the indisputable sign of black magic, and could (it was believed) be discovered by a witch-pricker like Paterson at INVERNESS (Southern Highlands).

After Barton had confessed all this, he was allowed to rest awhile, and woke laughing, saying that the Devil had appeared to him and rebuked him for confessing, reminding him of a promise that no man should take his life. He refused to give any more details of his satanic dealings, even when he was told that the fire was built, the stake set up, and the executioner on his way: he knew, he said, that he should not die that day. It seemed for a while that Barton was right, for on arrival at the prison the executioner suddenly fell dead. The authorities then, however, asked the executioner's wife to take over and strangle Barton:

> When the Warlock heard this, that a Woman was to put him to death; *O, crys he, how hath the Devil deceived me? Let none ever trust to his Promises.*

Barton's wife was accused at the same time, though the couple declared that neither had known that the other was a sorcerer. She confessed that one night she had gone to dance on the Pentland hills with the Devil leading the way in the likeness of a rough brown dog, playing on a pair of pipes, and carrying a candle stuck in his bottom under his wagging tail.

The promise made to Barton that no man should kill him, then evaded by having a woman perform the deed, is a good example of a misleading prophecy depending on a play on words. The same device was used by Shakespeare in MACBETH (p. 318), following Holinshed:

> And suerlie hereupon had he put Makduffe to death, but that a certeine witch, whome he had in great trust, had told that he should never be slain with man borne of anie woman.

When Macduff finally confronts his enemy, he declares, 'It is true, Makbeth, and now shall thine insatiable crueltie have an end, for I am even he that thy wizzards have told thee of, who was never born of my mother, but ripped out of her womb.'

See also WITCH-HUNTS (p. 270).

DELORAINE, BUCCLEUCH, SELKIRKSHIRE

In country districts of the Scottish Borders, tailors used to hire themselves out to neighbouring farmhouses for the day, returning to their village workshops at night. According to one of the stories collected by Sir Walter Scott's informant Thomas Wilkie, the farmer's wife of Deloraine in the Ettrick Forest once engaged a village tailor with his workmen and apprentices for a day, asking them to come in good time in the morning. This they did, and shared the family breakfast of milk and porridge. During the meal, one of the apprentices observed that the milk jug was almost empty, whereupon the farmer's wife slipped out at the back door with a basin. The lad had heard there was no more milk in the house, so he crept quietly after her and hid himself behind the door. He saw her turn a plug in the kitchen wall, whereupon a stream of milk poured out into the basin. When she turned the spigot again, the milk ceased to flow. Taking up the bowl, she returned to the tailors and they finished their breakfast.

About noon, one of the tailors complained of thirst and said he wished he had more milk as good as they had at breakfast. The apprentice said he could deal with that. As the farmer's wife was out of the way, he went out, twirled the plug, and filled the basin. But then, twirl as he might, he could not stop the flow. He called the other lads and they brought tubs and buckets they found in the kitchen, but these were soon filled. While the confusion was at its height, the farmer's wife reappeared, looking as black as thunder, crying that they had drawn the milk from every cow between the head of Yarrow and the foot.

The tailors slunk away abashed, and from that day on, the wives of Deloraine served their tailors nothing but mashed potatoes and cabbage.

This lively variation on the well-known tale of 'The Sorcerer's Apprentice' (who imitates his master's magic but cannot put a stop to it) hinges on the belief that witches could steal the milk from other people's cows by sympathetic magic, whether by milking a 'hair tether' or, as here, using a plug or spigot. Isobel Gowdie, executed for witchcraft in 1662, confessed to stealing milk from a cow with a hair tether: 'We plait the rope the wrong way in the devil's name, and thereby take with us the cow's milk,' and Marie Lamont of INVERKIP (Glasgow & Ayrshire) confessed at her trial that another woman had taught her to take milk by drawing a hair tether over the mouth of a mug, saying, 'In God's name, God send us milk, God send it, and meikle [much] of it.' The hair tether, such as is said to have been used by Scottish witches of the eighteenth century, was a tether made of hair from the tail of every cow the witch could possibly get at. She would plait the hair tether, tying a knot for each animal, then milk the rope, singing:

'Meare's milk, and deer's milk
And every beast that bears milk
Between St Johnston and Dundee
Come a' to me, come a' to me.'

The practice was not confined to Scotland. In Thorpe's *Northern Mythology* (1851) there appears the tale of a farmer at Caseburg in North Germany: he could get no milk from his cows and consulted a wise man, who detected that the culprit was a neighbour's wife. This woman had stuck a broom handle into the wall of her own cow-house and milked that. William Henderson, who retells Wilkie's tale of 'The Farmer's Wife of Deloraine' in his *Folk Lore of the Northern Counties of England and the Borders* (1866), notes another German example, that of a sermon

Thomas the Rhymer, a famous legendary figure, was also a real man whose family is thought to have lived in Earlston. As proof, people point to this gravestone, which can be found embedded in the church wall and reads 'AULD RYMR RACE LYES IN THIS PLACE'.

preached in Strasburg in 1508 and published in 1517, illustrated by a woodcut of witches milking pump handles.

Henderson also tells the story of two women, long suspected of witchcraft, who were seen by a farmer one Beltane morning brushing the May dew, traditionally a magical substance, off the pastures with a hair tether. At his approach, they fled, leaving the tether behind. He took it home and fixed it above his cow-house door. Next milking time, the dairymaids could not find pails enough to hold the abnormal flow of milk (which in this instance came from the cows themselves, not the tether) until the farmer took the tether down and burned it. There were numerous knots tied in the magical rope, each of which exploded like a pistol-shot as it was burned. Destroying the rope was the only way to break such a spell: in this case the tether had already been found, but if you needed to discover who had enchanted your cow, the recommended procedure in the sixteenth century was to put your husband's britches on the horns of the animal, one leg on either horn, give her a good clout with a stick and watch her run straight to the door of the guilty party.

There is a Scottish hair tether in the Folk-Lore Society's collection of artefacts housed at the Folk Museum, Cambridge, though the acquisition note concerning it does not say if it was made specifically for a folklore exhibition or was one that had actually been in use, by witches or otherwise.

See also WITCH-HUNTS (p. 270).

DRUMELZIER, PEEBLESSHIRE

When an early Baron of Drumelzier returned from the Crusades after some years, he found his wife with a new baby, which curious circumstance she explained by saying that she had been walking by the River Tweed one day when the spirit of the river had arisen to ravish her. This account was accepted by the baron, though with how much private conviction we cannot know. In the course of time the child inherited the title and became chief of the clan. Such was the popular story, still locally current in the early nineteenth century as a derivation for the family name of 'Tweedie', this having been the child's nickname.

Essentially this is a classical legend, the same told of Greek heroes such as Perseus or Theseus, sons begotten by the gods and mortal women. From the earliest times, river gods or spirits have been accounted powerful, potentially dangerous, and sometimes seductive, a combination which can be seen in stories of KELPIES AND WATER-HORSES (p. 364). Another tradition of Drumelzier is that Merlin's grave lies here, near the POWSAIL BURN.

EARLSTON, BERWICKSHIRE

Thomas the Rhymer is one of Lowland Scotland's most famous legendary figures,

stories of whose life and afterlife are told at EILDON HILLS and THE LUCKEN HARE, but he was also a real person, whose possible birthplace was at Erceldoune, now Earlston, and whose family name is said to have been Lermont or Learmont. According to the Bemerside Charter, held in the National Library of Scotland, the tower and lands of Erceldoune passed in 1299 from 'Thomas of Ercildoun', son and heir of 'Thomas Rimour of Ercildoun', to the Trinity House of Soltra (the Augustinian monastery of Soutra).

A gravestone believed to be that of Thomas's family is embedded in the wall of the church at Earlston, reading 'AULD RYMR RACE LYES IN THIS PLACE'. Other stones nearby date from the seventeenth century.

George Henderson, writing in 1856, says that the last inhabitant of what he calls the 'Rhymer's Tower', at the west end of Earlston, was Patrick Murray, a surgeon who 'pursued various studies of a philosophical kind, not very common in Scotland during the eighteenth century'. This is tamer than what Henderson tells us in an earlier article of 1834, where he gives a description of Murray as being 'a kind of herbalist, who, by dint of some knowledge in simples [herbal remedies], the possession of a musical clock, an electrical machine, and a *stuffed alligator*, added to a supposed communication with Thomas the Rhymer, lived for many years in very good credit as a wizard'.

EDINBURGH CASTLE

Except old sawes do faile,
  And wisards wits be blind,
The Scots in place must reigne,
  Where they this stone shall find.

This is how Raphael Holinshed translates the traditional prophecy relating to the Coronation Chair and the Stone of

Destiny, also known as the Stone of Scone. From the Holy Land to Spain, to Ireland, to Scotland, to England, to Scotland again – the Stone has been a frequent flyer, even if some of the journeys are doubtful. It is sometimes claimed to have been the biblical stone on which Jacob laid his head to dream of his and his people's future, and to have been taken to Ireland by a pharaoh's daughter, Scota, mythical progenitor of the Scots. That is unlikely to be true, but the stone may well have come with the original Scots from Ireland, perhaps around the end of the fifth century. After Kenneth II brought it to SCONE PALACE (Central & Perthshire) from DUN-STAFFNAGE CASTLE (Argyllshire & Islands) in 840, it was used for the inaugural ceremonies of thirty-four successive Scottish kings over four hundred years or so until 1296 when Edward I took it to Westminster Abbey. A daring raid by students in 1950 saw it restored to Scotland, but it was returned in 1951 (unless, as some say, what the English got this time was a faked copy), and finally handed back on 30 November 1996, St Andrew's Day. It is now in Edinburgh Castle.

See MACBETH (p. 318).

EDIN'S HALL BROCH,
BERWICKSHIRE

The largest Iron Age broch in Lowland Scotland is on the north-eastern slope of Cockburn Law. Signposted from the A6112 to Duns, and reached by footpath off the Oldhamstocks road, it can be visited at any time. Its massive proportions would suit an outsize tenant, and its name suggests a connection with the Etin, Old English *eoten*, a giant. J. Turnbull in 1882 mentioned the Etin who lived in this broch and was returning to it one day with his plunder, a bull and two sheep, shaking

from his shoe a 'pebble', in fact a vast boulder, when he drowned in the river.

Other sources claim the broch as the home of the Red Etin in one of the oldest Scottish tales of which we have a record. The title 'The Red Etin' is included in a list of songs and stories published in 1550, and the tale was one of those told in the early sixteenth century by the poet David Lyndsay to the young James V. Around 1827 the ballad collector Peter Buchan recorded it in manuscript, and Buchan's version was used as a basis for Robert Chambers's retelling in his revised edition of *Popular Rhymes of Scotland* in 1842.

There were once two widows, the story begins. One had two sons and the other had one son, and by and by it was time for the eldest of the two brothers to go and seek his fortune. His mother told him to bring water from the well to make a cake, but most of the water ran out of a hole in his pail and so the cake was small. Having baked it, his mother asked if he would take half of it with her blessing or the whole with her curse, and as it was so little he took it all. Before leaving he gave his brother his knife, telling him to look at it every morning. If it was clear and bright, its original owner was safe; if dim and rusty, evil would have befallen him.

On the third day of his journey, he met a shepherd. When he asked whose the sheep were, the man replied that they belonged to the Red Etin who had stolen the King of Scotland's daughter and feared no one, although one day he would meet his match:

> It's said there's ane predestinate
> To be his mortal foe;
> But that man is yet unborn,
> And lang may it be so.

Next the widow's son met a swineherd, and finally a goatherd, who gave him the same replies to his questions. The goatherd added that he should beware of the next beasts he met.

Sure enough, by and by the lad encountered some dreadful beasts with two heads and on every head four horns. Running away, he came to a castle where he asked for shelter. The old woman by the fire warned him that the castle belonged to the Red Etin, a merciless three-headed ogre. She hid him, but presently in came the Red Etin himself, crying:

Snouk but and snouk ben,
[Sniff in front and sniff behind]
I find the smell of an earthly man;
Be he living, or be he dead,
His heart shall be kitchen to my bread.

The Red Etin soon found the lad, and asked him three riddles. When he could not answer, the Red Etin knocked him on the head and turned him into a pillar of stone.

Next morning, the widow's second son looked at his brother's knife, and lo! the blade was rusty. He told his mother it was time for him to leave, and she sent him in his turn for water. All happened to this young man as had happened to his brother: he took the whole cake with his mother's curse, and in due course ended up as a pillar of stone in the Red Etin's castle.

The other widow's only son now determined to seek his friends, and for him things turned out differently. First of all, a raven told him there was a hole in his pail, so he patched the place with clay and returned with enough water for his mother to make a large cake, of which he took half with her blessing. On his travels he met an old woman who asked for a piece, and though he had not much he gave her some gladly. In return she gave him a magic wand, told him the answer to the Red Etin's riddles, and then vanished (being a fairy).

Like the other two, he met the shepherd,

One of the oldest recorded fairy tales of Scotland tells of the 'Red Etin', a giant who may have lived in Edin's Hall Broch. He kept dreadful two-headed, eight-horned beasts, as shown in this 1890 illustration.

the swineherd, and the goatherd, but heard a different final verse about the Red Etin:

> But now I fear his end is near,
> And destiny at hand;
> And you're to be, I plainly see,
> The heir to all his land.

When he encountered the two-headed eight-horned beasts he strode bravely through them, striking the first with his wand and laying it dead at his feet.

The old woman at the Red Etin's castle warned him what had happened to his friends, but he was determined to help them. Soon the Red Etin arrived, sniffed out the intruder, and asked him the three riddles. Thanks to the fairy's help he could answer them, the Red Etin's power was broken, and the lad chopped off his three heads with an axe.

He released several beautiful ladies imprisoned by the giant in the castle, including the Princess of Scotland, and restored the other boys to life by touching the stone pillars with his magic wand. All of them set out for the King of Scotland's court where the third lad married the princess, his friends married nobles' daughters, and they lived happily ever after.

EILDON HILLS, ROXBURGHSHIRE

Black's *Picturesque Tourist of Scotland* (1844) briefly mentions a tale of the hills:

> It is said that Eildon hills were once an uniform cone, and that the summit was formed into the three picturesque peaks, into which it is now divided, by a spirit, for whom Michael Scott was under necessity of finding constant employment.

There are many tales of MICHAEL SCOT, THE WIZARD OF BALWEARIE (p. 62)

including those set at AIKWOOD TOWER AND GLENLUCE ABBEY (Dumfries & Galloway) and BIGGAR (North East). Below Eildon Hills, legends of Sir Michael meet those of Thomas the Rhymer, for it was here that Thomas encountered the Fairy Queen, according to a romance of the fifteenth century and a ballad going back to at least the eighteenth. The mortal and the fairy lay together, and then – transformed from a beauty to a hag – she took him beneath the ground where he underwent a long dark journey. After this she pointed out to him the paths of good, evil, and mystery:

> O see not ye yon narrow road,
>   So thick beset wi thorns and
>   briers?
> That is the path of righteousness,
>   Tho after it but few enquires.
>
> And see not ye that braid braid road,
>   That lies across yon lillie leven?
> That is the path of wickedness,
>   Tho some call it the road to
>   heaven.
>
> And se not ye that bonny road,
>   Which winds about the fernie
>   brae?
> That is the road to fair Elfland,
>   Whe[re] you and I this night
>   maun gae.

In the Fairy Queen's own land, Thomas stays for three days, or so he thinks. After that time the queen takes him back to where the journey began, under the Eildon Tree, the site now marked by the Eildon Stone. The Queen teaches prophecies to Thomas, and bestows on him a tongue that cannot lie – hence another name for him, 'True Thomas' – and on his return to humanity he finds that his absence has lasted three mortal years.

Thomas of Erceldoune himself really lived in the thirteenth century, and by the

Rashin-Coatie

This Victorian illustration for 'Rashin-Coatie' – a Scottish version of 'Cinderella' – shows the heroine with her faithful helper, the red calf. Like Cinderella's Fairy Godmother, the calf presents her with a beautiful dress – but here it is so that she can attend kirk, rather than a ball.

There were once two sisters, one ugly and ill-natured, the other fair and good. The ugly one was the favourite of her parents, who starved their other daughter and sent her to herd cattle, but a red calf fed her every day with a fine dinner.

When her family found out her secret, they ordered the girl to kill the calf with an axe, but on the calf's instructions she killed her sister instead. The girl and calf ran away together, and as the girl had so few clothes they made her a coat of rushes, so after that she was called Rashin-coatie. The two of them went to the king's house, where Rashin-coatie was employed as a servant. At Christmas she was left behind to cook while the family went to kirk, but the calf made her a grand dress and slippers and sent her to kirk too. There the prince fell in love with her, and when she left she dropped one of her slippers which the prince kept.

Every lady in the land tried on the slipper, but it was too small for any of them. At last a henwife's daughter cut off her toes and made the shoe fit, and the prince was going to marry her until a little bird sang the truth to him. He found Rashin-coatie in the kitchen, and they were married and built a house for the red calf.

This precis of a story from Sir George Douglas's *Scottish Fairy and Folk Tales* (1896) suggests what Douglas himself calls 'a sense, stronger perhaps than is felt by any other nation, of fate and doom, of the mystery of life and death, of the cruelty of the inevitable . . .' Perhaps he states it a little too emphatically – there is plenty of merriment as well as melancholy in the Scottish repertoire – but a comparison of the Lowland 'Rashin-coatie' with the more familiar 'Cinderella' does indicate a different spirit. The henwife is a generally evil figure common to Scots and Gaelic tradition, while the fact that the heroine meets her prince not at a ball but at kirk is characteristic. Rather than a 'fairy godmother', the helper is a domestic beast, another common motif; in a Shetland version, 'Essie-Pattel an da Blue Yowe', it is a goat. In some tellings, the animal declares that it is the heroine's mother transformed to this shape.

Scotland has many versions of international tales, common throughout the Western world, which could be defined as fairy tales. Not all involve fairies, and folklorists tend to use the terms 'wonder tale' or 'tale of magic'. Scottish legends of fairies often imply an element of belief, being set in familiar places and associated with people known to the community. Wonder tales, on the other hand, are considered as fiction, their locations vague or fantastical like 'the Land of Enchantment' mentioned in some narratives, their characters generic rather than individual. In tales from the Lowlands and the Orkney and Shetland Islands, as in many European tales, the protagonist is usually of humble origin, either an anonymous 'poor lassie' or 'poor lad' or an all-purpose 'Jack', although in Orkney and Shetland there are variations on the name Essie-Pattel or Assipattle, as in the tale 'Assipattle and the Mester Stoorworm', supplied in Douglas's collection from WESTBROUGH.

The Gaelic hero or heroine, however, is often of royal blood, such as 'Lasair Gheug, the King of Ireland's daughter', a version of 'Snow White'. More characters in these tales are named, and the action is frequently set in specific but foreign lands such as France, Greece, or Lochlann (the old Gaelic name for Norway or more generally Scandinavia). These stylistic features reflect the influence of hero tales derived from the literature of the medieval aristocracy of Ireland, the Highlands, and the Western Isles, the most notable being the Fenian Cycle dealing with Fionn mac Cumhaill or FINGAL (p. 10) and his noble band of followers.

Tales from the Scottish Lowlands were collected in the 1820s by Peter Buchan and Robert Chambers, and in the 1850s John Francis Campbell of Islay began gathering Gaelic stories in the Highlands. Many Gaelic narratives were later printed in books and journals, and in the 1930s recordings as well as transcriptions began to be made, while from the 1950s onwards researchers from the School of Scottish Studies have collected hundreds of tales throughout Scotland, demonstrating a rich and varied narrative tradition.

See also EDIN'S HALL BROCH (Lothian & Borders); TRAVELLER TALES (p. 298).

early fourteenth century was remembered as a poet and prophet: it is not impossible that some of the verse-predictions associated with his name were actually composed by him. In his old age, according to some accounts, instead of dying he was recalled to fairyland, although other legends make him a 'sleeping hero' in the tradition of King Arthur, as at THE LUCKEN HARE.

See also BORDER BALLADS (p. 224).

ETTRICK WATER, SELKIRKSHIRE

In his *Poems* of 1721, Allan Ramsay mentions the spirit Shellycoat and defines it as follows:

One of those frightful Spectres the ignorant People are terrified at, and tell us strange Stories of; that they are clothed with a Coat of Shells, which make a horrid rattling, that they'll be sure to destroy one, if he gets not a running Water between him and it; it dares not meddle with a Woman with Child, &c.

Ramsay's reference to getting running water between oneself and the creature is a little puzzling, because Shellycoat was generally believed to live *in* the water. Sir Walter Scott writes of him in *Minstrelsy of the Scottish Border* (1802–3) as 'a spirit who resides in the waters, and has given his name to many a rock and stone upon the Scottish coast', and relates one of his pranks:

Two men, in a very dark night, approaching the banks of the Ettrick, heard a doleful voice from its waves repeatedly exclaim – 'Lost! Lost!' – They followed the sound, which seemed to be the voice of a drowning person, and to

their infinite astonishment, they found that it ascended the river. Still they continued, during a long and tempestuous night, to follow the cry of the malicious sprite; and arriving, before morning's dawn, at the very sources of the river, the voice was now heard descending the opposite side of the mountain in which they arise. The fatigued and deluded travellers now relinquished the pursuit; and had no sooner done so, than they heard Shellycoat applauding, in loud bursts of laughter, his successful roguery.

The leading of travellers astray was a trick ascribed to other impish spirits, including Will o' the Wisp, Puck, and Robin Goodfellow, of whom a loud mocking laugh is also a traditional attribute.

See also GORRENBERRY and LEITH.

EYEMOUTH, BERWICKSHIRE

In his 1856 book of Berwickshire rhymes, George Henderson includes a verse which he says 'has been in circulation for time immemorial':

I stood upon EYEMOUTH FORT,
    And guess ye what I saw?
FERNEYSIDE, and FLEMINGTON,
    NEWHOUSES, and COCKLAW,
The fairy folk o' FOSTERLAND,
    The witches o' EDENCRAW,
And the bogle in the BILLY-MYRE
    Wha' kills our bairns a'.

He notes that someone standing in the ruins of Eyemouth Fort would be disappointed if they expected to see all the places mentioned, since even in his day not all of them still existed, but he identifies as Fosterland Burn a stream which rises above Buncle Edge and runs into Billy Myre, a marsh.

The banks of this stream were a favourite haunt of the Fairies in bygone days – and we once knew an old thresher or barn-man, *David Donaldson*, or *Downieson*, by name, who, although he never *saw* one of those ærial beings, constantly maintained that he had frequently heard their sweet music in the silence of some summer midnight by *Fosterland Burn . . .*

Of the Bogle of Billy Myre, he says that in his own youth 'Jock o' the Mire' had been a terrible bogey, but that recent draining of the marsh had now banished the ghost.

Turning to the witches of Edencraw, or Auchencraw, Henderson says that 'like all other witches, they delighted in very wicked transactions', and quotes a further 'old Rhyme' in which he leaves coy blanks, some of which can be more easily filled in than others:

There's warlocks and witches in *Auchen-craw*
Wha neither fear God, nor regard the law;
They've l— a man, as I heard tell,
For whilk they'll a' be sent to h—!
In a barrel o' feathers they stappit his head,
And guddled [stabbed] the body till he was dead;
Then into the fire his —s they threw –
De'il ride the stang on the ill-deeded crew!

The 'stang' was a wooden pole on which people were carried – 'ridden' – as a punishment.

FAST CASTLE, BERWICKSHIRE

'The imaginary castle of Wolf's Crag has been identified by some lover of locality with that of Fast Castle,' writes Sir Walter Scott in the notes to *The Bride of Lammermoor* (1819). It certainly evokes a proper atmosphere for this most romantic of Scott's novels: the ruins, also known as Castle Knowe, are perched high above the sea on a crag connected to the mainland only by a narrow ridge, and 'a wilder or more disconsolate situation is difficult to conceive,' comments Black's *Picturesque Tourist of Scotland* of 1885.

Scott's story was inspired by history, but he changed the names of the characters and shifted the scene from west to east Scotland. These precautions did not entirely satisfy the living descendants of those concerned, who would have preferred not to give new publicity to 'so disastrous and distressing a family anecdote'.

There were political motives behind the 'Dalrymple legend' on which the novel was based. In the mid seventeenth century, James Dalrymple, first Lord Stair, had risen rapidly to power, and his enemies attacked him through the reputations of his daughter and particularly his wife, represented in lampoons and memoirs as a witch who gained preferment for her family through hellish compacts. A mocking 'Inscriptione for Lord Stair's Tomb' (meaning her son), written in Lady Stair's lifetime, describes her as a daughter of Beelzebub:

Whose malic oft wes wreckit at home,
On the curst cubs of her owne womb.

The bare facts of the tragedy that befell Lord Stair's daughter Janet were that on 12 August 1669 she married, on 24 August she was taken from her parents' house to her bridal home, and on 12 September she died. The story was embroidered to say that Janet had loved a Jacobite and pledged him her troth, but under the influence of her domineering father and even more of her mother became engaged to a prosperous Whig. On her wedding night, ghastly screams were heard: the bridegroom was found terribly wounded, and the bride crouched in a corner, quite insane. She died a fortnight later, he not for another thirteen years, but he never told anyone what had happened.

The most popular explanation was that the bride herself had been the attacker. Others thought it more likely that Janet's first lover had slipped in through the window to wound his rival, and Janet, seeing this, had lost her wits. A supernatural slant was given by those who claimed that the girl had called on the Devil to take her if she broke faith with her first love, and that when the Fiend claimed her he mauled the husband into the bargain. The fourth theory, implying a quite different series of events, is that the bride, marrying against her mother's will, received a parental curse and was stabbed by her husband, he then being the one to go mad.

Scott renames his heroine Lucy, and makes his climax a Gothic scene of blood and madness:

... one of the company, holding his torch much lower than the rest, discovered something white in the corner of the great old-fashioned chimney of the apartment. Here they found the unfortunate girl, seated, or rather couched like a hare upon its form – her head-gear dishevelled; her night-clothes torn and dabbled with blood, – her eyes glazed, and her features convulsed into a wild paroxysm of insanity. When she saw herself discovered, she gibbered, made mouths, and pointed at them with her bloody fingers, with the frantic gestures of an exultant demoniac.

Female assistance was now hastily summoned; the unhappy bride was overpowered, not without the use of some force. As they carried her over the threshold, she looked down, and uttered the only articulate words that she had yet spoken, saying, with a sort of grinning exultation, – 'So, you have ta'en up your bonnie bridegroom?'

Sir Walter Scott's novel *The Bride of Lammermoor* (1819) is a tragic and bloody drama. In this 1830 frontispiece the doomed Lucy swoons in the arms of her father.

The popular tale remembered now is, inevitably, that preferred by Scott and later by Gaetano Donizetti in his still more famous operatic version of the tragedy, *Lucia di Lammermoor* (first performed in 1835).

GALASHIELS, SELKIRKSHIRE

The seventeenth-century writer on witchcraft, George Sinclair, reports a 'true Narrative' of what happened once to Margaret Wilson of Galashiels. What passed on other occasions, he admits, 'I cannot relate, since I want Information,' but on the night in question her uncle came to Master Wilkie, the minister of Galashiels, and told him that the Devil was in his house: a strange knocking could be heard around his niece's bed. The minister accompanied him, and found that what Wilson had said was true. When Margaret got up from her bed and sat down to supper, the knocking continued under her chair, 'where it was not possible for any Mortal to Knock up'. At prayer time, too, knocking came from beneath where she knelt.

When Margaret went back to bed and fell asleep, her body was lifted up in the air so that even strong men were not able to keep it down, and at the same time a scratching noise was heard, like long nails along her feather bed. When she woke, she told the minister that the Devil had been speaking to her, offering her gifts. The minister induced her to put her name to 'a Personal Covenant with God' which he found ready composed 'in that little Treatise, called the Christians Great Interest', but even after this the Devil tried hard to persuade her to break her covenant.

The minister then talked seriously to Wilson, asking him if he had committed any sin, 'and particularly he charged him with one thing, whereof there was a loud report'; we are not told what this accusation was, although a modern conclusion might be that he had been having relations with his niece, then twelve or thirteen years old, which is also, of course, the classic age for poltergeist phenomena. Whatever the rumour, Wilson firmly denied it, and Margaret soon left Galashiels for Edinburgh, later going into service at Leith, and finally marrying and settling down. 'I do not hear that ever she was molested after,' says Sinclair, which has an ambiguous sound now, though he means by the Devil.

GORMYRE, WEST LOTHIAN

A church tract of 1594 deplores the 'horrible superstitione' prevalent in Garioch and elsewhere 'in not labouring a parcel of ground dedicated to the devil, under the title of the *Guidman's Croft*'. The purpose was to divert the attention of Satan, referred to as the 'goodman' in the sense of the tenant of a place as opposed to the laird, although the title was used also to avert the bad luck which might follow from directly naming a supernatural being: similarly, the fairies were often referred to as 'people of peace' or the classical Furies as 'the kindly ones'.

The practice criticised in the sixteenth century had not died out around 200 years later. Sir James Young Simpson, the pioneer of chloroform, recounted in 1861 what happened when his great-uncle Thomas bought a farm at Gormyre:

> Among his first acts after taking possession was the enclosing of a small triangular corner of one of the fields within a stone wall. The corner cut off – *which remains to this day in the same state* – was the 'Goodman's Croft.'

In his *West Lothian Lore* (1976), William Fyfe Hendrie mentions this anecdote, and comments that even when trying to propitiate the forces of darkness, Thomas was a good man of business: the ground set aside for the Devil was the roughest and stoniest earth in the district.

Sir James had a more unpleasant story of superstition concerning his grandfather Alexander at TORPHICHEN.

GORRENBERRY, HERMITAGE WATER, ROXBURGHSHIRE

In his introduction to *Minstrelsy of the Scottish Border* (1802–3), Sir Walter Scott writes that Shellycoat is 'a freakish spirit, who delights rather to perplex and frighten mankind, than either to serve, or seriously to hurt them'. Shellycoat was named from his appearance, since 'he seemed to be decked with marine productions; and, in particular, with shells, whose clattering announced his approach.' He was supposed particularly to haunt the old house of Gorrenberry, but could also be met with on ETTRICK WATER and at LEITH.

GRASSMARKET, EDINBURGH

Tanner's Close no longer exists, which may not be a bad thing. Described as a squalid alley near the junction of the West Port and the Grassmarket, the close was named for the nearby tanneries where animal skins were cured. This is, or was, one of the smelliest industries going, but that did not stop people staying in the cheap lodging house run by William Hare. One of those who took up occupation in 1827 was William Burke. Shortly after he moved in, another tenant died owing Hare money; to recoup his loss the landlord decided to sell the body, and got his new lodger to help.

There was a brisk trade at this time in fresh corpses, which were badly needed by the medical schools and were in short supply, since most people did not like the idea of their loved ones being cut up by the doctors. Bodysnatching had become an important part of underworld life, and Burke and Hare found it quite easy to reach an arrangement with a respectable surgeon, Dr Robert Knox. Their new careers as 'resurrection men' had taken off.

Robbing graves involved hard physical labour, and it soon occurred to the pair that there were easier ways to get a saleable cadaver. A lodger of Hare's was taken ill, and was eased out of the world with the help of a dose of whisky and a pillow across his face; as before, Dr Knox paid liberally for the body.

The two proceeded to kill at least sixteen more people in less than a year, before the

law caught up with them. When the news broke, it was a grim sensation, and children chanted in the streets:

Up the close and doon the stair,
But and ben wi' Burke and Hare.
Burke's the butcher, Hare's the thief,
Knox the boy who buys the beef.

A 'but and ben' is a two-roomed house, but the phrase can also be used to mean 'back and forth'.

Burke's execution was a social event. Everyone whose house commanded a good view of the scaffold in the Lawnmarket was offering their windows for hire, and business was so brisk that Charles Kirkpatrick Sharpe and Sir Walter Scott had to make do with a shared window. After the hanging, the corpse was, justly enough, made the subject of a medical demonstration.

Hare, on the other hand, had been offered immunity from prosecution in return for testifying against Burke, and was only imprisoned for a short time. He then disappeared from public view, although it was said by some that he was lynched in Ireland, and by others that he ended his days as a blind beggar on London's Oxford Street. A whole body of folklore about 'burkers' or 'resurrection men' was soon current, and the visits of legitimate antiquarians to old churchyards became fraught with risk, as Robert Chambers found out at LEVEN (Central & Perthshire).

See also TRAVELLER TALES (p. 298).

GREENLAW MOOR, BERWICKSHIRE

In *Glimpses into the Past in Lammermuir* (1892), John Hutton Browne relates the experience of John Niel, a local man, which 'influenced his mind, and became to him and his family a reality'. On a journey through Greenlaw Moor, Niel saw 'a strange animal, with a strange rider on its back':

> This may have been the result of his imagination working on the effects of moorland and sky, or it may have been some optical illusion, but when he approached Dronshiel, he met Robert Wilson of Blacksmill, and seriously asked him if he had met this unearthly equestrian. This adventure was related to his family, and so convinced were they all of the truth of this report that it became a trial for them to cross this moor, lest some evil would befall them.

Their fears were justified. Some time later, John's son Henry, a tall and muscular blacksmith, set out to cross the moor, but never reached home. Although out on Greenlaw there was always the possibility of a sudden mist to bewilder a traveller, and there had been lives lost in snow, 'it was neither mist nor snow that Henry Niel encountered on that fateful night, as he approached the Foul burn near the Cattleshiel road.' Instead he may have been the victim of a delusion that he was at home and going to bed, for when he was found dead (of exposure, perhaps, though this is not spelt out) he had taken off most of his clothes. Although he had apparently started to dress again, he had put some articles back on the wrong way round.

A variation on this story was told at LONGFORMACUS.

Greyfriars Kirk, Edinburgh

A notable memorial at Greyfriars is the 'haunted mausoleum' of Sir George Mackenzie, known as Bloody Mackenzie.

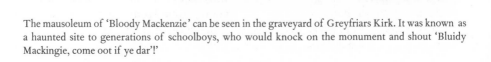

The mausoleum of 'Bloody Mackenzie' can be seen in the graveyard of Greyfriars Kirk. It was known as a haunted site to generations of schoolboys, who would knock on the monument and shout 'Bluidy Mackingie, come oot if ye dar'!'

Like the similarly nicknamed 'Bluidy Clavers' of DUNDEE (North East), Mackenzie had taken part in violent government suppression of the rebel Covenanters; both men were popularly supposed to be IN LEAGUE WITH THE DEVIL (p. 142), and the historian Charles Kirkpatrick Sharpe recorded in 1818 that Mackenzie was said to have died 'wasted by fountains of blood continually issuing from all parts', a divine punishment for his crimes against humanity.

In Robert Louis Stevenson's day, it was a game among the local schoolboys to knock and challenge Sir George to appear: 'Bluidy Mackingie, come oot if ye dar'!' The mausoleum was once used, however, as a refuge by a boy in hiding from the police. His friends brought him food there and at last he was able to smuggle himself on board a ship and escape abroad. 'But his must have been indeed a heart of brass,' comments Stevenson, 'to lie all day and night alone with the dead persecutor . . . When a man's soul is certainly in hell, his body will scarcely lie quiet in a tomb however costly; some time or other the door must open, and the reprobate come forth in the abhorred garments of the grave.'

The site of Mackenzie's memorial is ironically appropriate. The Covenanters he persecuted in the late seventeenth century were named for their support of the National Covenant, signed in 1638 in Greyfriars churchyard itself:

This covenant, or bond, was written on a parchment 'above an ell square,' [about 45 inches, or 113 cm] in which the subscribers swore to maintain Presbyterianism, and to resist what they designated 'contrary errors, to the utmost of their power.' After the document was signed in the church it was carried to the burying ground and spread upon a flat gravestone still extant, namely that of Boswell of

Auchinleck . . . and signed by as many as could approach. It is mentioned as an extraordinary instance of religious zeal, that hundreds not only added to their signatures the words *till death*, but actually subscribed it with their blood.

These details come from Black's *Picturesque Tourist of Scotland* of 1885, which goes on to mention, rather briefly and dismissively, the tradition of Greyfriars Bobby, 'a dog of typical fidelity'. Bobby probably gets more attention these days than the Covenanters, and has his own monument opposite the entrance to the church on the junction of George IV Bridge and Candlemaker Row. He was a Skye terrier belonging to John Grey, a farmer who died in 1858 and was buried in Greyfriars churchyard, after which the dog lived for the next fourteen years by the grave, being fed by local residents, who also built him a shelter. The Lord Provost of Edinburgh himself paid the annual dog licence, and Bobby was awarded the Freedom of the City.

HERMITAGE CASTLE, ROXBURGHSHIRE

It is said of the Castle of Hermitage that the measure of the iniquities perpetrated within it through the centuries cause it to sink ever deeper into the earth.

So writes Sir Walter Scott's informant Thomas Wilkie, referring to the career of the notorious Lord Soulis, who was said to use his servants worse than animals, drilling holes in their shoulders to harness them to the carts on which they had to drag the stones for his castle.

Numerous complaints of the lord's abominations were received by Robert the Bruce, who at last exclaimed, 'Boil him, if you please, but let me hear no more of him.' No sooner said than done: Soulis was seized, wrapped in a sheet of lead, and taken to the ancient stone circle at Nine Stane Rig, near Hermitage Water, where he was seethed in a cauldron. Robert Chambers wrote in the early nineteenth century that the cauldron was preserved by a Mr Pott of Pencryst, though John Leyden commented thirty years later that the said vessel was neither particularly large nor particularly old, and was in fact a cabbage pot.

A fourteenth-century source states that Soulis died at Dumbarton Castle, imprisoned there for his part in a plot to take the throne. It is only later that the boiling legend comes to be attached to him, almost certainly based on the tradition concerning John Melville, Laird of GLENBERVIE (North East).

Whereas Melville was merely disliked as a tyrant, Soulis was reputed to be a wicked magician. As a familiar he had a 'Redcap', a horrible Border bogey also known as Red-comb or Bloodycap or, in the story of COUT OF KEELDAR'S GRAVE, as 'The Brown Man of the Muirs'. This spirit was given to murdering travellers and draining their blood into his cap, or removing their brains while they slept. By this demon Soulis was protected against injury from rope or steel; to summon the spirit he would tap three times on an iron chest, but was forbidden to look at the form he raised. Once, however, he failed to turn away, and his doom followed, though his immunity from binding or wounding continued, and that is why he had to be wrapped in lead (not rope) and boiled (not executed).

Treasure was said to be hidden in or under the castle, but guarded by the demon for centuries after Soulis's death. John Leyden writes:

The door of the chamber, where Lord Soulis is said to have held his conferences

with the evil spirits, is supposed to be opened once in seven years, by that daemon, to which, when he left the castle, never to return, he committed the keys, by throwing them over his left shoulder, and desiring it to keep them till his return. Into this chamber, which is really the dungeon of the castle, the peasant is afraid to look; for such is the active malignity of its inmate, that a willow, inserted at the chinks of the door, is found peeled, or stripped of its bark, when drawn back.

This trick of stripping twigs of their bark is one reported of ghosts in other castle dungeons, such as SPEDLIN'S TOWER (Dumfries & Galloway).

HOLYDEAN, ROXBURGHSHIRE

William Henderson, writing in 1866, gives a story derived from the Wilkie manuscript collection of Border folklore. The tale is set in Holdean, probably what is now known as Holydean.

One day, tired from his work, the miller of Holdean fell asleep on some straw in his kiln-barn. After a while he was woken by a confused hubbub of voices, and looking down, he saw a number of feet and legs paddling about in the ashes of his fire as if enjoying the warmth. He distinctly heard a voice say, 'What think ye o' my feeties?' and a a second voice answer, 'An what think ye o' mine?'

Much astonished but unafraid, the miller threw down a large wooden hammer among them, stirring up the ashes, and asked them what they thought of his big hammer among all those legs of theirs:

A hideous rout at once emerged from the kiln amid yells and cries, which passed into wild laughter; and finally these words reached the miller's ears, sung in a mocking tone:

Mount and fly for Rhymer's tower,
    Ha, ha, ha, ha!
The pawky [artful] miller hath beguiled
    us,
Or we wud hae stown [stolen] his luck
For this seven years to come,
And mickle water wud hae run
    While the miller slept.

Although, as Henderson observes, the precise nature of the 'uncannie visitants' is not specified in the story, the clues suggest not witches but fairies. These often haunted mills, they were given to speaking in childish diminutives ('What think ye o' my feeties?'), and they frequently cast people into a long, enchanted sleep. The 'Rhymer's tower' is at EARLSTON, traditional home of Thomas the Rhymer, who makes appearances in other tales of fairy mischief such as that told at AUCHRI-ACHAN (North East).

HOLYROODHOUSE, EDINBURGH

The arms of Canongate, with their image of a white doe, preserve the legend of Holyrood's foundation. In about 1128, King David I, while hunting, was attacked by a stag when a cross descended from heaven into his hand. Seeing this, the stag fled in dismay. In a dream, David was then commanded to build a religious house on the site of the miracle, and thus came into being the Abbey of Holyrood.

The adjacent Palace of Holyroodhouse, dating from the end of the fifteenth century, became notorious as the site of a murder committed on 9 March 1566 in the presence of Mary, Queen of Scots. According to Sir Walter Scott's *History of Scotland* (1838), the queen was at supper in a small cabinet next to her bedroom, with

The blood of David Rizzio may still stain the floor of Holyroodhouse. He was believed by many to have been the lover of Mary, Queen of Scots, and was murdered in the palace on 9 March 1566.

the Countess of Argyll and some others, including David Rizzio or Riccio. Rizzio was an Italian musician, Mary's secretary, and widely rumoured to be her lover. Mary's husband Lord Darnley was passionately jealous, and had joined a conspiracy of Protestant lords to kill the Catholic interloper.

> Darnley suddenly entered the apartment, and, without addressing or saluting the company, gazed on Rizzio with a sullen and vindictive look; after him followed Lord Ruthven, pale and ghastly, having risen from a bed of long sickness to be chief actor in this savage deed; other armed men appeared behind.

Ruthven ordered Rizzio to come out.

> The miserable Italian, perceiving he was the destined victim of this violent intrusion, started up, and, seizing the Queen by the skirts of her gown, implored her protection. Mary was speedily forced by the king from his hold. George Douglas, a bastard of the Angus family, snatched the King's own dagger from his side, and struck Rizzio a blow; he was then dragged into the outer apartment, and slain with fifty-six wounds. The Queen exhausted herself in prayers and entreaties for the wretched man's life; but when she was at length told that her servant was slain, she said, 'I will then dry my tears, and study revenge.'

The 1844 edition of Black's *Picturesque Tourist of Scotland* reports that stains 'are still shown at the door of the apartment, said to be produced by the blood of the murdered man'. This claim is reworded and becomes more specific in subsequent editions: 'the exact spot where the body lay is pointed out and identified by marks of blood, still visible' (1865); 'the spot where the body lay being still marked by the stain of the blood' (1882).

Despite his atmospheric account of the crime, Scott himself was sceptical about its enduring traces. In *Chronicles of the Canongate* (1827), he introduces a Cockney detergent salesman who makes determined efforts to clean off the marks during a visit to Queen Mary's apartments. When the horrified guide puts a stop to his endeavours he retires 'muttering that he had always heard the Scots were a nasty people, but had no idea they carried it so far as to choose to have the floors of their palaces blood-boltered'. The hygienic scouring of an indelible bloodstain is an idea pursued and perfected by Oscar Wilde in *The Canterville Ghost* (1887).

See also THE THISTLE OF SCOTLAND (p. 252).

JEDBURGH, ROXBURGHSHIRE

Edgar Allan Poe's story 'The Masque of the Red Death' was inspired by macabre events said to have occurred at Jedburgh Castle in 1290 during the wedding of Alexander III. Holinshed's *Scottish Chronicle* (1576), in the English version by William Harrison, gives the legend:

> In the solemnization of the second marriage of king *Alexander*, as the bridegroome (according to the manner) led the bride in a dance, a great number of lords and ladies following them in the same dance, there appeared to their sight, as it were closing up the hindermost of the dancers, a creature resembling death, all naked of flesh and lire [meat], with bare bones right dreadfull to behold. Through which spectacle, the king and the residue of all the companie were so astonished, and put in such fright and fear, that they had quicklie made an end of their dance for that time.

In Poe's tale, the skeletal figure is a personification of a fatal disease which soon claims the courtiers. Poe (and several other writers) may have been misled by Holinshed's account, which runs together a mention of 'the first comming of the pestilence into Scotland' with a report of the marriage celebration, although the outbreak of plague occurred around eleven years earlier than the wedding. Such an apparition, however, could not but portend disaster. That same year, as the king was galloping along the cliffs at KINGHORN (Central & Perthshire), he fell from his horse and broke his neck, a disaster prophesied by Thomas the Rhymer. The day before, the Earl of March had asked Thomas what sort of weather they could expect:

> To whom the said *Thomas* answered, that on the morrow (before noone) should blow the sorest wind and tempest that ever was heard of in *Scotland* at anie time before.

When the morning dawned clear and bright, and continued so until nearly midday, the Earl remarked that Thomas had been mistaken. Thomas replied only that it was not yet past twelve, and immediately a messenger arrived bringing news of the king's death. Then said Thomas, 'That is the scathful wind and dreadfull tempest, which shall blow such calamity and trouble to the whole state of the whole realm of *Scotland*.'

This Thomas, adds Holinshed, was a man much renowned as a prophet, but whose predictions 'were ever hid and involved under the veil of dark and obscure speeches'. Other stories of the Rhymer are told at EARLSTON and THE LUCKEN HARE.

An altogether jollier character than the death's head at the feast was Archie Armstrong, official fool to James VI and I

(r. 1567–1625) and to his son Charles, whom he accompanied in his abortive attempt to negotiate marriage with the Spanish Infanta. He was allowed considerable licence at court: when the Spanish expedition was proposed, Archie indicated how rash he thought it by putting his jester's cap on James's head, and said that if Charles were allowed to return, he would give his hat to the King of Spain instead. He was popular with the Spanish, allowed to visit the princess and her ladies, and the King of Spain gave him a valuable chain and a suit of clothes (though Archie did not, presumably, hand over his cap in return).

In the *Book of Days* (1864), Robert Chambers writes that 'surprise is felt that one of the Armstrongs – that border clan remarkable only for *stouthreif* – should have ever found his way to court, even in so equivocal a position as that of the King's Jester.' ('Stouthreif' is robbery with violence, and the comment relates particularly to the famous Border reiver Johnnie Armstrong, summarily executed by James V at GILNOCKIE TOWER, Dumfries & Galloway.) 'The traditionary story on this point has been thus reported to us,' Chambers continues:

> A shepherd with the carcase of a sheep on his shoulders, was tracked by the officers of justice to a cottage in the moorlands, where, however, they found no one but a vacant-looking lad, who sat rocking a cradle, apparently altogether unconscious of their object. Searching somewhat narrowly, they at length found that, instead of a baby, the carcase of the missing sheep occupied the cradle.

They seized the rocker of the cradle and brought him to Jedburgh, where James VI had just arrived.

> Condemned to die for his crime, Archie Armstrong – for it was he – pleaded with

the king that he was a poor ignorant man – he had heard of the Bible, and wished to read it through – would his Highness please respite him till this should have been, for his soul's weal, accomplished. The good-natured monarch granted the prayer, and Archie immediately rejoined with a sly look, 'Then deil tak me an I ever read a word o't, as lang as my een are open!' James saw from this that there was humour in the man, and had him brought to court.

The story of the cradle which contains not a child but a dead sheep or a barrel of liquor is one told of many poachers and smugglers, and the ruse by which Archie gains his pardon is likewise a time-honoured piece of wit: the jester was clearly a notable character, about whom legends gathered.

Archie was finally sacked in 1637 by Charles I, having pushed his luck by mocking Archbishop Laud's intention to impose the Prayer Book on Scotland.

KELSO, ROXBURGHSHIRE

In Roxburgh Street, Kelso, there is a horseshoe embedded in the road, which is said to mark the spot where Prince Charles Edward's horse lost a shoe when he rode through the town on his way to Carlisle in 1745. He was also said to have planted a white rose in his host's garden, and descendants of 'Prince Charlie's White Rose' are or were alleged to survive in some gardens in the town.

Historical evidence confirms that the Bonnie Prince did indeed pass through Kelso on his way south, and spent a day there in November 1745. Whether his horse cast a shoe there and whether he planted a rose bush are not so certain: both the horseshoe and the rose tree are evocative symbols. Hoofprints of remarkable horses, or horses with remarkable riders, are said to survive imprinted on rock elsewhere, for example at Castle-an-Dinas in Cornwall, where King Arthur's steed left its mark, at Byard's Leap in Lincolnshire, commemorating a prodigious series of jumps made by a blind horse, and at SMOO CAVE (Northern Highlands), where the magician Donald Duibheal Mackay is said to have fled on horseback from the Devil. As for 'Prince Charlie's White Rose', Mary, Queen of Scots is similarly believed to have sown seeds of 'her' plant, the milk thistle (*Silybum marianum*), round her Scottish palaces and her English prisons.

That the horseshoe and the rose can be paralleled does not necessarily mean that these traditions are not historical: important people throughout the ages have made symbolic gestures in places whose inhabitants long remember the act.

KIRK YETHOLM, ROXBURGHSHIRE

For over a century, Kirk Yetholm near the English border was the royal court of the Scottish Travellers or gypsies. Here lived the Faas or Faws, whose forebear Johnnë Faw was recognised by James V in 1540 as 'Lord and Erle of Litill Egipt'. It was said that at the battle of Namur in 1695, a gypsy called Young defended the Laird of Kirk Yetholm, who rewarded him and his fellows with cottages in the village; an alternative account was that the laird was grateful for Wull Faa's recovery of his horse, stolen by Jacobites in 1715, but however the Travellers came to be there, by the nineteenth century their capital was famous. Queen Victoria herself called on Queen Esther Faa Blythe, last to bear the title, whose funeral in 1883 was attended by about 1,500 mourners.

TRAVELLER TALES (p. 298) are a significant element in Scottish folklore, and

The Thistle of Scotland

Why is the thistle the symbol of Scotland? One theory explains the plant's emblematic use as arising from the spear-like shape of its leaves, said to resemble the ranks of spears which the Scots used in battle. A more colourful explanation dates back to the eleventh century when a Danish army invaded the Highlands. According to the tale, the Danes tried to take the Scots unawares by walking barefoot, but when they encountered a field of thistles their anguished cries gave warning of their approach to the defenders, who attacked and defeated them. Another version of the story relates that even earlier, during the tenth century, Norsemen planned a midnight attack on a castle. When they stripped and tried to swim across the moat, they discovered that it had been filled not with water but with thistles, as a precaution against such an attempt. The naked warriors shrieked, alerting the guards, and the raid was repulsed. Since then the thistle has been highly regarded by all Scots, and was celebrated by James Rigg in 1897 in his poem 'To a Scotch Thistle':

> Strong on thy sabred citadel,
> In power thou guard'st thy crimson crown!
> What crawls, or creeps, or walks may tell
> The terrors of thy vengeful frown!

A question often asked is which is the 'true' Scottish thistle, and the answer is that there is probably no such thing. Any or all thistles can be taken as the national plant. The likeliest contenders for the role, since they are so common throughout Scotland, belong to the genus *Cirsium*: two species, the Creeping Thistle (*Cirsium arvense*) and the Spear Thistle (*Cirsium vulgare*), are both very widely found, and are both extremely prickly. Modern botanists use the name 'Scotch Thistle' as an alternative to Spear Thistle. A third species often mentioned is the Cotton Thistle (*Onopordum acanthium*), plants of which were carried in procession when George IV visited Scotland in 1822 and which from then onward was taken by many to be the 'Scotch Thistle', although in fact it is not native to Scotland.

As represented on coats of arms, the thistle is a stylised device, and does not accurately resemble any particular species. The plant was the badge of the House of Stuart, the family which reigned in Scotland from 1371, and coins bearing the thistle motif were minted from at least 1470 during the reign of James III. By 1503, when James IV married Margaret Tudor of England, the identification of the plant with the Stuarts and by extension with Scotland as a whole was well established. Ornamental thistles abound in documents recording the marriage, and the windows of Holyroodhouse in Edinburgh were decorated with a 'Chardon [thistle] and Rose interlassed', the rose being the badge of the Tudors. To celebrate the wedding, the poet William Dunbar wrote an allegory called 'The Thrissill and the Rois', in which James is depicted heraldically as the Lion, the Eagle, and finally the Thistle:

> Upone the awfull Thrissill scho beheld,
> And saw him kepit with a busche of
>   speiris.
> Concedring him so able for the weiris,
> A radius croun of rubeis scho him gaif,
> And said, 'In feild go furth and fend the
>   laif.'

> [Upon the awesome Thistle she
>   [Nature] looked,
> And saw him guarded with a bush of
>   spears.
> Considering him so able for the wars,
> A radiant crown of rubies she him gave,
> And said, 'In the field go forth and defend the rest.']

This sixteenth-century engraving shows James IV (r. 1473–1513) holding a thistle. The plant was the badge of the Stuart family, and has come to be seen as the symbol of Scotland.

The significance of the thistle in Dunbar's verse is protective, symbolising a king's duty to defend his country against invasion.

The highest order of chivalry in Scotland is the Order of the Thistle. The date of its founding is disputed, but it was certainly in existence by the reign of James V (1513–42). Its motto is *Nemo me impune lacessit*, 'No one provokes me with impunity' – or, in more colloquial Scots, 'Wha daurs meddle wi' me?' – an appropriately prickly message also used by the Royal Regiment of Scotland, the Scots Guards, and the Royal Scots Dragoons.

The leaves of thistles are painful but their down is soft, and was once commonly used to stuff bedding. There is a story that 200 years ago the Scottish thistle was brought to North America by a minister from Scotland who took with him his thistledown bed. When he arrived he found that feathers, a more comfortable filling, were plentiful, so he emptied out the thistledown. Scattered by the wind, the seeds germinated and filled the countryside with thistles.

Travellers themselves have been seen as legendary figures. Joseph Lucas writes in 1882 of his conviction that the gypsies are the prototypes of the fairies. His argument refers to fortune-telling, quite often practised by Travellers, and mentions the common slander that they stole children. He cites *A Discourse concerning the Nature and Substance of Devils and Spirits*, appended to the 1665 edition of Reginald Scot's *Discoverie of Witchcraft*, in which an account is given of men who claim to have feasted with the fairies in mountains and caves, and there met friends whom they know to have been dead for years and whose language they now cannot understand. 'The neighbours and acquaintances had, of course, run off and joined the Gypsies,' declares Lucas, and he goes on to quote from the *Discourse* the story of a man who was returning from market having failed to sell a horse, and on the way fell into conversation with a stranger who offered to buy the beast. This man told him that 'he himself was that person of the Family of Learmonts so much spoken of for a Prophet' – in other words, Thomas the Rhymer of EARLSTON.

> At which I began to be somewhat fearful, perceiving us in a road which I had never been in before, which increased my fear and admiration more. Well on we went till he brought me under ground I know not how into the presence of a beautiful woman that payd me the moneys without a word speaking; he conducted me out again through a large and long entry, where I saw above 600 men in Armour layd prostrate on the ground as if asleep: at last I found my self in the open field by the help of Moon-light in that very place where first I met him, and made shift to get home by three in the morning, but the money I received was just double of what I esteemed it, and what the woman payd me, of which at this instant I have several

pieces to show consisting of nine pences, thirteen pence halfpennies, &c.

Lucas maintains that this story 'without any doubt is a faithful narrative of a real event', and continues, 'Thomas the Rhymer was 27 years old in 1665, the date of the publication of Reginald Scot, and lived years after.' He is about three centuries out on the Rhymer's dates, and his grounds for believing that the slumbering warriors were Travellers seem flimsy in the extreme, but he concludes that 'I have not a shadow of doubt that his "Fairies" were Gypsies.' A more widely accepted interpretation would be that the sleepers were knights due to rise again when their country needs them, as at TOMNAHURICH (Southern Highlands).

LANGTON HOUSE, BERWICKSHIRE

George Henderson, in his *Popular Rhymes . . . of Berwick* (1856), gives a traditional rhyme, evidently a fairy work-song, which goes:

> Lift one, lift a',
> Baith at bak and fore wa' –
> Up and awa' wi' Langton House,
> And set it down in Dogden Moss.

Langton House, of which only the ruins now remain, is south-west of Duns, and Dogden Moss further to the south-west. Henderson learned the story explaining the rhyme as a boy, which takes it back to the eighteenth century. The fairies had a grudge against Langton and its inmates, and determined to carry it away:

> On a moonlight night at the end of autumn, they set to work to loosen the foundations, singing the song given above, and had just begun to lift the house, when one of the inmates woke up,

felt something like an earthquake, heard the singing, and ran to the window. He saw what the fairies were doing, and cried out, 'Lord, keep me and the house together, what's this o't?' At the prayer the fairies dispersed, and fled away through the air, leaving the house safe.

This is one of a number of stories concerning the magical transportation of buildings, most often churches. Sometimes this is understood as divine intervention, as at RUABHAL (Western Isles). In other cases the interference is said to be evil, the work of fairies, witches, or the Devil himself, and may be put a stop to by the ringing of church bells, the mention of God, or the opening of a Bible. Though interpreted here by the storyteller as a prayer, 'Lord, keep me and the house together, what's this o't?' (i.e. what's going on?) sounds more like an involuntary exclamation of surprise, but as it involves the Lord's name, this would work too. A more radical way of stopping a building being moved is mentioned at REILIG OGHRAIN (Western Isles).

LEITH, MIDLOTHIAN

Authorities differ on the nature of the water-spirit Shellycoat. The folklorist Lewis Spence, writing in 1948, describes him as 'gigantic, swift, malignant, delighting in blood and violence', and says that the rattling of his shell garment when he flew through the air would alarm the bravest. Katharine Briggs, on the other hand, writes in her *Dictionary of Fairies* (1977) that Shellycoat 'delights in teasing, tricking and bewildering human beings, without doing them actual harm', so resembling the Brag, a mischievous but basically harmless North of England bogey whose antics usually ended, like

those of Robin Goodfellow, with a horse-laugh, 'Ha! ha! ha!'

Shellycoat haunted the banks of ETTRICK WATER, where he would feign the cries of a drowning person and then jeer at the efforts of those who sought to rescue him, and another of his haunts was a large rock that once existed on the site of the present docks at Leith. Children would run round the stone three times, shouting:

'Shellycoat, Shellycoat, gang awa' hame,
I cry na yer mercy, I fear na yer name.'

Such bravado may have been ill-advised: it is said that Shellycoat once picked up a man at Leith and tossed him to and fro until he killed him. The spirit was powerless, however, without his coat of shells, which he used to take off and hide under a rock when he had performed a specially hard task; in this he is like the SELKIES (p. 404), helpless without their sealskins.

See also GORRENBERRY.

LINLITHGOW, WEST LOTHIAN

Edward I of England made use of Linlithgow during his invasion of Scotland, wintering there from 1301 to 1302 and fortifying the palace, which must then have been constructed almost entirely of wood: records show that he employed 107 carpenters on the building works and 80 ditchers, but not a single mason.

Edward II (r. 1307–27) also garrisoned the castle, but lost it back to the Scots. The English had grown so used to the visits of Farmer Binnie, who brought hay for their horses, that the guards no longer bothered even to challenge him, let alone to look at what he had in his cart. One day, the farmer stopped his wagon on the drawbridge directly under the portcullis;

throwing off their blanket of hay, Scottish soldiers leaped out to attack, while more were able to follow across the drawbridge, which could neither be pulled up and secured (with the haycart on top of it), nor protected by the portcullis (which had the haycart beneath it).

This wily manoeuvre was a mixed blessing to Robert the Bruce (r. 1306–29), who had insufficient men for a garrison and therefore had to destroy the palace to prevent it falling again into English hands. It was rebuilt under David II (r. 1329–71), but burned by the English in 1424, and did not until the reign of James VI (1567–1621) arise as it can be seen today.

St Michael's church at Linlithgow was the scene of one of Scotland's most famous predictions, delivered to James IV in 1513 as he was preparing for battle with the English forces. It is not clear whether the prophet was a man or a ghost, but the seventeenth-century writer George Sinclair describes the prophet as an 'apparition' which manifested itself while the king was at evensong:

> While he was at his Devotion, an Ancient Man came in, his Amber coloured Hair hanging down upon his Shoulders, his forehead high, and inclining to Baldness, his Garments of Azure colour, somewhat long, girded about with a Towel, or Table-Napkin, of a Comely and very Reverend Aspect.

This person approached the king with an air of clownish simplicity, and addressed him as follows: 'Sir, I am sent hither to entreat you, to delay your Expedition for this time, and to proceed no further in your intended journey: for if you do, you shall not prosper in your enterprise, nor any of your followers. I am further charged to warn you, not to use the acquaintance, company, or counsel of women, as you tender your honour, life,

and estate.' After this he withdrew. Sinclair continues:

> When Service was ended, the King enquired earnestly for him, but he could be no where found, neither could any of the Bystanders (of whom diverse did narrowly observe him, resolving afterwards to have discoursed with him) feel or perceive how, when, or where he passed from them, having in a manner vanished in their hands.

It was not known whether the king would have taken the warning to steer clear of women, since he ignored the first part of the apparition's good advice and marched forth to defeat and death at the battle of Flodden.

LINTON, ROXBURGHSHIRE

In the 1902 edition of Sir Walter Scott's *Minstrelsy of the Scottish Border*, a note is appended concerning a legend of Linton church:

> This small church is founded upon a little hill of sand, in which no stone of the size of an egg is said to have been found, although the neighbouring soil is sharp and gravelly. Tradition accounts for this, by informing us that the foundresses were two sisters, upon whose account much blood had been spilt on that spot; and that the penance imposed on the fair causers of the slaughter, was an order from the Pope to sift the sand of the hill, upon which their church was to be erected.

The writer adds, 'This story may, perhaps, have some foundation; for in the churchyard was discovered a single grave, containing no fewer than fifty skulls, most of which bore the marks of having been cleft by violence.'

William Henderson, writing in 1866, tells

a different version in which a young man killed a priest and was condemned to death for murder and sacrilege. His two sisters, who loved him dearly, pleaded for his life, and at last it was granted, on the condition that they would sift as much sand as would form a mound on which to build a church. This they succeeded in doing, and the church was built, although one of the sisters died as soon as her brother was freed, either from exhaustion or from overpowering joy at his release. 'The villagers point to the sandy knoll in confirmation of its truth, and show a hollow place, a short distance to the westward, as that from which the sand was taken.'

'Such is the version of the legend deemed the correct one at Linton,' remarks Henderson. Sometimes it was interwoven with the legend of the dispatching of a 'worm' or dragon that lived in a den east of Linton Hill. The worm used to slay the cattle with its venomous breath, and would sometimes emerge and coil around a nearby eminence still known in Henderson's time as Wormington or Wormiston. At last Somerville, Laird of Lariston, a brave and reckless man, volunteered to kill the beast. Having failed in one attack with ordinary weapons, he came up with a brilliant device, 'as the Linton cottagers testify to this day'. To the end of his lance he attached a small wheel, and on this he fixed a peat soaked in pitch. Setting fire to the peat, he thrust the lance down the worm's throat, suffocating the monster with the fumes of burning pitch. So violent were its death throes that the contractions of its coils left a permanent impression on the sides of Linton or 'Wormiston' Hill (in reality the terrace-like markings were probably created by miniature landslips).

As a reward for his bravery, the Laird of Lariston was granted extensive lands in the neighbourhood, and this is really the point of the story, a charter myth concocted or adopted by the Somerville family to account for their ownership of the manor of Linton. One inspiration for the tale may have been the Somerville coat of arms, containing a wheel which could have suggested the apparatus fixed to the laird's lance, and another was very probably the Somerville Stone above the door of Linton church. This is carved with an image now very worn but still just about decipherable as a knight facing two monsters, one of which he is attacking with his lance. In fact the 'knight' is thought to be St Michael defeating the Devil, often represented in medieval art as a dragon, although why there should be two beasts here is a question answered neither by iconography nor by the tale of the 'Linton Worm'.

A somewhat similar method of killing a monster is reported at WESTBROUGH (Orkney & Shetland Islands).

LITTLEDEAN TOWER, ROXBURGHSHIRE

Thomas Wilkie, a protégé of Sir Walter Scott, was a young medical student living at Bowden, near Eildon Hall, who put together a collection of Border customs, legends, and superstitions at Sir Walter's request. This later came into the possession of the folklore collector William Henderson. Wilkie's collection contains traditions current in the Borders in the eighteenth century, as in this pleasant ghost story attached to Littledean Tower, the unusual D-shaped remains of which can be seen in the valley of Tweed almost due south of Smailholm. Littledean Tower was said to have been long haunted by the spirit of an old lady, once its mistress, who had been a covetous, grasping woman, and oppressive to the poor:

Tradition averred that she had amassed a large sum of money by thrift or extortion, and now could not rest in her grave because of it. Spite of its ghost, however, Littledean Tower was inhabited by a laird and his family, who found no fault with their place of abode, and were not much troubled by thoughts of the supernatural world. One Saturday evening, however, a servant-girl, who was cleaning shoes in the kitchen by herself, suddenly observed an elf-light shining on the floor. While she gazed on it, it disappeared, and in its place stood an old woman wrapped in a brown cloak, who muttered something about being cold, and asked to warm herself at the fire.

The girl consented, and seeing that the old woman's shoes were wet, she offered to dry and clean them. The apparition, touched by her kindness, confessed herself frankly to be the ghost that haunted the house.

'My gold wud na let me rest,' said she, 'but I'll tell ye where it lies; 'tis 'neath the lowest step o' the Tower stairs. Take the laird there an' tell him what I now tell ye; then dig up the treasure, and put it in his hands. An' tell him to part it in two shares: one share let him keep, for he's master here now; the other share he maun part again, and gie half to you, for ye are a kind lassie and a true, and half he maun gie to the poor o' Maxton, the auld folk and the fatherless bairns, and them that need it most. Do this an' I sall rest in my grave, where I've no rested yet, and never will I trouble the house mair till the day o' doom.'

With that she vanished. Next morning the maid told her master what had happened, and took him to the place the apparition had described. The stone was removed and the treasure discovered, and divided according to instructions.

The servant-girl, so richly dowered, found a good husband ere the year had passed. The poor of Maxton, for the first time in their lives, blessed the old lady of Littledean; and never was the ancient tower troubled again by ghost or apparition.

Ghosts, like White Ladies, often act as treasure guardians, and have been known to reveal the whereabouts of their hoard in gratitude for kindness.

LIVINGSTON, WEST LOTHIAN

A gruesome tale is told of Livingston Place, the eighteenth-century mansion which replaced the old castle. In 1767 Sir William Cunningham inherited the house, and as he was greatly addicted to hunting he had new kennels built for the hounds of the Linlithgow and Stirlingshire Hunt, including a room for the huntsman next to the dog pens. One night the huntsman came home very drunk and mistook his way; instead of going into his own bedroom, he went into the kennels, where the dogs set upon him and tore him to pieces. Next morning, stated the records of the Hunt, nothing was left but his boots and a couple of scraps of cloth. William Fyfe Hendrie tells this shocker in his *West Lothian Lore* (1976), adding:

The truth of this incident might be questioned but it is given weight by the fact that all the fox hounds involved were immediately put down, a drastic move indeed and an expensive one for any hunt to undertake.

It is, however, demonstrably the same story as a Worcestershire tale set in a few different locations; in some of these, extra gore is added in the detail that not only the huntsman's boots are found but also his feet still inside them.

Longformacus,
Berwickshire

In his memoirs published in 1900, Augustus Hare tells of a haunt at what he calls Longmacfergus, near Dunse, which presumably is today's Longformacus. By way of authentication, he says, 'Mr and Mrs Spottiswoode lived there, who are the father and mother of Lady John Scott, and they vouched for the story.' He writes that the villagers of Longmacfergus were accustomed to do their marketing at the little town of 'Dunse', and though their nearest way home was to cross the burn at a point called 'the Foul Ford', they always took another and longer way, as the Foul Ford was universally thought to be haunted.

There was a farmer of 'Longmacfergus', who was well-to-do and highly respected. One evening his wife was expecting him back from the market at 'Dunse', but it was only after midnight, by which time she was much alarmed, that a violent knocking came at the door. When she let him in she was horrified to see his 'wild and agonized expression'. He told her he had come home by the Foul Ford, and that he must now die by morning. He begged her to send for the minister, 'the only person who could do him any good'. His wife sent for the doctor too, but he could do nothing. The minister, however, stayed for several hours, at the end of which the farmer died.

News of the tragedy naturally made the people of Longmacfergus even more afraid of the Foul Ford and for a few years no one tried to use it. Then there came a day when the dead farmer's son spent longer than usual drinking at Dunse, and when his cronies teased him for being too cowardly to go home the shortest way, he decided to risk it. This time, *his* wife sat

watching for his return, but all in vain, for he never came back. Next morning, neighbours who had gone to look for him found him lying dead on the bank above the Foul Ford. And oddly (a foolish fact, perhaps, says Hare, but always told as part of the story), though his body bore no marks of violence, and his coat was still on, his waistcoat was lying beside his body upon the grass, and his watch and money were still in his pockets.

At the funeral, the minister announced that, now a second death had occurred, he felt justified in revealing what the father had told him on the night that he died:

> He said that he had crossed the wooden bridge of the Foul Ford, and was coming up the brae on the other side, when he met a procession of horsemen dressed in black, riding two and two upon black horses. As they came up, he saw amongst them, to his horror, every one he had known amongst his neighbours in Longmacfergus, and who were already dead. But the man who rode last – the last man who had died – was leading a riderless horse. As he came up, he dismounted by the farmer's side, and said that the horse was for him. The farmer refused to mount, and all his former neighbours tried to force him on to the horse. They had a deadly struggle, in which the farmer seemed to get the better, for the horseman rode away, leading the riderless horse, but he said, 'Never mind; you will want it before morning.' And before morning he was dead.

The procession of the dead on horseback, leading an extra riderless horse, is mentioned elsewhere, for instance in Thomas Heywood's *Hierarchie of the Blessed Angels* (1635), although there the living man joins the procession and returns safely after three days. Tales like this may have influenced the story told to, and by, Hare, but it also seems very close to the plainer narrative concerning the blacksmith who died on GREENLAW MOOR, including the father-and-son relationship and the detail that the second dead man had taken off some of his clothes. As that account also relates to Foul Ford, and involves a strange horseman, it seems clear that one story, perhaps with an initial kernel of fact, has been developed in two ways.

LOTH STONE, EAST LOTHIAN

See TRAPRAIN LAW.

THE LUCKEN HARE, EILDON HILLS, ROXBURGHSHIRE

Between the southernmost and central peaks of Eildon is a little hill long known from its shape as the Lucken Hare. 'Lucken' means closed or compact, and here means that the hare looks as if it is crouching down. The hill is the setting for one version of a legend which Sir Walter Scott meant to use for a novel, and which he tells in the preface to the 1829 edition of *Waverley* as it was current in the Borders in his time.

A horse-coper called Canobie Dick (from Canonbie, Dumfriesshire) was riding over Bowden Moor one moonlit night with a pair of horses he had been unable to sell, when he met an aged man in antique costume who bought them both, paying for them in ancient golden coins. He asked the coper to bring more horses to that spot, which Dick did more than once, the last time hinting to the old man that there was no luck in a dry bargain. The old man thereupon led him up a narrow path to the Lucken Hare. Dick was startled to see the old man enter at the foot of the hill by a passage or cavern he had never noticed, though he knew the Lucken Hare well. Inside they came to stables filled with coal-black horses, and by each horse a sleeping knight in coal-black armour. At the far end of the great hall stood a table on which were lying a sword and a horn. The old man, who now revealed himself as the prophet Thomas of Erceldoune, told Dick that he who drew the sword and sounded the horn would be king of all Britain – but that everything hung on which he took up first. The coper seized the horn and blew a blast, and the thunderous peal it made woke the knights. Seeing them coming at him, he dropped the horn and tried to raise the sword, but heard a great voice proclaim:

Woe to the coward that ever he was
    born,
Who did not draw the sword before he
    blew the horn!

A whirlwind then carried Dick off and cast him down the bank, where he was found next morning by shepherds. He lived just long enough to tell his tale.

Thomas of Erceldoune, or Thomas the Rhymer, was held to have prophesied the reign of a great king, which some took to be Robert the Bruce, others Edward II of England. Through some confusion of ideas, Thomas the prophet came himself to be the prophesied leader. The 'sleeping warrior' legend is told of him at Dumbuck, near Dumbarton, and at TOMNAHURICH (Southern Highlands) as well as here at Eildon. In all three places, Thomas still lives in the fairy hill but comes out from time to time to buy horses of a special colour or kind for his host of warriors. When he has them all, the great battle will be fought and the king come into his own. The man who sells him the horses usually gets paid when he comes to the hill, inside which he sees the warriors sleeping.

This story was current by the seventeenth century, when it was told in *A Discourse concerning the Nature and Substance of Devils and Spirits*, added by an anonymous author to the third edition of Reginald Scot's *Discoverie of Witchcraft* (1665), and early in the nineteenth century John Leyden recorded a version in which the sleeping warriors are identified as King Arthur and his knights. This is how the legend runs in Northumberland and other places, but in Scotland Thomas is more usually the central figure.

See also EILDON HILLS.

MARY KING'S CLOSE, EDINBURGH

Edinburgh is a much haunted city, and Mary King's Close reportedly its most haunted street. In the eighteenth century it was built over, becoming part of the famous 'underground' of Edinburgh, and to descend into its hidden world is an eerie feeling, even as part of a guided tour.

In 1645 the plague struck Edinburgh, and very many residents of the crowded close perished of the disease. The street was probably quarantined – shut off entirely – and people like to imagine that it was then abandoned, but in fact once the pestilence had passed, the houses of the dead were soon in use again. They were, however, then said to be haunted, and in 1685 George Sinclair told a truly terrifying tale of what appeared to one Tom Coleheart and his wife.

The couple were warned when they moved in that the house was haunted: a man told their maid, 'if you live there, I assure you, you will have more Company than your selves.' She accordingly refused to stay, and Mrs Coleheart was frightened too, but Tom took the matter as a joke. He was soon to find out his mistake. Later the same day the ghosts started appearing, first to Mrs Coleheart, who saw the head and face of an old grey-haired man looking at her out of a small chamber opening off the bedroom. On seeing this she fainted. Tom maintained it had been her imagination, but that night he saw the same thing, and an hour later both of them 'clearly perceived a young child, with a coat upon it, hanging near to the old man's head'.

By and by a naked Arm appears in the air, from the elbow downward, and the hand stretched out, as when one man is about to salute another. [Tom] then skipt out of his Bed, and kneeling down begged help from heaven. The Arm had now come within its own length to him as it were to shake hands with him. Whereupon he immediately goes to his Bed again, and at the opening of the Curtain, it offered another salutation to him. The man and his wife embracing one another through fear, and still eying the naked Arm, they prayed the more earnestly.

Their prayers were unavailing. The arm and hand came still nearer, 'after a courteous manner, with an offer of acquaintance'.

They fell to prayer again, both of them being drowned with sweat, and in the mean time they saw a little Dog come out of that little Room aforenamed, which after a little time looking about, and towards the Bed, and the Naked Arm, composed it self upon a Chair, as it were with its nose in its tail to sleep. This somewhat increased their fever. But quickly after, a Cat comes leaping out from the same Room, and in the midst of the hall began to play some little Tricks. Then was the hall full of small little creatures, dancing prettily, unto which none of them could give a name, as having never in nature seen the like.

Looking back on this afterwards, Mr and Mrs Coleheart wondered 'that none of them had the wit to open the Door, and to flie from the house, which had been easier to have done, than to light the first Candle' – similar questions spring to mind watching many horror films. Even the next day they did not leave: deciding that their experience was a trial they had had to undergo, they stayed on in the house, 'concluding the worst was over as indeed it was'.

Mary King's Close was believed to hold other dangers. In the eighteenth century it was described as 'a disreputable quarter where the last dregs of the plague secreted themselves', and in the 1750s building work began to swallow the street. Some of it, however, remained in use as late as the Second World War when rooms there were converted into air-raid shelters.

Ghosts reported to haunt the close today include a lady in a long dark dress, and a 'short gentleman in a vaguely agitated state'. A group who spent the night in the underground rooms to raise money for charity complained in the morning of the noise from the party in the City Chambers above, saying that they had been unable to sleep for all the laughter and clinking of glasses; there had, of course, been no party. Several occurrences have been reported of electrical oddities, fires that switch themselves on and off, and a workman's drill which sprang into action although nobody was near it.

The most famous apparition of modern times was seen not actually in Mary King's Close but in the adjoining Allan's Close, one of the best-preserved parts of the underground streets. A psychic who visited the area with a television company reported seeing a little girl who had died of plague,

and who had lost her doll. A cameraman immediately went to buy a replacement doll, and there is now a collection of toys left under the bricked-up window where the lonely little ghost appeared.

MAXTON, ROXBURGHSHIRE

One of the stories recorded by Thomas Wilkie in his manuscript collection 'Old Rites and Ceremonies, and Customs of the Inhabitants of the Southern Counties of Scotland', and reproduced by William Henderson in 1866, concerns an encounter between a witch of Maxton and Laird Harry Gilles of LITTLEDEAN TOWER. Henderson writes:

The Laird (Harry Gilles) of Littledean was extremely fond of hunting. One day, as his dogs were chasing a hare, they suddenly stopped, and gave up the pursuit, which enraged him so much that he swore the animal they had been hunting must be one of the witches of Maxton. No sooner had he uttered the word than hares appeared all round him, so close that they even sprang over the saddle before his eyes, but still none of his hounds would give chase. In a fit of anger, he jumped off his horse and killed the dogs on the spot, all but one large black hound, who at that moment turned to pursue the largest hare.

Remounting to follow the chase, he saw the black hound turn the hare and drive it directly towards him.

The hare made a spring as if to clear his horse's neck, but the laird dexterously caught hold of one of her forepaws, drew out his hunting-knife, and cut it off; after which the hares, which had been so numerous, all disappeared. Next morning Laird Harry heard that a woman of Maxton had lost her arm in some unaccountable manner; so he went straight to

The 'Prentice Window' of Melrose Abbey is celebrated in legend and literature for its match-less beauty. The story goes that the master craftsman, in despair at the thought of being eclipsed by an apprentice who could produce such fine work, killed the youth in a fit of jealous rage.

her house, pulled out the hare's foot (which had changed in his pocket to a woman's hand and arm), and applied it to the stump. It fitted exactly. She confessed her crime, and was drowned for witchcraft the same day in the well, by the young men of Maxton.

That witches could transform themselves into hares is a commonplace of British tra-dition – there are numerous similar stories. That they could be wounded in that form was also a general belief, part and parcel of the general European superstition that wounds inflicted on their wer-animals would be reproduced on the human bodies of the witches and warlocks inhabiting them. Included in *The Book of Werewolves* (1865), a wide-ranging survey of the sub-ject by the historian Sabine Baring-Gould, is a story from the early seventeenth cen-tury very reminiscent of Harry Gilles's experience. A peasant in a Swiss village

near Lucerne was attacked by a wolf while he was hewing timber. He defended him-self and struck off its foreleg. The moment that the blood began to flow, the creature changed, and he recognised a woman he knew, who was accordingly burned alive.

MELROSE ABBEY, ROXBURGHSHIRE

The same story is told here as at ROSSLYN CHAPEL of the master who killed his apprentice for making finer work than he could do himself, in this case a window rather than a pillar. The 'Prentice Window', as it is known, is at the eastern end of the abbey, and dates from the four-teenth century. It is divided by four slen-der perpendicular bars, interwoven in the upper part with graceful stone tracery. An 1861 history of the abbey quotes Sir

Walter Scott's description of the 'match-less' design:

> Thou would'st have thought some
>   fairy's hand,
> 'Twixt poplars straight the osier wand,
>   In many a freakish knot had
>   twin'd;
> Then fram'd a spell when the work was
>   done,
> And chang'd the willow wreaths to
>   stone.

Below the window is said to lie Robert the Bruce's heart, which the hero had wished to be taken to the Holy Land. Sir James Douglas, carrying the embalmed heart to Jerusalem, was himself killed in Spain in 1330, and the heart was brought back to Scotland.

Also buried here, according to tradition, is MICHAEL SCOT, THE WIZARD OF BAL-WEARIE (p. 62). Black's *Picturesque Tourist of Scotland* of 1844 mentions the legend without identifying the grave:

> The door of entrance from the cloisters to the church is on the north side, close by the west wall of the transept, and is exquisitely carved . . . Through this door the 'monk of St Mary's aisle,' in the Lay of the Last Minstrel, is said to have conducted William of Deloraine to the grave of Michael Scott, after conducting him through the cloister.

There are, however, several other contenders for Michael Scot's burial place, including Burgh under Bowness in Cumbria and GLENLUCE ABBEY (Dumfries & Galloway), and no evidence supports one rather than another.

MID CALDER, WEST LOTHIAN

Between Mid Calder and the River Almond is Cunnigar of Midcalder, a hill sometimes called the 'witches' knowe'. In 1720 Patrick Sandilands, third son of James Lord Torphichen, declared that he had been bewitched by some women and a man from Calder, and five of those he accused subsequently confessed to heinous crimes including, in one case, having given her dead child to the Devil 'to make a roast of'. It seems, however, from the account in Charles Kirkpatrick Sharpe's *Historical Account of the Belief in Witchcraft in Scotland* (1884) that no executions took place. By the early eighteenth century such horrors were becoming rarer, although the last burning did not take place until 1727 in LOTH (Northern Highlands).

One entirely public-spirited activity said to have been undertaken by the Mid Calder witches was their 'taming' of the moon: every twenty-eight days they were said to fly up to turn the moon round, fearing that she might lose track of her proper movements since the new calendar had been introduced.

Anyone might have got confused, and probably many did. In 1582 the Pope had decreed a revised New Year (1 January instead of 25 March) and also that the days between 4 and 15 October should for that year be suppressed, this to adjust previous inaccuracy. Not everyone went along with the papal decision. Scotland adopted the 1 January New Year in 1600, while England and Wales resisted for another 150 years, so that during this time there were two British dating systems. Diarmaid MacCulloch, explaining all this beautifully in *Reformation* (2004), adds that a story of English rioters in 1752 demanding the return of their eleven days is only an eighteenth-century joke, and probably the story of the witches is a similar anti-papist gibe.

See also WITCH-HUNTS (p. 270).

MINCH MOOR, PEEBLESSHIRE

On the top of Minch Moor or Minchmuir is a spring, called the Cheese Well by Lewis Spence writing in the nineteenth century. According to Spence, the well 'is thought to be in charge of a fairy, to whom some offering must be made – a piece of cheese, or a pin'.

An anonymous collection of legends published in 1889 also refers to the Cheese Well, and expands on the characteristics of the fairies, calling them 'Daione Shie, or the Men of Peace':

> They are, though not absolutely malevolent, believed to be a peevish, repining, and envious race, who enjoy, in the subterranean recesses, a kind of shadowy splendour.

They live, the writer says, in green hills, especially those of a conical shape, on which their moonlight dances leave circular marks, sometimes yellow and blasted, sometimes deep green. It was dangerous to sleep in these fairy rings, or even to step inside them after sunset, and it was sometimes accounted unlucky to pass such spots as these, or caverns, waterfalls, and springs considered as fairy haunts, without performing some ceremony to avert the displeasure of the elves; hence the cheese left at the Minch Moor well.

MITTENFU' STANES, LONGFORMACUS, BERWICKSHIRE

Uphill from the Whiteadder Water is a chambered cairn known variously as the 'Mittenfu' Stanes', 'Mittenfull of Stones', 'Deil's Mitten', and 'Mutiny Stones', which has a legend to account for its origin:

The devil had been employed to make a cauld [dam] on the Tweed at Kelso, and as it required an enormous quantity of stones to carry out the work, he crossed the Lammermuirs to the sea coast at Dunbar and carried them on his back, and on some heavy journeys he stowed them carefully away about his person, and flew o'er the hilltops to his destination. In one of his journeys the night was dark, and there was no sign of moon or stars, and through the murky air he sped resolutely on his way; but miscalculating the position of one of the heights, he grazed one of his hands on the whinstone hillside, and thinking no more of this little accident, he reached a point above Byrecleugh, when his 'mitten' burst and down fell its contents, which to this day are called the 'Mittenfu' Stanes.'

This account comes from *Glimpses into the Past in Lammermuir* (1892) by John Hutton Browne, who adds that another local belief was that underneath this pile of stones the hide of an ox, filled with gold pieces, had been buried, and if anyone had the courage to dig for it, the gold would be found there.

MUSSELBURGH, EAST LOTHIAN

The *Edinburgh Topographical, Traditional and Antiquarian Magazine* (1848) tells a story of a fraudulent miracle performed at the shrine of Our Lady of Loretto in Musselburgh in 1558. The shrine had been founded, in the words of the anti-Catholic writer, by 'one Thomas Douchtie, who, in 1533, having brought an image of the Virgin Mary with him, turned hermit, and set up an establishment for himself', although other sources suggest that it existed from the late fifteenth century. It was a famous site in its day, visited by James V, who made a pilgrimage there on foot from Stirling Castle in 1536, but more often resorted to by women, since a gift at the shrine was said to result in a trouble-free birth.

Meanwhile, at the Convent of St Catherine of Siena, which has given its name to the Edinburgh district of Sciennes, the nuns used to pasture a flock of sheep tended by a boy 'who had the faculty of turning up the whites of his eyes in such a manner as to create an impression on the part of the spectators, that he was altogether blind'. This talent impressed the nuns so much that they told some senior churchmen who came to watch, and saw how the boy could be used. They advised the nuns to find another shepherd, and meanwhile to hide the boy away until everyone else had forgotten about him. The lad was kept 'in pious restraint' for seven or eight years, during which time he was educated in the part he had to play.

> The Roman Catholic clergy had become very much alarmed at the progress of the Reformation . . . With the view of keeping public attention alive, they now and then gratified the natives with something out of the common run. As the priests had little fear of detection, they determined to work the miracle with all fitting solemnity, and with that view fixed upon the Chapel of Loretto, near Musselburgh, as the scene of the drama.

A pregnant lady sometimes identified as Mistress Meldrum, but more often as Lady Cleish, was present when the 'miracle' was performed upon the former shepherd.

> After the various ceremonies used on such occasions, the impostor was desired to shut his eyes, whereupon the officiating priests bade him re-open them, announcing, at the same time, his restoration to sight. Having obeyed their command, to the astonishment of the beholders, he seemed to see just as well as

any of those present. He then descended from the scaffold, rejoicing greatly, blessing God, Saint Mary, and all the saints, priests, and friars.

Although Lady Cleish was a Catholic, her husband was a devout Protestant, and he smelt a rat. He persuaded the shepherd to go with him to an inn at Edinburgh, where he locked the door and threatened the man's life unless he told the truth. (Cleish does not seem to have considered that the confession, under these circumstances, might itself have been unreliable: he knew what he wanted to believe.) The shepherd told the whole story, and Cleish decided on a dramatic exposure:

> 'Go with me to the cross, and in few words, after you have cried O yes! thrice, tell the people you were never blind; but that you were hired by the priests to feign yourself to be such, and that there was no miracle wrought upon you yesterday. Tell them, therefore, to believe no longer in these blind guides, but take directly to the true religion; and when you have thus spoken, we shall quickly run down the close opposite to the cross, where my servant will be waiting with two horses in the Cowgate, and if we were once mounted, I defy all the kirk men in Edinburgh to overtake us before we get to Fife.'

The plan sounds rather comic, but seems to have worked: Cleish and the shepherd escaped, and at least one cleric was converted 'from the errors of popery'. He was the Reverend John Row, who later wrote a church history including a statement said to have been made by the shepherd himself, giving details of how he used to 'flype up the lids of my eyes, and cast up the whyte of my eyes, so that anie bodie wold have trowed that I was blind'.

We are not told what happened to the shepherd: one hopes he made a good thing out of telling his experiences, since they had taken up about eight years of his life. By 1848 there remained 'but an unpicturesque fragment' of the nunnery, and the site is now occupied by St Catherine's Place, south of the Meadows; at Musselburgh an earth-covered cell is all that is left of the shrine. Cleish, and the Reformation, had things their own way.

NEWHAVEN, MIDLOTHIAN

Eve Simpson writes in 1908 of a giant willow tree which once stood by the sea in Newhaven, visible for miles around. Legend has it that long ago a fisherman's wife sat one cold day holding her baby in its wicker cradle, watching for her husband's boat. At length she saw it approach, and ran towards the shore, carrying the child with her, but a sudden blizzard sprang up and when it had passed no sail was visible. Realising that she was a widow, she sank down in a faint: the snow came and covered her and the baby, and both froze to death.

The baby's cradle, however, had been woven of fresh willow, and one of the wands took root and sprouted. An old woman prophesied that the tree would grow into a landmark for sailors, and would flourish while the village prospered. It would fall either when the fishing trade left Newhaven, or when 'great decked boats fit to face the German Ocean even in winter' set sail from the harbour.

As the nineteenth century wore on, trawling began to encroach on the profits from traditional fishing. One night a big branch of the willow tree fell; this was taken as a bad omen, and threats were made to attack the trawlers, but the sensible minister of Newhaven reminded the people of the 'saving clause' in the prophecy, and not only encouraged them to build bigger boats but lent them money

to do so. At last a fleet of decked craft, headed by the *James Fairbairn* (named after the minister), sailed from the harbour. When the last of the obsolete small boats was finally superseded, 'the huge, prophetic willow, first watered by the young widow's storm of tears, fell in the sixties of last century, its mission fulfilled.'

The minister seems to have been a canny man of business as well as a diplomat. One suspects that he may have made up the second part of the old woman's prediction on the spot. Trees are often linked with the prosperity of a place or a family, as at DAL-HOUSIE CASTLE, but a let-out clause like the one related here makes destiny a coward.

NEWTON, WEST LOTHIAN

Michael Turnbull, writing in 1996, tells the story of Margaret, daughter of Sir John Herries of Newton, a religious and beautiful young lady of the fourteenth century who fell in love with a Cistercian monk from Newbattle Abbey. She met him secretly at a little farm, whose owner, a widow, also had a Newbattle monk for a lover. Margaret's father threatened to kill her if she did not end the affair, and one night when he found her room empty he went to the farmhouse. Unable to gain entry, he set light to the thatched roof, causing a fire which killed nine people including his daughter, the widow, and both monks.

A 'grey lady' used to be seen 'in what remains of the old monastic cellar under the present house', but in 1990, while building works were taking place, some skeletons were discovered thought to have been those of monks buried in the precincts of the abbey. The bodies were later reinterred in what Turnbull describes as 'a moving ecumenical service', in the

James VI (1567–1625) took a personal interest in eradicating witchcraft, since he himself was the object of an attempted murder by sorcery in 1590. *Newes from Scotland* (1591) hailed him as Satan's worst enemy in the world, and this image from the broadside shows him presiding over the trial of the North Berwick witches.

presence of the abbot of the Cistercian Abbey of Nunraw, and after that the 'grey lady' was seen no more.

The account raises questions of location: what house exactly has the 'old monastic cellar' underneath it? If it is a house in Newton, why should monks from New-battle Abbey, quite a distance away, be buried there? Turnbull cites Sir Walter Scott's 'Gray Brother' as his authority for the story of Margaret Herries, but Scott gives the father's name as Heron and never mentions that of the daughter, so some other source must be involved.

The story as told by Scott relates to a house near Lasswade called Gilmerton Grange, residence of the old nurse of a girl who was carrying on an affair with the abbot of Newbattle. The girl's father, a gentleman named Heron, 'formed a reso-lution of bloody vengeance, undeterred by the supposed sanctity of the clerical char-acter, or by the stronger claims of natural affection'. He piled dried thorns and wood against the house, and then one dark and windy night when his daughter and her lover were inside he set fire to the wood. The house was burned, with all its inmates, and the dwelling 'reduced to a pile of glowing ashes'.

This narrative forms a preamble to Scott's unfinished ballad 'The Gray Brother', and poses a further puzzle: Scott says that the house 'now called Gilmerton Grange' was 'originally named Burndale' from these events, but if it was called Burndale because Heron burned it down (most unlikely – a house was probably called Burndale because it stood near a burn in a dale) then that can't have been the original name.

The tale probably originated as anti-Catholic scandal: stories of monks or nuns breaking their vows of chastity were popular in the eighteenth and nineteenth centuries.

NORTH BERWICK

Over the winter of 1589–90, James VI was a guest of the Danish court, celebrating his marriage to Anne of Denmark. On the journey back to Scotland with his new bride, his ship encountered storms so terrible that witchcraft was thought to be the cause. The search for suspects was quickly underway, and the first major witch-hunt in Scotland revealed a coven of some 300 whose alleged intent was to destroy the king. Determined to stamp out this treasonable sorcery, James took charge of the trials conducted in Edinburgh in 1590–91, and the Danes held parallel trials in cooperation, a development unique in the history of European witch-hunting.

Among those accused was the king's own cousin, Francis Stewart, Earl of Bothwell. Most of the others were women, including Agnes Sampson, whose confession embraced matters so 'miraculous and strange' that James decided it was a tissue of lies. Agnes was concerned to convince him that she was speaking the truth – she had already been tortured, and if suspected to be lying would probably have been put to further 'tests'. She therefore apparently repeated to him words which had passed between him and Anne on their wedding night, and which could have been known to no one else. This was enough to force acceptance of her account, and Agnes was condemned to death.

Among other matters in her long statement, Agnes said that she and around 200 other witches had travelled across the sea in sieves to North Berwick kirk to meet Satan, who was accustomed to 'carnally use them, albeit to their little pleasure, in respect to his colde nature'. In order to sink the king's ship, she and others had christened a cat, tied to it parts of a dead man, and then cast it into the sea. This had

raised the wind, and Agnes said that only the king's great faith had saved him. She had also collected the venom of a black toad, with which she had meant to sprinkle a piece of James's used linen and by this means bring him to a painful death – a transference spell, since the poison would never have touched James's skin, only something that had once been in contact with it. This plan was foiled, however, since Agnes could not get the king's attendant to let her have any of his things.

Many elements in Agnes's narratives, such as travel in a sieve and sex with the Devil, are classics of witchcraft trials on the Continent, themes which later cropped up in Britain as the scare spread. The prosecutors of witches knew what evidence they were looking for; as reports circulated, it would have become known to the 'witches' themselves what details were expected from them, and so the self-reinforcing epidemic continued.

The king's direct involvement in hunting down the witches gained him a reputation as a strong leader: an English broadside, *Newes From Scotland* (1591), reported that James was Satan's worst enemy in the world. James went on to express his hatred of witches and the damage they did to the country in his treatise *Daemonologie* (1597), the only demonological work in Europe penned by a king. After his succession to the English throne in 1603, James's interest in the subject greatly subsided, and he even came to question some of his earlier convictions, but his image as an adversary of demonic conspirators lived on. The three witches in Shakespeare's MACBETH (p. 318) may have been included deliberately to please the king.

Witchcraft officially became a crime with the introduction of the Witchcraft Act in 1563, repealed in 1736. Throughout this period and for some while after it, belief in witches was found at all levels of

Witch-Hunts

From the mid sixteenth to the early eighteenth centuries, nearly 4,000 people were tried in Scotland for witchcraft, and around half were sentenced to death. Criminal prosecution began with the Witchcraft Act of 1563, and two witches were burned within a fortnight of the legislation. Thousands of individual trials followed, most executions being staged events, public demonstrations that witchcraft was not tolerated in a God-fearing society.

Although suspects could be young women, men, or even children, the stereotype of the witch in Scotland as elsewhere in Europe was an older woman, poor, and disliked by her community. Witches were said to possess the 'evil eye', and to perform harmful magic — 'malefice' or *maleficium* — by uttering curses or incantations. They were blamed for illness, death, and general misfortune. On the coast they stood accused of creating storms, sinking ships, and scaring off fish, while in agricultural areas they were reputed to steal milk from their neighbours' cows, prevent hens from laying, and ruin crops. Continental ideas about witchcraft added key elements: witches could perform their magic alone, but were also thought to gather in larger covens called sabbats. During the night they flew through the air to these meetings and paid homage to their master, as related in the trial of Barbara Napier in 1591:

> And the Devil sprang up in the pulpit, like a mickle [big] black man, with a black beard sticking out like a goat's beard, clad in a black tatty gown, and an evil-favoured skull-bonnet on his head. And having a black book in his hand, called on every one of them, desiring them all to be good servants to him and he should be a good master, and they should have enough and never want.

Most importantly, the notion that witches had entered into the Demonic Pact, a contract with Satan, made them terrifying and powerful. It also meant that they were heretics, an offence considered more heinous than any other. The Pact involved a ceremony during which the witch would renounce his or her baptism and receive the Devil's mark, produced by a nip from Satan. The mark was generally thought to be hidden in the genitals or under the armpit, or to be an area of skin insensitive to pain. Discovery of this mark, through pricking the witch's body with a needle, could be used as evidence of guilt, as it was at INVERNESS (Southern Highlands). Some witches sealed the pact by having sexual intercourse with the Devil, though it was reportedly an unpleasant experience.

Confessions were sometimes extracted by torture, the most common form being sleep deprivation, called 'waking' or 'watching' the witch.

Those who admitted their guilt were often persuaded to name others.

Belief in fairies featured in many such confessions and was interpreted by the inquisitors as evidence of consort with demons, little distinction being made between different types of supernatural being or different types of magic. A number of individuals declared their powers to be fairy-derived, and some claimed to have had long-term relationships with fairies. Bessie

'And the Devil sprang up in the pulpit, like a mickle black man . . .' So it was alleged in the trial of Barbara Napier for witchcraft in 1591.

Dunlop, tried in 1576, admitted to numerous meetings with a resident of fairyland named Thome Reid, and had seen the fairy troop riding by RESTALRIG LOCH (Lothian & Borders). Andrew Man from Aberdeenshire had actually fathered children with the Fairy Queen, according to his confession in 1598, and Elspeth Reoch from Orkney admitted in 1616 to having had a sexual relationship with a fairy man.

Even performers of benevolent charms were liable to accusations of witchcraft. Agnes Sampson was known as the 'wise woman of Keyth' before she was caught up in the 1590–91 witch-hunt at NORTH BERWICK (Lothian & Borders), and the healer Bessie Wright was pursued in 1628 by the presbytery of Perth as an 'abuser of the people'.

Early modern Scotland was tainted by the witch-hunts. The desire to cleanse society of a perceived evil sent many unfortunate souls to an untimely death. Five peaks of intensive witch-hunting have been distinguished: 1590–91, 1597, 1629–30, 1649, and the most virulent in 1661–2, with over 600 cases and approximately 300 sentences of death. The last woman executed was Janet Horne of LOTH (Northern Highlands), in 1727, and nine years later the Witchcraft Act was repealed, but belief in sorcery persisted long afterwards, proving the tenacity and enduring power of the witch figure.

See also INVERKIP; PAISLEY; POLLOK (Glasgow & Ayrshire); DALMENY; DELORAINE, SAMUELSTON; TORPHICHEN; WEST BOW; YARROWFORD (Lothian & Borders); BRIMS NESS; SCRABSTER (Northern Highlands); COLVADALE; STROMNESS; TINGWALL (Orkney & Shetland Islands).

society, from the common man or woman up to the king himself. While accusations generally originated at village level, frequently reflecting communal tensions, the ordinary person could not lawfully punish a witch. Prosecution required judicial sanction, and witch-hunting was, strictly speaking, a ruling-class activity.

In proportion to its population, Scotland was among the worst affected nations during the European campaign against witchcraft, with some 3,837 known trials and around 2,000 executions. Eighty to eighty-five per cent of those acccused were female. The areas most concerned were the Lowlands and Scots-speaking parts of the country, with the Highlands and Gaelic-speaking regions largely exempt. Why the period and country were marked with such fear of witchcraft is difficult to determine, although it is significant that post-Reformation Scotland was experiencing a period of heightened social control. The Devil was ascribed greater prominence in world affairs, and witchcraft was seen as the prime act of social deviance, representing chaos and evil. The figure of the witch was deemed not only as dangerous to the individual, but as a threat to society and the State, and ultimately as the enemy of God.

See also WITCH-HUNTS (p. 270).

PEASTON, EAST LOTHIAN

Sometime in the seventeenth century, the minister of Peaston in the parish of Ormiston had a servant called Isabel Heriot, described in George Sinclair's *Satans Invisible World Discovered* (1685):

She was of a low stature, small and slender of Body, of a Black Complexion. Her head stood somewhat awry upon her Neck. She was of a drolling and jearing humour, and would have spoken to Persons of Honor with great confidence.

She was a hard worker, but for all that the minister took a dislike to her, since she was irreligious and refused to profit by his teaching. Accordingly she was dismissed and went to work elsewhere, but after some time she returned and 'was sometimes haunting the Ministers house, but without his knowledge'. She then became ill and died in the winter of 1680, but her haunting of the house was not at an end.

Three or four days after she had been buried, at about midnight, her ghost was seen, wearing her white grave-clothes, walking from the chapel towards the house. A few nights later stones were cast at the house, and the minister himself was nearly hit by one of them as he came in at the back door. This seemed to indicate that the ghost was responsible, since when the living Isabel had been turned out of the house, she had violently thrown a stone at the same door.

More disturbance followed: the ostler felt something grip his heel in the stable, and later had an old horse-comb, which had been missing for several years, thrown at him. The horses were often found in the mornings sweating, as if they had been ridden during the night. A burning coal was found under a bed, and one of the family had his night-cap taken off and found it next morning full of ash and cinders. 'If the Devil could have done more, surely he would have done it,' says Sinclair, adding that after somebody mockingly remarked that the minister should drive away the Devil with prayers, no further trouble came to the family.

There was, however, a further manifestation to the woman who had seen the spectre first on its way from the kirk to the house: this time it was in the minister's yard. 'Never was one Egg liker to another than this Apparition was like to her,' reports Sinclair, who surmises that it was the Devil in the likeness of Isabel rather than the spirit of the woman herself. The ghost was collecting stones, and the woman who saw her exclaimed, 'Wow! Whats thou doing here, Isabel Heriot?' Isabel replied that she had stolen a golden Jewish shekel from the minister and sold it, and that she had agreed with the Devil to destroy the minister, or if not him, then the schoolmaster. 'After this conference, the Woman began to be feared; and came running home in haste.'

That appears to be the last that was heard of Isabel Heriot. One of Sinclair's closing comments in the tale, however, deserves to be quoted by every folklorist: 'If I have erred in some circumstances, or in any other thing, I am to be excused, since I was not an eye witness.'

PEAT LAW, SELKIRKSHIRE

A poor man of Peat Law (formerly Peatlaw) once fell asleep in the middle of a fairy ring. Suddenly he found himself dragged at top speed through the air, and before he well knew what had happened he was in the middle of Glasgow. His coat had been left on the Hill of Peatlaw, and his blue bonnet was found sticking on the top of the steeple of Lanark kirk. He came across a carter who knew him, and travelled back to Selkirk more slowly than he had come.

This account is given in Sir Walter Scott's *Minstrelsy of the Scottish Border* (1802–3) but the phenomenon of the *sluagh* or 'fairy host' appears in far earlier accounts. The anonymous *Discourse concerning the Nature and substance of Devils and Spirits* appended to the 1665 edition of Reginald Scot's *Discoverie of Witchcraft* includes the following:

And many such have been taken away by the sayd Spirits, for a fortnight or month together, being carryed by them in chariots through the Air, over Hills, and Dales, Rocks and Precipices, till at last they have been found lying in some Meddow or Mountain bereaved of their sences, and commonly one of their Members to boot.

The poor man of Peatlaw, however, was unharmed. Scott comments that his tale of being carried off by the fairies 'was implicitly believed by all, who did not reflect that a man may have private reasons for leaving his own country, and for disguising his having intentionally done so'.

Other tales of those carried away by the fairies were told at INVERESRAGAN (Argyllshire & Islands) and DALNACARDOCH (Central & Perthshire).

PEEBLES

In *Minstrelsy of the Scottish Border* (1802–3), Sir Walter Scott tells the story of the minister of Peebles known as Mass John Scott, the 'Mass' signifying his skill in laying or 'reading down' ghosts. Mass John is said to have lost his life while contending with an obstinate spirit. This was the fault of a young clergyman, who, out of conceit, rashly started the ceremony of exorcism without waiting for Mass John to arrive. As the youth was not strong enough to master the ghost, it began to master him. Sir Walter observes, 'It is the nature, it seems, of spirits disembodied, as well as embodied, to increase in strength and presumption in proportion to the advantages which it may gain over an opponent.'

The young clergyman lost courage, and things got so bad that as Mass John approached the house he saw slates and tiles flying off the roof as if in a whirlwind. On entering, he saw that all the wax-tapers used in the conjuration were out except one, which had already burned blue in the socket. Blue flames were a traditional sign of a ghostly presence, as at BALCOMIE CASTLE (Central & Perthshire), and many stories of exorcisms

Tradition holds that where the Powsail Burn meets the River Tweed, the wizard Merlin is buried at the foot of a thorn tree.

ratchet up the tension by describing how candle after candle flickers and dies, leaving only one to be wielded by the most skilled practitioner present. In this case Mass John's experience was sufficient to bring the spirit to reason, but while saying a word of advice or admonition to the younger man, he allowed the ghost to have the last word, something always to be avoided when dealing with a ghost. 'This fatal oversight occasioned his falling into a lingering disorder, of which he never recovered.'

POWSAIL BURN,
PEEBLESSHIRE

When Tweed and Powsaill meet at
    Merlin's grave,
Scotland and England that day ae [one]
    king shall have.

The Powsail Burn is sometimes marked on maps as the Drumelzier Burn. In times of low water it meets the Tweed to the east of the churchyard at Burnfoot Pool in DRUMELZIER, in which the wizard Merlin is said to be buried beneath an ancient thorn tree: in 1603, on the day when the Union took place, it is reported that the waters overflowed and joined at the small tumulus marking the grave, a juncture, wrote Robert Chambers in 1827, which never took place either before or since. Either he is being sarcastic or he changed his mind, since in the 1870 edition of his *Popular Rhymes of Scotland* he says, 'In reality, there is nothing in the local circumstances to make the meeting of the two waters at that spot in the least wonderful, as Merlin's grave is in the *haugh* or meadow close to the Tweed, which the river must of course cover whenever it is in flood.'

The Scottish Merlin, also known as Wild

Merlin (Merdwynn Wyllt), may not be the same as Arthur's Merlin: two sets of traditions seem to be combined, one from Arthurian legend, the other concerning Lailoken, a prophet said to have roamed the Scottish Lowland forests towards the end of the sixth century. A fifteenth-century manuscript tells how Lailoken met St Kentigern (St Mungo of GLASGOW, Glasgow & Ayrshire) in the wilderness, and told the saint that he roamed half-naked in penance for having caused a bloody battle. Another source tells roughly the same story but identifies the naked visionary as Merlin and the man of God as Waldhave, a twelfth-century abbot of MELROSE ABBEY, who 'describes himself as lying upon Lomond Law; he hears a voice, which bids him stand to his defence; he looks around, and beholds a flock of hares and foxes pursued over the mountain by a savage figure, to whom he can hardly give the name of man':

He was formed like a freike all his four
    quarters;
And then his chin and his face haired so
    thick,
With haire growing so grime, fearful to
    see.

He tells Waldhave that he is doing penance, 'pours forth an obscure rhapsody concerning futurity', and concludes:

'Go musing upon Merlin if thou wilt;
For I mean no more, man, at this time.'

Sir Walter Scott comments that this is exactly similar to the tale told of Kentigern. In explanation of why Merlin is chasing animals, he adds an anecdote taken from a 'curious poem' in which the magician, having fled to the forest in a state of distraction, sees in the stars that 'his wife, Guendolen' is about to marry again. He has foretold this before and warned her to keep the new bridegroom out of his way, but has promised her a wedding present:

Accordingly he collected all the stags and lesser game in his neighbourhood; and, having seated himself upon a buck, drove the herd before him to the capital of Cumberland, where Guendolen resided. But her lover's curiosity leading him to inspect too nearly this extraordinary cavalcade, Merlin's rage was awakened, and he slew him with the stroke of an antler of the stag.

This account seems to mingle the figure of Arthur with those of Merlin and Lailoken.

Geoffrey of Monmouth relates that Merlin's sister, wishing to trick the prophet, once introduced a page to him in three different disguises, asking each time how he would meet his death. The first time Merlin said that the page would die by a rock, the second time by a tree, and the third time by water. Merlin's sister thought that she had caught him out, but events proved him right: the page fell from a rock into a river, was run through the body by a projecting piece of wood, and drowned. Other accounts say that this triple death was what the Scottish Merlin predicted for himself and then suffered when he was pursued and stoned, fell into the River Tweed, and was impaled on a stake to which fishing nets were attached.

It is not uncommon for a seer's prediction to come to be applied to the prophet himself. The same thing happened in the case of Thomas the Rhymer as told at THE LUCKEN HARE. Legend is fluid stuff: oral and written narratives often diverge, coming to be associated with different places and people, and famous figures like Merlin, Arthur, and Kentigern attract to themselves stories from many sources.

RESTALRIG LOCH,
MIDLOTHIAN

In *Letters on Demonology and Witchcraft* (1830), Sir Walter Scott gives the story of Bessie Dunlop from around 1570. Bessie had recently given birth, and her new baby and her husband were both very ill. A stout woman came into her hut, sat down on a bench, and asked for a drink, which she was given. She then told Bessie that her baby would die but that her husband would recover, which predictions came true.

A short while after this, Bessie was driving her cows to pasture when she met a man who saluted her courteously. He told her that her stout visitor had been the Queen of the Fairies, and that he was now commanded to attend Bessie; he identified himself as Thome or Tom Reid, and said he had died at the battle of Pinkie in 1547. He was, Bessie said later, a respectable elderly-looking man with a grey beard, who wore a grey coat and breeches, white stockings, and a black bonnet.

Thome promised Bessie riches and plenty if she would deny Christianity, and in spite of her steadfastly refusing to do so, he continued to visit her regularly over the next four years, appearing whenever he was summoned thrice. He gave her advice to pass on to her neighbours about their sick cattle or stolen possessions and often urged her to visit fairyland with him, sometimes trying to pull her by the apron, but she always resisted.

Having once ridden to Leith, while tethering her horse at Restalrig Loch:

> . . . there came ane company of riders bye, that made sic din as heaven and eard had gane together; and incontinent they rade into the loch, with mony hideous rumble. Tom tauld her it was the gude wights [good folk, i.e. fairies] that were riding in middle-eard.

When she was accused of witchcraft in 1576, Bessie confessed all this. Her account is confusing in some ways – the visit from the Queen of the Fairies and the first meeting with Thome in particular are difficult to reconcile, since Thome too predicted the death of her baby and the survival of her husband – but she maintained that she had never abandoned her religion, and had never hurt anybody. None of this helped her: in the climate of the time, an association with spirits or fairies was never innocent, and Bessie was convicted and burned.

See also WITCH-HUNTS (p. 270).

ROSLIN CASTLE, LASSWADE,
MIDLOTHIAN

In one of his collections of Highland folk tales, published in 1964, Ronald Macdonald Robertson writes, 'To this day can be heard on dark and stormy nights the baying of a dog in the woods, near Roslin Castle, Midlothian.'

The legend he had heard was that on 24 February 1302, the wooded glen near Roslin or Rosslyn Castle echoed all day to the grim sounds of battle between the Scots and the English. An English soldier who fell in the fight had with him a large hound, which turned savagely on his master's slayer and was killed by the Scot. That night, as the Scottish troops rested in Roslin Castle, the ghost of a hound suddenly appeared in the guardroom, to the terror of the soldiers. Night after night it appeared, and the Scots named it 'The Mauthe Doog'. Finally it was the turn of the dog's killer to stand guard, and he had to carry the keys of the castle down a dark and winding passage that led to the captain's room. Suddenly a fearful cry and the snarling of a hound was heard coming from the passage. The soldier emerged, unwounded but terror-stricken. He told no one what had happened to him: in fact he never spoke again, and died three days later. 'After that, the hound vanished from the castle. Nevertheless, its baying is still occasionally heard.'

Although described as the ghost of a dog, the story of this hound is virtually that of the Moddey Dhoo (Moddey Doo, Mauthe Doo) of Peel Castle, Isle of Man. In 1864, George Waldron described the apparition that used to haunt the castle as 'a large black spaniel with curled shaggy hair'. It had been seen in every room, but particularly in the guard chamber, 'where, as soon as the candles were lighted, it came and lay down before the fire in the presence of all the soldiers, who at length, by being so much accustomed to the sight of it, lost great part of the terror they were seized with at its first appearance'. They were still careful, however, not to swear or speak profanely in its presence, as they believed it was an evil spirit only waiting its chance to do them some harm.

The Moddey Dhoo was always seen to emerge in the evening from a passage leading to the captain's apartment, and to return the same way at dawn. The soldiers therefore looked on this place as its 'peculiar residence', and when they locked the castle gates at night and delivered the keys to the captain they undertook this duty in pairs so as not to find themselves alone with the phantom.

One night, a fellow being drunk, and by the strength of his liquor rendered more daring than ordinary, laughed at the simplicity of his companions, and, although it was not his turn to go with the keys, would needs take this office upon himself to testify his courage. All the soldiers endeavoured to dissuade him, but the more they said, the more resolute he seemed, and swore that he desired nothing more than that the *Mauthe Doo* would

follow him, as it had done the others, for he would try if it were Dog or Devil.

Having boasted and blasphemed for some time, he snatched up his keys and went out of the guardroom.

In some time after his departure, a great noise was heard, and no one had the boldness to see what had occasioned it, till the adventurer returning, they demanded the knowledge of him; but as loud and noisy as he had been at leaving them, he was now become sober and silent enough, for he was never heard to speak more; and though all the time he lived, which was three days, he was entreated by all who came near him, either to speak, or if he could not do that, to make some signs, by which they might understand what had happened to him, yet nothing intelligible could be got from him, only that, by the distortion of his limbs and features, it might be guessed that he died in agonies more than is common in a natural death. The *Mauthe Doo* was, however, never seen after in the Castle, nor would anyone attempt to go through that passage, for which reason it was closed up, and another way made. – This happened about 1666.

The Mauthe Doo was never seen again in the castle, but nobody would ever venture down the passage again, and at last it had to be closed up and another way made to the captain's room.

Sir Walter Scott elaborated on Waldron's story of the Mauthe Doo in *Peveril of the Peak* (1822), where, possibly because he mistook Doo (Gaelic *dubh*, 'black') for 'dog', he calls him the Mauthe Dog. This is almost certainly how Robertson's 'Mauthe Doog' arrived in Scotland, rather than being original to Roslin. That being said, the Manx tale, once it had been popularised by Scott, may have been grafted onto an earlier tradition of a Black Dog haunting the Roslin woods. Especially significant is

A nineteenth-century engraving of the 'Apprentice's Pillar' in Rosslyn Chapel. As at Melrose Abbey, a master is said to have killed his apprentice in jealousy over such exquisite work.

the fact that he can be heard on dark and stormy nights, like the Norfolk Shuck or Shock whose baying was said by the local fishers to be a storm-warning.

Though many Black Dogs are said to be the ghosts of people, only a few are accounted for as the ghost of dogs, though here again East Anglia provides parallels, in Shuck as accounted for at Bacton in Norfolk, and 'Chuff' at Walberswick in Suffolk.

ROSSLYN CHAPEL, MIDLOTHIAN

It is said that the master-builder of the Chapel, being unable to execute the design of this pillar from the plans in his possession, proceeded to Rome, that he might see a column of a similar description which had been executed in that city. During his absence, his apprentice proceeded with the

execution of the design, and, upon his master's return, he found this finely ornamented column completed. Stung with envy at this proof of the superior ability of his apprentice, he struck him a blow with his mallet, and killed him on the spot.

So Black's *Picturesque Tourist of Scotland* (1844) relates one of the many traditions of Rosslyn Chapel. In the early nineteenth century, an old lady named Annie Wilson used to show visitors around and tell them the legend. One of her audience, who wrote to the *Gentleman's Magazine* in 1817, found Annie's delivery 'harsh and discordant', but was unable to stop her flow:

. . . if any thing in the way of interruption comes across her, she commences once more her elegant demonstration, her narrative of the Apprentice's Pillar, with 'his head bearing the scar just aboun the brow that his master made upon it, his mother's head represented as if bewiling the death of her son, and the apprentice's maister's head, just before he was hangit.'

By the time this correspondent heard her, Annie had already acted as guide to Rosslyn for many years, and had 'puttit three gude men anunder the yearth' (buried three husbands). Francis Grose, who recounts the legend in *The Antiquities of Scotland* (1789–91), may well have been treated to her guided tour. He remarks that what was pointed out as the apprentice's head, its wound 'marked with red oker', was that of a bearded old man; but details don't spoil a good story.

'The jealous craftsman' is an international theme. Similar stories are told of MELROSE ABBEY and of Rouen Cathedral, where the rose window in the north transept is said to have been made by an apprentice whose master took a hammer to his head. At Lincoln Cathedral two windows are involved: when the master saw that the window made by his apprentice was finer than his own, he threw *himself* off the scaffolding in rage. From here the trail leads to accounts of SUICIDAL ARTISTS AND ARCHITECTS (p. 156).

Until very recently, the tale of the Apprentice's Pillar was probably the best known legend attached to Rosslyn Chapel. Since the publication of Dan Brown's *Da Vinci Code* (2003), however, visits to the chapel have greatly increased. The idea that the chapel contains a secret connected with the Templars did not originate with Brown, but has achieved wide circulation through the book and film.

Jedburgh was on his way to one of the sheep markets held at Hawick at the end of every year to sell off sheep for slaughter. As he was passing over the side of 'Rubislaw' nearest the Teviot he was suddenly alarmed by a frightful and unaccountable noise which seemed to come from a multitude of female voices. He could see nothing of the speakers but he heard howling and wailing mingled with shouts of mirth and merriment, and he made out the words, 'O there's a bairn born, but there's naething to pit on't.' The outcry was evidently occasioned by the birth of a fairy child, at which most of the fairy women rejoiced, while a few lamented the lack of anything to wrap the baby in.

Much astonished at finding himself in the midst of invisible beings in a wild moorland place, far from help should help be needed, the poor man, hearing the lament over and over again, stripped off his plaid and threw it down on the ground. No sooner had he done so, than it was snatched up by an invisible hand, and the lamentations ceased, but the sounds of joy were redoubled.

Guessing that he had pleased the invisible beings, the poor man lost no time in continuing on his way to Hawick market. There he bought a sheep which proved a remarkably good bargain, and returned to Jedburgh. He never had cause to regret the loss of his plaid, for every day after that his wealth multiplied and he died a rich and prosperous man.

See also AUCHENGRUITH (Dumfries & Galloway).

RUBERS LAW FORT, ROXBURGHSHIRE

It is a good thing to befriend fairies, as this story from *Folk-Lore and Legends: Scotland* (1889) shows. A poor man from

ST BOSWELLS, ROXBURGHSHIRE

The manuscript collection of Border customs, legends, and superstitions compiled for Sir Walter Scott by Thomas Wilkie in the early nineteenth century records a death portent. Wilkie says that about seven years earlier a farmer's wife who lived on the banks of the River Ale, near St Boswells, was looking out of the window when she thought she saw a funeral party approaching. She at once mentioned this to some neighbours who were with her in the house:

They ran out to look, but came back, and sat down again, saying she must be mistaken, for there was nothing of the kind to be seen; the woman felt restless, however, and out of spirits; she could not help going to the window again, and again she saw the funeral moving on. Her friends ran out-of-doors and looked along the road, but still could perceive nothing; a third time she went to the window, and exclaimed, 'It is fast coming on, and will soon be at the door.' No other person could discern anything; but within half an hour a confused noise was heard outside, and the farm-servants entered, bearing her husband's lifeless body. He had died suddenly, by a fall from his cart.

The travel writer Augustus Hare, always intrigued by supernatural phenomena, tells a similar story in his memoirs for 1874:

When Mr Macpherson of Glen Truim was dying, his wife had gone to rest in a room looking out over the park, and sat near the window. Suddenly she saw lights as of a carriage coming in at the distant lodge-gate, and calling to one of the servants, said, 'Do go down; some one is coming who does not know of all this grief.'

The servant, however, stayed by Mrs Macpherson's side, and as the carriage came nearer the house they saw it was a hearse drawn by four horses. Many figures sat on the carriage.

As it stopped at the porch door, the figures looked up at her, and their eyes glared with light; then they scrambled down and seemed to disappear into the house. Soon they reappeared and seemed to lift some heavy weight into the hearse, which then drove off at full speed, causing all the stones and gravel to fly up at the windows. Mrs Macpherson and the butler had not rallied from their horror and astonishment, when the nurse watching in the next room came in to tell her that the Colonel was dead.

Tales of the 'death-coach' are widely known throughout Britain: another example is told at BALLATER (North East).

St Catherine's Well, Edinburgh

The pious Queen Margaret of Scotland (c. 1046–93) once sent one of her ladies on an errand to Mount Sinai, to bring back some holy oil from the tomb of St Catherine of Alexandria. As the lady approached Edinburgh, having carried out her mission, she dropped the container in the grounds of Liberton House; where the oil was spilt, a black spring known as 'the oily well' rose from the ground. An alternative legend says that Saint Catherine was being carried by angels from Alexandria to Mount Sinai, on a route (somewhat roundabout) which took them over Scotland, when a drop of oil distilled from her body dropped into the Liberton Well. Whatever the origins of the spring, a chapel was built there, and the black tarry water became renowned for its curative properties.

Bituminous beds of shale below the ground give the liquid the dark colour which led to the substance being called 'balsam of brimstone'. It contains a variety of soluble sulphates, chlorites, alkalis, and calcareous carbonates, and was considered effective for healing sprains, burns, and skin complaints.

Improved by James I and VI in 1617, then defaced by Cromwell in 1650, the well-house can still be visited, but in 2006 looked rather neglected.

See also SAINTS OF SCOTLAND (p. 490); SCOTLAND'S HOLY AND HEALING WELLS (p. 44).

ST TRIDUANA'S WELL, RESTALRIG, MIDLOTHIAN

St Triduana or Tredwell was one of those chaste ladies whose piety led them to self-mutilation. A pagan prince adored her fine eyes, and in response she plucked them out and presented them to him, speared on a thorn. Her shrines have been traditionally resorted to by those suffering eye complaints. The same legend is told of St Lucy and of St Medana, whose eyesight was miraculously restored; St Triduana's apparently was not.

East of Edinburgh city centre is Restalrig Loch, site of St Triduana's Well. A fifteenth-century hexagonal chapel once stood here, but was destroyed in the 1560s after the General Assembly of the Presbyterian Church of Scotland decreed that it was 'a monument of idolatrie'. The crypt which contains the well, however, survived, and was restored in the early twentieth century; Janet Bord writes that it is one of the finest well buildings still in existence, and there is a plentiful supply of water, indeed so much so that it has to be regularly pumped to prevent flooding. The building may be visited by appointment and pilgrims may drink the water, at their own risk.

The saint also had a shrine at ST TREDWELL'S LOCH, on Papa Westray (Orkney & Shetland Islands) and one at Caithness, where in the twelfth century, according to the Orkneyinga Saga (c. 1200), she healed

Bishop Jon, who had been mutilated by Harald, Earl of Orkney.

See also SAINTS OF SCOTLAND (p. 490); SCOTLAND'S HOLY AND HEALING WELLS (p. 44).

SAMUELSTON, EAST LOTHIAN

One of many stories of witchcraft from the area is told by George Sinclair in his tract on sorcery, Satans Invisible World Discovered (1685). This witch was a man, one Sandie Hunter or Hamilton, known as Hattaraik 'by the Devil, and so by others, as a Nick-name':

> He was much given to Charming, and cureing of Men and Beasts by Words and Spels. His Charms sometimes succeeded, sometimes not. On a day herding his kine upon a Hill side in the Summer time, the Devil came to him in form of a Mediciner and said Sandie, you have too long followed my trade, and never acknowledged me for your Master. You must now, take on with me, and be my servant and I will make you more perfect in your Calling. Whereupon the man gave up himself to the Devil, and received his Mark, with this new name.

After this, Hattaraik became famous for his charms and cures of men and beasts, and travelled through the country selling his skills:

> Whatever House he came to, none durst refuse Hattaraik an alms, rather for his ill, than his good.

One day he came to Samuelston, where some people were setting off on horseback. A young gentleman, brother of Lady Samuelston, struck him, saying, 'You Warlok-Cairle, what have you to do here?' whereupon Sandie went away grumbling threats. When the young man was coming home after dark, he met with somebody or something 'that begat a dreadful consternation in him, which for the most part, he would never reveal'. The next morning he was mad, and had to be restrained for several days. His sister called for Hatteraik, and asked him what he had done to her brother William. He admitted that he had punished the young man, and she promised the magician food if he would perform a cure. In order to do so, he required one of William's shirts: 'What Pranks he plaid with it cannot be known. But within a short while the Gentleman recovered his Health.'

When Hatteraik came to receive his wages, he told Lady Samuelston that her brother would soon leave the country and not return: believing the warning, she got William to make over all his property to her, thus defrauding her other brother George.

Hatteraik was eventually convicted of witchcraft, and burned on Castle Hill, Edinburgh. The 'Mark' he received from the Devil was the witch-mark, considered proof positive of witchcraft (*see* INVERNESS, Southern Highlands), and his request for the shirt is also standard magical practice, a garment worn by the victim being necessary for either curse or cure.

See also WITCH-HUNTS (p. 270).

SELKIRK

It was long ago the custom of sutors (shoemakers), on winter mornings, to begin their work before daylight came. Early one morning, a sutor who lived in the Kirk-Wynd, and whose shop was the nearest of all the shoemakers in Selkirk to the church, was visited while he was working by a stranger who asked for a pair of shoes to be ready at the same time on a certain day. At the time appointed, the stranger duly arrived, paid for his shoes, and departed.

When he left, the sutor, thinking there was something odd about his customer's appearance and manner, gave way to his curiosity and followed to see where he would go. To his astonishment, he went to the kirkyard and disappeared into a grave. Happening still to have his awl in his hand, the sutor stuck it into the grave so that he would know it again, and, returning with a gaggle of his neighbours in daylight, opened the grave and found the shoes inside the coffin. Forgetting (or ignoring) the fact that they were no longer his property, he took them home with him.

> Next morning, as he was sitting at work, the stranger suddenly stood before him, with a countenance whose ferocity almost froze his blood. He accused him of having taken away that which had been bought and paid for. 'You have thus,' he continued, 'made me a world's wonder; but I shall soon make you a greater.' So saying, he dragged the unhappy sutor to the church-yard; and at day-light poor Crispin's body was found torn limb from limb upon the grave which his curiosity had so unjustifiably violated.

'Crispin' was not the sutor's name but a generic term for shoemakers and leather-workers, from their joint patron saints Crispin and Crispinian. The story, told by Robert Chambers in *The Picture of Scotland* (1827), deploys a number of folk-tale motifs, including the taboo against violating a grave, and punishment of tradesmen for false dealing.

SMAILHOLM TOWER, ROXBURGHSHIRE

On a rocky outcrop commanding a wide view of the Border country stands the tall, rectangular fortalice of Smailholm Tower, probably erected in the sixteenth century, its upper part added perhaps a hundred years later. Sir Walter Scott knew it as a boy, having stayed for a time at the neighbouring farmhouse of Sandyknowe, the home of his paternal grandfather. Later, he made it the setting of his ballad *The Eve of St John*, and also described in it one of the preliminary epistles to *Marmion*:

> . . . still I thought that shatter'd tower
> The mightiest work of human power.

In *Border Antiquities* (1818), he tells us that 'there was somewhere about the tower, a human scull, possessed of such extraordinary powers of self-motion, that if carried to any distance it would be found next morning in its usual repository.'

The same idea underlies what is said of 'screaming skulls' in England, that if moved they will cause disturbance until returned to their rightful place. The notion of things returning of their own accord seems to go back to traditions of self-returning stones, a belief which can be dated as early as *c*. 800 CE in the writings of Nennius. He describes a stone in Brecknockshire, supposed to bear the hoofmark of Arthur's horse, which if carried away will return to its place the next day. Legends of this kind are fairly common in England and Wales but are notably lacking in Scotland, although St Fillan's bell was said to return to its place in the churchyard near ST FILLAN'S POOL (Central & Perthshire).

SOUTRA MAINS, MIDLOTHIAN

Chambers's Journal in 1888, after describing Soutra as a deserted and ruinous village, goes on to describe a 'solitary house by the roadside' known as Lowrie's Den:

> It was formerly a small inn, and was the scene of a murder at the beginning of the century. Two gypsies had quarrelled while drinking in the kitchen. During the

struggle, one of them drew a knife; his wife called out, 'Strike laigh [low], Rob!' which the ruffian did, stabbing his victim to the heart. The murderer at once fled. Sir Walter Scott – then a young man – coming up at the time, gave chase, and after following him a couple of miles, he was captured with the help of a neighbouring blacksmith, and handed over to the authorities, by whom he was afterwards tried and hanged. Even before this, however, the place had a sinister reputation: several packmen or pedlars had mysteriously disappeared. No clue to their fate was got until one warm summer morning, many years after, the goose-dub or small pond opposite the door became completely dry and exposed a number of human bones, revealing the gruesome secret.

The second part of the story is notably similar to that of the MURDER HOLE (Dumfries & Galloway) given in *Blackwood's Magazine* in 1829. As the *Blackwood's* version is the earlier by nearly sixty years, it may be that Chambers added the bones in the pool to a separate story about Walter Scott and the gypsies.

TORPHICHEN, WEST LOTHIAN

Alexander Simpson, who farmed at Slackend near Torphichen (then spelt Torpichen) in the late eighteenth century, was the grandfather of the renowned man of medicine Sir James Young Simpson. Alexander was known for his skill in healing, and was much sought after in the district for his veterinary talent. He believed in the power of magical ceremonies, as a tale passed on in the family shows all too vividly:

> When he failed to heal his four-legged patients, he concluded the witches were interfering with him by baffling his remedies, and had to be exorcised. A murrain

fell upon the cattle about Torpichen. Alexander Simpson was unable to save them. He decided therefore that to frustrate the malignant devices of the Evil One a cow must be interred alive. And interred it was! David Simpson, who assisted at this barbarous piece of superstition, told James he was for a long time afterwards haunted by the remembrance of the earth heaving after the grave was closed in.

If magpies flew over a field Alexander was sowing, he would stop work for the day, and he would turn back from market if a cat or hare crossed his path. He always finished his furrows by ploughing in a semi-circle, so as not to let the witches get an even aim at him as he followed the plough, and any flint arrowheads which he unearthed 'were proof to him that evil spirits warred with the tillers of the ground' – these relics were very widely regarded as being 'elf-shot', or fairy arrows.

One day a beggar-woman was turned away empty-handed from the door, and cursed the house as she left. When Alexander came home for dinner and was told of the maledictions, he immediately seized a knife and set off in pursuit until, catching up with the woman, he slashed her lengthwise across the forehead to remove the curse. This was a well-known technique for dealing with witches, known as 'scoring abune [above] the breath', also employed for instance in the Shetlands, as mentioned at COLVADALE (Orkney & Shetland Islands). *See also* WITCH-HUNTS (p. 270).

TRAPRAIN LAW, EAST LOTHIAN

The Iron Age hill-fort at the summit of this prominent dome-shaped hill is said to have been the ancient capital of Lothian. From it in 1919 was unearthed the Traprain Treasure, about 160 pieces of mainly fifth-century Roman silver, probably the buried loot of a robber, now in the Museum of Scotland, Edinburgh.

At the foot of the hill stands the Loth Stone, supposedly marking the grave of 'King Loth', after whom Lothian is said to be named. Early in the sixth century, according to the legend, Loth's daughter Thenew or Thanea had a love affair with a shepherd, and her furious father had her thrown from the top of the hill. The princess survived, but was then set adrift on the Firth and carried to Culross, where she gave birth to a baby, Kentigern, later to become St Mungo of GLASGOW (Glasgow & Ayrshire). Her lover meanwhile slew the tyrannical father with an arrow.

WEST BOW, EDINBURGH

'It is certain,' wrote Sir Walter Scott in 1830, 'that no story of witchcraft or necromancy, so many of which occurred near and in Edinburgh, made such a lasting impression on the public mind as that of Major Weir.' In the mid seventeenth century, Weir and his sister occupied a house in the West Bow. In Scott's youth the building was used for storage, for nobody would consent to live in a spot so notoriously haunted, and hardly anyone would even approach the place for fear of seeing or hearing the ghosts; by the time Scott wrote his account the place was in the course of being demolished.

Weir was a well-born Covenanter, and in 1649 was commander of the City Guard of Edinburgh, with a reputation for religious zeal:

He was peculiar in his gift of prayer, and, as was the custom of the period, was often called to exercise his talent by the bedside of sick persons, until it came to be observed that, by some association, which it is more easy to conceive than to explain, he could not pray with the same warmth and fluency of expression unless when he had in his hand a stick of peculiar shape and appearance, which he generally walked with. It was noticed, in short, that when this stick was taken from him, his wit and talent appeared to forsake him.

Other things about Weir began to attract attention. In an account given to George Sinclair in 1685, it was mentioned that one day he found some men drinking when they should have been working:

After a gentle reproof, one of them replyed, that some of their number being upon duty, the rest had retired to drink with their old Friend and Acquaintance Mr Burn. At which word, he started back, and casting an eye upon him, repeated the word *Burn* four or five times.

It was conjectured that he was thinking of 'some other thing, which this equivocal word might signify, as *burn in a fire*': that, in fact, he foresaw his own damnation and torment in the flames of hell.

Despite these aberrations, Weir was still a respected figure, and it was not until he began to tell people about his 'particular sins' and 'abominations' that he was finally arrested along with his sister, who 'advised the two Magistrates to secure his Staff especially'.

During the time of his imprisonment, he was never willing to be spoken to, and when the Ministers of the City offered to pray for him, he would cry out in fury, *Torment me no more, for I am tormented already*. One Minister . . . asking him, if he should pray for him? was answered, *not at all*. The other replyed in a kind of holy anger. *Sir I will pray for you in spite of your teeth, & the Devil your master too.*

The Major was said to have committed bestiality and to have had an incestuous relationship with his sister. She too confessed at great length, saying among other things that she and Weir had travelled together in a 'Fiery chariot' to Dalkeith, where they had been told of the outcome of the battle of Worcester.

Weir was executed, possibly by being burned alive, in April 1670, and his sister too was condemned to death, in her case by hanging. On the scaffold she had to be restrained from stripping off her clothes, wishing, she said, to die with the greatest shame possible. Her last words were significant of the religious fanaticism which had perhaps contributed to her and her brother's insanity:

'There are many here this day, wondering and greeting [crying] for me, but alace, few mourns for a broken Covenant.'

Sinclair comments on the tragic but fascinating story, 'Horrible sins covered with Religion, bring utter despair at the last.'
See also WITCH-HUNTS (p. 270).

WHITEKIRK, EAST LOTHIAN

Like Tyninghame monastery and Auldhame church, the church at Whitekirk is supposed to have been founded by St Baldred of the BASS ROCK. The village was known in earlier times by the name 'Fairknowe', and a document said to be preserved in the Vatican Library relates the history of 'the Chapell of Our Lady at Fairknowe':

In 1294, when Edward First of England had defeated the Scots army near Dunbar, many of the army fled into that castle, then commanded by Black Agnes, Countess of Dunbar, who, seeing the number within so great that the place must soon be surrendered, rather than fall into the hands of her enemies, made her escape by water in the night in order to have gone to Fife. But she, receiving a hurt while getting into the boat, and the wind being against her, was obliged to be landed on that part of the shore nearest to Fairknowe, to which she was carried. The English, however, ravaging the country, they were obliged to halt while a party of them passed, during which time, being in great agony, she prayed to the Holy Mother for relief, when an hermit came and told her, if she had faith to drink of that holy well she would find relief: which she did, and had no sooner done drinking than she was perfectly recovered from all bruises and made whole.

In gratitude she built and endowed a chapel and chantry, at which a great number of miracles took place. In about 1355, English sailors are said to have despoiled the shrine, and one man 'snatched a ring from the Virgin's image so rudely as to mutilate the finger it belonged to, when forthwith a crucifix fell from above and dashed his brains out'. It was recorded, moreover, that a ship bearing loot from this and other sacred places was wrecked in a storm off Tynemouth.

The site became hugely popular, attracting over 15,000 pilgrims in the year 1413 alone. The future Pope Pius II made a pilgrimage there in about 1435, from which 'he had anything but benefit in the flesh, whatever else he gained,' since the walking ten miles and back barefoot on the frozen ground gave him chronic rheumatism from which he never recovered.

The White Chapel, as it had been renamed in 1430, continued prosperously until 1540, when, in the words of the anonymous writer of the Vatican document, 'the cup of vengeance was full and heresy had covered the north':

Oliver Sinclair, being poisoned by the letters written to his master by that infamous wretch his uncle, Henry VIII of England, asked leave of his King to built him an house near the White Chapell, which the other too easily granted, in building of which he pulled down the pilgrims' houses, and made use of the stones for his own house. Times growing worse instead of better . . . the pilgrims were no more safe. The offerings . . . were seized upon, and the shrine was beat to pieces. That Holy Chapell also shared the fate of many more, and was made a parochial church for the preaching of heresy, and by them called 'Whitekirk.'

The church building survives, mostly fourteenth century with eighteenth-century additions, but Black Agnes's 'holy well' has never been found, though many searches have been made.

WHITTINGEHAME, EAST LOTHIAN

Robert Chambers writes in his *Popular Rhymes of Scotland* (1826), 'It is supposed to be not yet a century since the good people of Whittinghame got happily quit of a ghost, which, in the shape of an "unchristened wean", had annoyed them for many years.' His informant had got the tale from an old woman of Whittingehame who claimed to have seen the ghost. Her story (as retold by Chambers) was this:

An unnatural mother having murdered her child at a large tree, not far from the village, the ghost of the deceased was afterwards seen, on dark nights, running in a distracted manner between the said tree and the churchyard, and was occasionally heard crying. The villagers believed that it was obliged to take the air, and bewail itself, on account of wanting a *name* – no anonymous person, it seems, being able to get a proper footing in the other world.

Nobody dared to speak to the unhappy spirit until one night a drunkard, reeling home, met the ghost. Full of Dutch courage, he addressed it familiarly:

'How's a' wi' ye this morning, Short-Hoggers?' cried the courageous villager; when the ghost immediately ran away, joyfully exclaiming:

'O weel's me noo, I've gotten a name; They ca' me Short-hoggers o' Whittinghame!'

And since that time it has never been either seen or heard of.

The name given to the little apparition by the drunkard indicates that it wore 'short-hoggers' or short stockings without feet, which Chambers thought very probable, 'considering the long series of years during which it had walked'. Footless stockings were generally taken to signify poverty – the rich Macdonalds were said to have called Duirinish the 'Country of the Footless Stockings' as a gibe against the inferior land there – so the state of the ghost's footwear may have meant that when it was alive it was poor.

Although categorised as a ghost, 'Short-hoggers' has much in common with a Brownie, a similar tale being told of CLOCHFOLDICH FARM (Central & Perthshire), or a fairy. The taboo on speaking to fairies was well known, as in the story set at SANDRAY (Western Isles), and an international tradition identifies all fairies as unbaptised children.

WOODHOUSELEE, MIDLOTHIAN

The present house of Woodhouselee is several miles distant from the old mansion, the ruins of which can be seen in a glen beside the river. The old house was owned by Hamilton of Bothwellhaugh, but after the battle of Langside in 1568 it was seized by Sir James Ballenden, one of the favourites of the Regent Moray. Margaret, Bothwellhaugh's wife, was turned out into the night almost naked, together with her new baby; before morning, according to Black's *Picturesque Tourist of Scotland* (1844), she had become 'furiously mad'. She was said to have died from this brutal treatment, her ghost being reported to haunt not only the old house, but also, according to Sir Walter Scott, the new one:

This spectre is so tenacious of her rights, that, a part of the stones of the ancient edifice having been employed in building or repairing the present Woodhouselee, she has deemed it a part of her privilege to haunt that house also; and, even of very late years, has excited considerable disturbance and terror among the domestics.

This, he continues, is a remarkable vindication of the 'rights of ghosts'. The phantom always appears in white, and with her child in her arms, and appears thus in Scott's ballad 'Cadyow Castle':

What sheeted phantom wanders wild, Where mountain Eske through woodland flows, Her arms enfold a shadowy child – Oh, is it she, the pallid rose?

The wildered traveller sees her glide, And hears her feeble voice with awe – 'Revenge,' she cries, 'on Murray's pride! And woe for injured Bothwellhaugh!'

The legend is a little deflated by a note to T. F. Henderson's 1902 edition of Scott's *Minstrelsy of the Scottish Border*, to the effect that the lady was alive and sane thirty years after the battle of Langside.

YARROWFORD, SELKIRKSHIRE

There was once a blacksmith of Yarrow-foot (Yarrowford on modern maps) who had two apprentices, a pair of brothers, both steady, healthy lads. After a few months, however, the younger of the two began to grow pale and thin, lose his appetite, and show other signs of failing health. Though his brother often asked what ailed him, he would not say.

At last, however, he burst into tears, confessing that he was worn to a shred and would soon be brought to his grave by his mistress (the blacksmith's wife), who was in reality, though no one suspected it, a witch. Night after night she would come to his bedside and put on him a magic bridle which changed him into a horse. Mounting him, she would gallop for many a mile to the wild moors where she and other vile creatures held their revels. There she would keep him all night and in the morning ride him home. When she took off his bridle he would be in his own true form, but so tired he could barely stand. And thus he passed his nights while his brother was sound asleep.

The older brother immediately said he would risk a night with the witches, so put the younger one in his own place next to the wall and lay awake until the witch-woman's arrival. She entered, bridle in hand, flung it over his head, and up he sprang, a fine hunter. Leaping on his back, she then rode him to the witches' trysting place, which this time was a neighbouring laird's cellar.

While she and the rest of the witches were drinking the laird's claret and sack, the boy/horse, who had been left in an empty stall in the stable, rubbed his head against the wall until he had loosened the bridle and got it off. Now in his own shape, he hid at the back of the stall until his witch-mistress came within reach, when he

flung the bridle over her head 'and behold, a fine grey mare!' Together they dashed off, through hedge and ditch, until looking down he noticed that she had lost a shoe from one of her forefeet. Taking her to the first smithy that was open, he had new shoes fitted on both forelegs, then rode her up and down a ploughed field until she was exhausted. Finally he rode her home, and pulled off the bridle just in time for her to creep into bed before her husband woke and went to work.

The blacksmith of Yarrowfoot got up as usual, but his wife complained of being ill. He woke his apprentices, and the elder brother went out and came back with a doctor, who wanted to feel his patient's pulse. She flatly refused; losing patience, her husband pulled off the bedclothes and to his horror saw that she had horseshoes nailed to both her hands. Her sides, too, bore evidence of the kicks the apprentice had given her as he rode her up and down the field.

The brothers now revealed what had taken place and the next day the witch was tried by the magistrates of Selkirk and condemned to be burned to death. As for the younger apprentice, he got back his health by eating butter made from the milk of cows fed in the kirkyard, 'a sovereign remedy for consumption brought on through being witch-ridden'.

The boy's reluctance to tell his brother what has been going on is the nub of the story – the witch is his boss's wife and he dare not speak out against her. This is part and parcel of the international tale type known to folklorists as 'The witch-ridden boy'. The concept of being witch-ridden in the form of a horse or other beast of burden is an extremely old one. Often the transformation takes place after a youth who takes lodging with a witch eats cheese she gives him, as in stories told by Homer (850–800 BCE), Apuleius (born c. 125 CE), and St Augustine (354–430 CE), the general theme being connected with notions of the causes of nightmare.

In some medieval and modern versions of the story, the cheese is replaced by eggs, but most often, in tales from the Middle Ages on, the transformation is effected by a magic bridle, as mentioned by witnesses in British and European witch-trials. Men and women could be enchanted in this way. In 1672–3, Anne Armstrong, a young woman from Northumberland, said in her deposition that she had been transformed into a horse by means of a magic bridle and ridden to a witches' meeting. Somewhat like the blacksmith of Yarrowfoot's apprentice, she was unable to speak of her ordeal until, in her case, she was disenchanted, and able to tell others the witches' names and wicked deeds.

See also WITCH-HUNTS (p. 270).

Every night for months, the blacksmith's wife of Yarrowford turned her husband's apprentice into a horse and rode him to the moors, but at last her witchcraft brought her to the stake. Thousands of witch-burnings were carried out in Scotland and on the Continent during the sixteenth and seventeenth centuries. This sixteenth-century German woodcut shows such an execution, with a demon descending to carry off the soul of a sorceress.

NORTH EAST

*The counties of Aberdeenshire, Angus, Banffshire,
Kincardineshire, Moray, and Nairnshire*

ABERDEEN

In Aberdeen there once lived a young couple, Mary and John Nelson. Mary was pregnant, and around midnight, just as she was about to give birth, there came a terrible noise and all the candles went out. When a light was struck, Mary was found a lifeless corpse.

At the funeral, the minister said as soon as he saw the body that it was not Mary but something the fairies had left in her place. Nobody believed him, however, and the body was buried.

Some while later, John was out after dark and heard music. He saw a veiled woman dressed in white, and asked why she was walking so late; she raised her veil, and he recognised his wife. Crying, she told him that she was not dead but had been stolen by the fairies along with her child; what he had buried was no more than a piece of wood. The only person who could rescue her was her brother Robert, a captain on a merchant ship, to whom John would find a letter if he looked in her room the next Sunday morning. She had been warned that she would suffer for speaking to her husband, but to prevent that, she said, he should ride up the hill and 'threaten to burn all the old thorns and brambles that is round the moat, if you do not get a firm promise that I shall get no punishment'.

John did as he was told, and a voice told him 'to cast away a book that was in his pocket, and then demand his request'. He refused to part with his book and carried his point, upon promising that no harm should come to the thorn bushes, 'at which he heard most pleasant music'.

The letter left for Robert, who came home from sea a few days later, asked him to come to the moat, where he would see Mary with several others. He was to take hold of her and not let go, no matter what happened, until cockcrow. This Robert did, although the moat seemed to be on fire, dreadful thunder was heard, and terrible beasts and demons appeared to come towards him. As the cocks began to crow, he found his sister in his arms, and brought her home to her husband.

John and Robert then thought they would destroy the moat, in revenge for the child who was still missing. No sooner had they reached this decision, however, than a voice spoke, promising that they should have the child safe if they promised to leave the place unharmed, bushes, brambles, and all. When they agreed to this, the boy appeared on his mother's knee, 'which caused them to kneel and return thanks to God'.

This tale is quoted in Sir Walter Scott's *Minstrelsy of the Scottish Border* (1802–3) 'from a broadside still popular in Ireland'. It is similar in some respects to that of Tamlane (*see* CARTERHAUGH, Lothian &

Borders), but is a striking story in its own right, not least in its unexplained details. The book that John will not throw away is presumably a Bible, and the fact that the letter cannot be found until Sunday must be because of the sacred character of the day, but why can only Mary's brother, and not her husband, redeem her?

ABERDEEN UNIVERSITY

In 1824, an account appeared in print of Aberdeen students ganging up on an unpopular sacrist (a term used at Aberdeen University for a porter). The man, named as Downie, was subjected first to a mock trial in a black-draped room and then to an 'execution'. The strokes of the axe were simulated by flicking his neck with a wet towel, so convincingly that the man died of shock, and the body had to be secretly buried.

The tale was probably not a true one: no mention appears in college records of any official called Downie, nor are there any reports of a sacrist's sudden death or disappearance. Nonetheless the story received wide circulation, being reprinted several times in the nineteenth century and early twentieth, and orally current into at least the 1970s. The phrase 'airt and pairt in Downie's slaughter' (art and part in Downie's slaughter) became proverbial in Aberdeen, meaning 'confederates will not inform', and a cry of 'Fa [who] killed Downie?' was used to taunt students.

Associated with the story from at least 1852 was 'a hollow piece of ground near Powis, still known by the name of Downie's Howe' (which disappeared in 1926 when the land was developed as a dairy). This was said variously to be the place of the counterfeit execution and that of the burial. 'Downie', however, appears in many Scottish place-names, derived from *dun* (hill).

The death of Downie results from a 'fatal jest', a theme which appears in seventeenth-century Italian tales of a man slain by a mock execution, and in later British legends of people who go mad or die when their friends hide behind tombstones or gallows and impersonate ghosts. A similar trick was played on a man near HILLFOOT FARM in Dollar (Central & Perthshire), but there the victim only gave up drink, and could thus be said to have profited by his experience.

AIRLIE, ANGUS

A story in the *Celtic Review*, quoted by Walter Gill in 1932, tells of a house at Airlie where oatcakes baking on the hearthstone often disappeared. 'It was thought proper to pull down the cottage altogether, and then it was accidentally found out that the hearthstone was the roof-stone of an underground house, into which the cakes had fallen through a crevice.' Gill goes on to comment:

> The Airlie affair belongs to the 18th century, and it is easy to imagine the local folks of that period (or a much later period, for that matter) maintaining that the fairies had indeed taken the cakes found mouldering below, and had extracted from them their essential food-qualities.

Cakes which vanish from the hearth appear in other tales, and sometimes the interference of the fairies is more obvious: in a story from Shetland, for instance, the hearthstone is slowly lifted and a hand from below is seen to snatch a cake. Fairies were very often said to live underground, either beneath human houses as at MYRTON

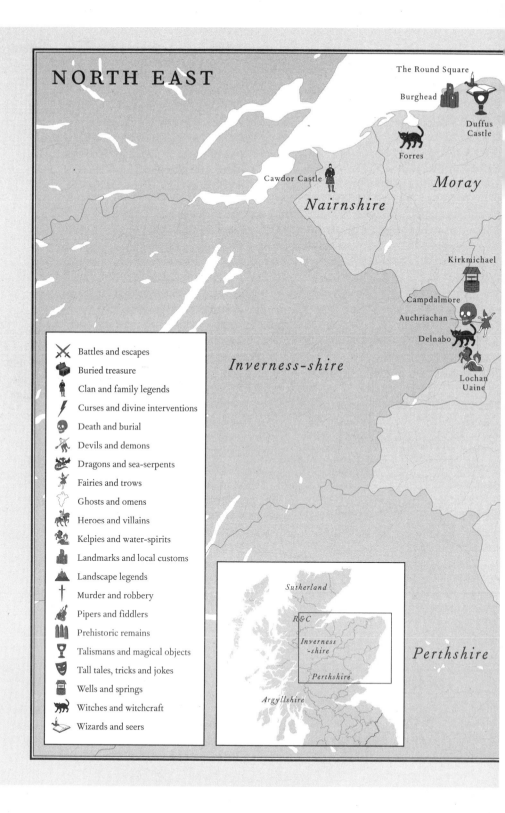

NORTH EAST

The Round Square

Burghead

Duffus
Castle

Forres

Moray

Cawdor Castle

Nairnshire

Kirkmichael

Campdalmore

Auchriachan

Delnabo

Inverness-shire

Lochan
Uaine

⚔	Battles and escapes
🧰	Buried treasure
🧍	Clan and family legends
⚡	Curses and divine interventions
💀	Death and burial
😈	Devils and demons
🐉	Dragons and sea-serpents
🧚	Fairies and trows
👻	Ghosts and omens
🐴	Heroes and villains
🐎	Kelpies and water-spirits
🏛	Landmarks and local customs
⛰	Landscape legends
†	Murder and robbery
🎻	Pipers and fiddlers
🗿	Prehistoric remains
⚱	Talismans and magical objects
🎭	Tall tales, tricks and jokes
📦	Wells and springs
🐈‍⬛	Witches and witchcraft
📖	Wizards and seers

Sutherland

R & C

*Inverness
-shire*

Perthshire

Perthshire

Argyllshire

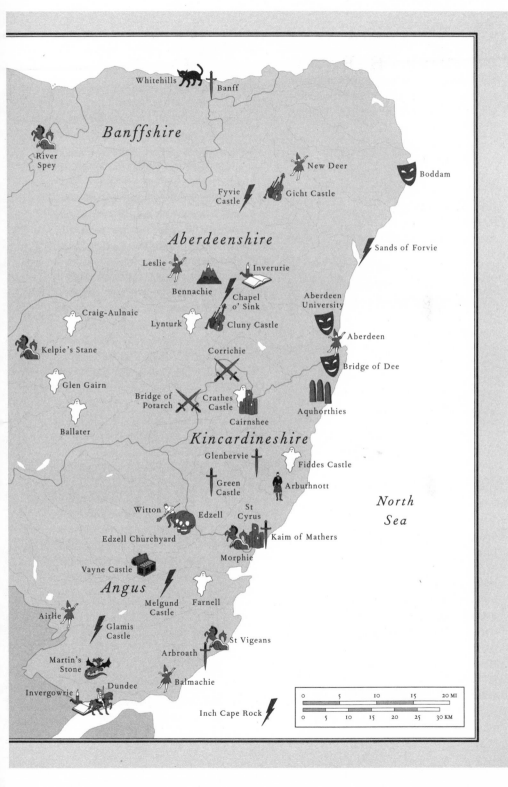

Whitehills · Banff

Banffshire

River Spey

New Deer · Boddam

Fyvie Castle · Gicht Castle

Aberdeenshire

Leslie · Inverurie

Bennachie · Chapel o' Sink · Aberdeen University

Craig-Aulnaic · Lynturk · Cluny Castle · Sands of Forvie

Kelpie's Stane · Corrichie · Aberdeen

Glen Gairn · Bridge of Dee

Bridge of Potarch · Crathes Castle · Aquhorthies

Ballater · Cairnshee

Kincardineshire

Glenbervie · Fiddes Castle

Green Castle · Arbuthnott

Witton · Edzell · St Cyrus · *North Sea*

Edzell Churchyard · Kaim of Mathers

Vayne Castle · Morphie

Angus

Melgund Castle · Farnell

Airlie

Glamis Castle

Martin's Stone · St Vigeans

Arbroath

Invergowrie · Dundee · Balmachie

Inch Cape Rock

| 0 | 5 | 10 | 15 | 20 MI |
| 0 | 5 | 10 | 15 | 20 | 25 | 30 KM |

CASTLE (Dumfries & Galloway), or in mounds such as the HILL OF DURCHA (Northern Highlands). Some of these legends are connected with souterrains, stone chambers constructed below ground level which are found in various parts of Britain. Dating from the last centuries BCE, they may have been built like ordinary cellars for storage, but in eastern Scotland particularly were identified as 'Picts' or 'Pechs' houses'. The Picts were often confused with the fairies, and it is possible that memories of the surviving race did contribute to fairy legend: *see* PICTS, PECHS, AND PIXIES (p. 430).

Gill's remark about extracting the 'essential food-qualities' from the cakes refers to the idea that fairies could take the 'foison' (goodness, nourishing qualities) from something while leaving it looking outwardly the same; they could also kidnap a person or animal but leave in its place a 'fairy stock', outwardly identical but in fact lifeless, as they tried to do at NEW DEER.

AQUHORTHIES, KINCARDINESHIRE

A special type of stone circle known as 'recumbent' is found in this part of the country, distinguished by a massive block lying flat and flanked by two upright stones. A good example is found here, near Banchory-Devenick. It is said that a local man removed one of the stones to serve as a hearthstone, but was afterwards so disturbed by strange noises in the night that he put it back where he had found it. Similar stories are told of many stone circles, but a more unusual tale concerning Aquhorthies is given in an 1813 agricultural survey:

Close to the principal druidical circle there are two parks of extraordinary fertility, although much incumbered with large masses of stone interspersed through them. The ground of these parks has been very long remarked for its productiveness; and the tradition of the country is, that in the time of the *Picts*, soil had been brought to these parks, all the way from Findon, a distance of two miles; and that this was done by ranging a line of men along the whole distance, who handed the earth from one to the other.

Elsewhere, buildings are said to have been constructed by handing stones along a line of men or sometimes giants as at the CAVE OF RAITTS (Northern Highlands), but it is less common to find land being improved in this way. It was remarked in 1985 that the fields around the Aquhorthies circle still have some of the best soil in the area.

ARBROATH, ANGUS

The precipitous coast around Arbroath is notable for a number of 'deep and dismal caves', one of which was said to have been the haunt of a family of cannibals in the late fifteenth century. Their story is given in Robert Lindsay of Pitscottie's *History and Chronicles of Scotland* (1570s), and was quoted with modernised spelling by Robert Chambers in 1827:

About this time there was apprehended and taken, for a most abominable and cruel abuse, a brigand, who haunted and dwelt, with his whole family and household, out of all men's company, in a place of Angus, called the Fiend's Den. This mischievous man had an execrable fashion to take all young men and children, that either he could steal quietly, or take away by any other moyen [means], without the knowledge of our people, and bring them home and eat them; and the more young they were, he held them the more tender and the greater delicate. For which damnable abuse he was burnt, with his wife, bairns, and family, except a young lass of one year old, which was saved and brought to Dundee, where she was fostered and brought up: but, when she came to woman's years, she was condemned and burnt quick [alive], for the same crime her father and mother were convicted of.

It was said that when the young woman was brought out to the place of execution, a great crowd, mainly of women, gathered to curse her. She turned to them with a furious and maddened expression, and told them, 'Give me credit and trow [believe] me, if ye had experience of eating man's and woman's flesh, ye would think the same so delicious, that ye would never forbear it again.' She died unrepentant.

This account is one of those which may have contributed to the Ayrshire legend of SAWNEY BEAN THE CANNIBAL (p. 200).

ARBUTHNOTT, KINCARDINESHIRE

In the graveyard at Arbuthnott lies James Leslie Mitchell, better known as the author Lewis Grassic Gibbon. His fictional village Kinraddie is largely based on Arbuthnott, and the opening pages of *Sunset Song* (1932) give a pen-portrait which may not have been greatly relished by local readers:

Next door the kirk was an olden tower, built in the time of the Roman Catholics, the coarse creatures, and it was fell old and wasn't used any more except by the cushat-doves and they flew in and out the narrow slits in the upper storey and nested all the year round and the place was fair white with their dung. In the lower half of the tower was an effigy-thing of

Cospatrick de Gondeshil, him that killed the gryphon, lying on his back with his arms crossed and a daft-like simper on his face . . .

The original of 'Cospatrick de Gondeshil' is a thirteenth-century member of the Arbuthnott family variously named as Hew, Hugo, or James, but also known as 'Blundus' or 'Le Blond', whose effigy lies in the chapel apse at Arbuthnott. According to legend he killed a wild boar that was causing destruction in the nearby Den of Pitcarles, and was rewarded by large estates. Variations on this story are told of many old families throughout Britain, some accounts involving boars but others mentioning wolves, bears, or occasionally supernatural animals such as the gryphon.

In Sir Hew's case, an extra 'proof' of the tale was a stone preserved at Arbuthnott House, said to be the missile with which the boar was killed, but in fact a cannonball which was fired at Inverbervie by a French privateer during the Napoleonic wars.

AUCHRIACHAN, STRATH AVON, BANFFSHIRE

A story told by Grant Stewart in 1823 and included by Katharine Briggs in her *Dictionary of British Folk-tales* (1970–1) tells of the tacksman or tenant of the farm of Auchriachan in Strath Avon, who was searching for his goats on a hill in Glen Livat when he suddenly found himself enveloped in a dense fog. Night came on, and still the fog persisted, and he began to give himself up for lost. Then suddenly, not far off, he saw a light. Hurrying towards it, he found that it came from a strange-looking building, and the door being open he went in. There he was much surprised to meet a woman whose funeral he had recently attended. She told him that the place belonged to the fairies, for whom she kept house, and that his only hope of evading them was to hide. She concealed him in a corner, and presently a troop of fairies came in calling for food. One of them mentioned the 'miserly' tacksman of Auchriachan, and how he had cheated them by using charms taught him by his grandmother.

> 'He is now from home,' said he, 'in search of our allies, his goats, and his family have neglected to use the charm, so come let us have his favourite ox for supper.' The speaker was Thomas Rimer, and the plan was adopted with acclamation. 'But what are we to do for bread?' cried one. 'We'll have Auchriachan's new-baked bread,' replied Thomas; 'his wife forgot to cross the first bannock.' So said, so done.

The ox was brought in and slaughtered before the tacksman's very eyes, and while the fairies were cooking it, the woman provided him with the chance to slip away.

The mist had cleared, and the moon was bright, so he soon reached home. His wife produced a basket of newly baked bannocks with milk to drink but his mind was still running on his ox. He asked who had tended the cattle that night, and finding it was one of his sons, asked if he had used the charm. No, he had forgotten.

> 'Alas! alas!' cried the tacksman. 'My favourite ox is no more.' One of the sons asked how that could be, seeing that he had seen him alive and well less than two hours before.
>
> 'It was nothing but a fairy stock,' cried the father. 'Bring him out here.' The poor ox was led forth, and the farmer, after abusing it and those that had sent it, felled it to the ground. The carcase was flung down the brae at the back of the house, and the bread was sent after it, and there they both lay untouched, for it was

observed that neither cat nor dog would put a tooth in either of them.

Although Thomas the Rhymer is here far from his homeland at EARLSTON (Lothian & Borders), his predictions feature in several traditions of the region, including those of BENNACHIE and FYVIE CASTLE. In this story, however, he does not figure as a prophet but merely as a fairy mischief-maker.

Briggs comments that help and warning from a mortal imprisoned in fairyland is a common feature of such tales. She adds that goats are supposed to be on good terms with the fairies, and possessed of 'more cunning and knowledge than their appearance bespeaks', although some might argue that a goat looks cunning enough for anything.

BALLATER, ABERDEENSHIRE

Ballater, on the River Dee west of Aberdeen, is the setting for a tale told by the Traveller Stanley Robertson, recorded in 1976. Stanley was well known as a storyteller and singer, and was very interested in the supernatural; he said his grandfather had known the people concerned in this spine-chiller, and Alan Bruford of the School of Scottish Studies comments that although the names may be invented, 'the locality is the true one'.

Sometime in the nineteenth century, a family of Travellers called MacDonald lived at Ballater. Their caravan was a beauty, painted in green and gold, and it was known as the Evening Star. The MacDonalds had only one son, Johnnie, who was about twelve years old but already earned an independent living by trading and hunting.

One night, Johnnie was far from home and tired. A big carriage came along the road, drawn by six white horses, and he waved it down, hoping for a lift. The coachman, a tall thin man, said he had some collections to make, but he let the boy get up beside him. Johnnie could see a young woman sitting inside the coach, and as the journey continued they picked up a stout woman in a flowing white gown, an old man, and a beautiful girl. None of them replied to Johnnie when he wished them good evening, and he thought it even more strange that none of them greeted each other when they got into the carriage.

Finally they stopped at a house where the coach driver said he was early. He left Johnnie to wait for him, but the boy was cold and so he climbed inside the carriage. None of the people said hello; they just stared at each other, glassy-eyed. Johnnie thought maybe they were on their way to a madhouse, so he got out again and went to shelter from the rain under the eaves of the house. Looking inside, he saw an old man lying on a bed. A woman was crying, and a minister was there who said the man had died, but just then the coachman entered the room and waved his hand, and the corpse got up and walked out to the waiting carriage.

Now Johnnie realised the truth: 'This is the Angel o Death's here!' he thought. The coachman said his next collection was in Ballater, but Johnnie wanted to get away, so he asked the coachman to stop about half a mile out of the town. Just as the coach was drawing off into the night, Johnnie shouted after it to ask whereabouts in Ballater the collection was to be made, and was appalled to hear the reply that it was at the Evening Star, his mother's and father's caravan.

He ran as fast as he could, but when he came to the caravan he saw it was ablaze. He started to cry and scream, thinking that his family were all dead, but then he saw his father and mother alive and coming to meet him. He told them what had happened to him, and asked them why the Angel of Death had come and left empty-handed. Maybe he didn't, his mother said: 'Princie, the dog, wis in the caravan fin [when] the caravan caught fire, sae the Angel o Death didnae gang awaa empty-handed efter aa.'

Another tale of the 'death-coach' was told at ST BOSWELLS (Lothian & Borders). *See also* TRAVELLER TALES (p. 298).

BALMACHIE, NEAR CARLUNGIE, ANGUS

Scotland has a number of stories of the abduction of women by fairies. Usually the substitute is a log or another simulacrum left in her place, but sometimes it is a fairy woman, as in this story from an 1889 collection of Scottish legends.

In the old days, when it was the fashion for men to wear swords, the Laird of Balmachie, an estate north of Carlungie, one day travelled to Dundee, leaving his wife ill in bed. Riding home in the twilight and having left the high road, he was crossing the little knolls known as the Cur-hills near Carlungie when he met a troop of fairies carrying something or someone on a litter. On impulse, he rode close to the litter, laid his sword across it and commanded, 'In the name of God, release your captive.'

Fairies could never endure 'cold iron', and the troop immediately dispersed, leaving the litter on the ground. Inside, the laird found his own wife, wearing her nightdress.

Wrapping his coat around her, he carried her home on his horse before him and left her downstairs in the care of a friend while he went to his wife's bedroom. There, apparently, she still lay in bed, fretful and complaining of neglect. Pretending to be sympathetic, he suggested she get out of

Traveller Tales

Gypsies probably originated in northern India, but the first arrivals in Europe, in the early fifteenth century, were believed to be natives of Egypt. These 'Egyptians' became known as 'gypsies', and by many other names too, of which 'Travellers' is the most widely applicable. Travellers, in this sense, came to Scotland around the beginning of the sixteenth century, and became an established presence, with their own 'capital' at KIRK YETHOLM (Lothian & Borders).

Storytelling remained an important part of life among Travellers for much longer than in settled communities, where from the nineteenth century people became reliant on print and later on the radio or gramophone for their entertainment. On the road or around the campfire, however, the old tales continued in oral circulation and could be told at epic length: in the 1950s, the Traveller Bella Higgins remembered that her father could start a story at six in the evening and not finish until six the next morning. From 1951, when the School of Scottish Studies was founded and set about the systematic collecting of folklore, a rich vein of tradition was found among the Travellers. Several anthologies have been published, and recordings made of gifted storytellers such as Betsy Whyte, Duncan Williamson, and others.

Whereas house-dwellers tend to preserve localised traditions anchored to familiar landmarks, Travellers show a perference for more universal themes, timeless 'wonder tales' set in magical realms. Even when the plots are internationally known, the narratives may be claimed as 'old Traveller stories' and slanted towards the experience of audience and teller: Cinderella, for example, may appear as a Traveller girl who marries a rich gentleman with help from her magic granny; and fairies, in mainstream Scottish tradition usually tricksy if not downright dangerous, are more likely to feature as helpful spirits, perhaps reflecting fellow feeling with a race shunned by the rest of the population.

Tales told among the Travellers often provided education as well as amusement. Duncan Williamson wrote in the 1980s that from about the age of six children would hear stories of fortune and adventure: 'A traveller child is taught . . . to obey his parents, go his own way in the world and look for a living, not to expect too much, not to be a thief or murderer and not to be bad or the devil will get him.' Devil stories and ghost stories, he says, are more suitable for older boys and girls: 'Younger ones would be too easily frightened by them.'

This applies also to 'burker' tales, a genre almost exclusive to Scottish

Gypsies arrived in Scotland in the sixteenth century, and their skill as storytellers has been celebrated ever since. This photograph from the early 1900s shows gypsy children listening to the stories of an elderly family member.

Travellers, of which a fine example is contained in Williamson's *Fireside Tales of the Traveller Children* (1983). A 'burker' is a bodysnatcher, named after Burke and Hare, the murderers who lived near GRASSMARKET in Edinburgh (Lothian & Borders). Travellers, writes Williamson, 'still believe that there are plenty of body-snatchers alive at this present moment', who will kill them and sell their corpses for medical research, 'though the demand for bodies is no' as much as it was in the olden days'. Williamson's father told him what he claimed was a personal experience. Lost late at night when a little boy, he saw a beautiful pair of leather boots lying near a graveyard. He picked them up and put them across his shoulder, and later he knocked at the door of a house. The people welcomed him in, but he was horrified to see that they all had *red hair*. 'I remember all the things that my daddy and mummy told me about red-haired people – they swore that they were burkers!' (The tradition of red-heads as evildoers has a long history: pictures of Judas frequently show him with red hair.) Soon a coach arrived, driven by a man in a tailcoat and a top hat, typical burker gear. The boy was locked into the cow's stable, but got out through a skylight. As he climbed he dropped the boots he had found. 'But as the boots fell, I looked – ooh, I nearly fell off too – there were legs in the boots cut from below the knee! Raw bloody legs, and they fell right at the cow's nose!' The kidnappers concluded that their cow had eaten the boy, all but his shins. 'And that is the God's honest truth – that really happened,' finished Williamson's father. He never explains why the legs were in the boots, but the gory touch probably helped make this his children's favourite tale.

See also BALLATER (North East); RANNOCH MOOR (Central & Perthshire).

bed so it could be made, but she said she couldn't get up. The laird then had a fire lit in the room and lifted his 'wife' as if to put her near it for warmth, but instead he threw her onto the flames, 'from which she bounced like a sky-rocket, and went through the ceiling, and out at the roof of the house, leaving a hole among the slates'.

He then brought his real wife back into her room and she told him that, a little after sunset, the nurse had left her, 'for the purpose of preparing a little candle'. (This is probably an error in the printed text for 'a little caudle' — a milky drink, and a much more likely thing for the nurse to be preparing.) As soon as the nurse was out of the room, a gang of fairies came in through the window, took the laird's wife out of bed and carried her away as they had entered. After that she could remember nothing until she saw the laird's face and found herself lying in the litter.

The hole through which the false wife escaped could never be kept mended. Every year a storm would blow the slates from that place alone, without touching any other part of the roof.

Probably the laird's wife was in bed because she had just given birth: although nothing is said in this story about the baby, the fairies are most likely to have wanted the woman as wet nurse to their own off-spring, and may have wished to kidnap the child too, as at ABERDEEN.

BANFF

A gallows once stood in Low Street where the Biggar Fountain is now. Here, in 1700, was hanged James MacPherson, as famous for his fiddle music as for his robberies.

MacPherson operated under some sort of licence or protection from the Laird of Grant, and was sometimes said to be Grant's illegitimate son by a gypsy girl, although it may have been the patronage which gave rise to the rumour, rather than the relationship which led to the patron-age. Either way, MacPherson's gang was able to carry out its thefts unhindered for some time; some accounts claim that they helped the poor, and they certainly helped themselves. Their technique was to visit the fairs and markets held periodically in Elgin, Forres, and Banff, where they would cut menacing figures with their muskets, broadswords, and dirks. They would not, however, attack then and there, but would watch to see how the cattle sales turned out, then follow whoever had done the best business to where they could more safely be menaced into giving up their earnings.

The Laird of Braco was determined to capture the bandit leader, and had his men in place at the Banff fair where he could be certain that James would put in an appearance, as he duly did. MacPher-son could perhaps have fought or run, but a woman leaned out from a window above him and dropped a blanket over his head, blinding him at the vital moment.

The sentence was death, and although a reprieve was issued it came too late. The story goes that Braco knew of the con-cession, and had the town clock put for-ward by a quarter of an hour to forestall the messenger bringing the news. As the clock struck, James died, but either in prison or at the very foot of the gallows he had composed his final tune, then offering his fiddle to anyone who would have it. No one stepped forward, and the robber broke the instrument in pieces — 'over the head of the executioner', says one account, though that seems highly unlikely.

'MacPherson's Lament' circulates in several versions, including one by Robert Burns ('MacPherson's Farewell'). A rendition recorded in 1960 combines elements from that traditionally written by James himself and from Burns's text: the last verse obviously post-dates the execution.

Fareweel, ye dungeons dark and strang,
MacPherson's day will no' be lang,
Upon the gallows tree I'll hang.
Sae rantingly, sae wantonly,
And sae dauntingly gaed he,
He played a tune and he danced it roond,
Below the gallows tree.

It was by a woman's treacherous hand
That I was condemned to dee,
Below a ledge at a window she stood,
And a blanket she threw ower me . . .

The reprieve was coming over the brig
o' Banff,
To let MacPherson free;
But they pit the clock at a quarter afore
And hanged him to the tree.

BENNACHIE, ABERDEENSHIRE

The mountain of Bennachie, rising abruptly above the surrounding country, is strikingly visible for many miles around. It was said in days gone by to have been guarded by a giant, Jock o' Bennachie, known familiarly as 'Little Johnnie' despite his enormous height. His bed, a space between two crags, was known as 'Little John's Length', and a bare patch on the north-west of Craig Shannock was pointed out as the place where Jock dried his shirt.

Jock had epic battles with another giant, Jock o' Noth, Noth being a hill to the north-west of Bennachie in the parish of Rhynie, Strathbogie. A boulder thrown by Jock o' Bennachie at his enemy landed on Tap o' Noth, and such was the giant's strength that the stone showed the impression of his gigantic fingers. Jock o' Noth prepared to retaliate, and had picked up a great rock to hurl back, when Jock o' Bennachie stuck out his foot and stopped it. The rock therefore stayed on Tap o' Noth, bearing the mark of Jock's toe.

Finally Jock o' Bennachie was put under a spell, and is understood to be awaiting his release from a locked cave somewhere on the mountain. This puts him in the category of other 'sleeping heroes' such as Thomas the Rhymer (*see* THE LUCKEN HARE, Lothian & Borders), who himself is said to have prophesied:

Scotland will never be rich, be rich,
Till they find the keys of Bennachie;
They shall be found by a wife's ae son,
    wi' ae e'e, [only son, with one eye]
Aneath a juniper tree.

This sounds more like hidden treasure than a hidden giant, and it seems likely that two or more legends have mingled. A variant on the verse has it:

A mither's ae son wi' ae e'e,
[A mother's only son with one eye]
Sall fin' the keys o' Bennachie
[Shall find the keys of Bennachie]
Aneath a rash buss
[Underneath a clump of rushes]
I' the backward o' Tullos.
[Behind Tullos.]

Tullos is to the eastward of the Mither Tap, one of the highest summits of the mountain, on the road leading from Blairdaff to Pittodrie. One man is said to have found the key sticking from the lock, but was unable to turn it (perhaps he had one eye too many: the legend does not say). He hung his hat on the key to mark the place and went to find help, but when he returned he could find neither hat nor key.

BODDAM, ABERDEENSHIRE

A traditional tale linked with several Scottish ports and fishing villages tells how in the eighteenth century their residents hanged a monkey because they believed it to be a French spy. Greenock is one location named, its citizens tricked by their neighbours in Port Glasgow who had dressed the monkey up in uniform. Although there was a French naval squadron in the Greenock area around 1760, the supposed date of the episode, there is no other evidence to back up the story, and a variant tells that it was the people of Port Glasgow who committed the deed out of frustration at missing a public execution.

Another contender is Boddam, its claims supported by a popular song with the refrain 'And the Boddamers hung the monkey O!' In an article in the *Scots Magazine* in 1982, James Drummond maintains the primacy of Boddam as the original site of the story, but the evidence is not on his side: the printed sources linking the tale with Boddam post-date those for Cullen in Banffshire, and indeed those for Hartlepool in England.

In most of its versions, 'Hanging the Monkey' is an example of what folklorists call a *blason populaire*, a joke told by one community against another, usually a near neighbour. The Boddam version, for instance, was apparently most often mentioned by natives of Peterhead. There is, however, an alternative motive sometimes cited here for the hanging: that the animal was the sole survivor on a wrecked ship. As the legal status of a wreck differed depending on whether any living thing was on board, the summary execution could thus be seen not as a gullible act but as a cunning ploy to justify plundering the vessel.

BRIDGE OF DEE, ABERDEEN

George Henderson Kinnear, writing his *History of Glenbervie* in 1910, gives a story of early nineteenth-century bodysnatchers or 'resurrection men'. In order to learn anatomy, young men in training for the medical profession needed corpses to dissect; these, however, were not readily available in times when dead bodies were considered sacred and a complete set of organs was thought necessary for the ultimate day of resurrection. Thus the practice arose of robbing the graves of the newly buried, since it was of course essential that the cadaver should be in a reasonably fresh condition. Notoriously, Burke and Hare had their own methods of ensuring this in GRASSMARKET (Lothian & Borders). The men in Kinnear's tale had not gone to those lengths: they had done no more than dig up a body from a churchyard near Glenbervie in Kincardineshire.

When the body had been dug up, it required caution to get it conveyed to its destination, which in this part of the country was usually the medical school of Aberdeen. In this case the two grave-robbers had dressed the corpse and propped it between them in their carriage, but were then unwise enough to stop for a drink, and called for a 'stirrup cup' to be brought out to them. The landlady was surprised that they had only ordered two drinks between three people. 'Oh, this one does not drink,' was the flippant though honest reply. The lady was no fool: although this took place after dark, she must have had to come right up to them to give them their order. She became suspicious and arranged for them to be followed.

Knowing they were pursued, the two men threw the corpse off the Bridge of Dee. They had been identified, however, and would now be under suspicion; one or both of them found it prudent to leave the country.

The story might be true, but has the ring of an urban legend. The crimes of Burke and Hare made a strong impression on the popular imagination in the early nineteenth century, and many tales of 'burkers' were told, particularly among Travellers (*see* TRAVELLER TALES, p. 298), some featuring a black coach driven by a gang of medical students in top hats. As the folklorist Katharine Briggs comments, this is a kind of successor to the death-coach featured in stories such as that told by Stanley Robertson about BALLATER, but she also includes in her *Dictionary of British Folk-Tales* (1970–1) a lighter-hearted anecdote of a horse and carriage which drew up outside an inn one night, the passengers being two men and a veiled woman. The men got out, leaving the woman alone, and the inn's ostler went up and said to her what a cold night it was. He got no answer, and when he looked closer he saw she was a corpse. He carried the body into the stable, took off her veil and cloak, and put them on himself. Then he got into the trap in the woman's place and was sitting bolt upright just like the woman when the men came back. They jumped in, one each side of him, and noticed no difference.

After they had travelled some way, however, one said to the other, 'D'ye ken that body's getting warm?' The other said, 'I was just thinking the same.' Then the ostler piped up, 'If ye had been as lang in Hell as me, ye'd be warm too!' The men ran for their lives, and the ostler kept the pony and trap.

BRIDGE OF POTARCH, ABERDEENSHIRE

Black's *Picturesque Tourist of Scotland* (1844) describes the Brig or Bridge of Potarch, twenty-four miles (38 km) from Aberdeen, where the old south and north road, still used at that time by drovers, crosses to the Cairn O'Mont, Fetter Cairn, and Brechin. 'The Dee, where it is spanned by this bridge, is hurried between two rocks, which leave but a space of twenty feet for its ample waters.' The story follows of 'a caird, or gipsey, called John Young' who was pursued for murder and escaped 'by leaping this wild chasm'.

The feat could have been a real one, but there are many similar stories of heroic jumps across rivers or ravines, including the famous SOLDIER'S LEAP (Central & Perthshire). Some such traditions may be based on history, but many more must be mythical. The 'caird' John Young was in any case a figure of local legend, being 'the same to whom was attributed the bold practical joke of releasing all the prisoners in the jail of Aberdeen, (himself included,) and placarding the door with the advertisement "ROOMS TO LET."'

BURGHEAD, MORAY

Close to the Pictish promontory fort of Burghead is an ancient rock-cut basin, twenty steps below ground, supplied with water by a spring. 'All trace of it, and well-nigh all memory of it, had vanished till the year 1809,' reports James MacKinlay. In that year extensive works were taking place at Burghead harbour, and the workmen wanted more water.

A hazy tradition about the existence of a well, where the ground sounded hollow when struck, was revived. Digging operations were begun, and, at a depth of between twenty and thirty feet below the surface, the basin was discovered.

A narrow ledge runs around the pool, and more steps lead down into the water itself, which contains a semicircular pedestal. The original purpose of the tank may have been to supply water to the fort, and it has also been suggested that it was once used as a baptistery, since there is known to have been an early Christian church nearby. The site may, however, have had a grimmer use for executions by drowning, a method apparently favoured by the Picts.

Tradition was evidently valued in Burghead. Writing of local ceremonies in 1908, Eve Simpson records the annual making and burning of the 'clavie', a ceremonial torch. On Christmas Eve the clavie was made by sawing a barrel in two and attaching it to a long pole. The half-barrel was then filled with wood dipped in tar, and piled so as to form a hollow pyramid. Into the central hole a burning peat was placed, then when the wood was alight more tar was added, and the barrel lifted onto a man's shoulders; if he fell or stumbled, that was a bad omen. 'In bygone times one strong man was selected to carry the clavie around the town, but now the post of honour is shared among several of the able-bodied,' says Simpson, and adds that only the older part of Burghead was by her day encircled, since the whole town had grown too big.

After the circle was complete, the clavie was taken to a hillock called the Doorie, where it was placed on a stone and more fuel added. It had once been the custom to keep the fire going all night until the next dawn, but by Simpson's day it was allowed to blaze there for only a short while before the barrel was rolled down the hill, with everyone trying to snatch a burning brand. Those who succeeded would take their trophy home, where it would protect the house from misfortune for a year.

It was also the custom to visit the ships in the harbour:

Indeed as late as 1875 the clavie was carried on board one vessel about to make her first voyage. Grain was showered on her deck, and then with a sprinkling of fire and water she was named *Doorie*.

Annual fires were lit in many rural communities, such as CAIRNSHEE, and of course in Scotland and England bonfires are still usually lit on 5 November and sometimes on New Year's Eve. The Burghead ceremony had some interesting features, carefully noted by Simpson, including the fact that no metal hammer was allowed to be used in the clavie's construction, and the fire could only be lit by a peat already burning, not by a match. Use of steel or iron was prohibited among the fairies and in certain magical rites, and the use of 'living fire' also indicates a connection with ceremonials such as the lighting of the *Teine-Eiginn* or 'need-fire', carried out at the beginning of the nineteenth century in HOUSTRY (Northern Highlands).

CAIRNSHEE, KINCARDINESHIRE

The name *cairn sithe* (pronounced 'cairn shee') signifies the fairies' mound, and like many other Scottish hills with similar names, this one has a large cairn on the summit, dating from the Bronze Age. There was a long-standing custom for the shepherds and cattleherds to light a great bonfire here on Midsummer Eve, the purpose being 'to exorcise evil spirits and ensure the safety of the flocks'.

By 1900 the ceremony was supposed to have been performed 112 times, according to Archibald Watt's account in *Highways and Byways Round Kincardine* (1985). Assuming there were no gap years, that would take it back to 1788. Now, in 1787 Alexander Hog, a well-off local man, made his will, mentioned in the *Statistical Account* of 1845, including a bequest of ten shillings a year (in those days quite a large sum) 'to the herds round the hill of Cairnshea, to make a midsummer fire on that hill, where the donor himself had once kept cattle'. Did Hog's dying wish start off the whole tradition? It seems more likely that he was remembering a pleasant annual ceremony of his own youth, and that the total of 112 bonfires lit by 1900 was an invented figure based on the date of the will. Whatever the truth of its origins, the yearly event kept going until the 1920s or 1930s, but then lapsed.

CAMPDALMORE, STRATH AVON, BANFFSHIRE

There was once a woman who lived in the Camp-del-more of Strathavon, whose cattle were seized with a murrain, or some such fell disease, which ravaged the neighbourhood at the time, carrying off great numbers of them daily. All the forlorn fires and hallowed waters failed of their customary effects; and she was at length told by the wise people, whom she consulted on the occasion, that it was evidently the effect of some infernal agency, the power of which could not be destroyed by any other means than the never-failing specific – the juice of a dead head from the churchyard.

The woman was reluctant to disturb the dead, but seeing more and more of her cattle die, at length in desperation she resolved to try out the remedy, and with difficulty persuaded a neighbour to accompany her. They set out a little before midnight, being the hour at which the head must be taken from the grave. The nervous neighbour refused to enter the churchyard, but agreed to stay at the gate until her friend's mission was accomplished.

The woman bravely set to with her spade. After a good deal of hard labour, she raised the first skull that she found and was about to take it when a hollow, wild, sepulchral voice exclaimed, 'That is my head; let it alone!' Not wishing to upset the skull's owner, she returned it to the grave and took up a second. 'That is my father's head,' bellowed the same voice. The wife of Camp-del-more, wishing to avoid disputes, took up another skull but the same voice instantly said, 'That is my grandfather's head.'

> 'Well,' replied the wife, 'although it were your grandmother's head, you shan't get it till I am done with it.'
> 'What do you say, you limmer [thief]?' says the ghost, starting up in his awry habiliments. 'What do you say, you limmer?' repeated he in a great rage. 'By the great oath, you had better leave my grandfather's head.'

The woman now told the ghost of her cattle's sickness, and they came to an understanding that she was allowed to take the skull, provided she brought it back by cockcrow.

On leaving the churchyard, she found that her friend had fainted on hearing the dispute with the ghost, and it took a deal of trouble to restore her, which was a nuisance as there were only two hours before the head had to be returned. Taking her friend on her back, the woman therefore carried her up the hill to the nearest house, left her there for the night, then returning home with all speed, made the 'dead bree' (broth) from the head, returned the skull to its guardian, and restored the grave to its former state. Her cattle speedily recovered, and as long as she had any of the bree, all sorts of diseases were of short duration.

The tale is taken from a collection of

The trunk of Cawdor's ancient thorn tree, guardian of
the family fortunes, can still be seen in the castle's Thorn
Tree Room.

Scottish folklore and legends published
anonymously in 1889. Similar stories often
involve a 'dare', and sometimes the voice
claiming the skull is that of a practical
joker. The would-be grave-robber sometimes goes mad from the shock, but here
the woman is acting from necessity, not
bravado, and her courage is rewarded.

CAWDOR CASTLE, NAIRN

Cawdor Castle is traditionally said to have
been constructed around a hawthorn tree,
whose preservation was believed to be
bound up with the family fortunes. The
trunk of this ancient tree is still shown at
Cawdor in the Thorn Tree Room.

The original castle was a medieval tower
house, built on rock by William, Thane of
Cawdor, by royal licence received from
James II in 1454. Lachlan Shaw, writing in

or before 1760, is the earliest printed
authority for the legend concerning what
he calls 'the Tower of Calder':

> Tradition beareth, that the Thane was
> directed in a dream to build the Tower
> round a hawthorn-tree on the bank of the
> brook. Be this as it will, there is in the
> lowest vault of the Tower the trunk of a
> hawthorn-tree, firm and sound, growing
> out of the rock, and reaching to the top of
> the vault. Strangers are brought to stand
> round it, each one to take a chip of it, and
> to drink to the *Hawthorn-tree* – *i.e.*, 'Pros-
> perity to the Family of Calder.'

Two other old hawthorn trees once grew
in a line with the castle, one in the garden
and another at the entrance. The first fell
around the beginning of the nineteenth
century and the second was blown down
in 1836, but both feature in a more elaborate version of the dream tradition given in

1859 by Cosmo Innes in his *Book of the Thanes of Cawdor*:

> Shaw omits . . . part of the legend which is yet vouched by the constant tradition of the castle – how the Thane resolved to build a tower of fence [defence], but hesitating as to its site, was admonished in a dream to bind the coffer containing the treasure he had collected for the purpose on an ass; to set the animal free, and to build his tower wherever it stopped; how the treasure-laden ass stopped exactly at 'the third hawthorn tree,' and how the castle was there built accordingly.

Innes does not explain the precise role of the three hawthorn trees in the story, but Charles Beard in his *Lucks and Talismans* (1934) says that the ass wandered until it came to the banks of a pleasant stream where three hawthorn trees grew. 'At the first it looked; against the second it rubbed itself; but beneath the third it lay down.' This bears a close resemblance to a common narrative theme where an animal determines the burial place of a saint.

Whether the lengthier version of the legend is the original, truncated by Shaw as Innes supposed, or whether it is someone's 'improvement' on the earlier, simpler tradition, is uncertain. That an improver may have been at work is suggested by the proliferation of 'proofs' of the truth of the story. By the time of Cosmo Innes, visitors were being shown not only the hawthorn tree itself but the very chest in which Thane William kept his treasure. Innes remarks, 'Even those who are sceptical enough to question the mythical history must confess that the tree is still standing rooted in the castle vault, and that beside it lies the coffer, albeit no longer full of gold or silver.' However, the tree and the coffer are two separate issues. Shaw's editor J. F. S. Gordon accepted the nub of the tradition – that the castle was

built round an existing tree – as historical: 'The Donjon or Vault is about 10 feet high, and the Hawthorn reaches to the top. There is no doubt that the walls must have been built around it.' The coffer, on the other hand, in fact an old iron chest dating from the seventeenth century, is transparent window-dressing, placed in the vault to corroborate the more elaborate version of the story. It is probably of a piece with 'King Duncan's chain-armour', in Gordon's time displayed in the same vault as 'proof' of the tradition that Duncan was murdered at Cawdor.

Charles Beard says that when strangers were brought to drink to the hawthorn, 'The usual form of the toast is or was "Freshness to the Hawthorn Tree of Cawdor".' Shaw's account makes it clear that toasting the hawthorn was tantamount to toasting the health and prosperity of the family, and that the hawthorn of Cawdor was to some extent regarded as a talisman or 'luck' on whose preservation depended the continuance of 'the house', in the twofold sense of the structure and the dynasty living within it.

See also GLAMIS CASTLE; MACBETH (p. 318).

CHAPEL O' SINK, GARIOCH, ABERDEENSHIRE

Leslie Grinsell, citing an article by F. R. Coles written in 1901, relates of this prehistoric site that 'In early days an attempt was made to build a chapel within the stone circle, but . . . each night the walls sank out of sight, and the building began anew every morning, until eventually the unlucky work was abandoned in despair.' Similar traditions are connected with certain stone circles known locally as 'Sunken Kirk' in the Border regions.

Other churches were said to have been

swallowed up by the earth not only while they were being built, but with all the congregation inside. The parishioners of ST VIGEANS feared such a fate, but were spared.

CLUNY CASTLE, ABERDEENSHIRE

In 1396, rivalry between Clan Kay and Clan Chattan was so violent that a solution had to be found. It was agreed that thirty of each clan should fight to settle the matter once and for all, and the battle continued until only one of Clan Kay's thirty was left, while the eleven survivors from Clan Chattan were so badly wounded that they could not hold their swords.

At the climax of the fighting a piper appeared in the air above Clan Chattan, playing wildly on a set of crystal bagpipes, and then vanished, letting the pipes fall to the ground. There they shattered, except for the chanter (the melody pipe), which was only cracked and was retrieved by the piper of the Clan Chattan, in whose family it remained a cherished treasure for many generations, a talisman whereby the prosperity of the clan was assured. It was known as the Black Chanter (Feadan Dubh) and is sometimes said to have been made of the tropical hardwood *lignum vitae*, a material probably as rare as crystal in fourteenth-century Scotland, and one which makes more sense of the name.

In the early eighteenth century the chanter was borrowed from Cluny, the head of Clan Chattan, by the Grants, following an attack by three MacDonalds of Glencoe. Although they so greatly outnumbered the aggressors, seven Grants had been killed, sixteen wounded, and the rest put to flight: those who fled had to walk round the church every Sunday carrying wooden swords with straw ropes attached, saying, 'We are the cowards that ran away.'

The chief of Clan Grant, desirous to wipe out this disgrace, applied to Cluny for the loan of the chanter. With this as a mascot, Grant felt that his men would overcome any enemy, and indeed the war notes of the pipes roused their spirits to such a pitch that it was said thereafter that 'no one ever saw the back of a Grant'.

The treasure was not returned until 1822, and in its absence the fortunes of Clan Chattan declined drastically. Arriving at Culloden Moor in 1746 too late to affect the outcome of the battle, they were nevertheless punished for their part in the rebellion: Cluny Castle was burned down, a price was set on Cluny's head, and for ten years he remained a fugitive. Another version of the legend omits the loan to the Grants, and tells that the Duke of Cumberland was warned by an aged witch before the battle of Culloden that if he waited for the Black Chanter to arrive with Clan Chattan he would be defeated. He attacked at once, and was successful.

Other chanters are said to have been magical gifts with supernatural powers, as for instance at LOCH FINLAGGAN (Western Isles), while Lord Reay's piper at TONGUE HOUSE (Northern Highlands) was given his chanter by the Devil.

CORRICHIE, KINCARDINESHIRE

I wis our quine had better friends,
I wis our countrie better peice;
I wis our lords wid na' discord,
I wis our weirs at hame may ceise!
Murn ye highlands, and murn ye leigh-
    lands
I trow ye hae meikle need;
For thi bonny burn o' Corichie
His run this day wi' bleid.

Mary, Queen of Scots (1542–87), who watched her
half-brother James Stewart lead her forces to victory
at Corrichie.

'The Ballad of the Battle of Corrichie' was first printed in the *Scots Weekly Magazine* in July 1772. It laments the encounter on 28 October 1562 between George Gordon, fourth Earl of Huntly, and the forces of Mary, Queen of Scots, led by her half-brother James Stewart. It was a quarrel that one could say had been forced on Mary: Huntly had refused her entry to her own castle at Inverness, and had possibly planned to abduct her. As the time of conflict approached, however, Huntly's enthusiasm – along with his support – was waning, and it was only the fact that he overslept that prevented him from withdrawing from the field. Even before that, the earl had apparently had less stomach for a fight than his wife, a dominant personality reputed, like many another strong woman, to be a witch. She had, it was said, been assured by her demon familiars that her husband would end the day unwounded at the Aberdeen Tolbooth.

The prophecy was fulfilled. In the *Diurnal of Occurrents*, printed from a late sixteenth-century manuscript, it is recorded that in the conflict Huntly was taken prisoner by one of the queen's guard and put on horseback to be brought before Mary, but as soon as he was mounted 'he bristit and swelt' – burst and swelled, i.e. suffered a stroke, perhaps – and died.

His unmarked body was taken to Aberdeen as foretold, his forces were trounced by the queen's men, and according to tradition Mary herself watched the whole from the hill of Meikle Tap, sitting in a hollow of the rock afterwards called the Queen's Chair. A spring between the stone and the battle-ground was known as the Queen's Well, and a more modern memorial is the granite stone erected in 1951 by the Deeside Field Club, bearing the inscription *Cuimhnichibh latha Coire-Fhroichidh* (Remember the day of Corrichie).

CRAIG-AULNAIC, STRATHDON, ABERDEENSHIRE

A male and a female ghost once haunted the wilds of Craig-Aulnaic. The ghost-woman used to shriek frightfully at night, disturbing the whole district, and one day James Gray, the tenant of the nearby farm of Balbig, Delnabo, complained to her of the noise. She explained that she had always resided in Craig-Aulnaic, whereas the man, while alive, had dwelt on a mountain in Glenavon. Now he was dead, however, he had taken a fancy to Craig-Aulnaic, and tormented her cruelly in order to drive her away.

This seemed quite unjust to James, and he asked whether any weapon could be used against the ghost-man. She told him that the only way her enemy could be wounded was if he were shot with silver or steel through a mole on his left breast. As James was a champion archer, he was quite prepared to try, and told her to come to him the next time her fellow spirit troubled her.

This was not long in happening. Being stronger and swifter than a living woman, the female ghost carried James to her persecutor's haunt, and they confronted the other ghost, a huge spirit. The mole was large in proportion to the rest of him, and James was able to hit it with his arrow; the ghost gave a great groan and vanished 'like the smoke of a shot'.

In gratitude the ghost-woman promised to serve James in any way he liked. First, though, she wanted to borrow his horses to move her belongings back into her old home. To test her, James pointed out a herd of deer and told her those were his horses, and to put them back in his stables when she had finished with them. Hardly had he reached his own house when the ghost arrived, complaining about his 'horses', which had broken half her furniture and given her untold trouble to stable. James assured her that next day they would be tame enough (meaning that they would then be venison).

The ghost proved very useful to James and his family, but unfortunately, in the way of such spirits, she had a habit of straying into other people's houses and often ate whatever food she found there. One day at the Hill of Delnabo she entered the miller's house and made free with some fish roasting on a gridiron. The miller's wife, enraged, tipped a cauldron of boiling water over the poor ghost, who fled screaming and was never seen again.

These spirits, which can perform household tasks and can also be wounded and scalded, sound more like Brownies or other semi-domesticated creatures such as the Urisk. Tales were told at GLEN FINCASTLE and LOCH SLOY (both Central & Perthshire) of a Brownie attacked with boiling water and an Urisk hurt by hot ashes.

CRATHES CASTLE, KINCARDINESHIRE

An outstanding example of the sixteenth-century Scots baronial style of architecture, Crathes has everything you would look for in a castle, the massive dignity of its original double square tower holding its own amid the picturesque pinnacles, turrets, and gargoyles. At the top of the castle is a 'curious effigy' of an early Scot wearing a three-cornered hat and a gold-decorated coat.

The castle and grounds are now owned by the National Trust for Scotland, but the Burnetts of Crathes retain title to the remarkable heirloom known as the Horn of Leys. Made of ivory set with jewels, and attached to a length of tasselled green silk of the time of Charles II (the material so delicate that it cannot be touched), the horn is said to have been the gift of Robert the Bruce to Alexander Burnard, the first Laird of Crathes, in 1323. Along with the instrument came the lands of Crathes and the office of Royal Forester of Drum, making it a 'horn of tenure', the only one in the possession of a Scottish family.

On the third floor of the castle is the 'Green Lady's room', rumoured to be haunted by the ghost of a girl who had an affair with a servant and became pregnant. When the girl disappeared she was generally thought to have gone away with the servant, who had been dismissed, but in the eighteenth century workmen took up the hearthstone in the room and found human bones beneath it, supposed to have been those of the unfortunate woman and her baby. After this, the haunting is said to have begun.

Tales of the ghost were probably inspired by the painted panels in the room, one of which shows a girl dressed in green with a child in her arms. The Green Lady has apparently not been seen for some time, though there have been reports of strange noises in her part of the castle. Some sources claim that when she appears it is a signal that a member of the Burnett family will die, giving the ghost a premonitory function like that of the Irish banshee.

DELNABO, BANFFSHIRE

One of the best witch-tales in Scotland, 'The Witches of Delnabo', is related in W. Grant Stewart's *Popular Superstitions and Festive Amusements of the Highlanders of Scotland* (1823). 'In the time of my grandmother,' begins the narrator, the farm of Delnabo, near Tomintoul, was divided between three tenants. All three were capable and hard-working, and at first all

were equally well off, but in time one became visibly poorer. His wife wondered why this should be so, and said she would do anything in her power to help her husband. One of the other wives then said that if she did exactly as she were told, she and her family would never be poor again. That night she was to come and meet the other two women, leaving beside her husband in bed her broom, 'well known for its magical properties'. It would resemble her so exactly that he would not be able to tell the difference: their own husbands had been perfectly satisfied with brooms in their beds for years.

The woman hurried home and consulted her husband, who realised that the other women must be witches and offered to meet them in her place. At midnight, dressed in his wife's clothes, he joined them at the agreed spot, where they welcomed the 'bride', as they called him. Each was carrying a fir torch, a broom, and a riddle (sieve), and they presented him with the same. They then set out along the banks of the Avon to Creag Poll nan Eun, 'the Craig of the Bird's-pool', where they forded the river.

Around the pool a hundred torches were flaming, so that the pool looked as if it were on fire. Fearful yells came from those taking part in the 'hellish orgies', and the man saw hags steering to and fro in their sieves, using brooms as oars, each holding a burning torch and 'halloing and skirling [shrieking] worse than the bogles'. At times they bowed to 'a large ugly black tyke' – the Devil – who was perched on a high rock 'bowing, grinning, and clapping his paws'. The wives of Delnabo told the 'bride' to speed them across the water in their master's name, but as soon as they had steered out of their depth, he cried, 'Go, in the name of the Best' (instead of 'the Beast' as they had undoubtedly instructed him).

Instantly the spell was broken and the witches sank. The torches all went out and the company fled, 'in such forms and similitudes as they thought most convenient'. The farmer went home, got his own clothes back on, and began his day's work. His neighbours did likewise, but towards breakfast-time they began to wonder why their wives were still abed. The farmer said he suspected they would not rise that day at all. This surprised the other two, who said they had left the women in good health when they had got up. 'Find them now,' was the reply, and the two men ran to their homes, where they were greatly astonished to find brooms in place of their wives. The third man told them to look in Poll nan Eun for the women, and when they dragged the pool they found the corpses, together with shattered sieves and brooms. This was enough to let the men know the truth, and 'the witches of Delnabo' were never mentioned by their families again. Needless to say, the less prosperous farmer got back his comfortable living and was soon doing nicely.

Many themes from stories of this kind were derived from Scottish witchcraft trials, in turn largely based on Continental formulae. This tale contains several such classic motifs: the witches' Sabbath, their homage to the Devil, the Devil appearing as a black dog, the witches transforming themselves into other shapes, their crossing water in a sieve, and their verbal charm being the reverse of a Christian one.

See also WITCH-HUNTS (p. 270).

DUFFUS CASTLE, MORAY

The English antiquary John Aubrey tells us that the cry of 'Horse and Hattock' is the password for being carried through the air by fairies. He gives a story sent him by 'a Learned Friend' in Scotland, Dr James Garden, who wrote to him in 1695 saying that he had heard 'long ago' concerning a forebear of Lord Duffus:

> That upon a time, when he was walking abroad in the Fields near to his own House, he was suddenly carried away, and found the next Day at *Paris* in the *French* King's Cellar with a Silver Cup in his Hand; that being brought into the King's Presence and question'd by him, Who he was? And how he came thither? He told his name, his Country, and the place of his Residence, and that on such a Day of the Month (which proved to be the Day immediately preceding) being in the Fields, he heard the noise of a Whirlwind, and of voices crying *Horse and Hattock* (this is the Word, which the fairies are said to use when they remove from any place) where-upon he cried (*Horse and Hattock*) also, and was immediately caught up, and transported through the Air, by the Fairies to that place, where after he had Drunk heartily he fell a-sleep, and before he awoke, the rest of the Company were gone, and had left him in the posture wherein he was found. It's said, the King gave him the Cup which was found in his Hand, and dismiss'd him.

Dr Garden adds that he went to some trouble to ascertain the then Lord Duffus's opinion of the tradition – this was James Sutherland, the second Lord (d. 1705). He heard from Mr Steward, the tutor of his lordship's eldest son, that Lord Duffus thought:

> That there has been, and is such a Tradition, but that he thinks it fabulous; this account of it, his Lordship had from his Father, who told him, that he had it from his Father, the present Lord's Grandfather,

There is yet an old Silver-Cup in his Lord-ship's Possession still, which is called the Fairy Cup; but has nothing Engraven upon it except the Arms of the Family.

'Horse and Hattock' is a fine version of a fairly widespread tale which has been attached to the ruined fourteenth-century castle of Duffus among other places. A very similar story was told in Cornwall in the nineteenth century of a farmboy who joined in the piskies' cry of 'I'm for the King of France's cellar,' and before whisking back to Cornwall again pocketed a silver goblet as a memento. This goblet is said to have remained in the possession of the farmer's family for several genera-tions, but disappeared prior to the 1850s.

The legend was evidently told in both cases to explain the existence of a particu-lar cup as a family heirloom. But its gen-eral background is not as simple as this might sound: there is a nod here to tales of the theft of a valuable cup or other vessel from fairies, such as the tale of Luran the butler boy of MINGARY CASTLE (Argyll-shire & Islands), and also to later tradi-tions of flight with the fairies, as at DALNACARDOCH (Central & Perthshire). Steward himself claimed to have wit-nessed the phenomenon at first hand:

He reports, that when he was a Boy at School in the Town of Forres, yet not so Young, but that he had Years and Capacity, both to observe and remember that which fell out; he and his School-fellows were upon a time whipping their Tops in the Church-yard before the Door of the Church; though the Day was calm, they heard a noise of a Wind, and at some dis-tance saw the small Dust begin to arise and turn round, which motion continued, advancing till it came to the place where they were; whereupon they began to Bless themselves: But one of their number (being

it seems a little more bold and confident than his Companions) said, Horse and Hat-tock with my Top, and immediately they all saw the top lifted up from the Ground; but could not see what way it was carried, by reason of a Cloud of Dust which was raised at the same time: They sought for the Top all about the place where it was taken up, but in vain; and it was found afterwards in the Church-yard, on the other side of the Church. Mr *Steward* (so is the Gentleman called) declared to me that he had a perfect remembrance of this matter.

The schoolboy was lucky that nothing worse happened: using a charm without proper experience is a dangerous thing to do, as any sorcerer's apprentice knows.

DUNDEE, ANGUS

Dundee was the birthplace of John Graham of Claverhouse (*c.* 1649–89), who became first Viscount Dundee. He was sheriff-depute of Dumfriesshire at the time when the government of Charles II was imposing episcopacy on Scotland. In this office he was employed to suppress the dissenting Covenanters, a charge he fulfilled so rigorously that, like General Tam Dalyell of THE BINNS (Lothian & Borders) and Sir Robert Grierson of Lag, he was said to be IN LEAGUE WITH THE DEVIL (p. 142).

The Covenanters believed (or put about as propaganda) that Claverhouse had got from Satan a charm which made him invulnerable to lead bullets. This led to colourful accounts of his death at the battle of Killiecrankie, Perthshire, in 1689. John Howie wrote in 1796:

The battle was very bloody, and by Mackay's third fire, Claverhouse fell, of whom historians give little account; but it

John Graham of Claverhouse, Viscount Dundee (c. 1649–89), was known to many as 'Bluidy Clavers' for his part in suppressing religious dissent. Others, like Sir Walter Scott, admired his gallantry and good looks, and called him 'Bonnie Dundee'.

has been said for certain, that his own waiting-servant taking a resolution to rid the world of this truculent bloody monster; and knowing he had proof of lead, shot him with a silver button he had before taken off his own coat for that purpose.

Some ascribed Claverhouse's invulnerability specifically to a coat off which bullets were said to bounce like so many hailstones. In 1810, R. H. Cromek described jackets made 'at a certain time of a March moon' of water-snake skins, called 'warlock feckets' and still remembered in his day:

Tradition has arrayed the brave persecutor Claverhouse in a lead proof jacket. He rode through a hail of bullets unhurt, pushing on his career of victory; but at length was marked out by one of those very men whom he had proscribed and persecuted. His charmed fecket could not

resist a 'silver sixpence' from the mouth of a Cameronian's fusee!

Claverhouse's jacket was made not made of snakeskin, however, but of pressed deer-hide so thick that it might be dented but not pierced. Those who like rational explanations of popular beliefs may still see the jacket in Glamis Castle.

Tradition also said that Claverhouse rode a great black horse given him by the Devil, who had ripped it from the womb of its dam. In a note to *Old Mortality* (1816), Sir Walter Scott explains:

This horse was so fleet, and its rider so expert, that they are said to have outstripped and coted, or turned, a hare upon the Bran-law, near the head of Moffat Water, where the descent is so precipitous that no merely earthly horse could keep its feet, or merely mortal rider could keep the saddle.

Scott, unlike most of his contemporaries, greatly admired Claverhouse and commemorated him in the song 'Bonnie Dundee'. The only portrait in Scott's library was of Claverhouse, and when Scott's friend Joseph Train saw the picture in May 1816, he was astonished by the 'beautiful and melancholy' face of a man whom he had been taught to believe was an incarnate fiend. Scott thought it a disgrace that one 'every inch a soldier and a gentleman' should be remembered as 'bluidy Clavers'. However, as Scott's editors remarked in 1993, his attempts to improve Claverhouse's image in the eyes of the early nineteenth-century Scots were 'like trying to rehabilitate Hitler or Richard III'.

EDZELL, ANGUS

The Lindsays of Edzell are said to have been prone to deep and protracted trances. This condition is reported of more than one member of the family, including Sir William Lindsay of Covington, who was laid out for dead and would have been buried had not his great-granddaughter observed 'his beard to wagg'.

A more dramatic story is told by Andrew Jervise in 1853 of a lady whose name 'tradition has failed to preserve', but who was laid in the tomb so loaded with rich and valuable jewellery that the sexton could not bear to think of such wealth lying idle. Accordingly he made his way by night to rifle the corpse, but could not pull off her rings:

These he eyed with great admiration, and having failed to gain them by ordinary means, the idea of amputation flashed across his relentless heart, and instantly the fatal blade of his large knife made a deep unhallowed incision.

This roused his victim, who groaned and stirred. The terrified sexton fainted, but the lady, disentangling herself from her shroud, helped him to his feet and led him out of the vault. She was so delighted at finding herself alive that she let him keep the jewels.

This story is a pleasant version of 'The lady restored to life', an international theme which does not usually feature such a gratefully recovered corpse: at KINGHORN (Central & Perthshire), the woman concerned was said never to have smiled again.

A less romantic tale concerns Euphemia, a poor relation of the Lindsays who came from Guthrie and later lived in Cortachy. She was known as 'Sleepin' Effie Lindsay' because on several occasions she was unconscious for a fortnight or more at a time, and all attempts to arouse her were in vain. After a final attack lasting six weeks she died, and this startling fate may have helped give rise to the story of the mistakenly buried Lindsay lady.

EDZELL CHURCHYARD, ANGUS

Major James Wood, who lived near Edzell, was roughly contemporary with the notorious Major Thomas Weir of WEST BOW (Lothian & Borders), and like Weir was said to have been desperately wicked. In fact, the deeds of one major may have been imputed to the other, since Andrew Jervise, writing in 1853, says that he has 'direct and opposite proofs of the engagements and doings' of the last ten years of Wood's life.

However exemplary the reality, the legends were lurid. A young bride-to-be who crossed the ford near Wood's house was pounced upon by him and assaulted; she struggled free, but only to fall into the river and drown. When he was on his deathbed, it was said that his cursing was such that dough was stuffed into his mouth to keep him quiet, and that he actually died of suffocation. Against all this, Jervise cites Wood's status as elder of the Church, his acting as witness to the baptism of several children 'of families of known respectability', and the virtuous character of his wife – although it should be noted that none of this disproves rape or blasphemy.

On Wood's death, it was said of him as of the reiver at LOCH CON (Central & Perthshire) that the Devil in the shape of a raven came for his soul, and when his body was carried to Edzell churchyard, the story goes that it was put down for a while and then proved so heavy that it could not be carried any further. The minister prayed, 'Lord! whoever was at the beginning of this, let him be at the end of it,' an oblique prayer which nonetheless did the job, since the corpse turned miraculously light. No one else would be buried near him, nor even have their coffins carried on the same poles, until an eccentric schoolmaster named Bonnyman insisted, when his own death was approaching, that he should share not only the major's coffin-bearers, but even his grave. Many people went to look when Bonnyman was buried, and some said that they saw amid Major Wood's remains the very dough which had choked him.

FARNELL, NEAR BRECHIN, ANGUS

South of Brechin is the village of Farnell, which now has a bridge over the stream where before there was only a ford. About two centuries ago, says R. Macdonald Robertson in *More Highland Folk-Tales* (1964), this ford was haunted by a ghost. According to Robertson's informant, this was the ghost of a man murdered at the

ford along with his horse, in consequence of which, out of revenge or for malicious pleasure, he plagued the district for some miles around, never doing real harm, but enjoying the fear he caused.

Some way from the ford was a cottage, by Robertson's time a ruin, which was once the home of a young girl, her parents, and her married sister, whose husband was away. On a cold and stormy night of early winter, the sister, who was pregnant, drew near her time. She was suffering badly, and her prospects looked grim unless a doctor or a midwife could be found. The parents were elderly and infirm, and their horse too was old and lame. The younger sister determined against all persuasion to go for help, though Brechin was a long way off and the ford would be high from the rain.

She was at the door, ready to go, when they saw a solitary horsemen. They all shouted and he looked round.

'Would you be going to Brechin?' they asked.

'No,' came the reply. 'But ye must be in sore need to travel this night; I can go that way.'

He told the girl to get up on his horse behind him, and asked if she was afraid. She was, she replied: mostly for her sister, but partly because of the ghost. She thought she would die of fear if she met him.

Encouragingly, he told her not to worry. The doctor would reach her sister in time, and all would be well. 'As to the second, well, there are ghosts and ghosts, and that ghost you will not meet this night!'

Hardly breaking stride, his horse crossed the torrential water at the ford and it seemed no time at all before they were at Brechin. The rider was reluctant to wait near the lighted window of the doctor's house: he said that he would be on his way, leaving the girl to travel back home with the doctor.

> She thanked him with all her heart, saying: 'I was real feared that I would meet the ghost.'
> 'There was no fear for that,' came the reply. 'I myself am the Ghost of Farnell!' And with that both horse and rider vanished.

Katharine Briggs notes that the tale shows clearly the narrow division between ghosts and Brownies, the latter being often said to ride for a midwife at need, sometimes with a passenger who was frightened of meeting the very creature who was helping them. A similar case is recorded at DALSWINTON (Dumfries & Galloway).

FIDDES CASTLE, KINCARDINESHIRE

Fiddes Castle is a sixteenth-century tower house, and appears in the poem 'Thrummy Cap, A Legend of the Castle of Fiddes', written in 1796 by John Burness, cousin of Robert Burns. Burns praised his relation's work as 'the best ghost story in the language'.

'This legend has long enjoyed a great popularity amongst the peasantry in the North East of Scotland,' writes George Henderson Kinnear in his *History of Glenbervie* (1910), although there may not have been a 'legend' before Burness invented one. The tale tells of two men walking on a stormy winter day:

> Ane was a sturdy bardoch chiel,
> An' frae the weather happit weel
> Wi' a mill'd plaiden jockey coat,
> An' eke, he on his heid had got
> A Thrummy Cap, baith large an' stout . . .
>
> [One was a sturdy fearless chap
> And from the weather well wrapped up

> With a mixed woollen jockey coat,
> And also on his head had got
> A hairy cap, both large and stout . . .]

'Thrums' are ends of threads or scraps of frayed cloth, and a cap made out of such scraps is called a 'thrummy cap'. 'Thrummy Cap' is also a nickname for the Devil, signifying his hairy head or perhaps his horns, and a ghost of that name was said to haunt METHIL (Lothian & Borders). The hero of Burness's poem has no devilish or otherworldly qualities, although he is shortly to encounter a ghost.

When he and his companion John seek shelter at a mansion house (i.e. Fiddes Castle) they are warned that the only free room is frightfully haunted. John is nervous, but Thrummy himself declares that as long as the bed is warm and dry, neither ghost nor devil will disturb his rest. In the middle of the night they are thirsty and Thrummy goes to look for water. When he gets downstairs he sees an uncanny apparition in the cellar: sitting astride a cask of ale is a figure just like himself, wearing clothes exactly resembling his own. It is a ghost, but Thrummy happily drinks with his double and takes some ale to John. At last the men go to sleep again, but are woken by a dreadful row in the next room. Thrummy goes to see what is happening, and finds two more ghosts ganging up on his recent drinking partner in a game of football:

> These speerits seemed to kick a ba',
> The ghaist against the ither twa;
> Whilk close they drove, baith back an' fore,
> Atween the chimla an' the door.

Thrummy joins in to help out the lone ghost, who is so impressed with his boldness that he tells Thrummy the story behind the haunting. The spirit was once overseer of the property, but cheated the present laird by hiding the title deeds to

Macbeth

Ah, me, alas for this fine story, with all its pathetic details and its appropriate and poetic justice! Those 'pestilent fellows,' the antiquaries, have been at their old tricks again, and picked it so clean, that only the very barest of bones remain.

So the writers of *Picturesque Scotland* (1887) mourn the spoiling of one of the country's most colourful sagas by a tiresome insistence on fact. Research had demonstrated that Shakespeare's *Macbeth*, based largely on the sixteenth-century chronicles of Hector Boece and Raphael Holinshed, bore little resemblance to history. Macbeth's reign had been a stable and mostly popular one; the figure of Banquo was a fabrication.

The last point was a vital one. In the time of Boece and Holinshed, Stewarts or Stuarts were established on the Scottish throne. Their ancestor was actually a steward – hence the name – in the household of David I (r. 1124–53), but both writers instead traced the dynasty back to Banquo, whose siring of a string of kings is predicted, in Holinshed, by three women in strange and wild apparell, resembling creatures of elder world'. This fated line must have been felt to confer more cachet than descent from a court official.

By Shakespeare's day, a Stuart reigned over both England and Scotland. Moreover, the king had written a treatise on demonology, had presided over withcraft trials, and was said to have himself been the victim of an attempted murder by enchantment at NORTH BERWICK (Lothian & Borders). *Macbeth* was written three years after the Union of the Crowns under James VI and I in 1603, and was partly intended to honour the new English king. The recasting as hags of the 'weird sisters' (a phrase from Holinshed) was in the spirit of the times, and Shakespeare's references to their practice are in accord with beliefs then current: his witches can raise winds and sail the sea in sieves, and like fairies or ghosts will not speak until first spoken to.

Shakespeare's borrowing from legend was matched by what legend took from him. The homicidal tyrant of the play is celebrated in association with many places around Fife, Perth, and Inverness. Sites known as 'Macbeth's Castle' are located near Inverness and on Dunsinane Hill, where Macbeth is said to have fought Malcolm Canmore, while at Lumphanan, where he may have really died, there is a 'Macbeth's Stone' and a 'Macbeth's Well'. Lady Macbeth is remembered as a tormented murderess whose ghost haunts TORVEAN MOTTE (Southern Highlands), and again Holinshed can be assumed to have inspired Shakespeare with

An image from 1831 of the three witches in *Macbeth*. One of the play's main sources, Holinshed's *Scottish Chronicle* (1576), mentions 'weird sisters', but identifies them as nymphs, fairies, or even 'the goddesses of destinie'. It was not until Shakespeare's 1606 reworking that they became malign hags.

his account of a woman 'verie ambitious, burning in unquenchable desire to beare the name of a Queene'.

Macduff, too, appears in a number of Fife legends. Both Dunimarle Castle and a castle at Cupar are mentioned as being where Lady Macduff and her children were butchered by Macbeth's assassins, and Tayport and Earlsferry are named as places from which Macduff was taken across the water when fleeing from his enemy. Neither of these incidents, by the way, can be considered as historically true, although in the late nineteenth century it was said that the descendants of the Earlsferry boatmen were still known.

An odder rumour is reported by Robert Chambers in 1827 relating to the Stone of Scone:

> Macbeth, from an implicit faith in the sacred character of the stone, and that the possession of it would insure the continuance of his sovereignty, transferred it to a close concealment in his fortress, substituting in its place a similar stone, which has ever since been accepted as the real one.

The Stone was taken to Westminster Abbey by Edward I in 1296. Seven hundred years later it was restored to EDINBURGH CASTLE (Lothian & Borders), but in the meantime it had been stolen (or reclaimed) by Scottish students in 1950 and returned to England the following year. Chambers's tale may have contributed to the widely believed tradition that what London got back in 1951 was a fake, the true Stone remaining hidden in Scotland.

See also LUNDIN LINKS STANDING STONES; NEWBURGH (Central & Perthshire); FORRES; GLAMIS CASTLE (North East); GRENISH STONE CIRCLE (Southern Highlands).

the estate. He now shows Thrummy where to find the deeds, sewn up in a leather ball, and suggests he offer them to the laird for fifty guineas, which Thrummy promptly does, and all ends happily.

The ghost which cannot rest until it has shown someone where to find something valuable is an international theme of folklore, as is the concept of the Doppelgänger – usually a much darker omen than it appears here – but the poem as a whole seems to owe more to literary invention than to legend.

The author John Burness (1771–1826) had an erratic career as baker, publisher's salesman, and soldier; he was a member of the Angus Fencible Volunteer Corps of Infantry when he wrote 'Thrummy Cap'. 'His name and works were once almost as well-known throughout Scotland as those of his more distinguished kinsman . . . but they have been allowed to drift almost to oblivion,' comments Archibald Watt in *Highways and Byways Round Kincardine* (1985), adding that 'Like his cousin he was not destined for worldly fortune partly on account of an injudicious marriage and partly on account of a love for intoxicating liquor.'

FORRES, MORAY

How far is't call'd to Forres? What are these,
So wither'd and so wild in their attire,
That look not like th'inhabitants of the earth,
And yet are on't?

Shakespeare places the three witches' first meeting with Banquo and Macbeth in the neighbourhood of the former royal burgh of Forres, and tradition locates the fateful encounter more precisely by a small stone circle on a hill near the town, known as Knock of Alves. Duncan and Macbeth may have used Forres Castle as a hunting seat, and a further link with *Macbeth* is provided by Sueno's Stone, a sandstone monolith elaborately carved in the Celtic tradition. Preserved at the east end of the town, it is said to commemorate an eleventh-century battle with the Norwegian leader Sweyn, also mentioned by Shakespeare (although there was more than one Norwegian chief of that name who attacked Britain).

Shakespeare may have based his story of witchcraft partly on the fate of King Dubh, or Duff, who reigned in the mid tenth century and was believed to have been put under a spell. George Sinclair tells the story in *Satans Invisible World Discovered* (1685):

> While the *King* was about the setling of the Countrey, and punishing the Troublers of the Peace, he began to be sore afflicted in his Body with a new and unheard of Disease, no Causes of his Sickness appearing in the least. At length, after that several Remedies and Cures were made use of to no purpose, a Report is spread, the authors thereof being uncertain, that the *King* was brought to that sickness and Trouble by Witches.

The king was getting thinner and thinner, weaker and weaker, every day. There seemed to be no cause of the disease and no remedy, in spite of all the doctors' efforts, and therefore his illness was attributed to black magic. After a while, 'all men being vehemently intent upon the Event, news came to *Court* that *Night-meetings* were kept at *Forres* a town in *Murray*, for taking away the life of the *King*'; this was generally believed, Sinclair says, since no better explanation could be found. Reliable messengers were therefore sent to Donald, the governor of Forres Castle, a

Fyvie Castle, built in the thirteenth century, was cursed by the prophet Thomas the Rhymer because stones taken from a nearby religious house were used to extend it.

man in whom the king had great confidence:

This man having gotten some knowledge of the business from a certain young *Wench*, whose Mother was under a bad report of being skilful in this *Black-Art*, found out and discovered the whole matter. The young *Harlot* is taken, because she had spoken some words rashly anent the *Kings* sickness, and that within a few dayes his life would be at an end. Some of the Guard being sent, found the Lasses Mother, with some Haggs, such as her self, roasting before a small moderate fire, the *Kings Picture made of Wax*. The design of this horrid Act, was that as the Wax by little and little did melt away, so the *Kings Body* by a continual sweating, might at last totally decay. The *Waxen-Image* being found and broken, and those old *Haggs* being punished by death, the *King* did in that same moment recover.

Perhaps not for very long: his reign was only from 962 to 967.

See also MACBETH (p. 318).

FYVIE CASTLE, ABERDEENSHIRE

According to Aberdeenshire tradition, Fyvie Castle was visited by the prophet Thomas the Rhymer (*see* EARLSTON, Lothian & Borders). The gate had stood 'wall-wide' for seven years and a day in expectation of his coming. At last he appeared before the walls, and a fearful storm burst over the castle, but around where Thomas stood there was dead calm as he pronounced his curse. This curse was reported in two versions by Walter Gregor in *Notes on the Folk-Lore of the North-East of Scotland* (1881). One version reads:

Fyvie, Fyvie, thou'se never thrive,
As lang's there's in thee stanes three:
There's ane intill the highest tower,
There's ane intill the ladye's bower,
There's ane aneth the water-yett,
And thir three stanes ye'se never get.

[Fyvie, Fyvie, you'll never thrive,
As long as there's three stones in you:
There's one in the highest tower,
There's one in the lady's bower,
There's one beneath the water-gate,
And these three stones you'll never get.]

The variant specifies the stones very similarly, but specifies that they come from 'harryit kirk's land' – despoiled church property. This makes the reason for the malison clearer. The castle was originally a peel tower, built in the thirteenth century and given by Robert III in 1390 to Sir James Lindsay, murderer of the 'Whyte Lyon' at GLAMIS CASTLE, later passing to Henry de Preston, who began to enlarge it using stones from a nearby religious house he had demolished. Putting materials from sacred buildings to secular use was generally considered unlucky, as was taking stones from ancient sites like GRENISH STONE CIRCLE (Southern Highlands).

According to one version of the story, during de Preston's improvements three stones fell into the River Ythan and were lost. Two were later retrieved, but one beneath the water-gate to the river has never been found. Another version has it that the three stones were boundary markers between the Fyvie estates and the church lands, and that two were built into the castle while the third, again, fell into the Ythan. More recent sources make Thomas specify that the stones should be reunited, rather than simply removed from the property, and point to the 'Weeping Stone' today kept in a perspex case in the Lady's Chamber at the castle. It is said to be never dry, shedding tears from

loneliness at being separated from its two companions.

Whichever version is preferred, the fortunes of Fyvie have not been good, if by that one understands an unbroken succession in the male line. Henry de Preston's heir was his daughter, and since that time the castle has several times passed to a different family.

GICHT CASTLE, ABERDEENSHIRE

The ruined castle of Gicht by the left bank of the River Ythan, east of Fyvie, is associated with a lost treasure in a tale narrated in the 1950s by Robert Stewart Aberdeen of New Deer, who had heard it from his father. The events took place 'maybe jist after Prince Charlie's time, 1745'. There was supposedly a treasure buried at the bottom of a deep pool in Gicht, and two local clans dared each other to go down into the pool to find it.

One night, men from one clan, three brothers and their father, met there. The first brother, who had always wanted to go down and see what was in the pool, jumped into the water, and found under it a stairway. He was down for ten minutes or less and, when he came up, was badly mauled and bleeding, and could hardly speak. Nevertheless, his father 'got onto him, like' and told him to go down again, but he said not for anything in this world would he go down the pool again.

Now the younger brother said he would try it, and he went down and the same thing happened to him, and he said it was the Devil that was down there.

The third brother, who was a piper, now said he would go down to see what was in the pool, 'jist to make ye scorns', if he found nothing down there for them to be so scared of.

'I'll gae doon,' and he says, 'if it is the Devil,' he says, 'or something no-right,' he says, 'I'll play a lament. And if everything's aa right,' he says, 'I'll play a march-pipe march.'

So he went into the pool and took his pipes down with him. It's understood, says the narrator Robert, that there was not water all the way down, but when you got in just so far, there was a passageway leading up to the castle, 'maybe this castle, Castle of Gicht'. The piper jumped in and was down a long time, and then they heard a lament, and he never came up again.

Not long before he told this story, when he was working on the Hill of Gicht at harvest, Robert had met two Aberdeen boys who were camping there, but knew nothing of the story.

An' I says, 'How did ye enjoy it up there?' and they said, 'We're enjoyin' it fine,' – but they couldnae get peace at night, and I says, 'Why?'
'Well,' he says, 'it was all right for the first night, but the second night,' he says, 'the pipes played aa night – a lament – played a lament the whole night,' he says.

When Robert told his father this, his father said, 'Look, I told ye, but ye wadnae believe me aboot this thing.' He had heard the pipes himself, and so had a lot of different people. It was only at certain times of the year, 'maybe when the deed happent, or that'.

A slightly different version of the story was collected a few years later, in 1961, from Geordie Stewart of Huntly. He names the entrance of the tunnel as 'Meg's Spot' (although he admits there is no sign of a hole there) and identifies the explorers as two pipers named MacAllister who 'cam doon fae the north' (i.e. they weren't locals, who might have known better). One of them ventured a little way along the passage from the river, but was afraid

to go on. His brother, furious at the idea of 'a MacAllister afraid', made him go back down. The first brother said he would play his bagpipes in the tunnel, and 'if the bagpipes stop ye'll ken fine that there's something wrong.' The pipes played for a long time, but in the end they stopped, and 'of course he never cam oot.' The second piper searched for him in vain, and in guilt for having sent his brother to his death he committed suicide.

Like Robert, Geordie ends his story with the report that the bagpipes can still sometimes be heard, but 'I've been doon there at aa hoors, aa times . . . an I never heard it.'

The story of the musician (often but not always a piper) who disappears underground is told in many places, for instance at CLACH-THOLL (Argyllshire & Islands).

GLAMIS CASTLE, ANGUS

Legend attracts legend. Glamis Castle's reputation as the most haunted house in Scotland – perhaps in all Britain – has gathered around it a bewildering array of hauntings historical and romantic.

From the very beginning, the castle came under supernatural attack. The original plan was to build on the nearby Hill of Denoon, associated (later, if not at the time) with the fairies, but each time the foundations were laid the work was undone by earthquake or whirlwind. Finally a 'dark, prophetic cry' was heard: 'Build not on this enchanted ground; 'Tis sacred all these hills around . . .' The architects took the hint and moved operations. This story has many parallels: 'disputed sites' of castles and particularly churches are reported all over Britain and beyond.

More localised is the tradition connecting the castle with MACBETH (p. 318),

Glamis Castle is said to be the most haunted house in Scotland – perhaps in all Britain. Ghosts encountered there have included a grey lady, a black pageboy, and a 'tongueless woman', while the 'secret chamber' of Glamis remains a mystery to this day.

whose ghost is said to haunt the castle in expiation of his murder of Duncan; in the nineteenth century, the very room was shown in which the deed was done. Shakespeare locates the murder only at a castle in Inverness, but Macbeth's titles as Thane of Glamis and of Cawdor have led to associations with both places (although the historical Duncan was killed in battle).

An older report is that Malcolm II was the victim – the fourteenth-century chronicler John of Fordun relates that the king was slain treacherously at Glamis, though sources closer to the date of Malcolm's death in 1034 imply that he met a natural end – while according to the fifteenth-century *Book of Pluscarden*, the man stabbed here 'when naked in bed and unsuspecting' was the Lord of Glamis known from his pallor as the 'Whyte Lyon', murdered in 1382 by Sir James Lindsay of Crawford. Thus began a feud between the Lindsays and the Lyons, Earls of Strathmore, that lasted with intervals for nearly 300 years. Prior to his death, the Whyte Lyon is said to have acquired a famous heirloom, the Lyon Cup, by some dark means. Although counted as a 'luck' necessary to the survival of the Lyon family, its possession has not kept misfortune at bay: it is sometimes said that the odd happenings at Glamis are attributable to its influence.

In 1537 Janet Douglas, widow of the sixth Lord Glamis, was convicted of practising witchcraft against the life of James V. She died at the stake on Castle Hill, Edinburgh, in 1537; too late it was discovered that the witnesses against her, a rejected suitor and her own son, had perjured themselves. It is possible that these events gave rise to the story that the castle is haunted by the wraith of a witch, surrounded by the flames in which she died, though Janet Douglas is also said to appear as a 'grey lady' in the family chapel.

Other ghosts have little or no background to account for their reputed appearances: the black pageboy who sits outside one of the bedrooms; the 'tongueless woman' tearing at her mouth; the lunatic spectre who follows the 'mad Earl's walk' along the rooftop – these crop up in relatively modern collections, but none of them have the resonance of the story of the 'secret chamber' of Glamis.

Unembellished, the tradition is that there is one room in the castle which has never been identified, although it has a window – or to put it another way, there are more windows on the outside than can be found from the inside. There is something about this bare mystery which is peculiarly uncanny, and perhaps the elaborations spoil it, but they are too rich to leave out.

A brief reference comes from Sir Walter Scott, who spent a night at Glamis in 1791:

> I was conducted to my apartment in a distant corner of the building. I must own, that as I heard door after door shut, after my conductor had retired, I began to consider myself too far from the living, and somewhat too near to the dead . . . In a word, I experienced sensations, which, though not remarkable either for timidity or superstition, did not fail to affect me to the point of being disagreeable, while they were mingled at the same time with a strange and indescribable kind of pleasure, the recollection of which affords me gratification at this moment.

There can be few better descriptions of the joy of ghost stories. Scott also says that the castle contains 'a secret chamber, the entrance of which, by the law or custom of the family, must only be known to three persons at once, viz. the Earl of Strathmore, his heir apparent, and any third person whom they may take into their confidence'. If Scott himself was that third person, he keeps counsel, describing the room only as 'a curious monument of the peril of feudal times', implying that it was used purely as a refuge.

Other nineteenth-century writers give more florid stories, of which there are three principal variants: one is of gamblers turned to stone by the Devil and then condemned to dice till Judgement Day in a room that none will ever be able to find; and a second of refugees from a clan feud, given asylum but then left to starve, the sight of whose mouldering bones so horrified a later owner that he had the room walled up.

The third legend, and the most often repeated, is that of a grotesque child born 200 or 300 years ago and concealed in a chamber constructed within the thickness of the walls. As each heir to the earldom came of age he was told the terrible truth and shown the monster – immensely strong with a hairy, barrel-like body, tiny arms and legs, and no neck. This unfortunate creature is said to have lived until the 1920s, for all that time the rightful earl, but never acknowledged or seen by anyone but the acting earl and a factor.

The sister-in-law of the twelfth earl wrote to Lord Halifax in the 1870s:

> It appears that after my brother-in-law's funeral the lawyer and the agent initiated Claude [the new earl] into the family secret. He went from them to his wife and said: 'My dearest, you know how often we have joked over the secret room and the family mystery. I have been into the room; I have heard the secret; and if you wish to please me you will never mention the subject to me again.'

In 1879, the raconteur Augustus Hare visited the castle and enjoyed the thrill:

> As we drove up to the haunted castle at night, its many turrets looked most eerie and weird against the moonlit sky, and its windows blazed with red light.

The earl, says Hare, 'has an ever sad look', and told his friend the Bishop of Brechin that 'in his unfortunate position *no one* could ever help him'. He had added a wing to the castle for the children and servants, since 'The servants will not sleep in the house, and the children are not allowed to do so.'

Unconnected with the 'secret' is a story relayed by Hare of a visitor to Glamis looking out of a window by moonlight, who saw a carriage drive up and pause for a moment. The driver glanced up, with 'a marked and terrible face'. The earl said there had been no late arrival that night. Subsequently, in a hotel in Paris, the man saw the face in a lift. He drew back, and at once the lift fell, killing all its inmates. Hare confesses that he had heard this story often before 'without definition of place', and as this version reached him in the 'happened to a friend of a friend' style of urban myth, it may have been no more than association which led Hare, or Eustace Cecil who told him, or Lady Trevanion who told Cecil, to attach the episode to Glamis. Legend attracts legend.

GLEN GAIRN, ABERDEENSHIRE

The valley of the River Gairn, which rises in Invercauld Forest and runs east to join the Dee just above Ballater, is the setting for a haunting story told by John Higgins in 1955.

A young man was going to meet his sweetheart as he did every Sunday night, when he saw a white lady standing by a gate. She told him that she had been standing there for over a year and knew that his girlfriend was unfaithful 'for she's carryin' on with another chap', and sent him to where he could hear for himself his girl talking to the man.

'Now you've found out for yourself,' said the white lady, and then asked if the boy would meet her every night for a week. He agreed, but went home miserable over how his girl had played him false.

Over the next few days his parents noticed how he was moping, but because they saw him going off every night to meet his sweetheart, as they thought, they couldn't understand what was wrong. Finally they sent the foreman of their croft after him to see what was happening.

The man followed the lad for a while, and then saw him lift his arm as if he were putting it round a girl, and heard him talking to himself. 'Gode bless me!' the foreman exclaimed. 'Has he gone off his heid?'

He went to tell the boy's father what he had seen, and that finally the boy had gone into an old ruined hut.

The next night the father went himself, and saw the same thing, but this time when the boy began talking he could hear a girl talking back to him – though he could still see nobody there. '"Gode bless me!" he says, "I hope," he says, "he didna dae the ither lassie in!"'

The boy meanwhile had entered the ruin and found a fire burning and a table spread with wine and food. He dined there with the white lady, and afterwards when they had walked for a while she said he must be sure to meet her the next day, as it was the last time. As he left her, a thought occurred to him:

'I hope,' he says, 'it's not a ghost I'm speakin' to, and not makin' dates with.'
'Oh no,' she says, 'it's not a ghost,' she says. 'I'm always here.'

Next day when he set off, both his father and his mother followed and they saw him meet the lady, still invisible to them, and heard her speaking to him. The mother in turn now thought that perhaps 'he'd done his sweetheart in', but when she made enquiries she found that the girl was alive and well.

The lad and the white lady dined as before until midnight, and as he was going home she told him not to come there again, but that she would come up to him in the morning.

When morning came, they heard a knock at the door and there was the lady. She told the boy and his parents that 'a long time back' her jealous brother had got a witch to put a spell on her to turn her into a ghost, 'and the first man as could carry on and make love to her for a week would break her enchantment.'

The story is unusual in that, unlike the ballad of 'Sweet William's Ghost', which also concerns a spectral lover, this one seems to have a happy ending. Although Katharine Briggs in her notes to the story says that the week's intimacy with a mortal 'lays' the ghost, the enchanted woman has clearly not been dismissed to the Other-world. She is at pains to say that she was once a young lady, 'jist what I'm now', surely meaning that she has been restored to life. John Higgins's story ends with the explanation of how her enchantment was broken, and it is left to the hearer to supply a conclusion – perhaps we can assume that the white lady, restored to her human form, will be united with her saviour and lover.

What is given here is the briefest synopsis of a long story which anyone interested in the flavour and manner of traditional storytelling would do well to read in the original. The transcribed text is given in Katharine Briggs's *Dictionary of British Folk-Tales* (1970–1).

GLENBERVIE, KINCARDINESHIRE

A particularly gruesome death is said to have been suffered by John Melville, Laird of Glenbervie, in the early fifteenth century. George Henderson Kinnear, writing in 1910, quotes from the undated account of the Reverend Mr Charles, a former schoolmaster and later a minister. Although such professions are often mentioned to signify trustworthiness in a narrator, Kinnear observes sedately that 'Of late, considerable doubt has been thrown on the authenticity of the story.'

> The tradition is this, and affords a sad specimen of the barbarity of the times of James I. About 1420, Melville, the Laird of Glenbervie and Sheriff of the Mearns, had, by a strict exercise of his authority, rendered himself obnoxious to the surrounding barons, who, having teased the King by repeated complaints against him – at last in a fit of impatience, the King said to Barclay, Laird of Mathers, who had come with another complaint, 'Sorrow gin that Sheriff were sodden and supped in bree.'

'As your Majesty pleases,' said Barclay, and at once assembled the Lairds of Lauriston, Arbuthnott, Pitarrow, and Halkerton for a hunting match in the Forest of Garvock, to which they also invited Melville.

> And having privately got ready a large kettle of boiling water in a retired place, they decoyed the unsuspecting Melville to the fatal spot, knocked him down, stripped him, and threw him into the boiling kettle. And after he was boiled or sodden for some time, they took each a spoonful of the soup.

The murderers had to take active measures to escape punishment, since the king had not meant anything like this to happen (any more than Henry II of England said he had meant Becket to be killed in 1170, when he asked who would rid him of the 'troublesome priest'). Barclay is said to have built himself the fortress known as KAIM OF MATHERS, 'on a perpendicular and peninsular rock sixty feet above the sea, where, in those days, he lived quite secure'. Arbuthnott was able to claim the benefit of the 'law of the clan Macduff', which allowed pardon for homicide to anyone within a certain degree of kinship to the Thane of Fife if they visited Macduff's Cross at NEWBURGH (Central & Perthshire). The fate of the other conspirators is unknown, but the field where the horrid deed was carried out was still known in 1910 as Brownie's Leys, 'because from the murderous deed then perpetrated it was long supposed to be haunted by spirits called Brownies'. Later accounts give several alternative names for the field: Sheriff's Kettle, Brownie's Kettle, Brownie's Hollow, or Fairies' Hollow. None of these appear on modern maps, but the site appears to be near Laurencekirk.

Virtually the same story was told of the evil Lord Soulis at HERMITAGE CASTLE (LOTHIAN & BORDERS). Soulis seems to have deserved his horrible fate a little better than Melville, although it is questionable whether in fact it befell either of them.

GREEN CASTLE, KINCARDINESHIRE

The large Iron Age ring fort of Green Castle, otherwise known as Queen's Castle or Finella's Castle, is said also to have been the site of an early medieval fortress, seat of the maomor or 'great officer' of the Mearns. Here, it was said, Kenneth III was assassinated around the end of the tenth century. The antiquarian Robert Chambers, writing in 1827, gives an account of the murder drawn from fourteenth- and fifteenth-century chronicles:

Having excited the implacable hatred of a powerful lady, named Fenella, by killing her son in a rebellion, she put on a courteous face, and invited him to her castle, where she had prepared a singular engine, for the purpose of putting him to death. Under pretence of amusing him with the architectural elegance of her mansion, she conducted him to the upper apartment of a tall tower, where, in the midst of splendid drapery and curious sculptures, she had planted a statue of brass, holding a golden apple. This apple, she told him, was designed as a present for his majesty, and she courteously invited him to take it from the hand of the image. No sooner had the king done this, than some machinery was set in motion, which, acting upon an ambuscade of crossbows behind the arras, caused a number of arrows to traverse the apartment, by one of which the king was killed.

Fenella left the castle before the murder was discovered by the king's attendants, who broke down the door and found their master weltering in his blood.

It was said that Fenella then made for another castle of hers at a wild place on the coast, called Den-Fenella. Being pursued, she concealed herself among the branches of the trees, and as thick forest stretched all the way from one castle to the other, she was able to swing herself along for a distance of around ten miles, and pass over the very heads of her bewildered pursuers. Different accounts can be found of what happened to her after that: some say that she was captured and burned, some that she was at last brought to bay near Lauriston Castle, where she chose death over captivity and threw herself from the crags onto the rocks beneath, while a third version holds that she escaped to Ireland.

INCH CAPE ROCK, ANGUS

East of Dundee Harbour is the Inch Cape Rock, also known as the Bell Rock. Only

Before the Bell Rock Lighthouse was built, a bell was fixed to the spot to warn sailors to steer clear. Southey's ballad 'Ralph the Rover' (1802) tells of a buccaneer who cut down the bell for sport, but was later wrecked on the very rock.

the top is visible at low water, and the rock has been responsible for many shipwrecks. According to tradition a bell was once fixed to it by one of the abbots of Arbroath, to act as a warning to sailors by ringing in the wind, but was removed by a pirate who perished a year later when his own vessel foundered on the rock. Southey's ballad 'Ralph the Rover' (1802) tells the story of how in malicious sport Sir Ralph cuts down the bell. He sails away and thinks no more of the matter, but after he has made a profitable voyage he heads back to Scotland on a dark, misty night. His men listen out vainly:

'Canst hear,' said one, 'the breakers roar?
For methinks we should be near the
    shore.'
'Now, where we are I cannot tell,
But I wish we could hear the Inchcape
    Bell.'

They hear no sound, the swell is strong,
Though the wind hath fallen they drift
    along;
Till the vessel strikes with a shivering
    shock,
'Oh Christ! It is the Inchcape Rock!'

Sir Ralph the Rover tore his hair,
He curst himself in his despair;
The waves rush in on every side,
The ship is sinking beneath the tide.

But even in his dying fear,
One dreadful sound could the Rover
    hear;
A sound as if with the Inchcape Bell,
The Devil below was ringing his knell.

INVERGOWRIE, ANGUS

The 'Ewes' or 'Yowes' of Gowrie were described by Robert Chambers in 1826 as 'two large blocks of stone, situated within high-water mark, on the northern shore of the Firth of Tay, at the small village of Invergowrie'. An ominous prediction concerning them is recorded:

When the Yowes o' Gowrie come to
    land,
The Day o' Judgment's near at hand.

Chambers explains the tradition:

The prophecy is ancient, perhaps by Thomas the Rhymer, and obtains universal credit among the country people. In consequence of the natural retreat of the waters from that shore of the firth, the stones are gradually approaching the land, and there is no doubt will ultimately be beyond flood-mark. It is the popular belief, that they move an inch nearer to the shore every year. The expected fulfilment of the prophecy has deprived many an old woman of her sleep; and it is a common practice among the weavers and bonnet-makers of Dundee, to walk out to Invergowrie on Sunday afternoons, simply to see what progress 'THE YOWES' are making!

As foretold, one of the rocks is now stranded. Other prophecies made by Thomas the Rhymer are mentioned at BENNACHIE, FYVIE CASTLE, and INVERURIE.

INVERURIE, ABERDEENSHIRE

Mark, in yon vale, a solitary stone,
Shunned by the swain, with loathsome
     weeds o'ergrown!
The yellow stone-crop shoots from
     every pore,
With scaly, sapless lichens crusted o'er:
Beneath the base, where starving hem-
     locks creep,
The yellow pestilence is buried deep,
Where first its course, as aged swains
     have told,
It stayed, concentered in a vase of gold.

John Leyden gives the following notes to this poem, which appears in his *Scenes of Infancy* (1803):

Tradition still records, with many circum-stances of horror, the ravages of the pesti-lence in Scotland. According to some accounts, gold seems to have had a kind of chemical attraction for the matter of infection, and it is frequently represented as concentrating its virulence in a pot of gold. According to others, it seems to have been regarded as a kind of spirit or monster, like a cockatrice, which it was deadly to look on, and is sometimes termed 'THE BAD YELLOW.'

Remarking that according to the chroni-cler Wyntoun, Scotland was first afflicted with the plague in 1349, Leyden continues that in many parts of Scotland 'the peas-ants point out large flat stones, under which they suppose the pestilence to be buried, and which they are anxious not to raise, lest it should emerge, and again con-taminate the atmosphere.'

One such place, according to Leyden, was the Bass of Inverurie, a mound said once to have been a castle which had been walled up and covered with earth because the inhabitants had the plague. There was a prophecy concerning the site, attrib-uted (like many others in the region) to Thomas the Rhymer:

Dee and Don, they shall run on,
And Tweed shall run, and Tay;
And the bonny water of Ury,
Shall bear the Bass away.

Alarmed by the implications of this verse, the citizens of Inverurie buttressed the mound against the river on whose banks it stood, since if the prediction were fulfilled and the mound washed away by the stream, the plague would be released once more.

See also BESSIE BELL'S AND MARY GRAY'S GRAVE (Central & Perthshire).

KAIM OF MATHERS, KINCARDINESHIRE

'Kaim' can be used simply to mean a camp or fortress, but also describes 'a pinnacle resembling a cock's comb'. The dwelling known as 'Kaim of Mathers' is mentioned in George Robertson's 1813 survey of Kincardineshire as being 'pitched, like an Eagle's nest, on the point of a rock pro-jecting into the sea', about six miles north of Montrose. 'Part of the fabric is still very entire; but at present, would be con-sidered as one of the most dreary habita-tions imaginable.'

The castle was of old the residence of the Barclays, and the tradition concern-ing it is that a fifteenth-century Barclay built it as penance for his part in the murder of the Laird of GLENBERVIE. 'I should rather conjecture,' writes Robertson, 'that if he was amenable to justice for this shocking deed he had of his own accord, fled to it as a place of refuge.' The traditionary origin of the Kaim of Mathers has, however, often been cited in 'proof' of the sheriff's horrible fate. Robertson is sharp enough to see the fallacy in pointing out a landscape feature in support of a legendary tale: it is, of course, the landscape which partly inspires the legend.

KELPIE'S STANE, ABERDEENSHIRE

Once when the River Don was in flood, a man needed to cross it to attend a relative's deathbed. The river had a resident Kelpie, a dangerous water-spirit which could, however, appear harmless or even helpful. This creature appeared and offered to carry the traveller across the swollen stream; the man agreed, but when they got to the middle of the river the Kelpie tried to drown him. Luckily he managed to escape and scrambled up onto the riverbank. Baulked of his prey, the angry Kelpie threw a large boulder after him, which rests on the bank and is still known as the Kelpie's Stane.

See KELPIES AND WATER-HORSES (p. 364).

KIRKMICHAEL, BANFFSHIRE

Some springs and wells are guarded by Kelpies or Water-horses, others by dragons like the one whose defeat is said to be recorded at MARTIN'S STONE. According to James MacKinlay's *Folklore of Scottish Lochs and Springs* (1893), St Michael's Well in the parish of Kirkmichael once had for its guardian spirit a much smaller animal:

> It showed itself in the form of a fly that kept skimming over the surface of the water. This fly was believed to be immortal.

The *Statistical Account of Scotland* (1791–9) also mentions this spring and its magical properties:

> If the sober matron wished to know the issue of her husband's ailment, or the love-sick nymph, that of her languishing swain, they visited the well of St Michael. Every movement of the sympathetic fly was regarded in silent awe; and as he appeared cheerful or dejected, the anxious votaries drew their presages; their breasts vibrated with correspondent emotions.

One wonders how to tell a dejected fly from a cheerful one. Possibly because of the difficulty, the well lost its reputation and by the end of the eighteenth century it lay 'neglected, choked with weeds, unhonoured, and unfrequented', although the writer of the article in the *Statistical Account* met an old man who said that if he were young and strong enough he would weed it, plant it, and 'once more, as in the days of youth, enjoy the pleasure of seeing the guardian fly skim in sportive circles over the bubbling wave, and with its little proboscis, imbibe the Panacean dews'.

LESLIE, ABERDEENSHIRE

In the mid seventeenth century, Alexander Mowat was minister of Lesley (now Leslie), and was described by his contemporary Dr James Garden as 'a Person of great Integrity and Judgment'. Mowat related an anecdote of 'flight with the fairies' to Garden, who in turn passed it on to the antiquary John Aubrey in a letter of 1695. Mowat had heard the Earl of Caithness tell the following story:

> That upon a time, when a Vessel which his Lordship kept for bringing home Wine and other Provisions for his House, was at Sea; a common Fellow, who was reputed to have the Second-sight, being occasionally at his House; the Earl enquired of him, where his Men (meaning those in the Ship) were at that present time? the Fellow replied, at such a place, by Name, within four Hour Sailing of the Harbour, which was not far from the place of his Lordship's Residence: The Earl asked, what Evidence he could give for that? The other replied, That he had lately been at the place, and had brought away with him one of the Seamens Caps, which he delivered to his Lordship.

When the four hours were up, the earl himself went to the harbour where he found that the ship had just come in. One of the sailors was minus his cap, and was asked how he had come to lose it:

> Answered, that at such a place (the same the Second-sighted Man had named before) there arose a Whirl-wind which endangered the Ship, and carried away his Cap: the Earl asked, if he would know his Cap when he saw it? He said he would; whereupon the Earl produced the Cap, and the Seaman owned it for that, which was taken from him.

SECOND SIGHT (p. 474) is often considered purely as clairvoyance, but here is evidently associated with powers like those of Calum Clever, who brought information from Fort William to INVERESRAGAN (Argyllshire & Islands) in the course of a game of shinty.

LOCHAN UAINE, BANFFSHIRE

In *Folklore of Scottish Lochs and Springs* (1893), James MacKinlay writes that near the boundary between Aberdeenshire and Banffshire 'is a small sheet of water called Lochan-Wan, *i.e.*, Lamb's Loch'. The place he means is probably Lochan Uaine, 'the Little Green Loch': 'lamb's' would be *uain*, and both words sound very like 'wan'. This may stand as an example of the difficulties in locating places mentioned in nineteenth-century and earlier sources, which tend to give anglicised phonetic spelling of Gaelic names and may also supply fanciful translations, none of which will be familiar to modern map-readers.

In this case, the reference to lambs is understandable, since the region was formerly sheep-farming territory, and according to an article on 'Guardian Spirits of Wells and Lochs' published in *Folk-Lore* in 1892, each farmer in the area had to sacrifice a lamb every year or risk half his flock being drowned in the loch. While there are many traditions in Scotland, and indeed elsewhere, of water-spirits claiming regular victims, this sounds very much like a fictionalised version of some customary annual rent paid by the tenants to the landlord each lambing season.

The legend continues that an attempt was once made to break the spell by draining the loch, but each day a channel was dug for the water, the same night the work was undone:

> A watch was set, and at midnight of the third day hundreds of small black creatures were seen to rise from the lake, each with a spade in his hand. They set about filling up the trench and finished their work in a few minutes.

Fairies or demons were often said to prevent buildings being erected in certain places, as they did at MELGUND CASTLE. This story shows more clearly their function as guardians of the landscape, concerned to prevent interference with lochs and other features.

The same article gives a similar report of 'Lochann-nan-deaan' between Corgarff and Tomintoul, a loch believed to be bottomless 'and to be the abode of a water-spirit that delighted in human sacrifice':

Notwithstanding this bloody-thirsty spirit, the men of Strathdon and Corgarff resolved to try to draw the water from the loch, in hope of finding the remains of those who had perished in it. On a fixed day a number of them met with spades and picks to cut a way for the outflow of the water through the road. When all were ready to begin work, a terrific yell came from the loch, and there arose from its waters a diminutive creature in shape of a man with a red cap on his head. The men fled in terror, leaving their picks and spades behind them. The spirit seized them and threw them into the loch. Then, with a gesture of defiance at the fleeing men, and a roar that shook the hills, he plunged into the loch and disappeared amidst the water that boiled and heaved as red as blood.

The spirit's headgear is interesting. An unpleasant bogey known as Redcap or Bloodycap was known to haunt the Borders, and one of his kind was servant to the devilish Lord Soulis of HERMITAGE CASTLE (Lothian & Borders). Redcap was not, however, generally said to be a water-spirit, and perhaps the guardian of Lochann-nan-deaan is a relation of KELPIES AND WATER-HORSES (p. 364). He may not have been able to defend his watery home for ever: no loch seems now to match the description given, so perhaps

the draining operation was tried again with more success.

LYNTURK, ABERDEENSHIRE

A Green or White Lady was reputed to haunt the Linn of Lynturk, a picturesque waterfall on a small stream dividing the lands of Lynturk, a mansion in central Aberdeenshire, from those of Tonley. Her last appearance, reported by Alexander Smith in *A New History of Aberdeenshire* (1875), was as follows:

The Laird of Kincraigie had dined with his neighbour the Laird of Tullochs, and as he returned home late at night, mounted on a spirited horse, and attended by a faithful dog, he was passing on the brink of the dell above the linn, when suddenly the apparition seized the bridle of his horse, and exclaimed, 'Kincraigie Leslie, I've sought you long, but I've found you now.' The dog, however, fiercely attacking the spectre, it quitted the bridle for a moment, and the horse dashed off at the top of his speed, while his terrified master could see the spectre and the dog tumbling down in mortal struggle to the very bottom of the dell. Kincraigie was thus saved, and his generous canine friend returned next day, showing evident marks of the perilous strife in which he had been engaged.

This fearsome being shares the malevolent character of a very few White Ladies, rather more Green, and almost all Kelpies. Though spoken of as an 'apparition' and a 'spectre', suggesting that she is thought to be a ghost, she is corporeal enough to be vulnerable to the dog's attack, and is revealed as at least partly a fairy by her dress, green and white being fairy colours. When Mistress Page in *The*

Merry Wives of Windsor (Act 4, scene 4) proposes to dress her daughter and little son 'and others of like growth' as 'urchins, ouphs and fairies, green and white' in order to delude Falstaff, the trick could only be expected to work if Falstaff (and Shakespeare's audience) understood this to be traditional lore concerning fairies.

MARTIN'S STONE, TEALING, ANGUS

In Strathmartin, in Forfarshire, is a spring styled the Nine Maidens' Well. These maidens were the daughters of a certain Donewalde or Donald in the eighth century, and led, along with their father, a saintly life in the glen of Ogilvy in the same county. Their spring at Strathmartin must have been well looked after, for it had as its guardian, no less formidable a creature than a dragon. We do not know whether there was any St George in the vicinity to dispute possession with the monster.

So wrote James MacKinlay in 1893, apparently unaware of the greatly elaborated story given by Robert Chambers in his *Popular Rhymes of Scotland* (1826). According to this, there lived at Pittempton near Dundee a peasant (unnamed in this version, but we may as well call him Donald) who had nine daughters, all of them beautiful. One day the eldest went to fetch water from the well a little way from the house, and did not come back. The second daughter was sent to look for her, but neither did she come back. The third daughter followed the second and so it went on, until all nine girls had gone to the well and not one had returned. Only then did Donald go himself to see what had become of his children, and on reaching the well he found a dragon with blood-stained jaws.

The horrified father gathered all his neighbours to fight the dragon, which ran away. First in pursuit was the sweetheart of one of the girls, a young man called Martin: he chased the fearsome reptile through a marsh called Baldragon, then further north where Martin hit him with a club, the onlookers crying out 'Strike, Martin!' as he did so. The dragon crawled a little further and was then killed.

To mark the spot where the monster met its end a stone was set known as 'Martin's Stane', whereon the following rhyme was claimed to represent the dragon's epitaph:

> I was temptit at Pittempton,
> Draiglit [wetted] at Baldragon,
> Stricken at Strike-Martin
> And killed at Martin's Stane.

The inspiration of most of this is a Pictish cross-slab in a field at Balkello, carved with pictures of outlandish beasts. The rhyme (which does not appear on the cross-slab) 'explains' various local place-names, including Strathmartin, pronounced 'Strike-Martin'.

This is not the only Nine Maidens' Well in Scotland: there is another at Newburgh in Fife said to be sacred to 'The Nine Virgins, daughters to St Donewald'. Evidently traditions of this saint and his daughters have combined with the story inspired by the carved stone to produce the complex legend told of Strathmartin. On the other hand, the *Statistical Account of Scotland* (1791–9) gives the significant detail that the girls went to the well on a Sunday, which means that far from being saintly, they were breaking the Sabbath and deserved their dreadful fate. This is gilding the legendary lily: the well guarded by a dragon is a very ancient motif which needs no moral.

MELGUND CASTLE, ANGUS

The low position of Melgund Castle is accounted for by the tale that an attempt was first made to build it on a neighbouring hill, but the walls raised during the day were demolished every night by invisible hands. A watch was set one night for the vandals, but instead of catching any human malefactors, the guard heard only an unearthly voice instructing them to:

> Big [build] it in a bog,
> Whare 'twill neither shake nor shog
>   [jog].

They obeyed, and continued construction in the marsh below, where there was no further obstruction of their work. This is one of many stories of buildings moved by supernatural interference; sometimes, as at RUABHAL (Western Isles), this is understood as the work of God, sometimes as that of devils or fairies, as in the case of LANGTON HOUSE (Lothian & Borders). Here it is not clear who is objecting to the castle's original position, but the workmen were probably wise to concede the point.

At the bottom of one of the towers of Melgund, wrote Robert Chambers in 1827, 'there is a deep hole, supposed to communicate with a subterraneous passage, leading from the castle':

> This passage, which was closed up a few years ago, on a cow having fallen into it, is a subject of infinite wonderment and speculation among the people, who report it to be the depository of prodigious treasure, and have a thousand stories concerning it. One of their legends is so unutterably horrible, as almost to make the flesh creep. They tell that the last laird of Melgund, having spent all his fortune, in one night, at cards, left the room in which he had been playing, and deliberately went, with his whole family, into this awful pit, and was never more heard of!

A young man was once tempted to explore the tunnel in the hope of finding treasure. His friends waited eagerly for his return, hoping that he would tell them strange and wonderful things, but when he emerged he was found to be a changed character. Once adventurous and cheerful, he was now despondent and withdrawn, and kept away from company as much as he could.

> The only information he could ever be brought to give, was, that he had gone a great way under ground, and had seen such sights, as, he blessed God, he could never expect to see on earth again.

He was lucky to come out alive. Others who entered such underground passages, like the piper who ventured into the tunnel beneath CULROSS ABBEY (Central & Perthshire), were never seen again.

MORPHIE, KINCARDINESHIRE

The Stone of Morphie or Morphy is said to mark the grave of a Danish king, Camus, defeated in battle by Malcom II (r. 1005–34). During a hurricane in the mid nineteenth century the stone fell down, and while it was being re-erected a skeleton was found beneath it, 'of large dimensions'. J. C. Watt, writing in 1914, surmises that the monolith once formed part of a circle, adducing the 'immense number' of stone circles and tombs found in the neighbourhood, and adds that 'some years ago' he sent a friend to photograph the stone, 'but it was doing duty at the core of a cornstack at the farm of Stone o' Morphy'.

The Stone is associated not only with the Danes but with the menacing Kelpie, said to have carried it. Archibald Watt notes in 1985 that 'you can still see his fingerprint on the stone where he grasped it', a motif more commonly associated with the Devil or a giant than the Kelpie, which usually appeared as a horse, although it could also manifest in human form. This Kelpie haunted the Ponage (or Poundage, or Pontage) Pool in the Esk, and was celebrated in a poem of 1826 by George Beattie:

> When ye hear the Kelpie howl,
> Hie ye to the Ponage-pool;
> There you'll see the Deil himsel'
> Leadin' on the hounds o' Hell.

Here the Kelpie is described as a 'stalwart monster, huge in size':

> Behind, a dragon's tail he wore,
> Twa bullock's horns stack out before;
> His legs were horn, wi' joints o' steel,
> His body like the crocodile.

'It is a well-authenticated fact,' notes Beattie, 'that, upon one occasion, when the Kelpie had appeared in the shape of a horse, he was laid hold of, and had a bridle, or halter, of a particular description, fastened onto his head. He was kept in thraldom for a considerable time, and drove the greater part of the stones for building the house of Morphie. Some sage person, acquainted with the particular disposition of the animal, or fiend, or whatever he may be called, gave orders that at no time should the halter be removed, otherwise he would never more be seen.' A maidservant, however, happened to go into the stable and took pity on the beast, taking off the bridle and giving it some food. The Kelpie then laughed and immediately went through the back of the stable, but leaving no mark whatever in the wall. As he went he proclaimed:

> O sairs my back, and sair my banes,
> Leadin' the Laird o' Marphie's stanes;
> The Laird o' Marphie canna thrive
> As lang's the Kelpie is alive.

The curse had its effect: no trace of Morphie Castle now survives.

See KELPIES AND WATER-HORSES (p. 364).

NEW DEER, ABERDEENSHIRE

The nineteenth-century writer Walter Gregor tells a sinister story of an attempted fairy kidnapping:

A man in the parish of New Deer was returning home at night. On reaching an old quarry much overgrown with broom he heard a great noise coming from among the broom. He listened, and his ear caught the words 'Mak' it red cheekit an red lippit like the smith o' Bonnykelly's wife.' He knew at once what was going on, and what was to be done, and he ran with all his speed to the smith's house and 'sained' the mother and her baby – an act which the nurse had neglected to do. No sooner was the saining finished than a heavy thud, as if something had fallen, was heard outside the house opposite to the spot where stood the bed on which the mother and her baby lay. On examination a piece of bog-fir was found lying at the bottom of the wall. It was the 'image' the fairies were to substitute for the smith's wife.

To 'sain' something is to bless it – more specifically, to make the sign of the cross over it (the word is related to 'sign'). 'Bog-fir' is the kind of hard, black, fossilised wood often recovered from bogs by archaeologists. Its antique appearance would be suitably uncanny for a 'fairy stock' substituted for a supernaturally kidnapped woman, a motif widely distributed throughout Britain and parts of Europe, occuring for example in late medieval Icelandic romance. A similar tale is told of WALLS (Orkney & Shetland Islands); in another, set at Lerwick in Shetland, the 'stock' is kept and used as furniture.

In another story, Gregor gives the reason why 'saining' mothers after childbirth should be necessary. He says that fairies valued human milk highly to nourish their own infants, and this was why they attempted to carry off unsained and unchurched mothers. One mother was so spirited away, and very shortly, despite all the care and attention lavished on her by the fairies, she was almost exhausted. She asked to be returned to her home and promised to give them instead the best mare in milk that her husband owned. The fairies granted her request and the mare was duly led to the fairy hillock and left there. The animal disappeared, but after a time was returned, so thin and weak that she could hardly stand.

The ritual of 'churching' was still practised in many parts of Britain into the second half of the twentieth century – one of the present authors was so churched in her Norfolk village in 1960. The purpose was understood as being to cleanse women from physical and spiritual impurity following childbirth, in order that they might be readmitted to Holy Communion. Many modern women considered this insulting, and the service was allowed to lapse, although the actual words of the service (which can be found in the Book of Common Prayer) merely give thanksgiving for the preservation of the mother's life.

RIVER SPEY, MORAY

The folklorist Lewis Spence wrote in 1948 that the Spey had a reputation for blood-thirstiness:

> The demon which presided over it was nameless, the ominous pronoun 'she' denoting, as perhaps nothing else could, the fear and dislike which this river inspired in the dwellers on its banks. That the Spey demanded at least one victim every year was proverbial.

One might ask why the word 'she' is felt necessarily to denote fear and dislike.

Other writers attribute a more specific shape to the Spey's 'demon': a beautiful white horse was said to walk along the riverbank, accompanying travellers until they grew tired and climbed on its back. Then it would immediately gallop off with them and plunge into a deep pool, hapless rider and all. On stormy nights, the whinnying of the wicked horse (evidently a Kelpie) could be heard.

The Traveller and storyteller Betsy Whyte was told of no evil spirits, but as a child she had a surprising experience by the river when she saw that the light summer rain coming down was full of tiny frogs, so many that soon they were running all over her and her friends. 'Have you never seen a shower of puddocks before?' asked her mother. 'God bless me, bairns! I thought you would all have kent about that.' Yet, Betsy adds, she has never seen one since.

See also KELPIES AND WATER-HORSES (p. 364).

This sixteenth-century woodcut shows a rain of frogs like that seen near the River Spey by Traveller and storyteller Betsy Whyte as a child in the 1930s.

The Round Square, Gordonstoun, Moray

In folk tradition, learned men are often said to be wizards, as in no other way could they have acquired their knowledge. Such tales are told, for instance, of the medieval scholars Roger Bacon and MICHAEL SCOT, THE WIZARD OF BALWEARIE (p. 62). A comparative newcomer is the inventor Sir Robert Gordon (1647–1704), owner of Gordonstoun House, now a celebrated public school. Sir Robert, who devised a sea pump bought by Samuel Pepys after he became secretary of the Admiralty in 1672, was said to be a warlock who had sold his soul to the Devil. As told in 1968 by Henry L. Brereton, warden of Gordonstoun, the story goes that in 1665, when he was seventeen, Robert was sent to the University of Padua. Here he was excited by the new scientific theories, but suspected that God was inclined to keep to himself the secrets of the universe. He therefore decided to take a scholarly shortcut by summoning the Devil.

In a darkened room, he duly recited the infamous Black Mass, and the Devil appeared, willing to tell all in exchange for a human soul. Cannily, Sir Robert bargained for twelve months' credit before payment was due, and the Devil agreed. Robert was then possessed of more knowledge than any one man should have and on this account became feared and avoided.

Exactly a year later, as he was walking down a Padua street in full sunshine, a bearded fellow dressed all in black suddenly stood before him, and claimed his soul. 'Take my shadow instead,' said Robert, and the Devil, pleased by his ready wit, agreed – for the time being. Robert was to have twenty-five shadowless years until the Devil's debt fell due.

On the death of his father, Robert returned to Gordonstoun. He improved his estate and busied himself in his laboratory, not only inventing the sea pump, but carrying out many experiments. He is said among other things to have cooked a salamander for seven years in the hope that it would yield him scientific secrets. Fine wrought-iron work was produced in the Gordonstoun vaults, and it was rumoured locally that Sir Robert's smith was no mortal man but the Devil himself.

As the years passed and the time of reckoning drew near, Robert bent his mind to ways of escape. The barns and stables at Gordonstoun had burned to the ground a century before and he now planned new stables, to be arranged in a circle calculated magically to keep his soul safe when the Devil came. The fateful hour fell on a wild November night in 1704, and Robert had asked his friend the parson of Duffus to bear him company. They sat before a log fire in the old library of Gordonstoun House, where, as midnight struck, a great gust of wind swept through the room. They caught a glimpse of a cloven hoof beneath the billowing tapestry hangings, and heard a voice cry, 'Robert, your time has come!' But Robert, once again, was ahead of the game – he had set the clock an hour fast. The Devil left, promising to return in one hour.

The terrified parson now pleaded with Robert to seek sanctuary in the holiest place thereabouts, the old kirk of Birnie near Elgin, persuading him at last that his own 'Round Square' refuge was not strong enough to keep the Devil out.

Towards midnight, the parson of Birnie, the Reverend John M'Kean, who told his wife the story later, was on his way home when he was overtaken by Robert, who asked him the way to Birnie and then dashed onwards in the dark. Scarcely had the sound of his footsteps faded when

M'Kean was again overtaken, this time by a horseman, who asked if a man had passed that way. The Reverend Mr M'Kean, sensing the presence of evil, answered that he had not. The horseman rode on, and suddenly the silence was broken by a long-drawn piercing shriek. Presently the horseman reappeared from the darkness, and now across his saddle lay a human body. On either side ran a huge hound, and the one nearest M'Kean had its fangs buried in the neck of the corpse.

So, says Brereton, whether either Birnie or the Round Square would have saved Robert no man will ever know, for the Devil caught him between the two. What Brereton does not explain is why, having built the Round Square, Robert sat waiting for the Devil in Gordonstoun's old library.

In her *Dictionary of British Folk-Tales* (1970–1), Katharine Briggs points out that this is a Scottish version of Faust with the additional motif of the 'hunted soul', of which theme she gives other British examples. The running hounds, one of them savaging the body, are reminiscent of the mastiffs in John Dryden's poem 'Theodore and Honoria': he took the story from Boccaccio's *Decameron*, written in the fourteenth century. In later folklore it was located in the ancient forest of Whittlewood, Northamptonshire, probably because Dryden was a Northamptonshire man, but dogs worrying a corpse claimed by the Devil are found in another well-known Scottish story, 'The Witch of LAGGAN' (Southern Highlands).

At the same time, the tale of Sir Robert Gordon is a folk explanation of the origin of the Round Square, in line with a tradition that some houses were built without corners so that the Devil had nowhere to hide, or so that a bargain to meet the Fiend at one end of a building could not be fulfilled. Some English examples are the Round House at Bodham, Norfolk, and the Round Houses of Veryan, Cornwall.

Modern articles about Gordonstoun sometimes go so far as to compare it to Harry Potter's Hogwarts, but in Robert Gordon's time it was not a school, and there was never any suggestion that he trained wizards.

ST CYRUS, KINCARDINESHIRE

Kincardineshire worthies seem to have been prone to making idiosyncratic wills (*see also* CAIRNSHEE). Archibald Watt, writing in 1985, relates that when John Orr, the Laird of Bridgeton, died in 1847, he left a bequest of £1,000 to charity: the interest was to be divided in five parts, one-fifth to go to the old and needy, and the remaining four-fifths to be given annually as dowries to the tallest, shortest, oldest, and youngest brides married at St Cyrus. It was stipulated that each bride must be measured properly, having removed her shoes and let down her hair 'so that her tresses may hang loosely over her shoulder and add nothing to her stature'.

The reason was apparently that he had felt sorry for a poor young couple he had seen trudging through the snow to the church to be married, but whether the bride-to-be on that occasion was particularly tall or short is not recorded.

When the bequest was made, each dowry was a substantial sum of money, and even as late as 1960 it was a worthwhile sum. One couple who married in the late fifties reported that it was the equivalent of two weeks' wages. From the sixties, however, inflation devalued the prize so much that in 1991 it was decided that instead of the very small amount of money involved, the brides should receive a presentation vase.

ST VIGEANS, ANGUS

The Kelpie was a bogey beast who could when it suited him appear as a human, but his most common manifestation was as a horse. If anyone threw a bridle over his head on which the sign of the cross had been made, the Kelpie would then have no choice but to work as he was bidden, as he had to do at MORPHIE.

It was presumably by this means that the Kelpie was induced to carry stones for the building of St Vigeans church, which moreover was said to be supported below by bars of iron, the best metal to ward off magic. Under these a deep lake was reputed to lie, and in the *Statistical Account of Scotland* (1794) it is reported that holy communion was not celebrated in the church between the years 1699 and 1736:

> As the administration of the sacrament had been so long delayed, the people had brought themselves to believe, that the first time the ordinance should be dispensed, the church would sink, and the whole people would be carried down and drowned in the lake. The belief of this had taken such hold of the people's minds, that on the day the sacrament was administered, some hundreds of the parishioners sat on an eminence about 100 yards from the church, expecting every moment the dreaded catastrophe.

They were relieved, or perhaps disappointed, when nothing happened. The story is an interesting variation on the theme of 'sunken churches', since in this case the church does not sink at all: one that did was CHAPEL O' SINK.

There was evidently something about St Vigeans that made people connect it with the supernatural. A monk named Turnbull is reported in the *Statistical Account* to have lived in the church steeple, in two rooms surviving in 1754. 'He is said to have been frightened from his chambers by the devil appearing to him in the shape of a rat, and no Monk after him would be persuaded to reside in the steeple.'

Today the village of St Vigeans is most notable for its collection of Pictish carved stones, housed in a converted cottage near the church.

See KELPIES AND WATER-HORSES (p. 364).

SANDS OF FORVIE, ABERDEENSHIRE

Furvie, or Forvie, was once a separate parish, but is now part of the parish of Slains. Much if not most of it is now covered with sand. Tradition says that the proprietor to whom the parish belonged left three daughters as his heirs; they were, however, 'bereft of their property and thrown houseless on the world'. On leaving their home they uttered a dreadful curse:

> If evyr maydenis malysone
> Dyd licht upon drye lande,
> Let nocht bee funde in Furvye's glebys,
> Bot thystl, bente, and sande.
>
> [If ever maiden's curse
> Did light upon dry land,
> Let nought be found in Furvie's fields,
> But thistles, weeds, and sand.]

Their prophecy was shortly fulfilled. A nine-day storm hit the area, and the parish of Forvie became a sandy waste. 'This calamity is said to have fallen on the place about 1688,' added Walter Gregor in 1881. If he is right about the date, the cataclysmic sandstorm was followed only a few years later by another one which hit the coast of Moray in 1694, creating the Culbin Sands from what had been fertile cornfields.

VAYNE CASTLE, ANGUS

The ruined castle of Vayne stands on a rocky height overlooking the Noran. Writing in 1853, Andrew Jervise says that popular tradition ascribes its building to Cardinal David Beaton, and holds further that the cardinal resorted here 'for less consistent purposes than the fulfilment of his vow of celibacy'. A deep pool in the river was known as 'Tommy's Pot', after a son of Beaton's by Lady Vayne who fell over the precipice and drowned there.

All this, however, Jervise adds, is a fable. The sixteenth-century cardinal was deeply unpopular for his persecution of the Protestants, so much so that he was assassinated in 1546 and strung up from the battlements of his own castle at St Andrews in Fife, and for a long time after his death 'not only the most of the obscure retreats and fortalices in Angus were said to have been tenanted by him and his paramours, but almost everything bad and disreputable was ascribed to him'.

Various legends are associated with the ruins of Vayne. A deep dungeon is said to lie below, into which the last inhabitants of the castle threw their silver and gold before leaving, and of the many who searched for the chamber, only one found it. When about to descend in search of the treasure, he was 'forcibly thrust from the mouth of the yawning gulf by an uncouth monster in the shape of a horned ox, who departed in a blaze of fire through a big hole in the wall'. The doorway to the dungeon forthwith disappeared, and has never been discovered since.

The treasure guardian was evidently demonic, and a local rhyme makes the devilish connections of the castle more explicit:

> There's the Brownie o' Ba'quharn,
> An' the Ghaist o' Brandieden;
> But of a' the places i' the parish,
> The deil burns up the Vayne!

As if devils and debauched Catholics weren't enough, there is also said to be a Kelpie on the premises, which left its large hoofprint in a sandstone block near the castle, and tormented the people of Waterstone, a neighbouring farm. It played the same trick here as the spirit Shellycoat did at ETTRICK WATER (Lothian & Borders), calling for help in the voice of a drowning person in order to lure its victims to the water, and when any real case of drowning occurred, the Kelpie would try to mislead rescuers by shouting for the men of Waterstone from the wrong direction.

See KELPIES AND WATER-HORSES (p. 364).

WHITEHILLS, BANFFSHIRE

John Milne's *Myths and Superstitions of the Buchan District* (first printed in 1891) records an instance of early nineteenth-century witchcraft. A cow on a farm in Buchan became ill, and the local vets, baffled, declared that the sickness was due to enchantment.

Milne writes that at Whitehills in Banffshire lived a woman named Lillie Grant, reputed to be a clever witch doctor:

> Lillie came and saw the cow, which by that time was roaring, and trying to climb the walls. Lillie said the spell had taken too strong a hold for her to conquer, and frightened the people at the farm by telling them she was afraid the cow would speak before she died, and declare who was her tormentor. But the animal died, before that gift was given her. Lillie then offered to make the witch come and dance over the cow's grave. This the owner would not permit, but he allowed Lillie to stick the cow's heart full of pins and burn

it at a dykeside – an act which she declared would cause the witch as much pain as if her own heart were being treated in the same way.

Such rites and beliefs survived elsewhere too: at TORPHICHEN (Lothian & Borders), a cow was buried alive as a remedy for an outbreak of murrain, probably at around the same time that Lillie performed her spell in Buchan.

WITTON, WEST WATER, ANGUS

West Water flows east and south from between Glen Esk and Glen Clove to join the North Esk at Stracathro. In its glen, according to an unnamed informant cited by Andrew Jervise in 1853, the Devil had taken up his abode around the beginning of the eighteenth century. He had then entered into a series of contests with the Reverend Mr Thomson, a local minister, one of which began when a Witton farmer went to confront a neighbour with whom he had quarrelled. His wife tried to dissuade him from going, and asked who was to keep her company while he was gone. He replied, 'The devil if he likes!' All too soon after his departure, Satan himself rose from the floor. The terrified woman sent her son out a back way to fetch the minister, who came promptly to the house:

> When within a short distance of it, Mr Thomson, supposing that he felt the odour of 'brimstane smeik', was so impressed with the belief of the bona fide presence of Beelzebub, that he retraced his steps to the manse, and arrayed himself in his black gown and linen bands, and taking the Bible in his hand, went boldly forth to vanquish the master fiend! On entering the ill-fated chamber, he charged the intruder with the Spirit of the Word, when, in the midst of a volume of smoke, and uttering a hideous yell, he shrunk aghast, and passed from view in much the same mysterious way as he had appeared; and an indentation in the ground floor of the farmhouse was long pointed out as having been caused by the descent of Satan!

Although told in mockery, this story reflects accurately enough the belief that a man of God armed with a Bible could defeat an evil spirit. The minister was, however, finally vanquished when the Devil entered his manse in the shape of a black cat. Pursuing the beast, Thomson fell down the stairs, and never quite recovered. 'Although uniformly ascribed to Mr Thomson, these stories are scarcely in accordance with his real character,' adds the sceptical Jervise.

NORTHERN HIGHLANDS

The counties of Caithness and Sutherland

ACHADH A' BHEANNAICH, LATHERON, CAITHNESS

In an article published in *Folk-Lore* in 1898, Malcolm MacPhail describes 'a cairn overgrown with heather' a short distance east of 'Druidical' stones in the parish of Latheron. He translates its Gaelic name, Achadh a' Bheannaich, as 'the Mound of Blessing or Salutation'.

MacPhail, who visited the site in the winter of 1874, describes it as having in the middle a small enclosure resembling one of the so-called Druid altars to be seen in the Highlands. He tells its story as he heard it from a Caithness minister, 'an intimate friend, now deceased':

> When the principle Druid of that district had become so old and infirm that he could no longer perform the functions of his office, he was burnt alive on this altar as a sacrifice. While he was being offered, the young Druid who had been appointed his successor in office kept going round in the altar-smoke — *ex fumo dare lucem* — that he might catch the spirit of his predecessor as it took its flight.

This farrago of ahistorical nonsense sounds less like folk tradition than antiquarian speculation concerning Druids and 'wicker men'. Early antiquaries' notions of Druids were derived from Roman writers, but what the Romans said about them may have been largely 'spin' – anti-barbarian propaganda designed to shock 'civilised' Roman citizens into backing a policy of expensive military conquest.

ARDVRECK CASTLE, ASSYNT, SUTHERLAND

Ruined but romantic Ardvreck or Ardvrock Castle stands on the shores of Loch Assynt. The tower house was probably built in the early 1500s. According to Hugh Miller's *Scenes and Legends of the North of Scotland* (1835), it was once tenanted by 'a dowager lady, – a wicked old woman, who had a singular knack of setting the people in her neighbourhood by the ears'.

The story of 'The Wicked Lady of Ardvrock' is set in the mid eighteenth century. The dowager had been dropping hints about a couple who lived nearby; as a result the husband became suspicious of the paternity of his child and accused his wife of being unfaithful. When he started threatening to kill the baby, his wife summoned her two brothers to help her. The younger brother, who had spent some years in Italy, said that on the morrow they would have to visit the dowager at Ardvrock, confront her with someone as clever as she was and thus arrive at the truth.

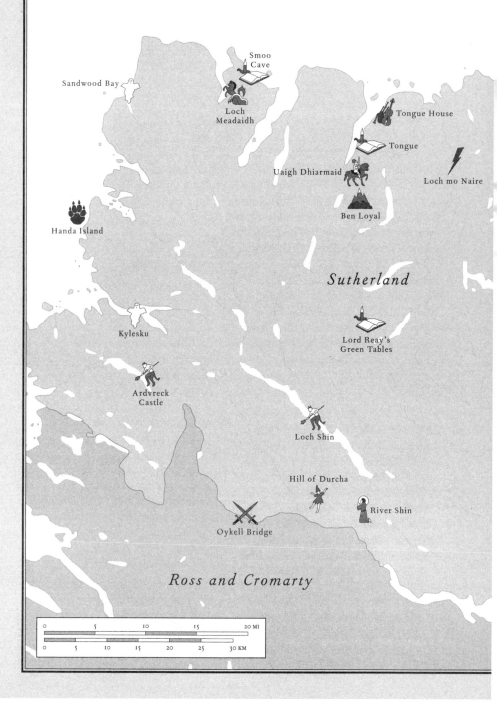

NORTHERN HIGHLANDS

Smoo Cave

Sandwood Bay

Loch Meadaidh

Tongue House

Tongue

Uaigh Dhiarmaid

Loch mo Naire

Ben Loyal

Handa Island

Sutherland

Kylesku

Lord Reay's Green Tables

Ardvreck Castle

Loch Shin

Hill of Durcha

River Shin

Oykell Bridge

Ross and Cromarty

| 0 | 5 | 10 | 15 | 20 MI |
| 0 | 5 | 10 | 15 | 20 | 25 | 30 KM |

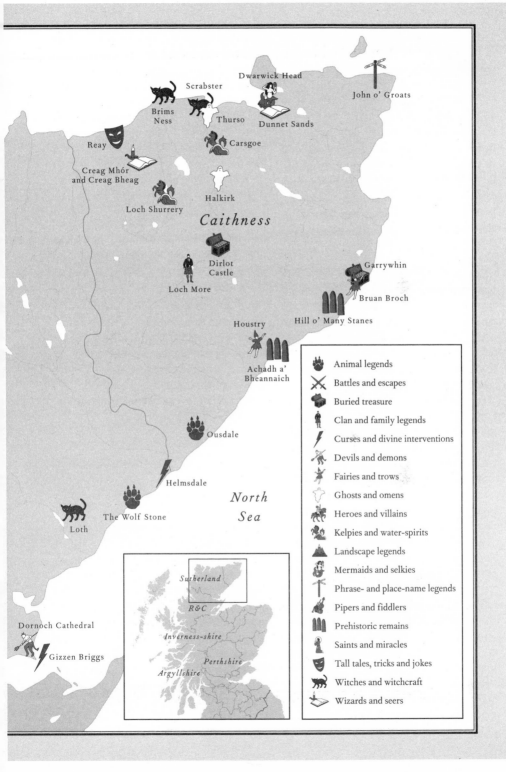

Dwarwick Head

Scrabster

John o' Groats

Brims
Ness

Thurso

Dunnet Sands

Reay

Carsgoe

Creag Mhór
and Creag Bheag

Halkirk

Loch Shurrery

Caithness

Dirlot
Castle

Garrywhin

Loch More

Bruan Broch

Hill o' Many Stanes

Houstry

Achadh a'
Bheannaich

Animal legends
Battles and escapes
Buried treasure
Clan and family legends
Curses and divine interventions
Devils and demons
Fairies and trows
Ghosts and omens
Heroes and villains
Kelpies and water-spirits
Landscape legends
Mermaids and selkies
Phrase- and place-name legends
Pipers and fiddlers
Prehistoric remains
Saints and miracles
Tall tales, tricks and jokes
Witches and witchcraft
Wizards and seers

Ousdale

Helmsdale

*North
Sea*

The Wolf Stone

Loth

Sutherland

R&C

Inverness-shire

Perthshire

Argyllshire

Dornoch Cathedral

Gizzen Briggs

At the castle they were civilly received, and the old lady appeared willing to reply to their questions. She even agreed when the younger brother proposed putting her accusations to the proof by summoning a mutual acquaintance. He proceeded to write with his finger on the stone floor of the great hall where they sat, and mutter in an unknown language. As he was doing this, the water of Loch Assynt began to heave and give off from its surface a thick mist that spread over the sky. Then they perceived a tall black shadowy figure standing beside the wall and the younger brother told the husband to question it – but quickly.

Nervously, the husband asked if his wife had been unfaithful. The shadow replied that she had, and as it spoke a huge wave rose from the loch and, dashing against the castle wall, broke the hall windows, while a tempest lashed roof and turrets, and the floor seemed to rise and fall like a ship in a storm.

The younger brother said to the old lady, 'He will not away from us without his bountith' (meaning a bounty or gift agreed to by contract). He asked who she could best spare, and the wicked old woman went to the door; as she opened it, a little orphan girl who was part of her household rushed into the room as if terrified by the tempest. 'No, not the orphan!' exclaimed the shadow. 'I dare not take her.' Another huge wave came crashing in, half filling the great hall, and the whole castle seemed on the point of falling. 'Then take the old witch herself!' shouted the elder brother. 'She is mine already,' said the shadow, 'but her term is not over. I will take someone that your sister will miss more.'

Even as it spoke, it vanished. When they got home, they were told of the death of the baby at the very moment the shadow disappeared. It was said that for five years

after, the grain produced in Assynt was black and shrivelled, and that the herrings forsook the lochs. At the end of that period, the castle of Ardvrock was consumed by fire, kindled no one knew how. The wicked lady perished in the flames, and after her death, things went on in their natural course – the corn ripened as before, and the herrings returned to the lochs.

This tale contains several traditional themes. The implication of the wife's younger brother having lived in Italy is that he had studied at the famous Black School at Padua attended by other Scottish magicians such as Donald Duibheal Mackay (see CREAG MHÓR AND CREAG BHEAG). The shadow summoned was the Devil, who as was customary arrived in a storm, and in accordance with the usual bargain carried off a soul as the price for his assistance. He was unable to take the orphan probably because she had been baptised: her innocence would not have protected her, as can be seen from the fate of the equally innocent baby.

BEN LOYAL, SUTHERLAND

Ben Loyal is an isolated mountain not far from Strath Naver, south of the Kyle of Tongue. Easily recognised from its four rocky peaks, and composed chiefly of granite, it is a so-called 'magnetic mountain', capable of distorting compass readings and creating the illusion that water and other substances or objects flow or roll uphill. The scientific reason for this is that it is full of iron ore; tradition adds that it has a great furnace at its heart in which the dwarves smelt their metal.

Not far off is a stone once known in Gaelic as 'the Stone of the Little Men'. If you left a silver coin there and a model or drawing of some metal object you wanted, when you returned that day week, you would find it waiting for you. This story, told by Otta Swire in 1963 without giving its source, has the air of being a fiction made up perhaps for children, based on the old tradition attached to Wayland's Smithy, Oxfordshire, where it was said that if a man left his horse and a piece of money, when he came back he would find the horse shod and the money gone.

It is curious that the dwarves are supposed to be terrified of noise except that of their own hammers. It is said that, when the first railway train went through Sutherland, because it was made of metal, the dwarves came out to watch. But the engine driver was from the south and, not knowing that they hated a din, let off steam in order to impress them. Since that time, no dwarves have been seen in Sutherland.

BRIMS NESS, CAITHNESS

In *Folk-Lore Gleanings*, published in 1937, the Reverend George Sutherland tells the story of Bell o' Brims, who lived on the west of Holborn Head. By the time she became widely known as a witch she was getting on in years, but few could surpass her in the knowledge of the Black Art. Like other witches, she helped herself to the milk from neighbours' cows, but her powers extended even further. One day she accosted the dairymaid at Brims Castle, saying that she could make the churning yield ten times as much butter as usual:

> Her offer was accepted, and when the butter came the quantity was so great that the churn could scarcely contain it, but it tasted somewhat fishy. The dairymaid asked her, 'Where did all this butter come from?' Bell said that she took it from a female whale that she saw out at sea.

Bell was distinctively dressed, habitually wearing an old linen coif, a tartan plaid pinned with a silver brooch, a red petticoat, and white woollen stockings. In her hand, she carried a sturdy walking stick. She had cronies in Orkney and to visit them would sail across the Pentland Firth on the back of a crab.

At that time, Rob Campbell was owner of the chief boat plying between Thurso and Tongue. He had the misfortune to fall foul of Bell and she swore that his next sea trip would be his last. Fully believing she had the power to bring this about, Rob did not put out to sea for months, but eventually he had to make a voyage to the west on urgent business, and set out on a fine summer's day. When he had rounded Holborn Head and was approaching Brims Ness, the weather suddenly became stormy. A tremendous squall nearly sank the boat, and ripped the sails to ribbons. Rob and his crew turned tail and made for home, but the hurricane continued. As the tide turned, the craft was swept onto the island of Stroma, where it capsized. Rob Campbell and all on board were drowned.

The shipwreck was, of course, the work of Bell, who, on the day she heard that Rob was to set out, filled a tub with water to represent the sea, and floated a small wooden bowl on it to stand for the boat. Then she put water into an earthenware jar and corked it up tight. This she placed beside a roaring fire, and having done so started reciting over and over again her cantrips. Once a sister hag on watch for the boat told her it was under way, Bell loosened the cork in the jar and allowed some steam to escape. The water in the tub then rippled, resembling a choppy sea. When the next blast of steam was released, the water in the tub became turbulent, and when she drew the cork completely out of the jar, the tub turned into a boiling cauldron and the bowl representing the boat was upset. Crazed with delight, Bell shouted, 'Robbie Campbell is awa' noo.'

After this, no one dared to deny Bell anything she wished. When she lay on her deathbed, the minister came in the hope that at the eleventh hour she might repent, but Bell only cursed him in the Devil's name and ordered him out of her sight.

The story of Bell is a version of one told a century earlier by the Reverend James Calder concerning Margaret or Meg Watt, the witch of Duncansbay. She dressed and behaved like Bell, and also rode on the back of a crab. Her magical ceremony for sinking the boat is the same, but instead of the earthenware jar she uses a bellarmine bottle or 'greybeard' – so called because of a bearded mask on it. These were often used as 'witch-bottles' for protecting against witchcraft and are still sometimes found hidden in or built into old houses. In Meg's case, the person she shipwrecks is Malcolm Groat, a descendant of the famous JOHN O' GROATS.

See also WITCH-HUNTS (p. 270).

BRUAN BROCH, LATHERON, CAITHNESS

In the parish of Latheron are the remains of a broch known as the fairy mound of Bruan. In 1937, the Reverend George Sutherland related that two men once passed the broch carrying a small keg of whisky for New Year celebrations. A door in the broch was open, and inside were fairies dancing to bagpipe music. One of the men wanted to join the dance and went in, but the other was more cautious and waited outside. A long time passed, and the waiting man called to the other, who replied, 'I have not got a dance yet.' After another while the man outside took his whisky and went on his way, expecting that his friend would be home by

morning, but next day he had still not returned, and the broch was closed, with no sign of a door, and no trace of the fairies. The man did not give up hope of his friend, however:

It was an old belief that in such a case the same scene would be enacted in the same place a year after, and accordingly on the anniversary of that day he went to the Bruan Broch. It was open, the music and dancing were going on as before, and his friend was there. He put some iron article in the door to prevent the fairies from closing it, as they are powerless in the presence of iron or steel. He went to the open door and said to his friend, 'Are you not coming home now?' His friend replied, 'I have not got a dance yet.'

The man outside told his friend that he had been a year in the broch, and that it was surely time for him to come home now, but his friend did not believe that he had been more than an hour or so inside.

The man then made a rush at his friend, seized him, and dragged him out by sheer force, and they set out for home together. It was difficult for him to realise that his sojourn with the fairies was such a prolonged one, but the fact that his own child did not recognise him, together with other changes that had taken place, convinced him.

The man who wanted to dance was lucky to have a loyal friend – some who enter a fairy mound never come out again. This is one of many similar tales told throughout Britain of the supernatural lapse of time in fairyland.

Caithness has numerous antiquities traditionally said to be fairy dwellings, among them a horned cairn known as the Fairies' Mound, or Cnoc na h-Uiseig. At the time of excavation it looked like a small green hill, but stone slabs breaking through the surface betrayed the cairn beneath, and also that it had at some time been disturbed. Local knowledge of the man-made constructions inside such seemingly natural mounds probably inspired the tradition that fairies lived in the 'hollow hills' and might still be encountered by those who entered.

CARSGOE, CAITHNESS

In a stretch of the River Thurso which runs by Carsgoe there are said to be very deep pools, called the 'deeps of Carsgoe'. A story relating to them is told by James Calder in *Sketches from John o' Groats* (1842):

> One very warm day in harvest, a young lad took it into his head to go down to the river to bathe. He had not been many seconds in the water, when he got into one of those ponds, and sank to the bottom. Seeing a door open, he entered, and found himself alone in a magnificent apartment, the walls of which sparkled with jewels and precious stones, while the floor seemed to be inlaid with silver. The youth was for a minute or two absolutely dazzled with the richness and brilliancy of the sight. In an adjoining apartment, apparently used as a kitchen, was an old dame parboiling salmon in a large kettle. The youth, whose appetite was whetted by the sight of such a tempting viand, asked her for a little of the fish, but she refused to give him any, upon which he seized her by the feet, threw her into the kettle, and brought away with him as much of the salmon as he could conveniently carry.

When he told the other reapers what had happened, they advised him to hide in the corn. Hardly had he done so when a troop of 'river sprites' arrived in pursuit, and threatened to flood the fields. The men at last told where the lad was hiding; he was carried off, and his body found next day floating on the river.

Aquatic spirits tend to be dangerous, as are rivers and lochs themselves. Many stories convey the moral that it is safer to stay away from the water.

CREAG MHÓR AND CREAG BHEAG, REAY, CAITHNESS

Sir Donald Mackay (1591–1649) led an eventful life. He was imprisoned for adultery and suspected of bigamy, led a regiment in the Thirty Years War (1614–48), and, having accused his lieutenant David Ramsay of treason, was challenged by him to single combat, though the duel was prevented by the intervention of Charles I. In 1628 he was created first Lord Reay, and a contemporary said of him that in his own estates 'he tyrannizes as if there were no law or king to putt order to his insolencies.'

After his death he became remembered in folk legend as a magician, Donald Duibheal or Dubhuail (pronounced Duival) Mackay, and many tales were told of his occult exploits, several of which are included by George Sutherland in his *Folk-Lore Gleanings* (1937). It was said that while serving as a soldier under Gustavus Adolphus of Sweden (1594–1632) he had met the Devil and been invited by him to attend the famous Black School of Padua. In return for his teaching, the Devil required that the last student to leave at the end of the session should be forfeit to him as payment. As they filed out, it happened to be Mackay who was the last one out of the door and the Devil tried to grab him, but the canny Mackay turned round and pointed to his shadow, saying, 'De'il tak' the hindmost.' The Devil accordingly seized hold of the shadow and before he realised he had been tricked, Mackay himself had got safe away. The story is a local version of an international tale known as 'Escape from the Black School', in which a student of the Dark Arts deceives his satanic master into taking shadow for substance, a ploy also attributed to MICHAEL SCOT, THE WIZARD OF BALWEARIE (p. 62) and Sir Robert Gordon of THE ROUND SQUARE (North East).

When Mackay returned to the Reay country, people soon noticed that he cast no shadow and therefore must be uncanny. The Devil meanwhile had pursued his prey all the way from Italy, and they had a fisticuff fight which ended with Mackay giving the Devil a beating and getting from him a swarm of little demons or fairies who did all his work, ploughing his land, harvesting and threshing his corn, and so forth. This was all very well, but when he had run out of jobs for them they still clamoured for employment, and Mackay found himself almost at his wits' end trying to occupy his troublesome assistants.

One idea that occurred to him was to get his imps to drain the loch on the east side of Clash Breac in Broubster, where a pot of gold was said to be hidden. They set to with a will, but when the Cailleach of Clash Breac saw what was happening she shouted to the workers, 'In the name of God, what are you doing here?' At once the imps vanished, unable to bear mention of the sacred name. In fury, Mackay picked up a spade and split the Cailleach's head with it.

> The unfinished work is still to be seen in the form of a deep ravine extending for about two hundred feet in the direction of the loch, but not reaching it. On the north side of this ravine there is a standing stone with the top part of it cleft in twain. This is said to be the Cailleach with her cloven skull now turned into stone.

Spoil from the canal dug by the imps was flung up to make the conspicuous steep-sided hills of Creag Mhór and Creag Bheag ('big crag' and 'little crag') south-east of Reay. As to the 'loch on the east side of Clash Breac', this probably refers to an area east of Cnoc na Claise Brice, not a loch but a bog, a fact which could have been cited as 'proof' that the imps had partly succeeded in their drainage works. The petrified Cailleach is Clach Clais an Tuire, a standing stone south-east of Loanscorribest.

The Cailleach, as the guardian of deer and other wild animals, may have resented the imps' interference with the landscape. It is not explained, however, why she, a supernatural being, is able to speak the name of God when the imps cannot bear to hear it. The Cailleach of LOCH AWE (Argyllshire & Islands) was also said to have been turned to stone, and more legends concerning this spirit or goddess are given in GUARDIAN OF THE WILD (p. 352).

Other stories of Donald Duibheal Mackay are set at DUNNET SANDS, LORD REAY'S GREEN TABLES, SMOO CAVE, and TONGUE HOUSE.

DIRLOT CASTLE, CAITHNESS

The ruins of Dirlot Castle stand on a rock pinnacle rising sheer from level ground at the edge of a deep pool in the River Thurso. According to a local story recorded by the Reverend George Sutherland in 1937, the pool contains a secret:

> A Dirlot tradition tells of a valuable treasure that was sunk in a deep pool in the river close to the castle. This was done to prevent it from falling into hands hostile to those of its owner. Later on attempts were made by good swimmers to recover the treasure by diving into the pool, but all that was ever seen again of anyone that

made the attempt was some of the internal organs of the divers floating on the surface of the pool. This circumstance suggests that the water horse was the guardian of that submerged treasure.

KELPIES AND WATER-HORSES (p. 364) appear in many Highland legends, though Sutherland says that such traditions, once common in Caithness and Sutherland, were by his time almost unknown. He describes the Water-horse as a malignant being that lived in freshwater lakes and often took the form of a beautiful horse, which would be seen quietly grazing at the margin of the lake. Its quietness and seeming friendliness would tempt young men to try and ride him, but once a rider was on his back, the horse would gallop into the lake and disappear into its depths. 'In a little while the heart and lungs of the rider would come to the surface of the water, and be driven by wind and wave to the shore.'

The Water-horse might also appear as a handsome young man or beautiful young woman, or as an aged crone looking as if she needed help. In whatever form it appeared, to touch it was fatal, for your hand would stick fast and you would be dragged to the water. The only parts of you likely to be seen again were some of your internal organs floating to land, a feature of the legend included in several versions of the traditional tale.

In her *Legends of the Pentland Firth* (1977), Henrietta Munro gives a back-history accounting for the Dirlot treasure, building on the tradition that it was sunk in the pool to prevent it from falling into the hands of enemies. According to her version, the chief of Clan Gunn went raiding near Thurso and came back to the castle with bags of gold, but the rival clan of the Keiths arrived to try to seize it. Gunn put the gold in a kettle (not the modern kind, but a large cauldron) and left it with his wife while he and his men fought the Keiths. The Gunns were defeated, and to prevent the Keiths taking the gold the chief's wife hurled the kettle over the castle wall. It fell down the cliff and into the pool, which was so deep that no trace of the gold has ever been found.

This 'historical' version, which gives no hint of the supernatural treasure-guardian, may be a rationalised reworking of the story. Most traditional treasure legends are handed down without circumstantial explanations of how the treasures came to be hidden.

DORNOCH CATHEDRAL, SUTHERLAND

Dornoch Cathedral was founded in the thirteenth century by Gilbert de Moravia, Bishop of Caithness, who later became patron saint of the cathedral and the diocese. The building was heavily 'restored' in 1835–7, and the atmosphere there today is not nearly as eerie as it must have been at the time of the following story, included in Alasdair Alpin MacGregor's *Peat-Fire Flame* (1947).

In Dornoch once lived a tailor who declared that he believed in neither ghosts nor witches. To prove it, he proposed to sit alone in the cathedral one night and knit a pair of hose. So one evening he went and sat cross-legged before the altar as twilight came on, and took up his knitting. While he sat plying his needles in the small hours, a human skull rose to his sight and began to roll towards him. When it was within arm's length of the tailor, it said, 'My fleshless and bloodless head rises to greet you.'

'Wait a minute till I've finished my hose,' said the tailor, plying his needles even more vigorously than before. 'My great head and my fleshless and bloodless body

Guardian of the Wild

The legendary Cailleach was said to haunt woodlands and wild places. She sometimes gave her blessing to huntsmen, but could bring bad luck to farmers.

The Cailleach (pronounced 'kaliach') was a giantess. The poet John Hay Allan wrote in 1922 that 'she could step with ease and in a moment from one district to another,' and that when offended she sent floods from the mountains which destroyed the corn and hid low ground under water. One legend tells how she made the whole of Scotland from earth and rock which she carried from Norway. As she raised her foot to cross the ocean she dropped some pebbles which formed the Hebrides, and the island of Ailsa Crag fell through a hole in her apron. Enormous stones in the Forest of Mar in Aberdeenshire were the remains of her palace, and rocks at the Fall of Connel were stepping stones by which her goats crossed Loch Etive in Argyllshire. At Ben Duirinish on the shore of the loch, relates K. W. Grant in *Myth, Tradition and Story from Western Argyll* (1925), a place called Cruidhean, meaning 'hooves', is named for a relic of her passing:

> The Cailleach, when hotly pursued by her enemies, urged her steed to leap across from Ben Cruachan. On alighting, the forefeet of the horse left an impress on the rock, which may still be seen.

She was sometimes called the Cailleach-uisge, meaning 'water-woman', and was described as frequenting dark caves and woods. Wanderers in the Highland forests would sometimes see her cleaning fish by a stream, a colossal woman wearing a variegated kerchief over her long grey hair and a yellow plaid around her shoulders. She was widely respected as the guardian of wild animals, although this function included allowing them to be culled: at BEINN A' BHRIC (Argyllshire & Islands), she even rewarded a young man for singing a bold song in her honour by granting him supernatural skill in hunting deer.

The seasons especially connected with her power were winter and early spring, when she was considered magically to preserve the deer through the harsh weather. Her protection, however, did not extend to human beings, for whom the cold months represented hardship and hunger. In autumn, the first farmer of the district to finish cutting his corn would make a straw doll called the *cailleach* and send it to his nearest neighbour. He in turn, when he had completed his harvest, would pass the doll to the next, and the farmer who got it last would have an imaginary 'old woman', the Cailleach, to feed for the year. In *Superstitions of the Highlands and Islands of Scotland* (1900), John Gregorson Campbell emphasises the importance attached to the symbol, and the unavoidable nature of the curse:

> The fear of the Cailleach in harvest made a man in *Saor-bheinn*, in the Ross of Mull, who farmed his land in common with another, rise and shear his corn by moonlight. In the morning he found it was his neighbour's corn he had cut.

Belief in the Cailleach as in other nature spirits, declined over the years, as reflected in her physical manifestation. Campbell writes that she was last seen in about 1880 in Lochaber. 'Age had told severely upon her. Instead of being "broad and tall," she had become no bigger than a teapot!' This shrinking reminds one of the Grecian Sibyl to whom Apollo promised anything she wished in return for her sexual favours. She asked for as many years of life as were grains in a handful of dust, but lacking the foresight you might expect of a prophetess, she did not ask for everlasting youth. She shrivelled with age, getting older and older, and smaller and smaller, until they put her in a bottle that hung at Cumae. When children asked her what she wanted, all she said (in Greek) was, 'I want to die.'

By the late twentieth century, however, the cult of the Cailleach had not yet vanished. In about 1975, the folklorist Anne Ross visited Tigh na Cailliche, a shrine in Killin, Inverness-shire containing three stones known as the Cailleach, the Bodach (her husband), and the Nighean (their daughter). Every May Day they were taken out and placed facing down the glen, and every Hallowe'en they were returned to their home. Bob Bissett, a shepherd, had taken care of the shrine and the ceremony, and when he died the new shepherd said he fully intended to continue with the ritual.

See also LOCH AWE (Argyllshire & Islands); BEINN A' GHLÒ (Central & Perthshire); CREAG MHÓR AND CREAG BHEAG (Northern Highlands); CORRYVRECKAN (Western Isles).

rise to greet you!' persisted the skull. 'Wait, I tell you,' said the tailor, 'till I've finished my hose.'

As the tailor spoke, the skeleton rose higher and higher until it could be seen from top to toe. But not until the tailor had finished his hose did he set eyes on the skeleton. Then to be sure he fled from the cathedral, with the skeleton close behind him, and slammed the door. The skeleton's pursuit of the tailor suddenly brought to a standstill, in frustration it seized hold of the doorposts. It is said that, up to the time of the cathedral's restoration, the imprints of his skinny fingerbones could be seen on the doorposts.

Similar tales are told of BEAULY (Southern Highlands) and of the old chapel of KILNEUAIR (Argyllshire and Islands), where the mark of the Devil's hand can still be seen on the wall.

DUNNET SANDS, CAITHNESS

After creating CREAG MHÓR AND CREAG BHEAG, the fairies or imps employed by the wizard Donald Duibheal Mackay undertook their biggest job: trying to bridge the Pentland Firth. Mackay set them to weaving ropes of sand from Dunnet Bay, and they managed to make the main rope which would support the bridge, but when they tried to stretch it from shore to shore it broke in half. The fairies were furious with Donald for setting them too hard a challenge and would have torn him limb from limb if he had not turned himself quickly into a black horse and galloped off at lightning speed into the town of Thurso.

Once fairies have put their hands to a task they cannot leave it undone, so they are doubtless still there on Dunnet Sands trying to make ropes. Like other stories of Donald Duibheal Mackay, this resembles a legend associated with that other famous northern magician Sir Michael Scot, who kept his own familiars similarly occupied near BALWEARIE CASTLE (Central & Perthshire). The tale is generically known as 'Ropes of Sand' from the task given to the industrious imps – obviously an impossible one, since although sand may by the action of wind and waves (or demons) be sculpted into rope-like strands, the shape will last only until the next tide.

DWARWICK HEAD, CAITHNESS

In *Sketches of John o' Groats* (1842), the Reverend James Calder says that a mermaid had occasionally been heard singing around the Caithness coast. Ideas about her were mostly the same as about other British mermaids – half-woman, half-fish, she was commonly seen sitting on a rock, combing her long yellow hair – but she had one less usual characteristic, which was that before any great national calamity or war she would be seen washing a bloody shirt. It was said that several people had seen her doing this 'before the late French war' (the Napoleonic Wars). She was very shy, and if she saw anyone looking at her would slip into the sea. If approached unawares, however, and spoken to civilly, she had been known to reply, and even to grant three wishes to the person who addressed her.

A young lad one day came on her disporting herself in a sandy pool between Murkle and Castlehill. He contrived to get into conversation, and was so pleasing to her that they began having regular meetings at that spot. This went on for some time, and the young man grew very rich, though no one could tell where all his wealth came from. He began cutting a dash with the girls, giving them necklaces of diamonds and pearls that had been gifts to him from the mermaid. By and by, he began to forget the regular meetings, and when he did go he always asked for jewels and money. The mermaid had sharp words to say about his love of gold, and finally became outraged at his treachery in giving her presents to other women. One evening, she showed him a beautiful boat, which, she said, would take him to a cave in Dwarwick Head where she kept the wealth of all the ships ever lost on Dunnet Sands. At first he hesitated to go, but his love of money prevailed and off they set for the cave.

> And here, says the tradition, he is confined with a chain of gold, sufficiently long to admit of his walking at times on a small piece of sand under the western side of the Head, and here, too, the fair siren laves herself in the tiny waves on fine summer eves; but no consideration will induce her to loose his fetters of gold, or trust him one hour out of her sight.

She was probably wise. A similarly greedy merchant of DUMBARTON (Central & Perthshire) not only deserted his mermaid lover but took with him most of her treasure.

GARRYWHIN, ULBSTER, CAITHNESS

A man and his son once lived by the hill of Garrywhin, and earned their living by making and selling a special brand of whisky and a special kind of ale which had a delicate heathery taste quite unlike other liquors. While the old man and his son readily acknowledged that they made their drinks with heather, exactly how they did this was a mystery. Other people

Robert Louis Stevenson (1850–94) was one of Scotland's best-loved poets and storytellers. In his poem 'Heather Ale' (1890) he tells a legend of the last of the ancient and mysterious Picts.

experimented with heather but had no success, and although everyone guessed that the man and his son worked and stored their goods in a cave in the precipitous cliff-face to the west of Garrywhin, no one else knew where the entrance was.

At last a group of curious and envious neighbours determined to learn the truth, and having failed to persuade the old man to tell them his secret, they threatened him with death.

> The old man said to them, 'If I should tell you, my son would kill me for doing so; kill my son and then I shall think over the matter.' They killed his son. The old man then said to them, 'Now, kill me also; no one else knows our secret, and it will die with me.' They killed him, and so the secret remained a secret.

Though the people searched every inch of the precipice, no trace of the cave or the heather whisky and ale stored in it was ever found.

A version of this story was made famous by Robert Louis Stevenson's poem 'Heather Ale' (1890), subtitled 'A Galloway Legend' – it is a tale told of several different places in Scotland, and is sometimes known as 'The Last of the Picts', as the old man and his son are often said to be survivors of that supposedly hidden race (see PICTS, PECHS, AND PIXIES, p. 430).

The Reverend George Sutherland, recording the Garrywhin tradition in the 1930s, quotes 'an old doggerel':

> If ye search Garrywhin,
> Very weel oot, and very weel in,
> Very good whisky you will fin'.

However, nobody has searched well enough yet, and the secret of Garrywhin remains a secret.

Sutherland adds that the cliff seems to have remained under supernatural guardianship until at least the end of the nineteenth century, when a young man met a mysterious stranger at Garrywhin. The stranger asked him to look at the cliff and say if he saw anything unusual. The young man looked, and saw nothing untoward. Then the stranger gave him 'a pencil with a small glass in one end of it' and told him to look at the cliff through the glass. He did so, and to his horror saw a large hairy beast slowly scaling the vertical cliff-face like a fly on a pane of glass. Terrified, he fled. To his dying day he believed that both the stranger and the big hairy beast were supernatural, but the strange pencil with the glass in the end sounds rather like an illusory device. One wonders if the vision was some kind of trick, or perhaps no more than an insect crawling over the end of a small telescope.

GIZZEN BRIGGS, DORNOCH FIRTH, SUTHERLAND

The Gizzen Briggs (spelt variously) is a name derived from old Norse gisnar, 'leaky', and brygga, 'bridge', and applied to a turbulent stretch of water above a quicksand at the entrance to the Dornoch Firth. The Gaelic name, Charles Bentinck recorded in 1926, is Drochaid an Aobh, which he translated as the Spectres' or Water Kelpies' Bridge. ('Kelpies', here and in a few other instances, is used in a loose sense to mean something like 'imps' – the spirits involved do not seem to have much in common with homicidal KELPIES AND WATER-HORSES (p. 364).)

The origin-legend of the place is that the fairies or water-kelpies built a bridge across the firth, which was nearly complete when somebody walked across it and called upon the name of God. At this, the structure collapsed and a perilous shoal began to accumulate around the wreckage.

In 1809 a ferry sank at the Gizzen Briggs with the loss of many lives – one hundred, says Joanna Close-Brooks in 1986, but she seems to have rounded it up, judging by an account from nearly a century earlier contained in Miss Dempster's 1888 article on 'Sutherlandshire Folklore':

> X. came to ask a tenant of ours to cross the ferry with him, and to go to Tain, for the fair held there. The man refused, because he had been warned of God in a dream that many would be drowned by the capsizing of the boat. X. laughed at him, went to Tain, and was among the eighty-eight persons drowned the following day. This happened on 16th August, 1809.

In 1937, Alasdair Alpin MacGregor wrote that in his day the Gizzen Briggs still presented a danger to water traffic:

I well remember how, when I was holidaying as a school-boy near Tain, some twenty years ago, the auxiliary engine of a small sailing-vessel laden with timber and coal, making for Bonar-Bridge, at the head of the Dornoch Firth, failed, and how the vessel consequently was carried out by the tide, and swept into the Gizzen Briggs and perdition. My recollection is that, despite frantic efforts to reach the doomed ship by life-boats from both sides of the Firth, the crew perished, and the skipper was rescued only after he had clung to the top-mast for three days and three nights. This mishap filled the countryside with a sense of tragedy; and everyone spoke freely of the fate that had befallen both vessel and crew at the evil hands of the Gizzen Briggs kelpies.

Another tale told of the Gizzen Briggs, and mentioned by both MacGregor and Dempster, is that of a wicked sea captain who built a ship called the *Rotterdam* in which he hoped to conquer the world. So big was the vessel that on its deck there was a garden full of fruit, flowers, and livestock, and when she was launched her captain said, 'I now fear nor God nor man.' He entered the Dornoch Firth in the hopes of finding a north-west passage, but being ignorant of the place he ran his ship upon the quicksands, where she sank. It is said that her topgallant sail can still be seen fluttering above the waves.

> Her crew and her captain must be still alive, for in calm weather they may be heard praying and singing psalms to avert the judgment of the Last Day, when the master of the Rotterdam will be punished.

Dempster hints that the captain may have been a slave trader, but the sin for which he suffers is probably that of blasphemy. There are echoes here of the legend of the 'Flying Dutchman', condemned to sail the seas until the Day of Judgement unless (in Wagner's version) he wins a woman's faithful love.

HALKIRK, CAITHNESS

Among other accounts of death-lights, wraiths, and apparitions in *Folk-Lore Gleanings* (1937), the Reverend George Sutherland tells that shortly after the funeral of a Halkirk miller, his family were sitting round the fire when the dead man appeared among them, walked past them into the 'ben end' (back room) of the house, and was then seen no more that night.

> For several nights running this occurred at the same hour each night. The miller had a son who was a bank accountant. He was communicated with about the matter, and came home. He said that if he would see the ghost, and recognise him as being indubitably his father, he would follow him into 'the ben end' of the house with a light, and ask him what he wanted. Punctual to his time the ghost came, and the son followed him with a light into the other room and asked him what he wanted. The ghost pointed to one or two corn measures, which were stowed away below a bed, and bade his son to burn them. They were false measures. The miller's spirit could not rest until they were destroyed. This was done, and the ghost appeared no more.

This is one of many local legends concerning fraudulent tradesmen who in life sold short measure or adulterated goods, another being the dairymaid of CRAIL (Central & Perthshire). Because of their unfair dealing their spirits were condemned to 'walk' after death, either as a divinely imposed penance or simply from an uneasy conscience.

HANDA ISLAND, SUTHERLAND

Mrs D. Ogilvy's *Book of Highland Min-strelsy* (1846) relates how wolves were once objects of terror. 'We are told that the tract of country called Ederachillis, on the west coast of Sutherland, was so infested by them that they even rifled the corpses from the graves, and the inhabitants were obliged to convey their dead to the neighbouring island of Handa, as the only safe place of sepulture.' A poem follows:

On Ederachillis' shore
The grey wolf lies in wait, –
Woe to the broken door,
Woe to the loosened gate, . . .
He climbeth the guarding dyke,
He leapeth the hurdle bars,
He steals the sheep from the pen,
And the fish from the boat-house spars;
And he digs the dead from out the sod,
And gnaws them under the stars.

That wolves preyed on dead human flesh was widely rumoured in the eighteenth and nineteenth centuries. The tradition concerning Handa is not unique: the same was said of Green Island, Loch Awe-side, in Argyllshire, as well as of the small island of St Mungo, off its west coast, and of an island in Loch Maree, Ross. The islands were said to have been appropriated for use as burial-grounds when wolves abounded, as the beasts could not swim. In Athole a different wolf-deterrent was reported in 1792 – a custom of burying the dead in coffins made from five flagstones.

Anglo-Saxon sources speak of wolves, along with ravens, hanging about battlefields. Whether wolves eating corpses after a battle was a poetic convention or historical truth, the same kind of report was circulating in school textbooks at the

It is said that inhabitants of the west coast of Sutherland once had to bury their dead on the island of Handa, to prevent the bodies being dug up and eaten by wolves. Such burials must have presented a challenge, judging by this nineteenth-century engraving of the island.

end of the eighteenth century and into the nineteenth: 'Wolves have sometimes been seen following armies, and repairing in numbers to the field of battle, when quitted by the combatants; where they devour all the bodies which they find exposed, or but negligently buried.' This is William Mavor, in *Natural History for the Use of Schools*, first published in 1799 and running to several editions.

The danger, said Mavor, was that 'When once accustomed to human flesh, they ever afterwards shew a particular predilection for it; and thus they have been known to prefer the shepherd to his flock.' This scare had little if any evidence to support it, at least as far as Britain was concerned.

See also THE WOLF STONE.

HELMSDALE, SUTHERLAND

Helmsdale Castle, overlooking the town from the mouth of the river, already needed reconstruction in the sixteenth century, and in the later twentieth was demolished so that a new bridge could be built to carry the coastal road over the water. The castle's decline was blamed on a sixteenth-century curse.

The castle once belonged to the Sinclairs, who had resigned their earldom of Orkney to the King of Scotland in 1470, but kept their mainland estates and the earldom of Caithness. According to the story told by Otta Swire in *The Highlands and their Legends* (1963), Isobel Sinclair entertained the Earl and Countess of Sutherland here in 1567 and, once she had them under her roof, set about poisoning them so that her son, the Earl of Caithness, might succeed also to the Sutherland earldom. Her plan misfired, however, for not only did the Earl and Countess succumb to her machinations, but her son died too, having accidentally drunk some of the poison.

This tragedy turned Isobel's brain and she made an end of herself, but not before she had cursed the castle and all who lived in it: hence its eventual abandonment and ruin.

HILL OF DURCHA, NEAR LAIRG, SUTHERLAND

Like other parts of the British Isles, but perhaps more especially the Highlands, Sutherland has its tales of the disparity between mortal and fairy time. Despite its title, Henry Bett's *English Myths and Traditions* (1952) includes a characteristic story set near the south-east end of Loch Shin. He writes that a man returning from Lairg sat down to rest on the hill of Durcha, near an opening in the ground:

He heard sounds of merriment from below, and went in. He was not seen again, and another man who had been in his company was accused of making away with him. He asked for a year and a day's grace, and solemnly promised he would vindicate himself by then. He watched the opening in the hillside, and finally saw his companion come out with a troop of fairies. All of them were dancing. The man who had been accused seized his friend and held him. The rescued man said peevishly, 'Why could you not let me finish the reel, Sandy?' He could not believe that he had been with the fairies for a twelvemonth until he had reached home, and seen his wife with a child in her arms a year old.

The man's holding on to his friend when he came out of the hill is not the throwaway detail it may seem: this was the traditional way to redeem someone from the fairies, used for instance by Sandy Harg of NEW ABBEY (Dumfries & Galloway) to rescue his wife. Other stories of the supernatural lapse of time in fairyland are set at BRUAN BROCH and MAIDEN CASTLE (Central & Perthshire), and at TOMNAHURICH (Southern Highlands).

The 'hill of Durcha' was clearly a fairy mound, a hillock in which the fairies had their dwelling. Often these were ancient cairns, but which of the many prehistoric sites around Lairg this one may have been is open to question. As well as brochs, stone circles, hut circles, and odd mounds, the parish contains numerous cairns and chambered cairns, any one of which might qualify as a fairy dwelling.

HILL O' MANY STANES, MID CLYTH, CAITHNESS

Unique in Britain to Caithness and Sutherland are multiple rows of small standing stones set out in parallel lines or fan shapes, thought to date from the early Bronze Age. They are found sometimes in the neighbourhood of cairns, that is, burial sites, and may have had a religious function, though in the 1970s Professor Alexander Thom argued that they were used to calculate the movements of the moon.

Whatever their original purpose, such rows are still a fantastic sight. The best preserved run down the southern slope of a low hill at Mid Clyth known as the Hill o' Many Stanes. They are small flat slabs, wedged upright with their broad faces aligned in more than twenty rows, fanning out slightly towards the southern end. Today about 200 stones remain, but it is thought that the pattern could once have involved 600 or more.

A popular belief that gold was hidden beneath the stones may have led to the removal of some, and others have been destroyed by agriculture or removed for building, but as in the case of stone circles, it was said to be dangerous to interfere with them. A farmer at Bruan is said to have removed one of the Mid Clyth stones to use as the lintel above the fireplace of a kiln. When the fire was lit, the stone burst into flames but remained mysteriously unconsumed. This made him so fearful that he hastily returned the stone to the exact place in the row that he had taken it from.

HOUSTRY, CAITHNESS

In the family of the Reverend George Sutherland, a minister from Mull, was preserved a 'need-fire log' used in Houstry around 1810. The story that went with it, quoted in an 1898 article on 'Sacred Fire' in *Folk-Lore*, related that David Gunn, a crofter, had taken building materials from

a broch. To interfere with such fairy habitations was held to be extremely unlucky, and the resulting misfortune did not fall on Gunn alone but on the whole community, in the form of a cattle-plague. The 'wise heads' of the district decided that a *Teine-Eiginn* or need-fire was required, and Sutherland relates the procedure:

A branch was cut off a tree in a neighbouring wood, the bark was stripped off, and it was carried to a small island, which I know well, in the Houstry Burn. The pure limpid water was flowing round it on all sides, and cut the island off from the impurities, and from all the transactions of common life. Every fire in the district was quenched, the life of the community, with all its doings and responsibilities, was symbolically quenched with it. The community repaired to the neighbourhood of the island. Fire was produced by the friction of pieces of wood, and from this sacred fire the fires of the houses were kindled, and life was entered upon anew.

No doubt the ritual stayed in the memory: it was by that time unusual, not to mention frowned on by the Kirk.

A more detailed account of what may be an even later occurrence is given in Donald Mackay's *This Was My Glen* (1965), citing information from Alisdair Sinclair, who was born in around 1820 and claimed to have a vivid recollection of seeing the ceremony in his youth. It is possible that this was indeed a first-hand report. Mackay himself suspects, however, that Sinclair changed the venue and date of the Houstry occurrence 'and put himself in as an observer to add verisimilitude to his story'.

However that may be, Sinclair places the scene of the ceremony on a small island in the Forss Water near the point where it leaves LOCH SHURRERY. As in the earlier story, the *Teine-Eiginn* was kindled to cure an outbreak of cattle dis-ease caused by upsetting the fairies, the culprit being a crofter in the Lieurary area who thought he would improve his land by top-dressing with soil from a fairy hill, although everyone warned him against it. He ignored not only his neigh-bours' advice but even a visit from a spec-tral woman who commanded him to stop his 'greedy and evil work'; when he con-tinued as before, she returned to tell him that he would find two dead oxen in his byre next morning.

That was the beginning of a terrible epi-demic affecting all the herds of the area. Someone was sent to Houstry to fetch 'second-sighted Sandy', known in Caith-ness for his powers of warding off evil. He came at once and ordered all the fires in the neighbourhood to be put out. Then he went to the island in the Forss Water where he erected two posts, with a cross-piece like a door frame. Sandy inserted a bar of wood through a hole in the middle of the crosspiece and set two men to turn it, to kindle a flame in the old way. They were told to wear only pure wool and no iron about their persons, not even a hob-nail in their boots. All day they worked, and still no spark came, and Sandy decided that something was wrong. He ordered a house search to be made next day, but word came back that every hearth was cold.

> Then Sandy disappeared to return later with some of his spell-breaking appli-ances. With water and silver he performed in silence a mysterious rite for divining where the evil influence came from. Anx-iously the people watched his serious countenance, and their hopes bounded when he jumped to his feet and set off at a smart pace, calling on the spectators to follow him.
>
> He went straight to Achscrabster, to a cottage there, where lived an old woman,

reputed to be familiar with the practice of the Black Art. Sandy demanded why she kept fire hidden in her house, but she denied the charge.

> 'Ye needna,' said Sandy, proceeding to the spot where he found in a pot a number of live embers.

Next day the fire-kindling ritual was begun again, and this time a spark came easily. Once the fire was going, the cattle were driven through the smoke and were cured, though the land which had been dressed with fairy soil never grew any-thing again, and the crofter who had caused the trouble left the area.

The story is interesting not only as an account of the kindling of the need-fire, but as a description of the proceedings of what south of the border would be called a 'conjuror' or cunning man. Sandy's spell using 'water and silver' is not further explained, but 'scryers' of the Tudor period and later were accustomed to pour clean water into a silver bowl and watch for an image to form. The use of clean water and silver, like the men's obligation to wear pure wool, is symbolic: all three represented purity. Iron, especially 'cold iron', forged without heat, was believed to be inimical to fairies and witches, and here was evidently forbidden in ritual magic.

JOHN O' GROATS, CAITHNESS

'From Land's End to John o' Groats', meaning from one end of Britain to the other, would not have nearly such a ring to it were it not for the memorable names. While the first is self-explanatory, the second has long given travellers cause to wonder. Although Wikipedia asserts con-fidently that, 'The town takes its name from Jan de Groot, a Dutchman who obtained a grant for the ferry from the Scottish mainland to Orkney,' this is not documented history. The first mention of the Grot or Groat family is from the early seventeenth century, recording a grant of land in Caithness to John Grot made in 1496, and subsequent references are made to the family as running the ferry.

Britain has many 'charter myths', stories invented at a later date (notably in the fifteenth century) to supply the want of documentation in the feudal period, and so to justify someone's right to a particular property or business. That the original ferryman was 'Jan de Groot, a Dutchman', may be true, or may simply be part of the traditional story told to account for the name of the place – which, by the way, used to be written 'John o' Groat's', short for 'John o' Groat's House', though as James Calder objected in 1861, 'The stranger who visits the spot is naturally disappointed, when instead of the house which his imagination had pictured, he sees nothing but a small green mound which is pointed out as the site on which it stood.' A verse by an unnamed tourist is quoted in the *Scottish Antiquary* in 1894:

> I went in a boat
> To see John o' Groat
> The place where his house doth lie;
> But when I got there
> The hill was bare
> And the devil a stone saw I.

Traces of the historical Groats, however, can still be seen: in the porch of St Drostan's church, Canisbay, is a tombstone commemorating various family members, though unfortunately the inscription was recut in the nineteenth century.

A tale first printed in the 1790s tells that in the reign of James IV (1488–1513) three brothers, Malcolm, Gavin, and John de Groat, arrived from Holland. In the course of time there came to be eight different landowners called Groat, all of whom gathered once a year to celebrate the anniversary of their coming to Caithness. On one occasion a violent quarrel broke out as to who should have precedence on entering, sit at the head of the table, and so forth. John, by now of great age, intervened, pledging himself to resolve the matter, and by the time the next gathering took place he had built an octagonal house with eight doors, inside which stood an octagonal table. The head of each Groat family could thus enter through his own door, no one could be said to sit in an inferior position to anyone else, and so peace was restored. In the *Statistical Account of Scotland* (1791–99), it is stated that the remains of the table had been seen by many people then still living.

Another story, purporting to be traditional and told by Robert Mackay in 1829, was that the ferryman ancestor of the Groats was forever arguing over fares until the magistrates intervened and fixed the rate at fourpence (one groat) for each passenger, after which the ferryman, whose name was John, became known as 'Johnny Groat'.

The best-known legend about John o' Groats must be that it is the most northerly point of mainland Britain, an honour which in fact belongs to Dunnet Head. John o' Groat's *house* was, however, the most northerly dwelling, while it stood.

KYLESKU, SUTHERLAND

Ronald Macdonald Robertson was an enthusiastic collector of folklore and clan legend. His books make good reading, although it is a pity that he gives so few references for his tales. One of these he calls 'The Curse of Kylesku'.

After a shipwreck, a keg of whisky was washed ashore at Kerrachar Bay and carried to the old ferry house at Kylesku (later the Kylesku Hotel) by a fisherman nick-named 'Tordeas', who took it upstairs. It was Saturday night, and Tordeas asked some of his friends in to help him drink the liquor. One of his boozing compan-ions was a 'seer' who foretold disaster to come, but the other men paid no attention. A drunken quarrel followed, which became violent. Tordeas pointed out that it was nearly midnight, approaching 'the Lord's Day', but his son was in a fury and threw the old man down the stairs, break-ing his neck. Tordeas died promising that he would return to have his revenge.

A few weeks later the son was drowned in Loch Glencoul, but Tordeas still did not sleep easy in his grave: Robertson wrote in 1961 that 'to this day' his ghost appears in the hotel at midnight on the anniversary of his death. The last person to see the ghost, according to Robertson, was Professor C. M. Joad in the 1950s, and 'it is believed that the curse of Kylesku still manifests on occasions, even unto the present time.'

LOCH MEADAIDH, DURNESS, SUTHERLAND

Found all over the Highlands in one form or another is the tale of a woman who encounters the Water-horse, a ferocious but sometimes alluring beast. The story outlined by John Gregorson Campbell in *Superstitions of the Highlands and Islands of Scotland* (1900) tells how a young woman herded her cattle to a lonely part of the hill. While they were there, a young man came that way and set out to woo her. Reclining on the ground where she sat, with his head in her lap, he fell asleep, and, when he stretched himself in slumber, she saw he had horse's hooves instead of feet. Gently lulling him so as not to wake him, she gradually shifted his head onto the ground. Taking out her scissors, she then cut away the part of her clothes still trapped beneath him and hurried off. The Water-horse made a most terrible outcry when he woke and found her gone.

Campbell gives several variations on this story, saying that in Sutherland it was set at Loch Meadaidh (he spells it 'Meud-haidh'), south of Durness and Sangomore, and that in this case the woman detected the Water-horse not by his hooves but by the sand in his hair. As she made her escape, she looked back and saw him tear-ing up the earth (as a horse might) in his fury. In Campbell's time, the descendants of the woman involved were still pointed out. He adds in a note:

> Such was the terror inspired by a report that the Water-horse of Loch Meudhaidh had made its re-appearance that the natives would not take home peats that they had cut at the end of the loch by boat (the only way open to them), and the fuel was allowed to go to waste.

See also KELPIES AND WATER-HORSES (p. 364).

LOCH MO NAIRE, STRATHNAVER, SUTHERLAND

William Henderson, writing in 1866, reports the marvellous powers of healing of Loch mo Naire, said to be particularly effective on the first Mondays in February, May, August, and November. In February and November there were not many visi-tors, probably because of the inclement weather, but the Reverend D. Mackenzie, minister of Farr, told Henderson that in May and August a great many people made pilgrimages to the loch from all over the north of Scotland and even from the Orkneys. The votaries had to be on the banks of the loch at midnight, plunge in

Kelpies and Water-horses

The many tales of the Kelpie make it clear that this was one of the best-known and most widely feared Scottish monsters. It was a beast that haunted water, and was commonly seen in the form of a horse – but was it, as one might imagine, the same creature as the Water-horse? Some say not:

> The Kelpie that swells torrents and devours women and children has no representative in Gaelic superstition. Some writers speak as if the Water-horse were to be identified with it, but the two animals are distinctly separate. The Water-horse haunts lochs, the Kelpie streams and torrents.

In *Superstitions of the Highlands and Islands of Scotland* (1900), John Gregorson Campbell is clear on the difference, and many of his fellow experts agree, but other folklorists or their sources are happy to talk of Kelpies in Highland lochs or Water-horses in Lowland rivers. The eminent scholar Katharine Briggs gives a story localised in Glen Keltney, Perthshire, of seven little girls out walking on Sunday who saw a pretty horse grazing by the loch:

> One after another they got on its back which gradually lengthened itself so that there was room for all. A little boy with them noticed this and refused to join them. The horse turned its head and suddenly yelled out 'Come on little scabby-head, get up too!' The boy ran for his life and hid among the boulders where the Kelpie could not get at him. When it saw this it turned aside and dashed into the loch. Nothing of the seven little girls but their entrails came to land.

The fact that the girls were caught on a *Sunday* makes this a moral tale: they should not have been riding pretty horses on the Sabbath. Elsewhere, rumours of aquatic demons were used to warn children away from water, while for older girls the message was to beware of strange young men. A gruesome legend in George Henderson's *Survivals in Belief among the Celts* (1911) is representative of the Water-horse's ways. A young woman on the island of Barra had been flirting with a handsome youth, and as they sat on the grass he laid his head in her lap and went to sleep. She noticed water-weed in his hair and became suspicious, so cut off the piece of her skirt on which his head rested and tiptoed away, but that was not the end of the story:

> A considerable time after, on a Sunday after Mass, a number of people were sitting on the hill and she along with them. She noticed the stranger whom she had met on the hill approaching, and she got up to go home so as to avoid him.

He made up to her, notwithstanding, and caught her, and hurried off and plunged with her into the lake, and not a trace of her was ever found but a little bit of one of her lungs on the shore of the lake.

Again it is a Sunday (perhaps she should not have been out in company on the holy day), and again the floating body part makes the girl's fate all too clear.

The Kelpie did not invariably look like a horse: at MORPHIE (North East) it is described as a reptilian monster, and at CONON HOUSE (Southern Highlands) it appears as a woman. Its most common manifestation, however, was in equine shape. In a brief tale reported by Walter Gregor in *Notes on the Folk-Lore of the North-East of Scotland* (1881), a Highlander, inspecting his horses beside a lonely loch, was surprised to see a grey beast that did not belong to the herd:

This nineteenth-century picture of the Kelpie shows its horse-like head, hooves, and tail, and makes very clear its menacing strength.

He looked, and in the twinkling of an eye, he saw an old man with long grey hair and a long grey beard. The horse he was riding on immediately started off, and for miles, over rocks and rough road, galloped at full speed till home was reached.

Gregor includes this story in his description of the 'Waterkelpie', but as he sets it beside a loch, the grey-haired apparition was probably what Campbell would call a Water-horse. As with all questions of language, there is no definitive right or wrong: terminology does change, and all one can do is bear in mind that writers may use the same word to mean different things.

See also LOCH VENACHAR; POWGUILD (Central & Perthshire); KELPIE'S STANE; THE RIVER SPEY; ST VIGEANS; VAYNE CASTLE (North East); DIRLOT CASTLE; LOCH MEADAIDH (Northern Highlands); LOCH NESS (Southern Highlands); LOCH NA MNA; ORSAY (Western Isles).

three times and drink a little of its water, then throw a coin in 'as a tribute to its presiding genius'. They had to get out of sight of the loch before sunrise, otherwise their labour would be in vain.

None of this would work, however, if you were a Gordon of Strathnaver. The reason for this, and for the loch's miraculous properties, is given by Miss Dempster in a long article of 1888 on the folklore of Sutherland, where she tells of an old woman of Strathnaver who had inherited a magical white stone. One of the Gordons of Strathnaver wished to perform a spell and asked to borrow the stone, but the woman refused.

When he saw that she would not lend it or give it up he determined to seize her, and to drown her in a little loch. The man and the woman struggled there for a long time, till he took up a heavy stone with which to kill her. She plunged into the lake, throwing her magic stone before her, and crying, 'May it do good to all created things save to a Gordon of Strathnaver.' He stoned her to death in the water, she crying, '*Manaar! manaar!*' [*Mo Naire! Mo Naire!*] ('Shame! shame!') And the loch is called the Lake of Shame to this day.

A very similar tale is given by William Walsh in *Curiosities of Popular Customs* (1898), although he comments that Loch mo Naire does not really mean 'the loch of shame' but 'the serpent's loch', *nathair* (serpent) being pronounced similarly to *naire* (shame).

In the version referring to the old woman's 'white stone', there may be some collation with the white stone sent to Inverness by St Columba to cure King Brude's Druid, or with the prophetic pebble found by the Brahan Seer of STRATHPEFFER (Southern Highlands). Walsh, however, refers to the magical objects as 'bright crystal stones'. The medicinal virtues of rock-crystal were celebrated from classical times: in the sixteenth, seventeenth, and eighteenth centuries it was variously prescribed, ground and mixed with water or wine or spirits of vitriol, for the cure of dizziness, dysentery, dropsy, scrofula, melancholy, and constipation. Mixed with honey, it was recommended for nursing mothers to improve lactation.

Another healing lake is ST TREDWELL'S LOCH (Orkney & Shetland Islands).

LOCH MORE, CAITHNESS

In his *History of Caithness* (1861), James Calder mentions Reginald Cheyne, who flourished about the beginning of the fourteenth century. Being very fond of the chase, he often stayed in a hunting lodge near where the River Thurso runs from Loch More, and it was said that he had 'some kind of a machine fixed in the mouth of the stream' for catching salmon, a Heath-Robinson-sounding apparatus in which the motion of the fish would set up vibrations in a cord running to a bell in the castle.

Calder tells an anecdote of Cheyne 'which is believed to be strictly founded in truth'. Being the last of his family in the male line, Cheyne was extremely anxious to have an heir to inherit his properties. However, the first baby born to Lady Cheyne was a daughter, and he was so exasperated that he gave orders for the infant to be drowned. Lady Cheyne, however, with the help of a faithful servant, managed to smuggle the child out of the castle and into the care of a nurse. Her next baby also being a daughter, Cheyne gave the same order, but this child, too, was preserved. After this she had no more children, a source of bitter disappointment to Cheyne, who could not but see it as a punishment for the

This 1738 portrait demonstrates why the young Charles Edward Stuart (1720–88) was known to his admirers as 'Bonnie Prince Charlie'. At Kelso (Lothian & Borders), a horseshoe still embedded in the road is identified as one cast by the prince's horse when he rode through the town in 1745, on his way to confront the English forces.

Robert the Bruce (1274–1329), shown here with his first wife Isabella in a picture from 1591, wanted his heart to be buried in Jerusalem, but it is believed to lie at Melrose Abbey (Lothian & Borders). Separate heart-burial was not uncommon at the time. The heart of the thirteenth-century king John Balliol is buried at Sweetheart Abbey (Dumfries & Galloway) in the grave of his wife Devorguilla.

Beautiful painted panels adorn the 'Green Lady's room' at Crathes Castle (North East), and may have inspired the story of a ghost haunting the apartment. The manifestations are said to have begun after workmen dug up human bones from beneath the hearth.

This picture from *Costume of Great Britain* (1805) shows the traditional clothes of a Scottish shepherd. On the hill of Cairnshee (North East), shepherds and cattleherds used to light a bonfire every Midsummer Eve, reportedly 'to exorcise evil spirits'. In 1787 a local man left money in his will to keep up the custom, which lasted well into the twentieth century.

Witches are often imagined with broomsticks, as in this late eighteenth-century picture. At Delnabo (North East), two neighbours invited a young wife to join their nightly coven, and told her that if she left a broom in bed her husband would never notice the difference. Their own husbands, they said, had been happy with brooms in their beds for years.

'All hail, Macbeth!' An Austrian artist's impression from 1835 of the doomed warrior's first meeting with the witches shows a turbulent coastal landscape, although Shakespeare sets his scene on a 'blasted heath' near Forres (North East).

Now a ruin, Ardvreck Castle (Northern Highlands) was once home to a 'Wicked Lady' who spread rumours that a neighbouring woman had played her husband false. When the woman's brothers challenged the evil old lady, a black shadow rose from Loch Assynt to answer their questions, and finally both castle and lady were burnt in a consuming fire.

Smoo Cave (Northern Highlands) looks just the sort of place you might meet the Devil. Here the wizard Donald Duibheal Mackay escaped from Satan by the skin of his teeth, warned by his little dog.

Variously said to have housed a pair of giants, a dwarf, a hermit, or a troll, the Dwarfie Stane (Orkney & Shetland Islands) is in fact a chamber tomb, carved from sandstone about four thousand years ago.

The Ring of Brodgar at Stenness (Orkney & Shetland Islands) was once the site of betrothal ceremonies. Couples first visited the nearby Stones of Stenness, where the girl would pray, and then came here for the man to do likewise. Finally each pair would go to the Stone of Odin, now destroyed, and join hands through the hole in the monolith while they made their vows.

An impressive monument set up in 1812 commemorates a sixteenth-century murder and the decapitation of the seven slayers. According to some accounts their heads were carried to Inverness in a basket, but began to leap about and make a noise. To keep them quiet they were washed in a spring, thereafter known as the Well of the Heads (Southern Highlands).

Colourful legends and customs are connected with many of Scotland's Holy and Healing Wells. At this 'cloutie' or 'clootie' well near Munlochy, pilgrims hang rags (clouts) around the site as offerings, hoping for a cure or making a wish, and since it is thought to be unlucky to interfere with the rags, they are rarely removed.

Robert Burns (1759–96), Scotland's most famous poet, took inspiration from his country's history and legends. His ballad 'MacPherson's Farewell' (1788) revised lyrics attributed to James MacPherson, a riotous bandit with a taste for music who was executed at Banff (North East) in 1700. The robber's personality may have struck a chord with Burns, himself known to appreciate wine and women as well as song.

Do the bagpipes have their own language? At Trotternish (Western Isles), a piper once ventured into a deep cavern. Who or what he met there was never known, but the message of his music was understood by the listeners as a lament for his dreadful fate. For a long while it echoed from underground, until finally all was silent.

crime he had committed, and became consumed with remorse. The two infants, meanwhile, grew and flourished, and received the best education that was to be had.

> After a lapse of eighteen years, Lady Cheyne, with the concurrence of her husband, got up a grand entertainment at Christmas, to which all their friends and acquaintances throughout the county were invited. Among the female guests on this occasion were two young ladies, whose extraordinary beauty and elegance of manners excited the admiration of the company. Reginald in particular was greatly struck with their appearance, and as he had never seen them before, he asked his wife whose daughters they were? After some little hesitation, she said they were his own. This unexpected announcement affected him so much that, for a minute or two, he could not articulate a word. When he had recovered, he embraced his two daughters with the most affectionate tenderness, and finally gave way to his pent-up feelings in a flood of tears.

Whether this tale of the lost heiresses is strictly true or not, Reginald Cheyne, before his death in 1350, did indeed divide his estate between his two daughters, Marjory and Mary.

LOCH SHIN, SUTHERLAND

The folklore collector Alasdair Alpin MacGregor gathered much of his material 'when wandering at various times through the Highlands and Hebrides with a notebook and a camera'. His book *The Peat-Fire Flame* (1947) includes a story of Loch Shin, where the Devil was said to fish from a particular stone a few feet out in the water. One night a boy and girl were making their way home by the loch when on the very stone they saw an angler, and a yellow dog with him.

The girl told the lad to go and ask if the man had trout, and would he give them a couple for supper. Summoning up his courage, the boy approached quietly and asked the fisherman if he had caught anything. Before the other could answer, the girl interrupted and asked if they could have a trout or two from the loch.

At the sound of human voices, the angler rose from the stone and blazed in a flame that set fire to the heather and ran to the young couple's feet. Stricken with terror, they hurried home and told what they had seen. Everyone agreed that the angler had been none other than 'the Great Mischief Himself' – in other words, Satan.

LOCH SHURRERY, CAITHNESS

In his *Superstitions of the Islands and Highlands of Scotland* (1900) John Gregorson Campbell describes the Water-bull (*Tarbh Uisge*), which unlike the Water-horse (*Each Uisge*) was harmless. It was seldom seen, living in lonely little moorland lochs and only emerging at night, when it would be heard lowing and would come among the farmer's cattle. The offspring resulting from these night-time encounters were described as 'knife-eared' because their ears looked as if their tops had been cut off: the Water-bull itself had no ears at all, 'and hence its calves had only half ears'.

Writing in the 1930s, the Reverend George Sutherland gives an account of such a Water-bull in Loch Shurrery. A cattleman in the neighbourhood was tending his herds when he suddenly saw a great form rising to the surface of the water and turning its head this way and that, as if scanning its surroundings. It then swam ashore, shook itself violently, sending showers of water from its body, and gave a mighty bellow. Alarmed, the ordinary cows fled, led by the black bull of their herd, but when they had gone a little way off they stopped and allowed the bellowing beast to catch them up.

Their own black bull resented his intrusion and offered fight. The fighting had not gone far, however, till the black bull prudently retired from the fray, and went for safety to a distant hill top, bellowing furiously as he went. The water bull rounded up the herd and brought them back to their pasture ground, and was so gentle and friendly that himself and the cattle were soon on the best of terms. The cattleman followed the example of the black bull and made a bee-line to the nearest house. The water bull left several reminders of that day's visit. Long after, the owners of the cattle loved to point out to friends and visitors the crop-eared offspring of the water bull – the result of his visit on that day.

Sutherland adds that crosses between Water-bulls and land cattle were generally better stock than pure-bred land animals. Mixed-breed cattle descended from sea-cows were also said to live in the Hebrides, as described at AN T-ÒB (Western Isles).

LORD REAY'S GREEN TABLES, SUTHERLAND

Lord Reay's Green Tables is the name given to a series of flattish hillocks on the moors through which the road runs from Lairg to Tongue. Lord Reay, the magician otherwise known as Donald Duibheal Mackay, some of whose exploits are described at CREAG MHÓR AND CREAG BHEAG, is said to have called them up out of the peat after he had recklessly invited the Devil to dine. He did not want the Devil in his castle, for there, if he gave the Devil the place of honour, it would put the other guests in his power; on the other hand, he could scarcely insult Satan by seating him in second place. The ingenious Lord Reay solved the problem by creating a separate table for each guest out in the open air, so that no one dined with the Devil and the Devil was given no offence.

LOTH, SUTHERLAND

The last burning of a Scottish witch took place at Dornoch in 1727. She was Jonet or Janet Horne, an old woman from the parish of Loth. It was said, wrote Charles Kirkpatrick Sharpe in 1884, that after she was brought out to execution, the weather being very cold, 'she sat composedly warming herself by the fire prepared to consume her, while the other instruments of death were making ready.'

On a historical note, in England witches were generally hanged, the flames being inflicted only on those also accused of murdering their husbands (considered as high treason – like an attempt on the king's life). Scotland, however, like Germany, burned its witches. Often they were strangled first and only their dead bodies consigned to the flames, but some were burned 'quick', meaning alive.

Janet was accused among other things of having ridden her daughter, who had been turned into a pony and shod by the Devil, making the poor girl lame ever after in both her hands and her feet. This affliction (which sounds like arthritis) was inherited by the girl's son. The riding of a woman or more often a man magically metamorphosed into a horse or donkey is an old tale, going back at least to the second century CE when *The Golden Ass* was written by Lucius Apuleius, describing a man's transformation by a witch into the ass of the title.

In some stories the spell is effected by the victim's accepting cheese or eggs at the hands of the witch, but from the Middle Ages on it was mostly by means of a magic bridle. In a pamphlet of 1595, it is reported that a certain Judith Philips cheated a wealthy man who wanted to meet the Queen of the Fairies. She saddled, bridled, and rode him, then made off with his valuables as he waited in expectation of the queen. A magic bridle also appears in the legend set at YARROWFORD (Lothian & Borders), where a blacksmith's wife repeatedly changed a boy into a horse.

The theme is connected with the notion of being 'hag-ridden'. The sensation of pressure on the chest during nightmares is explained in popular tradition by the idea of a hag or witch sitting on the person's chest or belly, inflicting terrible dreams and leaving their victims exhausted. In Scandinavia, the tormentor is a supernatural being known as the Mara, meaning 'mare'. Real horses, too, might be ridden by witches on their nightly excursions, an explanation of night sweats (probably brought on by the animals having eaten too much green-stuff). To protect the stables, it was customary to hang up hag-stones, flints with natural holes in them.

See also WITCH-HUNTS (p. 270).

OUSDALE, LANGWELL, CAITHNESS

A curious piece of cryptozoology is attached to Ousdale. The Scottish physician-turned-naturalist Sir Robert Sibbald (1641–1722) describes a creature he calls the Lavellan (Gaelic *la-bhallan*), peculiar to the far north, which was reputed to be able to harm cattle from forty yards away (37 m). He writes:

Monster or legend? The breath of the water-shrew or Lavellan was rumoured to be fatal, the only remedy being to drink water in which its head had been boiled.

Lavellan, Animal in Cathanesiâ frequens, in Aquis degit, capite Mustelae sylvestri simile, ejusdemque coloris Bestia est. Halitu Bestiis nocet. Remedium autem est, si de aquâ bibant, in quâ ejus caput coctum sit.

Translated, this means roughly: 'Lavellan, an animal numerous in Caithness, is a wild beast that lives in the rivers, having a head like that of a woodland weasel, and being of the same colour. The breath of these creatures is fatal. However, there is a remedy – drinking some of the water in which its head is cooked.'

You might think from this that the Lavellan was a formidable monster. However, in 1769 the Welsh traveller and naturalist Thomas Pennant visited 'Ausdale', where he formed a notion of what the Lavellan was – 'from description, I suspect [it] to be the Water Shrew-mouse . . . I believe it to be the same animal which in *Sutherland* is called the Water Mole.'

While it is true that the saliva of the water-shrew (*Neomys fodiens*) is toxic, enabling it to kill small creatures with a bite and creating a burning sensation on a human hand, it could not do any serious harm to something as large as a cow even at close range, let alone from a distance: the animal is only about 10 cm long (less than 4 inches). This is no doubt why 'Rob Donn', the famous eighteenth-century bard of REAY, mentions the tradition in a satirical song, 'Mac Rorie's Breeches' (translated from the Gaelic by Alexander Carmichael in 1900), in which the poet warns against allowing the trouserless man into the countryside lest the water-shrew should come and strike him:

> Do not allow him from townland,
> To moorland nor woodland,
> Lest the water-mole should come
> And rub on him.

He is poking fun at a large legend about a tiny beast.

OYKELL BRIDGE, SUTHERLAND

The Scandinavian history of Sutherland is attested by the name of the district – Old Norse Suðrland, 'the south land' – south, that is, from the point of view of the Norsemen of Orkney and Caithness. An episode from the epic past is recorded in the Orkneyinga Saga, written by an Icelander probably around 1200, where it is said that Sigurd Eysteinsson the Powerful, Earl of Orkney, met his end in a curious fashion.

In the ninth century, control of Orkney and Shetland was given to Sigurd by his brother Rognvald, Earl of More in Norway, and he had the title of earl bestowed on him by King Harald Fine-Hair. Joining forces with Thorsteinn the Red, Sigurd conquered the whole of Caithness, as well as much of Argyllshire, Moray, and Ross and Cromarty, and in about 890 it was arranged that he would come to a certain place to negotiate with Mælbrigt, Earl of the Scots. Neither side trusted the other, and the upshot was a battle. The conflict was fierce and before long Mælbrigt and all his men were dead. Sigurd had their heads strapped to the saddles of his troops as a mark of triumph, and from his own saddle hung the head of Mælbrigt, whose nickname was Tonn ('tooth') on account of a fang that projected from his mouth. As Sigurd spurred his horse, this tooth pierced the calf of his leg; the wound swelled and grew very painful, and from this soon came his death.

Either Mælbrigt or Sigurd is said to have been buried in a mound on the banks of the River Oykell. Some accounts say that Sigurd got nearly as far as Dornoch before he collapsed, and was interred at Cyderhall, known as late as 1230 as Siwardhoth or Siward's Howe.

REAY, CAITHNESS

By no means all local legends preserved in the north concern the supernatural. The eighteenth-century bard Robert Mackay, known as 'Rob Donn', was well known in his lifetime and remembered long afterwards; a snippet of his poetry is given in translation at OUSDALE.

A tale told in 1829, based on information given by Rob's surviving daughter, relates how Rob was accused of poaching and appeared before Mr Mackay of Bighouse, Lord Reay's man of business. (This is of course a much later Lord Reay than the magician Donald Duibheal Mackay, whose career is described at CREAG MHÓR AND CREAG BHEAG.) When Rob offered as security for his future good behaviour Mr Mackay's own son, a suggestion which was declined, he said sarcastically, 'Thanks be to Him who refuses not His Son as surety even for the chief of Sinners!'

The anecdote was too good to be forgotten, and was repeated and improved on. In a version related to John Dixon by James Mackenzie in 1886, it is Lord Reay himself who sends for Rob, and asks him to find a security that he will kill no more deer.

Leaving the room, Rob meets Lord Reay's son:

> 'Will you,' said Rob to the boy, 'become security for me that I will not kill more deer on your father's property?' 'Yes,' replied the boy. Rob caught him by the hand and took him to Lord Reay. 'Is that your security, Robert?' said his lordship. 'Yes,' said Robert, 'will you not take him?' 'No, I will not,' answered his lordship. 'It is very strange,' replied Rob, 'that you will not take your own son as security for one man, when God took his own Son for all the world's security.'

RIVER SHIN, SUTHERLAND

Otta Swire, writing in 1963, gives a sentimental religious tale concerning the River Shin, which flows from the foot of Loch Shin to Invershin, north-west of Bonar Bridge. A couple of miles from the river's mouth are the Falls of Shin, up which salmon can still be seen leaping – a dramatic spectacle – and it is them that the story concerns.

It is said that the river never freezes and the reason for this is that, one clear moonlit winter's night, Christ came walking along the river, pleased by its beauty and

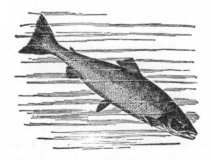

According to legend, Christ blessed the River Shin for the sake of the salmon which lived there.

that of the landscape around. Then he noticed that the fish in the river were troubled by something. Calling a large salmon to him, he asked what the matter was, and the salmon answered that they could smell a black frost coming and they were worried that the river, their home, might freeze. Against that they had no defence. Taking pity on the salmon, Christ stretched his hands over the river and blessed it, saying, 'The waters of this river will never freeze again.' And since that day, no one has ever known the River Shin to freeze.

SANDWOOD BAY, CAPE WRATH, SUTHERLAND

Sandwood Bay, an isolated beach on Sutherland's north-west coast, is haunted by the ghost of a sailor, as testified by several witnesses in the 1940s and '50s. Ronald Macdonald Robertson met some of those concerned, and tells their stories in his *Selected Highland Folktales* (1961).

One night Sandy Gunn, a small landholder on the Kinlochbervie estate, was out with two friends looking for a missing sheep. On the deserted beach they saw in the moonlight a man with hairy beard and whiskers. He was utterly unknown to them. Two weeks later, a boat was wrecked off the bay and the body of one of the crew was washed up just between the two rocks where the man had been seen. Gunn and his two friends immediately recognised the corpse as their stranger. The date of this first apparition – in this case a wraith of one about to die, rather than the ghost of one already dead – is not given, but must have been before December 1944 since Robertson records this as being when Sandy Gunn himself died.

Later came a manifestation on 8 August

1949, when a party of visitors on a fishing expedition walked across the dunes, led by a gillie from the Garbet Hotel in Kinlochbervie. A 'gillie' or 'ghillie' was originally a Highland chief's attendant, and the word is now used for a man accompanying huntsmen or anglers: this was therefore a local resident who knew the territory and might have heard about Sandy Gunn's experience, although Robertson does not mention that possibility. All members of the party saw a man in sailor's cap and tunic, but when the gillie approached he found no one there, nor even any prints in the sand. Similarly, in July 1953, some visitors from Edinburgh were having a picnic near the bay when they saw a big bearded sailor who then vanished, leaving no footprints behind him.

A further incident, undated, occurred when a crofter and his son were gathering firewood from the beach as daylight faded. Their horse became uneasy, and suddenly a man in seaman's uniform appeared and shouted at them to leave his property alone. Terrified, they dropped the wood and fled, but retained a clear impression of the man with his beard, boots, cap, and brass-buttoned tunic.

These occurrences might be related to the haunting of Sandwood Cottage, a house that was ruined by the time Robertson wrote of it. Sandy Gunn – the same man to whom the mysterious 'sailor' first appeared – once spent a night there and heard footsteps pacing from room to room, though 'perfectly convinced that there was no living creature – human or animal – with him in the cottage that night'. Robertson ends his story of the uncanny happenings associated with Sandwood Bay by saying that an 'Edinburgh citizen of high integrity' was sent a piece of wood from the staircase of Sandwood Cottage, and strange phenomena followed in her own house, including falling china, thumps and knockings by night, and the sound of footsteps.

> On one occasion she sensed a strong smell of alcohol and tobacco-smoke, and caught the dim outline of a bearded sailor, who shook the curtains violently before vanishing.

Robertson says that the lady in question had no knowledge of the hauntings when she received the piece of wood, but one wonders why in that case she wanted the souvenir. And how did she recognise the 'dim outline' as that of a sailor? This sort of embroidery tends to devalue an account, suggesting details supplied by hindsight rather than direct experience.

SCRABSTER, CAITHNESS

There are many stories throughout the British Isles dealing with the phenomenon known as 'repercussion', whereby wounds inflicted on a witch who has assumed the shape of an animal will remain on her body when she returns to human form. Some such tales, like that set at LOCH BAILE A' GHOBHAINN (Argyllshire & Islands), are humorously macabre – not so this chilling account from the eighteenth-century historical records of Thurso.

On 24 March 1719, the sheriff-depute of Caithness reported the following to Robert Dundas of Arniston, the king's advocate. In December of the previous year, William Montgomerie or Montgomery, a mason of Burnside, Scrabster, petitioned the sheriff, saying that his house had been several times so infested with cats that it was unsafe for himself and his family to stay there, and the servant had panicked because 'The catts were speaking among themselves.'

Driven to desperate measures, Montgomerie

had killed two of the cats, and thought he had wounded more of them. On 12 February, the sheriff-depute received word that:

> . . . one Margaret Nin-Gilbert, in Owst, living about ane mile and ane half distant from Montgomery's house, was seen by some of her neighbours to drop at her own door one of her leggs from the midle, and she being under bad fame before for witchcraft, the legg, black and putrified, was brought to me; and immediately thereafter I ordered her to be apprehended and incarcerated . . .

On being questioned, Margaret Nin-Gilbert confessed that she had been in compact with the Devil. Her statement implicated several others, who were then

Cats were traditionally associated with witchcraft. In the early eighteenth century a mason from Scrabster complained that his house was infested with the animals, which were 'speaking among themselves'.

seized and imprisoned, 'except two, who died the night of the encounter with the catts in Montgomerie's house, or a few days therafter'. Margaret Nin-Gilbert herself died in prison about two weeks after her first confession.

By this time, sick and no doubt nearly crazed, she had declared that the Devil had appeared to her 'in the likeness of a great black horse, and other times riding on a black horse, and that he appeared sometimes in the likeness of a black cloud, and sometimes like a black hen'. She herself had visited Montgomerie's house in the shape of a cat, and he 'had broke her legg either by the durk or ax, which legg since has fallen off'.

In the late eighteenth century, the traveller Thomas Pennant heard a similar tale of a young man in Thurso who was tormented by witches in the form of cats. Eventually he decided to give battle, and when they next attacked he slashed to right and left with his sword and cut off what he believed to be a cat's leg. He said that they never troubled him again, but that he could not tell what part of the witch would have been wounded had he cut off the cat's tail. Pennant regarded this story as probably 'the last instance of national credulity', but it is likely that it was inspired by the occurrences reported at Scrabster.

Another case from the Thurso district is mentioned in connection with this tale, dealing with a maker of illicit whisky who was having problems with the fermentation of his liquor. He had noticed that at times a strange cat would enter and sit on the edge of tub, dip in her paw and then lick it. He became certain it must be a witch, so, when next she appeared, he grabbed a scythe and cut off one of her paws, which dropped into the tub. When the vessel was emptied, out fell a human hand. Enquiries were made, and it was discovered that a certain old woman had suddenly taken to her bed. He went to see her and offered to shake her hand, but she said that she had burned it and had it well wrapped up. The case was brought before a commission of local ministers and officials, and the folklorist Alexander Polson commented in 1907 that the evidence 'revealed a humiliating amount of superstition'.

See also WITCH-HUNTS (p. 270).

SMOO CAVE, DURNESS, SUTHERLAND

Even after he had escaped from the Black School at Padua, as told at CREAG MHÓR AND CREAG BHEAG, Donald Duibheal Mackay was still pursued by his old master. One day Mackay went to explore the great Smoo Cave, a huge limestone cavern near the north coast, south-east of Durness – but the Devil got news of his intentions and was waiting for him there. Some say that Mackay fled, leaving his horse's hoofmarks by the cave entrance. In Otta Swire's 1963 account, however, Mackay had reached the second cavern when his dog, who had raced ahead of him into the third and innermost chamber, came back 'howling and hairless', warning Mackay who he could expect to see if he went further. Just at this moment, dawn broke and the sound of cockcrow was heard. The Devil and the three witches who were with him realised their time on earth was up, blew holes in the roof, and escaped: this is said to be the origin of the holes through which the Smoo Burn runs into the caverns.

The unfortunate dog's experience is like that of the piper's hound at CLACH-THOLL (Argyllshire & Islands), whose master set out to explore a subterranean passage and was never seen again. In many such sto-

ries the dogs alone escape but with all their hair singed off, a sure sign of a fiery diabolical encounter. It is interesting that here the Devil, like the ghost of Hamlet's father, is dismissed from the world by 'the bird of dawning', the cock announcing the end of night. Nor is this the only Shakespearean echo sounded: the 'three witches' accompanying the Devil are probably an addition with a literary inspiration.

THURSO, CAITHNESS

In his *History of Caithness* (1861), James Calder writes that it was not until 1800 that a bridge was built across the river at Thurso. Before that time people either crossed in a little skiff or forded the river, both of which could be dangerous in bad weather, and in 1756 a merchant named Richard Sinclair was drowned. Associated with his death was a classic instance of SECOND SIGHT (p. 474), recorded in 1763 in *A Treatise on the Second Sight, Dreams and Apparitions*:

In the [year] 1756, RICHARD SINCLAIR, then a merchant in the town of *Thurso*, returning at even home with his servant, as they came to the river close by the town, found it was swelled by a fall of rain, and much increased by the tide, which was in: the latter seemed averse to ford, which his master observing, lighted and gave him his own horse, and mounted his servant's horse, with which having entered the river, was soon carried by the flood out of his saddle, and was drowned. His wife knowing nothing then of the matter, as she was going from one room to another in her own house, saw Mr *Sinclair* go up the stair to his own room, and called to a servant-maid to bring him a candle and make up the fire; but after the servant had brought the light in great haste, found no person within: In less than an hour the noise was through the town, that the gentleman was drowned.

'I had this account from a person that came to the town next day,' adds the writer.

The appearance of someone's wraith as announcement of his or her death is a widespread theme in the annals of the supernatural. In this case Mistress Sinclair might not have been the only person gifted with the Sight: there is some ambiguity about what happened at the ford, and it may be that Sinclair's servant too had a premonition, or that his horse did. If it was the servant's horse giving trouble, the master might have decided that he (perhaps a more experienced rider) could control it better. This interpretation would fit the common belief that animals are more psychically sensitive than humans.

See also ANNANDALE (Dumfries & Galloway).

TONGUE, SUTHERLAND

A doctor named Farquhar once lived at Tongue in Sutherland. According to an oral tradition recorded by John Gregorson Campbell in *Superstitions of the Highlands and Islands of Scotland* (1900), he gained his talent for healing after meeting a stranger who showed great interest in the walking stick he carried. He asked Farquhar to go to the tree from which the stick had been cut, and look in a hole beneath the tree's roots where he would find a white serpent. This he was to boil, and then give the resulting broth, without touching it, to the stranger. Although he carried out his instructions, Farquhar happened to touch the hot juice with his finger, scalding himself, and then put his finger in his mouth. 'From that moment he acquired his unrivalled skill as a physician, and the juice lost its virtue.'

The burnt finger in the mouth that con-

fers a gift is a tale also told of FINGAL (p. 10). As well as legend, however, the story contains echoes of traditional folk medicine. By way of background, Campbell mentions a man in Applecross (Ross and Cromarty) who used to cure epilepsy with water in which he kept a live snake, and he also notes that one cure for the sting of a serpent was the water in which the head of another snake was put, like the remedy for the venomous breath of the 'Lavellan' reported at OUSDALE.

TONGUE HOUSE, SUTHERLAND

Many, many years ago, in the household of Lord Reay was a talented piper who could play a pibroch (set of variations) no other person knew. The piper had a son who was also a good musician, but the father would never play the pibroch all through if he knew the son could be listening.

Then one day Lord Reay asked for a performance of the pibroch for the distinguished guests then assembled at Tongue House. Thinking his son was away on the hill, the old man played his pibroch in front of the windows. But his son was not on the hill – he was working in the garden, where he heard and memorised the notes.

When the pibroch was done, the piper was summoned to the drawing room to take a dram with the company and left his pipes lying on a bench. His son took them up and played the pibroch perfectly: his father was so furious that he rushed outside, seized the chanter, and broke it against the wall. At once a swarm of black beetles came and gobbled up the bits and then disappeared as fast as they had arrived.

This Lord Reay was none other than the magician Donald Duibheal Mackay. The piper had learned the pibroch from the Devil, when his master was studying the Black Arts in Italy, and had presumably acquired the magic chanter from the same source. As the tune could only be played on that particular instrument, it is now lost.

See also CREAG MHÓR AND CREAG BHEAG; DUNNET SANDS; LORD REAY'S GREEN TABLES; SMOO CAVE.

UAIGH DHIARMAID, TONGUE, SUTHERLAND

The Arthurian narrative of Tristan and Iseult is based on the Irish tale of Diarmaid and Grainne, known from the ninth century. Diarmaid was the nephew of the great chief Fionn mac Cumhaill, and Grainne was Fionn's young wife. The two of them came under an enchantment, fell in love, and eloped.

In Scottish legend Fionn became FINGAL (p. 10), and traditions of Diarmaid or Diarmid too were widely known in Scotland. More than one place claims to be his burial-ground: there is a Diarmaid's Grave in Argyllshire, and another in Tongue with the Gaelic name Uaigh Dhiarmaid ('Diarmaid's Grave'), although archaeologists now believe this to be a clearance heap rather than a cairn as was evidently once supposed. The tale attached to it is told in an 1888 article on Sutherland folklore:

> Once upon a time there was a king in Sutherland whose lands were ravaged by a boar of great size and ferocity. This boar had a den, or cave, in Ben Laighal, and that was full of the bones of cattle and of men.

The king swore that he would give his daughter to the man who should rid the country of the monster, which had great white tusks, bristles a foot long, and eyes glowing red like fire. The task proved beyond Fingal or Ossian or any other hero, until Diarmaid arrived. Seeing the king's daughter, he said to himself that she must be his.

> Before the dawn of next day he had gone forth. He reached the boar's den and saw the monster lying, like a boat lies on the shore, long and broad and black. Drawing a shot from his bow he killed it on the spot. All the king's servants turned out and dragged the monster home with shouting. The king's daughter stood in the gate, like a May-morning, and smiling. But the king's heart was evil, and his face grew dark. Now that the boar was dead he would go back from his word, but he dared not do so openly. So he said to Diarmid that he should not have his daughter to wife till he had measured the body of his foe, by pacing it from snout to tail, and also backwards from tail to snout.

Diarmaid said he would gladly do so. He paced the beast from head to tail without taking any harm, but when he came to measure it backwards his bare foot was pierced by one of the boar's huge bristles. That night Diarmaid sickened and died, and he was buried beside the boar's den.

Versions of this legend are widely told, and it is often reported that Diarmaid's uncle Fionn engineered his death. The crest of the Campbells, who claim descent from Diarmaid, is said to commemorate the victory over the boar. In Welsh and Breton romance, Tristan too was said to have fought a monster (usually a dragon) to win Iseult, while the warrior wounded and slain by his dead foe has Scandinavian parallels, for instance in the story told of Earl Sigurd at OYKELL BRIDGE.

The Wolf Stone, Lothbeg, near Brora, Sutherland

At Lothbeg, on the east coast of Sutherland between Helmsdale and Brora, is the Wolf Stone. According to its inscription, it marks the place near which 'the last wolf in Sutherland' was killed by the hunter Polson in or about 1700.

A detailed account of the episode is given by William Scrope in *The Art of Deer Stalking* (1839). By the end of the seventeenth century, people supposed that wolves were already extinct in the area; nevertheless, a time came when ravages were committed among the flocks, and howling had been heard at night. The local inhabitants turned out in force to scour the countryside, but they found nothing until a man named Polson from Wester Helmsdale went to search around Glen Loth. He took with him only two young lads, one of them his son, the other a vigorous herd boy.

Polson was an old and experienced hunter. Following his instinct, he went straight to the rugged terrain around the Sledale burn. Here, after closely scrutinising the place, he found a fissure in a jumble of rocks which he guessed might lead to a cavern in which the wolf had its lair.

A stone at Lothbeg records the killing of the last wolf in Sutherland in about 1700.

Nothing happened when stones were thrown down between the rocks, and Polson then kept guard while the two lads squeezed through the gap. At the end of a narrow passage they found a small cavern. The floor was covered in animal bones, feathers, and eggshells, and here too were five or six lively little wolf cubs. The lads called up this news to Polson in some trepidation, and were told to destroy them.

As he heard the feeble howls of the dying cubs, Polson saw a full-grown wolf, evidently the mother, which had approached unobserved. Maddened by the cries of her young, she leaped forward, and Polson, who had propped his gun against a rock when helping the boys through the crack, instinctively threw himself on her and caught her by her long bushy tail. Her forequarters were already in the fissure, and so as not to alarm the boys, he silently wound the tail round his left arm and hung on tight, while the mother wolf twisted and scrabbled with all her strength to get down and save her babies.

In the midst of this singular struggle . . . his son within the cave, finding the light excluded from above for so long a space, asked in Gaelic and in an abrupt tone, 'Father, what is keeping the light from us?' 'If the root of the tail breaks,' replied he, 'you will soon know that.' Before long, however, the man contrived to get hold of his hunting knife and stabbed the wolf in the most vital parts he could reach. The enraged animal now attempted to turn and face her foe, but the hole was too narrow to allow of this; and when Polson saw his danger he squeezed her forward, keeping her jammed in, whilst he repeated his stabs as rapidly as he could, until the animal, being mortally wounded, was easily dragged back and finished.

Another version of this tale, told in Gaelic by the Duke of Sutherland's head forester in 1848 to John Francis Campbell, does not mention the hunter Polson. It says that a woman living in a little town in Sutherland lost one of her children, and though people searched the hills for three days they could not find him. After they had given up looking, a young lad coming home late past a big cairn of stones heard a child crying, and went up to the cairn, where in a hole under a big stone he saw the boy and two young wolves with him. Frightened that the mother wolf would come, he went home to the town, and in the morning came back with two others to the hole. The story then proceeds much as in the Polson version, and ends with the wolf and her young ones being killed, and the boy being taken home to his mother. According to the forester the boy's family were alive in his grandfather's time, and it was said that they were never like other people.

Campbell comments on the likeness of this to the story of Romulus and Remus being suckled by wolves, and mentions the evidence that wolves really carry off and suckle children. Several reports were published in the nineteenth century of feral children raised by wolves, particularly in India. W. H. Sleeman, an English soldier, wrote 'An Account of Wolves Nurturing Children in their Dens', mentioning an incident of February 1847 in which a boy was discovered at Sultanpoor living in a wolves' lair, and such cases provided inspiration for Rudyard Kipling's *Jungle Book* (1894), in which Mowgli dwells happily for years with the wolves.

See also HANDA.

ORKNEY & SHETLAND ISLANDS

BRINDISTER, MAINLAND, SHETLAND

A farmer of Brindister had not yet cut his corn, although it was late in the season, and he remarked one evening that he would give his best ox to have his crop safely harvested. Not long after, a friend of his passed his farm one night, and was surprised to see a couple working in the cornfield and chanting strange words. He went at once to tell the farmer, who realised that the people in his field must be trows who would expect his ox in payment for their work. His friend, however, armed himself with an axe, hid himself above the stable door, and struck down the male trow when he arrived to take the ox.

'It is said that the blood from the trow ran down over the rigs [fields] and after that the corn on the land used to grow red,' concludes this story, narrated by William Laurenson of Aith, Fetlar. As the folklorist Katharine Briggs remarks, 'It is surprising that this ruthless murder and bargain-breaking did not entail a fiercer punishment.'

In a similar story told of Windhouse on Yell, the farmer did not have such a crafty or violent friend. Having wished that his field was harvested even if it cost him the best ox in his possession, he got up next morning to find the field cut and the ox dead.

See also THE GREY NEIGHBOURS (p. 410).

BROCH OF HOULLAND, MAINLAND, SHETLAND

See THE TROWIE TUNES OF SHETLAND (p. 390).

BURNSIDE, CULLIVOE, YELL, SHETLAND

A tale of 'the last of the trows' was recorded in 1978, told by Tom Tulloch of North Yell. 'This was one of the last, if not the last trowie lived at Yell,' he begins; 'it was in a knowe at Burnside in Cullivoe.'

There was at that time a famous fiddler in Cullivoe, Rabbie Anderson, and every year he would be invited by the trows to play to them on Old Yule Eve. He knew better than to eat or drink anything while he was with them, and he never told anyone else where he went on that night, but it was noticed that everything always went well with him, and whatever he undertook was successful.

And then there was one winter that he never saw anything of the trows – they never met him or invited him. Rabbie was worried at this for he was wondering how it would affect his prosperity in the coming year. So one night getting on for Yule he summoned up his courage and went to the trowie hill.

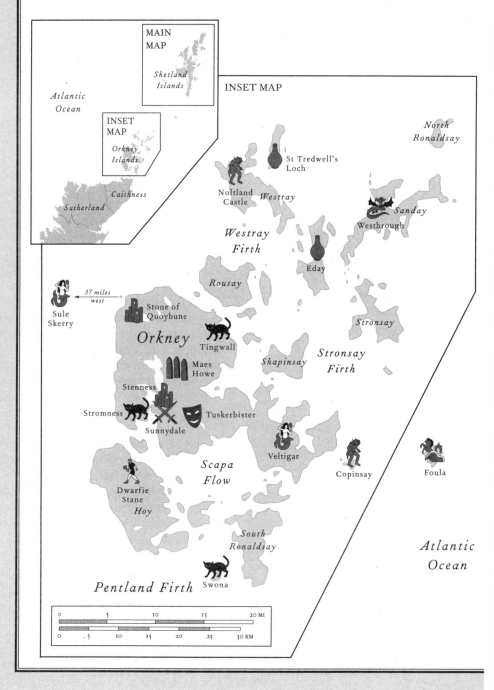

ORKNEY & SHETLAND ISLANDS

MAIN
MAP

*Shetland
Islands*

INSET MAP

*Atlantic
Ocean*

INSET
MAP

*Orkney
Islands*

Caithness

Sutherland

*North
Ronaldsay*

St Tredwell's
Loch

Noltland
Castle

Westray

Sanday

Westbrough

*Westray
Firth*

Eday

Rousay

Stronsay

Stone of
Quoybune

37 miles
west

Sule
Skerry

Orkney

Tingwall

Maes
Howe

Shapinsay

*Stronsay
Firth*

Stenness

Stromness

Tuskerbister

Sunnydale

Veltigar

Copinsay

Foula

*Scapa
Flow*

Dwarfie
Stane

Hoy

*South
Ronaldsay*

Swona

Pentland Firth

*Atlantic
Ocean*

0	5	10	15	20 MI
0	5	10	15	20	25	30 KM

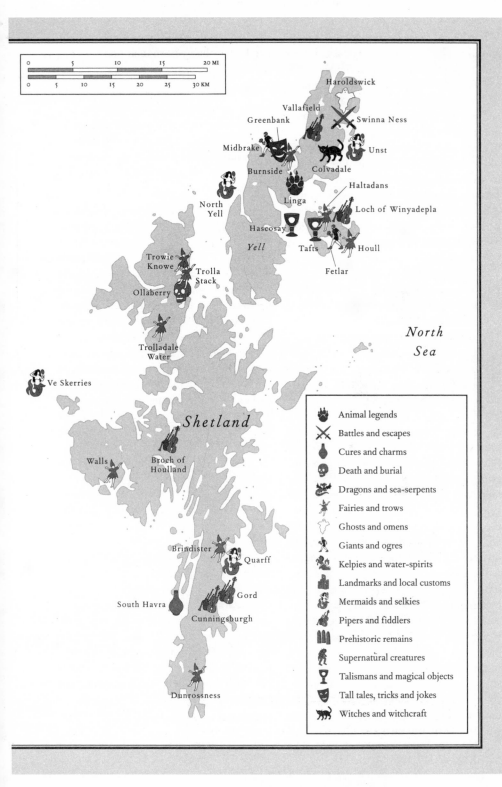

Haroldswick

Vallafield

Greenbank · · · · · · · Swinna Ness

Midbrake · · · · · · · Unst

Burnside · · · Colvadale

Linga · · · Haltadans

North Yell · · · Loch of Winyadepla

Hascosay

Yell

Tafts · · · Houll

Fetlar

Trowie Knowe

Trolla Stack

Ollaberry

Trolladale Water

Ve Skerries

North Sea

Shetland

Walls · · · Broch of Houlland

Brindister · · · Quarff

Gord

South Havra

Cunningsburgh

Dunrossness

Scale	
0 5 10 15 20 MI	
0 5 10 15 20 25 30 KM	

Animal legends
Battles and escapes
Cures and charms
Death and burial
Dragons and sea-serpents
Fairies and trows
Ghosts and omens
Giants and ogres
Kelpies and water-spirits
Landmarks and local customs
Mermaids and selkies
Pipers and fiddlers
Prehistoric remains
Supernatural creatures
Talismans and magical objects
Tall tales, tricks and jokes
Witches and witchcraft

When he got there he saw nobody except an old woman by the fire. He asked what had happened to all the rest of the trows, and she said he might well ask – a minister had come to Cullivoe, and he had preached and prayed so much that the trows could not stand it: 'they got no peace and all had to clear out to Faeroe.' She felt she was too old to start all over again in a new place, so she had stayed where she was. 'And that was the last of the trows that was ever told about in North Yell.' The minister in question was supposed to be the evangelical preacher James Ingram, who lived to the age of 103.

Tales of 'the last of the fairies' or 'the fairies' farewell' are told in many places, as for instance at BURROW HEAD FORTS (Dumfries & Galloway).

See also THE GREY NEIGHBOURS (p. 410).

COLVADALE, UNST, SHETLAND

A fishing boat started one summer morning from the Broch of Colviedell (Colvadale), intending to remain at sea for two days. But the men had scarcely launched their craft when a white gull came hovering overhead, and as soon as the boat was fairly under way the bird alighted on the rigging. Folding its wings, it fixed its dark eyes upon the crew and sat motionless overhead. Night came down, but still the bird remained watching the fishermen at their work. About midnight a sudden squall came on, which grew into a storm that lasted two nights and a day; during all that time the little boat lay tossing among the billows, with the white bird sitting upon the mast. When the storm abated the boat made for land, and not until she reached shore did the bird take wing. One of the men said that the bird should be given the best of their fish, since she had never left them in their trouble, and had probably been their preservation:

'. . . for yesterday, when we were in the heart of the storm, I saw an old woman sitting on the water, a little way from the boat, and *she appeared not good*. But of course she had no power to come nearer us while the bird stayed by us. No doubt *she* was a witch, and the bird was a good spirit.'

This story is told in *The Home of a Naturalist* (1888), a memoir by the Reverend Biot Edmonston and his sister Jessie Saxby of their life in the Shetlands. Saxby, who wrote other works on folklore, was greatly interested in magical practice, and wanted to know how a woman became a witch. She was told by more than one person that the only rite necessary was for the candidate to wait for a full moon, go alone to the seashore at midnight, and lie down on the beach below the flood-tide mark. She had to put her left hand under the soles of her feet and her right hand on top of her head and repeat three times, 'The muckle maister Deil tak what's atween dis twa haunds.' The Devil then appeared and settled the bargain by shaking hands. Once the ceremony had been performed, there was no retracting: the woman was the Devil's servant, and he gave her power on land and sea.

One safeguard against the malice of a witch was to flyte with (scold) them, but more effectual was to scratch them 'abune der breath' – literally 'above the breath', and in practice usually on the forehead. Faith in this protection was widespread: Saxby and Edmonston were told of a man who scratched his cousin's brow, believing her to be a witch, and in TORPHICHEN (Lothian & Borders) a farmer gashed a beggar with a knife to remove her curse on his house.

See also WITCH-HUNTS (p. 270).

COPINSAY, ORKNEY

In his *Folklore of Orkney and Shetland* (1975), Ernest Marwick says that the little island of Copinsay once had a strange inhabitant 'known, for lack of a better name, as a brownie'. Now a bird sanctuary, the island is so small that when it was farmed it only had a single tenant. This solitary farmer had just gone to bed one night when he saw in the corner an ugly naked creature with a wet, leathery, slightly phosphorescent skin:

> This being was somewhat smaller than a man, and much grosser in its features: the crown of its head was flat and bald; instead of hair and beard it had wet, slimy seaweed.

The farmer tried to eject the creature, using a book of psalms, a steel razor, an iron crook, and finally his fists. None of this had any effect, and when the thing continued to grin and make friendly gestures the man tried to understand what it was saying. It told him its name was Hughbo; it had always lived in the sea, but now it wanted to stay on land and would work for its keep. The farmer agreed, and Hughbo became a valued servant.

Some time later, the farmer married. He had carefully prepared his bride to meet Hughbo, and far from being frightened she became very fond of him – so fond that she worried about him getting cold in the night. 'She was also worried by the extent of his nakedness, which was massive and unashamed.' Accordingly she made him a warm cloak and hood and left the garment out for him, with the usual sad result. Instead of going about his accustomed tasks, Hughbo howled dismally:

> 'Hughbo's gotten cloak and huid,
> So Hughbo can do no more guid.'

He rushed out into the darkness and was seen no more. This is of course typical Brownie behaviour, and the rhyme is a clear echo of that used at GLENDEVON (Central & Perthshire), but the name 'Hughbo' points in a different direction. In Old Norse, *haug-búi* or *haug-búinn* is a 'mound-dweller', and from this came the *hogboy* or *hogboon*, once the prevalent supernatural being of the Orkney and Shetland Islands though now largely forgotten. 'At one time,' writes Marwick, 'almost every mound in Orkney had its hogboon,' and he quotes a late nineteenth-century mention of the Hogboy said to inhabit Maes Howe.

The Hogboy insisted on offerings such as milk and ale being poured over his mound. In the light of all this, it is suggestive to read John Brand, minister of Borrowstounness (Bo'ness, as it is now usually known), writing in 1701 that every family in Orkney and Shetland had a Brownie or evil spirit to whom it was customary to give a 'sacrifice' of buttermilk or unfermented malt:

> My Informer a Minister in the County told me, that he had conversed with an old Man, who when young used to Brew, and sometimes read upon his Bible, to whom an old Woman in the House said, that Brouny was displeased with that Book he read upon, which if he continued to do, they would get no more service of Brouny.

The man refused either to give up his Bible or to leave an offering for the Brownie. The first and second brewings of his beer turned out badly, but the third was very good, and after that the Brownie left the household alone.

Brand might have heard stories of the Hogboy and linked them to the Brownie, a creature which would have been more familiar to a mainland Scot.

CUNNINGSBURGH, MAINLAND, SHETLAND

See THE TROWIE TUNES OF SHETLAND (p. 390).

DUNROSSNESS, MAINLAND, SHETLAND

Some trowie tales from Dunrossness were printed in the 1950s in the *Shetland Folk Book*. The editor, E. S. R. Tait, knew the narrator, Kirrsie Smith, and comments that she 'was surely one of the last persons in Shetland to have a firm belief in trows'. One of her stories tells how the trows bath their babies: 'Aks you Mistress Jemson an' shø'll tell you 'ats no fabble,' begins Kirrsie ('Ask Mrs Jemson and she'll tell you that's no fable').

When Mrs Jemson was little she went to stay with her Aunt Keatie. There was a keg of water kept in the house, which was filled every afternoon from the nearby well, but when her aunt asked her to get some water, she found the keg was dry. The trows had taken the water to wash their children, declared Kirrsie: they liked water from the spring best, but if the water had been used to make bland (a mixture of water and whey, often drunk in the islands) then they would just use the bland to bath their babies.

A similar tradition is mentioned by John Gregorson Campbell at LARGS (Glasgow & Ayrshire), and a Shetland tale of the same sort is told by Biot Edmonston and Jessie Saxby in 1888. One Saturday night a boy was sleeping by the fireplace, as his bed was needed for some unexpected guests. Now the trows require that every hearth shall be swept clean on Saturday evening, that no one shall go near it during the night, and above all that plenty of clean water must be in the house. All these things had been neglected, so when the trows came they were enraged. The noise they made awakened the boy:

> What should he see but two Trow-wives seating themselves not far from where he lay. One carried a baby, the loveliest little creature that ever was seen, only that it had three eyes instead of two – the extra one being in the middle of the forehead.

The trows looked for water but found none, so they took some sowans (water used to soak oatmeal) from a keg, put it in a basin, and washed in it first their baby and then the baby's clothes. After that they poured it back into the keg, saying that was all the owners deserved for not having clean water in the house.

Having finished their washing they spread the clothes on their feet and stretched them out to the fire to dry. The boy knew they couldn't leave as long as he kept his eyes on them, so he watched them closely for so long that they began to get nervous. One of them stuck the tongs in the flames until the metal glowed red, then approached the boy and pointed the tongs at his eyes, grinning hideously. He blinked and screamed, and the trows fled while he had his eyes shut.

When the family went to the keg for their sowans in the morning, they found nothing there but dirty water.

See also THE GREY NEIGHBOURS (p. 410).

DWARFIE STANE, HOY, ORKNEY

Rock-cut chamber tombs are reasonably common in the Mediterranean, but the only one in Britain is to be found on Hoy. The massive sandstone block was carved out around 4,000 years ago, forming a space that has been said to look like a bedroom with a hole in the top. The legend in the late sixteenth century was that one giant was imprisoned here by another and gnawed his way out through the roof, though when Martin Martin visited the site around a hundred years later he heard the tradition that a giant couple had found shelter here. His description is most domestic:

> . . . at one of the ends within this Stone there is cut out a Bed and Pillow, capable of two Persons to lie in: At the other opposite end, there is a void space cut out resembling a Bed, and above both these there is a large Hole, which is suppos'd was a vent for Smoak.

Considered as a worked stone it is immense, and the obvious labour involved in cutting it must have suggested giant strength. As accommodation, however, the Dwarfie Stane would hardly be comfortable for any but a very small giant and his wife, especially if she was pregnant as suggested by the hollowing of her side of the bed. John Brand, writing in 1703, doubts the tale that a giant couple 'had this stone for their Castle':

> I would rather think, seeing it could not accomodate any of a Gigantick stature, that it might be for the use of some Dwarf, as the Name seems to import, or it being remote from any House might be the retired Cell of some Melancholick Hermite.

A number of travellers from at least the eighteenth century onward have added graffiti to the tomb, inside and out. One name is that of the well-known antiquary Hugh Miller, and another that of 'a Persian gentleman', Guilemus Mounsey, who apparently slept a couple of nights in the stone in 1850, and gave the Hoy locals a fright when he appeared from inside in his flowing eastern robes.

Sir Walter Scott probably visited in August 1814, and refers to the site in *The Pirate* (1821):

> The lonely shepherd avoids the place, for at sunrise, high noon, or sunset, the mis-shapen form of the necromantic owner may sometimes still be seen sitting by the Dwarfie Stone.

The 'necromantic owner' is named as Trolld, 'a dwarf famous in the northern sagas'. By this Scott means a troll, an ogre-like being that figures prominently in Scandinavian legend, but which has mutated in Orkney and Shetland lore into the trow or trowie, much closer to a fairy.

See THE GREY NEIGHBOURS (p. 410).

EDAY, ORKNEY

G. F. Black, writing on the folklore of the Orkney and Shetland Islands in 1903, explains that toothache in Sanday was called 'The Worm' from the idea that the pain was caused by a worm in the tooth or jawbone. To cure the disease a charm called 'Wormy Lines' was used, written on a slip of paper which had to be sewed into the clothes of the sufferer and kept there 'as long as the paper lasts':

> Peter sat on a marble stone weeping,
> Christ came by and said, 'What aileth thee, Peter?'
> 'O, my lord, my God, my tooth doth ache!'
> 'Arise, Peter, go thy way, thy tooth shall ache no more!'

John Brand, writing 200 years earlier in 1703, gives an account of a charm performed at a distance upon a person living in Eday. According to what Brand was told by 'an Honest Man worthy of Credit', at the exact time when the charm was performed, 'there fell a living Worm out of the Patients Mouth, when he was at Supper':

> This my Informer knew to be a Truth, and the Man from whose Mouth it fell is yet alive in the Isle of *Sanda*. Whether this Worm was generated in the corrupted part, and so fell out by the Devils means, at the using of the Charm; or the Worm was brought by an evil Spirit . . . to the mouth, and thence falling down, I shall not determine.

Although the spell mentioned by Black involves a written paper, which does not seem to be the case in Brand's report, the charm used was probably similar. Such pieces of folk medicine had a long survival in the islands.

FETLAR, SHETLAND

'Of all our hundred isles, big and little, Fetlar is perhaps the most eerie, as it certainly is where the folk-lore has been most carefully preserved,' wrote Jessie Saxby in 1932. She had spent a long lifetime gathering Shetland traditions and folklore; being the ninth child of a ninth child, she was considered to be 'within privileged lines' and therefore got a good deal of information from members of certain families, including a supply of old tales from a Fetlar woman called Hannah-Kitty.

Hannah-Kitty's story of the giant Fluker describes him as peaceable and friendly, but very ugly. He sometimes came from his Hadd (lair) in the cliffs to visit the houses, but the women objected to his visits:

> This, after a time, enraged Fluker and he stole a little boy he found playing by the shore. He carried the child to his Hadd, but no one saw him do so, because he was a wizard as well as a giant, and cast a thick mist over Fetlar so that nothing could be seen.

It was supposed that the child had dropped into the sea, and the mother went along the crags wailing for her little boy.

> So pitiful were her cries that Fluker's heart was melted and he hastened to his Hadd with the intention of letting the boy go. But the boy had vanished!

A Fetlar story told of a mermaid who stole a human child from the giant Fluker. In the quarrel which followed, both giant and mermaid were killed.

A mermaid had stolen the child in her turn, and hidden him in a ruined broch. A little later, however, when a boat happened to pass nearby, the boy was seen and returned to his mother. Fluker was enraged when he found out what had happened. He and the mermaid had a great quarrel:

> He threw rocks at her, and she tossed waves into his cave smothering him in a short time. But one of the rocks he flung struck her on the tail, and she sank dead in the sea. Thus they both perished.

The rock which Fluker flung, says Saxby, was known in her day as 'The Mermaid's Baa' (ball).

There is a tradition in Scottish legend of giants as kidnappers. Another such attempt was ultimately foiled by Fionn mac Cumhaill, also known as FINGAL (p. 10).

FOULA, SHETLAND

G. F. Black, compiler of a 1903 collection of Orkney and Shetland folklore, was told that 'until within recent years' it was common on Foula for mothers putting their children to bed at night to tell them to be good 'or the Noggle will come and take you away'. The *nökk* or *nykk* is a Scandinavian water-spirit which may appear as a horse, and from this comes the Noggle, spelt variously Nygel, Nyugl, Neogle, or Nuggle, reported to take equine form 'with the exception of his tail, which was said to resemble the rim of a wheel, but which he cunningly kept concealed between his hind legs'.

The Noggle was often seen in mills, where he would hold the mill wheel and keep it from turning. When the miller went to discover what the trouble was he would find a beautiful pony, saddled and bridled, but should he mount on its back it would make off full tilt until it reached the sea, where it would throw the rider in and then vanish in a flash of flame.

Although he could turn himself into a flame, the Noggle could also be driven away by fire. A story was repeated of a man and his sister walking one dark night beside a stream and holding flaming torches, 'a very common mode of lighting up the path in the Shetland country districts in winter'. Some sparks from their brands blew into the water, and 'a creature like a Shetland horse' rose in the middle of the burn and rushed downstream to the sea.

One of Black's informants referred to the Noggle as a 'trow', evidently using this as a generic term for a supernatural creature; from the above account the Noggle seems very similar to KELPIES AND WATER-HORSES (p. 364).

W. Traill Dennison of WESTBROUGH, who told the story of the Mester Stoor-worm, recorded the legend of another monster, Nuckelavee, evidently yet another variation on the Noggle:

> His home was the sea; and whatever his means of transit were in that element, when he moved on land he rode a horse as terrible in aspect as himself. Some thought that rider and horse were really one, and that this was the shape of the monster.

One starlit night a man named Tammie was walking between the sea and a deep freshwater loch when he saw a huge shape before him, and was sure it was no earthly thing. He could not bypass it and was too frightened to turn his back on it, and so walked slowly forward. To his horror he found that it was the dreaded Nuckelavee:

> The lower part of this terrible monster, as seen by Tammie, was like a great horse with flappers like fins about his legs, with a mouth as wide as a whale's, from whence

came breath like steam from a brewing-kettle. He had but one eye, and that as red as fire. On him sat, or rather seemed to grow from his back, a huge man with no legs, and arms that reached nearly to the ground.

Most horrible of all, the creature was skinless: his surface was made up of raw red flesh, black blood running through yellow veins, and white sinews twisting and stretching as he moved his arm to grab for his prey. Tammie remembered that Nuckelavee was said to dislike fresh water, and ran as fast as he could towards the rivulet connecting the loch with the sea.

> Tammie knew, if he could only cross the running water, he was safe; so he strained every nerve. As he reached the near bank, another clutch was made at him by the long arms. Tammie made a desperate spring and reached the other side, leaving his bonnet in the monster's clutches. Nuckelavee gave a wild unearthly yell of disappointed rage as Tammie fell senseless on the safe side of the water.

Fresh running water was always a protection against fairies and witches, but not effective against the Kelpie; nor could it have been a bar to the Shetland Noggle, since this creature was sometimes seen in a burn. Nuckelavee is a sort of composite ogre, and Dennison's detailed account is perhaps over-elaborate: other bogey beasts are sometimes said to be skinless, but their flayed appearance is not usually described in such graphic terms.

GORD, MAINLAND, SHETLAND

There are many tales of the trows luring fiddlers into their mounds to play to them. There they would pass a year, or a year and a day, or many years, always returning home quite unconscious of time having passed, and sometimes bringing with them a fairy tune. One such piece of music, known as 'The Fiddler o' Gord', was recorded in 1977 as performed by the fiddle-player and storyteller George Peterson, who told the story that goes with the tune.

A fiddler one night went away to the crags to fish, and was coming home with his catch when he passed a certain knowe. Seeing a light shining from it, he took a closer look and there were the trows dancing inside, so he went in, and the knowe closed behind him with nothing to show that there had ever been a doorway.

All night his family waited for him to come home with the fish, and in the morning they searched for him, but not a thing did they find. In the end it was decided that he had fallen over the cliffs into the sea. As time went by his family grew up and moved away, and after a hundred years had passed there was a new family living in his house.

One winter night the new family was round the fire when a ragged old man with a long white beard came in, carrying a fiddle. 'What are you doin here?' he cried. 'Dis' my house: you've got to get oot o hit.' Everyone laughed – except the grandfather, who sat smoking his pipe. The man with the fiddle demanded to know where his folk were, and the grandfather asked what the man was called. When he heard the answer, he said that a man of that name had once been there, 'long, long afore my day', but had disappeared one night and had never come home.

Now the laughing stopped, and everyone knew there was something odd going on. The man with the fiddle asked again where his folk were, and the grandfather by the fireside said they were all dead.

> 'Well then,' he says, 'if that's the case, then,' he says, 'A'll go an join them.'

He turned and went out. There was one boy who hadn't laughed at the man, and he followed. He saw the old fellow with the fiddle go to the back of the kale yard, where he looked up at the Merry Dancers shining in the northern sky. He lifted his fiddle to his neck and played a tune once or twice, and then all of a sudden he collapsed. The boy ran to where he lay, and there he found the remains of a man who had been dead for a hundred years.

> And he aalways minded that tune, and when that boy grew up he could play that tune, and that tune's been handed doon to this day.

The 'Merry Dancers' are the aurora borealis. The Shetland folklore collector Jessie Saxby writes that these merry or pretty dancers were once regarded with fear, and were talked of as 'the fighting lasses' in reference, no doubt, to the Valkyries, but by her time had a more peaceful reputation:

> It has often been asserted that when the air is calm and the sky cloudless you can hear the swish of the Pretty Dancers as they glide about the northern sky like ladies in rustling silks.
> There was an old reel called the Pretty Dancers' Reel. The music was wild, the steps of the dance slow and gliding, the 'figures' simple and graceful.

See also THE GREY NEIGHBOURS (p. 410); THE TROWIE TUNES OF SHETLAND (p. 390).

gig outside the pub while they were drinking. The horse, being hungry and thirsty, stamped his feet against a barrel of porter, broached the keg, and drank the lot.

When the men set out for home, they soon realised there was something wrong with the horse, and before long the poor animal collapsed and appeared dead. To make the best of a bad job, the men flayed the horse and walked home with the skin.

Later that night, or the next morning, they heard a noise outside and there was the flayed horse tramping around, 'but he appear't to be very cowld'. As it happened, several sheep had been killed not long before, to be salted down for the winter, and in this emergency the men had the idea to use their skins. The sheepskins grew on the horse as if they had been his own, with the extra happy result that the horse became more profitable than ever before, since they could now collect as much wool from him every year as from five or six ordinary sheep.

The tale probably originates in Ireland (note that the horse gets drunk on the typically Irish drink porter), but is found throughout Scotland in various forms and is particularly popular on Yell. A not dissimilar story was told as a true anecdote to one of the present writers: in Saxony, a goose supposed to be killed for Christmas came round after its feathers were plucked and walked out of the fridge complaining. The repentant owner knitted it a jacket, and it lived a long and satisfactory life.

GREENBANK, NORTH YELL, SHETLAND

Tom Tulloch of Yell, who told the story of the giant at Erne's Knowe, near MIDBRAKE, also supplied the School of Scottish Studies with a tale of some men who went to Greenbank and left their horse and

HALTADANS, FETLAR, SHETLAND

The trows of the Shetlands were in some respects very like fairies. They were for instance fond of music, though their preferred instrument was the fiddle rather than the bagpipes favoured by fairies in

The Trowie Tunes of Shetland

At dances in the Shetlands, fiddlers still play tunes said to have been learned from the fairies, or trows as they are known in the islands. Local tradition preserves the stories of how the pieces were first heard. In one such tale, set in the 1790s, a carpenter from Cunningsburgh in the mainland is said to have been making his way home by moonlight, having finished work on a new boat and stayed to celebrate. Coming towards the head of Aith Voe where a stream runs into the bay, he heard music and saw light coming from a chink in the side of a green mound. Wedging his carpenter's adze into the gap to widen it, he looked inside, where a trows' dance was in full swing. Fortunately, perhaps, the trows did not notice that they were being spied on, and the man listened until he had the tune by heart. Afterwards, being also a fiddler of some skill, he was able to play the music he had heard, which became known as Aiths Rant (a 'rant' is a lively tune).

In some cases, the men who eavesdropped on the trows are remembered by name. Hakki Johnson was a fiddler of the early nineteenth century who was rumoured to become a little strange when the moon was full – 'no aa dere' (not all there) – a reputation which helped give him credit as the recipient of fairy inspiration, since such weak-minded individuals were generally thought to be more liable than others to otherworldly influence. Late one night or early one morning, Hakki was coming home to Tumblin from a party in Aithsting when he heard music coming from the old ruin known as the Broch of Houlland. He memorised the tune, handed down as the Wast Side Trows Reel. The story is suspiciously similar to that connected with Aiths Rant, even down to the location: the Broch of Houlland overlooks another bay called Aith Voe. The tune, however, is different, and in this case can be identified as an old German melody.

The story of VALLAFIELD or the Trowie Reel, a variant on the same legend, is also said to date from the early nineteenth century. Three of the trowie tunes, then, are said to have been heard under similar circumstances between about 1790 and 1810. Why did the music of the Otherworld sound so clear at around this time? Part of the answer may lie in the development of traditional music in Shetland. Fiddle-playing had come to the islands in the eighteenth century, and perhaps the wild, hypnotic power of the new rants and reels was felt to verge on the supernatural. The popularity of the

The fiddle arrived in the Shetland Islands in the eighteenth century, and its music exerted such intoxicating power that many popular fiddle tunes were said to have supernatural origins. Pictures often show fiddlers sitting raised above the rest of the company, as in this 1869 illustration of a rural dance.

instrument must have led to professional competition between fiddle-players, and who could doubt the expertise of a man who had learned his music directly from the trows?

It may be, however, that the musicians did not invent their stories so much as give a mythical gloss to the process of inspiration. The tale of Gibbie Laurenson is a case in point. One night Gibbie brought a load of corn to the watermill of Fir Vaa, a place with a bad reputation. There were stories of an old woman being torn to pieces by the trows there, and so Gibbie had every reason to be cautious when, sitting dozing by the fire, he saw a troop of trows come in with their children. He did not stir, even when one trow woman hung a nappy on his leg. Before they left, the little people discussed what to do with the human. 'Oh,' said one, 'he's no an ill body. Tell Shanko ti gie him a tün.' The tune they played was memorised by Gibbie and passed into the fiddle repertoire as Winyadepla, the name of a nearby loch.

At the 'clack mills' of Shetland, visiting crofters saw to the grinding of their own corn without the assistance of a miller. Not only was Gibbie half-asleep, in what is called the hypnagogic state when otherworldly experiences are often reported, but he was by himself in a place filled with the noise of the rushing torrent. Night, loneliness, and water are the common themes of these stories. For Gibbie in the mill, Hakki Johnson above the bay, or the carpenter of Cunningsburgh by the stream, the shifting, changing sounds of sea or river seem to have provided the background within which the musicians could begin to hear fairy notes.

See also GORD: HALTADANS.

the rest of Scotland. They would sometimes lure a musician inside their hill
where he would remain unconscious of
the passing of time until he was released
after a year and a day or longer.

In other stories, rather than entering the
mound the fiddler rests outside, where he
overhears the trows' own music. Several
tunes are said to have been passed on in
this way, including one from VALLAFIELD
and another known as the Hyltadans or
Haltadans, dating back to the mid seventeenth century. According to tradition, a
man from Cùlbenstoft was going towards
the sea one night when he heard the trows
dancing to a song he later wrote down.
This is one of the simplest of THE TROWIE
TUNES OF SHETLAND (p. 390), and the earliest. It must have begun as a song-tune
before it was adapted for the fiddle, since
the instrument only came to the islands in
the eighteenth century.

The tune survived but not these particular trows, who carried on dancing too long
and were caught by the sunrise. They
were turned to stone – 'as a punishment',
according to some sources, although this
is probably a later addition to the story,
referring to legends of human dancers in
mainland Britain who suffered this fate for
dancing on the Sabbath. The trows, however, were closely associated with the
Scandinavian troll, traditionally said to be
petrified by the sun's rays.

What remains of the dancers can still be
seen at Haltadans: an outer circle of stones,
originally standing but now fallen, and an
inner circle of earth and stones. At the
centre are two standing stones (there may
once have been a third) said to have been the
fiddlers who played for the trows. The name
of the tune and the site, 'Hyltadans' or
'Haltadans', means 'halting dance': trows
were traditionally said to have a particular
stumbling or limping way of dancing.

See also THE GREY NEIGHBOURS (p. 410).

HAROLDSWICK, UNST, SHETLAND

Biot Edmondston and his sister Jessie were
told by their Shetland nurse in the nineteenth century that a spirit could not rest
until its body was buried or 'dissolved',
presumably by either fire or water, and
that if any wicked deed had been done by
the deceased, the ghost needed to tell those
it met. It could not, however, speak until
spoken to by a living person. Mentioning
the name of the dead person would count
as addressing the ghost, which would then
appear to the one who 'called' it.

These beliefs are very widespread: a
story of a ghost which waits until it is
addressed is told at NORRIE'S LAW (Central
& Perthshire). To illustrate the point,
Edmondston and Saxby give an account of
a boat built at Haroldswick which was
launched on its maiden voyage to Burrafiord. Rounding the headland at Skau,
the boat met another whose skipper asked
what they were going to do; they said they
were lying by for a while to get bait. The
second boat went to sea but ran short of
bait themselves and had to return; when
they came back to Skau, they found pieces
of the boat, with her oar and mast, lying
strewn about the sea. Back on shore they
met the wives of the crew, who asked if
they had seen anything of the new boat.
Then they knew that the men on board
must have died, and the skipper told the
women to go home to their children: 'your
lads'll come when they can, pür fellows!'
The story continues in what must be the
words of the Edmondstons' nurse:

There was no more of it but sorrow till
some days later, when some people saw
the six men who had been in the boat at
the south end of the island, near a well-
known Trow-haunt. They looked just as
they had been in life, only for the *kind o'*

something in their faces that was no' just earthly atagether.

After that they were often seen by day and night, always the six of them together, walking with their faces turned to the sea. At last a woman had the courage to speak to them while they were passing by her house. She called the skipper by his name, but when he replied his voice was 'like a clap of thunder' and she could not understand him.

She said, 'Moderate your speech, for I'm no' fit to stand it.' Then the man spoke quite naturally.

He told her that Madge Coutts, a witch who disliked the men, had come into their boat, and they knew by her looks that she was planning their deaths. They managed to knock her off the gunwhale into the water, but instantly she dived under the boat and got into it on the other side in the form of a large black ox. Lowering her head, she drove her horns into the boat until it fell to pieces.

The skipper explained that the reason the men kept appearing now was because of dishonest dealing between himself and a brother of his, and he begged the woman to set things right. She did so, and the six men were seen no more.

It was remembered that upon the day of the accident Madge Coutts was seen going in at her own chimney in the form of a grey cat, and that immediately afterwards a sulphur-tainted smoke was seen ascending.

The witch's attack in animal form is similar to the story told at EILEAN TRODDAY (Western Isles) of the death of Iain Garbh.

HASCOSAY, SHETLAND

The Knockin'-stane was a very precious heirloom. If a family moved from one place to another (which seldom happened) the Knockin'-stane always accompanied them.

All sorts of ill-luck was sure to come to those who were foolish enough to neglect such an important item of the house furnishings. It was said to have been in use in the days of the Pechs, long before the Viking Age, and, of course, before the invention of corn-mills. The Knockin'-stane is a large and heavy lump of rock, solid, and roughly shaped and hollowed till it resembles a huge bowl. Into this the corn was placed to be bruised by the mill, or beetle, a thick stick with a round or over-shaped end. The Knockin'-stane usually lived in the barn, and he was much valued, being always supposed to have special virtues of his own – a treasure indeed.

So wrote the Shetland folklore collector Jessie Saxby, in 1932. Her forebears, the Edmonstons of Hascosay, had their own Knockin'-stane which came mysteriously back into her possession long after the ancestral house had passed out of the hands of the family. She surmises that 'a kindly trow must have had sympathy with some feelings of mine, and transported the relic to Baltasound, for here it is, and I hope "the luck" with it.'
See also SOUTH HAVRA.

HOULL, FETLAR, SHETLAND

An old man, sitting out of doors one summer evening, saw a party of Trows coming lightly over the marshy ground close by. As they skipped along they sang, 'Hupp horse handocks, and we'll ride on Bulmints.' The old man instantly called out, 'I'll ride with you.' Thereupon they carried him off and kept him for a twelvemonth, and then they put him back on his own roof, but he never told what he had seen or heard while visiting Trowland.

This story, told by the Edmonstons' nurse in the nineteenth century, is a short (and slightly garbled) version of a tale recorded in the seventeenth century set at DUFFUS CASTLE (North East). The fairy password, given in the earlier narrative as 'Horse and Hattock', has here become 'Hupp horse handocks', while another version, told at East Yell Parochial School in around 1865, has 'Up hors, up hedik'. Instead of the impenetrable 'we'll ride on Bulmints', the East Yell story gives, 'Up will ridn bol-wind': 'bulwands' are dock stems. Else-where, fairies were said to ride on pieces of straw, like those who took the 'Black Laird of Dunblane' with them at MEN-STRIE (Central & Perthshire).

The Yell narrative is set at Houll, and says that the man carried off by the trows landed in Delting on the roof of a house where a woman was giving birth. When her baby was born she sneezed three times: if nobody had 'sained' her, the fairies would have been able to take her with them, leaving an image behind in her place. It is implied that it was the sneez-ing which put her in the trow's power, although in other stories fairies are able to abduct women and children whether or not they have sneezed. In this case, how-ever, the man said, 'Gyud save him an her,' and the blessing caused the trows to vanish. After doing so they raised such a strong wind that the man was not able to get home for a fortnight, by which time his family had quite given up hope of seeing him again. This is clearly related to tales of the fairy 'sluagh' like that told at NUNTON (Western Isles), but includes the still common idea that someone who sneezes should be blessed.

See also THE GREY NEIGHBOURS (p. 410).

LINGA, SHETLAND

On the little islet of Linga, off the coast of Yell, there is supposed to be a small green circle, once known as the 'Bear's Bait' or 'Bear's Ring'. It is said to have been made by a bear walking round the pole to which it was tethered. The story of how the bear came to be there was given the title 'A Shetland Saga' in *The Scotsman* in 1895; the events described are said to have taken place towards the close of the reign of Harold Fairhair (d. 933), King of Norway, but the historical context seems rather to be the thirteenth and fourteenth centuries, when Orkney and Shetland farmers paid a land tax, called *skatt*, direct to the Norwegian king.

In those days, a udaller (freeholder) of the name of Jan Teit, a powerful and hot-tempered man, lived on Fetlar. One summer morning, a longship arrived in Shetland. It was the king's officer sent to collect the *skatt* due to the crown, in the form of produce. All the local udallers were summoned to pay their tax, each bringing his own *bismar*, or weighing beam, to weigh the produce he was offer-ing. It would then be weighed on the gov-ernment *bismar*, in order to prevent fraud.

To this gathering came Jan Teit, bring-ing butter as part of the tax. He weighed out the required quantity, but when it was checked on the official scales, the collec-tor declared it to be underweight. Jan insisted that his *bismar* was correct and he was being cheated, but the collector remained unmoved. Their altercation grew heated and ended with Jan hitting the tax collector over the head with his *bismar* and killing him.

Jan Teit was taken to Norway as a pris-oner and brought before the king, his head and feet bare. Although it was unlawful to appear before the king carrying weapons, Jan had managed to conceal his axe beneath the white cloak he wore as a sup-plicant.

According to some accounts, Jan had knobbly double-joints in both hands and feet; according to others, his feet were disfigured with bunions. The king now studied his bare feet for a time, then burst out laughing. When Jan asked why he was laughing, the king replied, 'Never have I seen a man with joints as ugly as thine.' 'Well,' answered Jan, 'I would not wish to give you offence and this at least can be mended,' and he drew his axe out from under his cloak and chopped at the offending joints. The king, amazed at his audacity and courage, had his axe taken from him, saying:

> 'I'm not surprised you slew my commissioner when you have so little concern for your own person. You deserve death for your crime in Shetland, yet a bold man like you deserves a chance at life. You can have your freedom on this condition. Out in the forest is a bear who has killed many people. He is so strong that no one dare face him. Bring me that bear and we shall let bygones be bygones.'

A wise woman told Jan, 'As butter has been your undoing, it shall be your salvation.' Taking the hint, Jan used drugged butter to tempt the bear, trapped it, and led it to the king's court; a strange pair they made, the bear still staggering from the drugs, and Jan hurpling along on his injured feet.

Though the king was entertaining guests, Jan marched in unbidden and said, 'Here is the bear you asked for.' The king admitted that he had not really expected Jan to return, but that he had done well. All he asked now was that when Jan went home he would take the bear with him and care for it until it died of natural causes.

Jan agreed, but when he got the bear home to Fetlar the people did not welcome it. He was therefore obliged to take the beast to Linga and chain it to a post, where it spent its days walking round and round, creating a circle by its tread.

LOCH OF WINYADEPLA, FETLAR, SHETLAND

See THE TROWIE TUNES OF SHETLAND (p. 390).

MAES HOWE, ORKNEY MAINLAND

Maes Howe or Maeshowe is among the finest chambered tombs in Europe, dating from around 2700 BCE. It was said to be inhabited by a creature known as a Hogboy (see COPINSAY), but human beings too left their mark on the site. When it was excavated in 1861, the archaeologists found they were not the first on the scene: Vikings had broken in, about 700 years earlier, and left graffiti on the walls. The presence of the twelfth-century vandals is recorded in twenty-four runic inscriptions, two of which refer to 'Jorsalafara' – literally, 'Jerusalem-farers', or crusaders.

The sort of thing people write on walls hasn't changed all that much over the centuries. 'Thorny bedded; Helgi writes it' – perhaps the tomb, macabre though it might seem, was where the locals did their courting, or perhaps the men were thinking of happier times: 'Ingigerd is the most beautiful of women,' says one inscription.

Also carved here is a picture of an animal usually interpreted as a dragon, and some of the writings relate to buried treasure. The poem *Beowulf* tells of a hoard guarded by a dragon in a barrow containing a secret passage, and it has been suggested that on entering Maes Howe the Vikings drew the dragon and wrote the runes because they were so vividly reminded of the episode. There may, however, have been some factual element: one of the inscriptions states

A Victorian engraving of the ancient chambered tomb
at Maes Howe. Just visible on the walls is graffiti, left
by twelfth-century Vikings who boasted of their
sexual conquests and referred to buried treasure.

that treasure was concealed north-west
of the barrow, and in 1858 a cache of
Viking silver ornaments was found at
Sandwick, some way north-west from
Maes Howe.

Particularly interesting is an inscription
in large, even runes, informing us that
these were cut 'with the axe which
belonged to Gaukr Trandilsson in the
South of Iceland'. The carver does not
add his name, but Hermann Pálsson of
Edinburgh University has used centuries-
old Icelandic poetry to establish his identity: he was Thórhallr Ásgrímsson, named
in the Orkneyinga Saga as captain of the
ship that brought Earl Rognvaldr Kali
back from crusade to Orkney late in
1153, and great-great-great-grandson of
Ásgrímr Ellitha-Grímsson, named in Njáls
Saga as the slayer of Gaukr Trandilsson.
The axe of the victim was kept as an heirloom by the killer's family for six generations, around 200 years, and was brought

to Orkney by a direct descendant of
Ásgrímr. The tracing of its history is an
astounding example of archaeological and
scholarly detective work.

MIDBRAKE, YELL, SHETLAND

A boy was sent out to the hill to check on
the cows, and found the herd near the
Erne's Knowe (the name means 'Eagle's
Knoll') a little way north of Midbrake. He
took a bannock out of his pocket to eat,
but he dropped it and it rolled down the
side of the knoll. That seemed a good
game to him, so he rolled it up and down
a few times and at last it disappeared in a
clump of heather. Looking among the
heather for the cake, he found a big hole
leading into the hill, and the further he followed the bigger it got, until he found
himself in a large cave. There was a giantess there, but the boy could tell she was

blind and couldn't see him. She was laying the table for a huge meal.

After a while the giant came home with the treasure he'd collected that day. He sat down to dinner, but all the time he was eating he kept lifting his head and sniffing, and finally he said:

'Fee faw fam,
I feel the smell o an earthly man,
But be he livin or be he deid
I'se hae his heid wi my sopper bried!'
[I'll have his head with my supper bread]

The giant searched the cave and soon found the boy, but decided he was too thin to eat yet, so the giantess tied the boy up and every day she fed him, until one morning the giant found that the boy's wrist had become as fat as his own little finger. He said he'd be ready to eat that evening, and then he went out to hunt.

The giantess put a cauldron of water on the fire, and after a while she asked the boy to climb on her shoulder and see if the water was boiling. But the boy said he couldn't tell, so he suggested *she* should get up on *his* shoulder, and he pitched her forward into the water, and boiled her till she was done. Then he laid her out on the table, and climbed up into the roof of the cave.

When the giant came home he sat down to table and starting eating the old wife, and though he said it was tough he finished it off and fell asleep afterwards, lying back in his chair and snoring with his mouth wide open. The boy had some little stones, and he threw them down into the giant's throat so that they choked him to death.

The boy climbed down, gathered the best of the giant's treasure, and went home, and his family lived rich and happy ever after.

This tale, which has clear echoes of 'Hansel and Gretel' and 'Jack and the Beanstalk', was narrated in North Yell

dialect in 1975 by Tom Tulloch of Gutcher. The teller suggested that the moral was not to play with your food, though, as the editors point out in their notes, 'as the final result is wealth for the boy's whole family it hardly seems a clear warning!'

NOLTLAND CASTLE, WESTRAY, ORKNEY

On the birth or marriage of any of the Balfours, a glow was said to rise around the family's home at Noltland Castle. (At ROSSLYN CHAPEL (Lothian & Borders) something similar was said to mark the death of one of the Barons of Roslin.) By the early nineteenth century, however, the castle had 'for a century been left to the undisputed possession of the Brownie', who had in his day been a paragon, according to David Vedder in a passage quoted by R. Menzies Fergusson in 1883:

. . . a more painstaking and industrious drudge never wielded flail or sickle, spade or pitchfork. He would even construct and repair bridges, was a very Macadam at roadmaking, hauled up boats above high-water mark during storms, and procured instantaneous medical assistance to the lady of the castle.

Brownies are very often said to help with farm work, and stories of their fetching doctors or midwives for women in labour include that told at DALSWINTON (Dumfries & Galloway).
See also BROWNIES (p. 80).

NORTH YELL, SHETLAND

The *Shetland Times* for 21 July 1961 printed an article entitled 'Did the mermaid exist?'

reporting the alleged capture of a mermaid by fishermen in 1833. The account was found among 'old documents' by Lady Nicholson, and is a deposition sworn by William and Daniel Manson and John Henderson of Cullivoe, North Yell, in the presence of Arthur Nicholson of Lochend, Justice of the Peace. In the beginning of July, the men were deep-sea fishing a long way from land. About midnight, they took up a strange creature on their hook:

> From the navel upwards it resembled a human being – had breasts as large as those of a woman. Attached to the side were arms about 9 inches long, with wrists and hands like those of a human being, except that there were webs between the fingers for about half their length.

The animal was about three feet (0.9 m) long, its arms and breasts covered by round fins growing from its shoulders. It had a short neck and a head of about a man's size but more pointed at the top, small blue eyes more like those of a human being than those of a fish, no nose but two nostrils for blowing through, and a large thick-lipped mouth with no chin, although the lower jaw projected a little further than the upper. It had no ears. The front of the animal was covered with white skin and the back was grey. It had a long flexible bristle on each side of its head, and another between its nostrils:

> When the men spoke the animal answered, and moved these bristles, which led them to suppose that the creature heard by means of them.

They also noted that there was no hair on its body, which was soft and slimy. They did not notice what kind of teeth it had, or sexual organs, but said the creature was

The Brownie of Noltland Castle was a model of his kind, working tirelessly in all weathers, and even bringing the doctor for his mistress. By the early nineteenth century, he was said to be the only inhabitant of the ruined building.

very nearly round at the shoulders with a kind of hollow space between its shoulder bones. Its body tapered off towards the tail, which resembled that of a halibut, and was flat and consisted of two lobes which, when extended, might be six inches (15 cm) together wide.

Arthur Nicholson's account goes on to add, 'There is an old opinion among fishermen that it is unlucky to kill a mermaid and therefore, after having kept it in the boat for some time, they slipped it,' and he concludes, 'All of which is the truth, so help me God.'

The skipper of the fishing boat also described this event to a Mr Edmonston. The year 1833 seems too early for this to have been the Shetland naturalist and author quoted at COLVADALE and elsewhere, but it may have been another member of this Hascosay family. Edmonston sent an account to the Natural History Department at Edinburgh University, saying:

> Not one of the six men dreamed of a doubt of its being a mermaid . . . The usual resources of skepticism that the seals and other sea animals appearing under certain circumstances operating upon an excited imagination and so producing an optical illusion cannot avail here. It is quite impossible that six Shetland fishermen could commit such a mistake.

The story as reported does not give the impression of a hoax, and one suggestion is that this was the result of a collective hallucination. Otherwise, the accepted 'scientific' explanation of mermaids is that they are members of the sirenians, a marine family that comprises manatees, dugongs and Steller's sea-cow (thought to be extinct). The most likely candidate in this case is the dugong, which has a bilobate tail, a relatively hairless body, and two front flippers. It has also been seen suckling its young while standing half out of the water. None of the sirenians, however, are indigenous to Scottish waters.

OLLABERRY, MAINLAND, SHETLAND

Brucie Henderson of Arisdale, South Yell, was recorded in 1955 telling what the *Shetland Folk Book* describes as 'A Shetland Version of the Legend of Don Juan', referring to the climax of the original tale, when the libertine rashly invites a statue to dinner. His guest duly arrives, to claim the soul of his host.

In Henderson's story, a bridegroom was going to church in Ollaberry to hear himself 'proclaimed' (i.e. his banns read), and came upon a skull lying in the graveyard. He kicked the skull, and said, 'I'm marryin on Thursday, you bogger. Come ta my wedding on Thursday.'

The skull replied:

> 'Remember, man, as thou pass by,
> As thou is now, so once was I;
> As I am now, so thou shalt be.
> Remember, man, that thou must dee.'

The man paid no attention, but went into the church and heard himself proclaimed and then went home. On Thursday afternoon he was married, and all the guests at the wedding were dancing away until midnight, when it was time for supper. A knock came at the door, and when the best man opened it he found a stranger there asking to speak to the bridegroom. The bridegroom went out, and the guests heard him talking, and then he shut the door.

> An he never cam back an he never cam back.

After a while the bride got anxious, and half the wedding guests went looking for the groom, but he was nowhere to be found. The story was told all over Shetland of the bridegroom who disappeared from his house on his wedding day. The years rolled by, the people left the area, and after a century only the black-faced sheep were left on the land, apart from one old woman who lived alone in the house where the wedding had happened. She was just on her way to bed when a knock came at the door, and in came the bridegroom, just as he had been a hundred years before. The old woman cried, 'God surround me an ma hoose dis nicht! Who ida world are you, an what are you come in here ta torment me aboot?'

The bridegroom said, 'A'm come in ta torment you in no ways at all.' He asked if she had been at his wedding, and said he had been called out about an hour ago to speak to a man.

> 'No, no! I can mind my midder telling da story,' she says. 'It wis before I was born,' she says, 'at dis took place. An,' she says, 'probably my midder's midder and faider was at dat wedding.'

Oh, was that right? said the man. Yes, it was, said the old woman, and he must be the bridegroom who left his own wedding, and he was the bridegroom who kicked the skull. He said he was, and he vanished down through the floor.

The skull's verse or something very like it is a common epitaph on nineteenth-century gravestones, but the idea behind it dates back a good deal further than that: in ancient Rome, 'memento mori' (remember you must die) was traditionally whispered to the emperor to remind him of the vanity of human triumph.

QUARFF, SHETLAND

At the end of the seventeenth century, a boat was passing Quarff with several men on board when they saw something like a head appearing above the water. At first it was some way away from them, but when it came nearer they could see that it had the face of an old man with a long beard.

> The sight was so very strange and affrighting, that all in the Boat were very desirous to be on Land, tho the Day was fair and the Sea calm; a Gentleman declaring, (as a Minister in Company with them, and saw this sight informed me,) that he never saw the like, tho he had travelled through many Seas.

This account by John Brand in 1703 sounds as if it might refer to one of the Blue Men of THE MINCH (Western Isles). His next tale, however, is much more mermaid-like:

> I heard another remarkable story like unto this, that about 5 Years since, a Boat at the Fishing drew her Lines, and one of them, as the Fishers thought, having some great Fish upon it, was with greater difficulty than the rest raised from the Ground, but when raised it came more easily to the surface of the Water upon which a Creature like a Woman presented it self at the side of the Boat, it had the Face, Arms, Breasts, Shoulders, &c. Of a Woman, and long Hair hanging down the Back, but the nether part from below the Breasts, was beneath the Water, so that they could not understand the shape thereof.

The two fishermen were amazed, and one of them drew a knife and brutally thrust it into her breast. She cried, as they thought, 'Alas,' and fell backwards. The fishing hook, so large that it had passed through her chin and out at her upper lip, gave way, and she disappeared.

> The Man who thrust the Knife into her is now dead, and, as was observed, never prospered after this, but was still haunted by an evil Spirit, in the appearance of an

old Man, who, as he thought, used to say unto him, *Will ye do such a thing who Killed the Woman*; the other Man then in the Boat is yet alive in the Isle of Burra.

Brand was told the story by a couple who said they had heard it from the bailiff of the place from which the boat came. He made enquiries of several other people, some of whom had never heard the tale, 'yet some said that they had heard thereof, and judged it to be very true.'

St Tredwell's Loch, Papa Westray, Orkney

St Tredwell's Loch was at one time famous, wrote James MacKinlay in 1893, 'partly from its habit of turning red whenever anything striking was about to happen to a member of the Royal Family'. The omen of water appearing like blood is reported of other lakes, rivers, and springs in Britain and Europe: a fountain near the Elbe in Germany was believed to run red when war was approaching, and a spring at Kilbarry on Barra in the Western Isles was said to produce drops of blood in advance of war and fragments of peat if peace was to remain unbroken.

St Tredwell or Triduana was one of those chaste ladies whose piety led them to self-mutilation: when a pagan prince admired her fine eyes, she plucked them out and presented them to him speared on a thorn, and her shrines and wells were traditionally resorted to by those suffering from eye complaints. The loch too was renowned for its healing properties. The Reverend John Brand, writing in 1703, heard from the minister of Westray that patients would walk round the loch 'so many times . . . as they think will perfect the Cure, before they make any use of the Water', and that they did so in silence, believing that if they spoke this would

stop the treatment working. He gives some examples of cures:

> As a certain Gentleman's Sister upon the Isle, who was not able to go to this Loch without help, yet returned without it, as likewise a Gentleman in the Countrey who was much distressed, with sore Eyes, went to this Loch and Washing there became sound and whole, tho he had been at much pains and expence to cure them formerly.

The former minister of Westray had vouched for these reports, but Brand is unwilling to call them miraculous: he attributes the results either to imagination or to the 'Aid and assistance of Satan'. He notes that only a very few people were healed even when they did all that was required of them, including circling the loch, washing themselves in the water, and leaving old clothes or rags as a tribute at the site.

Brand's scepticism notwithstanding, popular belief in the powers of the loch was evidently still strong in his time.

See also SAINTS OF SCOTLAND (p. 490); SCOTLAND'S HOLY AND HEALING WELLS (p. 44).

South Havra, Shetland

In *Shetland Folklore* (1981), James Nicolson reports the once-common tradition that because no mice lived on 'Havera' its earth could be used as a charm, sprinkled under cornstacks to protect them from infestation. A laird came one day for a bag of soil, and was handed the usual amount by the island's owner. Having stowed it away in his boat, the laird announced, 'You are now my tenant, for the earth you have just handed over symbolizes the isle itself.' The procedure, Nicolson explains, was part of the old ceremony of 'sasines' in which legal possession of property passed from one to another: the seller would hand to the purchaser a handful of earth and stones as a symbol of the transaction. 'Unfortunately for the particular story regarding the island of Havera,' he adds, 'historians assert that the tale has no foundation whatsoever.'

The island in question is probably South Havra, but Little Havra and North Havra could also have been mouse-free. The naturalist George Low wrote in 1813 that the Common Mouse was found 'everywhere, except in a few of the lesser islands, which our country sages tell us gravely are privileged, and neither cat nor mouse will live in them, even though brought thither':

> They add further, the earth of these isles brought thence kills them wherever they are. When an honest gray-headed man told me this, I desired to let me have a little of the earth of his isle, to make the experiment, but this he would by no means grant; this would, in his opinion, take away the virtue from the rest.

John Brand remarked in 1703 that 'in the Isles of *Burra* and *Haskashy* no Mice are to be found, yea if they take some dust or Earth out of these Isles to other places where they are, they will forsake such places, where the dust is laid', but things had clearly changed on Hascosay by the nineteenth century, when Jessie Saxby records meeting a young man she knew by the seashore. He was carrying his fishing gear and obviously hurrying to join his friends at the boats, so she was surprised to see him coming back only a short while later. He looked annoyed, and she asked him what was wrong:

> Then he smiled and looked a bit sheepish and replied, 'Well, I don't *really* believe some old notions, but well – a mouse ran across me road, and the men said I must not come with them after *that*.'

Vermin would have been a real problem on islands where grain was in short supply and could not easily be replenished, and it is not surprising that mice were regarded as unlucky.

STENNESS, ORKNEY MAINLAND

Several eighteenth- and nineteenth-century sources describe ceremonies performed at the Ring of Brodgar and the Stones of Stenness. On the first day of the New Year, young people of the neighbourhood used to meet in the Kirk of Stenness, taking enough food with them to last four or five days. Pairs of lovers would then leave the rest of the party and go to the Stones of Stenness, known as the Temple of the Moon, where the women would pray to Odin that he would enable them to perform the promises they made to the men; after that the couples would go to the Temple of the Sun (the Ring of Brodgar) where the men made similar prayers. They would then go to the Stone of Odin, a standing stone with a round hole in it through which the couples would clasp hands and plight their troth, 'a pledge of love which was to them as sacred as a marriage vow'.

The *Archaeologia Scotica* (1792) records the case of a young man who had got a girl pregnant and then deserted her:

> The young man was called before the session; the elders were particularly severe. Being asked by the minister the cause of so much rigour, they answered, you do not know what a bad man this is; he has broke the promise of Odin. Being further asked what they meant by the promise of Odin, they put him in mind of the Stone at Stenhouse with the round hole in it; and added, that it was customary, when promises were made, for the contracting parties

to join hands through this hole, and the promises so made were called the promises of Odin.

It was further said that a child passed through the hole when young would never shake with palsy in old age. When visiting the stone, it was customary to leave an offering of bread, cheese, a piece of cloth, or a pebble.

The Ring of Brodgar and the Stones of Stenness can still be seen, although many of the stones have fallen and are embedded in the ground. The Stone of Odin, however, was removed in around 1814 by a farmer, not a native of Orkney, who was annoyed by the number of visitors coming to see it. He is said to have used the stone to build a cow-house, and although no supernatural punishment is reported to have followed, two unsuccessful attempts were made by aggrieved neighbours to set fire to his property.

STONE OF QUOYBUNE, BIRSAY, ORKNEY MAINLAND

'In the parish of Birsay there is a "Druidical Stone" with a rather strange and tragic history attached to it,' wrote R. Menzies Fergusson in 1883. This is the Stone of Quoybune, which is said to walk or move towards the Loch of Boardhouse every New Year's Eve as the clock strikes twelve. When the edge of the loch is reached it quietly dips its head into the water, and then returns to its post.

In Fergusson's day it was considered unsafe for anyone to stay and see this happening. Many stories circulated of people who dared to watch and who next morning were found dead beside the stone, like a young Glaswegian whose curiosity impelled him to stay out on 31 December:

As time wore on and the dread hour of midnight approached, he began to feel some little terror in his heart, and an eerie feeling crept slowly over his limbs. At midnight he discovered that, in his pacing to and fro, he had come between the stone and the loch, and as he looked towards the former he fancied that he saw it move. From that moment he lost all consciousness, and his friends found him in the grey dawn lying in a faint. By degrees he came to himself, but he could not satisfy enquirers whether the stone had really moved and knocked him down on its way, or whether his imagination had conjured up the assault.

Another tale was that one December a ship was wrecked on Birsay, and all on board were drowned except one man, who then found shelter in a cottage close by the stone. Hearing the story of its yearly march, he resolved to see the phenomenon for himself; in spite of all remonstrance he went out on the evening of Hogmanay and sat on top of the very stone itself.

There he awaited the events of the night. What these were no mortal man can tell; for the first morning of the new year dawned upon the corpse of the gallant sailor lad, and local report has it that the walking stone rolled over him as it proceeded to the loch.

This is one of several legends of standing stones, usually megalithic monuments, which move, sometimes to go and drink, at midnight or dawn, often on particular days. The tradition is quite common in Brittany, Wales, and southern England, but is almost unknown in Scotland, although on Rousay the Yetnasteen ('Stone of the Giants') is said to go and drink in the Loch of Scockness every New Year's morning.

Leslie Grinsell remarks in *Folklore of Prehistoric Sites in Britain* (1976) that if it were

Selkies

Beneath the sea, according to tradition, there lives a race of people like humans but more beautiful. In their enchanted kingdom they have air to breathe, but in order to pass through the ocean which separates them from mankind they have to take on another form, usually that of a seal. On land they can remove their magical skin, but if they lose it they must remain where they are.

In *Superstitions of the Highlands and Islands of Scotland* (1900), John Gregorson Campbell relates a tale of a man who fell in love with a seal-woman or selkie and stole her skins. Without it she could not return to the ocean, and he persuaded her to be his wife. The couple had children and lived together for many years, but one day she found the sealskin where he had hidden it. Putting it on, she immediately dived into the waves and was never seen again.

In Campbell's time, people said to trace their ancestry from the seal-woman still lived on North Uist and were known as 'the MacCodrums of the seals', a rumour which lasted at least until the 1930s, when Canadian members of the family reported that their ancestor was supposed to have been found as a child after a shipwreck, wrapped in a sealskin coat. This is modern rationalisation: the older legend goes back to the eighteenth century, when John MacCodrum (*c.* 1695–1781), a North Uist poet, was widely believed to be descended from the selkies.

Similar stories of cross-breeding between seals and humans were told in many places, particularly in Ireland and the Orkney and Shetland Islands. An article on Orkney folklore by W. Traill Dennison published in 1893 gives a story 'said to have happened in the last bygone century' to an heiress of the islands. He gives her the pseudonym Ursilla, withholding her real name 'because her descendants are still among us'. She was a handsome and strong-minded girl whose husband proved a disappointment (he may have been impotent).

> And she was not the woman to sit down and cry over sorrow; she determined to console herself by having intercourse with one of the selkie folk.

When she shed seven tears into the sea, a handsome bull seal appeared. They began a regular affair, and Ursilla gave birth to several babies, every one with webbed hands and feet. The midwife clipped the webs – 'She showed the shears that she used to my grandmother,' said Dennison's informant – but the result was that they grew into a 'horny crust' on the palms and sóles of the children, something inherited by later generations. 'Whatever may be thought of this tale, its last sentence is quite true,' maintains Dennison, who interprets the tale as an imaginative explanation for

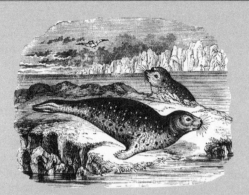

Seals were widely supposed to be supernatural
creatures that could shed their skins and appear on
land as beautiful human beings.

this 'strange phenomenon visibly seen' on Ursilla's descendants. He himself met one of the family who could not bind a sheaf of corn because of
the horn on his hands.

The many legends of selkies reflect the importance of seals in the
economy of the islands and coastal areas, where they were much hunted
for their flesh and particularly their valuable skins. In *The Fairy Mythology* (1850), Thomas Keightley tells of a fisherman who lived near John
o' Groats in the Northern Highlands and specialised in the killing of
seals. One evening, having spent the day hunting, he was visited by a
stranger who said that if the man accompanied him, he could make a profitable sale of skins. Eagerly the fisherman went with the stranger to the
shore, where he found himself seized and plunged into the depths of the
ocean. At last they came to a cavern crowded with seals, where the fisherman found to his horror that he himself had been transformed into a
seal. His strange guide showed him a knife, and asked if he recognised it;
he could not deny that it was the very tool he used to kill and skin his
prey. He was then told that one of the seals he had wounded earlier that
day was the guide's father, and that only the man who had inflicted the
wound could heal it. The terrified fisherman laid his hand upon the
injured seal, which was instantly made whole. Then, having sworn that
never again would he kill a seal, he was carried back to land where he
resumed his human form, and was rewarded by his selkie guide with a
generous present.

See also SULE SKERRY; UNST; VE SKERRIES (Orkney & Shetland Islands).

not for the frequent association with calendar customs, he would regard these supposed movements 'as mere conundrums invented by parents to sharpen the wits of children' – like the legend, or joke, of the stone lions outside the Fitzwilliam Museum in Cambridge for whose roars generations of children have waited in vain.

STROMNESS, ORKNEY MAINLAND

Bessie Miller of Stromness used to sell favourable winds to sailors. Her fee was sixpence, for which 'she boiled her kettle and gave the bark advantage of her prayers'; the wind she asked for was sure to arrive, although sometimes the sailors had to wait a while for it. By the time Sir Walter Scott visited her in 1814 she was very old:

> The woman's dwelling and appearance were not unbecoming her pretensions; her house, which was on the brow of the steep hill on which Stromness is founded, was only accessible by a series of dirty and precipitous lanes . . . She herself was, as she told us, nearly one hundred years old, withered and dried up like a mummy. A clay coloured kerchief, folded round her head, corresponded in colour of [sic] her corpse-like complexion. Two light blue eyes that gleamed with lustre like that of insanity, an utterance of astonishing rapidity, a nose and chin that almost met together, and a ghastly expression of cunning, gave her the effect of Hecate.

Hecate, goddess of magic, controls the witches in Macbeth. Bessie Miller, however, maintained that she used no 'unlawful arts'.

A later 'wind agent' of Stromness was Mammie Scott, widely remembered in the late nineteenth century. A captain bound for Stornoway called on her for help in his voyage, and was given a scarlet thread with three knots in it: if he did not get enough wind he was to untie the first knot; if he wanted still more, he should untie the second; but on no account should he untie the third, or disaster would follow. He set out, and finding that the breeze was light, soon untied the first knot. The wind strengthened, but was not enough for him, so he untied the second knot. A brisk gale swept the boat round Cape Wrath, and soon the entrance to Stornoway harbour was reached. The captain now felt that he was near enough the end of his voyage to risk untying the third knot, but was swiftly punished for his curiosity when a hurricane arose which blew him straight back to Hoy Sound. An almost identical story is told by Benjamin Thorpe in Northern Mythology (1851) of a German sorceress, and the theme can be traced back to the episode in Homer's Odyssey in which Aeolus presents the sailors with a bag of wind which some of them foolishly untie, believing it to contain gold.

Mammie had skills other than raising wind: she was said to be able to drive people mad. A young woman from one of the southern islands lost her reason, but regained it when her sweetheart bribed Mammie. Another couple were less fortunate: when the wife became insane, reportedly by Mammie's influence, her husband tried to restore her wits by towing her through the sea tied to his boat, a treatment which she survived but which did her no good. R. Menzies Fergusson, writing about this episode in 1883, calls the proposed cure 'original and remarkable', but it closely resembles the technique used to help lunatics at ST FILLAN'S POOL (Central & Perthshire).

Another story related of Mammie makes her sound far more of a 'real' witch than Bessie Miller. One day she visited Caithness and said she had a grievance against some men who were ferrying a stranger across the Pentland Firth. She borrowed a tub of water and set a small wooden bowl floating in it, stirring the water with her finger until the bowl went under. 'Aye, there they go; but I'm sorry for the puir strange laddie that's wi' them,' said Mammie. Sure enough, the men's boat sank and all on board were drowned. The technique used by Mammie was that employed by the foster-mother of Iain Garbh at EILEAN TRODDAY (Western Isles). *See also* WITCH-HUNTS (p. 270).

SULE SKERRY, ORKNEY

In the 1850s, Captain Thomas sent a ballad to the Society of Antiquaries of Scotland, written down by him from the dictation of an old lady of Snarra Voe, Shetland. The ballad begins with a woman nursing a child and singing to it that she knows little of its father, and less of where he is now.

> Then ane arose at her bed-fit,
> > An a grumly [surly] guest I'm
> > sure was he:
> 'Here am I, thy bairnis father,
> > Although that I be not comelie.

> 'I am a man, upo the lan,
> > An I am a silkie in the sea;
> And when I'm far and far frae lan,
> > My dwelling is in Sule Skerrie.'

Silkies or SELKIES (p. 404) are seal-people. When they take off their sealskins they appear like human beings and may then mate with humans. The woman says that it was not well done of 'the Great Silkie of Sule Skerrie' to have given her a child, and he pays her a purse of gold as a nurse's fee. One day, says the Silkie, he will teach his little son to swim:

> 'An thu sall marry a proud gunner,
> > An a proud gunner I'm sure he'll be;

> An the very first schot that ere he
> > schoots,
> > He'll schoot baith my young son
> > and me.'

Thomas comments that the ballad is 'too regular and well constructed to be very old'. Dr Otto Anderson, who noted the music in 1947, maintains that it is 'a very ancient melody', but tune and words of course are separate issues. There is another version entitled 'Sealchie Song' among the unpublished manuscripts of John Francis Campbell, sent to him by the minister of North Ronaldsay, Orkney, in 1859, suggesting that it was in fairly wide circulation by the mid nineteenth century. In that text the woman threatens the seal that her husband will shoot him and the child, but he defies her:

> 'I fear nae livin' proud gunner
> > I fear nae mortal man' quo he
> 'For pouther winna burn i' saut
> [For powder will not burn in salt]
> > Sae I an' thy young Son'll gae free.'

Sure enough, when the gunner takes a shot at the seals he hits his wife instead, and the silkie father and son 'Wi heavy hearts took tae the sea', a more rounded though perhaps less haunting ending than that supplied to Thomas.

SUNNYDALE, ORKNEY MAINLAND

In *Rambling Sketches in the Far North* (1883), R. Menzies Fergusson tells of the battle of Summerdale, which probably took place at what is now known as Sunnydale. In 1529 Lord Henry St Clair invaded the Orkneys, supported by the Earl of Caithness and a force of 500 men. They landed at Orphie, and in their march towards Stenness they met a witch, who walked before them unwinding two balls of thread, one red and the other white. When the red ball was wholly unwound, she told them that whichever party's blood was first shed would be defeated. Soon the earl's men saw a boy herding cattle and immediately slew him, finding out too late that he was a native of Caithness. As predicted, in the battle which followed the Orcadians triumphed, attacking the invaders with a hail of stones which appeared miraculously on ground which was ordinarily empty of. them. The invaders were beaten back into the Moss of Bigswald (Bigswell) and vanquished.

The only Orcadian killed, it was said, fell after the battle was done at the hand of his own mother. He had taken the clothes of a slain Caithness warrior, and as he returned home in the evening, his mother, thinking he was one of the enemy, hit him with a stone in the foot of a stocking.

SWINNA NESS, UNST, SHETLAND

The earth here is considered too sacred to put a spade into, because the Vikings had fought so many bloody battles on the land. A man dug a small bit of ground and sowed corn, but when it grew it was found that the stalks were filled with blood, and the ears dropped salt tears instead of dew.

Near Burrafiord, a place with a similar legend was known as the 'death-rig' or 'field of the dead'. Anyone who dug there was liable to terrible misfortune. Once a woman dared to dig up a portion of the death-rig, and shortly afterwards her cow died. She ignored the warning, dug again next year, and sowed corn. 'Then her husband died, and after that she let the rig alane.' The supposition is that the death-rigs are battlefields.

SWONA, ORKNEY

The little island of Swona, west of the southernmost tip of South Ronaldsay, has given its name to the whirlpool known as the Wells of Swona, in the Pentland Firth. In *More Legends of the Pentland Firth* (1979), Henrietta Munro tells the story of its origin.

A witch once took a fancy to a dark and handsome young man and wanted him for her lover. When she asked him to go to the beach with her, however, he refused, as his sweetheart was at that moment on her way to join him. Concealing her anger, the witch persuaded the young man and his girl to come out with her in her boat. As they approached Swona, she worked a spell on the boat and it overturned. The young man caught his girl's hand in an attempt to save her, but at the same moment the witch caught hold of his to drag him under the waves and into her power. The three were so entangled that they could not be pulled apart. The young man and his sweetheart were drowned, but the witch is still struggling to get free, and it is her frantic churning of the waters that causes the Wells of Swona.

TAFTS, FETLAR, SHETLAND

Several versions have been recorded of a story concerning a brass pannikin, 'Da Ferrie's Brass Pan', once treasured by a family at Taft (which appears on modern maps as Tafts) in the belief that it had originally belonged to the trowies or fairies. As given in the *Shetland Folk Book* (1957) the tale comes from a woman 'belonging to the family', and tells how a Fetlar lad was riding one night on a red mare and leading a grey foal. While passing the hill of Stakaberg he heard a voice saying:

Trira rara gonga
Du at rides da red
An rens da gre
Tell du Tüna Tivla
At Füna Fivla
'Es fain e da feyr
An brunt her.

[Trira rara gonga
Thou that ridest the red
And runnest the grey
Tell thou Tüna Tivla
That Füna Fivla
Has fallen in the fire
And burnt her.]

The first line means nothing in any language; the rest of the original is in the Shetland dialect, which in many ways resembles Lowland Scots but contains a large number of Norse words.

When the lad came to Taft he went into the byre, where a trow was milking the cows into a copper pan. The boy repeated the words he had heard, and at once the trow hurried away, crying out that her child Füna Fivla at Stakaberg was burned. In her haste the trow dropped her vessel: 'People say the pan is still in the house, some say built in the wall, and the family never afterwards lacked milk.'

Other tellings give slightly different words for the verse, sometimes garbling the names of the trows to make nonsense lines: clearly some tellers knew the dialect better than others. The ultimate fate of the copper pan also changes from version to version, and it is sometimes said to have vanished one day when the family forgot to leave food in it for the trows, or when they neglected to 'sain' it, i.e. bless it with the sign of the cross.

The story is a localised version of an international legend concerning spirits who leave a house on hearing of the death of one of their kind, while the fanciful names and message couched in rhyme relate it to the tale of 'The King of the Cats', a version

of which is told at APPIN HILL (Argyllshire & Islands). In this case, the story has been linked with the widespread theme explaining a family heirloom as something given by or stolen from fairies.

See also THE GREY NEIGHBOURS (p. 410).

TINGWALL, ORKNEY MAINLAND

John Brand wrote in 1703 of a hill near Tingwall known as the Knop of Kebister or Luggie's Knowe, home of 'a Varlet or Wizard' called Luggie. When the weather was too stormy for boats to go to sea, Luggie would go to the top of the hill and let down his fishing line into a hole, from which he would bring up any fish he chose. Nor did his talents end there: when fishing at sea, he could catch his fish ready-gutted and roasted. These seem harmless enough skills, but were considered to be 'done by the Agency of evil Spirits, with whome he was in Compact and Covenant', and Luggie was convicted of witchcraft and burned near Scalloway.

See also WITCH-HUNTS (p. 270).

TROLLA STACK, MAINLAND, SHETLANDS

See THE GREY NEIGHBOURS (p. 410).

TROLLADALE WATER, MAINLAND, SHETLANDS

See THE GREY NEIGHBOURS (p. 410).

TROWIE KNOWE, MAINLAND, SHETLANDS

See THE GREY NEIGHBOURS (p. 410).

The Grey Neighbours

The trolls of Scandinavian mythology were hideous ogres, but in legends of the Orkney and Shetland Islands they became the trows, much more like fairies.

When Norsemen settled Shetland and Orkney they brought with them their mythology, echoes of which can still be heard there. From the ninth century until the end of the Middle Ages, the language of the islands was Norn, a branch of the West Scandinavian tongue which developed into modern Norwegian, Icelandic, and other languages: later, increasing contact with Scotland fostered a dialect resembling Lowland Scots but including many Norn words and phrases. Some of these refer directly to the trolls, misshapen creatures of Scandinavian folklore, whose haunts are commemorated in place-names such as Trolla Stack and Trolladale Water, while epithets like *trollet* ('deformed') and *trollmolet* ('surly' – literally 'troll-mouthed') indicate that they were thought of as grotesque and sulky.

As legend and language in the islands changed, trolls became known as 'trows' or 'drows' and took on more fairylike characteristics, although they were still often called the 'grey neighbours' or 'grey folk', as opposed to more southerly elves, whose typical colour was green. The greyness of the trows harks back to the original mountain-dwelling trolls, who resembled rocks and were turned to stone if caught by sunrise. This is said to have happened to a party of trows at HALTADANS, although in other tales they were merely 'day-bound', unable to return to their home until the next night. They were sometimes described as having three eyes, and when dancing were said to 'henk' or 'lunk' – limp or stumble – words associated specifically with the trows that appear in place-names such as Hinkie's Knowe in Sandsting and Lunkshoull in Yell. They lived in hillocks or cairns like the Trowie Knowe, a chambered tomb on the Shetland mainland.

Jessie Saxby, who was brought up in Shetland in the mid nineteenth century and wrote in detail about its folklore, was fascinated by the trows. She spent hours listening to an old man's 'endless yarns', and concluded that although the name 'trow' had been superseded by 'fairy', 'the characteristics of the race have never changed, and a Shetland fairy is quite different from Shakespeare's English dainty creatures.' The point is debatable: *A Midsummer Night's Dream* begins with Oberon and Titania quarrelling over a changeling boy, and the trows were much given to stealing children. Saxby relates a tale of a midwife visiting a young mother:

> As she neared the door she saw a small man *in grey* crossing the little kail-yard at the back of the house. He carried a heavy burden on his back, and a smaller one in his arms, and the old woman guessed the truth at once. Hurrying indoors with many misgivings she found a dead changeling and a mad wraithe [*sic*] where the mother and baby had been.

The husband had neglected to leave crossed straws on the threshold or a circle of pins in the pillow, either of which would have protected his wife. Similar thefts were attempted but foiled at WALLS and HOULL, and at BRINDISTER cattle rather than humans were targeted.

Not all the trows' visits were so motivated. Sometimes they came into a house for warmth or to wash their babies, as they did for instance at DUNROSSNESS. They liked to find a neat kitchen and a supply of clean water, and would reward good housekeeping but might bewitch a messy household.

Occasionally they left things behind. Such objects, like 'Da Ferrie's Brass Pan' at TAFTS, always brought luck to their new owners, and were sometimes medically valuable. A woman once saw some trows nursing one of their kind which they said had jaundice, pouring water on the sick one out of a small wooden bowl called a 'cap'. The woman invoked God and the trows fled, leaving the trophy, which was later used in cases of human disease. People would pay a shilling to borrow the trows' cap: it was not always effective, but Jessie Saxby's nurse had been cured of jaundice in childhood by this method. Another example was a tiny jar or 'pig' acquired from the trows by a couple named Farquhar. People came from miles around to use the ointment it contained, and yet the jar never became empty. The Shetland folklorist John Spence wrote in 1899 that he was in possession of 'Farquhar's pig', and Jessie Saxby in 1932 claimed likewise, admitting, however, that 'there are quite a number of these pigs in existence purporting to be the original and so mine is probably as genuine as the rest.'

See also BURNSIDE; DWARFIE STANE; GORD; VALLAFIELD (Orkney & Shetland Islands); THE TROWIE TUNES OF SCOTLAND (p. 390).

TUSKERBISTER, ORKNEY MAINLAND

A classic story of quick wits scoring off authority was recorded in 1969 from Gilbert Voy, a 75-year-old native of Orkney. He sets the story in 'Tissiebist', a misspelling or perhaps an older name for Tuskerbister in Orphir.

A poor man of Tissiebist had many children to provide for, and what with the potato crop failing and the sheep dying, he had his work cut out. One dark December night, however, he was away from home on a mysterious errand, and after that there was a strange sheep in the family's possession. The minister suspected theft and, sure enough, one day he overheard one of the children singing a song:

'Me father's stol'n the parson's sheep
An' we'll hae mutton an' puddin's tae
    eat,
An' a mirry Christmas we will keep,
But we'll say nethin' aboot it.

For if the parson gets tae know,
It's ower the seas we'll have tae go,
And there we'll suffer grief an' woe
Because we stole fae the parson.'

The sly minister offered the boy new clothes and half a crown if he would sing the same song in church the next Sunday. The little boy agreed, but he was more cunning than the minister. At the service, when the parson invited him to sing to the congregation, he gave the same tune with altogether different words:

'As I was walkin' oot one day
I spied the parson very gay:
He was tossin' Molly in the hay –
He turned her upside down, sir.

A suit o' claes and half a croon
Was given tae me be Parson Broon

Tae tell the neighbours all aroon'
What he hed done tae Molly!'

The tale of the bribed boy who sings the wrong song is told in many countries – the earliest surviving version comes from sixteenth-century Spain. Details vary, but the hypocrisy of the minister and the triumph of the naughty child are constant elements.

UNST, SHETLAND

A story included in a late nineteenth-century collection of folk tales illustrates the traditional belief in SELKIES (p. 404), people of the ocean who wore sealskins to visit the land. One day a fisherman of Unst encountered a group of these sea-people dancing on the sandy shore; when they saw him, the gathering broke up and each dancer seized a sealskin and plunged into the sea. But the fisherman had taken up a skin lying a little apart from the rest, and when he returned from hiding it, the shore was deserted except for one beautiful girl searching desperately for the skin, her only means of returning home. Guessing that he had taken it, she begged for its return. He asked her to marry him and at length in despair she consented.

She made him a good wife and was a good mother to her children, but she was always searching for something and on moonlight nights would steal down to the water and with a long cry summon a big dog seal to the edge of the water, where they would talk together earnestly in an unknown tongue. One day, when the fisherman was out in his boat, the children were playing hide-and-seek round the peat stacks. One of them found an old sealskin hidden away and ran with it to his mother. She kissed her children tenderly and bade them a hurried goodbye, then hastened down to the shore with the skin in her hand. The fisherman returned to find the children crying at the loss of their mother. He ran after her to the shore and was just in time to see her slip on the coat and join the big bull seal who had come up to greet her. At the despairing cries of her mortal husband, she turned as they swam away and said gently, 'Farewell, and all good fortune go with you. I like you well enough, but I always loved my first husband best.'

VALLAFIELD, UNST, SHETLAND

The Trowie Reel, also called Vallafield, is said to have been overheard outside a trowie hill early in the nineteenth century by one Sandy Winwick, on his way home from Colvadale to the Westing in Unst.

In the shelter of Gulla Hammar, a rock face on the west side of Vallafield, he stopped to have a smoke. It was beginning to get dark, and when he heard music on the air he was first enraptured and then frightened. Jumping to his feet, he grabbed his pocket-knife, 'and as his fingers touched the steel the music ceased'.

Running home as fast as he could, he told the story to his family and sang the tune to his daughter, who played it on her fiddle. This is a 1951 retelling of the story, adding a good deal of circumstantial detail to versions of 1888 and 1899, the latter recorded by John Spence, who claimed that his informant was the very man who had heard the trows' tune.

The trows of Shetland seem to have been particularly careless in allowing their music to be learned by human performers, but it was not unknown for fairy melodies to be passed on in this way in the rest of Scotland. A few even had lyrics attached, although they could be disappointing. 'One of these, which the writer heard,

seemed to consist entirely of variations upon the word "do-leedl'em",' John Gregorson Campbell reports in *Superstitions of the Highlands and Islands of Scotland* (1900). If such songs fell short of the sublime, that was probably the responsibility of the musicians, who liked to endow compositions with an otherworldly origin. It enhanced their status in the community, and in later years, when the folklorists and ethnomusicians came calling, a fairy tune was a special thing that could only be passed on after a generous helping of beer.

See also THE GREY NEIGHBOURS (p. 410); THE TROWIE TUNES OF SHETLAND (p. 390).

VE SKERRIES, SHETLAND

The Ve Skerries were believed to be the particular retreat of the seal-people or SELKIES (p. 404). They were also hunting grounds for fishermen who landed there to attack the seals. A story is told of a boat's crew that landed at one of the Stacks, stunned a number of animals, and stripped them of their skins. Leaving the carcasses on the rock, they were about to set off for Papa Stour when a great storm blew up. The men ran to the boat, but one imprudently lingered and was trapped by the waves.

Abandoned on the skerry, he saw those seals who had escaped coming back to help their friends, now deprived of their skins and helpless. The mate (or in another version the mother) of one of them struck a bargain with the marooned fisherman: she said she would carry him back to Papa Stour if he would then find and return her beloved's sealskin. The man, frightened to travel through the storm, asked if he might cut holes in the skin of her shoulders and flanks as hand-holds.

Two holes are cut in the Silky's skin by the rescued man to hold on by, and the truth of his story is proved some weeks afterwards to the incredulous people by the body being found upon the shore, having the two holes in the skin by which the fisherman had held.

G. F. Black, or his informant Captain Thomas, runs this story together with the ballad of 'The Great Seal of SULE SKERRY', but the narrative there is quite different.

VELTIGAR, TANKERNESS, ORKNEY MAINLAND

In *The Well at the World's End* (1956), Norah and William Montgomerie tell the tale of a young man called Johnnie Croy from Volyar, probably the farm known today as Veltigar. The name derives from Old Norse, 'vol' or 'vel' from *vollr*, meaning a valley, and 'gar' or 'yar' from *garth*, an enclosure.

One day when Johnnie went to the shore to look for driftwood he heard the sound of singing, and looking over the rocks he saw a mermaid combing her hair. Creeping up behind her, he sprang forward and kissed her. She knocked him over with one flip of her tail and dived into the sea, but in her hurry she dropped her comb. Johnnie found it at his feet and picked it up.

'Give me my comb!' cried the mermaid, but Johnnie refused, saying that she must come and live with him on land. She answered that she could not bear the rain and snow, nor the sun, nor the smoke from the fire in his house, and invited him instead to come with her and be made 'chief of the Fin-folk'. He tried to tempt her, promising that she should be mistress of his house at Volyar where he had cows and sheep and plenty of money, but she saw her own people coming and swam out to sea.

When Johnnie's mother heard what had happened, she told him he was a fool to fall in love with a mermaid, but that if he really wanted her he must keep her comb. This he did, and one morning he was awakened by the sound of music in his room and found the mermaid by his bed.

'I've come for my comb,' said she. Once more he refused, and asked her to stay and be his wife. This time she agreed, on the condition that after she had lived with him for seven years he should come with her to see her own people, and so they were married.

The mermaid made the best wife in all the countryside, and the best mother too. Seven children were born to the couple, and their home at Volyar was a merry one. As the end of the seven years approached the family made ready for their voyage, but before midnight on the day before they set out Johnnie's mother made a wire cross, heated it on the fire, and laid it on the bare bottom of the youngest child, although he screamed like a demon.

In the morning, Johnnie's wife found only six of her children waiting with her husband by the boat. She sent servants to fetch the baby, but they returned empty-handed, saying that four men could not lift the cradle. Then the mermaid herself went back to the house, and found that she could not move the cradle either. She tried to lift the baby out, but a terrible burning ran up her arms that made her scream. She returned to the boat with tears streaming from her eyes, and as they sailed away, those on the shore heard her lamenting for her bonny boy. 'Away, far away, sailed the boat, no one knows where. Johnnie Croy, his braw young wife, and their six bairns were never seen again by mortal eye.'

It was by no means unknown for a mermaid to marry a mortal man, although a more usual conclusion would be for her finally to return to the sea alone, leaving all her family behind. The means adopted by Johnnie's mother to preserve her youngest grandchild must be considered as muscular Christianity at its most brutal: by marking the baby with the sign of the cross she would have guarded him against any supernatural interference. The sympathies of the authors seem to lie with the mermaid, who is stated to have been a wonderful wife and mother, and perhaps they mention this particularly ungentle procedure to make their point more sharply.

WALLS, MAINLAND, SHETLAND

It was a common belief that the trows used secretly to carry off people and animals and leave in their place some deformed or defective creature. Sometimes, though, they left the effigy of the stolen person, or in the case of a cow or other farm animal, a lifeless mass. At one time there were several people in Shetland who sold charms and other contrivances to prevent this happening, but now and then an ordinary person took it upon themselves to deal with the trows.

One winter night, an old crofter in the parish of Walls was coming home across the hills in darkness. He was close to his outer gate when he met a gang of trows carrying a bundle between them. 'He felt a thrill of apprehension as he saw the bundle, but he allowed them to pass and hurried on down towards his cottage.'

As soon as he entered the cottage he saw that his wife was gone, and that the trows had left an effigy instead of her, in her accustomed chair. Quick as thought, he seized the effigy and flung it into the fire – which in a Shetland cottage was usually in the middle of the living-room floor, the smoke (or most of it) escaping through a round hole in the roof called the 'lum'.

The effigy at once caught fire, rose flaming in the air in a cloud of smoke, and vanished through the lum. As it disappeared, the real wife walked in at the cottage door, safe and sound, and the trows never troubled this man or his family again.

This story was told in 1895 in the *Scottish Review*, and is very like a tale from Lerwick included by Sir George Douglas in his *Scottish Fairy and Folk Tales* (1896) with the sinister title 'Mind the Crooked Finger', the words the man hears the trows saying. His wife has a crooked finger, and he realises that they are preparing her image. With great presence of mind he takes a Bible and a steel knife, frightens away the trows, and is then left in possession of his own wife plus the image left by the trows, which he keeps and uses as a (surely rather macabre) piece of furniture.

See also THE GREY NEIGHBOURS (p. 410).

WESTBROUGH, SANDAY, ORKNEY

W. Traill Dennison of Westbrough, Sanday, supplied a story to Sir George Douglas for his *Scottish Fairy and Folk Tales* (1896) called 'Assipattle and the Mester Stoorworm'. 'Assipattle' was an Orcadian name for a youngest son, and Dennison says that in his youth he himself, being the youngest son of the family, was sometimes called Assipattle. The literal translation is 'Ash-paddle', implying that the boy lies by the hearth and idly pokes the fire; the very similar name Askeladd (Ash-lad) is used in Norwegian folk tales to the same effect, and Cinderella is a female version, though perhaps in her case it is implied that she has to sweep the hearth rather than lying about on it.

Like all youngest sons, Assipattle turned out to have heroic capacities when put to the test, as demonstrated in this tale when

In a tale from Westbrough a great sea-serpent was overcome by the boy Assipattle, who killed it by thrusting a burning peat into its stomach.

the Stoorworm came to the country where his family lived. A stoorworm is a great sea-serpent, and this was the master and father of all stoorworms, and so was named the Mester Stoorworm. The only way to keep the monster quiet was to feed it seven virgins every Saturday morning, and soon the supply of virgins was running short. The king was told that now he had no choice but to sacrifice his only daughter, Princess Gemdelovely, to the monster.

The king sent out messengers to every part of the country, offering the hand of his daughter in marriage to any champion who would come and kill the Stoorworm. When Assipattle said he wanted to fight the monster everyone laughed at him, but he took his father's swift horse and rode off in the night. When he came to the seashore he found a hut with a fire from which he stole a burning peat, carrying it in an old pot. Then he went outside again and saw the king's boat on the water; having tricked the guard into getting out of the boat, Assipattle hopped in himself, and pushed out from the land.

He could see the Stoorworm's head before him like a great mountain, but he

wasn't afraid. The sun was rising, and as the monster woke it yawned. Assipattle rowed a little closer, and when the next yawn came his boat was swept into the creature's mouth and down its throat, until the mast stuck in its gullet. Assipattle jumped out and ran on until he came to the Stoorworm's liver. He cut a hole in the liver and put in the peat, blew until the oil of the liver caught fire, and then quickly ran back to the boat.

When the Stoorworm felt the heat of the fire in his inside, he began to spew as if he would have brought up the bottom of his bowels. Then there arose from his huge stomach terrible floods.

One of these floods caught the boat, snapped the mast, and flung boat and man out onto the land.

The king and all the people were watching, and they saw the death agonies of the Stoorworm. As its head fell a number of its teeth fell out, and these teeth became the Orkney Islands; then its head rose and fell again, shedding more teeth, which became the Shetland Islands; finally its head rose and fell and shed one last set of teeth, which became the Faroe Islands. Then the monster coiled itself up into a great lump, which became Iceland, and died. The king embraced Assipattle and called him his son, and everyone rode back to the palace.

Assipattle and Gemdelovely were king and queen, and lived in joy and splendour. And, if not dead, they are yet alive.

'Many of our old tales conclude with this sentence,' adds Dennison. 'In our old dialect it ran thus: "An' gin no' deed, dei'r livin' yet."' When a boy in Orkney, he says, he heard many versions of this tale. It is a fine story, of which this is no more than a brief synopsis: the full version, full of incident, drama, and humour, is well worth reading.

WINDHOUSE, YELL, SHETLAND

See BRINDISTER.

SOUTHERN HIGHLANDS

The counties of Inverness-shire and Ross & Cromarty

BEAULY, INVERNESS-SHIRE

In his *Witchcraft and Second Sight in the Highlands and Islands of Scotland* (1902), John Gregorson Campbell tells the tale of 'The Grey Paw', commenting that it is 'perhaps the most widely known and most popular story in the Highlands'. A very similar legend is told, for instance, of DORNOCH CATHEDRAL (Northern Highlands), but Campbell's rendition is such a fine one that it demands quoting at length.

In the church at Beauly monastery, strange sights and sounds were seen and heard by night, and none who went there to watch in the churchyard or within the church itself ever returned alive. A courageous tailor made light of the matter, and laid a bet that he would go any night and sew a pair of hose in the haunted church.

As he began his task, the moonlight streamed in through the windows, and at first all was silent.

At the dead hour of midnight, however, a big ghastly head emerged from a tomb and said, 'Look at the old grey cow that is without food, tailor.' The tailor answered, 'I see that, and I sew this,' and soon found that while he spoke the ghost was stationary, but when he drew breath it rose higher. The neck emerged and said, 'A long grizzled weasand that is without food, tailor.' The tailor went on with his

work in fear, but answered, 'I see it, my son, I see it, my son; I see that and I sew this just now.'

He made a great effort to speak slowly, dragging out the words for as long as possible, but at last he had to draw breath.

The ghost rose higher and said, 'A long grey arm that is without flesh or food, tailor.' The trembling tailor went on with his work and answered, 'I see it, my son, I see it, my son; I see that and I sew this just now.' Next breath the thigh came up and the ghastly apparation said, 'A long, crooked shank that is without meat, tailor.' 'I see it, my son, I see it, my son; I see it and I sew this just now.' The long foodless and fleshless arm was now stretched in the direction of the tailor. 'A long grey paw without blood, or flesh, or muscles, or meat, tailor.'

The tailor had nearly finished his work. He answered, 'I see it, my son, I see it, my son; I see that and I sew this just now,' while he took the last few stitches. When he could speak no longer, the ghost spread out its long bony fingers and clutched the air in front of him, saying, 'A big grey claw that is without meat, tailor.' The final stitch was in, and the tailor sprang for the door.

The claw struck at him and the point of the fingers caught him by the bottom against the doorpost and took away the piece. The mark of the hand remains on the door to this day. The tailor's flesh shook and quivered with terror, and he could cut grass with his haunches as he flew home.

BEINN A' BHRIC, LOCHABER, INVERNESS-SHIRE

The deer of the Highlands and Western Isles are said to be guarded by a spirit known as the Cailleach (pronounced 'kaliach'). One of her haunts was the mountain of Beinn a' Bhric in Lochaber. In 1925, K. W. Grant wrote that in Glen Nevis she used to milk the does, especially in the 'dead' months of winter.

The huntsman heard her song as she milked her deer; for all Highland milkmaids were wont, in times past, to charm the milk from cattle by keeping time with their fingers to a ringing lilt. The song of the Cailleach was unlike that of every other milkmaid; it was peculiar to herself, and unique in every respect.

The hunters knew that if one of them caught a glimpse of her, he would shoot no game that day. Once a young man, hearing that she was out on the mountain, determined to brave her. All day he hunted, but never a trace of a hind did he light upon. When evening came he lit a fire, and out of bravado sang a song:

The grizzled Cailleach, tall and stern,
Swift she glides o'er peak and cairn.

After he had completed a few verses the Cailleach approached, and told him that she had come to give him luck in hunting:

'To-morrow, as I milk my deer, watch thou, and whichever of the deer becomes restive, I will strike with the knob of my fetter. (A fetter was made of plaited

horse-hair with a loop at one end and a knob of hard wood at the other for fastening it.) Note it well; take good aim, and thou shalt have good luck.'

The man obeyed, and from that day forward he never hunted in vain.

See also GUARDIAN OF THE WILD (p. 352).

BLACK ROCK GORGE, ROSS AND CROMARTY

For part of its course the River Allt Grand or Auldgrande runs through a deep channel, the walls so close together that branches of trees from either side meet above the chasm. Where a bridge spans the gully, 'the observer, if he can look down on the gulf below without any uneasy sensation, will be gratified by a view equally awful and astonishing' of the dizzy depths, precipitous rocks, and inaccessible caverns where the sunlight never reaches. Even where the water is invisible, the river's voice echoes like a wild, imprisoned spirit.

Having set the scene, Hugh Miller, writing in 1835, goes on to tell the sinister tale of a lady said to have lived in the early seventeenth century at the house of Balconie, within a few miles of the chasm. She was a solitary woman, regarded by those who knew her with mingled fear and respect, and she liked to take long walks alone by the river. Suddenly, however, she seemed eager to make friends with one of her own maids, a simple Highland girl who was more perturbed than flattered by the attention, but had no choice but to accompany her mistress as she was asked. When she was with the lady, she felt always as if she were in the presence of a creature from another world.

One evening the two women walked together to the chasm: the place Miller

SOUTHERN HIGHLANDS

Sutherland

Ross & Cromarty

Inverness -shire

Perthshire

Argyllshire

Ross and Cromarty

🐾 Animal legends

⚔️ Battles and escapes

⚡ Curses and divine interventions

💀 Death and burial

😈 Devils and demons

🐉 Dragons and sea-serpents

🧚 Fairies and trows

👻 Ghosts and omens

🧍 Giants and ogres

🐴 Heroes and villains

🐎 Kelpies and water-spirits

🏰 Landmarks and local customs

🔺 Legendary beings

🎻 Pipers and fiddlers

🪨 Prehistoric remains

🧎 Saints and miracles

👹 Supernatural creatures

🎭 Tall tales, tricks and jokes

🗄️ Wells and springs

🐈‍⬛ Witches and witchcraft

📜 Wizards and seers

Dun Telve
and Dun Troddan

Kintail

Glen Mallie

Lochaber

Argyllshire

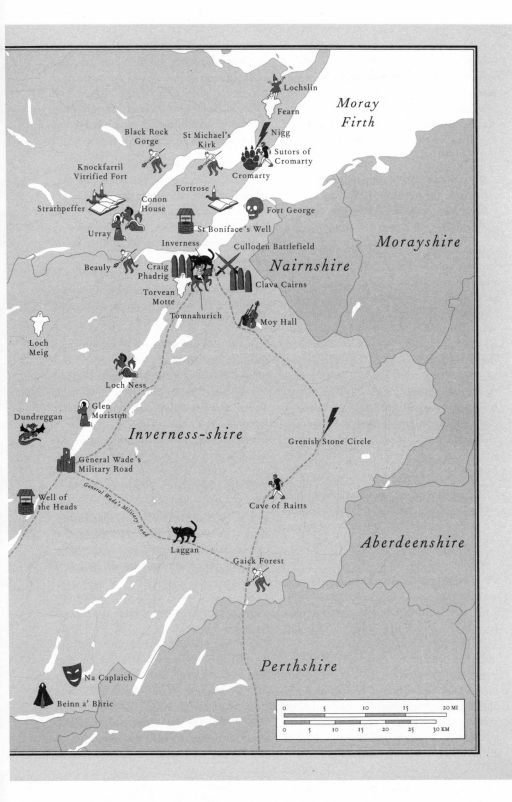

Lochslin

Fearn

Moray
Firth

Nigg

Black Rock
Gorge

St Michael's
Kirk

Sutors of
Cromarty

Knockfarril
Vitrified Fort

Fortrose

Cromarty

Conon
House

Strathpeffer

Fort George

Urray

St Boniface's Well

Morayshire

Inverness

Culloden Battlefield

Beauly

Craig
Phadrig

Nairnshire

Clava Cairns

Torvean
Motte

Tomnahurich

Moy Hall

Loch
Meig

Loch Ness

Glen
Moriston

Dundreggan

Inverness-shire

Grenish Stone Circle

General Wade's
Military Road

Well of
the Heads

General Wade's Military Road

Cave of Raitts

Aberdeenshire

Laggan

Gaick Forest

Perthshire

Na Caplaich

Beinn a' Bhric

| 0 | 5 | 10 | 15 | 20 MI |

| 0 | 5 | 10 | 15 | 20 | 25 | 30 KM |

means is probably what is marked on modern maps as 'Black Rock Gorge', a little way above Balconie Point. The girl was feeling more than usually nervous, while the lady was silent and melancholy. As the sun was going down they reached the brink of the abyss. The girl stopped, but the lady advanced.

> 'O no Ma'am, not nearer,' said the terrified girl, 'the sun is almost set, and sad sights have been seen in the *gully* after nightfall.'

The lady said she would show her a path leading to the water, one of the finest places in the world: 'I have seen it a thousand times, and must see it again tonight.' She dragged her reluctant companion forward, but suddenly a man appeared and addressed the lady: 'Your surety,' he said, 'must be a willing one.' The girl stayed where she was, while the lady and the man went on together. Twice the lady turned to speak to the girl, but could say nothing: her expression was despairing, and she clasped her hands in agony. Then, pausing a third time, she threw from her the household keys she wore at her belt.

> The keys struck, in falling, against a block of granite, and sinking into it as if it were a mass of melted wax, left an impression which is still pointed out to the curious visitor.

For ten years from that evening, the lady was seen no more. After that time, a Highland man named Donald, servant to a woman who lived in the neighbourhood, went fishing one day near the chasm. He hid some of his catch under a bush, meaning to give them to his mother, and when his mistress asked him if he had brought all the fish home, he said he had not been able to catch any more, 'devil a one'. The phrase was common parlance for 'none at all', but to name the dark powers was always risky. When Donald returned to the burn, he found the fish gone. A faint trail showed that they had been dragged off in the direction of the chasm, and Donald, following, found himself on a narrow precipitous path which led eventually down to an immense cavern.

> As he entered, two gigantic dogs, which had been sleeping one on each side of the opening, rose lazily from their beds, and yawning as they turned up their slow heavy eyes to his face, laid themselves down again. A little farther on there was a chair and table of iron apparently much corroded by the damps of the cavern. Donald's fish, and a large mass of leaven prepared for baking, lay on the table; in the chair sat the lady of Balconie.

Donald was astonished. He remembered the lady well from ten years earlier, and offered to take her home to Balconie, but she replied that she was fixed to her seat, and all the Highlands could not raise her from it. She said, 'The fish you have denied to your mistress in the name of my jailor, and his they have become, but how are you yourself to escape?'

All the while the dogs were eyeing him. The lady took the dough from the table and threw half to each dog, and while they were occupied Donald ran from the cavern and scrambled back up the path. No one ever saw the lady of Balconie again.

Like the wicked lady of ARDVRECK CASTLE (Northern Highlands), the lady of Balconie has sold her soul to the Devil. Her attempt to lure or force the maid into the chasm is so that she can give another soul to her master, probably to delay her own imprisonment. In her notes to the story, Katharine Briggs comments that 'The witch, like the fairies, evidently had to pay a tribute to Hell': this refers to stories like that of Tamlane at CARTERHAUGH

(Lothian & Borders), where a 'teind' or tithe of souls is said to be taken from fairyland every seven years.

CAVE OF RAITTS, LYNCHAT, INVERNESS-SHIRE

The Cave of Raitts, a little way off the main road near Lynchat, is horseshoe-shaped and roofed with large slabs of stone, and is sometimes claimed to be an old 'Pechts' house'. The semi-subterranean, low-roofed souterrains or earth-houses, probably once used for storage, are often popularly identified as having belonged to the Pechts or Picts, sometimes equated with the fairies (*see* PICTS, PECHS, AND PIXIES, p. 430).

The structure may look low from outside, but as its other name An Uaimh Mhor ('the Great Cave') implies, it is actually quite ample, and another tradition more suitable to its size is that it was built by giants. According to Alexander MacBain, writing in 1922:

> The women carried the excavated stuff in their aprons and threw it in the Spey, while the men brought the stones, large and small, on their shoulders from the neighbouring hills. All was finished by morning, and the inhabitants knew not what had taken place.

A similar legend is reported of DUN TELVE AND DUN TRODDAN.

CLAVA CAIRNS, CROY AND DALCROSS, INVERNESS-SHIRE

A little way east of Inverness are three circular chambered cairns of an unusual type, each surrounded by a stone kerb and a ring of standing stones. While the passages of most chambered tombs in Scotland face approximately east or south-east, those at Clava face south-west towards the midwinter sunset, an alignment which may have had symbolic significance.

Although archaeological evidence dates them to the third millennium BCE, tradition connects the tombs with a later period. They have been said to mark the burial place of the family of the sixth-century Pictish king Brude, and Otta Swire suggests in *The Highlands and their Legends* (1963) that this theory may have been inspired by the digging up of a gold rod during some drainage operations near the site. She does not mention when this discovery was made, but in any case the area had pre-existing associations with King Brude, whose castle is said to have been at nearby CRAIG PHADRIG. Brude himself was one of St Columba's most important converts to Christianity, and was buried on Iona, sacred to the saint.

See also GRENISH STONE CIRCLE.

CONON HOUSE, ROSS AND CROMARTY

The Kelpie of the River Conon is, or was, a highly dangerous spirit. According to Hugh Miller, writing in 1854, it usually appeared 'as a tall woman dressed in green, but distinguished chiefly by her withered, meagre countenance, ever distorted by a malignant scowl'. She would leap out of the stream when travellers were passing and point at them with a skinny finger or beckon them to follow. On one occasion a Highlander's journey took him at nightfall to the banks of the river, where he was seized by her. Although the lad who was with him tried to help as the man clung to a tree, she was too strong for them both, and the unfortunate traveller was dragged into the middle of the current and drowned.

Another story told of the Conon's Kelpie is that long ago, when the little church by the ford across the river near Conon House was still standing, a party of reapers were cutting the corn on an autumn day near the false ford where the water ripples over seeming shallows just before sweeping down into the deep pool below. They heard a voice crying out, 'the hour but not the man is come,' and looking at the river they saw the Kelpie standing in the false ford. She cried once again and plunged into the depths. As she vanished they heard the sound of drumming hooves and a rider came full pelt down towards the false ford. Half a dozen men jumped out of the corn and ran to catch hold of him. They told him what the Kelpie had said and explained the dangers of the ford, but still he spurred on like a madman. They pulled him off his horse, carried him struggling and shouting to the church, and locked him in, telling him they would come back when the hour of danger was past. When the Ill Hour was over, back they came and called out to him but there was no answer. They went into the church and found the traveller lying near the door with his head in an old stone trough filled with water. He had fallen in a fit and drowned while they waited for the hour to pass.

The tale is an old one. A version was told by Gervase of Tilbury in his *Otia Imperialia* (*c.* 1200) of a deep pool in the Rhône near Arles, where a figure like a man was seen running along by the river for three days, calling out the words, 'The hour is passed, and the man does not come.' On the third day, the figure raised its voice higher than before and a young man ran to the bank, plunged in, and was swallowed up, after which the voice was heard and the figure seen no more.

Many stories in Britain and Scandinavia involve the idea that certain rivers claim a life once a year or once in seven years:

here, as at RIVER SPEY (North East), the stream is personified as a woman. KELPIES AND WATER-HORSES (p. 364) are more often said to be male, but are always considered highly dangerous.

CRAIG PHADRIG, INVERNESS AND BONA, INVERNESS-SHIRE

Some ancient forts, mostly from the Iron Age, had ramparts constructed from a double wall of stone with layers of wood and rubble sandwiched between. If the timber were set on fire as it might be during an enemy attack, certain types of stone melted and fused other stones together. The great lumps of heated, cooled, and solidified rock have patches that glitter like glass, giving rise to the term 'vitrified' forts.

Folklorists used to speculate that these were the origin of the glass castles of tradition. David MacRitchie, in 1891, wrote that 'when one hears some wild story of a dreaded giant or ogre living in a castle surrounded with walls of glass', one knows that such a castle could not have existed, but that the real glass castles may have been vitrified forts. He cites the example of a famous glass castle said to stand on Tor Inis or Tory Island off the north coast of Ireland, but as castles of glass appear in fairy tales in places where no vitrified forts exist, this no longer seems a workable proposition, however tempting such a rationalisation may appear.

Craig Phadrig, a wooded hill west of Inverness, is crowned by a vitrified fort. Radiocarbon-dating suggests that its ramparts were originally built in the fifth or fourth century BCE, although they may have been strengthened around 500–600 CE. It has been proposed that Bridei or Brude, King of the Picts (*c.* 555–84), lived here, as it is recorded that he had a royal palace near the River Ness. There is a King Brude Road on the way here from Inverness.

Brude was visited by St Columba, who wanted permission to continue his work of Christian conversion, but the saint and his companions were refused entry. Then, says Columba's biographer Adomnan (627–704), Columba made the sign of the cross on the great doors, knocked and laid his hands on them, and immediately their bolts shot back of their own accord. Brude is supposed to have been converted by this miracle, and he and his retinue in the fort were all baptised.

A local tradition said that this baptism took place at the foot of a fir tree growing at the centre of the fort. In 1963, Otta Swire noted:

> This tree was still growing, one of the finest and largest Scotch firs that I ever saw, when Craig Phadraig was sold to the Forestry Commission in the 1920's and much strong feeling was aroused by their decision to fell it as part of a clearance scheme.

See also SAINTS OF SCOTLAND (p. 490).

CROMARTY,
ROSS AND CROMARTY

Hugh Miller's *Scenes and Legends of the North of Scotland* (1835) includes an unusual tale of a 'meteor'. Miller locates the events at a bay west of Cromarty, and dates the story to around the middle of the seventeenth century.

A captain whose vessel was moored in the bay was sitting alone on deck one night, waiting for his crew to return from shore. All lights of the houses were out, except at one cottage about two miles west of Cromarty. Suddenly a hissing noise was heard overhead, and the shipmaster saw a falling star, apparently heading for the cottage:

It increased in size and brilliancy as it neared the earth, until the wooded ridge and the shore could be seen as distinctly from the cottage as by day. A dog howled piteously in one of the out-houses, an owl whooped from the wood. The meteor descended until it almost touched the roof, when a cock crew from within. Its progress seemed instantly arrested; it stood still; rose about the height of a ship's mast, and then began again to descend. The cock crew a second time. It rose as before, and after mounting much higher, sunk yet again in the line of the cottage. It almost touched the roof, when a faint clap of wings was heard, as if whispered over the water, followed by a still louder note of defiance from the cock. The meteor rose, as if with a bound, and continuing to ascend until it was lost among the stars, did not again appear.

Not until the next night, that is, when the captain saw exactly the same thing happen. The day after, he visited the cottage, where 'partly out of curiosity, partly from the desire of possessing so interesting a bird', he bought the cock, and then set sail before nightfall.

When he returned to the coast about a month later, he saw that the cottage had vanished; all that was left was a heap of blackened stones. He was told that it had burned to the ground, no one knew how, the very night he had left the bay. Feeling responsible for the destruction, he had the cottage rebuilt and furnished. 'About fifteen years ago,' Miller finishes his story, 'there was dug up, near the site of the cottage, a human skeleton, with the scull and the bones of the feet lying together, as if the body had been doubled up when committed to the earth; and this discovery led to that of the story, which, though at one time often repeated, and extensively believed, had been suffered to sleep in the memories of a few elderly people for nearly sixty years.'

That the 'falling star' is some sort of evil spirit is strongly implied, since it is repelled by the crow of the cock, a sound very often said to dismiss devils and witches, as it did for instance at SMOO CAVE (Northern Highlands). It seems that whoever lived in the cottage did not know of their danger, or at least not that the cock was protecting them, or surely they would not have sold the bird to the captain.

CULLODEN BATTLEFIELD, INVERNESS-SHIRE

On 16 April 1746, Prince Charles Edward Stuart ('Bonnie Prince Charlie') launched his final bid for the crown, and was decisively defeated by the Duke of Cumberland's troops. The fighting actually took place in the centre of Drummossie Moor or Muir, Culloden being a little way to the north-west, but the latter name has become firmly attached to the event. The area is described in Black's *Picturesque Tourist of Scotland* (1844) as being 'as grim and shelterless a waste as vengeance could desire for an enemy's grave', though whether the 'enemy' in question is the fallen Highland or the fallen English troops, the book does not specify.

The Brahan Seer of STRATHPEFFER is said to have predicted the battle about a hundred years before it took place, exclaiming, 'Oh! Drummossie, thy bleak moor will, ere many generations pass away, be stained with the best blood of the Highlands. Glad am I that I will not see that day, for it will be a fearful period; heads will be lopped off by the score, and no mercy will be shown or quarter given on either side.' The Seer generally preferred an oblique style, and one suspects that this uncharacteristically direct 'prophecy' is a later invention, but it is not the only tale of a vision associated with the

site. In his journey through Scotland in 1769, Thomas Pennant describes a 'sort of divination, called *Slinneanachd*, or reading the *speal-bone*, or the blade-bone of a shoulder of mutton well scraped', a ritual also mentioned in a story told in the twentieth century at RODEL (Western Isles). Pennant records that:

> When Lord *Loudon* was obliged to retreat before the Rebels to the isle of *Skie*, a common soldier, on the very moment the battle of *Culloden* was decided, proclamed [*sic*] the victory at that distance, pretending to have discovered the event by looking through the bone.

The prince's army was at a disadvantage on the level ground against Cumberland's cavalry and artillery, and it is said that about a thousand Highlanders were slain at Culloden, while on the other side a figure of 300 included all those killed, wounded, and missing. In 1881, stones bearing the names of the clans involved were set up by Duncan Forbes of Culloden, and later a stone was added to commemorate the English dead. In 1836, however, when the writer William Howitt visited the battlefield, the mass graves were almost indistinguishable from the greensward about them. Howitt saw that in many places the turf was broken up by digging, and his guide, a local man called Wully Mackenzie, told him that this was from souvenir-hunting: 'scarcely a party came there but was desirous to carry away the fragment of a bone as a relic.'

> 'What,' said we, 'are the bones soon come at?' 'Yes,' he replied, 'in some places they lie within a foot of the surface.' These graves have been dug into in hundreds of places, yet you can scarcely turn a turf but you come upon them. He dug out a sod with his knife, and throwing out a little earth, presently came to fragments of the crumbling bones of the skeletons of 1746.

An eighteenth-century depiction of the battlefield at Culloden, showing the slaughter of the Jacobite forces. The Brahan Seer is said to have predicted a century before the battle that the 'bleak moor' would one day be stained with Highland blood.

Mackenzie said that one traveller had carried off a quantity of bones, but had afterwards been 'continually tormented by his conscience and his dreams'. He had eventually returned the bones, at great expense, and had them buried again.

Howitt talked at length with Mackenzie's family, who told him that the original name of the battlefield, Drummossie Moor, had now been quite superseded by the name Culloden, but that a wild track towards Badenoch at the edge of the moor was still called 'Drumossie'.

> They assured us, with the utmost gravity, that a battle would some day be fought *there*. We inquired how they knew that. They replied, because it had been repeatedly seen. On a summer's evening, people going across that moor had suddenly on various occasions found themselves in the very midst of the smoke and noise of a battle. They could see the various clans engaged, and clearly recognise them by their proper tartans; and on all these occasions the Laird of Culdethel, a neighbouring gentleman, was conspicuous on his white horse.

The Mackenzies were not to be convinced that this was imagination. 'They were perfectly satisfied that a battle was to be fought on Drumossie, and that the Laird of Culdethel would be in it – though with whom the clans would fight, and for what, they could not pretend to tell.' Howitt calls this a 'singular second-sight sort of superstition', but phantom armies and battles have been reported in several other places: in England, the battle of Edgehill was said to be spectrally re-enacted not only at the site itself but also at Claydon House, and the siege of Ticonderoga was witnessed from halfway across the world at INVERAWE HOUSE (Argyllshire & Islands).

DUN TELVE AND DUN TRODDAN, INVERNESS-SHIRE

T. M. Murchison was minister of Glenelg in the 1930s, and his mother's people had been shepherds in the area for many generations. His parish history was compiled partly from oral tradition gleaned from his relations and older parishioners. 'The most famous antiquities in Glenelg,' he records, 'are the two brochs or so-called "Pictish towers" in Glenbeg.' At one time apparently there were at least two more, but of these only 'a heap of jumbled boulders and stones' remained by his time. Dun Telve and Dun Troddan, however, still stand. It is said that when the brochs were being built, stones were handed from the quarry along a chain of men, a tradition reported of other buildings, such as the homestead which originally stood on the site of Rothesay Castle in Bute.

A 'broch' or 'brugh' is an archaeological term for the late prehistoric round towers found chiefly in the Orkney and Shetland Islands and the Western Isles and on the adjacent Scottish mainland. They are round stone-built towers, and are often popularly supposed to have been built by the Picts or Pechts, sometimes identified with the fairies (*see* PICTS, PECHS, AND PIXIES, p. 430). Here, however, the brochs are associated with Fionn mac Cumhaill or FINGAL (p. 10) and his followers the Fianna, said to have lived in these brochs and resorted to Skye for their hunting. The women of the band, says Murchison, never took food in the presence of their menfolk, but nevertheless remained healthy and beautiful, and the men wondered how the women managed to live on so little nourishment. One day, therefore, while the other men went to Skye, a warrior named Gairidh (pronounced Gary) pretended to be ill and was left lying on his bed, intending to watch the women.

He fell asleep, however, and the women promptly took strong wooden pegs and fastened Gairidh's seven locks tightly to the bottom of the bed, to keep him out of the way, and then they proceeded to feast on the finest food that glen or river could produce. Gairidh suddenly awoke, was irritated to find he was fastened to the bed, leapt to his feet with a mighty effort, and in so doing left every lock of his hair and the skin of his skull on the bed. Mad with pain, Gairidh rushed out, gathered brushwood which he placed around the locked door, and set fire to the dwelling with the women inside, so that none escaped.

Over in Skye, Fionn and the hunters saw the smoke rising and knew some terrible disaster had taken place. They hurried back, vaulting on their spears over the narrow channel to the mainland. One of them named Reithe did not leap far enough and was drowned, and the name of the place from which he jumped, Kylerhea, is said to be derived from Caol-Reithe, 'the Narrows of Reithe'. Fionn and his men found their women dead and Gairidh missing, but at last he was discovered skulking in a cave and was punished.

An almost identical tradition was reported of KNOCKFARRIL VITRIFIED FORT by Hugh Miller in 1835, and used by him to account for the name of Glen Garry, said to be where the murderer was torn to pieces. The tale is a better fit for Glenelg, much nearer to Glen Garry, and Murchison adds further local detail: at Kylerhea, he says, you can see the marks made by the warriors' feet as they jumped across the water, and at Bernera nearby is a site called Iomair nam Fear Mora ('the Ridge of the Big Men'), pointed out as the burial place of the 'Fingalians' (the Fianna or Fenians).

It is said that once upon a time a bold man began ploughing up the place, in defiance of local warnings. He turned up a human skull, which was so big that it easily fitted over the head of the biggest man present (alleged to be the Rev. Colin MacIver, minister of Glenelg from 1782 to 1829). Just at that point, however, a terrible storm of thunder and lightning arose, and the ploughing speedily ceased and the skull of 'Gairidh' or some other Fingalian was promptly buried again.

The Fianna were commonly said to be of giant size, so the finding of an unusually large skull may have helped to associate them with the site.

DUNDREGGAN, INVERNESS-SHIRE

Otta Swire tells us that Dundreggan, at one end of Glen Moriston, is said to mean the dun of the great beast or dragon. It may have been so called because the skeleton of some huge prehistoric creature was really found here. One legend goes that this was the site of a great battle between a dragon and the Gaelic champion Fionn mac Cumhaill or FINGAL (p. 10), who finally slew the reptile with the help of his dog Bran and buried it where it fell. The folklorist John Francis Campbell noted in 1872 that this story 'is part of the Dragon Myth, which is the widest spread of all myths known to me': he records that the tale of a fight between a man, a hound, and a water dragon is localised at several places in Scotland, and was told to him in the Western Isles on Barra and Uist.

A 'dun' is an archaeological term for a small stone-walled defensive homestead of the Iron Age, found mostly in western and central Scotland. Many such sites have become grown over and are now grassy

Picts, Pechs, and Pixies

Between the third and ninth centuries the Picts dominated much of Scotland, but remarkably little is known of this once-powerful tribe. Later ages imagined them as 'noble savages', as shown in this nineteenth-century engraving, and it was suggested that memories of their presence contributed to legends of the fairies.

The Picts are among the most mysterious of peoples. Between the third and early ninth centuries CE they controlled much of Scotland, yet very little is known about this dominant tribe. They were probably of partly Celtic origin, but spoke neither Brythonic (like the Britons) nor Goidelic (like the Irish). Their language remains untranslated, although several Pictish inscriptions survive, carved in an alphabet known as Ogam. Likewise obscure is the significance of the many ornately decorated stones and slabs found in their territory, some of which can be seen for instance at MEIGLE (Central & Perthshire).

Their power-base may have stretched as far as Orkney and Shetland, and certainly tales of them were told in the islands. Biot Edmondston and Jessie Saxby, writing on Shetland folklore in 1888, quote a statement that 'The first folks that ever were in our isles were the Picts, and they were said to come from a place in France called Picardy.' This is an imaginative but certainly fictional derivation. The Latin name *Picti*, meaning 'painted men', has been interpreted as referring to the warriors' use of woad or tattoos, but Viking invaders in the eighth century called them 'Petts' or 'Pechts': as the Scandinavians were not Latin-speakers, this may suggest that 'Picti' and 'Pechts' were respectively Latinate and Norse adaptations of the name that the Picts called themselves.

Much speculation has arisen from the common use in Scotland of the term 'Pechs' to refer to the fairies. The word is cognate with *puca*, *phooka*, *puci*, and *spuk*, Irish, Icelandic, and German words meaning elf or hobgoblin, and from which derive the English 'spook' and 'pixie' as well as Shakespeare's 'Puck'. The similarity to 'Pechts' and 'Picts' is therefore probably misleading, but a tempting rationalisation of legend is that tales of fairy folk related to the Picts, imagined as not only declining in power but dwindling in size. In the late nineteenth century the scholar David MacRitchie proposed this theory, arguing that the notion of fairy spirits stemmed from memories of a small and fugitive race, living mostly underground.

This thesis is at variance with the archaeological evidence, which does nothing to support the idea that the Picts were or became dwarfish, while the mounds and barrows MacRitchie cites as dwellings are mostly burial places. Earth-houses such as those at AIRLIE (North East) and CAVE OF RAITTS (Southern Highlands) were used by the living, but probably only for storage. Other 'proofs' were later exploded: an islet at the northern end of Lewis was known as Eilean Daoine Beaga ('the Little Men's Isle') because tiny bones were unearthed there in the sixteenth century and said to be those of pygmies, but in the twentieth century they were found to be the remains of seabirds.

Traditions of aboriginal peoples may indeed contribute to the idea of fairies, but it is an oversimplification to equate the historical Picts with the supernatural Pechs. The latter were, however, often described as a race which used to inhabit the land in times gone by. The antiquary Robert Chambers wrote in 1870, summarising many accounts he had heard:

> Long ago there were people in this country called the Pechs; short wee men they were, wi' red hair, and long arms, and feet sae braid, that when it rained they could turn them up owre their heads, and then they served for umbrellas.

Although diminutive, they were said to have been very strong. Chambers went on to give a version of the story 'Heather Ale', localised in other tellings at places including GARRYWHIN (Northern Highlands). An old Pech refused to give up the secret of the drink he alone could make, and was imprisoned for his obstinacy. He lived to an enormous age, becoming bedridden and blind:

> Maist folk had forgotten there was sic a man in life; but ae night, some young men being in the house where he was, and making great boasts about their feats o' strength, he leaned owre the bed and said he would like to feel ane o' their wrists, that he might compare it wi' the arms of men wha had lived in former times.

As a joke they held out a thick bar of iron. He snapped it in two with his fingers as if it had been a pipe stem, commenting that it was a fair bit of gristle, but nothing to the wrist bones of his days. 'That was the last o' the Pechs.'

hillocks, but in some cases stones are visible and in others it has been discovered through digging that there are structures beneath the surface: it is therefore a common tradition that these are or were dwellings of the fairies, often said to live underground.

Like many another dun, therefore, Dundreggan was rumoured to be a fairy mound. The elves who lived here were always anxious to carry off the mothers of newborn babies, to act as wet nurses to their own children. It is told that Ewan Macdonald of Dundreggan was out seeing to his livestock on the same night as his wife had their first-born son. A sudden gust of wind passed by and as it shook him he thought he heard in it the sigh of his wife, just as she had sighed before their child was born. Recognising the sound, he flung his knife into the wind in the name of the Holy Trinity, and his wife dropped safely to the ground beside him.

Sometimes women were taken as wet nurses along with their own newborn infants. One night, a man out late on the hillside heard plaintive singing coming from the knoll of Dundreggan. Stopping to listen, he heard a woman's voice singing over and over:

'I am the wife of the laird of Balmain,
The Folk have stolen me over again.'

Hurrying to the laird's house, he learned that the laird himself was away and his wife and baby son were missing.

Worried by what he had heard at Dundreggan, he went to find a priest, who duly came back with him to the knoll, blessed it, and sprinkled it with holy water. Suddenly there was a noise like thunder, the moon came out from behind a cloud, and they saw the laird's wife lying on the grass with her own baby in her arms. She had no idea of how she had got there, but was as weary as if she had come a long distance. A comparable story is told of John and Mary

Nelson at ABERDEEN (North East).

Why the fairies could not suckle their own babies is never explained in such stories, any more than why they should have had such a hankering after human children. It is sometimes suggested that they stole babies so that they could use them to pay their 'teind' or tithe of souls to hell, as mentioned at CARTERHAUGH (Lothian & Borders), but it is also possible that they wanted healthy new breeding stock. On one level, these legends were obviously told to explain death in childbirth and infant mortality, very common in the days before modern medicine, but they also reflected the idea of the fairies as in decline and eager to infuse new vigour into their ailing race.

FEARN, ROSS AND CROMARTY

In his *Scenes and Legends of the North of Scotland* (1835), Hugh Miller tells a story of a wicked stepmother:

In a now ruinous cottage with an old elm tree beside it, in the parish of Fearn, high on the hillside, there once lived a farmer, and a harsh one-eyed woman, his wife. He had a son of four, and a daughter of six, the children of a former wife, to whom the stepmother was bitter and unkind.

She beat her stepchildren, and would never let them have anything but a few rags to cover them in bed, though their real mother had left plenty of sheets and blankets. When winter set in, the children used to lie shivering with cold.

Then for a week they were found closely wrapped in some of their mother's best blankets, and for all their stepmother's threats and beatings, the children could tell her nothing of how it came about. The blankets were taken away, and locked fast in a great storechest; but it was in vain, in the morning they were found again on the children's bed, and all they could tell of the matter was, that they had been very cold when they fell asleep, and warm and comfortable when they awoke.

One night, when her brother had fallen asleep, the little girl stayed awake with cold and fear. Near midnight she saw a lady in white come in and go to the locked chest, which flew open at her approach. She took out the blankets, and wrapped them closely around the children.

She kissed the boy, and would have kissed the girl, when she looked up, and saw the face of her dead mother. Then the lady went away, without opening the door.

As in the fairytale of 'Cinderella', one wonders what the *father* was doing to let such cruelty go on. But this story has a happy ending. Miller concludes, 'In the morning, when the girl related her story to her stepmother, its effect was such that her severity was tempered for the rest of her life.'

FORT GEORGE, INVERNESS-SHIRE

See SUICIDAL ARTISTS AND ARCHITECTS (p. 156).

FORTROSE, ROSS AND CROMARTY

Coinneach Odhar of STRATHPEFFER was known as the Brahan Seer, and was as celebrated in the Highlands as Thomas the Rhymer of EARLSTON (Lothian & Borders) was in the Lowlands. He has been called the Isaiah of the North on account of his predictions. In his *Prophecies of the*

Brahan Seer (1877), Alexander Mackenzie reports that Coinneach (Kenneth) 'was sought after by the gentry throughout the length and breadth of the land', and his utterances were widely relayed and interpreted long after his lifetime. Many required considerable ingenuity in their explanation. One passage, translated from Gaelic, reads:

The day will come when English mares, with hempen bridles, shall be led round the back of Tomnahurich.

This Mackenzie understands as a 'prophecy, 150 years before the Caledonian Canal was built, that ships would some day sail round the back of Tomnahurich Hill'. Similarly, Kenneth's declaration that 'the day will come when the Big Sheep will overrun the country until they strike the northern sea' was said to refer to the Highland clearances, and his vision of the hills of Ross being 'strewed with ribbons' is 'generally accepted', writes Mackenzie, as finding its fulfilment in 'the many good roads' constructed in later years.

Near the Chanonry Lighthouse at Fortrose, a plaque commemorates Kenneth's death in the mid seventeenth century. According to this:

Many of his prophecies were fulfilled and tradition holds that his untimely death by burning in tar followed his final prophecy of the doom of the house of Seaforth.

Kenneth was a dependant of the Seaforth family. Tactlessly, he revealed to Lady Seaforth that her husband was having an affair in Paris, and his punishment was to be 'inhumanly thrown, head foremost, into a barrel of burning tar, the inside of which was thickly studded with sharp and long spikes driven in from the outside'. Mackenzie comments that 'The time when this happened is not so very remote as to lead us to suppose that tradition could so grossly blunder as to record such a horrible and barbarous murder by a lady so widely and well-known as Lady Seaforth was, had it not taken place,' a claim which need not be taken too seriously, since tradition is only too capable of such blunders. Before Kenneth's doom, as mentioned on the plaque, he foretold that the Seaforths would before too long 'end in extinction and in sorrow', and said also that a raven and a dove would fly over his ashes. If the dove were first, that was a sign that he would go to heaven, Lady Seaforth to hell, and so it turned out. A similar tradition was reported of MICHAEL SCOT, THE WIZARD OF BALWEARIE (p. 62).

See also CULLODEN BATTLEFIELD; KNOCKFARRIL VITRIFIED FORT.

GAICK FOREST, INVERNESS-SHIRE

The deer forest of Gaick was not formally created until 1814, but the isolation of this wild, mountainous tract of land had long made it a favoured haunt of wild game. On 31 December 1800, Captain MacPherson of Balychroan, accompanied by several other men, was passing the night there in a lonely hut used by hunters when an avalanche or whirlwind occurred, levelling the hut to the ground and scattering far and wide the bodies of the men who had been in it. When people came to look for the missing hunters next morning, a deep blanket of snow lay over

A contemporary portrait of General George Wade (1673–1748), responsible for opening up the Highlands with modern roads in the early eighteenth century.

the land, broken here and there by a dead man's hand sticking out of it.

News of the catastrophe ran through the Highlands and was still talked of in the Hebrides when the Reverend John Gregorson Campbell was collecting traditions in the late nineteenth century. By this time, people had woven superstition around the event and come up with a supernatural explanation.

Captain MacPherson, known as 'the Black Officer of Ballychroan', was said to be a 'dark savage' of a man who had abandoned his wife and children and had rooms beneath his house whence the cries of tortured prisoners could be heard by passers-by at night. The story now told was that a little while before his death the captain had been staying overnight with some other men in the hut. There they had been disturbed by strange noises, and a violent knocking on the roof.

> First came an unearthly slashing sound, and a noise as if the roof were being violently struck with a fishing rod. The dogs cowered in terror about the men's feet. The captain rose and went out, and one of his attendants overheard him speaking to something, or someone, that answered in the voice of a he-goat. This being reproached him with the fewness of the men he had brought with him, and the Black Officer promised to come next time with a greater number.

The servant who overheard this conversation adamantly refused to go on the next hunting expedition, on the last night of 1800. This was a wise precaution, for of those who went, not one returned.

When their dead bodies were being brought back from the deer forest, the elements were in a tumult, betraying the Devil's hand in events. As long as the Black Officer's body was carried first in the line the tempest halted all progress, but when the order of the corpses was changed the storm slackened enough to let the procession continue.

GENERAL WADE'S MILITARY ROAD, INVERNESS-SHIRE

In 1724, General George Wade was appointed Commander of the Forces in North Britain. He was given the task of restoring order to the Highlands following the Jacobite risings of 1715 and 1719, and realised that the first thing necessary was to improve communications between the various military posts. Between 1725 and 1733, he built some 250 miles (400 km) of roads in the Highlands, linking the four barracks at Fort William, Fort Augustus, Inverness, and Ruthven with each other and with Crieff and Dunkeld in the south.

The roads, though narrow, could support wheeled traffic, and the difference between these and the tracks hitherto in use gave rise to a contemporary couplet:

> If you'd seen these roads before they
> were made,
> You'd lift up your hands, and bless
> General Wade.

Antiquaries would be less inclined to give their blessing, commented Robert Chambers (himself an antiquary) in 1827, since one of the general's roads went smack through a Roman camp at Ardoch.

This is all a matter of history, but the general's name leads irresistibly to an association with the Yorkshire giant Wade mentioned by the sixteenth-century English antiquaries John Leland and William Camden, and in later tradition said to have built Wade's Causeway between Musgrave and Pickering Castles so that his wife could cross the moors to milk her enormous cow. (The road was in fact constructed by those other great communications experts the Romans.) This Wade's name is usually derived from that of Wada, a North European sea-being who in England became renowned as a builder. It is tempting, however, to surmise that into the rich mix of themes woven generation by generation into Britain's older legends there may more recently have been added some memory of General Wade's work in the Highlands.

GLEN MALLIE, INVERNESS-SHIRE

According to John Gregorson Campbell, Glen Mallie was the haunt of an Urisk, an unusually inquisitive member of its shy race:

> The Urisk of the 'Yellow Water-fall' in Glen Màili, in the south of Inverness-shire, used to come late every evening to a woman of the name of Mary, and sat watching her plying her distaff without saying a word. A man, who wished to get a sight of the Urisk, put on Mary's clothes, and sat in her place, twirling the distaff, as best he could. The Urisk came to the door but would not enter. It said:

> 'I see your eye, I see your nose,
>   I see your great broad beard,
> And though you will work the distaff,
>   I know you are a man.'

There does not seem to be any reason why the Urisk would not visit a man as such: presumably this particular Urisk felt it had developed a relationship with Mary and was comfortable with her but uneasy with a stranger. It was probably right to be wary, judging by what happened to another Urisk in Thomas Keightley's tale related at LOCH SLOY (Central & Perthshire).

GLEN MORISTON, INVERNESS-SHIRE

A short way south-west of Dundreggan, before the A887 bends and crosses the River Moriston, there is a cairn said to have been built by visiting pilgrims who added to it stone by stone. They came to honour the memory of the itinerant Presbyterian preacher Finlay Munro, who was preaching here in 1827. His text was Amos 4:12, which catalogues the punishments visited on Israel for oppression and idolatry and threatens worse to come: 'Therefore thus will I do unto thee, O Israel: and because I will do this unto thee, prepare to meet thy God, O Israel.' In Munro's sermon, 'Israel' could easily be understood to stand for the Episcopalians in Scotland, and behind them the English government.

Some local boys, possibly Catholics, challenged his words and called him a liar, to which he answered, 'As a proof that I am telling the truth, my footprints will forever bear witness on this very ground I stand on.' Just as he said, on the spot where he had stood his footprints were left indelibly in the ground. It became the custom for visitors to stand in the marks, and people claimed that the hair stood up on the back of your neck when you did so. Janet Bord, in *Footprints in Stone* (2004), reports that the prints were vandalised in the 1990s, but her latest information was that they were becoming visible again.

GRENISH STONE CIRCLE, DUTHIL, INVERNESS-SHIRE

Stones from religious sites, whether ancient or modern, should not be removed. Such is the prevalent belief, recorded at FYVIE

CASTLE (North East) and HILL O' MANY STANES (Northern Highlands) among other places. C. G. Cash, in 1906, recorded that a stone from the circle at Grenish was once taken to be used as a lintel over the doorway of a byre, but when it was in place the cattle were afraid of entering. Consequently it was taken back to the circle and an ordinary slab used instead, which the cattle were happy to pass.

It is not surprising that the Grenish Stone Circle should be supernaturally protected, if it was truly the crowning place of the Pictish kings. This tradition was reported by Otta Swire in 1963: 'The last to be crowned there was King Brude, so the old gardener we had at Kingussie told me.' He had been told this as a boy by his grannie, who came from Aviemore, and she heard it from *her* grannie, who got it from *her* grannie, a noted wise woman or witch. According to the gardener's grannie, when a Pictish king died, all who hoped to succeed him gathered at the circle, where the Druids invoked the spirits who told them which claimant to crown and other things besides. When the spirit was summoned at the death of the forty-eighth king, he told them to crown Brude but he would be the last they crowned. Thinking this meant the downfall of the Pictish kingdom, they asked more questions but only got an enigmatic answer: 'Living die, Dying live.'

When the king was crowned it was customary to raise three spirits, and for the king to ask each a question, the first of which must be 'What of my reign?' When Brude asked this question, he couldn't understand the reply: the spirit was that of an Irish champion who spoke only Gaelic, while Brude spoke the Pictish language. Fortunately a bilingual Druid was on hand to translate, telling Brude that one greater than he would come out of the sea, rule in his kingdom above him, and make him great. The prophecy referred to the coming of St Columba and his conversion of King Brude to Christianity.

As with a number of Otta Swire's stories, it is uncertain if this is a popular tradition or a romantic fiction. In some respects it sounds suspiciously like the revelation to MACBETH (p. 318) of Banquo's royal descendants, although it is of course entirely possible that Shakespeare based his scene on a report of ancient Scottish custom.

INVERNESS

One of the most interesting figures in Inverness's colourful history, though hardly one of the most attractive, was 'Paterson the Pricker'. Like the self-styled 'Witch-finder General' Matthew Hopkins of Essex, the roughly contemporary Paterson made a business (and a profit) out of detecting witches. Although in some respects Paterson was evidently unusual, the method used was a common one: that of sticking a pin into any spot or blemish found on the supposed witch's skin. This would be the 'witch-mark' left as a sign of the bargain with the Devil. If the victim felt no sensation and no blood flowed from the wound, he or more often she was adjudged to be a witch.

In his local and family history, the seventeenth-century Inverness minister James Fraser records that:

There came then to Inverness on[e] Mr Paterson, who had run over the kingdom for triall off witches, and was ordinarily called the Pricker, becaus his way of triall was with a long brasse pin. Stripping them naked, he alleadged that the spell spot was seen and discovered. After rubbing over the whole body with his palms he slipt in the pin, and, it seemes, with shame and fear being dasht, they felt it not, but he left it in the flesh, deep to the head, and desired them to find and take it out. Itt is sure some witches were discovered, but many honest men and women were blotted and broak by this trick.

Fraser comments that Paterson made a great deal of money, enough to keep two servants, and was at last 'discovered to be a woman disguised in mans cloathes'. It is an intriguing but not a unique story of a woman playing a man's part in a man's world: other females were known to have adopted a bloodthirsty male role, perhaps the most notorious being Anne Bonny who in the eighteenth century joined a pirate crew under 'Calico Jack' Rackham and, while on board she coincidentally met another disguised woman, Mary Read.

See also WITCH-HUNTS (p. 270).

KINTAIL, ROSS AND CROMARTY

A shepherd in Kintail, living alone in a bothy far from other houses, lit a bright cheerful fire one evening and threw himself on his bed of heather. About twenty cats then entered and sat around the fire, holding up their paws and warming themselves.

One went to the window, put a black cap on its head, cried 'Hurrah for London!' and vanished. The other cats, one by one, did the same. The cap of the last fell off, and the shepherd caught it, put it on his own head, cried 'Hurrah for London!' and followed. He reached London in a twinkling, and with his companions went to drink wine in a cellar.

The shepherd got drunk and fell asleep. When he woke in the morning the cats were gone. The owner of the cellar had him arrested, and he was taken before a judge and sentenced to death.

At the gallows he entreated to be allowed to wear the cap he had on in the cellar; it was a present from his mother, and he would like to die with it on. When it came the rope was round his neck. He clapped the cap on his head, and cried 'Hurrah for Kintail!' He disappeared with the gallows about his neck, and his friends in Kintail, having by this time missed him, and being assembled in the bothy prior to searching the hills, were much surprised at his strange appearance.

'This is a fair specimen of the popular tale,' commented John Gregorson Campbell in *Witchcraft and Second Sight in the Highlands and Islands of Scotland* (1902). He added that in Skye the adventure was claimed by a man nicknamed 'Topsy-Turvy' (But-ar-scionn) as having occurred to himself, and that after coming home, he made the gallows into a weaver's loom; in Argyllshire the hero made it the stern and keel of a boat, 'which may be seen in Lorn to this day'. Campbell also knew the story from Harris and the Monach isles, west of Uist. To this can be added various related tales where someone uses a password to travel with fairies or witches, like the Black Laird of Dunblane at MENSTRIE (Central & Perthshire), and the associated theme of the 'fairy host' or *sluagh* as at PEAT LAW (Lothian & Borders).

KNOCKFARRIL VITRIFIED FORT, FODDERTY, ROSS AND CROMARTY

On the summit of Knockfarril or Knockfarrel there stands a perfect specimen of a vitrified fort, one of those Iron Age buildings whose stone walls were once fused by fire so that they gleam. In the mid nineteenth century the site was visited by Alexander Mackenzie, who had devoted much time to studying the prophecies of

Coinneach Odhar, the Brahan Seer of STRATHPEFFER:

> On the summit of the hill we met two boys herding cows, and as our previous experience taught us that boys, as a rule – especially herd boys – are acquainted with the traditions and places of interest in the localities which they frequent, we were curious enough to ask them if they ever heard of *Coinneach Odhar* in the district, and if he ever said anything regarding the fort on Knockfarrel.

The boys took him (he seems to have been referring to himself in the plural) to the interior of the fort and pointed out what they called 'Fingal's Well', which they said had been used by the inhabitants until FINGAL (p. 10) one day drove them out and placed a large stone over the well. He had then jumped to the other side of the Strathpeffer valley. 'There being considerable rains for some days prior to our visit, water could be seen in the "well," but one of the boys drove down his stick until he reached the stone, producing a hollow sound which unmistakably indicated the existence of a cavity beneath it.'

According to the boys, the Brahan Seer had foretold that if ever the stone was taken from its place, Loch Ussie would ooze up through the well and flood the valley below 'to such an extent that ships would sail up to Strathpeffer and be fastened to *Clach an Tiompain*', an upright stone like a pillar near the Strathpeffer Wells. This was particularly interesting to Mackenzie since he knew of the Seer's unfulfilled prediction that 'the day will come when ships will ride with their cables attached to *Clach an Tiompain*'. The lads said that this would happen after the stone had fallen three times.

> 'It has already fallen twice,' continued our youthful informant, 'and you can now see it newly raised, strongly and carefully

propped up, near the end of the doctor's house.'

The fact that the stone had 'already fallen twice', with its suggestion that the event foretold would soon come to pass, is typical of nineteenth-century writing about the Brahan Seer's pronouncements. Another of his statements was that 'the raven will drink its fill of men's blood from off the ground, on the top of the High Stone in Uig.' The High Stone is on top of a mountain in Skye, and John Gregorson Campbell writes in *Superstitions of the Highlands and Islands of Scotland* (1900) that 'it is ominous of the fulfilment of the prophecy, that it has fallen on its side.'

See also CULLODEN BATTLEFIELD; DUN TELVE AND DUN TRODDAN; FORTROSE.

LAGGAN, INVERNESS-SHIRE

Often told in the Badenoch district of the Highlands was the story of 'The Witch of Laggan'. A hunter who made a habit of persecuting witches once sheltered from a storm in a mountain bothy in the forest of Gaick. A cat came in, and the hunter was hard put to it to calm the dogs he had with him. The cat admitted that she was a witch, but implored his help 'from the cruelty and oppression of her sisterhood'. Taking pity on her, he invited her to come in and sit, but she asked him first to tie up his hounds and handed him a hair rope with which to do it. He pretended to tie them, but fastened the rope to a beam.

The cat then came and sat by the fire but soon began to grow enormously. At last she changed shape into the Witch of Laggan, told the hunter that his last hour had come, and sprang at his throat. When the hounds leaped to his help she cried, 'Fasten, hair, fasten,' but hearing the beam crack she knew she had been tricked. The dogs set their jaws on her and 'never loosed their hold, until she demolished every tooth in their heads', after which she metamorphosed into a raven and flew over the mountains, leaving the dogs to crawl back to their master and die.

When the hunter went home, his wife told him, 'I have been seeing the Goodwife of Laggan, who has been just seized with so severe an illness, that she is not expected to live for any time.' The hunter went to the witch, uncovered her wounds, and accused her in front of all her friends who were gathered round her bed (having supposed her to be a virtuous woman). She confessed her crimes, and then expired.

That same night, a neighbour of the Wife of Laggan was returning from Strathdearn and had just entered the forest of Monalea when he met a running woman dressed in black who asked him urgently how far she was from the churchyard of Dalarossie, and whether she could reach it by midnight. He replied that she might, and she ran on. Soon the traveller encountered two black dogs, which seemed as if they were hunting something, and finally he met 'a stout black man' on a black horse, who asked if he had seen the woman and the dogs, and whether the first dog would overtake her before she reached the churchyard. 'He will, at any rate, be very close upon her heels,' answered the traveller, and before he had got the length of Glenbanchar, he was overtaken by the rider returning with the woman lying in the saddle in front of him, the dogs' teeth clamped to her body. If she had managed to enter the churchyard, she would have been safe, but 'it seems the unhappy Wife of Laggan was a stage too late'.

The horseman, from the black horse and two black dogs, was evidently the Devil come to claim his own. A similar fate befell the wizard Robert Gordon at THE ROUND SQUARE (North East).

LOCHABER, INVERNESS-SHIRE

Many reports of the Glaistig describe her as a fairly benevolent being, somewhat like a Brownie (*see* THE MAIDEN OF INVERAWE, p. 24). A quite different account was given by Alexander Carmichael in 1900: his 'glaistic' is a vicious creature, half woman, half goat, frequenting lonely lakes and rivers. 'She is much dreaded, and many stories are told of her evil deeds.'

Big Kennedy (Maenalrig Mor) of Lianachan in Lochaber was coming home one night when he saw the Glaistig. He captured her and brought her home with his sword-belt round her waist, and in the morning he took his coulter (cutting blade of a plough) and heated it in the fire. He asked the Glaistig to swear on the iron that she would never again molest anyone on his land, nor be seen in Lochaber either by day or by night. Doing as she was bid, the Glaistig burned her hand to the bone.

With a shriek of agony she flew out at the window and through the mist of the morning to the hillside beyond, and there she put out three bursts of the blood of her heart, which are still visible in the discoloured russet vegetation of the spot, and with each burst of blood the glaistig uttered a curse on Big Kennedy and on his seed for ever:

Growth like the fern to them,
Wasting like the rushes to them,
And unlasting as the mist of the hill.

The descendants of Big Kennedy of Lianachan say that the curse is still upon them, writes Carmichael.

From an etymological point of view, it is interesting to note that 'coulter', derived from Latin *culter* ('knife'), was used in the Scots language in the seventeenth and eighteenth centuries to mean 'cautery', an instrument used to cauterise (burn to stop bleeding). The coulter of a plough may once have been the most readily available large piece of metal for this purpose. In this story, however, it does not staunch the flow of blood but rather provokes it.

LOCH MEIG,
INVERNESS-SHIRE

Of all the folk beliefs surrounding 'cold iron', perhaps the most unexpected is one recorded by John Gregorson Campbell in *Superstitions of the Highlands and Islands of Scotland* (1900): 'A man who secreted iron, and died without telling where, could not rest in his grave.'

He illustrates this with the following story of 'Meigh in Lochaber', by which he probably means Loch Meig. The area was haunted by a ghost which was in the habit of meeting anyone who was out late:

An old man, having taken with him a Bible and made a circle round himself on the road with a dirk, encountered it, and, in reply to his inquiries, the ghost confessed to having stolen a plough-share (*soc a' chroinn*), and told where the secreted iron was to be found. After this the ghost discontinued its visits to the earth.

The significance of the dirk being used to mark the protective circle is that this, too, was cold iron or steel, powerful against fairies, ghosts, witches, and all forms of evil. People also swore oaths on their dirks because this form of iron was the readiest to hand, and an oath sworn on cold iron was the most binding of any.

The tale of the 'Apparition of ARRAN' (Argyllshire & Islands) also concerns a man whose spirit cannot rest because he has stolen plough-irons.

LOCH NESS,
INVERNESS-SHIRE

Loch Ness has some mysterious and even terrible characteristics. It never freezes; its water produces dysentery in a stranger; it is usually agitated violently when any other part of the world is undergoing the phenomenon of an earthquake; and, narrow though it be, it is found, at a very little distance from its verge, to be from sixty to a hundred and thirty-five fathoms deep. The last of its qualifications is the cause of the first, but the rest are inexplicably wonderful.

So wrote Robert Chambers in 1827, and Hugh Miller in 1835 agreed about the sympathetic disturbance of the waters: 'the waves of Loch Ness undulated in strange sympathy with the reeling towers and crashing walls of Lisbon during the great earthquake of 1755.' He attributes this to the long hollow line of the valley forming part of an immense fissure in the crust of the earth.

Neither of these nineteenth-century writers mentions the monster, whose immense fame is of quite recent date, although its first appearance is recorded in the seventh century by St Columba's biographer Adomnan. According to him, Columba was on his missionary travels when he saw a man being buried by the River Ness who had been mauled by a 'water-beast'. The saint ordered one of his companions to swim to the opposite bank to fetch a boat that was moored there, and a monk dived into the water. His splashing aroused the beast, which came roaring up from its lair and made for the man, jaws agape, but Columba calmly made the sign of the cross and ordered it to turn back. At his words the monster fled, terrified.

Loch Ness is twice as deep as the average depth of the North Sea, and its waters

The Loch Ness Monster

Reports of a 'monster' sighted in Loch Ness first appeared in local Highland papers in May 1933, and were picked up by the national press later the same year. The *Daily Mail* was sufficiently convinced to run the headline NOT A LEGEND – BUT A FACT.

The story rapidly took hold of the nation's imagination. The alleged physical attributes of the monster – the long neck and small head, with the rest of the body showing above the water in a succession of humps – exhibited a striking resemblance to the 'sea-serpent' which had already figured in news reports of the early 1930s, and it is significant that one of the first 'experts' to appear on the scene was Lieutenant-Commander R. T. Gould, whose book *The Case for the Sea-Serpent* had appeared in 1930. Gould's report of his investigations into the Loch Ness phenomenon was published in *The Times* on 9 December 1933, giving the monster an apparent scientific credibility and greatly enhancing its worldwide fame.

Believers in the monster like to point out the existence of earlier traditions of creatures living in the loch and the River Ness, and to claim that these give their Nessie an authentic family history. It is true that there were stories in existence long before 1933, including the well-known incident in Adomnan's *Life of St Columba* which tells how the saint vanquished a beast that lurked in the River Ness, simply by making the sign of the cross. Later tales from the early nineteenth century onwards described a Kelpie which inhabited the loch and enticed unwary travellers to their doom. These accounts bear little resemblance to the 1933 Loch Ness Monster, and the assumption that there is a direct link from the sixth-century saint through the nineteenth-century Kelpie to Nessie, though tempting, should not be accepted without careful consideration. That a story can survive, relatively unchanged, over 1,500 years of oral tradition is a theory which is at best unproven, and perhaps inherently unlikely. A different take on this scenario is that once an item of lore has been recorded in writing, the written version can be used to refresh the tradition or even to create it. Anyone familiar with Adomnan's text could have introduced the story into the locality at any time.

Similarly, there is no evidence of a causal connection between the Kelpie story and the 1933 monster, and certainly the serpentine Nessie is quite dissimilar to the equine Kelpie in both appearance and habits. Nothing like the Monster is mentioned in any nineteenth- or early twentieth-century source, including local guidebooks aimed at tourists and works devoted to

Scottish water-lore. This argues strongly against the legend's existence at that time, and it seems that Nessie's story was born in the 1930s by a sort of spontaneous combustion.

The biggest mystery surrounding the Loch Ness Monster is how the tale achieved such worldwide renown, not only taking off so quickly in 1933, but continuing ever since to be disseminated and discussed. One crucial factor seems to be the immense power of the mass media, but in addition to gullible or manipulative journalists, a body of people clearly existed who were willing and indeed determined to believe in the monster. It is these enthusiasts who have undertaken well-publicised and increasingly hi-tech investigations, who have written the countless books and articles which have kept the story in the spotlight, and who have propounded the theories of prehistoric survivals and sea-serpents. Media interest has waxed and waned but never completely faded away, as there is always a new exploration about to be launched, or a new documentary purporting to solve the 'mystery'.

This photograph of Nessie, allegedly taken by Colonel Robert Kenneth Wilson in 1934, was later revealed to be a fake.

On present evidence, it seems highly likely that the idea of a Loch Ness Monster was simply invented in about 1930. Despite countless amateur hunters and tourists pounding daily round the loch's shores with cameras and binoculars, there have been no convincing photographs or film of the monster, no physical remains, and no plausible explanation of how such a creature, or colony of creatures, came to be in the loch or could have survived there. The cryptozoologists and other monster-supporters have had over seventy-five years to make their case and prove the existence of anything more unusual than an upturned boat or a playful seal, and have signally failed. There is no stopping the tourist industry's 'Loch Ness Monster', but it is time to rephrase the *Mail*'s headline with NOT A FACT – BUT A LEGEND.

See also MINGARY (Argyllshire & Islands); LOCH NESS (Southern Highlands); KELPIES AND WATER-HORSES (p. 364).

are peat-stained and dark. It is not surprising that it is said to harbour strange creatures: reports of its monster form a staple of cryptozoology (the modern investigation of possibly real, possibly imaginary creatures also including the Yeti), but before such pursuits became popular there were tales of a Kelpie and an associated legend of the 'Willox Ball and Bridle'. The 'Ball' is or was half of a glass ball of unknown purpose (possibly a fishing float). Of its supposed origin, Walter Gregor wrote in 1881: 'It was hidden for untold ages in the heart of a brick, and was cut from its place of concealment by a fairy, and given generations ago to an ancestor of the present owner as a payment for a kind service.' The 'Bridle' is described as a small brass hook, said to have been cut from the Kelpie's harness:

> This kelpie had been in the habit of
> appearing as a beautiful black horse,
> finely caparisoned, on a well-frequented
> road in the Highlands. By his winning
> ways he allured unwary travellers to
> mount him. No sooner had the weary,
> unsuspecting victim seated himself in the
> saddle than away darted the horse with
> more than the speed of the hurricane, and
> was plunged into the deepest part of Loch
> Ness, and the rider was never more seen.

A Highlander was returning home one night when he saw the horse beside him. He knew what the beast was and what it had done, and instead of getting on its back he drew his sword in the name of the Father, Son, and Spirit, and struck at its head. Down fell a small hook, which the man caught up. He ran home as fast as he could, outdistanced the enraged Kelpie, and kept his prize.

The procedure for using the 'Willox Ball and Bridle' was to pour a small amount of water into a basin, put the 'ball' in it and turn it round three times, saying, 'In the name of the Father, of the Son, and of the Holy Ghost'. This performance was repeated with the 'bridle', and sometimes the sword supposed to have struck the Kelpie's head was waved over the water to the accompaniment of the same formula. The water then had the power to cure all manner of disease, and Gregor notes that the healing power lay in the objects themselves, not in the person performing the ceremony. Although he does not say so, the recitation of the names of the Holy Trinity was itself regarded as a powerful conjuration, and this, perhaps combined with the touch of metal, was what would have defeated the Kelpie.

See also KELPIES AND WATER-HORSES (p. 364); THE LOCH NESS MONSTER (p. 442); SAINTS OF SCOTLAND (p. 490).

LOCHSLIN, ROSS AND CROMARTY

A folk tale from Hugh Miller's nineteenth-century collection is cited by Katharine Briggs as an example of fairies punishing wrongdoing. Many years ago, writes Miller, a woman of Tarbat was walking along the shores of Lochslin carrying a large roll of newly woven linen, generally called a 'web'. It was then just as common for farmers to grow flax for clothing as corn for food, and it was necessary in the preparation of the flax to leave it spread out on the fields, protected by little more than the honesty of the neighbours.

> To the neighbours of at least this woman
> the protection was incomplete; – the very
> web she carried was composed of stolen
> lint. She had nearly reached the western
> extremity of the lake, when feeling
> fatigued, she seated herself by the water
> edge, and laid down the web beside her.
> But no sooner had it touched the earth
> than up it bounded three Scots ells into the

air, and slowly unrolling fold after fold, until it had stretched itself out as when on the bleaching-green, it flew into the middle of the lake, and disappeared for ever.

A 'Scots ell' is about a yard: three Scots ells therefore would be roughly nine feet or 2.74 m, giving an idea of the cloth's dramatic ascent.

MOY HALL, INVERNESS-SHIRE

Donald MacLeod of Hamer, Skye, under the resonant pseudonym 'Theophilus Insulanus' ('Theophilus' from Greek, meaning 'one who loves God', 'Insulanus' Latin for 'islander'), wrote a collection of stories of second sight and the supernatural in 1763. One of these gives an account of the Rout of Moy seventeen years earlier:

> Patrick MacCaskill . . . declared to me, That, in the evening before the Earl of Loudon attempted to surprize the young Pretender, at the Castle of Moy, Donald MacCrummen, piper to the independent company, (commanded by the young Laird of MacLeod,) talked with him on the street of Inverness, where they were then under arms, to march, they did not know whither, as their expedition was kept a secret: And that, after the said Donald, a goodly person, six feet high, parted with him about a pistol-shot, he saw him all at once contracted to the bigness of a boy of five or six years old, and immediately, with the next look, resume his former size. The same night Mac-Crummen was accidentally shot dead on their long march.

'Donald MacCrummen' is Donald Bàn MacCrimmon, traditionally identified as the last of the renowned MacCrimmon pipers, and thus symbolising the end of the ancient Gaelic culture associated with

the family. A lament for Donald's passing came to stand for a more generalised nostalgia, and is given here in a late nineteenth-century translated version:

> No more, no more, no more, for ever,
> In war or peace, shall return Maccrimmon;
> No more, no more, no more for ever
> Shall love or gold bring back Maccrimmon!

A little later, reports began to circulate that Donald Bàn had foreseen his own death. Many legends were associated with the MacCrimmon family, said to have been given a magical chanter by the fairies. Not the least unlikely tale, given that Mac-Crimmon's employer MacLeod was fighting on the Hanoverian side, related how Donald Bàn as he lay dying on the moor had composed and played a magnificent salute for Prince Charles Edward Stuart.

See also BORERAIG; TROTTERNISH; LOCH FINLAGGAN (Western Isles).

NA CAPLAICH, NEAR LOCH OSSIAN, INVERNESS-SHIRE

A. D. Cunningham tells a story in his *Tales of Rannoch* (1989) of a shepherd and his wife who were once making their way from Rannoch to Loch Treig up the old track now known as the Road to the Isles. They had come a long way and their mare was getting tired, and just as they were breasting the hill in sight of Loch Ossian a storm broke overhead with violent gusts of wind and icy sleet. The shepherd and his wife were soaked to the skin, and soon the woman became so numb with cold she could not keep her seat on the horse.

The shepherd got her down and laid her beside a large rock. He knew she could not last for the length of time it would take him to get help, so he knocked the mare on the head, disembowelled her, and placed the woman inside.

When he returned with others to aid his wife, they found her still alive and got her to warmth and shelter, where she revived. This event gave its name to the spot where it happened, Na Caplaich, 'the Mare'. The rock is on the path from Meall na Lice, less than half a mile from the modern youth hostel.

Though the event sounds historical, this story of taking shelter inside a horse is told of more than one place in Britain and also, perhaps originally, of the Alps, where Elsone or Aelsine, Archbishop of Canterbury (d. 959), is said to have perished of cold despite warming his feet in his horse's carcass. This story was current by the seventeenth century. It may be that successive travellers *really* had recourse to this expedient, though it meant sacrificing the beast that would be needed to carry them out of the wilderness if they survived. On the other hand, the legend may be the equivalent of a modern 'urban myth', a scare or horror story passing from mouth to mouth and located for verisimilitude in different remote places. Cunningham, the writer cited above, was for many years Expeditions Master at Rannoch School, and this sort of tall tale must have been excellent on a walk – this is a time-honoured way for oral folklore to be shared around, at foot pace and within sight of a particular landmark.

NIGG, ROSS AND CROMARTY

In his youth, Donald Roy was irreligious and greatly addicted to sport, taking part in games at his local club even on the Sabbath. He was a farmer and owned a small herd of black cattle, one of which he found dead on his threshold as he returned one Sunday evening. Next Sunday, after playing as usual, he found the body of another cow lying in exactly the same place, and began to wonder if this was a sign. The week after that, an important match was due to take

place (Hugh Miller, telling the story in 1835, does not specify exactly what game is in question, but it might be football). Donald took part and performed particularly well, but as he returned home he saw a fine cow, which he had bought only a few days before, fling herself down to expire at his feet with a horrible bellow. Donald now realised that this was God's judgement: 'I have taken *his* day, and he takes *my* cattle.' He never played at the club again, and at the age of twenty-three he was ordained an elder of the Church. He died in January 1774, aged 109.

'There are several stories still extant regarding him,' Miller tells us, 'which show that he must have latterly belonged to that extraordinary class of men (now extinct) who, living as it were on the extreme verge of the natural world, and seeing far into the world of spirits, had in their times of darkness to do battle with the worst inmates of the latter, and saw in their seasons of light the extreme bounds of the distant and the future.'

One on occasion, it is said, that when walking after nightfall on a solitary road, he was distressed by a series of blasphemous thoughts, which came pouring into his mind, despite of all his exertions to exclude them. Still, however, he struggled manfully, and was gradually working himself into a better frame, when looking downwards he saw what seemed to be a little black dog trotting by his side. 'Ah,' he exclaimed, 'and so I have got company; I might have guessed so sooner.' The thing growled as he spoke, and bounding a few yards before him, emitted an intensely bright jet of flame, which came streaming along the road until it seemed to hiss and crackle beneath his feet. On he went, however, without turning to the right hand or the left, and the thing bounded away as before, and emitted a second jet of flame.

'Na, na, it winna do,' said Donald. The thing had first tried to loose his hold of God and was now trying to frighten him, but he knew both God and the Devil too well for that. The appearance, however, went on bounding ahead and spurting out flame by turns until Donald reached the outer limits of his own farm, when it vanished.

A black dog was quite a common manifestation for the Devil, said to have taken a similar form at DELNABO (North East). Another tale of Donald Roy is told at URRAY.

ST BONIFACE'S WELL,
MUNLOCHY,
ROSS AND CROMARTY

See SCOTLAND'S HOLY AND HEALING WELLS (p. 44).

ST MICHAEL'S KIRK,
ROSS AND CROMARTY

Hugh Miller told a story in 1835 of an old woman living in Cromarty in the early eighteenth century whose enjoyment and suffering seemed linked in a strange way to the fortunes of her neighbours, for she was happy when those around her were miserable, and miserable when they prospered. It was not surprising, therefore, that her neighbours regarded her with dislike and contempt. She was a born troublemaker, and in her company families became divided, and lovers estranged.

She was working as a reaper for a Cromarty farmer, and her partner in the field was a poor widow, struggling to support three children. Years earlier, the malicious old lady had done her best to prevent this woman's marriage. 'Those whom the wicked injure, they never forgive,' and the old woman now worked with demoniac fury to

exhaust the widow, but to everyone's surprise the widow kept up and even seemed less tired that the other reapers when evening came. For the last two hours, the wicked woman had seemed dreadfully agitated, and was heard muttering to herself.

The next morning, the old woman was absent. The only one who went to enquire for her was the widow, who found her enemy in a high fever. All day she got worse, and shortly before midnight she died.

That night a solitary traveller was making his way along the southern shore of the bay when he heard a faint noise like that of the wind in an autumn wood. Fearing the presence of an evil spirit he crossed himself and stood still, and in the fitful moonlight he saw a tall figure gliding along the road from the east. A hollow voice demanded whether it was possible to reach Kirk-Michael before midnight. 'No living person could,' answered the traveller, and the figure groaned, and was out of sight in a moment. The sound as of falling leaves continued, and another figure came up, this one on horseback, and asked the same question. But before the traveller could reply, the horseman had vanished, and a shriek of torment and despair reached him. Suddenly the moon shone out brightly, and from the west there appeared a gigantic rider on a pale horse, with a female shape bent double before him. Two dogs were tugging, one at the head, and the other at the feet, and as they passed, the traveller saw in the moonlight that the woman's features were those of the old woman who, unknown to him, had died a few minutes before.

Versions of the same legend are told of Sir Robert Gordon at THE ROUND SQUARE (North East) and the Witch of LAGGAN. This rendition has some wonderfully evocative details: the whispering of dead leaves falling in an autumn wood is just the sound one might imagine a ghost to make.

'Kirk-Michael' is probably what appears on modern maps as St Michael's Kirk, a ruined church overlooking Udale Bay on the Cromarty Firth. The building has been disused since 1767 and is in a state of collapse, but there are plans to renovate it.

STRATHPEFFER,
NEAR DINGWALL,
ROSS AND CROMARTY

In the seventeenth century there lived in Strathpeffer a farmer named Kenneth Mackenzie, known as Coinneach Odhar (spelt differently in different sources), which means 'Dun' or 'Sallow' Kenneth. He is also and most famously known as the Brahan Seer, and his dreadful fate is recorded at FORTROSE, where he is said to have been burned to death in a barrel of tar.

A fascinating account of his career and prophecies was given in 1877 by Alexander Mackenzie, who collected stories of the Seer from many different sources. Kenneth's gift of divination was said to come from possession of a magical stone, which he is reported to have acquired in various ways: one tale is that the ghost of a Norwegian princess revealed the stone's existence to his mother. Another account is that one day Kenneth went to sleep on 'a little knoll' (clearly a fairy mound) and woke to find his head resting on a small round stone with a hole in the middle of it. Looking through the hole with one eye, he found he could see what was hidden from other men, but at the same time he became blind in that eye. In *Superstitions of the Highlands and Islands of Scotland* (1900), John Gregorson Campbell relates yet another version in which Kenneth took eggs from a raven's nest and boiled them, intending to put them back and find out how long the bird would sit before it despaired of hatching them. When he returned he found the oracular

stone in the nest (and maybe his ghastly end was delayed revenge on the part of the raven, a bird known to have magical properties of its own).

Perhaps the Seer's most famous prediction related to 'the last of the Seaforths'. When condemned to death by Lady Seaforth, Kenneth announced:

'I read the doom of the race of my oppressor. The long-descended line of Seaforth will, ere many generations have passed, end in extinction and in sorrow. I see a Chief, the last of his house, both deaf and dumb. He will be the father of three fair sons all of whom he will follow to the tomb.'

This was said to have come to pass in 1815 on the death of Francis, Lord Seaforth, who had had his own experience of SECOND SIGHT (p. 474) at the age of twelve when scarlet fever broke out at his school. Lying in the sickroom, he had seen a hideous old woman enter the room and stare at one of the other boys.

She then passed to the foot of the next boy's bed, and, after a moment, stealthily moved up to the head, and taking from her wallet a mallet and peg, drove the peg into his forehead. Young Seaforth said he heard the crash of the bones, though the boy never stirred. She then proceeded round the room, looking at some boys longer than at others. When she came to him, his suspense was awful. He felt he could not resist, or even cry out, and he never could forget, in after years, that moment's agony, when he saw her hand reaching down for a nail, and feeling his ears.

After that, however, she left. Although the nurse laughed at the story, the doctor took it more seriously and wrote down what Francis told him, and later those boys whom he had described as having a peg driven into their foreheads were those who died of the fever, those she passed by recovered, and those she looked at or touched suffered to some degree. Francis himself was left almost stone deaf.

In later years, Francis's three sons all died young, and after his third bereavement he became unable or unwilling to speak, communicating only by signs or in writing. When he died, leaving his estate to be inherited by his eldest daughter, the Brahan Seer's last prophecy was held to have been fulfilled.

See also CULLODEN BATTLEFIELD; KNOCK-FARRIL VITRIFIED FORT.

SUTORS OF CROMARTY, ROSS AND CROMARTY

A legend of the origin of the British people was recorded (or partly invented) by the seventeenth-century Laird of Cromarty Sir Thomas Urquhart. In a remote age, according to Urquhart, Diocletian the King of Syria had thirty-three daughters who all killed their husbands on their wedding night. As a punishment the princesses were loaded into a ship and cast adrift, at last arriving on the coast of uninhabited Britain. Here they lived until a race of demons became enamoured of them and took them as wives, producing a race of giants, the aborigines of the island ('if indeed the demons have not a prior claim,' noted Hugh Miller in 1835, relaying Urquhart's story). These giants were eventually exterminated by Brutus, but not before they had achieved some remarkable feats:

> There is a large and very ponderous stone in the parish of Edderton, which a giantess of the tribe is said to have flung from the point of a spindle across the Dornach frith; and another within a few miles of Dingwall, still larger and more ponderous, which was thrown from a neighbouring eminence by a person of the same family, and which still bears the marks of a gigantic finger and thumb impressed on two of its sides. The most wonderful, however, of all their achievements was that of a lady, distinguished even among the tribe as the *cailliach-more* [*cailleach-*

This illustration from John Gregorson Campbell's book *The Fians* (1891) shows an intruder venturing into the chamber of Fingal and his sleeping warriors.

mhór], or great woman, who from a pannier filled with earth and stones, which she carried on her back, formed almost all the hills of Ross-shire. When standing on the site of the huge Ben-Vaichaird, the bottom of the pannier is said to have given way, and the contents falling through the opening, produced the hill, which owes its great height and vast extent of base to the accident.

The Sutors of Cromarty are said to have been the work stools of two giants, shoemakers to the whole tribe. They worked together, having only one set of tools, which they threw across the firth to each other. A 'soutar' being a shoemaker, the two promontories in turn became known as the 'Sutors'.

These tales may be drawn from classical mythology – the daughters of Danaus, like those of 'Diocletian', killed their husbands on their wedding night. The story of the intermarriage between mortals and demons recalls Genesis 6:4: 'There were giants in the earth in those days; and also after that, when the sons of God came in unto the daughters of men, and they bare children to them, the same became mighty men which were of old, men of renown,' the 'sons of God' being often identified as the fallen angels.

Miller comments on the common belief that 'the race of men is degenerating in size and prowess with every succeeding generation, and that at some early period their bulk and strength must have been gigantic', an opinion also held by Alasdair Challum of GLEN ERROCHTY (Central & Perthshire). In fact as far as we can tell the reverse has been the case, better nutrition having led to an increase in human stature. The idea that past races were smaller than modern man has inspired its own folklore: tales of the fairies are sometimes said to derive from memories of 'little people',

surviving from prehistoric times. *See* PICTS, PECHS, AND PIXIES (p. 430).

TOMNAHURICH, INVERNESS-SHIRE

Tomnahurich is the anglicised form of Tom na h-Iubhraich, said variously to mean 'Hill of the Yew Tree' and 'Boat Mound'. Black's *Picturesque Tourist of Scotland* (1844) translates the name as 'hill of the fairies', but there seems no ground for this other than wishful thinking. Rising out of what was formerly swampland, the hill is generally thought to be an isolated hard core of rock, but others have believed it to be at least in part a dun or hill-fort, though as the site has been put to use as a graveyard it can no longer be excavated.

Of it the Welsh folklorist Sir John Rhys wrote in 1901:

> I was told the other day of a place called Tom-na-Hurich, near Inverness, where Finn and his followers are resting, each on his left elbow, enjoying a broken sleep while waiting for the note to be sounded, which is to call them forth.

He adds, 'What they are then to do I have not been told.'

Finn is the Irish hero Fionn mac Cumhaill, or in Scotland FINGAL (p. 10), who lies here accompanied by the Fianna or Fenians. John Gregorson Campbell writes:

> There is a huge chain suspended from the roof, and if any mortal has the courage to strike it three times with his fist, the heroes will rise again. A person struck it twice and was so terrified by the howling of the big dogs (*donnal na con mòra*) that he fled. A voice called after him, 'Wretched mischief-making man, that worse has left than found.'

This is almost exactly what is told of Arthur

and his knights at many a 'sleep site' in Britain. Such 'sleeping heroes' are usually said to wait in enchanted slumber until the day they are needed to save their land from some enemy. Meanwhile, they are sometimes inadvertently woken when someone enters their chamber and in ignorance sounds a horn lying near them. In England, Arthur sleeps mainly in a cluster of sites in the north, including Brinkburn Priory, Dunstanburgh Castle, and Sewingshields Crags in Northumberland, and The Sneep, Allansford, County Durham. In Scotland, he is supposed to wait beneath ARTHUR'S SEAT (Lothian & Borders). Gigantic warriors were said to lie in Craigiehowe Cave near Munlochy in Ross and Cromarty until wakened by a horn: as both Arthur and Fionn were imagined in folk tradition to be giant-sized, this legend could belong to either. It is not a peculiarly British tradition. On the Continent, several historical kings lie asleep, waiting the day of their return, and older than any of these is the ecclesiastical legend of 'The Seven Sleepers of Ephesus'.

Magicians and prophets as well as heroes were associated with the hill of Tomnahurich. Robert Chambers in 1827 reported a belief that the man buried here was MICHAEL SCOT, THE WIZARD OF BALWEARIE (p. 62), but more often the site is linked to Thomas the Rhymer of EARLSTON (Lothian & Borders). Campbell quotes the Uist bard MacCodrum as saying:

'When the hosts of Tomnaheurich come,
Who should rise first but Thomas?'

The story of Thomas himself as the prophesied leader seems to have arisen from a conflation of 'sleeping hero' traditions with his own prophecy about the coming of a great king. It is told also of Dumbuck, near Dumbarton, and in Sir Walter Scott's tale of 'Canobie Dick', set on THE LUCKEN HARE (Lothian & Borders).

In *The Fairy Mythology* (1850), Thomas

Keightley gives the story of the Fiddlers of Strathspey, two musicians who took lodgings in Inverness around the end of the sixteenth century and were offered double their usual fee by a grey-haired old man to come with him and play their instruments. He led them out of the town to a strange-looking dwelling, where they played all night for the dancers.

When morning came they left the place and were greatly surprised to find themselves coming out of a small hill. On reaching Inverness, they could recognise nothing and nobody – everything was so changed. While they were in a state of amazement over this, and the townspeople were equally astonished at their appearance, a very old man came up to them. On hearing their story, he said, 'You are then the two men who lodged with my great-grandfather, and whom Thomas Rimer, it was supposed, decoyed to Tomnafurach. Your friends were greatly grieved on your account, but it is a hundred years ago, and your names are now no longer known.'

It was the Sabbath day, and the bells were tolling. Awed at what had befallen, the fiddlers entered the church. They sat in silent meditation while the bell went on ringing, but the minute the minister began the service, they crumbled into dust.

This is a good example of the widespread theme of the 'supernatural lapse of time in fairyland', exemplified earliest in Britain by the twelfth-century tale of King Herla.

See also KIRK YETHOLM (Lothian & Borders).

TORVEAN MOTTE, INVERNESS AND BONA, INVERNESS-SHIRE

A little way north of Torvean Croft in the civil parish of Inverness and Bona is Torvean Motte, called in stories the hill of Torvean. According to Otta Swire, in *The*

Lady Macbeth is imagined here in an eighteenth-century engraving ceaselessly washing her hands, as her ghost is rumoured to do at Torvean Motte.

Highlands and their Legends (1963), this is traditionally said to be where Lady Macbeth is imprisoned, though unable to sleep away the centuries like FINGAL (p. 10) or King Arthur.

Once a boy herding goats on the hill lay down for a rest and awoke at dusk from a sleep, terrified to hear somewhere beneath him light footsteps, like those of a woman walking endlessly back and forth. This was Lady Macbeth, whose ghost is still sometimes seen, dressed in a kirtle of undyed wool, with a reddish-purple cloak over it, washing her hands in the River Ness nearby. According to some, she scrubs them with stones from the riverbed, while others says it is with leaves from a nearby alder tree.

This frantic scrubbing of her hands undoubtedly derives from Shakespeare's *Macbeth*, in which Lady Macbeth, having incited her husband to murder King Duncan, suffers from suppressed guilt, and, walking in her sleep, incessantly washes her symbolically bloody hands – 'Here's the smell of the blood still. All the perfumes of Arabia will not sweeten this little hand.' The haunt itself may also be attributable to Shakespeare's words in Malcolm's closing speech concerning the 'fiend-like queen, / Who, as 'tis thought, by self and violent hands / Took off her life'. Traditionally suicides are among those who cannot rest after death.

The ghost of Lady Macbeth is also said on occasion to pace slowly up and down the riverbank. If one person sees her, it is a sign of evil about to fall on the individual, but, if several people see her, it forebodes a national disaster. She is concerned especially with the Royal House and any of Macbeth's kindred.

The last time Otta Swire had heard of her being seen was by some visitors to Inverness, who mistook her for a film star on location. This was just before Princess Elizabeth and Prince Philip were due to fly to Africa, and when rumours got about of Lady Macbeth having been seen, there were fears concerning the royal plane. It landed safely, but when Elizabeth returned it was as the Queen. Lady Macbeth's appearance – if this is not, like many such 'traditions', an after-the-event fabrication – had heralded the death of Elizabeth's father, George VI.

See MACBETH (p. 318).

URRAY, ROSS AND CROMARTY

'On one of the days of preparation set apart by the Scottish church previous to the dispensation of the sacrament, it is still customary in the north of Scotland for the elders to address the people in set speeches on their experience of the truth of religion,' wrote Hugh Miller in 1835. The day was known as 'the day of the men'. When the elders of a parish were not sufficiently eloquent, they were called 'dumb elders', and their places would be taken for the occasion by more gifted preachers from nearby. Such was the case in the early eighteenth century in Urray, and one of those invited to attend was Donald Roy, the famous elder of NIGG.

Donald set out with three other elders, and towards evening they were passing a house on the outskirts of the parish when they met the housekeeper, who herself came from Nigg, and pressed them to spend the evening with her. Her mistress, she said, was a staunch Roman Catholic, but one of the best creatures that ever lived; her master was a kind man, of no religion at all. Both of them would make the four men very welcome.

Donald's companions wanted to refuse, but Donald thought that they must have been sent here for a reason, and persuaded the others to come inside. One of the rooms of the house had been converted by the mistress into a kind of chapel, with a small altar and twelve niches in the walls occupied by little brass images of the apostles. The lady was about to retire to her devotions here when the housekeeper told her of the guests, and asked that they should be allowed to worship in their own manner in one of the outhouses. Permission was given, and the lady then went to her chapel, but instead of kneeling before the altar she sat by a window.

And first there rose from the outhouse a low mellow strain of music, swelling and sinking alternately, like the murmurs of the night wind echoing through the apartments of an old castle. When it had ceased she could hear the fainter and more monotonous sounds of reading. Anon there was a short pause, and then a scarcely audible whisper, which heightened, however, as the speaker proceeded. Donald Roy was engaged in prayer. There were two wax tapers burning on the altar, and as the prayer waxed louder the flames began to stream from the wicks, as if exposed to a strong current of air, and the saints to tremble in their niches. The lady turned hastily from the window, and as she turned, one of the images toppling over, fell upon the floor; another and another succeeded, until the whole twelve were overthrown.

When the prayer had ceased, the elders were summoned to attend the lady, and found her eager to convert. The next morning the twelve images were flung into the River Conon.

Many years later, around the beginning of the nineteenth century, a fisherman dragging for salmon in a pool of the Conon found a little brass figure so richly gilt that for some time it was supposed to be made of gold; this event, according to Miller, was taken by local people to be 'an indubitable proof of the truth of the story'.

WELL OF THE HEADS, LOCH OICH, INVERNESS-SHIRE

On the shores of Loch Oich near Invergarry is the Well of the Heads, or Well of Seven Heads as it is called in *Black's Picturesque Tourist of Scotland* (1845). The well is supposed to take its name from an event in the 1660s. A monument to commemorate the episode was erected at the well in 1812; it shows a hand holding a dirk and seven heads, and inscriptions on different sides of the monument give an account of events in Gaelic, French, Latin, and English. The English version reads:

AS A MEMORIAL OF THE AMPLE AND SUM- MARY VENGEANCE, WHICH IN THE SWIFT COURSE OF FEUDAL JUSTICE INFLICTED BY THE ORDERS OF THE LORD MCDONELL AND A ROSS OVERTOOK THE PERPETRATORS OF THE FOUL MURDER OF THE KEPPOCH FAMILY, A BRANCH OF THE POWERFUL AND ILLUSTRIOUS CLAN OF WHICH HIS LORD- SHIP WAS THE NORMAL CHIEF.

THIS MONUMENT IS ERECTED BY COLONEL MCDONELL OF GLENGARRY XVII MAC-MHIC-ALAISTER HIS SUCCESSOR AND REPRESENTATIVE IN THE YEAR OF OUR LORD 1812.

THE HEADS OF THE SEVEN MURDERERS WERE PRESENTED AT THE FEET OF THE NOBLE CHIEF IN GLENGARRY CASTLE AFTER HAVING BEEN WASHED IN THIS SPRING AND EVER SINCE THAT EVENT WHICH TOOK PLACE EARLY IN THE SIX- TEENTH CENTURY IT HAS BEEN KNOWN BY THE NAME OF 'TOBAR-NAN-CEANN' OR THE WELL OF THE HEADS.

Seven heads are carved on top of the well, some bearded and some not.

Anne Ross in *Pagan Celtic Britain* (1993) fleshes out the story, saying that the seven heads of men responsible for the murders of two young MacDonalds were being taken in a basket to Inverness from Inverlair House, and on the way the party taking them stopped at Invergarry. The heads had grown restless in the basket and were leaping about and making a grinding noise as they clashed against one another. They were taken out and washed in the spring, which became known as 'Well of the Heads' on this account. She draws attention to similarly clashing heads in the Irish tale *Buil Suibhne*, in which Suibhne is pursued by five rough grey heads that clash together as they leap along the road behind him.

The MacDonald murders are thought to be historical; if the heads were indeed washed in the well before being presented to MacDonald of Glengarry, this was a curious repetition of a proceeding known from medieval Irish literature and might relate to the ancient Celtic practice of taking the heads of enemies as trophies. Similarly, in a ballad closely related to that of 'May Colven' set at GAMES LOUP (Glasgow & Ayrshire), the princess washes Heer Halewijn's head in a spring before taking it home.

In Scotland there are several other wells known as the Well of the Head or Heads, including Tobar nan Ceann, on Vatersay, Outer Hebrides, and Tobar a' Chinn, Torrin, on Skye. The name is explained in each case by a murder story involving a decapitated head, or heads being thrown in or washed in the well.

WESTERN ISLES

AN T-ÒB, HARRIS

Several sea-cows are said once to have come ashore at An t-Òb (Leverburgh) in South Harris. A sea-maiden who was in charge of the cows herded them back to the sea and away down the Sound of Harris, singing in Gaelic a song which Alexander Carmichael translates:

A low is heard in the sea of Canna,
A cow from Tiree, a cow from Barra,
A cow from Islay, a cow from Arran,
And from green Kintyre of the birches.

Carmichael reports that 'crimson-eared' and 'purple-eared' are terms applied to a species of cattle alleged to be descended from sea-cows. He thinks it likely that their ancestors were in fact the old Caledonian cattle which also had red ears: some of the island cows had one or both ears scalloped, and hence were sometimes known as 'notch-eared', a term also applied to the Caledonian herds.

At LOCH SHURRERY (Northern Highlands) the Water-bull was said to have no ears at all. He sometimes mated with the land-cows, producing calves with half-ears that looked as if their tops had been cut off.

ARDNADROCHAID, MULL

At Ardnadrochaid, not far from Craignure, lived a family called Lamont. They were served by a Glaistig who appeared in canine form. One day a band of cattle-reivers from Morven arrived across the Sound of Mull, intent on stealing as many Lamont cattle as could fit in their boat, but the Glaistig saw them landing and immediately started to drive the herd into the hills for safety. The reivers overtook them, however, at a spot called the Heroes' Hollow. The Glaistig then struck each of the beasts in turn, transforming them into grey stones rather than let the rievers take them. According to Alasdair Alpin MacGregor, recording this story in 1937, the stones are still to be seen in the Heroes' Hollow, their number attesting to the size of the Lamont herd.

Inconsolable for the loss of the cattle, the Glaistig pined away and died. The Lamonts buried her with all due reverence by the Sound of Mull, in a piece of ground traditionally used for burying unbaptised children: like unchristened babies, supernatural beings were thought to be excluded from entry into heaven, and so like them the Glaistig could not be be buried in consecrated ground.

Generally the Glaistig was said to dislike dogs (probably because they, like horses, could sense a supernatural presence), but in some tales she appears in their shape, or in that of an old grey mare. This particular Glaistig was unusual in being able to die, and her legend tends to support John Gregorson Campbell's view that Glaistigs

WESTERN ISLES

Atlantic Ocean

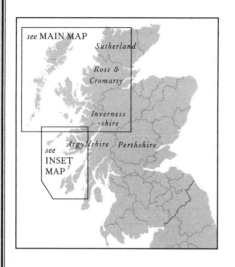

see MAIN MAP

Sutherland

Ross & Cromarty

Inverness -shire

Argyllshire *Perthshire*

see INSET MAP

Lewis

Callanish
Standing Stones

Eilean
Anabaich

Losgaintir

*South
Harris*

An t-Òb

Fladda-chuain

Rodel

North Uist

Dun
Buidhe

Ceallan

Nunton (Baile
nan Cailleach)

Stinky Bay
(Poll nan
Crann)

Ruabhal

Stilligarry

Dunvegan
Castle

Staoinebrig

Uisinis

Bornais

Beinn Mhor

*South
Uist*

St Brendan's
Church

Barra

Sandray

Pabaigh

Berneray

Legend

🐾 Animal legends

⚔ Battles and escapes

🏺 Cures and charms

⚡ Curses and divine interventions

💀 Death and burial

🧚 Fairies and trows

👻 Ghosts and omens

🐎 Heroes and villains

🐴 Kelpies and water-spirits

🗿 Legendary beings

🧜 Mermaids and selkies

🎻 Pipers and fiddlers

🗿 Prehistoric remains

🧍 Saints and miracles

👹 Supernatural creatures

🏆 Talismans and magical objects

🐈 Witches and witchcraft

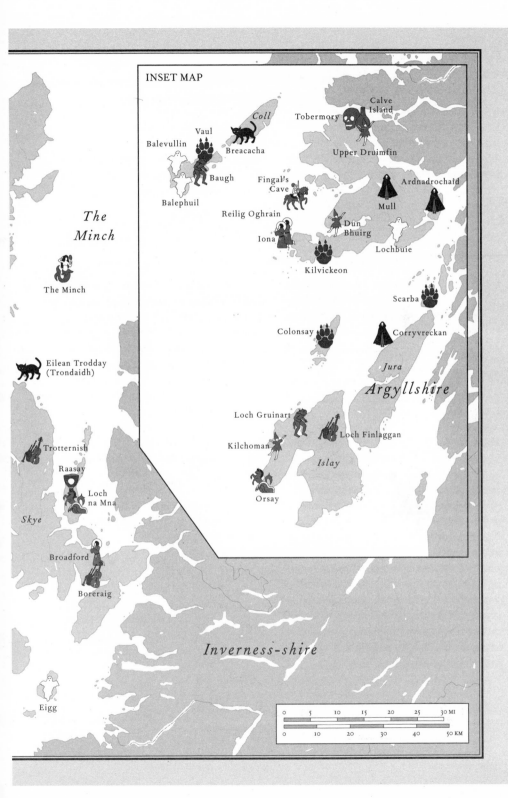

INSET MAP

Coll

Balevullin
Vaul
Breacacha
Baugh
Balephuil

Tobermory
Calve Island
Upper Druimfin
Ardnadrochaid
Mull

Fingal's Cave
Reilig Oghrain
Iona
Dun Bhuirg
Lochbuie
Kilvickeon

Scarba

The Minch

The Minch

Colonsay
Corryvreckan

Jura

Argyllshire

Eilean Trodday
(Trondaidh)

Loch Gruinart
Loch Finlaggan

Kilchoman
Islay

Trotternish
Raasay
Loch na Mna

Orsay

Skye

Broadford
Boreraig

Inverness-shire

Eigg

| 0 | 5 | 10 | 15 | 20 | 25 | 30 MI |

| 0 | 10 | 20 | 30 | 40 | 50 KM |

in general were originally human but had taken on fairy attributes. Another Glaistig was attached to the MacQuarry family at Ulva, where she looked after the cattle, and a third had her home in the Ross of Mull. A local man called Neil, who used to fish off the rocks of the Ross, was always followed as he made his way back of an evening with his catch by the voice of the Glaistig, saying 'Give me a cuddy, Neil!' Neil noticed that the oftener he gave her some fish, the oftener she asked, and sometimes she pestered him so much that by the time he got home he had hardly any left. This greedy apparition seems not to be attached to any particular family, and is more like the malign Glaistig described by Alexander Carmichael as haunting rivers and lakes in LOCHABER (Southern Highlands).

See also THE MAIDEN OF INVERAWE (p. 24).

BALEPHUIL, TIREE

People in the Highlands and Western Isles were often said to be gifted with SECOND SIGHT (p. 474) – the ability to see or sense events at a distance or yet to come. Lord Archibald Campbell was one of several writers who gathered stories about precognition, and he included some examples in his *Records of Argyll* (1885). One supplied by Alexander Brown from Balephuil or Baile-phuill told of an occasion when he was walking along and suddenly fell to the ground. He got up, but a few seconds later he fell down again. Thinking that he was being clumsy, he got up again and went on, but fell yet a third time.

I looked about me, and thought I saw the shadow of a woman standing at my side, and when I walked again I felt as if she touched my shoulder, and fell again; this time I walked or crawled on my knees to the house, the shadow following me, but

never touching me again. Next night I went to the wake of an old woman who had died on a farm. I was asked to go next day for strings for the coffin, and I carried the strings in the pocket which was on the side I was knocked down from. I have no other explanation to give of the phenomena, but that it was the old woman who died that was walking with me the previous evening and knocking me down.

Campbell heard another anecdote from John MacNiven of Barrapol, who was not himself a seer but had experience of people who were:

I was coming from Scarnish (*Sgairinis*) a few years ago, and had a horse and cart, and another man, John MacKinnon, Sandaig, with me. When about a quarter of a mile from Moss Church the dun mare stood, and would not move. After urging her on, I said –

'What can be wrong with her? She never refused to go on before.'

MacKinnon lifted his head and looked out, took hold of the reins, and said, 'Let her stand a little.' After three or four minutes he said, 'Drive her now.'

I said, 'Go on, Ellie.' She started at once. I said, 'I never saw her stand so before.'

MacKinnon said, 'How could she go on and a funeral passing us?'

It was, of course, a phantom funeral seen or sensed by the horse and by MacKinnon, who must have had the 'sight', but invisible to the other man. Such spectral processions have been reported in various parts of Britain, and were often interpreted as prognostications of funerals to come.

BALEVULLIN, TIREE

As well as tales of SECOND SIGHT (p. 474) from BALEPHUIL and Barrapoll, Lord Archibald Campbell heard various accounts, given to him 'as Facts', relating to a series of omens at Balevullin (which he spells Balevulin). Strange noises had been heard coming from the boat of one of the local crofters when no one was near it, and at other times two strangers had been noticed visiting the boat when it was beached, but when anyone looked for these men they could never be found. The rumour gained strength that the boat was destined to drown someone; this being confirmed by the local seers, the owner could persuade no crew to go out with the boat, and was obliged to offer it for sale.

> After lying a considerable time it was purchased by the sons of Neil MacDonald of Balemartin (*Baile-mhàrtuin*), with the full knowledge of all the rumours that were abroad about it. After they had had the boat in Balemartin for some time, some curious sights and noises were seen and heard about the boat, which made them regret their purchase, and they went to the Balevulin man to have the bargain made void.

The seller would not hear of it, and Mr Sproat, a lawyer, told the buyers that they could do nothing to compel the Balevullin man to take the boat back. Sproat dismissed their fears as superstitions, but it was some time before the MacDonalds would take the boat to sea. Eventually, however, they launched it again with a crew including one of their own sons. While they were fishing for lobsters the boat struck a rock at Hynish and capsized, and young MacDonald was drowned.

BARRA

In 1911 an old piper on the island of Barra told a story about a boy apprenticed to carpentry who was working with his master on a boat. He found he had forgotten a tool and ran back to get it from the workshop, where he disturbed a crowd of carpenter fairies hard at work in his master's absence. They scattered as he came in and one little fairy woman in her haste dropped her silk girdle. The boy picked it up and put it in his pocket, and when she presently came in search of it he refused to hand it over, until she offered in exchange to make him expert in his trade without further apprenticeship.

Next morning the boy got up early and fitted two planks into the boat. The work was so perfect that the master was amazed: whoever had done it, he said, knew the trade better than he did himself. The boy told how he had acquired his skill, and there the tale ends. Fairy gifts usually departed if they were spoken of, but some men, like the Islay smith at KILCHOMAN, kept their art, so this lad too may have retained his magic.

See also ST TREDEWELL'S LOCH (Orkney & Shetland Islands).

BAUGH, TIREE

BROWNIES (p. 80) were sometimes said to work with cattle. This was the case at Baugh, where the crofters were relieved of night-time duty by a Brownie who acted as herdsman between sunset and sunrise. No one ever saw him, though people sometimes watched, and one man endowed with SECOND SIGHT (p. 474) who stayed out late said next day that he had seen 'an impalpable creature' herding the cows away from the crops. The creature he saw was wearing little or no clothing, which made the man pity him, and he offered him a gift of shoes and breeches. The Brownie's response was:

> Shoes and breeks on Gunna,
>   And Gunna at the herding;
> But may Gunna enjoy neither shoes
>   nor breeks,
>   If he should herd the cattle
>   any more.

He then departed, and after that the people of Baugh had to look after their own herds. This is of course the standard reaction of a Brownie when offered clothes, but it is not so usual for one of these shy beings to volunteer his name. 'Gunn' and 'Gunnar' are used as Christian names in Norway today, and it might be that this Brownie, Gunna, came to Tiree with the Vikings.

BEINN MHOR, SOUTH UIST

Mary Macinnes of Benbecula told Alexander Carmichael in the mid nineteenth century that Beinn Mhor was always eerie because of the Loireag dwelling there. The Loireag is a small water-nymph or elf-woman, not particularly frightening in what she does, but dreaded for her uncanny nature. She is described as plaintive, stubborn, and cunning, and has a particularly keen ear for music. The women of the islands had to spend a lot of time making cloth, spinning the yarn, weaving it, and finally waulking or fulling it, a cleansing and thickening process involving soaking the material and stamping it with the feet; at this communal task there was usually singing, and the Loireag made her displeasure evident by spoiling the cloth if anyone sang out of tune, or even if the same tune were repeated too often.

Being particularly fond of milk, the Loireag would suck it from cows, goats, or sheep if she got the chance, and would put a spell on the creatures so they could not move away from her. A girl in Beinn Mhor once found a cow being sucked by the Loireag and tried to separate them, but was ignored by both the elf and the cow. She then fetched her father, described by Carmichael as 'a little cross carle [fellow]':

The little carle leapt out at the door in sparks of red fire, swearing at the impu-dent 'loireag' and at the cow. He threw a boulder at the 'loireag', wishing to kill her, but struck the cow instead and nearly killed her! He then seized the point of the cow's horn in the name of Columba the kindly, and immediately the cow leaped away from the 'loireag' and she leapt away from the cow. She betook herself up the corrie of Coradale, her tune in her mouth and her tongue in her cheek, mocking the little cross-grained carle and singing as she went.

Carmichael's informant finished on a note of nostalgia, saying that she remembered when the Loireag 'was wont to drive the people out of their heart-shrine with fear' but that since the people were driven from Beinn Mhor, 'there is no person there whom she can frighten or dismay unless the big sheep.'

BERNERAY

The late seventeenth-century writer Martin Martin was fascinated by the phenomenon of SECOND SIGHT (p. 474). He quotes many curious stories, including examples from Holland, the Isle of Man, and Wales, but mainly gleaned from his travels around the Western Isles. One notable tale relates to the island of EIGG, and several other accounts were supplied to him by his friend Sir Norman MacLeod of Berneray, one of which tells of an occasion when MacLeod and some friends were playing 'Tables', explained by Martin as 'a game called in Irish Falmer-more, wherein there are three of a side, and each of them throw the dice by turns'. (Sir Walter Scott and others interpret it as a version of draughts, but it does not sound very like the modern game.)

There happen'd to be one difficult Point in the disposing of one of the Table men;

this oblig'd the Gamester to deliberate before he was to change his Man, since upon the disposing of it, the winning or losing of the Game depended; at last the Butler who stood behind advised the Player where to place his Man, with which he complied, and won the Game.

Sir Norman was surprised, because he thought the butler could not play Tables, and asked the man how long it was since he had learned the game. He replied that he had never played in his life, 'but that he saw the Spirit *Browny* reaching his arm over the Players head, and touched the Part with his finger, on the Point where the Table-man was to be plac'd'.

This butler was probably the 'seer' involved in another episode when Sir Norman had gone to Skye on business without saying when he would be coming back to Berneray. In his absence his servants were all sitting in the main hall one evening, when 'one of them who had been accustomed to see the *Second Sight*' told the rest that they should move, because the hall would soon be wanted for others. It seemed very unlikely that anyone would come so late, but within an hour a messenger arrived to say that Sir Norman had just landed. Told what had happened, Sir Norman questioned the seer, who answered 'that he had seen the Spirit called *Browny* in Human Shape, come several times, and make a shew of carrying an old Woman that sat by the fire to the door, and at last seem'd to carry her out by neck and heels, which made him laugh heartily, and gave occasion to the rest to conclude he was mad to laugh so without any reason'.

BROWNIES (p. 80) are usually described as domestic spirits which work around the house or farm, are averse to gifts, and may get medical help at need, as in the tale of DALSWINTON (Dumfries & Galloway). It seems that sometimes they were also thought of as having second sight: John

Aubrey, writing in the seventeenth century about the Grant family of Strathspey, mentions a Brownie attached to the family that could see into the future.

BORERAIG, SKYE

On 2 August 1933, a cairn above Loch Dunvegan was raised to the MacCrimmons. The Gaelic inscription on the cairn is translated by Alasdair Alpin MacGregor as:

> The Memorial Cairn of the MacCrimmons, of whom ten generations were the hereditary pipers of MacLeod, and who were renowned as Composers, Performers, and Instructors of the Classical Music of the Bagpipe. Near to this spot stood the MacCrimmon School of Music, 1500–1800.

To this college, writes MacGregor, travelled pupils from all parts of Scotland and Ireland, and the course was an arduous one, lasting as much as ten years.

In charge of the college were the MacCrimmons: forefathers of Scottish music; inventors of *piobaireachd*, the great music of the pipes; composers of the famous tunes 'I Got a Kiss of the King's Hand', 'Too Long in this Condition', and many more. The origins of the family lie in Cremona, Italy, from which town they took their name, and they may have been related to the sixteenth-century philosopher Giordano Bruno. 'The MacCrimmons were never excelled or even equalled as pipers and composers of pipe music,' declared W. L. Manson in 1901.

Most of this is doubtful, to put it mildly. Although it is true that MacCrimmons were pipers to the MacLeods of Skye, much else that has been written about them is sheer fantasy. The story of the family's elevation to the status of unchallenged

The MacCrimmons of Skye were pipers to the clan
MacLeod, but how much of their fame is fact and
how much is legend?

emperors of the pipes is a fascinating one, told in detail by William Donaldson in *The Highland Pipe and Scottish Society 1750–1950* (2000). A 'secret' history of the MacCrimmons was said to have been written in 1826 but suppressed and then lost, an idea aired in correspondence in the *Oban Times* in the early twentieth century which then continued to develop more and more baroque features. The MacCrimmons were surmised to have links with the freemasons, and pipe music to encode theological mysteries.

One motive behind the rumours was cynical: an Australian whip-plaiter named Simon Fraser, the man who claimed to have seen the vanished 1826 book, made money from selling his privileged information. Profit, however, cannot account for why the MacCrimmon legend was adopted so eagerly. Symbolic of Highland culture as a whole, the myth of the MacCrimmons was an ambiguous one, providing at the same time a halo of antiquity for the music and a foreign origin for it: authority given with one hand, taken away with the other. Performers too are at once exalted and disempowered by the legacy of an 'authentic' tradition, which asserts, in Donaldson's words, 'the value of an ordered, historic legitimacy against a dangerously creative and uncontrolled present'.

Glorification of the MacCrimmons at the expense of all other pipers has been a largely nineteenth- and twentieth-century phenomenon, but tales of the family, both historical and fantastical, stretch back further than that. *See* MOY HALL (Southern Highlands), STIRLING (Central and Perthshire), and TROTTERNISH.

BORNAIS, SOUTH UIST

A woman at Bornais or Bornish, South Uist, put a protecting charm on Allan

Macdonald of Clanranald before he left to fight beside the Earl of Mar at Perth in 1715, but another woman, a widow from Staoinebrig, cursed him because he took her only son away to battle. She implored him to leave the lad, but he would not relent, and so she vowed that *Ailen Beag*, 'Little Allan', as Clanranald was called, would never return.

She baked two bannocks, a little bannock and a big bannock, and asked her son whether he would have the little bannock with his mother's blessing, or the big one with her malison. The lad said that he would have the little bannock with his mother's blessing, and as well as these she gave him a crooked sixpence, saying, 'Here, my son, is a sixpence seven times cursed. Use it in battle against Little Allan and earn the blessing of thy mother, or refrain and earn her cursing.'

At the battle of Sheriffmuir, neither bullets nor blows hurt Allan of Clanranald, but when the strife was hottest and the outcome still in doubt, the son of the widow of Staoinebrig remembered his mother's injunction, and that it was better to fight with her blessing than fall with her cursing. He put the crooked sixpence in his gun, aimed, and fired, and Clanranald fell.

> His people crowded round Clanranald weeping and wailing like children. But Glengarry called out, 'To-day for revenge, to-morrow for weeping,' and the Macdonalds renewed the fight. Thirsting for revenge they fell upon the English division of Argyll's army, cutting it to pieces and routing it for several miles.

The protective curse defeated by a silver bullet, here linked to Clanranald by Alexander Carmichael writing in 1900, is associated in legend with other military leaders, including Claverhouse of DUNDEE (North East).

BREACACHA, COLL

An encounter between a witch and a man of Coll named Hector McLean was described by Hector to John Gregorson Campbell. The narrative is included in *Witchcraft and Second Sight in the Highlands and Islands of Scotland* (1902), and tells how one evening Hector was about halfway along the mountain track from Arinagour to Breacacha when 'a black sheep came about his feet, and several times threw him down.' At last he took out a clasp-knife and threatened the animal, but it kept on knocking him over, and the knife closed on his own hand, giving him a nasty cut between finger and thumb.

> On coming to the large open drain or stream below Breacacha Garden, he stood afraid to jump across, in case the black sheep should come about his legs, and make him fall in the drain. He was now, however, within hail of his own house, and whistled loudly for his dog. It came, and was fiercely hounded by him at the sheep. Every time the dog made a rush and came too near, the sheep became an old woman, whom Hector recognised as one of his acquaintances, and jumped in the air.

The old woman asked Hector to call off his dog, and when he refused, promised that if he did so she would stand his friend in right and wrong. He did try to call the dog then, but it would not obey, so he caught it by the scruff of the neck, and it tried to turn on him. He promised to keep hold of it while the woman made her escape.

> The witch became a hare, and Hector called out to her, as she seemed to have such wonderful power, to 'add another leg to her stern, to make her escape the faster.'

She ran away as a hare, and when he released the dog it followed, and did not come home until the next morning. The next time the woman saw Hector, she blamed him for having let go of the dog, and said it had kept her on a rock all night.

Hector later went as a servant to Arileod farm nearby, and several times saw the same woman in her hare's shape, sucking milk from the cows. The dog chased her whenever it saw her. In the end he sought her out and accused her, upon which she lost her temper and threatened to punish him for spreading such stories about her. He said the proprietor of the island had offered a reward for discovery of the person who had been guilty of troubling the farm, and asked her to go to Arileod that night, 'so that people would not have it to say it was for him the evil had arisen'. She said she could not go that night, but would go the next night, 'and he would hear of it'. He did, because the next night she let out the cows and caused much mischief on the farm.

Witches were not the only supernatural residents of the district. Breacacha Castle had its own Glaistig or household spirit, described unflatteringly as 'a lump of a lassie' and generally rather an unattractive being: rather than yellow hair like other Glaistigs hers was white and reached to her ankles. Although she would do the housework when guests were expected, when they had arrived she would entertain herself by leading them astray in the night if they got up, so that they could not find their way back to their rooms. Tales were still told in the 1930s of how she would distress and even maltreat strangers who stayed at the castle, although those she knew she let alone.

John Gregorson Campbell, basing his judgement on extensive investigation and many oral accounts, declares Glaistigs to be women originally of the human race, put under enchantments so that they come to have a fairy nature.

See also THE MAIDEN OF INVERAWE (p. 24).

BROADFORD, SKYE

In the early days of Celtic Christianity, a priest was sent from Pabbay to preach in Skye. On his way through the forest near where Broadford now stands, he stopped to eat his lunch, and drove his walking stick into the ground beside him. Having finished his meal, he saw several small men and women standing around him. A little old man approached and knelt before the priest. When the priest asked who these people were, the old man said that they were the fairies, who had repented of their sins and wished to ask forgiveness.

The priest pitied the old man, but he had been taught that the fairies were the fallen angels who had been cast out of heaven by God, so he answered that he could not forgive them.

An old lady now knelt too, and argued from the Bible that 'there is more joy in heaven over one sinner that repenteth than a thousand righteous men.' The fairies, she said, had repented for many years. The priest was disturbed, but still he refused to forgive the fairies. 'Sooner would my ash stick turn into a tree than God would forgive you,' he declared, and walked away, leaving the stick standing in the earth. As he went he heard the fairies wailing behind him.

It was not for some time that he returned to the clearing. When he did so, he found that his walking stick had become a beautiful ash tree, and realised what this meant. He settled in the forest as a hermit and prayed for the fairies, and as the years passed he heard their wailing less and less, until one day all around him was silent.

The standing stones at Callanish on Lewis are known in Gaelic as Fir Bhreig or 'The False Men'. They are said to be giants who were turned to stone as punishment when they refused to build a church.

That day the people who brought him food found him lying dead with a blissful expression on his face.

The story, told by George Macpherson in *Highland Myths and Legends* (2005), is pleasant but highly sentimentalised. Much truer to type is a short tale quoted by Sir George Douglas in the late nineteenth century, located only at 'a quiet spot upon the Ross-shire coast' where an old man sat reading his Bible by the sea one summer evening:

A beautiful little lady, clad in green, drew near, and addressing him in a silvery voice, sought to know if for such as she Holy Scripture held out any hope of salvation. The old man spoke kindly to her; but said that in those pages there was no mention of salvation for any but the sinful sons of Adam. On hearing this, the fairy flung her arms despairingly above her head, and with a shriek plunged into the sea.

That fairies were concerned about their ultimate fate at the Day of Judgement was a belief recorded in the seventeenth century by Robert Kirk. *See* THE MINISTER AND THE FAIRIES (p. 112).

CALLANISH STANDING STONES, UIG, LEWIS

West of Stornoway an avenue of stones leads across the moors to a circle of thirteen pillars around a chambered cairn, about 4,000 years old. Fir Bhreig, 'The False Men', is the Gaelic name for the group. In Ireland, many standing stones are known as *far-breaga* or 'false man', these usually being solitary menhirs which from a distance look like people; their 'falseness' lies in their not being as human as they appear.

The Lewis pillars are said to be giants who refused to build a church for St

Kieran and were therefore turned to stone. Such retributory legends are common in folk tradition, and the meta-morphosed beings may be believed to recover their power of motion at certain times, becoming able to walk or even to dance. The sin for which they were petri-fied is often that of having danced on the Sabbath.

A second account of Callanish is that the stones were brought to Lewis in ships by a priest-king and set up there by black men under the guidance of priests in feathered robes, and another belief was that 'the Shining One' appeared there on mid-summer morning to walk the length of the avenue, heralded by the cry of the cuckoo, the bird of the Celtic land of youth Tir-nan-Og. It used to be the custom for local families to visit the stones on that day and on May Day, at first openly and then in secret when such practices were condemned by the Kirk.

It was said that once during a famine on the island a woman was so desperate that she went to the sea intending to drown herself, but saw a white cow which appeared from the waves and told her that she and all her neighbours should bring their milk pails to the stones of Callanish that night. When they did so, the cow provided each of them with a pailful of milk, and this bounty contin-ued until a witch brought a sieve instead of a pail. As the cow could not fill it how-ever hard she tried, she was milked dry, and was never seen on the island again. The power of witches to get abormal supplies of milk from cows, whether ordinary animals or magical ones, was well known, as related at DELORAINE (Lothian & Borders), and in England too there are tales of witches milking fairy cows into sieves.

CALVE ISLAND

Calve Island lies across the mouth of Tobermory harbour. At one time, appar-ently, so many rats were breeding there that the smallholders of the island subscribed sixpence each as a fee to Iain Pholchrain of Morven, said to be an expert in the 'Rat Satire' described by John Greg-orson Campbell in *Superstitions of the Highlands and Islands of Scotland* (1900):

> When a place is infested to a troublesome extent with rats or mice, and all other means of getting rid of the pests have failed, the object can be accomplished by composing a song, advising them to go away, telling them where to go, and what road to take, the danger awaiting them where they are, and the plenty awaiting them in their new quarters. This song is called the Rat (or Mouse) Satire, and if well composed the vermin forthwith take their departure.

Iain composed a long ode in which he told the rats to leave in peace and not lose themselves in the wood. (As they would have had a sea journey ahead of them, this seems an unneccessary instruction.) They were advised what houses to call at and which to avoid, the latter being those of the poet's friends, and tempting descrip-tions were given of what awaited them in the shape of butter, cheese, and meal. After this, it was said, there was a notice-able decrease in the rat population.

CEALLAN, GRIMSAY

'What I am going to tell you now took place a good many years before I was born, and it is true,' says the storyteller Peter Morrison, recounting in Gaelic in

1978 a case of the SECOND SIGHT (p. 474) that befell his grandmother, who lived on the island of Grimsay, in connection with a drowned woman whose relatives were still living in Morrison's time.

The body of the drowned woman had been searched for but not found, and it was concluded that she must have been carried off by the ebb-stream in the Minch. Then one night she appeared in a dream to Morrison's grandmother Mairi, telling her to get up and go and look for her in Lon Cait, a little bay at the furthest point of Ronay, opposite Ceallan. Mairi woke, and said to her husband, Donald Campbell:

'Goodness,' said she, 'what a dream I've had,' said she, 'about the woman who was drowned. She asked me to get up,' said she, 'and get help and go and we would find her body,' said she, 'in the wrack in Lon Cait in Ronay.'
'Oh,' said my grandfather, 'everyone is dreaming about her,' said he. 'I don't know,' said he, 'if it's the same sort of dream you've had, but it is a weight on everyone's mind,' said he, 'until she's found, and we can't stop thinking of her, and I'm sure,' said he, 'that that was what made you dream about her tonight.'

What he said sounded reasonable, so she went back to sleep.

Then again she dreamed that the drowned woman was asking for her help, and again she woke her husband, but he said it was too far to go to Lon Cait in the middle of the night. So she fell asleep again, but the drowned woman appeared for the third time. 'If you don't hurry,' she said, 'and get the people together, if this tide goes out with me . . . I shall never be found again.'
So Morrison's grandmother woke her husband again.

'Oh, I'm not going to budge,' said he.
'If you won't,' said she, 'I'm going for the neighbours.'

She did that, and she and Donald the Tailor rowed out to Lon Cait and found the woman's body just as the tide was beginning to lift. They brought her back and she was buried among her own people.

The family involved gave my grandmother a black calf as a reward for having done so well, and for years and years after that the cattle on my grandmother's croft were bred from that black she-calf, and the last of them may still have been there when I was born, but I can't say that for certain.

COLONSAY

The Macphies or MacDuffies were Lairds of Colonsay until the middle of the seventeenth century. In the story of 'Macphie's Black Dog' the laird is seen as a magical figure. The tale is related to the episode of the child-stealing giant vanquished by FINGAL (p. 10) when he acquired his dog Bran, and has been attached in various forms to many places in the Highlands. It was still in oral circulation in 1968, when a version set on Benbecula was recorded by the School of Scottish Studies, but this is an older rendition, translated from Gaelic in the late nineteenth century by John Gregorson Campbell and given the title 'The Black Dog's Day'.

The preamble relates how the young Lord of Moidart married a fairy wife, who fled away when challenged by Macphie of Colonsay. What follows may be understood as being her revenge for his interference, although the connection is never made explicit. After his encounter with the fairy, Macphie went home to his own island where one night he met an old man with a litter of puppies. One of them was so black and beautiful that he resolved to have it for his own, and the old man told him that although the dog would do him no more than one day's service, it would do that well.

The Black Dog grew remarkably large and handsome, but it would not hunt, and Macphie's friends advised him to kill it, because it was not worth its keep. Macphie told them to let it alone: the Black Dog's day would come yet.

One day, Macphie set out with a party of sixteen to hunt on Jura, then a deer preserve empty of men, with one place for hunters to stay known as the Big Cave. They called the Black Dog, but it would not come. 'Shoot it,' cried the men. 'No,' said Macphie, 'the Black Dog's day is not come yet.' The wind rose and the boat did not reach Jura.

The next day, again, the Black Dog was called but would not come, and again the boat did not get across, but on the third day the weather was fine, and although nobody called the Black Dog it leaped into the boat to join them. 'The Black Dog's day is drawing near,' said Macphie.

In the Big Cave that night the men all wished their sweethearts were there, but Macphie said, 'I prefer that my wife should be in her own house; it is enough for me to be here myself to-night.' He then saw sixteen women enter and approach the sixteen men; the lights went out, except for the fire in the middle of the cave. One of the women approached Macphie as if to attack him, but the Black Dog sprang at her and she fled.

A little while later Macphie heard a horrid noise overhead, and looking up he saw 'a Hand' coming down through a hole in the top of the cave:

The Black Dog gave one spring, and
between the shoulder and the elbow
caught the Hand, and lay upon it with all

its might. Now began the play between the Hand and the Black Dog. Before the Black Dog let go its hold, it chewed the arm through till it fell on the floor. The Thing that was on top of the cave went away, and Macphie thought the cave would fall in about his head. The Black Dog rushed out after the Thing that was outside. This was not the time when Macphie felt himself most at ease, when the Black Dog left him. When the day dawned, behold the Black Dog had returned. It lay down at Macphie's feet, and in a few minutes was dead.

When day dawned, Macphie looked around the cave and saw that not a man was alive but himself. Taking the Hand with him, he returned to Colonsay alone. No one in Islay or Colonsay had seen such a thing as the Hand before.

There only remained to send a boat to Jura and take home the bodies that were in the cave. That was the end of the Black Dog's Day.

CORRYVRECKAN

Between Scarba and the north end of Jura is the famous whirlpool of Corryvreckan, described by Martin Martin in 1703:

The Sea begins to boil and ferment with the Tide of Flood, and resembles the boiling of a Pot, and then increases gradually, until it appear[s] in many Whirlpools, which form themselves in sort of Pyramids, and immediately after spout up as high as the Mast of a little Vessel, and at the same time makes a loud report. These white Waves run two Leagues with the wind before they break; the Sea continues to repeat these various motions from the beginning of the Tide of Flood, until it is more than half Flood, and then it decreases gradually until it hath ebb'd about half an hour, and continues to boil 'till it is within an hour of low water.

The name Corryvreckan is supposedly derived from Breacan, a Scandinavian prince drowned here and buried in a cave on SCARBA. The other legendary figure associated with the eddy is the Cailleach Bhéarra, the personification of winter weather, said to wash her linen among the furious waves. In Martin's time it was said that when the white foam spouted highest, the Cailleach had 'put on her kerchief'; it was then reckoned fatal to approach her. *See also* GUARDIAN OF THE WILD (p. 352).

Another legend held that far below Corryvreckan lay an entrance to the home of the ocean-gods. Once, in a dreadful storm, a sow belonging to the underwater realm was tossed up in the turbulent sea. She swam ashore to Scarba and had nine piglets, from whom all the wild boar of Scotland were descended.

DUN BHUIRG, MULL

By the shore of Loch Scridain in Ardmeanach is Dun Bhuirg (the name combines the Gaelic and Norse words for a fort). Like other prehistoric forts, it was once thought to be inhabited by fairies. One day a woman living nearby was at her weaving and exclaimed, 'it is about time the people of the hill were coming along to give me a hand.' Suddenly she was overrun with fairies from the dun, who swiftly turned all the wool into cloth. When they asked for payment for their work, she shouted, 'Dun Bhuirg is on fire!' The fairies rushed off and were not seen again, but surprisingly did not punish her for the mean trick she had played on them.

This story from P. A. MacNab's *Isle of Mull* (1970) is a variant on an earlier tale

repeated all over the Highlands, set in several places with similar names. In around 1860, John MacLean of Tarbert in Argyllshire supplied John Francis Campbell with a version very like the one above, although the Argyllshire woman is not trying to avoid paying but is overwhelmed by the fairies' eagerness for work, like the wizard Donald Duibheal Mackay at CREAG MHÓR AND CREAG BHEAG (Northern Highlands). MacLean adds a verse spoken by the fairies while at their work and another when they depart in haste, mourning their possessions lost in the supposed fire, the latter translated by Campbell as:

My mould of cheese, my hammer, and anvil,
My wife and my child, and my butter crock;
My cow and my goat, and my little meal kist;
Och, och, ochone, how wretched am I!

A slightly different tale was told of the hill of Dunvuilg in Craignish, Argyllshire, where the call of fire is given by an envious neighbour of the woman whom the fairies are helping, and Campbell heard yet another version in Lewis 'from a medical gentleman, who got it from an old woman, who told it as a fact, with some curious variations unfit for printing'. These unprintable details may possibly have concerned throwing urine at the fairies, a technique adopted, for instance, at DUNVEGAN CASTLE.

DUN BUIDHE, BENBECULA

The Bean-nigh or Nigheag ('washerwoman' or 'little washer') is a spirit who presides over those about to die, and washes their shrouds in lakes or rivers while singing a dirge. She may be so absorbed in her task that she can be taken unawares, and will then grant her captor three wishes: it used to be said of anyone particularly successful that he had got the better of the washerwoman.

A follower of Clanranald of the Isles was going home alone one night to Dun Buidhe when he saw the washerwoman by a ford, 'washing and rinsing, moaning and lamenting'. Creeping up unseen and unheard, he seized her:

'Let me go,' said 'nigheag,' 'and give me the freedom of my feet, and that the breeze of reek coming from thy grizzled tawny beard is anear putting a stop to the breath of my throat. Much more would my nose prefer, and much rather would my heart desire, the air of the fragrant incense of the mist of the mountains.'

He said he would let her go in return for his three wishes: for the creek of his home town to have plenty of seaweed (used as fertiliser), for himself to get his chosen wife, and to know who the washer-woman's shroud was for. For Clanranald, was the answer. The man took the shroud on the point of his spear and threw it into the loch, then ran to his chief. Hearing the news, Clanranald ordered a cow to be killed and a coracle made from its hide, and when the boat was prepared he embarked on the waves, and never returned to Benbecula.

The man who brought the news was named as the Lad of the Wet Foot, because, explains Alasdair Alpin Mac-Gregor, retelling the story in 1937 from an earlier version, his duty was to walk in front of his chief and take the dew or rain off the grass. In this tale the Lad 'walked in front' in a more symbolic sense: his warning gave Clanranald the chance to prepare for his end with dignity, although death, once foretold, could not be escaped.

DUNVEGAN CASTLE, SKYE

The most ancient portion is said to have been built in the 9th century; another portion, consisting of a lofty tower, was added a few hundred years afterwards by Alastair Crotach, or the hump-backed son of William, who was slain at the battle of the Bloody Bay in Mull, and was head of the family in 1493. The lower and more lengthened edifice which conjoins these two was the work of Rory Mòr, who was knighted in the time of James VI.

So Black's *Picturesque Tourist* describes Dunvegan Castle, adding that it contains many relics of the past, among them the horn of Rory Mòr, a drinking cup, and a fairy flag.

The flag is also known as 'Macleod's Fairy Banner'. 'When unfurled, victory in war attends it, and it relieves its followers from imminent danger,' writes John Greg-orson Campbell in *Superstitions of the Highlands and Islands of Scotland* (1900), adding that 'These virtues it is to have only thrice, and it has already been unfurled twice. Many of the common people wanted it brought out at the time of the potato failure.' It was not brought out then, and so one may suppose that it has one triumph left. Every pregnant woman who sees the flag is said to be taken in premature labour, a misfortune which befell the English wife of a former laird in consequence of her curiosity to look at it; this also applies to cattle, and every cow that looks on the banner casts her calf. Campbell says that the flag is reputed to have been a gift from 'an Elfin sweet-heart'; Alasdair Alpin MacGregor, writing in 1937, expands on this, saying that one of the MacLeod chiefs was betrothed to a fairy who stayed with him only a short time, and when she returned to fairyland

At Dunvegan Castle many precious relics are preserved, including a fairy cup and a fairy banner.

left the flag with him as a keepsake. The spot where the lovers parted is at the point where the Portree, Dunvegan, and Vaternish roads converge, a little way from Dunvegan, and was still known in MacGregor's time as the Fairy Bridge.

MacGregor gives two more alternative accounts of the flag's origins. According to one, a fairy entered the castle and wrapped MacLeod's infant heir in the flag, singing a lullaby which was remembered for years and sung by every nurse of the MacLeods. The 'more generally accepted theory', he says, is that it came into the possession of a young MacLeod fighting in the Crusades. At a river the warrior met a fairy maiden who would not let him pass until he had wrestled with her. When he had overcome her, she presented him with the flag, which, she told him, when unfurled, 'would present the appearance of a great multitude of armed men'. She warned him to use it no more than three

times, and said that if it were misused, none of the MacLeod's cattle, horses, or sheep would give birth, and neither would any children be born to the family, a variation on the curse mentioned by Campbell.

The 'Fairy Cup of Dunvegan' is described in Black's as 'a chalice or drinking cup of oak, mounted with silver', and is said there to have been part of the spoil taken from an Irish chief called Nial Glundubh ('Nial of the Black Knees'). The legend attached to the cup, however, says that it was stolen from the fairies. An oral tale of the theft was still current in the 1950s when a version was recorded from Angus Macleod of North Uist. Angus told how a Harris man was out with his cattle when in reply to his own calls to the cows of 'Ho, ho! Stop here!' he heard a voice call back, 'Ho, ho! Stop here! A safe return to you and a safe journey to you!' Continuing on his way, he came to a green knoll where a door stood open. A beautiful woman welcomed him in, and a little old man gave him a golden cup of whisky to drink. The girl who had greeted him first told him that when he had finished the whisky the fairies would take the cup, and then he would be trapped for ever, so he moved step by step to the door, and when there was only one mouthful left in the cup he ran outside, with the fairies following.

When they got close, he cried, 'Ho, ho! May you come back safe, and may you go safe!' and each time he said that, the fairies stopped, giving him the chance to run further. At last he came to his own house, where his wife, alarmed by the noise, stood in the doorway.

'Flora, out with the chamber pot!' he shouted. She quickly returned and threw the urine over the fairies, who never troubled the man or his wife again.

Macleod of Dunvegan heard about the golden cup, and gave the man a farm in exchange for it. 'The cup is at Dunvegan still, to the present day; it may be seen by anyone who goes that way,' finished Angus: it still can.

EIGG

John Frazer, minister of Tiree and Coll, came across a number of instances of SECOND SIGHT (p. 474) in the islands. One of them he describes as 'strange and of certain truth and known to the whole Inhabitants of the Island of *Egg*'. One Sunday in 1685, after church, a man of Kildonan told everyone:

That they should all flit out of that Isle, and plant themselves some where else; Because that people of strange and different habits and Arms, were to come to the Isle an to use all acts of Hostility, as Killing, Burning, Tirling [stripping] and Deforceing of Women; Finally to

discharge all that the hands of an Enemy could do; but what they were, or whence they came, he could not tell.

At first nobody paid much attention, but he frequently begged people to remember what he had said, and after a while several families did leave Eigg, some going to Canna and some to Rhum. In June 1689, the visionary fell ill. The priest implored him 'to recant his former folly and his vain prediction', but he answered that they would very shortly find out the truth of what he had said, and then died. About two weeks later, a force of English soldiers under the command of Major Ferguson and Captain Pottinger arrived on the island, and Frazer, himself imprisoned by Captain Pottinger, found himself 'Eye witness' to the proof of the prophecy:

I did admire [wonder] to see it particularly verified; especially that of the different habits and Arms, some being clad with Red coats, some with White Coats, and Granadier Capes, some Armed with Sword and Pike, and some with Sword and Musket.

A slightly different account of what must be the same episode is given by Martin Martin in 1703:

One who had been accustomed to see the *Second Sight*, in the Isle of *Egg* . . . told his Neighbours that he had frequently seen, an Apparition of a Man in a Red Coat lin'd with Blue and having on his Head a strange sort of Blue Cap, with a very high Cock on the fore part of it, and that the Man who there appeared, was kissing a comely Maid, in the Village where the Seer dwelt; and therefore declar'd that a Man in such a dress would certainly debauch or marry such a Young Woman.

No foreigners being thought likely to visit Eigg, and the young woman in question having no intention of going elsewhere, the seer was generally mocked, and the story was even discussed on Skye, where Martin's friend Norman MacLeod heard it. Both of them being interested in second sight, he remembered to repeat it to Martin in Edinburgh in September 1688.

In about 1691, according to Martin's version, Major Ferguson was sent by the government with a troop of 600 men and some frigates, to chastise the islanders which had supported the Stuarts in the revolution of 1689. Eigg was not high on his list until one of his soldiers was killed by the crew of a boat from the island:

> ... upon Notice of which, the Major directed his Course to the Isle of *Egg*, where he was sufficiently reveng'd of the Natives; and at the same time, the Maid above mentioned being very handsome, was then forcibly carried on Board one of the Vessels, by some of the Soldiers where she was kept above twenty four Hours, and ravish'd, and bruitishly rob'd at the same time of her fine Head of Hair; she is since married in the Isle, and in Good Reputation; her Misfortune being pitied and not rekon'd her Crime.

Martin already believed in the reality of second sight, and this episode convinced the minister Frazer too. 'We know but too well,' he comments, 'that Necromancers & Magicians themselves have not only seen the shapes & forms of things, but likeways have allowed others to see the same, who had no skill of their Art.'

EILEAN ANABAICH, NORTH HARRIS

A man who lived at Eilean Anabaich once caught a mermaid, and to procure her release she granted him three wishes. The gifts were interesting ones: firstly, the man became a skilful herb-doctor, who could concoct remedies for incurable diseases, even the king's evil (scrofula), which as the popular name implies was usually only to be cured by royalty. Secondly, he became a prophet, specialising in telling the futures of women. His third wish was to obtain a remarkably fine voice, and he believed this too had been granted, but here the mermaid seems to have tricked him. 'This latter gift he had only in his own estimation; when he sang, others did not think his voice fine or even tolerable.'

According to John Gregorson Campbell in *Superstitions of the Highlands and Islands of Scotland* (1900), mermaids could be kept prisoner in the same way as SELKIES (p. 404), since they would sometimes take off their fishy tails, which could then be hidden by men who wanted the mermaids as wives. One such man from Skye kept his mermaid captive for a year, during which time she gave him 'much curious information', but declined to answer his final question:

> When parting he asked her what virtue or evil there was in egg-water (*i.e.* water in which eggs had been boiled). She said, 'If I tell you that, you will have a tale to tell,' and disappeared.

The mystery remains unsolved, but eggs are magical things, smooth-shelled and inscrutable, an obvious metaphor for a secret. Ogres and giants were sometimes said to hide their hearts in eggs, witches were believed to sail in eggshell boats, and the 'eggshell brewery' was a well-known test for fairy changelings, described in the story of KILCHOMAN.

EILEAN TRODDAY (TRONDAIDH)

Iain Garbh Mac Gille Chaluim of Raasay was drowned in April 1671, reportedly

Second Sight

Second sight is the ability to see events at a distance, either in space or in time. John Frazer, minister of Tiree and Coll at the beginning of the eighteenth century, compiled a collection of examples of the phenomenon. He was fascinated and convinced by the stories he heard, although wary of their possible demonic inspiration, commenting that 'God, who knoweth all things, no doubt imparteth much of the foreknowledge of things, not only to good angels, but also evil angels, for reasons well known to himself.' He asked an old woman of his parish how she knew things which later came true:

> She freely confessed, that her father upon his death-bed, taught her a charm, compiled of barbarous words, and some unintelligible terms, which had the virtue, when repeated, to present, some few hours after the proposition of a question, the answer of the same . . . I do not think it fit to insert the charm, knowing that severals [*sic*] might be inclined to make an unwarrantable trial of it.

In this account, second sight is in the nature of a spell which can be learned, an opinion also held by a student who wrote to the antiquary John Aubrey in the late seventeenth century. He had been informed by a visitor to Skye 'that any person that pleases will get it taught him for a pound or two of tobacco', but the student's father had been advised against the experiment by a man who had the sight and said that once anyone had learned the art, not a minute would pass without his seeing innumerable people around him, night and day, 'which perhaps he would think wearisome and unpleasant'.

Other people held that the gift was hereditary, but however it was said to be acquired, there was general agreement that it was unwelcome. Aubrey's correspondent remarked that those with the ability 'cannot foretell, much less prevent, what shall befall themselves', so that there was little advantage in it. Counter-charms were said to exist: Martin Martin writes in his *Description of the Western Islands* (1703) of a John Morison in Berneray who wore a plant called *Fuga daemonum* (St John's wort) sewn in the neck of his coat to keep away his visions, and would not let Martin unpick the seam for any money.

The reason why seers were so keen to be rid of their skill must have been because their premonitions were so commonly of death. Fatality was predicted in a great variety of ways. Sometimes, as at MOY HALL (Southern Highlands), the doomed one was seen shrinking to a tiny size; in other cases they appeared to be wrapped in winding sheets, the date at which they would die being judged, according to Martin, by the height of the shroud.

If it was not above the middle, they would live for a year or longer, but if it approached the head, 'Death is concluded to be at hand within a few days, if not hours, as daily experience confirms.' To see a spark of fire falling on someone's arm or breast foretold that the person would carry a dead child, while seeing a seat as empty when someone was sitting in it was a presage of their death soon afterwards. Sounds, too, might be involved: if a gifted one heard a cry like the voice of a particular person, that person would quickly die.

Occasionally second sight could affect the outcome of events. Some time in the seventeenth century, a nobleman put on a new coat and was at once begged to take it off, since another man saw a dagger sticking in it. A servant said that he would wear the coat, which was given to him, and before nightfall he was stabbed just where the dagger had been seen.

St John's wort (*Fuga daemonum*) was used as a charm against second sight by John Morison of Berneray. He sewed it into the neck of his coat to keep his visions at bay, and would not be persuaded to remove it.

Not every vision, however, was of doom. A more pleasant anecdote tells of Daniel Nicholson, a widowed minister in Skye. Archibald MacDonald, a renowned seer, perceived a young woman frequently by Nicholson's side, and said that she would be his second wife. Nicholson was sceptical, but a few years later he met one Mrs Morison in Bute, 'and from that moment fancied her, and afterwards married her'. His neighbours agreed that Archibald had described her exactly, and, says Martin, 'This story was told me above a year before the accomplishment of it.'

See also LOCH AN DAIMH (Central & Perthshire); ANNANDALE (Dumfries & Galloway); GRIEVEHILL (Glasgow & Ayrshire); ABBOTSFORD (Lothian & Borders); THURSO (Northern Highlands); BALEPHUIL; BALEVULLIN; BERNERAY; BAUGH; CEALLAN; EIGG (Western Isles); THE MINISTER AND THE FAIRIES (p. 112).

through the malice of his foster-mother. Telling the story in *Carmina Gadelica* (1900), Alexander Carmichael gives two related traditions, one of which tells how a gentleman out hunting in South Uist saw a cat on the wall of a bothy, and tried to shoot it. He tried two or three times, but although the powder in the pan flashed, the gun did not go off. Realising that the beast was uncanny, he put a silver stud in the gun and was aiming it when the cat changed into the form of a woman well known to him. She told him that she and many other witches were in the process of drowning Iain Garbh of Raasay, who was even then on the verge of death:

> 'His galley was full of cats and he was chasing them with his great broadsword, slashing them here and mauling them there, when he struck the sheet-rope a blow with his sword and the galley capsized. It is his own foster-mother who forced me to go there, and we were there a great swarm of cats.'

The other version of the tale is more detailed, starting on a clear calm day when Iain Garbh set out in his boat from Lewis. His foster-mother lived in Trondaidh (Eilean Trodday), a small remote island north of Skye, and she saw his boat from a distance. To help her she called on several famous witches of the islands, Yellow Foot and Gormshuil of Skye, and Black Doideag of Mull.

With these notorious sorceresses ready to take part, Iain Garbh's foster-mother began to raise a storm. She put milk in a large vessel, and floated a little vessel on the milk. A herd-boy stood in the doorway, where he could see both Ian Garbh's own boat and the little ship in the milk, while the woman herself stood by the fire and recited her spells.

The little vessel began to sway to and fro. The boy saw that it was going round

deiseil (sunwise) in the big pot, then being shaken and going round *tuathail* (widdershins), and finally capsizing and turning upside down. At that moment Iain Garbh's boat disappeared, and the boy could see it no longer.

Meanwhile on the boat, three ravens had appeared and were hovering about in the raging storm. More birds appeared, and soon there were twenty, which flew on board and turned into frogs. What with the ravens flying and the frogs leaping about, Iain Garbh was distracted, and forgot to keep a guard on his tongue.

> All the witches of Scotland were there, and all as busy as busy could be; but they could not sink the galley until Iain Garbh said: 'What the big brindled one (i.e. the devil) brought you here?'

A huge raven lighted on the gunwhale, and he drew his sword to kill it, but in his fury he drove the sword right through the boat to the keel. Holed below the waterline, the galley sank and Iain Garbh was drowned.

In Scotland in those days, the relationship of foster-mother and foster-child was considered particularly close: such a murder would have seemed against nature, as much if not more so than for a bloodmother and her own offspring. One storyteller said that the motive was money, but Carmichael's main text leaves the point obscure.

FINGAL'S CAVE, STAFFA

Suppose now the Giants who rebelled against Jove had taken a whole Mass of black Columns and bound them together like bundles of matches – and then with immense Axes had made a cavern in the body of these columns – of course the

The remarkable structure of Fingal's Cave, Staffa, invites comparisons with cathedral architecture, and has inspired some of the nineteenth century's most evocative music.

roof and floor must be composed of the broken ends of the Columns – such is fingal's Cave, [except that] the sea has done the work of excavations and is continually dashing there . . . the colour of the columns is a sort of black with a lurking gloom of purple therin – For solemnity and grandeur it far surpasses the finest Cathedrall.

The Romantic poet John Keats was not alone in comparing Fingal's Cave on Staffa to a cathedral, not simply because of its columns but because it evokes the kind of religious awe that stupendous works of nature can inspire. Keats was one of a line of poets and painters who found in Fingal's Cave something that answered to the spirit of the Romantic movement – the beauty tinged with savagery that could be sought in the high mountains, on the wild moors, or by the ocean.

The cyclopean pillars of Staffa, encompassed by angry seas, conjure visions of almost unimaginable antiquity and immeasurable force. The now uninhabited island bears witness to cataclysmic events about 60 million years ago, when subterranean volcanic activity found a vent along a line from Skye to Ireland, the effects of which can be seen at their most dramatic in Staffa and the Giant's

Causeway. Both are essentially composed of liquid basalt ejected to the surface, where it cooled and contracted into mainly hexagonal columns.

Staffa, whose name means 'Pillar Island', was so called by Vikings who settled along the western Scottish coast from the tenth century to the thirteenth, but as far as educated Europe was concerned it was 'discovered' on 13 August 1772 by the celebrated botanist Joseph Banks, who declared it one of the greatest wonders of the world. He added, 'The Giants causey [Causeway] in Ireland, or Stonehenge in England, are but trifles when compared to this island.'

Keats's image of giants as the builders of the stupendous cave echoed folk tradition. Already when 'discovered' by Banks it went by the name of the Dark Age warrior known in Ireland as Fionn mac Cumhaill and in Scotland as FINGAL (p. 10), the most popular Gaelic folk hero on both sides of the Irish Sea. In an eighteenth-century Highland cattle-blessing his name was invoked in the same breath as Christian saints: 'The safeguard of Fionn mac Cumhaill be yours . . . The shield of the king of the Fiann be yours.'

Fingal and his war-band the Fenians (the Irish Fianna) were imagined as giants. According to Hector Boece, writing in the sixteenth century, 'Fyn Makcoule' was a man of huge stature, seventeen cubits (about thirty feet, or ten metres) tall. In both Ireland and Scotland, Fionn/Fingal was connected with ancient forts, large boulders, standing stones, and megalithic tombs. In 1703, Martin Martin mentioned three stones, each of them about three foot (0.9 m) high, on the Skye coast:

... the Natives have a Tradition, that upon these Stones a big Caldron was set for Boyling *Fin Mack Coul*'s Meat. This Gigantick Man is reported to have been

General of a Militia that came from *Spain*, to *Ireland*, and from thence to those Isles.

Dr Johnson was shown a square stone said to be 'Fingal's Table' in a cave on Mull, and two standing stones at Lower Kilchattan on Colonsay are known as 'Fingal's Limpet Hammers', but the landscape features particularly associated with Fingal are those of the Giant's Causeway and Staffa. Irish bards told how the Giant's Causeway once reached right across the sea, placed there as stepping stones by the giants of Scotland and Ireland so they could visit one another. On Staffa not only Fingal's Cave but 'Fingal's Chair', a shallow niche in the columns beside the Causeway, is shown to visitors, who have only to sit in it to have their wishes fulfilled.

Fingal and the Fenians were the main characters in James Macpherson's 'Ossianic' verses of the 1760s, which he claimed were translations of ancient Gaelic originals written by Fingal's son Ossian or Oisín, but which Dr Johnson and others dismissed as forgeries. The furore over these poems focused the attention of literary Europe on the Gaelic west, and it was the Ossian epic as well as the extraordinary spectacle described by Banks that drew the Romantic poets and novelists to Fingal's Cave.

But the person who was to make it world-renowned was a musician – the young Felix Mendelssohn, who visited the cave in 1829 with his friend Klingemann, who later wrote:

We were put out in boats and lifted by the hissing sea up the pillar stumps to the famous Fingal's Cave. A greener roar of waves surely never rushed into a stranger cavern – its many pillars making it look like the inside of an immense organ, black and resounding, and absolutely without purpose, and quite alone, the wide grey sea within and without.

On Mendelssohn himself, aged twenty, these prodigious sights and sounds made a profound impression, and he was inspired then and there with the majestic theme which later became the Hebrides Overture, popularly known as 'Fingal's Cave'.

FLADDA-CHUAIN

In the 1960s Otta Swire wrote several books on Scottish folklore, including many tales told by her older relatives and neighbours in the Highlands. She had heard that the narrow, uninhabited island of Fladda-chuain ('Fladda of the Ocean') was once a sacred place, identified by some as the mysterious Tir-na n-Og, the Isle of Perpetual Youth, traditionally believed to lie somewhere in the western ocean, on which magical island it is always summer and the sun never sets.

The Druids allegedly revered Fladda-chuain, and this was why St Columba, when he brought Christianity to the islands, built a chapel there. On its altar lay a stone known as the Weeping Stone because it was perpetually wet. Although she does not directly connect these things, Otta Swire said in the 1950s that 'until fairly recently' fishermen used to land and pour three handfuls of seawater on the stone to procure favourable winds or stop severe flooding. She reports that by the time she was writing the Weeping Stone no longer existed, or at least was not to be found near the altar on which it once stood.

The story was told of a fisherman who always had bad luck at the fishing and was on the brink of ruin. He determined to go to Fladda-chuain, pour water on the Weeping Stone, and pray for better winds and good catches, but his boat was small and on the way to the island a whale appeared and with a flick of its tail over-

turned it. Clinging for dear life to the upturned boat, the fisherman called on St Columba for his help, and at once a white figure appeared on the water beside him. The saint scolded the whale for being so clumsy as to overturn a boat, particularly one on a pilgrimage to the island. He set it the penance of pushing the fisherman and his boat to their destination, and this the whale duly did. Ever after that, the fisherman's catches were so good that his good fortune became proverbial.

See also SAINTS OF SCOTLAND (p. 490).

IONA

See THE MAIDEN OF INVERAWE (p. 24); SAINTS OF SCOTLAND (p. 490).

KILCHOMAN, ISLAY

Years ago, begins a story supplied to John Francis Campbell in the mid nineteenth century, there lived on Islay a smith called MacEachern. He had one child, a son of about thirteen or fourteen, who was cheerful, strong, and healthy, but one day suddenly fell ill and took to his bed. Nobody could tell what was the matter with him: he seemed to be wasting away, although he had an extraordinarily large appetite.

A wise old man told the father that his son had been stolen by the fairies, and a changeling left in his place. The smith asked how he was to get his own child back:

'I will tell you how,' answered the old man. 'But, first, to make sure that it is not your own son you have got, take as many empty egg shells as you can get, go with them into the room, spread them out carefully before his sight, then proceed to draw water with them, carrying them two and two in your hands as if they were a great weight, and arrange when full, with every sort of earnestness round the fire.'

The smith obeyed; soon a shout of laughter came from the bed, and the seeming sick boy exclaimed, 'I am now 800 years of age, and I have never seen the like of that before.'

This proved that it was indeed a fairy, and the old man now told the smith how to get rid of the intruder by flinging him onto a large fire. When he did so, the changeling gave an awful yell and flew through the roof where there was a hole to let out the smoke.

Next the smith was instructed to visit a round green hill, carrying with him a Bible, a dagger, and a cockerel. He heard singing and dancing from the hill, and entered, sticking his dirk into the threshold. As he was carrying his Bible the fairies could not touch him, but they asked him with some displeasure what he wanted. When he replied that he had come for his son and would not leave without him, the fairies burst out laughing, waking the cock, which began to crow. The angry fairies seized the smith and his son and threw them out of the hill and the dirk after them.

For a year and a day after this, the restored boy did no work and hardly spoke a word, but at last, watching his father making a sword, he suddenly exclaimed, 'That is not the way to do it.' Taking the tools, he set to and soon fashioned a weapon the like of which had never been seen in the country before. From then onwards father and son worked together and became famous and rich.

'I have heard of the Islay smith, who could make wonderful swords, all my life,' declares Campbell. The smith, he says, was a famous character, probably a real person to whom the story had become attached, whose house was still pointed out, not far from the church of Kilchoman.

There are many popular elements in this tale. The 'eggshell brewery' is mentioned in Irish and French as well as Scottish legend as a means of inducing the changeling to laugh and betray the fact that it is not a child at all but a creature many centuries old. Writing of changelings in *Superstitions of the Highlands and Islands of Scotland* (1900), John Gregorson Campbell describes the usual development of such a 'mannikin', closely followed in the story of Kilchoman:

> The child grew up a peevish misshapen brat, ever crying and complaining. It was known, however, to be a changeling by the skilful in such matters, from the large quantities of water it drank – a tubful before morning, if left beside it – its large teeth, its inordinate appetite, its fondness for music and its powers of dancing, its unnatural precocity, or from some unguarded remark as to its own age.

Common, too, is the idea that someone who had lived with the fairies would gain supernatural knowledge or skill, as was said of Thomas the Rhymer of EARLSTON (Lothian & Borders), and smiths were often said to have supernatural powers, an old tradition linked to belief in the magical properties of iron, as referred to in the wife's verse at SANDRAY.

See also CAERLAVEROCK (Dumfries & Galloway); DUNDREGGAN (Southern Highlands).

KILVICKEON, ROSS OF MULL

Kilvickeon or Kilviceuen, a ruined chapel on the Ross of Mull, dates from the thirteenth century. Its last minister, before the parish was united with that of Kilfinichen in the seventeenth century, was an

Episcopalian named Kennedy who was said to have died in the following manner. His parishioners were carrying a new millstone to the mill, and Kennedy went to their help, first taking off his cassock and leaving it on the ground. In the evening a maidservant was sent to fetch the cassock, but found a large black dog lying on it which would not let her touch the garment. She went home, and refused to go back to the place – wisely, as it turned out, since the next ones who went were bitten by the dog, and ultimately twelve people, including the minister himself, died of hydrophobia.

'So shocking an event could not take place without superstition busying itself about it,' says John Gregorson Campbell in *Superstitions of the Highlands and Islands of Scotland* (1900), and soon it was reported that on Beltane night shortly before these events, the minister's serving man had been woken by the noise of someone trying to open his door, which was locked. He thought it was some young men who were courting and had come to the wrong place, so he kept quiet, but soon the door opened and a stranger entered without saying a word, and stood by the fire. The man saw that the stranger's feet were horse's hooves. A short while later the apparition left again, relocking the door behind it. The man then got up and went to an old man much esteemed for piety, who lived alone at the Dog Rock. The servant told what he had seen, and the good man concluded that evil was portended. Nothing would persuade the servant to stay another night at the minister's house, and it was arranged that he would sleep at the old man's hut and go to his work at the manse in daytime. It was shortly afterwards that the mad dog was found on the cassock, and the servant was the only one of the minister's household who escaped.

While it was a girl who avoided the dog in the first place, it was a man who was spared in the resulting legend. Details like this do of course often change in the telling and retelling of a story.

LOCH FINLAGGAN, ISLAY

The ruins of a castle once used by the Lords of the Isles can still be seen on an islet in Loch Finlaggan. This is the setting of a story supplied to Lord Archibald Campbell in the 1880s telling how MacDonald of the Isles employed a man known from his height as the Big Ploughman. One day, feeling hungry, the ploughman declared to the boy driving the horses, 'My good fellow, were it to be got in an ordinary way or magically, I would take food in the meantime, were I to have it.'

They then came to the side of Knockshainta (Cnoc-seunta), where an old man invited them to a table laden with food. The boy was frightened, but the Big Ploughman ate until he was full, after which the old man gave him a black chanter (a chanter being the vital part of a set of bagpipes, with the fingerholes). The ploughman, who had never played before, found himself an expert, and later when MacDonald heard him play, he made the ploughman his piper.

A young man called MacCrimmon came to the Big Ploughman to learn music, and began courting the ploughman's daughter. She let MacCrimmon try the black chanter, and when he found how well he could play on it, he begged her to let him borrow it for a few days more. Soon afterwards MacDonald of the Isles went to Skye, and MacCrimmon with him. The young man never came back, neither to marry the ploughman's daughter nor to return the chanter, and the people of Islay say that this was how the music went from Islay to the Isle of Skye.

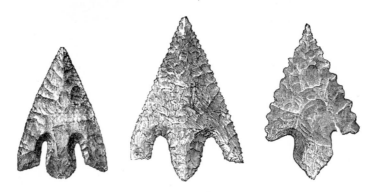

A battle at Loch Gruinart was won with the help of 'elf bolts' – prehistoric flint arrowheads like these, often associated with the fairies.

The rest is history – or is it? For more on the MacCrimmons of Skye, *see* BORERAIG and TROTTERNISH.

LOCH GRUINART, ISLAY

In August 1598, a bloody battle was fought at the head of Loch Gruinart between Sir Lachlan Mor MacLean of Duart and Sir James MacDonald of Islay. In the conflict, 280 of Sir Lachlan's men were killed, but only thirty MacDonalds, a result attributed by tradition to a strange warrior who took part.

Just before the battle, 'a certain tiny fellow of the brownie order, known as the Eighth Part Measure of a Carle [man], and sometimes as the Black Elf', offered his services to Sir Lachlan who, himself a sizeable man, refused with some scorn. The Eighth Part Measure then fair-mindedly offered himself to Sir James, who accepted gracefully, and said he would welcome the help of a hundred similar warriors.

All day the little man followed Sir Lachlan, who was wearing a suit of armour and thought himself safe. But when he finally raised his visor, the Brownie shot him in

the forehead with an 'elf-bolt' – a fairy arrow, as prehistoric flint arrowheads were generally called.

After the battle, Sir James asked who had killed Sir Lachlan, and the Black Elf spoke up that it had been himself. 'It was better for you and your clan that you had me with you than against you!'

Fairies did not care much for the rights and wrongs of a quarrel, but they minded very much about their dignity: it was notoriously unlucky to laugh at them or reject their offers of help.

LOCH NA MNA, RAASAY

Near Dùn Caan, the highest hill on Raasay, is Loch na Mna, 'The Woman's Loch', once haunted by a Water-horse which devoured a girl. James Boswell mentions the story in his journal of Dr Johnson's Hebridean tour, and John Gregorson Campbell includes it in *Superstitions of the Highlands and Islands of Scotland* (1900). According to Campbell the name of the loch derives from the monster's abduction of the woman. Nearby lived a man known as 'the big Smith' (An Gobha Mòr), who resolved to kill the predator and laid his plans carefully. First he built a hut next to the loch, with an opening leading down to the water. Then he waited until the wind was blowing towards the loch, and when the time was right he killed and roasted a sheep in the hut. The Water-horse, tempted by the savoury smell drifting on the breeze, made its way into the hut by the entrance left for it, and the smith, who had his irons ready in the fire, rushed with them at the beast and killed it.

Campbell reports that on examination, the monster proved to consist of nothing but grey clods of turf, or, according to others, a soft mass like a jellyfish. In *Minor Traditions of British Mythology* (1948), Lewis Spence quotes a description of the dead Water-horse as resembling 'a heap of starch, or something like it', and comments that this 'may be accepted as providing a popular notion of the composition of supernatural bodies'.

A comparable phenomenon is reported in a late nineteenth-century book on the Shetland Islands in a tale set in Unst but not specifically located:

Every year at Yule-time, a house was *troubled*, and no person could stay in it. At last a bold-hearted fisherman undertook to break the power of evil by remaining in the house during its afflicted period. He sat down in one of the rooms, and lighting a candle, began to read the Bible. Suddenly he heard a noise, as if dead meat were being dropped along the passage. Seizing his Bible in one hand and an axe in the other, he rushed to meet the supernatural foe.

The brave fisherman followed the thing out to the cliffs, and just as it was about to jump into the sea he said a holy word and threw his axe. Then he hurried back to get a friend, and the two men found the thing with the axe sticking in it. They covered it with earth, and dug a trench round it so that nobody could go near it. 'But,' asks a listener, 'what was it like?'

'The men called it a sea-devil, and all the description they could ever give of it was, that it resembled a large lump of grey *slub*' (jelly-fish sort of stuff).

'Had it a face?'

'No; it had no form at all.'

'How could it walk? It must have had *legs*, at least.'

'No; it had no legs nor wings, but it kept the man running, and run what he could, he could not go so fast as it.'

'What *could* it be?'

'That no human can tell. The men never could tell what it was like, but they called it a sea-devil, and they said it was the same thing which came up at the Haaf one day, and told the fishers that they must never go to sea on the fourth day of Yule, else evil would betide them.'

Giant squid or jellyfish are often cited in explanation of strange aquatic phenomena. Perhaps a theory could be devised to account for these happenings in scientific terms, as has been attempted in the case of the LOCH NESS MONSTER (p. 442).

See also KELPIES AND WATER-HORSES (p. 364).

LOCHBUIE, MULL

The best-known and most dreadful spectre in the West Highlands, writes John Gregorson Campbell in his *Witchcraft and Second Sight in the Highlands and Islands of Scotland* (1902), was the phantom of a headless horseman, which would appear whenever any of the Maclaines of Lochbuie were near death. The horse was a small black steed with a white spot on its forehead, and the marks of its hooves were not like those of other horses, but round indentations as if it had wooden legs.

Its rider was known as 'Hugh of the Little Head', a name which he got during his lifetime. A proverb quoted by Campbell is 'A big head on a wise man and a hen's head on a fool', and Hugh was apparently a case in point. By the time he was a ghost, of course, the name could be taken as a different sort of gibe, since by that time he had *no* head.

While he was alive, Hugh was a fearless fighter and was also known to have a particularly mean wife. One day, just before he was due to fight a battle with his uncle, the chief of Dowart, he came upon a fairy woman at the boundary stream, singing and rinsing clothes.

> Her long breasts, after the manner of her kind (according to the Mull belief regarding these weird women), hung down and interfered with her washing, and she now and then flung them over her shoulders to keep them out of the way. Hugh crept up silently behind her, and catching one of the breasts, as is recommended in such cases, put the nipple in his mouth, saying, 'Yourself and I be witness you are my first nursing mother.' She answered, 'The hand of your father and grandfather be upon you! You had need that it is so.'

She had foreknowledge of the battle, and told Hugh that if he and his men got butter with their breakfast without asking for it, they would be victorious. Hugh knew his wife's nature all too well: sure enough they were offered no butter, and Hugh went out to battle prepared for death.

> The sweep of a broadsword took off the upper part of his head. Instead of falling dead, he jumped on the top of his horse, a small black steed with a white spot on its forehead, and ever since is 'dreeing his weird' by going about to give warning when any of his race are about to die.'

One night a man of the Maclean family met Hugh, who spoke never a word but caught hold of the man to take him away. Maclean resisted, and in the struggle caught hold of a birch sapling. One after another the roots of the tree gave way, but as the last was yielding the cock crowed, and the spectre departed. 'The twisted tree may still be seen,' says Campbell, although he adds that the same story is told of a twisted tree near Tobermory, and another localised between Lochaber and Badenoch.

An 1889 collection of Scottish folklore records that the tomb of Hugh (here named as Ewen), showing his figure on horseback, was pointed out on Iona by guides who would tell his story. Perhaps the tale was partly inspired by the carving, as in the legend told of MARTIN'S STONE (North East).

LOSGAINTIR, HARRIS

Alasdair Alpin MacGregor's book of Scottish folklore, *The Peat-Fire Flame* (1937), includes much that is derived from earlier writers but also has some more recent stories. Within MacGregor's memory there lived at Niosaboist near Losgaintir (then spelt Nisabost and Luskentyre) a man who was an inveterate curser:

> One day a friend of mine, when on his way home from Kyles on a wild night with a pony and trap, halted at his house for some refreshment. On setting a plenitude of tea and oatcakes before the sojourner, the occupant stood aside with a large knife in his hand, as if at any moment he might have stabbed his guest in the back. He then delivered himself of one of his favourite Gaelic oaths: 'O, Son of the Devil, eat every morsel of that, or I'll stick this knife into you!'

This was the usual manner in which he welcomed storm-stayed friends to Nisabost.

It was prophesied during the man's lifetime that because of his constant blaspheming, when he was dead nothing would grow on his grave. This proved to be the case when he was buried at Luskentyre, says MacGregor: 'despite several attempts at manuring the surface of the grave, and sowing it with grass seeds, not a blade will spring upon it.'

Many sites are traditionally reported as 'barren ground' on which nothing, or only weeds, will grow. Sometimes they are battle-grounds, sometimes, as in this case, the graves of notorious sinners, although except for his oaths this man was said to be 'a thoroughly good fellow in other respects'.

THE MINCH

The strait between the island of Lewis and the Shiant Isles was known in the nineteenth century as 'the Stream of the Blue Men' (Sruth nam Fear Gorm), because it was inhabited by a strange race of creatures. A ship passing that way once found a blue-coloured man asleep on the waves; he was taken on board and tied up securely, but soon afterwards two more of his kind were seen following the ship, and their voices were heard. The captive leaped to his feet, broke his bonds 'like spider threads', and jumped overboard.

In *Superstitions of the Highlands and Islands of Scotland* (1900), John Gregorson Campbell gives a report of the Blue Men received from a person who was convinced that he had himself seen one. He described it as blue-coloured with a long grey face, and said that it followed his boat for a long time, floating out of the water as far as its waist. It was sometimes so close that he could have touched it, although he did not try to do so. The man told Campbell that Lucifer's followers had been driven out of Paradise in three divisions, one of which became the fairies and another the Blue Men; the third became the Merry Dancers, the Hebridean name for the aurora borealis. Some other accounts identify the fairies as the fallen angels, but elsewhere there is no mention of the Merry Dancers or the Blue Men being their fellow-spirits.

The 'Blue Men of the Minch' have provoked much theorising from later writers. Lewis Spence maintains that they are personifications of the sea itself, being the colour of the waves, while Malcolm Archibald surmises that the legend may have its origin in times when the Norsemen used slaves captured from North African ships: these Berbers would have worn blue, veiled clothes, like the Touareg, sometimes known as the 'blue men of the desert'. This explanation seems a little too inventive: the Vikings themselves never figure as supernatural sea-monsters, so why should their captives?

While the Blue Men slept the weather would remain fine, but they could conjure storms when they wished. They were sensitive to the spoken word, particularly rhyme, and were not dangerous to those who were able to charm them in verse. Something similar is reported of seals, which could be enticed by music and song.

MULL

St John's wort is a plant of magic powers, says John Gregorson Campbell, 'if found when neither sought nor wanted'. A young man named Callum found some of the plant when crossing the hills of Aird-mead-honach ('Middle Height') in Mull, and took some with him. Having swollen feet, he sat down to bathe them in a stream, and when he looked up he saw on the other side of the stream an ugly little woman with no nostrils, her feet resting against his own.

She asked him for some of the plant, but he refused. She then asked him to make snuff from it, and give her some. 'What could she want with snuff, when she had no nostril to put it in?' he asked her, and went on his way.

He did not come home that night. His family went to search for him next day, and he was at last found asleep by the side of a small hill. When he woke, he thought he could only have slept for a few minutes, because the sun was almost in the same position as when he had gone to sleep. In fact, he had been unconscious for more than twenty-four hours. His dog too, was sleeping in the hollow of his back, and was completely bald; it was thought that it had lost its hair in protecting its master from the fairies. A similar thing happened in some stories of musicians lost underground, as in one version of the legend of the Golden Cave at TROTTERNISH, when a dog emerged hairless from a subterranean encounter with the Devil.

These animals were luckier than one involved in another story told by Campbell, similar to the Mull tale above but without a precise location, in which a herd-boy is bathing his feet when a woman, this time beautiful but still without nostrils, appears on the other side of the water and asks him to pull a particular plant for her to make snuff. Again, the boy asks what need she has of snuff when she has no nostrils, and he refuses to cross the stream. When he goes home his stepmother gives him food and milk, but the dog eats it and dies. That brief tale has a number of interesting implications: the boy will not cross the water (which the fairy or demon probably cannot do, so he is safe with the stream between them), and the person who gives him the poisoned food is his stepmother, always an unchancy character.

NUNTON (BAILE NAN CAILLEACH), BENBECULA

Two men were tending the calves one night at Nunton in a building known as 'the long house'. They were talking in front of the fire when in rushed two dogs on a leash of silver bespangled with gold and jewels. The dogs tore round the house terrifying the cattle, and a voice was heard in the air outside calling:

'Slender-fay, slender-fay!
Mountain-traveller, mountain-traveller!
Black-fairy, black-fairy!
Lucky-treasure, lucky-treasure!
Grey-hound, grey-hound!
Seek-beyond, seek-beyond!'

The dogs then ran out of the building, and when the men followed they saw in the bright blue sky a great crowd of spirits, with hounds on leash and hawks on hand. The air was filled with music like the tinkling of innumerable silver bells, mingled with voices calling to the hounds. The words the men heard were the names of the dogs.

Telling this story in *Carmina Gadelica* (1900), Alexander Carmichael does not explain why the sky is blue when it is said to be night-time, but perhaps the light shining around the spirits is as bright as day. He says that the spirits are those of the departed on a hunting expedition, journeying westwards far beyond the islands to the Land under Waves, the Land of Youth, and the Land of Age, beneath the great western sea, and gives them the name of the *sluagh*, a word which means 'host' or 'multitude' and in folklore is usually applied to a travelling band of elves. Carmichael's 'spirits' seem to have much in common with fairies:

> According to one informant, the spirits fly about ... in great clouds, up and down the face of the world like the starlings, and come back to the scenes of their earthly transgressions ... In bad nights, the hosts shelter themselves ... behind little russet docken stems and little yellow ragwort stalks. They fight battles in the air as men do on the earth. They may be heard and seen on clear frosty nights, advancing and retreating, retreating and advancing, against one another.

The *sluagh* commanded men to follow them and throw fairy darts to kill whatever victims they pointed out. They were supposed to come from the west, and therefore, when a person was dying, the door and windows on the west side of the house were secured to keep them out.

Much of this lore, recorded by Carmichael in the late nineteenth century, is repeated in very similar terms in a tale from Angus MacMillan of Benbecula, who said, in the 1960s, that in the old days the window on the west side of a house would be left open to let out smoke from the fire, but with a bar of iron to repel the fairies:

> And it was said that the *sluagh* was going around and if they found the window open, with nothing blocking it, they would shoot anything, they'd kill anything that was in the house if there wasn't an iron bar across it, but if the bar was across it they couldn't do anything.

One man, continues Angus, came back very late one night, and when his wife asked where he'd been he said he'd visited Heisker and all the islands, having gone off with the *sluagh*. He had been told to shoot a girl milking the cows but hadn't

the heart to kill her, so he had shot at a hen instead and the girl had survived.

Many stories in which mortals are asked to throw elf-shot (prehistoric flint arrows) tell how the marksman misses the human target on purpose and shoots an animal instead. This ploy was resorted to, for example, by the weaver of BRIDGE OF AWE (Argyllshire & Islands), while at GORTAN (Argyllshire & Islands), Calum Clever avoided hitting any living creature.

ORSAY

'There is a small island off the Rhinns of Islay where there is a light-house now, but which was formerly used for grazing cattle only.' John Francis Campbell, writing in the 1860s, does not identify the island by name, but almost certainly he means Orsay. A man and a woman, he goes on, had charge of a herd of cattle there, and the woman was left alone one stormy night when her husband had gone to the mainland and could not return.

She was sitting at her peat fire, when suddenly she heard a sound as of living creatures all round her hut. She knew it could not be her husband, but thought it might be cows. However, glancing at the open window, she saw a pair of large, round, malignant eyes, and heard a low whining laugh.

> The door opened, and an unearthly creature walked in. He was very tall and large, rough and hairy, with no skin upon his face but a dark livid covering. He advanced to the fire and asked the girl what her name was. She answered as confidently as she could, 'MISE MI FHIN' – me myself. The creature seized the girl, and she threw a large ladle full of boiling water about him, and he, yelling, bounded out. A great noise ensued of

wild unearthly tongues, questioning their yelling companion as to what was the matter with him, and who had hurt him. 'Mise mi Fhin, Mise mi Fhin – me myself, me myself,' shouted the savage; and thereupon arose a great shout of laughter.

The girl rushed out in terror, turned one of the cows from its resting place, and lay down there, having first made a circle around herself. In the night she heard the rushing of many footsteps, loud laughter, and sounds of quarrelling. When morning came she was safe, protected by the circle she had drawn, but the cow she had disturbed was dead.

Campbell, or perhaps his informant the Reverend Thomas Pattieson, identifies the intruder as a Water-horse, and equates this with the Fuath, a water-spirit also said to haunt SOUTH UIST. The Orsay story is clearly similar not only to Homer's legend of Odysseus and the Cyclops, but to the tale told at LOCH SLOY (Central & Perthshire) of the mostly peaceful Urisk, and to a Sutherland story reported by Campbell of the Brollachan, said there to be the son of the Fuath. Readers will be most likely to have come across the shapeless but far from harmless Brollachan in two splendidly spooky books by Alan Garner, *The Weirdstone of Brisingamen* (1960) and *The Moon of Gomrath* (1963).

See also KELPIES AND WATER-HORSES (p. 364).

PABAIGH

John Francis Campbell gives a short story set on Pabaigh, narrated in Gaelic by Alexander M'Donald of Barra in 1859:

There came a woman of peace (a fairy) the way of a house of a man in the island of Pabaidh, and she had the hunger of motherhood on her. He gave her food, and that went well with her. She staid that night. When she went away, she said to him, 'I am making a desire that none of the people of this island may go in childbed after this.' None of these people, and none others that would make their dwelling in the island ever departed in childbed from that time.

It is fascinating to read what is quite obviously the same story in an oral version narrated almost exactly a hundred years later by Nan MacKinnon, again from Barra, included in Alan Bruford's and Donald MacDonald's collection of *Scottish Traditional Tales*:

There was a man living in Pabbay at one time and his wife was in child-bed. And what they used to give them in these times when they were in child-bed was porridge with butter, and he was making porridge for his wife this night. And when he had the porridge on the fire, a woman came in and sat on the bench. And she never spoke and neither did the man speak to her. But, anyway, when he had the porridge cooked, he asked her if she would take some porridge and she said she would indeed, and he gave her some porridge.

The woman ate all the porridge she was given and then got up to scrape the pot. The man asked her if she would like more, and she said she would. He made her countless pots of porridge, and finally she had eaten as much as she wanted.

'There now,' she said, 'that's what I ought to have had when I was in child-bed myself, and it was hunger,' she said, 'that was the cause of my death. But now,' she said, 'as long as a drop of your blood remains, no woman will ever die in child-bed if anyone related to you is attending her.'

And neither there did, and his descendants are still on this island.

Perhaps by the 1950s a ghost story would be more readily believed than a tale of fairies. Bruford and MacDonald comment that the story is told to account for the success of certain local families as midwives, but they do not mention the previous tale, and nothing is said to account for the curious fact that both these Barra storytellers locate their tales on Pabaigh.

RAASAY

Tales have been told since medieval times of cups or other objects stolen from the fairies, purporting to explain how a particular vessel came to be handed down in a family. MINGARY CASTLE (Argyllshire & Islands) had one such cup, and another was said to have been acquired by Hugh Macleod of Raasay, who was returning one day to his castle when he heard the sound of revelry through the open door of one of the fairy mounds. Hugh entered, to be greeted with shouts of 'Here's to you, Hugh,' or 'I drink to you, Hugh,' and was offered a cup of wine. Draining the liquor he fled with the cup, pursued by his hosts and the bright green fairy hound Farvann, as big as a two-year-old bullock, whose tail was sometimes plaited, sometimes curled over its back like a pig's. The reputation of that dog was that it was amazingly swift but only ever barked three times in the course of a chase, the last bark rendering the victim helpless from terror. Hugh Macleod managed to hide before the third bark and so escaped with the cup back to Raasay, where it remained.

It would have been wiser for Macleod to empty the wine on the ground rather than drink it, as tasting their food or drink was believed to put a mortal in the fairies' power. He was doubly lucky, being neither held in the fairy mound for centuries, nor savaged by the dog.

REILIG OGHRAIN, IONA

St Oran was a friend and follower of St Columba, and was buried in Icolmkill [Iona]. His pretensions to be a saint were rather dubious. According to the legend, he consented to be buried alive, in order to propitiate certain demons of the soil, who obstructed the attempts of Columba to build a chapel. Columba caused the body of his friend to be dug up, after three days had elapsed: when Oran, to the horror and scandal of the assistants, declared, that there was neither a God, a judgment, nor a future state! He had no time to make further discoveries, for Columba caused the earth once more to be shovelled over him with the utmost despatch. The chapel, however, and the cemetery, was called *Relig Ouran* [the burial place of Oran].

Writing in 1802–3, Sir Walter Scott gives this tongue-in-cheek version of a story taken more seriously nearly a hundred years later by Alexander Carmichael. Carmichael's account in the *Carmina Gadelica* shows Oran as a Christ-like figure who remains in hell for three days:

Contention and controversy awoke between Columba and Oran about the merits of heaven and the demerits of hell, the happiness of the good and the unhappiness of the bad. Oran said that he would put the matter to the test in the place whereon they stood, and that he would go for the space of three days and three nights down to the grave (hell). Digging implements were procured, and a grave was dug as deep down as Oran was high up. Oran went down into the grave, and the earth was filled over him.

Saints of Scotland

Christianity probably began to be established in southern Scotland in the period of the late Roman Empire, before 410 CE, spreading through the rest of the country over the next 300 years. The central figure of this period is Columba or Colm Cille (*c.* 521–97), the only one of the early saints of Scotland whose life is well documented. A member of Ireland's royal clan of Ui Neill, he might have had some claim to the throne, but instead chose a religious life. At the age of about forty he left Ireland with some companions and settled in Iona, where he founded an abbey which for centuries remained a major Christian centre of the British Isles.

His story, written around a hundred years after his death by St Adomnan, is full of miracle and marvel. He is said to have repulsed the attack of a water-beast at LOCH NESS (Southern Highlands), mastered the winds, restored the dead to life, and conquered 'innumerable hostile bands of demons making war against him'. A touching story relates that when an old man, he told his attendant that he was about to die. One of the monastery's horses leaned its head against him and seemed to weep; Columba would not allow his attendant to drive the animal away, but blessed it.

Medieval histories of the saints contain mostly legend. The Life of St Serf of Fife, for instance, was written in Latin around the twelfth century, and retold, with variations, by Andrew de Wyntoun in the early fifteenth century. These sources provide a wildly implausible story, according to which Serf, a Canaanite prince, made his way to Rome, where he was elected pope. Resigning the papacy, he walked across Europe and then over the sea, coming to land in the Firth of Forth. Another miracle associated with the saint took place in Airthrey, Stirlingshire, where according to de Wyntoun a thief stole and ate a ram, a beast the saint had reared and which used to follow him everywhere. The crime was soon discovered, when 'The schepe thare bletyd in hys wame' – bleated in the felon's stomach.

In the Middle Ages, tombs and shrines of the saints dotted the landscape of Scotland, and their statues and pictures filled the churches. Many were native to Scotland, their legends and cults linked to specific places, focuses for innumerable acts of pilgrimage. On the eve of the Scottish Reformation, the wealth of imagery was evoked by Sir David Lyndsay in 'The Monarchy' (1554), a poem which lists a host of saints and their emblems, and mentions the specific troubles they were supposed to help. St Tredwell or Triduana, whose legend was that she plucked out her own eyes, is shown holding them impaled on a thorn; her shrines at ST TRIDUANA'S WELL (Lothian & Borders) and ST TREDWELL'S LOCH (Orkney & Shetland Islands) were visited by those with eye complaints. St Mungo or Kentigern of GLASGOW (Glasgow & Ayrshire) was said to cure insanity, while St Margaret, queen of Scotland in the eleventh century, was believed to help women in childbirth.

At the Reformation most of the images and shrines were destroyed, but the cults of many saints survived, ancient prayers in their honour continuing in use in the Highlands and Western Isles. Many legends in the written accounts relate to landmarks which have proved more durable than the tombs and statues, including caves, holy wells, and rocks. Near the BASS ROCK (Lothian & Borders), for instance, are St Baldred's stone boat, his well, his cave, and a rock formation known as his cradle, while St Conval's Chariot at Inchinnan near Govan, a large stone said to have

St Columba was central to the spread of Christianity in Scotland in the sixth century, and tales of his many miracles were told throughout the country. This image is from a sixteenth-century Irish manuscript life of the saint.

brought the saint sailing up the Clyde, was for centuries the goal of pilgrims seeking cures, and can still be seen today. The continuing existence of these relics has meant that elements of the saints' medieval traditions have also survived as legends accounting for landscape features.

At Portpatrick in Galloway, quarrying has destroyed St Patrick's Well, but a remarkable tale describes how the saint was beheaded there, a spring appearing where his head fell. He then swam to Ireland, 'holding his head in his teeth'.

See also SOUTHEND (Argyllshire & Islands); OLD KILPATRICK; ST FILLAN'S CAVE (Central & Perthshire); ST NINIAN'S CAVE (Dumfries & Galloway); CUDDYHALL; ST CATHERINE'S WELL (Lothian & Borders); CRAIG PHADRIG (Southern Highlands); FLADDA-CHUAIN; REILIG OGHRAIN; ST BRENDAN'S CHURCH (Western Isles); SCOTLAND'S HOLY AND HEALING WELLS (p. 44).

After three days and nights the earth was removed. When he was uncovered, Oran said:

> 'Nor is heaven as is alleged,
> Nor is hell as is asserted,
> Nor is the good eternally happy,
> Nor is the bad eternally unhappy.'

As in Scott's version, Columba was appalled. He cried:

> 'Earth! earth on the eye of Oran,
> Before he wakes more controversy,
> Lest scandal should be given to the faith,
> Lest offence should be given to his
> brethren.'

In Scott's version, Oran's living burial is a human sacrifice, and although Carmichael makes the motive a religious experiment he ultimately draws the same conclusion:

> Probably human sacrifices were placed under the foundation-wall of St Oran's Temple, whether or not Oran was the name of the man sacrificed. Human sacrifices were placed under buildings in ancient Greece and Rome, and under buildings in modern England, Ireland, and Scotland. A well-known Greek case was that of the Bridge of Arta, which only stood secure after the master-builder had placed his own wife beneath the foundation.

Although theories like this were popular among nineteenth-century antiquarians, reports of 'pagan' rituals were greatly exaggerated if not entirely fabricated, particularly in relation to the Druids, whose ceremonies were thought to have influenced early Christian practice in the Western Isles. (*See also* ACHADH A BHEAN-NAICH, Northern Highlands.)

See also SAINTS OF SCOTLAND (p. 490).

RODEL, HARRIS

Angus Macleod of Harris, known as 'Angus the Tailor', told some local anecdotes in Gaelic to Kenneth Jackson of the School of Scottish Studies in 1951. One of them is a violent tale of a raid.

For centuries, says Angus, it was the custom in Harris to celebrate Hallowe'en with a night's dancing and music. One year many women had gathered in the house of an old man, but the young men were at another house and were expected to join the women after midnight. After supper, the old man put a sheep's jawbone in the fire and began to 'read' it. This was a traditional way of seeing events at a distance, described in 1763 by 'Theophilus Insulanus' (Donald MacLeod of Skye) as a 'kind of divination, by looking in the shoulder-blade of a sheep, goat, &c. as in a book, by which some skilful in that occult science, pretend to read future events', and was used for instance to envision the outcome of the battle of CULLODEN (Southern Highlands).

Suddenly the old man leaped up, shouting that enemies were at hand. He said he would try to hold them off as long as possible, and told the women to escape. They ran to find the young men and told them to arm at once, but though there was no delay, the defenders arrived too late. The old man was dead, having used all his arrows, and there was no sign of the enemy.

After a search, the oars of a boat were found in a hollow, still known in Angus's time as 'the Hollow of the Oars' (Lag nan Ràmh). The men hid the oars, and when they found the attackers, a band of Mac-Neills, a bloody battle ensued. Running to where they had left their oars, the MacNeills found them gone and had to jump into the sea at a place called 'the Battle of the Drowning' (Cath a' Bhathaidh).

The gallant old man was buried where he had fallen. 'To prove that this story is true,' Angus declares, 'Lag nan Ràmh is still there, and Cath a' Bhathaidh where the strangers jumped out into the sea.' This sort of detail is often included in oral narrative to link a story with a particular place, and local place-names are frequently explained in relation to similar legends.

When a new road was being made through Rodel or Roghadal in about 1910, Angus adds, the bones of a man were unearthed and buried in the graveyard. 'They recognised that it was the bones of the old man that they had found.' Although it is unlikely that the remains could have been identified, as the old man or at all, it is quite possible that some human bones were found and reburied in consecrated ground, and since Angus was born in 1895 this would have been within his memory.

RUABHAL, BENBECULA

Throughout the British Isles stories of church-building are told in which the stones for the structure are moved supernaturally to a new site. As Janet and Colin Bord comment in their *Secret Country* (1979), this demonstrates the significance attached in former times to the positioning of sacred or important buildings. In many cases the interference is demonic or mischievous, but occasionally it is understood as divine.

One such case involved St Torranan, a Christian missionary rejected by the Irish, who took to sea in his little coracle, prayed for guidance, and came to land in the creek of Cailigeo in Benbecula. Alexander Carmichael tells the story in *Carmina Gadelica*, his great collection of songs,

spells, and folklore from the Highlands and islands made in the second half of the nineteenth century, and includes a description of the landscape as seen from the central hill of the island, Rueval or Ruabhal, 'the Red Hill'.

> The summit commands an extraordinary view of fords and channels, islands, peninsulas and mainlands, seas and lakes, and of moors and machairs broken up and dotted over in the most marvellous manner with shallow pools, tarns, and lakes scattered broadcast beyond count, beyond number. Probably the world does not contain anything more disorderly than the distribution of land and water in and around Benbecula.

Attempting to bring a little order to this chaos, St Torranan decided to build his first church on Cnoc Feannaig ('the Knoll of the Hooded Crow') near his landing place, and began to collect stones on the hillock. Each morning, however, he found that overnight the stones had been taken to a small island in a loch nearby, and at length he understood that this revealed the will of God. His church was accordingly built on the island.

Carmichael notes that the church ascribed to St Torranan probably dated from the sixth century, when churches were usually constructed of wattles (woven rods and twigs), but since no wood was to be found on the island, stones had to be used instead. Most traditions of building materials moved by spirits involve stones, probably because the magical element is clearer: twigs could blow away in the wind, but stones could only be carried by powerful forces.

ST BRENDAN'S CHURCH, BARRA

Malcolm Maclean, a smith of Barra and 'a man of quiet wit', told a story of St

Brendan to Alexander Carmichael in the late nineteenth century. There was once a farmer called Domhull Dubh (Black Donald) who lived at Baile-na-creige, near St Brendan's church and burial place. Donald was inclined to ignore saints' days, and on the day of St Brendan, when others were at morning mass, he went out to plough:

> He chose a hollow out of sight, where he thought he might work unseen and unmo-lested of man, or of woman, or of tell-tale child, not thinking that the eye of Bren-dan would see him, nor that the wrath of Brendan would be upon him for disturb-ing his rest and breaking his day.

No sooner had he called his horses to go on than a magic mist came down, hiding the horses and the plough. Feeling that he might have offended the saint, Donald called out:

> 'Brendan! O Brendan!
> Lift off me the mist.'

The fog lifted, but instead of his horses he found that he had asses before him, and instead of his plough he now held his wife's distaff, while he himself had shrunk in size and was no bigger than a dwarf. He was greatly perplexed, but thinking to make the best of a bad job he called to the asses to go on. At once the mist descended. Again he cried out:

> 'Brendan! O Brendan!
> With God's will and men's wish,
> Lift from me the fog.'

The mist cleared once more, but now instead of asses he was driving a team of rabbits, and had his wife's spindle in his hand, while he himself was no bigger than a fairy man of the knoll. In spite of these disadvantages he yet again began to plough, and again the mist came down. Now truly contrite, he addressed the saint:

> 'Brendan! O Brendan!
> Listen to my prayer,
> With God's will and men's desire,
> Lift from me the fog.'

As his repentance this time was sincere, the saint relented. When the fog lifted, Donald had his own horses and plough and was himself again. Ashamed, he went home and from then on observed the holy days as he should.

See also SAINTS OF SCOTLAND (p. 490).

SANDRAY

The small island of Sandray, or Sann-traigh, south of Barra and Vatersay, was the scene of a story told in Gaelic in 1859 and printed by John Francis Campbell, in which a fairy borrows a kettle every day from a herdsman's wife until the herds-man, left for once on his own, is too fright-ened to let the fairy in. The kettle is taken magically, and the wife has to go and fetch it from the fairy mound, after which the fairy never comes to the house again.

The daily accompaniment of the lending is a verse spoken by the wife, translated by Campbell as:

> A smith is able to make
> Cold iron hot with coal.
> The due of a kettle is bones,
> And to bring it back again whole.

The traditional aversion of the fairies to 'cold iron' is sometimes referred by schol-ars to the relationship between Iron Age man and his Neolithic predecessors, to whom metalworking was perhaps an uncanny mystery. Whether or not such a connection is legitimate, it seems a fair assumption that a Neolithic and an Iron Age person would each have found the other equally surprising and unsettling, as is the case in this story with the fairies and the humans. The terrified herdsman bars the door against the 'woman of peace', as the fairy is called; a man in the fairy mound, seeing the human woman take the kettle, addresses her as 'Silent wife'. A similar motif occurs in a Manx legend in which a fairy man complains of a mortal housewife who lives above his house, 'The Dumb Woman from the Land of the Dead took my kettle.' In both cases the women say nothing because that was the recommended behaviour in dealing with the fairies, and their behaviour mirrors that of the fairy in the Sandray story who comes each day to the house in silence; to the fairies the world above ground is 'the Land of the Dead' because it is where the mortals live, while to human beings the underworld, the fairy realm, is considered in that bony light.

It was not considered unusual, however, for these two mutually distrustful races to borrow from each other, and the kettle or cooking vessel was one of the objects most often lent. In *Clan Traditions and Popular Tales* (1895), John Gregorson Campbell tells how the wife of a tenant farmer in a remote part of Lewis was visited one day while she was spinning by a little woman 'of reddish appearance' with two dogs. The little woman asked the farmer's wife for the loan of a small cauldron, and when this was granted, the dogs bore it away. Five days later it was returned, the little woman remarking that she could hear the farmer's wife singing songs above her dwelling. Sad to say, the good neighbourliness was put a stop to by the woman's husband, who told the minister what had passed, and on his advice pulled down his house, burning every scrap of the old thatch and pouring nine pails of charmed sea-water on the rafters. It often seems to be the human husbands who spoil the good relations between their wives and the fairies.

Scarba is probably named for the cormorant, *sgarbh* in Gaelic, a bird associated from ancient times with witches.

SCARBA

Scarba was the site of an early Christian settlement, and once had a population of around fifty. It is now uninhabited, and according to Otta Swire, writing in the 1960s, in her day it had a sinister reputation. There were rumours of strange forms flitting about the island on moonlit nights, and even when there was no moon, terrible cries could be heard coming from its cliffs, phenomena that could have had something to do with sea-birds. The name of the island is probably derived from *sgarbh*, meaning 'cormorant', a bird widely regarded as uncanny. From Roman times its appearance has been held to forebode storms, and it was said that the cormorant was a shape adopted by witches.

Scarba is not far from the whirlpool of CORRYVRECKAN, which according to Martin Martin writing in 1703 'hath its Name from *Brekan*, said to be Son to the King of *Denmark*, who was drowned

John Francis Campbell of Islay (1821–85) was a
pioneer in the collection of Gaelic folklore.
Among the tales he gathered from the Highlands
and Western Isles were legends of the Fuath, a
spirit said to protect the fish of South Uist.

here'. Otta Swire, telling the story, calls
Breacan a prince of Lochlann, the name
given in old Scottish legend to a sort of
general mythical Scandinavia, and usually
taken to mean Norway. Breacan loved the
daughter of the Lord of the Isles, but her
father disapproved of the match. Not
wishing, however, to anger the King of
Lochlann, he did not refuse outright, but
said that in order to win his daughter's
hand Breacan should prove himself a com-
petent sailor by anchoring his ship for
three days and nights in Corryvreckan.

The wise men of Lochlann advised Breacan to take three new cables, one made
from wool sheared from sheep which had
never before been shorn, another from

hemp grown in a graveyard, and the third
from the hair of pure virgins. The first
two were easily supplied, and to the third
every maiden in Lochlann contributed.

Prince Breacan anchored his ship by all
three cables in the whirlpool. After one
day and night of the turbulence, the first
rope snapped; after a second day and
night, the second gave way. Had all the
Lochlann girls been telling the truth, the
third cable would have held for the third
day and night, but alas, one had played
false. She was no maiden, the cable
snapped, and all on board the ship were
drowned except Breacan's hound, the
Grey Dog, which searched for its master's
body and dragged it ashore on Scarba.

Returning to the sea, the dog itself drowned between Scarba and Lunga, in a strait long called the Grey Dog's Sound.

A variant on the legend says that the Breacan who drowned was not from Lochlann but from Ireland, grandson of Niall of the Nine Hostages, and therefore kin to St Columba. When Columba and his monks passed near Corryvreckan on their voyage from Ireland to Iona, one of Prince Breacan's ribs floated up to greet his relative. The holy men would have been swallowed by the whirlpool if Columba had not brought with him a little soil from St Ciaran's grave which he scattered on the waters, calming their fury.

SOUTH UIST

The fish in the lochs and rivers of South Uist were believed to be under the protection of a spirit known as the Fuath. Anyone who fished there in spawning season was in danger. One man catching fish at this time met the Fuath in the shape of a huge black man, who threw him into a pool. Another saw something like a mill wheel bowling down the hill and hastily fled, leaving his fish behind. When he went the next day to get them, they had gone.

These stories embody real taboos, providing warnings against antisocial behaviour: it was obviously in everyone's interests to prevent over-fishing, particularly at spawning time. There is, however, considerable disagreement about the nature of the Fuath. It seems from the above instances that it was a bogey beast which could change its form and even appear as an inanimate object like a mill wheel, and the folklore collector John Francis Campbell says its child is the Brollachan; as the Brollachan has no shape of its own, that would suggest that its parent the Fuath is also shapeless. Campbell, who was told several Sutherland stories about the

Fuath, concludes that it is a water-spirit, and 'that there are males and females; that they have web-feet, yellow hair, green dresses, tails, manes, and no noses; that they marry men, and are killed by light, and hurt with steel weapons; that in crossing a stream they become restless'. From other tales, he goes on, it appears that they are hairy, have bare skin on their faces, and two large round eyes. This sounds very like the apparition at ORSAY, identified as a Fuath but also called a Water-horse.

Another veteran folklorist, John Gregorson Campbell, disagrees. The word *fuath*, he says, means literally 'aversion' or 'hatred', but in Ross-shire and elsewhere is commonly used to denote an apparition, ghost, or spectre, not specifically associated with water. He remarks that John Francis Campbell has fallen into the error of conjoining attributes ascribed in several stories, and representing the Fuath as a water-spirit.

The characteristics of any of these legendary beings – Urisk, Fuath, Brollachan, Brownie – are essentially fluid, changing from story to story and region to region. Since the creatures themselves are not available for scientific examination, their natures have to be deduced from the tales told of them: as narratives evolve, so the attributes of the beasts or spirits change over time and space.

STAOINEBRIG, SOUTH UIST

Angus MacEachain, a herdsman of Staoinebrig, was known in South Uist as 'Angus of the exorcisms'. In the late nineteenth century he told Alexander Carmichael the story of a cure he performed on a girl with jaundice, whose parents had sent for him. Having examined her, Angus announced that she was possessed of the demon of the jaundice, but that he would expel the demon and cure the girl.

He asked the girl's mother to light a big fire, her sisters to bring a tub of cold water, and her father to fetch the plough-irons, evil spirits being averse to iron. Angus then placed the plough-irons in the fire until they were red hot. The room was in darkness, and the patient's eyes were bandaged, 'that the eyes of the body might be subjective to the eyes of the mind'. The exorcist then directed that the girl should be placed with her bare back towards him, and that he should be left alone with her, after which he secured the door and made a clanging noise with the plough-irons, as if to drive away the demon. He then put the ploughshare back in the fire, and the coulter (the blade usually fixed in front of the ploughshare) in the cold water.

Then pretending to take the red-hot share out of the fire, he took the icy-cold coulter and placed it along the spine of the patient, loudly commanding the demon to depart. The girl screamed in evident agony, calling on the Mother of Christ and on the Foster-mother of Christ, and on her own mother, to come and rescue her from the brutal treatment of black Angus the father of evil, the brother of demons, and to see how her blood was flowing in streams and her flesh was burnt off her back, laying her backbone bare.

In a few days the girl was up and about, though Angus did not know whether it was due to her faith in the exorcism or to shock. 'She is grateful, but shy of me ever since, probably remembering the hard things she said. She will always believe that I exercised some occult power over the jaundice demon.'

STILLIGARRY, SOUTH UIST

The word *fride* was applied by the islanders of Uist to small gnome-like creatures which they said dwelt among the rocks. These rock-gnomes were supposed to eat and drink like humans, and it was proverbial that any crumbs which fell on the floor should be left where they lay: 'Let it be, many are the needy mouths awaiting it.'

MacVurich of Stilligarry (Stadhlaigeàrraidh), a man reputed to have magic powers, was losing his cattle through accident and illness. One day as he sat on a rock he heard a gnome mother singing to her child, telling it to hush, and when MacVurich's table was set, it would get something nice. MacVurich went to his kitchen where his housekeeper was making bread, and told her to leave the scraps of dough that fell from the board. From that day onwards he took bread and milk to the gnomes, and never again lost his cattle or sheep or horses.

It was reported of MacVurich that when he was born he was given three wishes by God. He was once returning to Uist from Moidart when the wind dropped, and soon ceased altogether. The men stuck knives in the mast and whistled for a wind, but no breeze came, and at last MacVurich's son begged his father to ask for a wind. MacVurich spoke a verse, and a wind rose, but the son, a 'lad without sense', thought it too gentle, and challenged his father to produce a stronger gale. MacVurich lost his temper, and demanded a wind from 'cold hell'. Instantly the storm broke, and it seemed that it would blow them to eternity. MacVurich's son then regretted what he had thoughtlessly asked:

'O father, father, weaken the wind or we are with the shellfish of the deep.'

'Thou blockhead, thou who didst ask me to seek the wind, away with thy senseless talk. I would not ask the third request of my God should she go to the tangles of the deep,' said MacVurich.

The crew were terrified: not a man among them could do a thing, save MacVurich himself and his servant Finlay, who in calm weather was treated as a figure of fun, but in this emergency proved a hero, bailing water while MacVurich steered. Eventually between the two of them they brought the boat to shore, where the men were so weak they could hardly stand. Even a dog which came from the ship lay down beside a lamb without troubling it. MacVurich said:

'The son of the hound and the son of the lamb
In the cold friendship of the snow,
It is the storm of the waves and the roar of the sea
That have made you lie down side by side.'

The three wishes for the wind, the third of which must not be used, are like the three knots tied in scarlet thread by Bessie Miller, the wind-witch of STROMNESS (Orkney & Shetland Islands), and also echo the Greek myth of Aeolus tying the winds in a bag as a gift for Odysseus, whose shipmates then foolishly unfastened the bag.

STINKY BAY (POLL NAN CRANN), BENBECULA

'Some seventy years ago,' wrote Alexander Carmichael in 1900, the islanders of Benbecula were cutting seaweed at Grimnis (Griminish) when a woman heard a splash out to sea. The weather was calm, so she looked up to see what had made the noise, and cried out in astonishment at the sight of a creature 'in the form of a woman in miniature' swimming in the sea. Everyone ran to look:

The creature made somersaults and turned about in various directions. Some men waded into the water to seize her, but she moved beyond their reach. Some boys threw stones at her, one of which struck her in the back.

A few days later she was dead, probably from the blow she had received. Her body was washed up at Cuile, Nunton, and examined minutely:

The upper portion of the creature was about the size of a well-fed child of three or four years of age, with an abnormally developed breast. The hair was long, dark, and glossy, while the skin was white, soft, and tender. The lower part of the body was like a salmon, but without scales. Crowds of people, some from long distances, came to see this strange animal, and all were unanimous in the opinion that they had gazed on the mermaid at last.

Duncan Shaw, factor for Clanranald, the sheriff of the district, ordered a coffin and shroud to be made, and the body was buried a short distance above the shore where it was found, according to Carmichael. Ronald Macdonald Robertson, retelling the sad little story in 1961, contradicts this detail:

Actually, the alleged mermaid was interred in the presence of a large assemblance of the Hebridean people in the burial-ground at Nunton, where her grave is pointed out to this day. I have seen it myself.

Up-to-date information suggests that the mermaid is buried *not* in the graveyard but on the border between Nunton and Griminish, in a bay known in Gaelic as Poll nan Crann ('Inlet of the Mast or Masts') and in English as Stinky Bay, from the prevailing smell of seaweed. Her burial site is to the north of the bay, just above the shore, about half a mile from Nunton graveyard. Robertson may have been shown a different spot, but in any case, seeing a grave

The Spanish galleon *Florida* was blown up at Tobermory in the late sixteenth century.
Legend soon gathered around the incident, and it was said that the ghost of a princess killed
on the ship haunted MacLean of Duart, asking for her bones to be returned to her homeland.

proves nothing about what is buried in it. As so often, the physical memorial is cited to demonstrate the truth of the story.

TOBERMORY, MULL

Lord Archibald Campbell in *Records of Argyll* (1885) gives a story 'in the original wording as sent to the Editor' concerning MacLean of Duart and a princess of Spain. The princess had fallen in love with a man she had seen in a dream, and knew he must be sought for in another country because she could not understand his language. Commandeering one of her father's frigates, she sailed to Holland, Denmark, Sweden, Norway, and finally Scotland.

Her plans were, at every place she stopped, that she had a dinner on board the ship, and inviting all the gentlemen that would be round that district to the dinner, to see if she would fall in with the one she saw in her dream.

When she came to Tobermory, one of the men who came to dinner was MacLean of Duart. As soon as the princess saw him 'she clasped her hands round his neck and kissed him', and after that 'MacLean stayed with her for some days.'

There was, however, a Mrs MacLean to be reckoned with. Hearing of her husband's affair with the princess, the wife set off for Tobermory, and employed a servant to blow up the Spanish ship, killing everyone on board – including the princess, whose body was found a few days later.

MacLean had sincerely loved the princess, and now, grieving, he buried her in Morvern. She later appeared to him in a vision, and told him to disinter her body and bury it instead in Kilmaluag in

Lismore. Some years after that, MacLean had another vision in which the princess asked him to dig up her bones yet again, wash them in a well at Kilmaluag, and return them to Spain, and this too he did. The King of Spain rewarded MacLean of Mull for bringing his daughter's remains:

> But after MacLean left, the king over-hauled the body of his daughter, and found one of her joints amissing. Then he got into a rage, and ordered two of his best frigates under way to destroy the Island of Mull, and MacLean with it. So the two frigates arrived in Duart Bay, and anchored there.

MacLean called in the Mull witches, who were called Doideagan, or Dodags. There were nine of them at work on their magical looms in Castle Duart making wind to blow the Spanish ships ashore, but the captain of the Spanish ships, whose (not very Spanish) name was Forester, was skilled in the Black Arts, and fought back. He saw the Dodags flying round his masts in the shape of crows, but he said he could beat them as long as Gormsuil, a witch from Lochaber, did not come. Hardly had he said this when Gormsuil appeared in the shape of a cat.

> Then Captain Forester gave up all hopes; the ships began to drive. They then got their axes to cut the cables; so the heads of the axes flew off the shafts over the side. Then the two frigates drove ashore at the back of Lismore, and sank there, and all hands perished. I understand that a few years ago one of her Majesty's gunboats lifted some of the guns that were on board these frigates.

John Francis Campbell mentions this tale briefly in the introduction to his *Popular Tales of the West Highlands* of the 1860s, with the detail that MacLean revenged the murder of his sweetheart by exposing his wife on the Lady Rock. Earlier than this,

however, Robert Chambers gives a story which is recognisably the same, but has accumulated less romantic paraphernalia. According to this, the *Florida*, a man-of-war belonging to the Spanish Armada, was left at Tobermory after the overthrow or wreck of its companions in 1588:

> Queen Elizabeth, at length hearing of the circumstance, despatched a person to procure its destruction. One Smollett, an ancestor of the novelist, is said to have been the person.

Smollett went to Mull as a cattle-dealer, and easily found his way on board the *Florida*, where he made friends with some of the crew and was able to see round the ship.

> He at length found a convenient time for his diabolical object, and placed some combustible substance in a situation where it was likely to produce the desired effect. He had travelled to a distance of six or eight miles, when he heard the explosion, and the spot where he stood is still marked for the execration of mankind. The ship was blown up, and nearly all on board perished.

MacLean of Duart is mentioned here as having borrowed some cannon from the *Florida* in order to attack a neighbouring chieftain on his own account, but nothing is said about the princess, whose story may have been partly inspired by that of 'The Spanish Lady's Love', another Armada-based romance set in England. In that tale, based on a ballad of the same name, several different noblemen were named in connection with a beautiful senorita who fell in love with a married man but generously sent him home to his wife.

Attempts were made to retrieve the treasure from the *Florida*, but apparently the most successful expedition was made by an English ship which then absconded with its booty and was never heard of again. In 1787 a diver named Spalding failed to find the wreck, the remains of the vessel having by then sunk into the mud and completely disappeared.

A related legend set at KIEL (Argyllshire & Islands) tells how the princess's ghost returned in search of her missing little finger.

TROTTERNISH, SKYE

The story of 'The Cave of Gold' is one of the most famous in Scottish legend. Martin Martin, writing of his journey round the Hebrides in 1695, records an early version, linking it to a big cave in Bornesketaig (Borgh na Sgiotaig) at the north end of Skye:

> The Natives told me that a Piper who was over curious, went into the Cave with a design to find out the length of it, and after he entered, began to play on his Pipe, but never return'd to give an account of his Progress.

He gives this cave no name, but a little later he mentions a 'Golden Cave' in Sleat, 'said to be seven Miles in length, from the West to East'. Other caves are named by later sources in connection with the legend, one in Harlosh, and another in Inverness-shire.

Martin's bald narrative could apply to any one of the 'lost pipers' of Scotland, but the Skye tale is more complex, and is made up of two distinct episodes. A good version of the first act is James Mac-Dougall's 'The Black Lad MacCrimmon and the Banshee': naturally the piper is often identified as a MacCrimmon, and the family's musical pre-eminence explained as having supernatural origins. This tendency probably became more pronounced in the nineteenth century as reports of the piping school at BORERAIG took on legendary proportions.

The MacCrimmons were once no better than other good pipers, MacDougall begins: it was the Black Lad who rose above all the rest. Yet as a boy he could hardly play at all, and was looked down on by his father and two brothers. One day when the Black Lad was alone, he took down the great bagpipes which his father called 'The Black Gate'. While he was trying to play, a banshee came to him and asked which he would prefer, success without skill or skill without success; similarly double-edged gifts were said to be offered by the Glaistig (see THE MAIDEN OF INVERAWE, p. 24). MacCrimmon replied that he would rather have skill without success, and at that she pulled a hair from her head and asked him to tie it round the chanter. Then she guided his fingers with her own on the chanter, and told him that he was now King of the Pipers: 'Thine equal was not before thee, and thine equal shall not be after thee.'

The sequel is darker. In the Uamh an Oir ('Cave of Gold'), a monster was said to lurk. The piper, whose notes could charm the most savage creature, ventured into the cavern playing a lament: he knew that he would not return. Those outside could hear the music as the piper went further and deeper, and then a terrible wail, 'Oh for three hands! Two for the bagpipe and one for the sword.' The beast was upon him, and his only defence was his music. The echoes continued for a long while, but in the end there was silence.

Many details emerge from other tellings. Often the bargain is struck from the beginning that the piper must on a given day enter the cave, to pay with his life for the fairy gift. What he meets inside is sometimes a wolf, 'the great grey she-one', but also appears as 'the green bitch'. Green being the fairy colour, this is clearly a supernatural terror. There are parallels to the ancient myth of Orpheus, who entered the Land of the Dead with only his music to protect him, and the names used in Mac-Dougall's version, 'The Black Lad' and 'The Black Gate', suggest a descent to hell. The same point is made in versions which mention a dog following its master into the depths only to emerge with no hair, scorched by the sulphur and brimstone of the pit which has swallowed the piper.

One question raised by the tale is how the message is conveyed that the piper wishes he had three hands, since he is playing all the while, not singing. 'Have the pipes a language?' asks W. L. Manson, writing in 1901 on the history of the Highland bagpipe. 'Through the great bulk of what has been written about the bagpipe there runs this idea of its power, this wild, fanciful notion that it has an actual language and that those who understand that language can converse by its means.' That power is itself uncanny, and is connected with the notion that the pipes were the favoured instrument not only of fairies but also of the Devil, as described at ALLOWAY (Glasgow & Ayrshire).

See also LOCH FINLAGGAN.

UISINIS, SOUTH UIST

A sinister tale of the living dead, narrated in Gaelic in 1953 and printed in translation in *Scottish Traditional Tales* (1994), is set in Uisinis, a hilly peninsula to the east of the highest hills of South Uist, now totally uninhabited. It is an atmospheric setting for the nearest Scottish equivalent to a vampire story.

Three hundred and fifty years ago, begins the narrator with rare precision, a man named MacPhail lived in Uisinnis (Uisinis) with his wife, his son and his son's wife, and their daughter. The little girl, who was nearly thirteen, was dumb.

In the course of time old MacPhail died, and his son went to the town to prepare for the funeral, leaving the three women alone in the house with the corpse.

At around one in the morning, MacPhail's wife was astonished to hear the dumb girl speak: 'Granny, Granny, my grandfather's getting up! He'll eat you and he won't touch me!'

Sure enough, the dead man was sitting upright. His widow jumped back and closed the door on him, but he was pushing from the other side, and she began to pile boxes in front of the door. He then began to dig his way out through the earth underneath the door, and his head and shoulders had just emerged when the cock crowed three times. At once the undead man fell lifeless and stayed where he was until the son returned.

He was lifted then and buried, but the hole he made underneath the doorway is still to be seen in the old ruins of the house where the thing happened in Uisinnis, and no one has ever been able to fill it in. The hole is known as 'MacPhail's Pit' to the present day. It's said that people tried more than once to fill it up with stones and earth, but next day it would be the same as before, and not one blade of grass ever grew there – nothing but a foul, dank mire.

The reason the old man will not eat his granddaughter is because she is of his own blood, unlike his wife and his daughter-in-law. The story is found in other versions on Harris and in Ross, linked to places where pits or large holes could be seen.

The dumb girl who becomes able to speak is likewise a recurrent theme. At POLLOK (Glasgow & Ayrshire), Janet Douglas regained her voice in order to accuse witches, and Sir Walter Scott uses the theme in *Peveril of the Peak* (1822), basing his character Fenella on 'Dumb

Lizzie', a woman who worked for Scott's own grandfather for several years before suddenly proving to have perfect command of her tongue. Lizzie, however, was only feigning dumbness, whereas here the granddaughter is presumably granted the power of speech at her moment of need.

UPPER DRUIMFIN, MULL

A man named Donald at one time carried the mail from Tobermory to the ferry for the mainland. Donald was a good deal given to drink, and consequently to loitering by the way. He once lay down to have a quiet sleep near a fairy-haunted rock above Druimfin (spelt Drimfin by John Gregorson Campbell, who tells this story) when he saw the rock open, and a flood of light pour out. A little man came to him and said in English, 'Come in to the ball, Donald,' but Donald fled, and never stopped till he reached the houses at Tobermory, two miles off. He said he heard the whizz and rustling of the fairies after him the whole way. The incident caused a good deal of talk in the neighbourhood, and Donald and his fright were made the subject of some doggerel verse:

'Rise, rise, rise, Donald,
Rise, Donald, was the call,
Rise up now, Donald,
Come in, Donald, to the ball.'

Recording this in *Superstitions of the Highlands and Islands of Scotland* (1900), Campbell comments in conclusion: 'It is well known that Highland Fairies, who speak English, are the most dangerous of any.'

VAUL, TIREE

A story set in Vaul tells how a man riding home at night, his young son seated behind him, was met by a number of cats. The boy had his hands clasped round his father, and the man, pressing them to his sides to make sure of the boy's hold, urged his horse to a gallop. The cats sprang, and, fastening on the boy, literally devoured him. When the man reached home, with his horse at full speed, he had only the boy's arms left.

This horrific story, reminiscent of the German legend of the Erle-King in which a boy riding with his father is stolen away although closely held in his father's arms, is told by John Gregorson Campbell in his *Witchcraft and Second Sight in the Highlands and Islands of Scotland* (1902). Campbell comments that the association of witchcraft with cats is of great antiquity, and mentions a Greek legend that Hecate herself, goddess of sorcery, chose on occasion to appear as a cat:

The association probably arose not so much from cats being the frequent, almost invariable, companions of the poor old women accused of witchcraft, as from the savage character of the animal itself. Its noiseless and stealthy motions, its persevering watchfulness, its extraordinary agility and tenacity of life, its diabolical caterwauling, prowling habits, deceitful spring, and the luminous appearance of its eyes in the dark, would alone suffice to procure it the name of unearthly; but when infuriated, glaring, bristling, and spitting, it forms a vivid representation of a perfect demon.

Campbell was evidently a dog man.

REFERENCES AND INDEXES

BIBLIOGRAPHY

ABBREVIATIONS
NQ for Notes and Queries
PSAS for Proceedings of the Society of Antiquaries of Scotland (Edinburgh)
TDG for The Transactions and Journal of the Proceedings of the Dumfriesshire and Galloway Natural History and Antiquarian Society
TGSI for Transactions of the Gaelic Society of Inverness (Inverness)

Agnew, Sir Andrew, *The Hereditary Sheriffs of Galloway* . . . 2 vols. (Edinburgh, 1893)
Allan, John Hay, *The Bridal of Caölchairn and Other Poems* (London and Edinburgh, 1822)
—, *Ancient Monuments in Scotland, a list corrected to 31 December 1976*, 4th edn (Edinburgh, 1979)
Anderson, A. O. and M. O., *Adomnan's Life of Columba* (London, 1961)
Anderson, Tom and Pam Swing, *Haand me doon ma Fiddle* (Stirling, 1979)
Archibald, Malcolm, *Scottish Myths & Legends* (1992; repr. Edinburgh, 1994)
Armstrong, Edward A., *The Folklore of Birds*, 2nd rev. edn (New York, 1970)
Aubrey, John, *Miscellanies*, 2nd edn (London, 1721)
Bailey, Brian, *Burke and Hare* (Edinburgh, 2002)
Baldwin, John R., *Exploring Scotland's Heritage: Lothian and the Borders* (Edinburgh: 1985)
Balfour, J. A., *The Book of Arran: Archaeology* (Glasgow, 1910)
Balfour, Michael, *Mysterious Scotland* (Edinburgh, 2003) [1997]
Barbour, John Gordon, *Unique Traditions Chiefly of the West and South of Scotland* (London and Glasgow, 1886)
Baring-Gould, Sabine, *The Book of Werewolves* (London, 1995) [1865]
Bauer, Henry H., *The Enigma of Loch Ness: Making Sense of a Mystery* (Urbana, 1986)

Beard, Charles, *Lucks and Talismans* (London, 1934)
Beath, David, *The Bishopshire and its People* (Kinross, 1902)
Beattie, George, *John of Arnha'* (6th edn, Glasgow, 1847) [1826]
Bede, Cuthbert, *see* Bradley, Edward
Beith, Mary, *Healing Threads: Traditional Medicines of the Highlands and Islands* (Edinburgh, 1995)
Bellenden, John, *see* Boece, Hector
Bentinck, Rev. Charles, *Dornoch Cathedral and Parish* (Inverness, 1926)
Beveridge, David, *Between the Ochils and Forth* (Edinburgh, 1888)
Bett, Henry, *English Myths and Traditions* (London, 1952)
Bittem, Bessie, *see* Stewart, Alexander
Black, Fiona, 'A Taste of Scotland, Historical Fictions of Sawney Bean and his Family', in *The Polar Twins*, ed. Edward J. Cowan and Douglas Gifford (Edinburgh, 1999) 154–70
Black, G. F., *County Folk-Lore 3: Orkney and Shetland*, ed. Northcote W. Thomas (London, 1903)
Black, William George, *Folk Medicine: A Chapter in the History of Culture* (London, 1883)
Black's *Picturesque Tourist of Scotland* . . ., 3rd edn (Edinburgh, 1844)
—, 4th edn (Edinburgh, 1845)
—, 16th edn (Edinburgh, 1865)
—, 23rd edn (Edinburgh, 1882)
—, 25th edn (Edinburgh, 1885)
Blair, Anna, *Tales of Ayrshire* (London, 1983)
Blair, Matthew, *The Paisley Shawl* (Paisley, 1904)
Blind, Karl, 'New Finds in Shetlandic and Welsh Folk-Lore', *Gentleman's Magazine* 252, January to June 1882, 353–71
'Blind Harry', *The Wallace*, ed. Anne McKim (Edinburgh, 2003)

Blythell, Rosemary, *The Real Bride of Lammer-moor* (Wigtown, 2007)

Boece, Hector (trans. John Bellenden, 1531) *The Chronicles of Scotland*, 2 vols., ed. R. W. Chambers and Edith C. Batho (Edinburgh and London, 1938–41)

The Book of Pluscarden, ed. F. J. H. Skene, 2 vols. (Edinburgh, 1877, 1880)

Bord, Janet, *Cures and Curses: Ritual and Cult at Holy Wells* (Loughborough, 2006)

—, *Footprints in Stone* (Loughborough, 2004)

—, *Holy Wells in Britain* (Loughborough, 2008)

—, *The Traveller's Guide to Fairy Sites* (Glastonbury, 2004)

Bord, Janet and Colin, *The Enchanted Land* (London, 1995)

—, *Mysterious Britain* (London, 1973)

—, *Sacred Waters* (London, 1985)

—, *The Secret Country* (London, 1976; pa. edn, 1978; repr. 1979)

Bovet, Richard, *Pandaemonium, or The Devil's Cloyster* (1684)

[Bradley, Edward], 'Cuthbert Bede', *The White Wife: with other stories, supernatural, romantic and legendary* (London, 1865)

Brand, John, *A New Description of Orkney, Zetland, Pightland-Firth and Caithness* (Edinburgh, 1703) [1701]

—, *Popular Antiquities of Great Britain*, rev. Sir Henry Ellis (1853 edn)

Bray, Elizabeth, *The Discovery of the Hebrides* (Glasgow, 1986)

Brereton, Henry L., *Gordonstoun: Ancient Estate and Modern School* (Edinburgh and London, 1968)

Briggs, Katharine, *A Dictionary of British Folk-Tales*, 2 pts in 4 vols. (London, 1970–1)

—, *A Dictionary of Fairies* (London, pa. edn 1977) [1976]

—, *The Fairies in Tradition and Literature* (London, 1967)

—, *Pale Hecate's Team* (London, 1962)

—, *The Personnel of Fairyland* (Oxford, 1953)

—, *The Vanishing People* (London, 1978)

Brockie, William, *The Gypsies of Yetholm* (Kelso, 1884)

Brown, Theo, *The Fate of the Dead* (Ipswich and Totowa, N.J., 1979)

Browne, John Hutton, *Glimpses into the Past in Lammermuir* (Edinburgh, 1892)

Bruford, Alan, (ed.), *The Green Man of Knowledge* (Aberdeen, 1982)

Bruford, A. J., and D. A. MacDonald (eds.), *Scottish Traditional Tales* (Edinburgh, 1994)

Buchan, David, *Scottish Tradition* (London, etc., 1984)

Burke, J. Bernard, *Family Romance*, 2 vols. printed as one, (London, 1853)

Burgess, J. J. Haldane, 'Some Shetland Folklore', *Scottish Review* 25 (1895) 91–103

Burness, John, *Thrummy Cap* (Brechin, 1832) [1796]

Burnham, Josephine M., 'A Study of Thomas of Erceldoune', *Publications of the Modern Language Association of America* XXIII (1908) 375–420

[Burns, Robert], *The Poetical Works of Robert Burns*, ed. J. Logie Robertson, Oxford Complete Edition (London, Edinburgh, Glasgow, New York, and Toronto, 1904)

[Burt, Edmund], *Letters from a Gentleman in the North of Scotland*, 2 vols., (London, 1754)

Butler's Lives of the Saints, 4 vols. (Aberdeen and London, 1956) [1756–9, rev. edn. 1926–38]

Calder, James T., *Sketch of the Civil and Traditional History of Caithness from the Tenth Century* (Glasgow, etc., 1861)

—, *Sketches from John o' Groats, in Prose and Verse* (Wick, 1842)

Camden, William, *Britain*, trans. Philemon Holland (London, 1610)

Campbell, Lord Archibald, *Records of Argyll: Legends, Traditions, and Recollections of Argyllshire Highlanders Collected Chiefly from the Gaelic* (Edinburgh and London, 1885)

—, *Waifs and Strays of Celtic Tradition, Argyllshire Series*, 5 vols. (London, 1889–95)

Campbell, John Francis, *Leabhar na Feinne* (London, 1872)

—, *Popular Tales of the West Highlands*, pa. edn in 2 vols. (Edinburgh, 1994) [1860–2]

Campbell, John Gregorson, *Clan Traditions and Popular Tales* (London, 1895) [vol. 5 of Campbell (1889–95)]

—, *The Fians* (London, 1891) [vol. 4 of Campbell (1889–95)]

—, *Superstitions of the Highlands and Islands of Scotland* (Glasgow, 1900)

—, *Witchcraft and Second Sight in the Highlands and Islands of Scotland* (Glasgow, 1902)

Campbell, Mary, and Mary Sandeman, 'Mid Argyll: an archaeological survey', *PSAS* 95 (1964) 1–125

Cargill Guthrie, James, *The Vale of Strathmore: Its Scenes and Legends* (Edinburgh, 1875)

Carlyle, Thomas, *Reminiscences*, ed. James Anthony Froude, 2 vols. (London, 1881)

Carmichael, Alexander, *Carmina Gadelica*, 2 vols. (Edinburgh, 1900)

—, *Carmina Gadelica*, 5 vols. (Edinburgh and London, 1928–54)

Cash, C. G., 'Stone Circles at Grenish, Aviemore, and Delfour, Strathspey', *PSAS* 40 (1906) 245–54

Chambers, Robert, *Book of Days*, 2 vols. (London and Edinburgh, 1864)

—, *The Picture of Scotland*, 2 vols. printed as one (Edinburgh, 1827)

—, *Popular Rhymes of Scotland* (Edinburgh and London, 1826)

—, *Popular Rhymes of Scotland*, New Edition (4th) (London and Edinburgh, 1870)

Chambers, William, *Exploits and Anecdotes of the Scottish Gypsies* (Edinburgh, 1886) [1821]

Chambers, W. and R., *Chambers's Journal of Popular Literature Science, and Arts* (London and Edinburgh, 1888)

—, *Domestic Annals of Scotland* (Edinburgh and London, 1891) [1861]

Cheviot, Andrew, *Proverbs, Proverbial Expressions and Popular Rhymes of Scotland* (Paisley and London, 1896)

Child, Francis J., *English and Scottish Popular Ballads*, 5 vols. (New York, 1957) [1882]

—, *English and Scottish Popular Ballads*, ed. Helen Child Sargent and George Lyman Kittredge (London, 1904)

Close-Brooks, Joanna, *Exploring Scotland's Heritage: The Highlands* (Edinburgh, 1986)

Cluness, Albert T., *The Shetland Isles* (London, 1951)

Coffey, Timothy, *The History and Folklore of North American Wildflowers* (New York, 1993)

A Collection of Rare and Curious Tracts on Witchcraft and the Second Sight (Edinburgh, 1820)

Corrie, John, 'Folk Lore of Glencairn', *TDG* 1890–1 (1891) no. 7, 37–45, 75–83

Cowan, E. J., 'The Darker Vision of the Scottish Renaissance: the Devil and Francis Stewart', in *The Renaissance and Reformation in Scotland*, eds. I. B. Cowan and Duncan Shaw (Edinburgh, 1983) 125–40

Cramond, W., 'The Groat Tombstone', *Scottish Antiquary* 8 (1894) 51–2

Crockett, Samuel Rutherford, *The Raiders* (London, 1894)

Cromek, R. H., *Remains of Nithsdale and Galloway Song, with Historical and Traditional Notices Relative to the Manners and Customs of the Peasantry* (London, 1810)

Crowe, Catherine, *The Night-Side of Nature, or, Ghosts and Ghost-Seers* (London, 1848; pa. edn, Wellingborough, Northamptonshire, 1986)

Crowl, Philip, *The Intelligent Traveller's Guide to Historic Scotland* (London, 1986)

Cruden, Stewart, *The Early Christian and Pictish Monuments of Scotland* (Edinburgh, 1973)

Cunningham, A. D., *Tales of Rannoch* (Author and Perth & Kinross District Libraries, 1989)

Cunningham, Allan, *Traditional Tales of the English and Scottish Peasantry*, 2 vols. printed as one (London, 1822)

Cunningham, Andrew S., *Upper Largo, Lower Largo, Lundin Links, and Newburn* (Leven, 1907)

Dale-Green, Patricia, *Dog* (London, 1966)

Dalgleish, Walter Scott, *Shakespeare's Macbeth* (Edinburgh, 1862)

Dante, *The Divine Comedy: Inferno*, trans. Dorothy L. Sayers (London, 1972) [1949]

Darton, Mike, *The Dictionary of Scottish Place-Names* (Moffat, 1990)

Darwin, Tess, *The Scots Herbal: The Plant Lore of Scotland* (Edinburgh, 1996)

Davidson, Thomas, *Rowan Tree and Red Thread* (Edinburgh and London, 1949)

Dawson, Robert, *Scottish Traditional Traveller Families: Published Sources* (Blackwell, 2002)

Defoe, Daniel, *A Tour Through the Whole Island of Great Britain originally begun by the Celebrated Daniel De Foe, continued by the late Mr. Richardson, Author of Clarissa, and brought down to the present Time by a GENTLEMAN of Eminence in the Literary World*: The 7th edition with very great Additions, Improvements, and Corrections, 4 vols., (London, 1769)

Dempster, Miss, 'The Folk-Lore of Sutherlandshire', *Folk-Lore Journal* 6 (1888) 149–89, 215–52

[Denham, Michael Aislabie], *The Denham Tracts, A Collection of Folklore by Michael Aislabie Denham, and reprinted from the original tracts and pamphlets printed by Mr. Denham between 1846 and 1859*, ed. James Hardy, Publications of the Folk-Lore Society XXXV, 2 vols. (London, 1892–5)

Dick, C. H., *Highways and Byways in Galloway and Carrick* (London, 1916)

Dinsdale, Timothy, *The Leviathans* (London, pa. edn, 1976) [1966]

A Discourse concerning the Nature and Substance of Devils and Spirits (anon.) appended to Scot (1665)

Discover Historic Clydesdale (Lanark, 1993)

A Diurnal of Remarkable Occurrents that have passed within the Country of Scotland (Edinburgh, 1833)

Dixon, John H., *Gairloch in North-West Ross-shire: Its Records, Traditions, Inhabitants, and Natural History . . .* (Edinburgh, 1886)

—, *Pitlochry past and present . . .* (Pitlochry, 1925)

Donaldson, William, *The Highland Pipe and Scottish Society 1750–1950: Transmission, Change and the Concept of Tradition* (East Linton, 2000)

Douglas, Sir George (ed.), *Scottish Fairy and Folk Tales* (London, 1977) [1896]

Drever, Helen, *The Lure of the Kelpie: Fairy and Folk Tales of the Highlands* (Edinburgh and London, 1937; repr. 1944)

Drummond, James, 'The Tale of the Monkey', *Scots Magazine* (October 1982) 62–70

Drummond, William, *The History of Scotland*, 2nd edn (London, 1681)

Dryden, John, 'Theodore and Honoria', *Fables, Ancient and Modern* (1700)

Dunbar, William, *The Poems of William Dunbar*, ed. Priscilla Bawcutt, 2 vols. (Glasgow, 1998)

The Edinburgh Topographical, Traditional and Antiquarian Magazine, September – December 1848 (Edinburgh, 1848)

Rev. Biot Edmonston and Jessie Saxby, *The Home of a Naturalist* (London, 1888)

Exploring Sunart, Ardnamurchan, Moidart and Morar, West Highland Series No. 10 (Oban, n.d.)

Edwards, A. J., 'Excavations at Reay Links and at a horned cairn at Lower Dounreay, Caithness', *PSAS* 63, ser. 6, vol. 3 (Edinburgh, 1929) 138–50

Ellis Davidson, H. R., 'The Sword at the Wedding', *Folklore* 71 (March 1960) 5

Fairweather, Barbara, *Highland Plant Lore* (Glencoe and North Lorn Folk Museum, n.d.)

Farmer, David, *The Oxford Dictionary of Saints*, 4th edn (Oxford, 1997) [1978]

Farnie, Henry, *Handy Book of the Fife Coast from Queensferry to Fifeness* (Cupar, c. 1860)

Fergusson, Lieut.-Colonel Alexander, *The Laird of Lag* (Edinburgh, 1886)

Fergusson, R. Menzies, *The Ochil Fairy Tales* (London, 1912)

—, *Rambling Sketches in the Far North* (London, Edinburgh, Glasgow, and Kirkwall, 1883)

Finaly, Ian, *The Lothians* (London, 1960)

[Fotheringham, W. H.], 'Orkney Charms', *NQ* 1st ser., vol. X, 220–21

Fraser, Antonia, *Mary Queen of Scots* (1969; repr. London, 1998)

Fraser, Gordon, *Wigtown and Whithorn: Historical and Descriptive Sketches, Stories and Anecdotes . . .* (Wigtown, 1877)

Fraser, James, *Chronicles of the Frasers 1666–99*, ed. William Mackay (Edinburgh, 1905)

Frazer, James George, *The Golden Bough*, abridged edn. (London, 1923) [1890]

Frazer, Rev. John, *A Brief Discourse concerning the Second Sight* (Edinburgh, 1707)

Gardner, Alexander, *Ballads of the Scottish Border* (Paisley, 1908)

Gavin, John, *The Dowry Brides of St Cyrus* (privately printed, c. 1997)

Gervase of Tilbury, *Otia Imperialia*, ed. Felix Liebrecht (Hanover, 1856)

[W.W. Gibbings, publisher], *Folk-Lore and Legends: Scotland* (London, 1889)

Gibbon, Lewis Grassic, *Sunset Song* (Edinburgh, 1995) [1932]

Gibson, William, *Reminiscences of Dollar and Tillicoultry and other Districts adjoining the Ochils*, 2nd edn (Edinburgh, 1883)

Gill, Walter, *A Second Manx Scrapbook* (London and Bristol, 1932)

Gomme, George Laurence, *Folk-Lore Relics of Early Village Life* (London, 1883)

Goodare, J. (ed.), *The Scottish Witch-Hunt in Context* (Manchester, 2002)

Goodare, J., L. Martin and J. Miller (eds.), *Witchcraft and Belief in Early Modern Scotland* (Basingstoke, 2008)

Gordon, Principal, 'Remarks made in a Journey to the Orkney Islands', *Archaeologia Scotica*, 3 vols. (Edinburgh, 1792–1831) vol. 1 (1792) 256–8

Gould, R. T., *The Case for the Sea-Serpent* (London, 1930)

—, 'The Loch Ness Monster: A Survey of the Evidence', *The Times* (9 December 1933)

[Graham, Dougal], *Ancient and Modern History of Buckhaven: The Collected Writings of Dougal Graham*, ed. George Macgregor, 2 vols. (Glasgow, 1883)

Graham, Patrick, *Sketches Descriptive of Picturesque Scenery on the Southern Confines of Perthshire* (Edinburgh, 1806)

Grant, Katherine Whyte, *Myth, Tradition and Story from Western Argyll* (Oban, 1925)

Grant Stewart, William, *The Popular Superstitions and Festive Amusements of the Highlanders of Scotland* (Edinburgh, 1823)

Gregor, Revd Walter, *Notes on the Folk-Lore of the North-East of Scotland* (London, 1881)

—, 'Guardian Spirits of Wells and Lochs', *Folk-Lore* 3 (1892) 67–73

Grimble, Ian, *The World of Rob Donn*, new rev. edn (Edinburgh, 1999)

Grinsell, Leslie, *Folklore of Prehistoric Sites in Britain* (Newton Abbot, London, North Pomfret, and Vancouver, 1976)

Grønneberg, Roy, *Shetland's Viking Heritage*, (Shetland Tourist Organisation, n.d.)

Grose, Francis, *The Antiquities of Scotland*, 2 vols. (London, 1789–91)

—, *Provincial Glossary*, 2 pts in 2 vols (London, 1787)

A Guide to the Island of Jersey (London, 1842)

Haining, Peter, *A Dictionary of Ghosts* (London, 1982; 2nd edn, Waltham Abbey, 1993)

Halifax, Lord, *see* Lindley, Charles

Hall, James, *Travels in Scotland* (London, 1807)

Hamilton, Judy, *Scottish Myths and Legends* (New Lanark, 2003; repr. 2006)

Hamilton, William, *The Ancient and Renown'd History of the Surprising Life and Adventures and Heroic Actions of Sir William Wallace* (Falkirk, 1785) [1721]

Hare, Augustus, *In My Solitary Life* (abridged last 3 vols. of Hare (1900)) (London, 1953)

—, *The Story of My Life*, 6 vols. (London, 1900)

Hartshorne, Emily Sophia, *Enshrined Hearts of Warriors and Illustrious People* (London, 1861)

Hatfield, Gabrielle, *Encyclopedia of Folk Medicine* (Santa Barbara, Cal., etc., 2004)

Henderson, Ebenezer, *The Annals of Dunfermline and Vicinity . . .* (Glasgow, 1879)

Henderson, George, 'The Popular Rhymes of Berwickshire', *History of the Berwickshire Naturalists' Club*, vol. 1 (Edinburgh, 1834) 145–52

—, *The Popular Rhymes, Sayings, and Proverbs of the County of Berwick* (Newcastle, 1856)

—, *Survivals in Belief among the Celts* (Glasgow, 1911)

Henderson, George, and Edward J. Cowan, *Scottish Fairy Belief: A History* (East Linton, 2001)

Henderson, Lizanne, 'Witch, Fairy and Folktale Narratives in the Trial of Bessie Dunlop', in *Fantastical Imaginations: The Supernatural in Scottish History and Culture* (Edinburgh, 2009)

—, 'The Survival of Witch Prosecutions and Witch Belief in South-West Scotland', *Scottish Historical Review*, vol. LXXXV, 1, no. 219 (April 2006) 52–74

Henderson, William, *Notes on the Folk Lore of the Northern Counties of England and the Borders* (London, 1866)

Hendrie, William Fyfe, *West Lothian Lore* (Perth, 1976)

Henshall, Audrey Shore, *The Chambered Tombs of Scotland*, 2 vols. (Edinburgh, 1963, 1972)

Herman, Arthur, *The Scottish Enlightenment* (London, 2006) [2001]

Hewett, Sarah, *Nummits and Crummits* (London, 1900; republ. Wakefield, 1976)

Hewison, James King, *Bute in the Olden Time*, 2 vols. (Edinburgh, 1893, 1895)

Hibbert, Samuel, *A Description of the Shetland Islands* (Edinburgh, 1822)

Historie of the Kennedyis, in *Historical and Genealogical Account of the Principal Families of the Name of Kennedy from an original MS*, ed. Robert Pitcairn (Edinburgh and London, 1830)

History of Lanark, and Guide to the Scenery, 3rd edn (Lanark, 1835)

Hobbs, Alexander, 'Downie's Slaughter', *Aberdeen University Review*, vol. xlv, 2, no. 150 (Autumn 1973) 183–191

Hobbs, Sandy, 'Errors, suicides and tourism', *Foaftale News*, 27 September 1992

Hobbs, Sandy, and David Cornwell, 'Hanging the Monkey', *Dear Mr Thoms . . .* 35 (1994) 17–20

—, 'Hunting the Monster with Iron Teeth', in *Monsters with Iron Teeth*, ed. G. Bennett and P. Smith (Sheffield, 1988) 115–37

—, 'Killer Clowns and Vampires', in *Supernatural Enemies*, ed. H. Ellis Davidson and A. Chaudhri (Durham, N.C., 2001) 203–17

—, 'Sawney Bean, the Scottish Cannibal', *Folklore* 108 (1997) 49–54

Hobsbawm, Eric, and Terence Ranger (eds.), *The Invention of Tradition* (Cambridge, 1983)

Hogg, James, *Winter Evening Tales*, 2 vols. (Edinburgh, 1820)

Holinshed, Raphael, *Scottish Chronicle; or, a Complete History and Description of Scotland*, 2 vols. (Arbroath, 1805) [1576]

Home, David Milne, *The Estuary of the Forth and adjoining Districts viewed Geologically* (Edinburgh, 1871)

House, Jack, *Down the Clyde* (Edinburgh and London, 1960)

[Howie, John], *Biographia Scoticana; or, a brief historical account of the lives, characters, and memorable transactions of the most eminent Scots Worthies*, 3rd edn (Edinburgh, 1796)

Howitt, William, *Visits to Remarkable Places* (London, 1840)

—, *Visits to Remarkable Places*, 2nd ser. (London, 1842)

Hughes, Mary Ann, *Letters and Recollections of Sir Walter Scott*, ed. H. G. Hutchinson (London, 1904)

Illustrations of the Topography and Antiquities of the Shires of Aberdeen and Banff, 5 vols. (Aberdeen, 1843–69)

Ingram, John Henry, *The Haunted Homes and Family Traditions of Great Britain*, 2 ser. (London, 1884)

Innes, Cosmo, *The Book of the Thanes of Cawdor 1236–1742*, Spalding Club (Edinburgh, 1859)

Irving, George, 'The Irvings of Hoddom', in *TDG* 1900–1905 (1906) 175–201

Irving, Washington, *Abbotsford and Newstead Abbey* (London, 1835)

Jack, John, *The Key of the Forth* (Edinburgh and Cupar, 1858)

Jackson, Kenneth, 'Four Local Anecdotes from Harris', *Scottish Studies* (Edinburgh) 3 (1959) 72–87

Jacobs, Joseph, *English Fairy Tales* (London, 1968) [1894]

Jakobsen, J, *The Place-Names of Shetland* (London and Copenhagen, 1936)

Jervise, Andrew, *The History and Traditions of the Land of the Lindsays in Angus and Mearns, with notices of Alyth and Meigle* (Edinburgh, 1853)

Johnson, James, *The Scots Musical Museum*, 6 vols. (Edinburgh and London, 1787–1803)

Johnston, James B., *Place-Names of Scotland*, 3rd edn (London, 1934; repr. 1970)

Johnstone, William, *The Bard and the Belted Knight* (Edinburgh, 1867)

'The Judgement and Justice of God Exemplified . . .', Appendix to Howie (1796)

'Just fancy that . . .', *Scottish Memories* (June 1993) 2

[Keats, John], *The Letters of John Keats*, ed. Hyder Edward Rollins, 2 vols. (Cambridge, Mass., 1958)

Keightley, Thomas, *The Fairy Mythology*, revised and enlarged edn (London, 1850)

Kightly, Charles, *Folk Heroes of Britain* (London, 1982; pa. edn, 1984)

Kinnear, George Henderson, *The History of Glenbervie, the Fatherland of Burns* (Edinburgh and Glasgow, 1910)

Kirk, Robert, *The Secret Common-Wealth*, ed. and commentary by Stewart Sanderson (Cambridge, 1976) [1691]

Kirkton, James, *The Secret and True History of the Church of Scotland* (Edinburgh, 1817)

Kunz, George Frederick, *The Magic of Jewels and Charms* (Philadelphia and London, 1915)

Laing, Alexander, *Notice of the Ancient Ecclesiastical History of Abernethy . . .* (Newburgh, 1861)

Lane, Alan, and Ewan Campbell, *Dunadd: An Early Dalriadic Capital* (Oxford, 2000)

Lang, Andrew, *Cock Lane and Common-Sense* (London and New York, 1894)

—, 'A Galloway Nursery Tale', *The Academy*, 17 October 1885, 257–8

—, 'Poltergeists', *Encyclopædia Britannica* (Cambridge, 1911), vol. 22, 14–17

—, *St Andrews* (London and New York, 1893)

Larner. C., *Enemies of God: The Witch-Hunt in Scotland* (London, 1981)

Law, Robert, *Memorialls . . . from 1638 to 1684*, ed. Charles Kirkpatrick Sharpe (Edinburgh, 1818)

Lees-Milne, James, *Ancestral Voices* (London, 1975)

Leishman, James Fleming, *Linton Leaves* (Edinburgh and London, 1937)

Leyden, John, *Journal of a Tour in the Highlands and Western Islands of Scotland in 1800*, ed. James Sinton (Edinburgh and London, 1903)

—, *Poems and Ballads* (Kelso, 1858)

—, *Scenes of Infancy: descriptive of Teviotdale* (Edinburgh, 1803)

[Leyden, John], *Scotish [sic] Descriptive Poems . . .* (Edinburgh, 1803)

Liestøl, Aslak, 'Runes', in *The Northern and Western Isles in the Viking World*, ed. Alexander Fenton and Hermann Pálsson (Edinburgh, 1984) 224–38

[Lindley, Charles, Viscount Halifax], *Lord Halifax's Ghost Book* (London, 1936)

Lindsay of Pitscottie, Robert, *The Chronicles of Scotland, 1436–1565* (Edinburgh, 1728)

'Loch Ness Monster: Drawings by Eye-Witnesses', *The Scotsman*, 15 November 1933

Lockhart, J. G., *Memoirs of the Life of Sir Walter Scott, Bart.*, 7 vols. (Edinburgh and London, 1837–8)

Low, Rev. George, *Fauna Orcadensis* (Edinburgh, 1813)

Lucas, Joseph, *The Yetholm History of the Gypsies* (Kelso, 1882)

Lyle, E. B., 'Thomas of Erceldoune: the Prophet and the Prophesied', *Folklore* 79 (1968) 111–121

MacArthur, John, *Antiquities of Arran* (Glasgow, 1861)

MacBain, A, *Place Names: Highlands and Islands of Scotland* (Stirling, 1922)

McConnochie, Alex, *Bennachie* (Aberdeen, 1890)

McCormick, Andrew, *The Tinkler-Gypsies* (Darby, Pa., 1973) [1907]

MacCulloch, Diarmaid, *Reformation*, pa. edn (London, 2004)

McCulloch, Gordon, 'Suicidal sculptors: Scottish versions of a migratory legend', in *Perspectives on Contemporary Legend*, vol. 2, ed. Gillian Bennett, Paul Smith and J. D. A. Widdowson (Sheffield, 1987) 109–16

MacCulloch, John, *A Description of the Western Islands of Scotland, including the Isle of Man*, 3 vols. (London, 1819)

Macdonald Robertson, R., *More Highland Folk-Tales* (Edinburgh and London, 1964)

—, *Selected Highland Folktales* (Argyll, 1998) [1961]

—, *Wade the River, Drift the Loch* (Edinburgh and London, 1948)

MacDougall, Rev. James, *Folk Tales and Fairy Lore in Gaelic and English* (Edinburgh, 1910)

McEwan, Graham J., *Sea Serpents, Sailors and Sceptics* (London, Henley, and Boston, 1978)

MacGregor, Alasdair Alpin, *The Peat-Fire Flame: Folk-tales and Traditions of the Highlands and Islands* (Edinburgh and London, 1937; repr. with corrections, 1947)

Mackay, Aeneas E. G., *A History of Fife and Kinross* (Edinburgh, 1896)

MacKay, Angus, *A Collection of Ancient Piobaireachd or Highland Pipe Music* (Edinburgh, 1838)

Mackay, Donald, *This was my Glen* (Thurso, 1965)

McKay, John G., *More West Highland Tales*, 2 vols. (Edinburgh and London, 1940, 1960)

Mackay, Robert, *History of the House of Mackay* (Edinburgh, 1829)

[Mackay, Robert], *Songs and Poems in the Gaelic Language, by Robert Mackay*, ed. Mackintosh Mackay (Inverness, Edinburgh, Glasgow, and London, 1829)

Mackenzie, Alexander, *The Prophecies of the Brahan Seer* (Inverness, 1877)

Mackenzie, W. M., *The Book of Arran: History and Folklore* (Glasgow, 1914)

MacKinlay, James, *Folklore of Scottish Lochs and Springs* (Glasgow, 1893; facs. repr.)

Maclagan, R. C., 'Sacred Fire', *Folk-Lore* 9 (1898) 280–1

McLaren, Moray, *Shell Guide to Scotland* (London, 1965)

MacLennan, Malcolm, *A Pronouncing and Etymological Dictionary of the Gaelic Language* (Aberdeen, 1979) [1925]

MacLeod, Dr Norman, and Rev. Dr Daniel Dewar, *A Dictionary of Gaelic Language in two parts* (Glasgow and London, 1831)

MacNab, P. A., *The Isle of Mull* (Newton Abbot, 1970)

McNeill, F. Marian, *The Scots Kitchen* (London and Glasgow, 1929; repr. 1937)

MacPhail, Malcolm, 'Folklore from the Hebrides', *Folk-Lore* 9 (1898) 84–93

Macpherson, George W, *Highland Myths and Legends* (Edinburgh, 2005) [2001]

MacQuarrie, Alan, *The Saints of Scotland: Essays in Scottish Church History AD 450–1039* (Edinburgh, 1997)

Macrae, Revd David, *Notes about Gourock* (Edinburgh, 1880)

MacRitchie, David, 'The Historical Aspect of Folk-Lore', *The International Folk-Lore Congress, 1891: Papers and Transactions*, ed. Joseph Jacobs and Alfred Nutt (London, 1892) 103–12.

MacTaggart, John, *The Scottish Gallovidian Encyclopedia* (London, 1824)

Manson, W. L., *The Highland Bagpipe, its History Literature and Music* (Paisley and London, 1901)

Martin, Martin, *A Description of the Western Islands of Scotland Circa 1695* (London, 1703)

Martin, W. G. W., *Pagan Ireland* (London, 1895)

Marwick, Ernest, *The Folklore of Orkney and Shetland* (London, 1975)

Mason, James, 'The Folk-Lore of British Plants', *Dublin University Magazine* 82 (1873) 313–28, 424–40, 554–70, 668–87

Matheson, William (ed.), *The Songs of John MacCodrum* (Edinburgh, 1938)

Matthews, John, and Bob Stewart, *Celtic Battle Heroes* (Poole, 1988)

Mavor, William, *Natural History for the Use of Schools* (London, 1800)

Maxwell Wood, James, *Smuggling in the Solway* (Dumfries, 1908)

—, *Witchcraft and Superstitious Record in the South-western District of Scotland* (East Ardsley, 1975) [1911]

Maybole: The Official Guide (Cheltenham and London, n.d. [c. 1964])

Metcalfe, W. M., *A History of Paisley 600–1908* (Paisley, 1909)

Miles, David, *The Tribes of Britain* (London, 2005; pa. edn, 2006)

Miller, D., 'The Castles of Caithness', in *The New Caithness Book*, ed. Donald Omand (Wick, 1989) 156–69

Miller, Frank, *The Poets of Dumfriesshire* (Glasgow, 1910)

Miller, Hugh, *My Schools and Schoolmasters* (Edinburgh, 1854)

—, *Scenes and Legends of the North of Scotland, or, The Traditional History of Cromarty* (London, 1835)

Miller, J., 'The Middle Ages', in *The New Caithness Book*, ed. Donald Omand (Wick, 1989) 78–90

Miller, Joyce, *Magic and Witchcraft in Scotland* (Musselburgh, 2004)

Miller, T. D., *Border Ballads and Balladists* (Galashiels, 1931)

Milliken, William, and Sam Bridgewater, *Flora Celtica* (Edinburgh, 2004) [2001]

Milne, Colin, *The Story of Gourock 1858–1958* (Gourock, 1958)

Milne, John, *Myths and Superstitions of the Buchan District*, 3rd edn (Aberdeenshire, 1987) [1891]

Miscellanea of the Rymour Club, 3 vols. (Edinburgh, 1912–19)

Monger, George, *Marriage Customs of the World* (Santa Barbara, Cal., etc., 2004)

Monteath, John, *Dunblane Traditions* (Stirling, 1835)

Montgomerie, Norah and William, *The Well at the World's End* (London, 1956)

Morris, Ruth and Frank, *Scottish Healing Wells* (Sandy, 1982)

[Morrison, Peter], *Scottish Tradition Cassette Series 5: Gaelic Stories told by Peter Morrison*, trans. D. A. MacDonald and A. J. Bruford (Edinburgh, 1978)

Mort, Frederick, *Renfrewshire*, Cambridge County Geographies (Cambridge, 1912)

Munro, Henrietta, *Legends of the Pentland Firth* (Thurso, 1977)

—, *More Legends of the Pentland Firth* (Thurso, 1979)

Murchison, Rev. T. M., 'Glenelg, Inverness-shire: Notes for a Parish History', *TGSI* 39–40 (1963) 294–333

'The Murder Hole. An Ancient Legend', *Blackwood's Edinburgh Magazine* 25 (February 1829) 189–92

Murray, A. H. James (ed.), *Thomas of Erceldoune*, Early English Text Society vol. LXI (London, 1875)

Murray, W. H., *The Companion Guide to the West Highlands of Scotland* (London, 1968; 7th edn, 1977; repr. 1985)

Myatt, L., 'Stone Rows and Stone Circles', in *The New Caithness Book*, ed. Donald Omand (Wick, 1989) 40–6

Napier, Mark, *Memorials and Letters illustrative of the Life and Times of John Graham of Claverhouse*, 3 vols. (Edinburgh, 1859–62)

The New Statistical Account of Scotland, 15 vols. (Edinburgh, 1845)

Newstead, Helaine, 'The Origin and Growth of the Tristan Legend', in *Arthurian Literature in the Middle Ages*, ed. Roger Sherman Loomis (Oxford, 1959) 122–33

Newton, Michael, *Savage Girls and Wild Boys* (London, 2002)

Nicholas, D., *The Young Adventurer* (London, 1949)

Nicholson, John, *Historical and Traditional Tales in prose and verse, connected with the South of Scotland* (Kirkcudbright, 1843)

Nicolson, James R., *Shetland Folklore* (London, 1981)

Nicolson, John, *Some Folk-Tales and Legends of Shetland* (Edinburgh, 1920)

Notman, Robert Black, *Restalrig Parish Church* (Edinburgh, 1976)

Oates, Caroline, 'Cheese Gives you Nightmares: Old Hags and Heartburn', *Folklore* 114 (2003) 205–25

Ogilvy, Mrs D., *Book of Highland Minstrelsy* (London, 1846)

Ó hógáin, Dáithi, *Fionn mac Cumhaill: Images of the Gaelic Hero* (Dublin, 1988)

—, *Myth, Legend and Romance: An Encyclopædia of the Irish Folk Tradition* (London, 1990)

Oldham, Tony, *The Caves of Scotland* (Bristol, 1975)

Omond, George W. T., *The Arniston Memoirs* (Edinburgh, 1887)

Opie, Iona and Peter, *The Oxford Dictionary of Nursery Rhymes* (Oxford, 1951)

Orkneyinga Saga, trans. Herman Pálsson and Paul Edwards (London, 1978; pa. edn 1981; repr. 1987)

Oxford Dictionary of National Biography, 60 vols. (Oxford, 2004)

Parsons, C. O., 'The Dalrymple Legend in The Bride of Lammermoor', *Review of English Studies* XIX (1943) 51–8

Parsons, Coleman O., *Witchcraft and Demonology in Scott's Fiction* (Edinburgh and London, 1964)

Paterson, James *History of the Counties of Ayr and Wigton*, 3 vols. (Edinburgh, 1863–6)

Pennant, Thomas, *A Tour in Scotland, 1769*, 2nd edn (London, 1772)

—, *A Tour in Scotland, and Voyage to the Hebrides, 1772*, 2nd edn (London, 1776)

Philip, Adam, *Songs and Sayings of Gowrie* (Edinburgh and London, 1901)

Philip, Neil, *The Penguin Book of Scottish Folktales* (London, 1995)

Polson, A., *Scottish Witchcraft Lore* (Inverness, 1932)

Polson, Alexander, 'Folklore', in *The County of Caithness*, ed. John Horne (Wick, 1907) 89–114

Porteous, A., *Forest Folklore, Mythology and Romance* (London, 1928)

Pratt, Rev. John Burnett, *Buchan*, 3rd edn (Aberdeen, 1870) [1858]

Ramage, Craufurd Tait, *Drumlanrig Castle and the Douglases* (Dumfries and London, 1876)

Ramsay, Allan, *The Ever Green*, 2 vols. (Edinburgh, 1724)

—, *Poems*, 2 vols. (Edinburgh, 1721, 1728)

—, *The Tea-Table Miscellany: or, a collection of choice songs, Scots and English*, 10th edn, 4 vols. printed as one (London, 1740)

Rankin, Ian, *Rebus's Scotland* (London, 2005)

Reader's Digest Field Guide to the Wild Flowers of Britain (London, etc., 1981)

Red Guide: The Complete Scotland, ed. Reginald J. W. Hammond, 11th edn (London, 1975)

Redworth, Glyn, *The Prince and the Infanta* (New Haven and London, 2003)

Reed, James, *The Border Ballads* (London, 1973)

Reid, Stuart, *Culloden 1746* (Barnsley, 2005)

[Renfrew], *A History of The Witches of Renfrewshire* (Paisley, 1809)

Rhys, Sir John, *Celtic Folk-Lore*, 2 vols. (1901; pa.edn, London, 1980)

Richards, Frederick B., *The Black Watch at Ticonderoga* (Glen Falls, NY, 1912)

Richardson, M. A., *The Local Historian's Table Book*, 5 vols. (London, 1841–6)

Rigg, James, *Wild Flower Lyrics and other Poems* (London, 1897)

Ritchie, Graham, and Mary Harman, *Exploring Scotland's Heritage: Argyll and the Western Isles* (Edinburgh, 1985)

Ritson's English Songs 3 vols. (London, 1783)

Rixson, Denis, *The Small Isles: Canna, Rum, Eigg and Muck* (Edinburgh, 2001)

Robertson, George, *General View of the Agriculture of Kincardineshire* (London, 1813)

Robertson, T. A., and John J. Graham (eds.), *Shetland Folk Book*, vol. 3 (Lerwick, 1957)

Robertson, William, *Ayrshire: Its History and Historic Families*, 2 vols. (Kilmarnock and Ayr, 1908)

—, *Historical Tales and Legends of Ayrshire* (London and Glasgow, 1889)

Robin Good-Fellow, His Mad Prankes, and merry jests (London, 1628)

Robinson, Mairi, *The Concise Scots Dictionary* (Aberdeen, 1985)

Ross, Anne, *Folklore of the Scottish Highlands*, rev. edn (Stroud and Charleston, 2000)

—, *Pagan Celtic Britain*, rev. edn (London, 1992; pa edn, 1993)

Royal Commission on the Ancient and Historical Monuments of Scotland, 7 vols. (Edinburgh and Glasgow, 1971–92)

Rye, Walter, *Recreations of a Norfolk Antiquary* (Holt and Norwich, 1920)

Sandford, Edmund, *A Cursory Relation of all the Antiquities & Familyes in Cumberland . . . circa 1675*, ed. Chancellor Ferguson, Cumberland and Westmorland Antiquarian and Archaeological Society Tract Series 1–6, 1882–92 (Tract no. 4, Kendal, 1890)

Saxby, Jessie M. E., *Shetland Traditional Lore* (Edinburgh, 1932)

Scot, Reginald, *Discoverie of Witchcraft* (London, 1665)

Scott, Sir Walter, 'Appendix to the General Preface', *Waverley* (Edinburgh, 1829)

—, *The Border Antiquities of England and Scotland*, 2 vols. (London, 1814–17)

—, *The Bride of Lammermoor*, in *Tales of My Landlord*, 3rd series, 4 vols. (Edinburgh, 1819), vols. 1–3

—, *The History of Scotland* (Paris, 1838)

—, *Letters on Demonology and Witchcraft* (London, 2001) [1830]

—, *Minstrelsy of the Scottish Border*, ed. T. F. Henderson, 4 vols. (Edinburgh and London, 1902) [1802–3]

—, *Old Mortality*, ed. Jane Stevenson and Peter Davidson (Oxford, 1993) [1816]

—, *Peveril of the Peak* (London, 1910) [1822]

—, *The Pirate* (London, 1877) [1821]

[—], *The Poetical Works of Sir Walter Scott*, Oxford Complete Edition, ed. J. Logie Robertson (London, etc., 1904)

—, *Redgauntlet* (London, 1877) [1824]

—, *Tales of a Grandfather*, First Series, 3 vols., 5th edn (Edinburgh, 1828)

—, *The Talisman* (London and New York, 1904) [1825]

The Scots Magazine (Edinburgh)

The Scottish Journal of Topography, Antiquities, Traditions, etc., 2 vols. printed as one (Edinburgh and London, 1848)

Screeton, Paul, *Who Hung the Monkey?* (Hartlepool, 1991)

Scrope, William, *The Art of Deer Stalking* (London, 1839)

Seeger, Peggy, and Ewan MacColl, *The Singing Island* (London, 1960)

Selby, J., *Over the Sea to Skye* (London, 1973)

Shakespeare, William, *Macbeth*, ed. Kenneth Muir (London, 1951; pa. edn, 1964; repr. 1989) [1606]

Sharpe, Charles Kirkpatrick, *A Historical Account of the Belief in Witchcraft in Scotland* (London and Glasgow, 1884)

Shaw, Lachlan, *The History of the Province of Moray*, enl. edn by J. F. S. Gordon, 3 vols. (Glasgow and London, 1882)

Shepherd, Ian A. G., *Exploring Scotland's Heritage: Grampian* (Edinburgh, 1986)

—, *Shetland Folk Book* 3 (Lerwick, 1957)

'A Shetland Saga', *The Scotsman*, 13 November 1895, 8, col. g–h

Shippey, Tom, 'Act like Men, Britons!', *London Review of Books*, (vol. 30, no. 15, 31 July 2008) 17–18

Sibbald, Sir Robert, *The History, Ancient and Modern, of the Sheriffdoms of Fife and Kinross*, new edn with notes (Cupar, 1803)

—, *Scotia Illustrata sive Prodromus Historiae Naturalis* (Edinburgh, 1684)

Simpkins, John Ewart, *County Folk-Lore 7: Fife* (London, 1914)

Simpson, Eve Blantyre, *Folk Lore in Lowland Scotland* (London, 1908)

—, *Sir James Y Simpson* (Edinburgh and London, 1896)

Simpson, Jacqueline, *British Dragons* (London, 1980)

Simpson, Robert, *History of Sanquhar*, new edn (Glasgow, 1865)

Sinclair, Charles, *A Wee Guide to Macbeth and Early Scotland* (Musselburgh, 1999)

Sinclair, George, *Satans Invisible World Discovered* (Edinburgh, 1685)

Skene, William F., *Celtic Scotland*, 3 vols. (Edinburgh, 1876–89)

Small, Revd Andrew, *Interesting Roman Antiquities Recently Discovered in Fife . . .* (Edinburgh, 1823)

Smith, A., *A New History of Aberdeenshire*, 2 pts (Aberdeen, Edinburgh, and London, 1875)

Smith, William, 'Mansie o' Kierfa and his Fairy Wife', *Old-Lore Miscellany of Orkney, Shetland, Caithness and Sutherland* 6 (1913) 19–21

Southey, Robert, *Minor Poems*, 3 vols. (London, 1815)

Speaight, George (ed.), *The New Shell Guide to Britain* (London, 1985)

Speirs, John, *Medieval English Poetry* (London, 1957; 2nd imp. 1958)

Spence, John, *Shetland Folk-Lore* (Lerwick, 1899)

Spence, Lewis, *British Fairy Origins* (London, 1946)

—, *Legendary London* (London, 1937)

—, *Minor Traditions of British Mythology* (London, 1948)

Stace, Clive, *New Flora of the British Isles*, 2nd edn (Cambridge, 1997)

Statistical Account of Scotland 1791–1799, ed. Sir John Sinclair, 21 vols. (Wakefield, 1979) [1791–9]

Stell, Geoffrey, *Exploring Scotland's Heritage: Dumfries and Galloway* (Edinburgh, 1986)

Stenlake, Richard, *Bygone Lanark* (Glasgow, 1990)

Stevenson, J. B., *Exploring Scotland's Heritage: The Clyde Estuary and Central Region* (Edinburgh, 1985)

Stevenson, Robert Louis, *Ballads* (London, 1890)

—, *Edinburgh: Picturesque Notes* (London, 1879)

—, *Ticonderoga* (Edinburgh, 1887)

Stewart, Alexander (Bessie Bittem), *Reminiscences of Dunfermline and Neighbourhood . . .* (Edinburgh, 1886)

Stewart, John, and Peter Moar, 'When the Trows Danced', in Tait (1951) 17–25

'Streamline', *Foretold: Stories of Modern Second-Sight* (Stirling, 1934)

Sutherland, Rev. George, *Folk-Lore Gleanings and Character Sketches from the Far North* (Wick, 1937)

Swire, Otta F., *The Highlands and their Legends* (Edinburgh and London, 1963)

—, *The Inner Hebrides and their Legends* (London and Glasgow, 1964)

—, *Skye: The Island and its Legends*, 2nd edn (Glasgow and London, 1961)

Tait, E. S. Reid (ed.), *Shetland Folk Book*, vol. 2 (Lerwick, 1951)

Tales of the Elders of Ireland (Acallam na Senórach) trans. Ann Dooley and Harry Roe (Oxford, 1999)

Taylor, Revd J. W., *Historical Antiquities of Fife . . .* 2nd edn (Cupar, 1868)

Temperley, Alan, *Tales of Galloway* (Edinburgh, 1979; pa. edn, 1986)

'Theophilus Insulanus' (Donald MacLeod), *A Treatise on the Second Sight, Dreams and Apparitions* (Edinburgh, 1763)

Thiselton Dyer, T. F., *Church-Lore Gleanings* (London, 1892)

—, *The Folklore of Plants*, facs. repr. (Llanerch, 1994) [1889]

—, *Strange Pages from Family Papers* (London, 1895)

Thomas, F. W. L., 'Ballad o' de Lathie Odivere', *PSAS* 1 (1851) 86–9

—, 'Dunadd, Glassary, Argyllshire: The Place of Inauguration of the Dalriadic Kings', *PSAS* 13 (1879) 28–47

Thompson, Francis, *The Supernatural Highlands* (London, 1976)

Thomson, David, *The People of the Sea* (London, 1980) [1954]

Thorpe, Benjamin, *Northern Mythology* (Ware, 2001) [1851]

Tocher: Tales, Song, Tradition, Selected from the Archives of the School of Scottish Studies (Edinburgh, 1971–)

Todd, R. Larry, *Mendelssohn: A Life in Music* (Oxford, 2003)

Towill, Edwin Sprott, *The Saints of Scotland* (Edinburgh, 1983) [1978]

Traill Dennison, W., 'Orkney Folk-Lore', *The Scottish Antiquary* 7 (1893) 171–7

Trotter, Robert de Bruce, *Galloway Gossip, or the Southern Albanach 80 Years Ago* (Dumfries, 1901)

Trubshaw, Bob (ed.), *Explore Phantom Black Dogs* (Loughborough, 2005)

Turnbull, J., 'On Edin's Hall', *History of Berwickshire Naturalists' (Field) Club* 9 (1882) 81–99

Turnbull, Michael, *Edinburgh and Lothians Holy Corners* (Edinburgh, 1996)

Underwood, Peter, *A Gazetteer of Scottish Ghosts*, 5th edn (Glasgow, 1982) [first pub. 1973 as *A Gazetteer of Scottish and Irish Ghosts*]

Vedder, David, *Poems, Legendary, Lyrical, and Descriptive* (Edinburgh, Glasgow, and London, 1842)

Vickery, Roy, *A Dictionary of Plant Lore* (Oxford, 1995)

Waddell, Rev. P. Hately, *An Old Kirk Chronicle: being a history of Auldhame, Tyninghame, and Whitekirk in East Lothian from Session Records, 1615–1850* (Edinburgh and London, 1893)

Wade, James A., *History of St Mary's Abbey, Melrose* (Edinburgh and London, 1861)

Walcott, Mackenzie E. C., *A Guide to the Mountains, Lakes and North-West Coasts of England* (London, 1860)

Waldron, George, *A Description of the Isle of Man* (Douglas, 1864)

Walker, Bruce, and Graham Ritchie, *Exploring Scotland's Heritage: Fife and Tayside* (Edinburgh, 1987)

Wallner, Suzanne, *The Myth of William Wallace* (Stuttgart, 2003)

Walsh, William, *Curiosities of Popular Customs* (London, 1898)

Warrack, Alexander, *Scots Dictionary* (London and Edinburgh, 1965) [1911]

Watson, William J., *The Celtic Place-Names of Scotland* (Edinburgh and London, 1926)

Watt, Archibald, *Highways and Byways Round Kincardine* (Aberdeen, 1985)

Watt, Francis, and Andrew Carter, *Picturesque Scotland* (London, 1887)

Watt, James Crabb, *The Mearns of Old: A history of Kincardine from the earliest times to the seventeenth century* (Edinburgh and Glasgow, 1914)

Weir, Tom, *Scottish Islands* (Newton Abbot, 1976)

Wentz, W. Y. Evans, *The Fairy Faith in Celtic Countries* (Oxford, 1911)

Westwood, Jennifer, *Albion* (London, 1985)

—, 'Friend or Foe? Norfolk Traditions of Shuck', in *Supernatural Enemies*, ed. H. Ellis Davidson and A. Chaudhri (Durham, N. C., 2001) 101–16

Westwood, Jennifer, and Jacqueline Simpson, *The Lore of the Land* (London, 2005)

White, T. H., *The Book of Beasts* (London, 1954)

Whyte, Betsy, *The Yellow on the Broom* (1979; repr. London, 1986)

Whyte, Donald, *Scottish Gypsies and Other Travellers: A Short History* (Blackwell, 2001)

Wilkie, James, *Bygone Fife* (Edinburgh and London, 1931)

—, *The History of Fife* (Edinburgh and London, 1924)

Wilkie, Thomas, 'Old Rites and Ceremonies, and Customs of the Inhabitants of the Southern Counties of Scotland' [nineteenth-century manuscript, cited in Henderson (1866)]

Williamson, Duncan, *Fireside Tales of the Traveller Children* (Edinburgh, 1986) [1983]

—, *The Broonie, Silkies & Fairies* (Edinburgh, 1985)

Wilson, Alan J., Des Brogan and Frances Hollinrake, *Hidden and Haunted: Underground Edinburgh* (Edinburgh, 1999)

Wilson, Roger J. A., *A Guide to the Roman Remains in Britain* (London, 1975)

Wilson, William, *Folk Lore and Genealogies of Uppermost Nithsdale* (Dumfries and Sanquhar, 1904)

Wodrow, Robert, *Analecta, or Materials for a History of Remarkable Providences*, 4 vols. (Edinburgh, 1842–3) [1701–31]

—, *The History of the Sufferings of the Church of Scotland*, 2 vols. (Edinburgh, 1721–2)

Wood-Martin, W. G., *Pagan Ireland* (London and New York, 1895)

Wordsworth, Dorothy, *Recollections of a Tour Made in Scotland A.D. 1803* (Edinburgh, 1874)

Wright, Gordon, Ian Adams and Michael Scott, *A Guide to Holyrood Park and Arthur's Seat* (Edinburgh, 1987)

Yeoman, Peter, *Pilgrimage in Medieval Scotland* (London, 1999)

REFERENCES

ARGYLLSHIRE & ISLANDS

Achinduin, Lismore Campbell (1885) 335–6. NM 8139 **Appin Hill, Argyllshire** Campbell (1900) 216; Grant (1925) 1–3. NM 9449 **Arran** Bradley (1865) 126–30; Campbell (1900) 246–7. NR 9637 **Auchindarroch, Argyllshire** Campbell (1900) 162; MacDougall (1910) 266–9; MacGregor (1947) 65. NN 0055 **Beinn Iadain, Morvern, Argyllshire** Campbell (1900) 81–3; MacLeod and Dewar (1831) 94, sub *bru-chorcan/bruth-chorcan*. NM 6955 **Benderloch, Argyllshire** Campbell (1900) 291, 303; Westwood (1985) 86; Westwood and Simpson (2005) 205, 207, 560–1. NM 9038 **Bridge of Awe, Argyllshire** Campbell (1900) 88–9. NN 0330 **Caisteal a Choin Duibh, Craignish, Argyllshire** Campbell and Sandeman (1964) site 164 (as *Caisteal nan Coin Duibh*); Ó hógáin (1990) 200; Swire (1963), 4. Fort: NM 8008 Standing stone and supporting stones: NM 8008 *Fingal* Campbell (1872) *passim*; Campbell (1889–95) vol. 2, 32–67; Campbell (1891) *passim*; Ó hógáin (1988) *passim*; Spence (1948) 72–82. **Carskiey, Kintyre, Argyllshire** Campbell (1885) 376–7; *A Guide to . . . Jersey* (1842) 28–34. NR 6508 **Castle Stalker, Argyllshire** Campbell (1900), 292–5; Campbell (1994) vol. 1, 448–50; Drever (1944), 113–20. NM 9247 **Clachan, Lismore** Campbell (1885) 321–2, 325–7; Ritchie and Harman (1985) 112; Rixson (2001) 183. NM 8643 **Clach-tholl, Port Appin, Argyllshire** Grant (1925) 1. NM 9146 **Coeffin Castle, Lismore** Campbell (1885) 329–33. NM 8544 **Creagan, Loch Creran, Argyllshire** McKay (1940, 1960) vol. 1, 488–9; *TGSI* vol. 20 (1897) 58; Trotter (1901) 231–3. NM 9744 **Deil's Cauldron, Bute** Hewison (1893, 1895) vol. 1, 20–3. NN 7723 **Dun Ghallain, Argyllshire** *Exploring Sunart . . .* (n.d.) 12; Hamilton (2006) 54; Macpherson (2005) 123–6; Swire (1963) 112. Dun Ghallain: NM 6560 Fas-

nacloich: NN 0247 **Dunadd, Argyllshire** Bord, *Footprints* (2004) 33; Campbell and Sandeman (1964) sites 261 and 623 (rock basin); Crowl (1986) 469–70; Lane and Campbell (2000) *passim*, esp. 26–7; Ritchie and Harman (1985) 13, 91, 126–7; *Royal Commission on the Ancient and Historical Monuments of Scotland*, vol. 6, 149–59; Skene (1876–89) vol. 1, 229–30; Thomas (1879) *passim*, esp. 31, n. 1; 36, n. 4; 37. NR 8494 **Dunollie Castle, Lorn, Argyllshire** Campbell (1900) 166; MacGregor (1947) 59–60, 62; Miles (2006) 132, 168–9, 180, 186; Ritchie and Harman (1985) 13, 65, 72, 77. NM 8531 **Dunstaffnage Castle, Kilmore and Kilbride, Argyllshire** Campbell (1900) 164–5; Campbell (1885) 90–1, 97; Grose (1789–91) vol. 2, 294; Ritchie and Harman (1985), 78–80. NM 8834 **Garbh Shlios, Argyllshire** Campbell (1900) 155–6; Grant (1925) 2–3. NM 7542 **Giants' Graves, Arran** Boece (1938–41) vol. 1, 300; Henshall (1963, 1972) vol. 2, 384–5, 394; Martin (1703) 217. NR 0425 **Glenstockdale House, Argyllshire** Grant (1925) 29. NM 9549 **Gortan, Lorn, Argyllshire** Campbell (1900) 26–7, 154; Davidson (1949) 50, 70–3. NR 7122 **Inveraray Castle, Argyllshire** [Lindley] (1936) 3–8. NN 0909 **Inverawe House, Loch Etive, Argyllshire** Campbell (1885) 136–43; Richards (1912) 23–4, 30–8; Stevenson (1887) 8–27; *thebeat.iloveny.com*. NN 0332 **The Maiden of Inverawe** Campbell (1900) 155–86; MacLennan (1979) 182; Thompson (1976) 146–7. **Inveresragan, Argyllshire** Campbell (1900) 72; Lees-Milne (1975) 246. NM 9835 Connel Ferry Station: NM 9234 **Kiel, Morvern, Argyllshire** Campbell (1900) 242; *The New Statistical Account of Scotland* (1845) vol. 7, Argyleshire, 498–9. NM 9039 **Kilchrenan, Loch Awe, Argyllshire** Campbell (1900) 84, 153. NM 9610 **Kilchurn Castle, Breadalbane, Argyllshire** Campbell (1885) 101–2, 104–5; Ritchie and Harman (1985) 72; Westwood (1985) 14–16, 220–3, 234–5, 312–13; Wordsworth (1874) 138–9, and

William Wordsworth, 'Address to Kilchurn Castle', 285–6. NN 1328 **Kildalloig, Kintyre, Argyllshire** Campbell (1885) 220; *Royal Commission on the Ancient and Historical Monuments of Scotland*, vol. 1, 71, 87–8. Kildalloig Dun: NR 6519 Kildalloig Fort: NR 7519 **Kilmaronag, Lorn, Argyllshire** Campbell (1885) 259–60. NM 9334 **Kilmichael Glassary, Argyllshire** Campbell and Sandeman (1964) sites 43, 75, 117, 174, 179, 190, 257, 388; Grinsell (1976) 224; Ó hógáin (1990) 296–7. Scodaig cup-marked stone: NR 7897 **Kilmore, near Oban, Argyllshire** Campbell (1900) 295. NM 8824 **Kilneuair, Kilmichael Glassary, Argyllshire** Bord, *Footprints* (2004) 193, citing information received from Andreas Trottmann; Chambers (1870) 64–6; Jacobs (1968) 86. NM 8904 **Kingarth, Bute** Hewison (1893, 1895) vol. 1, 266–8. NS 0956 **King's Cave, Blackwaterfoot, Arran** Balfour (1910) 213–18, citing James Robertson's *Tour of Scotland* (1768); Mackenzie (1914) 31; Pennant (1776) vol. 1, 206–7; Weir (1976) 9. NR 8831 **Kintraw, Argyllshire** Campbell (1889–5) vol. 1 (1889), 71–2. Kintraw: NM 8305 Gorlach: NM 8406 **Knap, Argyllshire** Campbell (1900) 172–3. NM 9248 **Largiebaan, Mull of Kintyre, Argyllshire** Campbell (1885) 221. NR 6114 **Loch Awe, Argyllshire** Bord (1995) 88, 102–3; Campbell (1900) 218; Grant (1925) 7–8, 9; MacCulloch (1819) vol. 2, 184–5. NM 9610 **Loch Baile a' Ghobhainn, Lismore** Campbell (1902) 33; Hewison (1893, 1895) vol. 1, 268. NM 8542 **Machrie Moor Stone Circle, Arran** Campbell (1900) 30–1; Martin (1703) 220. NR 9132 **Mingary, Argyllshire** Dinsdale (1976) 179–80; McEwan (1978) 61–2. NM 5063 **Mingary Castle, Argyllshire** Campbell (1900) 52–7; Ritchie and Harman (1985) 84. NM 5063 **Point House Cairn, Bute** Hewison (1893, 1895) vol. 1, 154–66. NS 0867 **Rockhill, Loch Aweside, Argyllshire** Campbell (1885) 166–9. Rockhill Farm: NN 0721 **Saddell Castle, Kintyre, Argyllshire** Bord, *Footprints* (2004) 120; Chambers (1870) 64–6; Jacobs (1968) 86; MacGregor (1947) 185–6. NR 7932 **Southend, Keil Point, Kintyre, Argyllshire** Bord, *Footprints* (2004) 65; Crowl (1986) 60–1; MacKinlay (1893) 80. NR 6908 *Scotland's Holy and Healing Wells* Bord (2006) *passim*; Bord (2008) 169–86; Ross (2000) 92–3. **Strachur, Argyllshire** Campbell (1885) 32–3; Ritchie and Harman (1985) 61. NN 1001 **Strontian, Argyllshire** Campbell (1900) 177, 179. NM 8161 **Torrylin (Torlin) Cairn, Arran** Balfour (1910) 142–3; MacArthur (1861) 22–3. NR 9621 **Toward Castle, Inverchaolin, Bute** MacGregor (1947) 243–6. NS 1268

Ugadale, Kintyre, Argyllshire Campbell (1885) 374–5; Darton (1990) 225; Watson (1926) 157–8. NR 7828 Port Righ: NR 8237

CENTRAL AND PERTHSHIRE

Aberfoyle, Perthshire NN 5201 **Aldie, Kinross-shire** Beveridge (1888) 302–3; Simpkins (1914) 113. NT 0699 **Balcarres, Fife** Wilkie (1931) 190–2. Balcarres House: NO 4704 **Balcomie Castle, Fife** *Robin Good-Fellow* (1628) 'F2'; Simpkins (1914) 41; Wilkie (1931) 315–16. NO 6209 **Balwearie Castle, Fife** Beveridge (1888) 238; Simpkins (1914) 56, 223–5. NT 2590 **Beinn a' Ghlò, Blair Atholl, Perthshire** Campbell (1900) 94, 125–6. NN 9673 **Bessie Bell's and Mary Gray's Grave, near Perth** Black's (1844) 324–5. NO 0329 **Boghall Farm, near Dollar, Clackmannanshire** *Scottish Journal* (1848) vol. 2, 275. Boghall: NS 9797 **Borestone, Stirlingshire** Chambers (1827) vol. 2, 40–3; *The New Statistical Account of Scotland* (1845) vol. 8, Stirlingshire, 316. NS 7991 Bannock Burn: NS 7791 Sauchieburn House: NS 7889 **Buckhaven, Fife** Black's (1845) 362; Simpkins (1914) 212, 260; Taylor (1868) vol. 2, 155–7; Wilkie (1931) 142–3. NT 3598 **Cardenden, Fife** Rankin (2005) 8; Simpkins (1914) 260–1. NT 2293 **Castle Law, near Abernethy, Perthshire** Laing (1861) 20; *The New Statistical Account of Scotland* (1845) vol. 9, Kinross, 60; Small (1823) 142–3; Walker and Ritchie (1987), 129. Castle Law hill-fort: NO 1815 Cairnavain (remains of): NO 0608 **Clochfoldich Farm, near Pitlochry, Perthshire** Briggs (1953) 127; Briggs (1967) 29; Briggs (1978), 184; Chambers (1826) 264. NN 8953 **Colzium House, Stirlingshire** Chambers (1864) vol. 1, 106. NS 7278 *Michael Scot, the Wizard of Balwearie* Camden (1610) *England*, 773; Campbell (1889–95) vol. 1, 47–53; Campbell (1900) 285, 288, 295–7; Dante (1972) Canto XX; [Denham] (1892–5) vol. 2, 118–19; Sandford (1890) 31; Scott, *Poetical Works* (1904) 66–7; Westwood and Simpson (2005) 367, 385–6, 413. **Craighall, Perthshire** *Gentleman's Magazine* (January 1731) 31–2. NO 0817 **Craiginnan, Clackmannanshire** *Scottish Journal* (1848) vol. 2, 276. NN 9600 Saddle Hill: NN 9601 **Crail, Fife** Mackay (1896) 100; Simpkins (1914) 6, 46. NO 6107 **Culross Abbey, Fife** Hall (1807) 49; Simpkins (1914) 6, 10, 47–8; Sinclair (1685) 212–13; Wilkie (1931) 24–5. NS 9886 **Dalnacardoch, Perthshire** Campbell (1900) 71–2.

Dalnacardoch Forest: NN 6775 **Denny, Stirling-shire** Buchan (1984) 88, 234. NS 8082 **Devil's Mill, Clackmannanshire** Beveridge (1888) 298–300; Chambers (1827) vol. 2, 337; Cheviot (1896) 197. NT 0299 Rumbling Bridge: NT 0199 **Dollar, Clackmannanshire** Black's (1844) 178–9; *Scottish Journal* (1848) vol. 2, 62–3. NS 9698 **Dreel Castle, Anstruther Easter, Fife** Chambers (1827) vol. 2, 204–6. NO 5704 **Dumbarton, Dunbartonshire** Davidson (1949) 218–19, citing J. Mitchell and J. Dickie, *The Philosophy of Witchcraft* (Paisley, 1839). NS 4175 **Dumyat, Clackmannanshire** Chambers (1827) vol. 2, 333. NS 8499 **Dunblane, Perthshire** Monteath (1835) 85–6. NN 7801 **Dunfermline, Fife** Chambers (1827) vol. 2, 180; Henderson (1879) 252–3; Home (1871) 49; Mackay (1896) 110; Stewart (1886) 143–4. NT 0887 **Dunfermline Abbey, Fife** Chambers (1827) vol. 2, 175–9. NT 0987 **Dunsinane, Perthshire** NO 2131 **Easter Wemyss, Fife** Black's (1845) 361–2; Wilkie (1931) 133. Court Cave: NT 3497 **Errol, Perthshire** Allan (1822) 335–8; Camden (1610) *Scotland*, 42; Holinshed (1805) vol. 1 306–8; Philip (1901) 67–83; Porteous (1928) 93; Pratt (1870) 56–8, 372–80. NO 2522 **Falkland, Fife** Chambers (1827) vol. 2, 186–91; Crowl (1986) 116–17. NO 2507 **Finlarig, Perthshire** Campbell (1885) 351, 354–5; Westwood (1985) 183–4. NN 5734 **Fossoway, Kinross-shire** Beveridge (1888) 305–6. Easter Fossoway: NO 0403 Middleton Fossoway: NO 0202 **Friarton Island, Perthshire** Chambers (1827) vol. 2, 355. NO 1221 **Glen Errochty, Atholl, Perthshire** Campbell (1900) 94–5. 'Sithean': NN 9065 **Glen Fincastle, Perthshire** Aubrey (1721) 212; Briggs (1970–1) B1, 207–8, 308; Scott (1902) vol. 1, 152. NN 8661 ***Brownies*** Bruford and MacDonald (1994) 377–82, 479; Campbell (1900) 184–94; Keightley (1850) 358–96; Westwood and Simpson (2005) 828–9. **Glendevon, Clackmannanshire** Keightley (1850) 358. NN 9904 **Hillfoot Farm, Dollar, Clackmannanshire** *Scottish Journal* (1848) vol. 1, 364. NS 9799 **Killernie Castle, Saline, Fife** Beveridge (1888) 238; Child (1904) no. 93, 196–9; Simpkins (1914) 231, 269–70; *Statistical Account of Scotland 1791–1799* (1979) vol. 10, 757; Wilkie (1931) 89–90. NT 0392 **Killin, Perthshire** Briggs (1970–1) B1, 236, 238, 272–4; Campbell (1900) 15–16, 147; Westwood and Simpson (2005), 102, 405, 565, 653. NN 5732 **Kinghorn, Fife** Farnie (*c.* 1860) 41; Jack (1858) 114–26; Mackay (1896) 33–4; Simpkins (1914) 120–1, 265. NT 2787 **Kinneston, Kinross-shire** Beath (1902) 41. NO 1901 **Kirkcaldy, Fife** Chambers (1827) vol. 2, 220–1; Mackay (1896)

272–3; Simpkins (1914) 3, 265–6. NT 2791 **Lag Uaine, Dunbartonshire** MacGregor (1947) 15–16. NN 2609 **Leven, Fife** Chambers (1827) vol. 2, 214–16. NO 3800 **Lingo House, Pittenweem, Fife** Herman (2006) 45; Wilkie (1931) 202. NO 5008 **Loch an Daimh, Perthshire** Cunningham (1989) 137–9. NN 4746 **Loch Con, Lower Rannoch, Perthshire** Campbell (1900) 295–6. NN 6867 **Loch Ericht, Perthshire** Cunningham (1989) 76. NN 5573 **Loch Katrine, Perthshire** Barbour (1886), 184–7. NN 4409 **Loch Leven, Kinross-shire** Beveridge (1888) 72; Black (1883) 161; Cheviot (1896) 240; Johnston (1970) 238; *Statistical Account of Scotland 1791–1799* (1979) vol. 18, 670. NO 4010 **Loch Sloy, Dunbartonshire** Campbell (1900) 195–9; Keightley (1850) 396, citing W. S. Rose in *Quarterly Review* (1825); Westwood and Simpson (2005) 828–9. NN 2812 **Loch Venachar, Perthshire** Graham (1806) 103–5; Leyden (1903) 13–14. NN 5605 **Lundin Links Standing Stones, Fife** Black's (1844) 363; Chambers (1827) vol. 2, 213–14; *The New Statistical Account of Scotland* (1845) vol. 9, Fife, 438–9; Walker and Ritchie (1987) 177–8. NO 4003 Orwell standing stones: NO 1504 **Magus Muir, Fife** Chambers (1827) vol. 2, 198–200; Crowl (1986) 244–5. NO 4515 **Maiden Castle, near Dollar, Perthshire** Bord, *Fairy Sites* (2004) 209; Rhys (1980), vol. 1, 157–8. NN 9702 **Meigle, Perthshire** Boece (1938–41) vol. 1, 380; Chambers (1827) vol. 2, 378–9; Cruden (1973) 14–17; 1 Kings 21:23, 2 Kings 9:35. NO 2844 **Melville's Manse, Anstruther Easter, Fife** Kirkton (1817) 188–90; Wilkie (1931) 294–301. NO 5704 **Menstrie, Clackmannanshire** Black's (1844) 178; Chambers (1827) vol. 2, 333–4; Fergusson (1912) 34–40; Monteath (1835) 81–5; Simpkins (1914) 315–16. NS 8496 **Methil, Fife** Farnie (*c.* 1860) 112–13; Simpkins (1914) 39–40; Wilkie (1931) 144–5. NT 3699 **Milnathort, Kinross-shire** Small (1823) 285–6. NO 1204 ***The Guidman o' Ballangeich*** Briggs (1970–1) B2, 66–8; Scott (1828) vol. 3, 33–9; Chambers (1827) vol. 2, 23–4; Simpkins (1914) 255–6; Wilkie (1931) 302–3. **Murthly, Perthshire** Briggs (1970–1) B1, 3. Murthly Castle standing stone: NO 0740 **Newburgh, Fife** Chambers (1827) vol. 2, 357–8; verbal information from Sarah Kelly, Perth Library. NO 2419 **Norrie's Law, Fife** Chambers (1826) 61–3; Chambers (1864) vol. 1, 337–8; Simpkins (1914) 1–3, 183–4; Wilkie (1931) 167–70. NO 4107 Auchindownie: NO 4205 Balmain: NO 4105 **Old Kilpatrick, Dunbartonshire** *Butler's Lives* (1956) vol. 1, 612–13; House (1960) 17–19, 74. NS 4773 **Orwell, Kinross-shire** *Scots Magazine* 18 (1756) 464;

Scottish Journal (1848) vol. 1, 67. NO 1404
The Pends, St Andrews, Fife Lang (1893)
306–8; Wodrow (1842–3) vol. 1, 104–5; verbal
information from St Andrews Library. NO 5117
Pitfirrane, Fife Richardson (1841–6) vol. 3,
239–40; *Scottish Journal* (1848) vol. 2, 273. NT
0686 **Powguild, Loch Gelly, Fife** Simpkins (1914)
47; Wilkie (1931) 97. NT 2192 Loch Gelly: NT
2092 **Quarrel Burn, Clackmannanshire** *Scottish
Journal* (1848) vol. 2, 273–4. NT 1859 **Rannoch
Moor, Perthshire** Philip (1995) 55–9. NN 3452 to
NN 3851 **St Andrews, Fife** Briggs (1970–1) B1,
111–113, 503; Kirkton (1817) 189–90; Lang (1893)
262–4; MacKinlay (1893) 120–2; Sibbald (1803)
80; Simpkins (1914) 5, 62; Wilkie (1931) 294;
Wodrow (1842–3) vol. 1, 102–4. NO 5015 to NO
5016 **St Fillan's Cave, Pittenweem, Fife** Boece
(1938–41) vol. 2, 273–4; Simpkins (1914) 235–6.
NO 5502 **St Fillan's Pool, Perthshire** Black's
(1844) 358; Bord (2006) 13–16; Bord (2008)
185–6; Bruford and MacDonald (1994) 288–91;
MacKinlay (1893) 123–6. NN 6925 **Schiehallion,
Perthshire** Bruford and MacDonald (1994) 473;
Campbell (1900) 94; Cunningham (1989) 70–1.
NN 7154 **The Minister and the Fairies**
Henderson and Cowan (2001); Kirk (1976).
Scone Palace, Perthshire Bruford and MacDon-
ald (1994) 223–5, 458–9. NO 1126 **Sheardale
Braes, Clackmannanshire** *Scottish Journal* (1848)
vol. 2, 274. NS 9596 **Soldier's Leap, Kil-
liecrankie, Perthshire** Black's (1844) 361–3;
Dixon (1925) 110–11; *Folklore* 87 (1976) 147. NN
9162 **Stirling** Donaldson (2000) 401–23; Fraser
(1905) 379–80. NS 7993 to NS 7994 **Stirling
Castle** Chambers (1827) vol. 2, 25–6. NS 7994
Tillicoultry, Clackmannanshire Chambers (1827)
vol. 2, 334–6; Gibson (1883) 155–6. NS 9298 **The
Trooper's Dubb, Kinross-shire** Chambers (1827)
vol. 2, 338; Robinson (1985) *sub* keltie; kilt (2);
Scottish Journal (1848) vol. 2, 275–6. NO 0601
Tullibole Castle: NO 0500 **Tullibardine,
Perthshire** Barbour (1886) 97–100; McNeill
(1937) 232. NN 9113 **Tullibody, Clackmannan-
shire** Simpson (1914) 316. NS 8695 **Wemyss
Castle, Fife** Briggs (1970–1) B1, 488–9; Simpkins
(1914) 36–9; Wilkie (1931) 137–9. NO 3497
Wester Durie, Fife Wilkie (1931) 88, 158. NO
3602

DUMFRIES & GALLOWAY

Annandale, Dumfriesshire Douglas (1977) 201–
7; Hogg (1820) vol. 1, 99–104. NY 1292

Auchabrick House, Kirkmaiden, Wigtownshire
Maxwell Wood (1975) 250–1; Westwood and
Simpson (2005) 107. NX 1236 **Auchengruith,
Dumfriesshire** Cromek (1810) 300. NS 8209
Auchneight, Mull of Galloway, Wigtownshire
Bord, *Fairy Sites* (2004) 196; Maxwell Wood
(1975) 151–4. Auchneight: NX 1134 Loup of
Grennan: NX 1339 Barncorkrie: NX 0936 **Bail
Hill, Dumfriesshire** Maxwell Wood (1975) 184;
Wilson (1904) 75. NS 7614 **Blackett Tower, Kirk-
patrick-Fleming, Dumfriesshire** William Scott
Irving, 'Fair Helen' (1814) in Miller (1910) 220–1.
Kirkpatrick-Fleming: NY 2770 **Bodesbeck Farm,
near Moffat, Dumfriesshire** Chambers (1826)
266–8; Cromek (1810) 332–3; Keightley (1850)
358–9; Scott (1902) vol. 1, 149. NT 1509 Bodesbeck Law: NT 1610 **Borgue, Kirkcudbrightshire**
Briggs (1970–1) B1, 182–3; Campbell (1994) vol.
1, 425; Henderson and Cowan (2001) 64–5. NX
6248 **Borron Point, Dumfriesshire** Cunningham
(1822) vol. 2, 259–82; Westwood and Simpson
(2005) 145. NX 9957 *Galloway Smugglers*
Chambers (1886) 57–68; McCormick (1973) 266;
Maxwell Wood (1908) *passim*; Temperley (1986)
271–87. **Buckland Glen, near Bombie, Kirkcudbrightshire** Maxwell Wood (1975) 269–72. Buckland Bridge: NX 7049 Monkland Hill: NX 7248
Burrow Head Forts, Whithorn, Wigtownshire
Cromek (1810) 310. NX 4634 **Caerlaverock,
Dumfriesshire** Campbell (1900) 38–9; Cromek
(1810) 308–9; Williamson (1985) 12–13, 43–65.
NY 0265 **Cardoness Castle, Anwoth, Kirkcudbrightshire** Agnew (1893) vol. 1, 222; Dick (1916)
137–8; Stell (1986) 101–2; Temperley (1986) 40.
NX 5955 **Claunch, Sorbie, Wigtownshire**
Maxwell Wood (1975) 253–4 NX 4348 **Closeburn
Castle, Dumfriesshire** Burke (1853) vol. 2, 200–
12; Grose (1789–91) vol. 1, 144, 150–3; Ramage
(1876) 185–6; Thiselton Dyer (1895) 183–5; Westwood (1985) 34–8; Westwood and Simpson (2005)
794. NX 9092 **Collin Farm, Rerrick, Kirkcudbrightshire** Lang (1911) 16, Bibliography;
Alexander Telfair, *A True Relation of an Apparition, Expressions, and Actings of a Spirit, which
infested the House of Andrew Mackie, in Ring-Croft
of Stocking, in the Paroch of Rerrick, in the Stewartry of Kircudbright, in Scotland, 1695*, repr. in
Law (1818) 267–77; Temperley (1986) 164;
Maxwell Wood (1975) 300, 321–43. NX 7951
Cowhill Tower, Dumfriesshire Cromek (1810)
232–48; Monger (2004) 38, 49–52, 99–101. NX
9582 **Craigdarroch, Dumfriesshire** Buchan
(1984) 73–4; Corrie (1891) 76. NX 7490 **Crawick,
Dumfriesshire** Wilson (1904) 17–29. NS 7710
Criffel, Kirkcudbrightshire Dick (1916) 13. NX

9561 **Dalbeattie Burn, Kirkcudbrightshire**
Cromek (1810) 229–32. Confluence of Dalbeattie
Burn with Urr Water: NX 8360 **Dalswinton,
Dumfriesshire** Cromek (1810) 334–6. NX 9835
Dowalton Loch, Wigtownshire MacRitchie
(1892) 106. NX 4046 **Drumlanrig Castle, Dum-
friesshire** Brown (1979) 69; Gervase of Tilbury
(1856) 12–13; 'The Judgement and Justice . . .'
(1796) 40 n.; Law (1818) lxxx. NX 8599 *In
League with the Devil* Fergusson (1886) *passim*,
esp. 6–10, 141–59; MacTaggart (1824) 241–3;
Maxwell Wood (1975) 226–32, 278–81; Vedder
(1842) 362–3; Westwood (1985) 7. **Dryfesdale,
Dumfriesshire** Chambers (1827) vol. 1, 216–17.
NY 1082 **Dunskey Castle, Portpatrick, Wigtownshire** Maxwell Wood (1975) 244–5. NX 0053
Ecclefechan, Dumfriesshire Carlyle (1881) vol.
1, 40–1; Fergusson (1886) 153–9. NY 1974 **Ericstane Hill, Dumfriesshire** Chambers (1827) vol.
1, 328; Scott (1877) [1824] 322, 565. NT 0612
Galdenoch Castle, Meikle, Wigtownshire
Agnew (1893) vol. 2, 164–6; Dick (1916) 349–50;
Maxwell Wood (1975) 245–8. NW 9763 **Gatehouse of Fleet, Kirkcudbrightshire** Campbell
(1994) vol. 1, 424–5. NX 5956 **Gilnockie Tower,
Canonbie, Dumfriesshire** Child (1904) no. 169,
413–18; Lindsay (1728) 145; Ramsay (1724) vol. 2,
190–6; Scott (1902) vol. 1, 339–41; Stell (1986) 90.
NY 3879 **Glencairn, Moniaive, Dumfriesshire**
Corrie (1891) 42–3. NC 7790 **Glenluce Abbey,
Old Luce, Wigtownshire** MacTaggart (1824)
457–8; Temperley (1986) 34, 131; Maxwell Wood
(1975) 15–16. NX 1959 **High Ardwell, Wigtownshire** Maxwell Wood (1975) 248–50. East and
West High Ardwell: NX 0845 **Kirkwaugh, Wigtownshire** Fraser (1877) 208–9. NX 4154 **Knockhill House, Hoddom, Dumfriesshire** Irving
(1906) 199; Stell (1986) 73. NY 1774 **Martyrs'
Tomb, Wigtown, Wigtownshire** Agnew (1893)
vol. 2, 141–3; Dick (1916) 189–94; Stell (1986)
139–40, 142; Warrack (1965) 89, 401; Wodrow
(1721–2) vol. 2, 505–7. Martyrs' Tomb and
Covenanters' Monument, stone post: NX 4456
Martyrs' Monument, Windy Hill: NX 4355
Moffat, Dumfriesshire NT 0906 *Suicidal Artists
and Architects* Sandy Hobbs Hobbs (1992);
McCulloch (1987). **Mote Hill, Dalry, Kirkcud-
brightshire** Lang (1885) 258. Norman motte:
NX 6281 **Murder Hole, Loch Neldricken,
Kirkcudbrightshire** Crockett (1894) 250–5;
Dick (1916) 169–71, 420–3; 'The Murder Hole'
(1829); Nicholson (1843) 48–59; Temperley
(1986) 125–30. NX 4483 **Myrton Castle,
Wigtownshire** Agnew (1893) vol. 2, 168–9;
Chambers (1891) 174–5; Dick (1916) 141–2;

The New Statistical Account of Scotland (1845) vol.
4, Wigtown, 226–7; Scott (1902) vol. 2, 359–60.
NX 3643 **New Abbey, Kirkcudbrightshire**
Cromek (1810) 305–6. NX 9666 **Palnackie,
Kirkcudbrightshire** Temperley (1986) 103–9. NX
8526 **Portencorkrie Bay, Wigtownshire** Maxwell
Wood (1975) 154–6. Portencorkrie: NX 0935
Barncorkrie: NX 0936 **Rerrick Parish, Kirkcud-
brightshire** Dick (1916) 77. NX 7851 area **Routin'
Bridge, Irongray, Dumfriesshire** Barbour (1886)
92–6; Temperley (1986) 93. NX 8778 **St Ninian's
Cave, Glasserton Parish, Whithorn, Wigtown-
shire** MacRitchie (1892) 105–6; Stell (1986) 135,
156; Yeoman (1999) 41–2. NX 4236 **Sanquhar,
Dumfriesshire** Maxwell Wood (1975) 284–7;
Simpson (1865) 56–7. NS 7909 **Spedlin's Tower,
Lochmaben, Dumfriesshire** Beard (1934), 237–8;
Chambers (1827) vol. 1, 214–15; Grose (1789–91)
vol. 1, 143–5; Law (1818) lxxx–lxxxii. NY 0988
Jardine Hall: NY 0987 **Sweetheart Abbey, New
Abbey, Kirkcudbrightshire** Crowl (1986) 382–3;
Gomme (1883) 39–40; Grose (1789–91) vol. 2, 9,
12; Hartshorne (1861) 66, 86–7, 121–3, 241; *Statistical Account of Scotland 1791–1799* (1979) vol. 2,
138; Stell (1986) 148–9; Thiselton Dyer (1892)
130–1, 134. NX 9766 **Tynron Doon, Nithsdale,
Dumfriesshire** Maxwell Wood (1975) 282–3; Stell
(1986) 122. NX 8294 **Whinnieliggate, Kirkcudbrightshire** Hatfield (2004) 225; Maxwell Wood
(1975) 40–3; *Reader's Digest* (1981) 147. NX 7252

GLASGOW & AYRSHIRE

Alloway, Ayrshire Chambers (1827) vol. 1, 291;
Grose (1789–91) vol. 2, 199–201; Manson (1901)
223–4. NS 3318 **Biggar, Lanarkshire** Chambers
(1827) vol. 1, 332–4. NT 0437 **Carfin Lourdes
Grotto, Lanarkshire** Bord (2008) 184;
www.carfin.org.uk. NS 7758 **Carnwath, Lanark-
shire** Chambers (1827) vol. 1, 339–40. NS 9846
Changue Forest, Carrick, Ayrshire Robertson
(1889) 140–7. NX 2382 **Cora Linn, Lanarkshire**
Darton (1990) 79; *History of Lanark* (1835) 156;
Stenlake (1990) 42. NS 8841 **Couthalley Castle,
Lanarkshire** Chambers (1826) 26–7. NS 9648
Craufurdland Bridge, near Kilmarnock, Ayrshire
Chambers (1870) 241–2. NS 4641 **Culzean Castle,
Maybole, Ayrshire** Black's (1845) 285–6; Briggs
(1970–1) B1, 298–9; Burns (1904) 18–25, 560;
Chambers (1870) 332–3; Grose (1789–91) vol. 2,
210; Oldham (1975) 39–41; Paterson (1863–6) vol.
2 (1864) 294–5; Stevenson (1985) 53. NS 2510
Dalry, Cunninghame, Ayrshire Barbour (1886)

132–3; Robertson (1889) 240–1. NS 2949 **Dolphinton, Lanarkshire** Briggs (1967) 32–3 NT 1046 **Dundonald Castle, Kyle, Ayrshire** Chambers (1870) 236–8; Opie (1951) 270–6; Spence (1937) 267–70; Westwood and Simpson (2005) 516–17; Wilson (1975) 310. NS 3635 **Finnieston Quay, Glasgow** Macpherson (2005) 113–14. NS 5765 **Firth of Clyde, Renfrewshire** Chambers (1826) 331; Cromek (1810) 229–33. NS 3274 **Games Loup, Carrick, Ayrshire** Child (1957) vol. 1, no. 4, 56–7; Dick (1916) 375–6. NX 1088 **Glasgow** Chambers (1827) vol. 1, 373–7; Chambers (1864) 105–6; Sinclair (1685) 219; Westwood (1985) 372–4. NS 5965 *The Vampire with Iron Teeth* Hobbs and Cornwell (1988); Hobbs and Cornwell (2001); Westwood and Simpson (2005) 620, 697. **Grievehill, near New Cumnock, Ayrshire** Wilson (1904) 77–9. New Cumnock: NS 6113 **Inverkip, Renfrewshire** Law (1818) lxx–lxxii; Macrae (1880) 8–12. NS 2071 **Kempock Stone, Inverkip, Renfrewshire** House (1960) 88; Macrae (1880) 6–12; Milne (1958) 4–5. NS 2478 **Knockdolian Castle, Colmonell, Ayrshire** Chambers (1870) 331–2. NX 1285 **Lady Glen, near Kilkerran, Ayrshire** Barbour (1886), 108–12. Kilkerran: NS 3003 **Lanark** *Discover Historic Clydesdale* (1993); Stenlake (1990) 19. NS 8843 **Largs, Ayrshire** Campbell (1900) 76–8. NS 2059 **The Lee, Lanarkshire** Beard (1934) 121–3; Black's (1844) 242–3; *History of Lanark* (1835) 114–17; *PSAS* 4 (1863) 223; Scott, *The Talisman* (1904) xvi–xviii, 460–1. NS 8547 **Logan, Kyle, Ayrshire** Maxwell Wood (1975) 24–5. NS 5820 **Maybole, Ayrshire** Barbour (1886) 124–31; Child (1904) no. 200, 483–5; Cromek (1810) 4; *Historie of the Kennedyis* (1830) 1–71, 91; *Maybole* (c. 1964) 9; Ramsay (1740) 427–8; Robertson (1889) 201–15; Robertson (1908) vol. 2, 25; Scott, *Poetical Works* (1904) 69–70. NS 3009 **Murdostoun, Lanarkshire** NS 8258 **Old King Coil's Tomb, Tarbolton, Ayrshire** Boece (1938–41) vol. 1, 21–45; Defoe (1769) vol. 4, 130–1 (Letter III); Grinsell (1976), 232–3; Johnson (1787–1803) vol. 5, 486–7; Kightly (1984) 56–93; *The New Statistical Account of Scotland* (1845) vol. 5, Ayrshire, 751–4; *Statistical Account of Scotland 1791–1799* (1979) vol. 6, 95; Robertson (1889) 111–23; Westwood (1985) 355–7. Colisfield Mains, cairn: NS 4426 Water of Doon: NS 3317 **Paisley, Renfrewshire** Blair (1904) 2; Chambers (1827) vol. 2, 7–9; Law (1818) xcii–xciii; Metcalfe (1909) 458–67; [Renfrew] (1809) 65ff, esp. 189–90. NS 4863 **Pollok, Glasgow, Lanarkshire** Davidson (1949) 115ff; [Renfrew] (1809) 35–51. NS 5362 *Sawney Bean the Cannibal* Black (1999); Hobbs and Cornwell (1997). **Sawney Bean's Cave, near Ballantrae, Ayrshire** NX 0987 **Strathaven, Lanarkshire** Chambers (1826) 59–60. NS 7044 **Tinto, Lanarkshire** Chambers (1826) 24–5; Chambers (1827) vol. 1, 331–2; *History of Lanark* (1835) 127. NS 9534 *William Wallace* 'Blind Harry' (2003) viiff; Campbell (1902) 193–4; Hamilton (1785) *passim*; Wallner (2003) 14–41. **Turnberry, Carrick, Ayrshire** Robertson (1889) 174–7. NS 2005 **Wallace's Cave, Lanarkshire** Crowl (1986) 104; *History of Lanark* (1835) 135, 152, 162; Stenlake (1990) 36. NS 4923

LOTHIAN & BORDERS

Abbotsford, Roxburghshire Crowe (1986) 148–9; Lockhart (1837–8) vol. 4, 139, 143; Martin (1703) 306; Parsons (1964) 73–7. NT 5034 **Aikwood Tower, Selkirkshire** Black's (1844) 101; Scott, *Poetical Works* (1904) 66–7. NT 4226 **Allanbank, Edrom, Berwickshire** Crowe (1986) 342–4; Hare (1900) vol. 4, 264, 266–7. NT 5247 **Arthur's Seat, Edinburgh** Shippey (2008) 17; Wright, Adams, and Scott (1987) 4, 36–7. NT 2772 **Athelstaneford, East Lothian** Boece (1938–41) vol. 2, 28–30; Crowl (1986) 492. NT 5377 **Barnbougle Castle, West Lothian** Underwood (1982) 55–6. NT 1778 **Barnhill's Bed, Minto, Roxburghshire** Black's (1844) 138; *The Lay of the Last Minstrel*, in Scott, *Poetical Works* (1904) 1–88: 7, 62. NT 5620 **Bass Rock, East Lothian** Bord (2008) 174; MacKinlay (1893) 74; Waddell (1893) 3. NT 6087 St Baldred's Well, East Linton: NT 5978 **Bedrule, Roxburghshire** Gibbings (1889) 99–100. NT 6017 **The Binns, West Lothian** Briggs (1962) 160; Hendrie (1976) 10, 83–6; Scott (1902) vol. 2, 245, 253. NT 0578 **Bow-Brig-Syke, Maxton, Roxburghshire** Henderson (1866) 273–4, citing Wilkie MS. Maxton: NT 6130 **Bowden, Roxburghshire** Henderson (1866) 159, citing Wilkie MS. NT 5530 **Bowland, Vale of Gale, Midlothian** Mackenzie (1877) 15–16; Underwood (1982) 47–8. NT 4439 **Brocklaw, Jedwater, Roxburghshire** Douglas (1977) 137–9. Brocklaw Rig: NS 8019 **Calton Hill, Edinburgh** Bovet (1684) 173; Briggs (1970–1) B1, 219–20; Scott (1902) vol.2, 356–8. NT 2676 **The Carlops, Peeblesshire** Black's (1844) 82; Ramsay (1721, 1728) vol. 2, 330. NT 1655 **Carterhaugh, Selkirkshire** Black's (1844) 101; Bord (2008) 170; Chambers (1827) vol. 1, 153; Scott (1902) vol. 2, 300–407. NT 4427 *Border Ballads* Child (1904) xi–xxxi; Gardner (1908) *passim*; Miller (1931) *passim*; Reed (1973) *passim*. **Cauldshiels Loch, near Abbotsford, Roxburghshire** Irving (1835) 101; Parsons (1964) 96; Stevenson (1879) 14. NT 5132 **Cockburn's Castle, Vale of Megget, Selkirkshire** Black's (1844) 103–4; Chambers (1827) vol. 1, 165–6; Scott (1902) vol. 3, 108–13. NT 2324 **Comiston, Midlothian** Stevenson (1879) 37. NT 2468 **Cout of Keeldar's Grave, Roxburghshire** Leyden (1858) 232–44; Scott (1902) vol. 4, 258–76. Remains of chapel: NY 4996 **Cramond Bridge, Midlothian** Briggs (1970–1) B2, 66–8 NT 1775 **Cranshaws Farm, Berwickshire** Henderson (1856) 65–6. NT 6962 **Cuddyhall, Blainslie, Roxburghshire** Chambers (1888) 257–9. NT 5543 **Dalhousie Castle, Midlothian** Ramsay (1721, 1728) vol. 1, 276. NT 3263 **Dalkeith, Midlothian** Scott (2001) 200–1. NT 3467 **Dalmeny, Midlothian** Holinshed (1805) vol. 1, 348–51; Sinclair (1685) 160–4. NT 1447 **Deloraine, Buccleuch, Selkirkshire** Davidson (1949) 58–9, 139–40, 166–8; Henderson (1866) 160–1; Thorpe (2001) 485. Wester Deloraine: NT 3320 Easter Deloraine: NT 3420 **Drumelzier, Peeblesshire** Chambers (1827) vol. 1, 189–90. NT 1334 **Earlston, Berwickshire** Burnham (1908) *passim*; Henderson (1834) 145–6; Henderson (1856) 147; Lyle (1968) *passim*; Murray (1875) *passim*; Westwood (1985) 452–8, 501–2. NT 5738 **Edinburgh Castle** Beard (1934) 150–62; Boece (1938–41) vol. 1, 25; Holinshed (1805) vol. 1, 36–9; Spence (1948) 48; Westwood (1985) 418–20. NT 2574 **Edin's Hall Broch, Berwickshire** Simpkins (1914) citing MS collection by Peter Buchan, in *Transactions of the Buchan Field Club*, vol. 9, part 2, 143–7; Turnbull (1882) *passim*; Westwood (1985) 363–7. NT 7760 **Rashin-Coatie** Bruford and MacDonald (1994) 1–31, 64–9; Douglas (1977) ix–xxxi, 17–20. **Eildon Hills, Roxburghshire** Black's (1844) 121; Child (1904) no. 37, 63–6: *The Lay of the Last Minstrel*, in Scott, *Poetical Works* (1904) 1–88: 10, 67; Parsons (1964) 96–8. NT 5532 Eildon Stone: NT 5634 **Ettrick Water, Selkirkshire** Briggs (1967); Ramsay (1721, 1728) vol. 1, 227; Scott (1902) vol. 1, 150. NT 4832 **Eyemouth, Berwickshire** Henderson (1856) 2–3, 54. NT 9464 **Fast Castle, Berwickshire** Black's (1885) 133; Blythell (2007) *passim*; Parsons (1943) *passim*; Parsons (1964) 141–5; Scott (1819) *passim*. NT 8670 **Galashiels, Selkirkshire** Davidson (1949) 113–14; Sinclair (1685) 200–2. NT 4836 **Gormyre, West Lothian** Hendrie (1976) 15; Simpson (1896) 21–2. NS 9772 **Gorrenberry, Hermitage Water, Roxburghshire** Scott (1902) vol. 1, 150; vol. 4, 248. NY 4797 **Grassmarket, Edinburgh** Bailey (2002) *passim*. NT 2573 **Greenlaw Moor, Berwickshire** Browne (1892) 94–7. NT

7048 to NT 7148 **Greyfriars Kirk, Edinburgh** Black's (1885) 43–5; Law (1818) lxxx; Stevenson (1879) 20. NT 2673 **Hermitage Castle, Roxburghshire** Chambers (1827) vol. 1, 104–10; Henderson (1866) 215–17; Howitt (1842) 554–62; Leyden (1858) 213–31; Scott (1902) vol. 4, 218–60; Thiselton Dyer (1895) 166–8, 276. NY 4996 Nine Stane Rig: NY 5297 **Holydean, Roxburghshire** Douglas (1977) 179–80; Henderson (1866) 158–9. NT 5430 **Holyroodhouse, Edinburgh** Black's (1844) 26–7, 29; Scott (1838) 267–8. NT 2773 *The Thistle of Scotland* Coffey (1993); Darwin (1996); Dunbar (1998) vol. 1, 163–8; vol. 2, 395–400; Fairweather (n.d.); Milliken and Bridgewater (2004); Rigg (1897); Stace (1997); Vickery (1995). **Jedburgh, Roxburghshire** Chambers (1864) vol. 1, 183–5; Holinshed (1805) vol. 1, 408–10; Redworth (2003) 101, 162; Scott (1838) 29; Thiselton Dyer (1895) 73–5. NT 6521 **Kelso, Roxburghshire** Nicholas (1949) 46; Selby (1973) 61–3; Westwood and Simpson (2005) 94–5, 442–3, 536–7. NT 7334 **Kirk Yetholm, Roxburghshire** Brockie (1884) 34–6; Chambers (1886) 4–5; Lucas (1882) *passim*; Scot (1665) appendix. NT 8328 **Langton House, Berwickshire** Henderson (1856) 68–9. NT 7653 Dogden Moss: NT 6849 **Leith, Midlothian** Briggs (1977) 362; Scott (1902) vol. 1, 150–1; Spence (1948) 17–18; Westwood (1985) 458–9. NT 2775 to NT 2876 **Linlithgow, West Lothian** Hendrie (1976) 20–1; Sinclair (1685) 39–40; Underwood (1982) 134–5. NS 9976 to NT 0076 **Linton, Roxburghshire** Briggs (1970–1) B1, 164–5; Henderson (1866) 256–8; Leishman (1937) 10–14, citing *The Memoirs of the Somervilles* (1680); Scott (1902) vol. 1, 140; Simpson (1980) 78; Westwood (1985) 470–2. Linton Hill: NT 7828 **Littledean Tower, Roxburghshire** Baldwin (1985) 70; Henderson (1866) 271–2. NT 6331 **Livingston, West Lothian** Hendrie (1976) 58; Westwood and Simpson (2005) 803. NT 0768 **Longformacus, Berwickshire** Hare (1953) 151–2. NT 6957 **Loth Stone, East Lothian** NT 5874 **The Lucken Hare, Eildon Hills, Roxburghshire** [Denham] (1892–5) vol. 1, 121–8; Hughes (1904) 112–13, 115; Philip (1995) 241–3, citing Scott (1829); Scott, (1902) vol. 1, preface; vol. 4, 79–137; Scott (2001) 82–7. NT 5432 Bowden Moor: NT 5332 **Mary King's Close, Edinburgh** Sinclair (1685) unpaginated postscript; Wilson, Brogan, and Hollinrake (1999) 2–22. NT 2674 **Maxton, Roxburghshire** Baring-Gould (1995) 66–7; Henderson (1866) 165–6, citing Wilkie MS. NT 6130 **Melrose Abbey, Roxburghshire** Black's (1844) 112–18; Scott, *Poetical Works* (1904) 64–5; Wade (1861) 306. NT 5434 **Mid Calder, West Lothian**

MacCulloch (2004) 549–50; Sharpe (1884) 194–5; Turnbull (1996) 93. NT 0767 **Minch Moor, Peeblesshire** [Gibbings] (1889) 185–8; Spence (1946) 177. NT 3633 **Mittenfu' Stanes, Lammermuir Hills, Berwickshire** Browne (1892) 76–7. NT 6259 **Musselburgh, East Lothian** *Edinburgh Topographical . . . Magazine* (1848) 159ff; Turnbull (1996) 6. NT 3573 **Newhaven, Midlothian** Simpson (1908) 134–8. NT 2577 **Newton, West Lothian** Scott (1902) vol. 4, 199–211; Turnbull (1996) 25–6. NT 0978 **North Berwick, East Lothian** Cowan (1983) *passim*; Davidson (1949) 46, 150–3; Goodare (2002) *passim*; Goodare, Martin, and Miller (2008) *passim*; Henderson (2006) *passim*. NT 5584 *Witch-hunts* Henderson (2009); Larner (1981). **Peaston, East Lothian** Davidson (1949) 224–9; Sinclair (1685) 144–54. NT 4265 **Peat Law, Selkirkshire** *A Discourse concerning . . . Devils and Spirits* (1665) Bk II, cap. iv, 51; Scott (1902) vol. 2, 378. NT 4431 **Peebles, Peeblesshire** Scott (1902) vol. 1, 145–6. NT 2540 **Powsail Burn, Peeblesshire** Chambers (1827) vol. 1, 193; Chambers (1870) 228–9; Scott (1902) vol. 4, 109–115; Westwood (1985) 460–1. NT 1333 **Restalrig Loch, Midlothian** Scott (2001) 91–5. NT 2875 **Roslin Castle, Lasswade, Midlothian** Briggs (1970–1) B1, 13; B2, 174; Hewett (1976) 39–41; Macdonald Robertson (1964) 36; Trubshaw (2005), 57–76: 58–9, 62; Waldron (1864) 12–13, 91–2; Westwood (2001) 102, 105; Westwood and Simpson (2005) 500–1. NT 2863 **Rosslyn Chapel, Midlothian** Black's (1844) 84; *Gentleman's Magazine* (September 1817) 209; Grose (1789–91) vol. 1, 44. NT 2763 **Rubers Law Fort, Roxburghshire** [Gibbings] (1889) 98–9. NT 5716 **St Boswells, Roxburghshire** Hare (1953) 49–50; Henderson (1866) 29, citing Wilkie MS. NT 5930 **St Catherine's Well, Edinburgh** Bord (2008) 175–6, 204; Turnbull (1996) 16ff. NT 2768 **St Triduana's Well, Restalrig, Midlothian** Bord (2008) 176–7; Farmer (1997) 480; Miller (2004) 146; Morris (1982) 96–8; Notman (1976) *passim*. NT 2875 **Samuelston, East Lothian** Davidson (1949) 244–5; Sinclair (1685) 122–5. NT 4870 **Selkirk, Selkirkshire** Chambers (1827) vol. 1, 155–6. NT 4729 **Smailholm Tower, Roxburghshire** Baldwin (1985) 74 (no. 35); Black's (1845) 121–2; Grinsell (1976) 60; Parsons (1964) 96–8; Scott (1814–17) vol. 2, 151. NT 6435 **Soutra Mains, Midlothian** Chambers (1888) 257–9. Soutra Mains Wood: NT 4558 **Torphichen, West Lothian** Hendrie (1976) 9–14; Simpson (1896) 11, 20–1. NS 9672 **Traprain Law, East Lothian** Finlay (1960) 14; Grinsell (1976) 219; Turnbull (1996) 10. NT 5874 **West Bow, Edinburgh** Scott (2001) 194–6; Sinclair

(1685) unpaginated postscript. NT 2673 **Whitekirk, East Lothian** Waddell (1893) 140–4. NT 6081 **Whittingehame, East Lothian** Briggs (1970–1) BI, 566; Chambers (1826) 9–10; Philip (1995) 423–4; Swire (1961) 61. Churchyard: NT 6073 **Woodhouselee, Midlothian** Black's (1844) 80, 237; Finlay (1960) 121, 156; Scott (1902) vol. 4, 178–98. NT 2364 **Yarrowford, Selkirkshire** Davidson (1949) 85–6; Henderson (1866) 154–8; Oates (2003) *passim*; Thorpe (2001) 240, 346, 584–6. NT 4030

NORTH EAST

Aberdeen Douglas (1977) 129–34; Scott (1902) vol. 2, 372–5. NJ 9007 **Aberdeen University** Hobbs (1973) *passim*; Westwood and Simpson (2005) 222. NJ 9210 **Airlie, Angus** Gill (1932) 209–10, citing MacRitchie, *Celtic Review*, iv, 319. NO 3150 **Aquhorthies, Kincardineshire** Grinsell (1976) 208; Robertson (1813) 81; Watt (1985) 24–5. NJ 9198 **Arbroath, Angus** Chambers (1827) vol. 2, 233–4. NO 6441 **Arbuthnott, Kincardineshire** Gibbon (1995) 7; Watt (1985) 116–20. NO 7975 **Auchriachan, Strath Avon, Banffshire** Briggs (1970–1) B1, 361–2; Briggs (1978) 175–6; Grant Stewart (1823) 127–34; Keightley (1850) 390–1. NJ 1818 **Ballater, Aberdeenshire** Bruford (1982) 63–7, 100–1, 109. NO 3795 to NO 3696 *Traveller Tales* Brockie (1884) 95; Bruford (1982) vii–x, 11–27; Bruford and MacDonald (1994) 1–31; Buchan (1984) 1–14; Williamson (1986) 10–16, 137–46. **Balmachie, near Carlungie, Angus** Bord, *Fairy Sites* (2004) 207–8; [Gibbings] (1889), 52–4. NO 5135 Carlungie NO 5136 **Banff** Archibald (1994) 69–71; Buchan (1984) 92, 126–7, 240; McLaren (1965) 95; Seeger and MacColl (1960) 77, 89. NJ 6964 **Bennachie, Aberdeenshire** Buchan (1984) 84–5; McConnochie (1890) 9–17, 61–2. NJ 6622 **Boddam, Aberdeenshire** Drummond (1982) *passim*; Hobbs and Cornwall (1994) *passim*; 'Just fancy that . . .' (1993) *passim*; Screeton (1991) *passim*. NK 1342 **Bridge of Dee, Aberdeen** Briggs (1970–1) B2, 13–14; Kinnear (1910) 136–9. NJ 9203 **Bridge of Potarch, Aberdeenshire** Black's (1844) 391. NO 6197 **Burghead, Moray** Bord (2008) 184; MacKinlay (1893) 98–9; Simpson (1908) 125–7. NJ 1169 **Cairnshee, Kincardineshire** *New Statistical Account* (1845) vol. 11, Kincardineshire, 177; Watt (1985) 151, 198. NO 7494 **Campdalmore, Strath Avon, Banffshire** [Gibbings] (1889) 189–92. NJ 1519 **Cawdor Castle, Nairnshire** Beard (1934) 144–6; Crowl

(1986), 525; Ellis Davidson (1960); Innes (1859), 18; Shaw (1882), vol. 2, 270. NH 8449 **Chapel o' Sink, Garioch, Aberdeenshire** Grinsell (1976) 20, 208. NJ 7119 **Cluny Castle, Aberdeenshire** Beard (1934) 189–91; Manson (1901) 228–9. NJ 6182 **Corrichie, Kincardineshire** *A Diurnal of Remarkable Occurrents* (1833) 74; Fraser (1998) 234–44. NJ 6902 to NJ 7002 **Craig-Aulnaic, Strathdon, Aberdeenshire** [Gibbings] (1889) 32–8. Strathdon: NJ 3513 **Crathes Castle, Kincardineshire** Watt (1985) 240–4; *www.aboutaberdeen.com*. NO 7396 **Delnabo, Banffshire** Douglas (1977) 185–9; Grant Stewart (1823) 170–8. NJ 1617 **Duffus Castle, Moray** Aubrey (1721) 158–60; Scott (1902) vol. 2, 366–7; *Shetland Folk Book* (1957), 3. NJ 1967 **Dundee, Angus** Cromek (1810) 281; 'The Judgement and Justice of God Exemplified . . .', Appendix to corrected and enlarged 3rd edn of [Howie] (1796) 38; Lockhart (1837) vol. 4, 37–8; Napier (1859–62) vol. 1, 283; Scott (1993) 467, 492, citing Lockart (1837) vol. 1, 254. NO 3931 **Edzell, Angus** Briggs (1970–1) B2, 83–7; Jervise (1853) 13–14. NO 6068 **Edzell Churchyard, Angus** Jervise (1853) 14–17. NO 6069 **Farnell, near Brechin, Angus** Briggs (1970–1) B1, 461; Macdonald Robertson (1964) 41–3. NO 6255 **Fiddes Castle, Kincardineshire** Burness (1832) *passim*; Kinnear (1910) 123–6; Watt (1985) 268–70. NO 8281 **Forres, Moray** Davidson (1949) 43–4, 254–5; Shepherd (1986) 122–3; Sinclair (1685) 100–2; Speaight (1985) 388. NJ 0359 to NJ 0458 area **Macbeth** Chambers (1827) vol. 2, 376–7; Dalgleish (1862) 9–20; Matthews and Stewart (1988) 143–186: Simpkins (1914) 126, 190–4, 257–8; Sinclair (1999) *passim*; Watt and Carter (1887) 165, 286–9. **Fyvie Castle, Aberdeenshire** Balfour (2003) 181–3; Beard (1934) 42–4; Gregor (1881) 109–10. NJ 7639 **Gicht Castle, Aberdeenshire** Briggs (1970–1) B1, 123–4, citing Hamish Henderson, School of Scottish Studies; Buchan (1984) 86–7. NJ 8239 **Glamis Castle, Angus** Beard (1934) 41–2, 242; *Book of Pluscarden*, vol. 2, 243; Bord, *Footprints* (2004) 143; Briggs (1970–1) B2, 208–10; Cargill Guthrie (1875) 1–79 *passim*; Haining (1993) 101–2; [Halifax] (1936) 25; Hare (1953) 113, 297–8; Ingram (1884) 99–100, 460, 466; Scott (2001) 230–1; Thiselton Dyer (1895) 99–101; Underwood (1982) 104–9. NO 3848 **Glen Gairn, Aberdeenshire** Briggs (1970–1) B1, 461–5, citing Hamish Henderson, School of Scottish Studies. NJ 3100 **Glenbervie, Kincardineshire** Kinnear (1910) 11–16; Scott (1902) vol. 4, 218–58. NO 7781 **Green Castle, Kincardineshire** Chambers (1827) vol. 2, 256–7; Robertson (1813) 190–3; Watt (1985) 350ff, 495. NO 6676 **Inch**

Cape Rock, east of Dundee, Angus Black's (1844) 373–4; Southey (1815) vol. 3, 148. NO 7626 **Invergowrie, Angus** Buchan (1984) 194; Chambers (1826) 96–7. NK 0651 **Inverurie, Aberdeenshire** Leyden (1803) pt 2, 53–4, 166–8. NJ 7721 **Kaim of Mathers, Kincardineshire** Robertson (1813) 194. NO 7664 **Kelpie's Stane, Aberdeenshire** Bord (1995) 32–3. NJ 2608 **Kirkmichael, Banffshire** *Illustrations . . . of Aberdeen and Banff*, vol. 2 (1847) 306–7; MacKinlay (1893) 182–3; *Statistical Account of Scotland 1791–1799* (1979) vol. 16, 303–4. NO 0860 **Leslie, Aberdeenshire** Aubrey (1721) 161–2; Crowl (1986) 244–5. NJ 5924 **Lochan Uaine, Banffshire** Gregor (1892); MacKinlay (1893) 156–8. NJ 1415 **Lynturk, Aberdeenshire** Smith (1875) pt 2, 887. NJ 6113 **Martin's Stone, Tealing, Angus** Brand (1853) vol. 1, 322; Chambers (1826) 262–4; Chambers (1864) vol. 1, 541; MacKinlay (1893) 181; Simpkins (1914) 13; *Statistical Account of Scotland 1791–1799* (1979) vol. 13, 640–1. NO 3737 **Melgund Castle, Angus** Chambers (1827) vol. 2, 251–2. NO 5456 **Morphie, Kincardineshire** Beattie (1847) 14, 17–18; Chambers (1826) 334; Watt (1914) xl–xli, 46, 374; Watt (1985) 462–4. NO 7164 **New Deer, Aberdeenshire** Gregor (1881) 62. NJ 8846 **River Spey, Moray** Bord (1995) 32–3; Spence (1948) 21; Whyte (1986) 31. NJ 3357 area **The Round Square, Gordonstoun, Moray** Brereton (1968) 64–75; Briggs (1970–1) B1, 132–4; Dryden (1700); Westwood and Simpson (2005) 495, 543–4. NJ 1869 **St Cyrus, Kincardineshire** Gavin (*c.* 1997) *passim*; Watt (1985) 479ff. NO 7464 **St Vigeans, Angus** *Statistical Account of Scotland 1791–1799* (1979) vol. 12, 173–4. NO 6342 **Sands of Forvie, Aberdeenshire** Buchan (1984) 196; Gregor (1881) 110; Speaight (1985) 387. NK 0327 **Vayne Castle, Angus** Jervise (1853) 200–3. NO 4959 **Whitehills, Banffshire** Milne (1987) 6–7. NJ 6665 **Witton, West Water, Angus** Jervise (1853) 128–30. NO 5670

NORTHERN HIGHLANDS

Achadh a' Bheannaich, Latheron, Caithness Grinsell (1976) 199; MacPhail (1898) 87. ND 2034 **Ardvreck Castle, Assynt, Sutherland** Miller (1835) 212–15. NC 2424 **Ben Loyal, Sutherland** Swire (1963) 190, 191–2; Westwood (1985) 228–31. NC 5748 **Brims Ness, Caithness** Calder (1842) 60–6; Sutherland (1937) 73–5. ND 4073 **Bruan Broch, Latheron, Caithness** Edwards (1929) 140; Henshall (1963, 1972) vol. 1, 271, 280–

1, 287; Sutherland (1937) 24–5. ND 3140 Fairies Mound, horned cairn, Lower Dounreay: NC 9968 **Carsgoe, Caithness** Calder (1842) 221. ND 1463 **Creag Mhór and Creag Bheag, Reay, Caithness** Munro (1977) 45–6; *Oxford Dictionary of National Biography* (2004) vol. 35, 504–6; Sutherland (1937) 77. NC 9963 Cnoc na Claise Brice: ND 0059 Marsh: ND 0159 Clach clais an Tuire: NC 9963 *Guardian of the Wild* Allan (1822) 332–3; Campbell (1900) 243–4; Grant (1925) 4–10; Ross (2000) 113–14; Spence (1948) 78–80; Thompson (1976) 126. **Dirlot Castle, Caithness** D. Miller (1992) 162; Munro (1977) 33–5; Sutherland (1937) 98–9. ND 1349 **Dornoch Cathedral, Sutherland** Bord, *Footprints* (2004) 120; Close-Brooks (1986) 115; MacGregor (1947) 184. NH 8090 **Dunnet Sands, Caithness** Sutherland (1937) 78–80. ND 2069 to ND 2271 **Dwarwick Head, Caithness** Calder (1842) 222–3. ND 2171 **Garrywhin, Ulbster, Caithness** Close-Brooks (1986) 166–7; Stevenson (1890) 123–9; Sutherland (1937) 111–13. ND 3141 **Gizzen Briggs, Sutherland** Bentinck (1926) 512; Close-Brooks (1986) 49; Dempster (1888) 154–5; MacGregor (1947) 116–17. NH 8287 **Halkirk, Caithness** Sutherland (1937) 32–3. ND 1359 **Handa Island, Sutherland** Mavor (1800) 70; Ogilvy (1846) 256–7. NZ 7215 **Helmsdale, Sutherland** Close-Brooks (1986) 11, 15, 50, 57; Swire (1963) 198. ND 0215 Telford bridge: ND 0315 **Hill of Durcha, near Lairg, Sutherland** Bett (1952) 30. Durcha: NC 5003 **Hill o' Many Stanes, Mid Clyth, Caithness** Close-Brooks (1986) 157, 161; Myatt (1992) 45. ND 3038 **Houstry, Caithness** Mackay (1965) 50–2; Maclagan (1898). ND 1534 Forss Water: ND 0360 Lieurary: ND 0762 Achscrabster: ND 0862 **John o' Groats, Caithness** Calder (1861) 10–11, 245–52; Close-Brooks (1986) 112–13; Cramond (1894) 52; Mackay, *History of the House of Mackay* (1829) 503n.; J. Miller (1992) 87. ND 3773 Dunnet Head: ND 2077 St Drostan's church: ND 3473 **Kylesku, Sutherland** Macdonald Robertson (1998) ix, 59–60. NC 2334 Kerrachar Bay: NC 1835 **Loch Meadaidh, Durness, Sutherland** Campbell (1900) 212–13. NC 4064 *Kelpies and Waterhorses* Briggs (1967) 57–8; Campbell (1900) 215; Gregor (1881) 66–7; Henderson (1911) 161–5. **Loch mo Naire, Strath Naver, Sutherland** Dempster (1888) 221; Henderson (1866) 132–3; Kunz (1915) 153–5; Swire (1963) 190; Walsh (1898) 624–6. NC 7354 **Loch More, Caithness** Calder (1861) 77–80; D. Miller (1992) 162; J. Miller (1992) 84; Munro (1979) 58–61. Loch More Castle: ND 0846 **Loch Shin, Sutherland** MacGregor (1947) 293. NC 4816 **Loch Shurrery, Caithness**

Campbell (1900) 216; Sutherland (1937) 99–100. ND 0455 **Lord Reay's Green Tables, Sutherland** Swire (1963) 189. Lairg: NC 5806 Tongue: NC 5956 **Loth, Sutherland** Bentinck (1926) 461–5; [Burt] (1754) vol. 1, 281; Oates (2003) *passim*; Sharpe (1884) 199–200. NC 9410 to NC 9711 area **Ousdale, Langwell, Caithness** Campbell (1900) 220–1; Carmichael (1900) vol. 2, 274; Grimble (1999) 98–103; Pennant (1772) 160; Sibbald (1684) pt 2, bk 2, 11; White (1954) 168–9. ND 0620 **Oykell Bridge, Sutherland** Close-Brooks (1986) 13; *Orkneyinga Saga* (1987) ch. 5, 27–8; Swire (1963) 195–6. NC 3800 **Reay, Caithness** Dixon (1886) 208; Mackay, *Songs and Poems* (1829), xviii–xxi. NC 9664 **River Shin, Sutherland** Swire (1963) 177. NH 5796 **Sandwood Bay, Cape Wrath, Sutherland** Macdonald Robertson (1948) 105; MacDonald Robertson (1998) 40–3. NC 2266 **Scrabster, Caithness** Davidson (1949) 69–70; Polson (1907) 109–10; Sharpe (1884) 180–94. ND 1070 **Smoo Cave, Durness, Sutherland** Dale-Green (1966) 54; MacGregor (1947) 174; Sutherland (1937) 75–7, 80; Swire (1963) 182–3. NC 4267 **Thurso, Caithness** Calder (1861) 34–5; 'Theophilus Insulanus' (1763), 30. ND 1168 **Tongue, Sutherland** Campbell (1900) 224–5; Ó hógáin (1990) 213–17. NC 5956 **Tongue House, Sutherland** Close-Brooks (1986) 73–4; Munro (1979) 30–2. NC 5959 **Uaigh Dhiarmaid, Tongue, Sutherland** Dempster (1888) 159–60; Newstead (1959) *passim*. NC 5852 **The Wolf Stone, Lothbeg, near Brora, Sutherland** Campbell (1994) vol. 1, 313–4; Newton (2002) 182–207; Scrope (1839) 370–2. Lothbeg: NC 9410

ORKNEY & SHETLAND ISLANDS

Brindister, Mainland, Shetland Briggs (1970–1) B1, 356–7; Burgess (1895) 100; Tait (1951) 5, 12–13. HU 4337 Windhouse, Yell: HU 4891 **Broch of Houlland, Mainland, Shetland** *See The Trowie Tunes of Shetland* HU 3454 **Buruside, Cullivoe, Yell, Shetland** Bruford (1982) 97. Cullivoe: HU 5402 **Colvadale, Unst, Shetland** Black (1903) 13; Edmonston and Saxby (1888) 205–6. HP 6205 **Copinsay, Orkney** Brand (1703) 112; Marwick (1975) 39–40, 148–50. HY 6101 **Cunningsburgh, Mainland, Shetland** HU 4411 **Dunrossness, Mainland, Shetland** Black (1903) 25–6; Edmonston and Saxby (1888) 209; Tait (1951) 1–2. HU 4022 **Dwarfie Stane, Hoy, Orkney** Black's (1865) 565; Black's (1882)

620; Brand (1703) 41–2; Grinsell (1976) 185–6; Martin (1703) 364; Scott (1877) [1821] 259. HY 2400 **Eday, Orkney** Black (1903) 143; Brand (1703) 62; Fergusson (1883) 122. HY 5531 **Fetlar, Shetland** Saxby (1932) 5, 47–9, 127. HU 6291 **Foula, Shetland** Black (1903) 189–93; Blind (1882) 368–70; Douglas (1977) 160–3. HT 9639 **Gord, Mainland, Shetland** Bruford and Mac-Donald (1994) 331–2, 472–3; Saxby (1932) 189–90; *Tocher* 26 (1977) 104–5. HU 4329 **Greenbank, North Yell, Shetland** Bruford and MacDonald (1994) 258–9, 461. HP 5304 **Haltadans, Fetlar, Shetland** Bord (1979) 104; Grinsell (1976) 183; Jakobsen (1936) 171–2, Inv no. 1226; Stewart and Moar (1951) 19–20. HU 6292 *The Trowie Tunes of Shetland* Anderson and Swing (1979) *passim*; Blind (1882) 369; Edmonston and Saxby (1888) 202; Grinsell (1976) 182; Hibbert (1822) 450; Marwick (1975) 34; Nicolson (1920) 13–19; Spence (1899) 151–2; Stewart and Moar (1951) *passim*. **Haroldswick, Unst, Shetland** Edmonston and Saxby (1888) 218–21. HP 6312 **Hascosay, Shetland** Saxby (1932) 185–8, 191. HU 5592 **Houll, Fetlar, Shetland** Edmonston and Saxby (1888) 201; Robertson and Graham (1957) 1, 5. HU 6590 **Linga, Shetland** Cluness (1951) 45–6; Grønneberg [n.d.] n.p.; Marwick (1975) 175–8, 204; Nicolson (1981) 21–2; 'A Shetland Saga' (1895) *passim*. HU 5598 **Loch of Winyadelpa, Fetlar, Shetland** HU 6493 **Maes Howe, Orkney Mainland** Black's (1865) 561–2; Grinsell (1976) 69, 186–7; Liestøl (1984) *passim*. HY 3213 **Midbrake, Yell, Shetland** Bruford and MacDonald (1994) 45–7, 443. HP 5305 **Notland Castle, Westray, Orkney** Fergusson (1883) 71–2. HY 4248 **North Yell, Shetland** McEwan (1978) 104–6. HP 5100 area **Ollaberry, Mainland, Shetland** Robertson and Graham (1957) 65–7. HU 3680 **Quarff, Shetland** Black (1903) 187–9; Brand (1703) 113–14. HU 4135 **St Tredwell's Loch, Papa Westray, Orkney** Black (1903) 6–7; Brand (1703) 58–9; MacKinlay (1893) 13–14, 145–7. HY 4950 **South Havra, Shetland** Black (1903) 15; Brand (1703) 111; Low (1813) 26; Nicolson (1981) 30–1; Saxby (1932) 191. South Havra and Little Havra HU 3526 North Havra: HU 3742 **Stenness, Orkney Mainland** Black (1903) 2; Fergusson (1883) 26–7; Grinsell (1976) 187–9; Gordon (1792) 263. Stones of Stenness: HY 3113 Ring of Brodgar: HY 2913 Stone of Odin: HY 2113 **Stone of Quoybune, Birsay, Orkney Mainland** Black (1903) 3–4; Fergusson (1883) 28–9; Grinsell (1976) 56–60, 189–90; Westwood and Simpson (2005) 57. HY 2526 **Stromness, Orkney Mainland** Fergusson (1883) 34–7, citing Walter Scott; Thorpe (2001) 445. HY

2509 *Selkies* Keightley (1850) 394–5; Matheson (1938) xvii–xliv; Spence (1948) 41–57; Thomson (1980) 215ff; Traill Dennison (1893) *passim*. **Sule Skerry, Orkney** Black (1903) 179–82; Child (1904) no. 113, 240; Thomson (1980) 215, citing unpublished manuscripts of J. F. Campbell. HX 6224 **Sunnydale, Orkney Mainland** Fergusson (1883) 43–4; *The New Statistical Account of Scotland* (1845) vol. 15, 67. HY 3010 Bigswell: HY 3311 **Swinna Ness, Unst, Shetland** Black (1903) 1; Edmonston and Saxby (1888) 224. HP 6509 **Swona, Orkney** Munro (1979) 19. ND 3884 **Tafts, Fetlar, Shetland** Black (1903) 34, citing Burgess (1895) 96–7; Robertson and Graham (1957) 4; Tait (1951), 6–7. HU 6192 **Tingwall, Orkney Mainland** Black (1903) 54–5; Brand (1703) 110–11. HY 4023 **Trolla Stack, Mainland, Shetland** HU 3782 **Trolladale Water, Mainland, Shetland** HU 3273 **Trowie Knowe, Northmavine, Mainland, Shetland** HU 3685 *The Grey Neighbours* Edmonston and Saxby (1888) 183–229; Grinsell (1976) 184; Nicolson (1981) 76–85. **Tuskerbister, Orkney Mainland** Bruford and MacDonald (1994) 207–8, 457–8; Buchan (1984) 60–1, 231–2. HY 3510 **Unst, Shetland** [Gibbings] (1889) 86–8. HP 6107 **Vallafield, Unst, Shetland** Campbell (1900) 138–9; Spence (1899) 151–2; Stewart and Moar (1951) *passim*. HP 6008 **Ve Skerries, Shetland** Black (1903) 179–82; Hibbert (1822) 566; Thomas (1851) *passim*. HU 1065 **Veltigar, Tankerness, Orkney Mainland** Montgomerie (1956) 101; additional information from *www.VisitScotland.org*. HY 5006 **Walls, Mainland, Shetland** Burgess (1895) 102–3; Douglas (1977) 123–4. HU 2449 **Westbrough, Sanday, Orkney** Douglas (1977) 58–72, 299–301. HY 6642 **Windhouse, Yell, Shetland** HY 4992

SOUTHERN HIGHLANDS

Beauly, Inverness-shire Campbell (1902) 194–7. NH 5246 **Beinn a' Bhric, Lochaber, Inverness-shire** Campbell (1900) 122; Grant (1925) 7, 10. NN 3164 **Black Rock Gorge, Ross and Cromarty** Briggs (1970–1) B1, 111; Miller (1835) 215–21. NH 5967 Balconie Point: NH 6365 **Cave of Raitts, Lynchat, Inverness-shire** MacBain (1922) 267–8; Swire (1963) 42–3. NH 7701 **Clava Cairns, Croy and Dalcross, Inverness-shire** Close-Brooks (1986) 159, 162; Swire (1963) 84–5. NH 7644 **Conon House, Ross and Cromarty** [Gibbings] (1889) 39–42; Keightley (1850) 466; Miller (1854) 193–5. NH 5353 **Craig Phadrig, Inverness-shire**

Black's (1844) 337; Close-Brooks (1986) 133, 138; MacRitchie (1892) 106–8; Swire (1963) 5–6. NH 6445 **Cromarty, Ross and Cromarty** Briggs (1970–1) B1, 152–3; Miller (1835) 18–21. NH 7867 **Culloden Battlefield, Inverness-shire** Balfour (2003) 164; Black's (1844) 554; Howitt (1840) 51–79; Mackenzie (1877) 7; Pennant (1772) 165; Reid (2005) *passim*; Westwood and Simpson (2005) 44–5. NH 7445 area **Dun Telve and Dun Troddan, Glenelg, Inverness-shire** Grinsell (1976) 54; Murchison (1963) 303–5. NG 8317 **Dundreggan, Inverness-shire** Campbell (1872) 29–30; Swire (1963) 251–2. NH 3114 **Fearn, Ross and Cromarty** Miller (1835) 363–4. NH 8377 *Picts, Pechs, and Pixies* Chambers (1870) 80–2; Philip (1995) 227–8; Spence (1946) 3–4, 115–19. **Fort George, Inverness-shire** NH 7757 **Fortrose, Ross and Cromarty** Campbell (1900) 272–3; [Gibbings] (1889) 5–8; Mackenzie (1877) *passim*. NH 7256 **Gaick Forest, Inverness-shire** Campbell (1900) 300–3. NN 7584 **General Wade's Military Road, Inverness-shire** Chambers (1827) vol. 2, 342–3; Close-Brooks (1986) 49–50; Swire (1963) 225; Westwood (1985) 343–6. NH 9243 area **Glen Mallie, Inverness-shire** Campbell (1900) 197–8. NN 0887 **Glen Moriston, Inverness-shire** Bord, *Footprints* (2004) 48, 195–6, and 239, n. 68, citing Andreas Trottmann, 'Well of the Phantom Hand', *Athene* 16 (Autumn 1997), 8, and recent information and local details also from Andreas Trottmann. NH 4216 **Grenish Stone Circle, Duthil, Inverness-shire** Cash (1906) 245–9; Swire (1963) 30–1. NH 9116 **Inverness, Inverness-shire** Davidson (1949) 30, 32–3; Fraser (1905) 446–7. NH 6644 **Kintail, Ross and Cromarty** Campbell (1902) 35–6. Kintail Forest: NG 9917 **Knockfarril Vitrified Fort, Fodderty, Ross and Cromarty** Campbell (1900) 272–3; Mackenzie (1877) 8–9. NH 5058 **Laggan, Inverness-shire** Grant Stewart (1823) 189–98; Polson (1932) 147–9. NN 6194 **Lochaber, Inverness-shire** Carmichael (1900) vol. 2, 287; MacGregor (1947) 2–3; Robinson (1985) 117. NJ 0759 **Loch Meig, Inverness-shire** Campbell (1900) 246–7. NH 3555 to NH 3557 **Loch Ness, Inverness-shire** Anderson (1961) 387–9; Campbell (1994) vol. 1, 489; Chambers (1827) vol. 2, 322–3; Gregor (1881) 38–9, 187–8; Miller (1835) 60. NH 5023 *The Loch Ness Monster* Bauer (1986); Gould (1930); Gould (1933); 'Loch Ness Monster' (1933); MacKinlay (1893). **Lochslin, Ross and, Cromarty** Briggs (1970–1) B1, 359–60; Miller (1835) 111–12. NH 8380 **Moy Hall, Inverness-shire** Donaldson (2000) 401–23; 'Theophilus Insulanus' (1763) 154–5. NH 7736 **Na Caplaich, near Loch**

Ossian, Inverness-shire Cunningham (1989) 65; Westwood (1985) 12–13. NN 3767 **Nigg, Ross and Cromarty** Briggs (1970–1) B1, 8–9; Miller (1835) 183–5. NH 8071 *St Boniface's Well, Munlochy, Ross and Cromarty* NH 6454 *St Michael's Kirk, Ross and Cromarty* Briggs (1970–1) B1, 152–3; Miller (1835) 413–17. NH 7166 **Strathpeffer, near Dingwall, Ross and Cromarty** Campbell (1900) 272–3; [Gibbings] (1889) 5–8; Mackenzie (1877) *passim*. NH 4858 **Sutors of Cromarty, Ross and Cromarty** Miller (1835) 25–31. NH 8067 **Tomnahurich, Inverness-shire** Black's (1844) 552; Campbell (1900) 270–1; Chambers (1827) vol. 1, 333; Grant Stewart (1823) 98–102; Keightley (1850) 387–8; Rhys (1980) vol. 2, 483–4; Swire (1963) 16; Watson (1926) 423. NH 6644 **Torvean Motte, Inverness and Bona, Inverness-shire** Shakespeare, *Macbeth*, 5.1. 30, 33, 41 and 5.9. 35–7; Swire (1963) 7. NH 6443 **Urray, Ross and Cromarty** Miller (1835) 188–90. Easter Urray: NH 5152 Old Urray and Wester Urray: NH 5052 **Well of the Heads, Loch Oich, Inverness-shire** Black's (1845) 353; Bord (1985) 9–10; Ross (1993) 147–8; inscription copied from monument by J W 1996. NH 3100

WESTERN ISLES

An t-Òb, Harris Carmichael (1900) vol. 2, 253, MacGregor (1947) 42–3. NG 0186 **Ardnadrochaid, Mull** MacGregor (1947) 63–4. NM 7236 **Balephuil, Tiree** Campbell (1885) 250–3; Philip (1995) 414. NL 9641 Barrapol: NL 9542 **Balevullin, Tiree** Campbell (1885) 250–3. NL 9546 Balemartine: NL 9841 **Barra** Wentz (1911) 106–7. NF 6700 area **Baugh, Tiree** MacGregor (1947) 46. NM 0244 **Beinn Mhor, South Uist** Carmichael (1900) vol. 2, 300–1; MacGregor (1947) 56–8. NF 8131 **Berneray** Aubrey (1721) 212; Keightley (1850) 396; Martin (1703) 300–70 *passim*, particularly 310, 332–3. NL 5580 **Boreraig, Skye** Donaldson (2000) 401–23; *Journal of the Folk-Song Society* 4 (1914) 157–60; Mac-Dougall (1910) 175–81; MacGregor (1947) 34–6; Manson (1901) 268; Philip (1995) 466–7. NG 6116 **Bornais, South Uist** Carmichael (1900) vol. 2, 26. NF 7329 **Breacacha, Coll** Campbell (1900) 166; Campbell (1902) 30–3; MacGregor (1947) 61; Philip (1995) 418–19. Breacacha Castle: NM 1553 **Broadford, Skye** Douglas (1977) 134; Macpherson (2005) 100–3. NG 6423 **Callanish Standing Stones, Uig, Lewis** Bord (1973) 26; Bord (1979) 34–5; Spence (1948) 145; Wood-Martin (1895)

302–3. NB 2133 **Calve Island** Campbell (1900) 225–6. NM 5254 **Ceallan, Grimsay** [Morrison] (1978) 1–2. NF 8856 **Colonsay** Bruford and MacDonald (1994) 318–19, 470–1; Campbell (1900) 109–22. NR 3893 **Corryvreckan** Martin (1703) 236–8; Swire (1961) 20–1; Swire (1964) 167. NM 6901 **Dun Bhuirg, Mull** Bord, *Fairy Sites* (2004) 215; Campbell (1994) vol. 1, 422–4; Grinsell (1976) 230; MacNab (1970) 208–9. NM 4226 **Dun Buidhe, Benbecula** Carmichael (1900) vol. 2, 226–7; MacGregor (1947) 298–300. NF 7955 **Dunvegan Castle, Skye** Black's (1844) 292; Black's (1855) 518–19; Campbell (1900) 5–6; Jackson (1959) 75–9; MacGregor (1947) 20–2; Philip (1995) 306–7. NG 2449 **Eigg** Frazer (1707) 6–9; Martin (1703) 331–2. NM 4686 *Second Sight A Collection of Rare and Curious Tracts . . .* (1820) *passim*; Martin (1703) 300–15; 'Streamline' (1934) 7; 'Theophilus Insulanus' (1763) *passim*. **Eilean Anabaich, North Harris** Campbell (1900) 201–2. NB 2005 **Eilean Trodday (Trondaidh)** Carmichael (1928–54) vol. 5, 300–1. NG 4478 **Fingal's Cave, Staffa** Boece (1938–41) vol. 1, 300; Keats (1958) vol. 1, 26 July 1818, 348–9; Martin (1703) 152–3; *Scots Magazine* 34 (1772), 637; Todd (2003) 216. NM 3235 **Fladda-chuain** Swire (1961) 40, 56–7. NG 3681 **Iona** NM 2824 **Kilchoman, Islay** Campbell (1900) 38–9; Campbell (1994) vol. 2, 418–20. NR 2163 **Kilvickeon, Ross of Mull** Campbell (1900) 298–300. NM 4120 **Loch Finlaggan, Islay** Campbell (1885) 337–8. NR 3867 **Loch Gruinart, Islay** Campbell (1895) 5–6; MacGregor (1947) 51–3. NR 2870 **Loch na Mna, Raasay** Campbell (1900) 209–10; Edmonston and Saxby (1888) 226–7; Spence (1948) 135–6. NG 5838 **Lochbuie, Mull** Campbell (1902) 111–19; [Gibbings] (1889) 72–5. NM 6125 **Losgaintir, Harris** MacGregor (1947) 306. NG 0899 Tràigh Niosaboist: NG 0597 Àird Niosaboist: NG 0598 **The Minch** Archibald (1994) 59–60; Campbell (1900) 199–200; Spence (1948) 30. NG 7381 **Mull** Campbell (1900) 103–5. NM 6233 **Nunton (Baile nan Cailleach), Benbecula** Bruford and MacDonald

(1994) 358–9, 476; Carmichael (1900) vol. 2, 257–8, 330–1. NF 7753 **Orsay** Campbell (1994) vol. 2, 532–5. NR 1651 **Pabaigh** Bruford and MacDonald (1994) 299, 467; Campbell (1994) vol. 2, 413. NL 6087 **Raasay** Beard (1934) 37–8; Campbell (1900) 57; Simpson (1908) 108–9. NG 5742 **Reilig Oghrain, Iona** Carmichael (1900) vol. 2, 315–17; MacNab (1970) 208; Scott (1902) vol. 4, 155. NM 2824 **Rodel, Harris** Jackson (1959) 85–7; Philip (1995) 305, 311–12; 'Theophilus Insulanus' (1763) 73–4. NG 0583 **Ruabhal, Benbecula** Bord (1979) 138–9; Carmichael (1900) vol. 2, 80–1. NF 8353 *Saints of Scotland* MacKinlay (1893); MacQuarrie (1997); Towill (1983); Yeoman (1999). **St Brendan's Church, Barra** Carmichael (1900) vol. 2, 232–4. NL 6087 **Sandray** Briggs (1967) 98–9; Campbell (1895) 83–6; Campbell (1994) vol. 1, 414–15; Gill (1932) 210; Philip (1995) 446–7. NL 6491 **Scarba** Armstrong (1970) 83; Swire (1964) 169–72. NM 7004 **South Uist** Bord (1995) 92; Campbell (1902) 188–9; Campbell (1994) vol. 1, 532. NF 7933 **Staoinebrig, South Uist** Carmichael (1900) 12–13. NF 7433 **Stilligarry, South Uist** Carmichael (1900) vol. 2, 280–1; MacGregor (1947) 58. NF 7638 **Stinky Bay (Poll nan Crann), Benbecula** Carmichael (1900) vol. 2, 305; Macdonald Robertson (1998) 150–1; verbal information from Inverness-shire Council. NF 7654 **Tobermory, Mull** Briggs (1970–1) B2, 605; Campbell (1885) 345–7; Campbell (1994) vol. 1, 24–5; Chambers (1827) vol. 2, 404–5; Martin (1703) 253–4, 302. NM 5055 **Trotternish, Skye** Donaldson (2000) 401–23; *Journal of the Folk-Song Society* 4 (1914) 157–60; MacDougall (1910) 175–81; Manson (1901) 87, 247–56; Martin (1703) 150–51; Swire (1961) 59–60, 134–6, 167–8. NG 4554 area Bornesketaig (Borgh na Sgiotaig): NG 3870 **Uisinis, South Uist** Bruford and MacDonald (1994) 309–10, 469; Scott (1910) 5–6. NF 8635 **Upper Druimfin, Mull** Campbell (1900) 63. NM 5253 **Vaul, Tiree** Campbell (1902) 39. NM 0448

INDEX OF MIGRATORY LEGENDS AND TALE TYPES

Jacqueline Simpson

The first catalogue of Migratory Legends was R. Th. Christensen's *The Migratory Legends* (1958), coded ML. This was devised for Norwegian folklore only, but has since been expanded to include material from certain other countries: ML SIT covers 'Suggested Irish Types', and numbers marked with an asterisk are taken from K. M. Briggs's *Dictionary of British Folk Tales* (1970–1). It should be noted, however, that several legends common in Scotland and elsewhere have not as yet been assigned a number. Significant examples are the tale of the bagpiper or fiddler who explores a tunnel and never returns (found throughout Britain and particularly prevalent in Scotland), the anecdote of the talented apprentice murdered by his jealous master (related in Germany, Sweden, and France, as well as in Britain), and the story of the bold tailor confronted with a skeleton or demon that appears piecemeal (told of many Scottish sites and also in the Isle of Man). Other recurrent themes are labelled not as 'tale types' but only as 'motifs', a more detailed form of classification although it includes quite broad descriptions such as 'The king in disguise' and 'The phantom funeral'. We have not attempted to list motif numbers for all tales included in this book, but the general index supplies many motifs and should enable the reader to find stories dealing with particular subjects.

ML 3000 Escape from the Black School 349–50

ML 3021* Impossible task for demon 54–5, 150–1

ML 3025 Carried by the Devil 48–9, 62–3

ML 3026* A contest between magicians 214

ML 3030 The white serpent 375

ML SIT 3036 The ship-sinking witch 347–8, 382, 392–3, 406–7, 408, 473, 476, 500–2

ML 3037* The milk-stealing witch 18–20, 185, 188, 232–4

ML 3040 The witch making butter 347–8

ML 3046* Man turned into witch's horse 288–9, 368–9

ML 3050 At the witches' Sabbath 170–1, 185, 188, 311–12

ML 3055 The witch who was hurt 37–8, 87, 262–3, 372–4, 463–4

ML 3057* The witch-ridden boy/girl 288–9, 368–9

ML 3061* Banning the rats 466

ML 3071* Devil as musician 170–1, 183–5, 231–2, 375–6

ML 4020 The unforgiven dead 103–4, 357

ML 4021* Troublesome ghost laid 4–5, 146–7, 164–6, 273–4 (variant)

ML 4025 The child without a name 286–7

ML 4030 The dead mother revisits her children 34–5, 432–3

ML 4050 The river claims its due 423–4

ML 4060 The mermaid's message 182, 473

ML 4075 Visit to fairyland 119, 127–8, 222–3

ML 4077* Caught in fairyland 93–4, 147, 389, 392

ML 4080 The seal woman 404–5, 412–15 (variant: mermaid)

ML 4081* The wounded seal 413–14

ML SIT 4086 The Water-horse as work horse 335–6, 340

ML SIT 4086B Riding the Water-horse 91, 331, 337, 350–1, 364–5, 387–8, 441–4

ML SIT 4091 Music taught by fairies 388–91, 481–2, 502–3

ML 5006* The flight with the fairies 7–8, 27–8, 67,

95–6, 119, 178–9, 220–1, 273, 312–13, 393–4, 438

ML 5020 Devil (or giant) throws rocks, creates hill, ditch, etc. 65, 102, 139, 171, 265, 301, 386–7, 449–50

ML 5050 The fairies' prospect of salvation 464–5

ML 5060 The fairy (variant: demon) hunter 439–40, 447–8

ML 5070 Midwife to a fairy (variant) 83

ML 5072* Visit to fairyland: time lapse 93–4, 237, 240, 348–9, 359, 388–9

ML 5080 Food from the fairies 481–2

ML 5081* Fairies steal food 295–6

ML 5082* Fairy borrowing 494–5

ML 5085 The changeling 132–3, 479–80

ML 5085* Woman stolen, stock left 7–8, 21–2, 34–5, 290–1, 297, 300, 336–7

ML 5086* Rescue from fairyland 6–8, 28–9, 223, 226, 290–1, 297, 300, 348–9, 359, 429, 432

ML 5087* The trows' bundle 159, 415

ML 6020 The grateful fairy mother 124, 218–19, 279, 488–9

ML 6035 House spirit assists in human work 18–20, 43, 56–7, 60–1, 78–9, 229–30, 295–6, 379, 397

ML 6045 Drinking cup stolen from fairies 39, 470–2, 489

ML 6060 Fairy cattle 367–8, 455, 464–5

ML 6070 Fairies send a message 4, 408

ML SIT 6071 'The fairy hill is on fire!' 177–8

ML 7010 The house-spirit's revenge for being teased or criticised 229–30

ML 7012* The house-spirit's revenge for negligence 64–5, 78–9

ML 7015 The new suit 56–7, 80–1, 93–4, 126–7, 180, 383, 459–60

ML 7016* Laying a Brownie 140–1

ML 7050 The ring in the fish 183–5

ML 7060 The disputed site for a church (or castle) 158–9, 176–7, 254–5, 335, 493

ML 7070 Church bells 77

ML 7080 Legends concerning the plague 56, 150–2, 330

ML 8000 The wars of former times 196–8, 217, 255–6, 370, 407–8, 462–3, 492–3

ML SIT 8009 The sleeping warriors 10–11, 216–17, 251, 254, 260–1, 301, 450–1

ML 8010 Hidden treasures 59–60, 97, 100–2, 177–8, 180–1, 203, 246–7, 341, 350–1

ML 8025 Robber tales 154–5, 158, 283

Folk tales in Antti Aarne and Stith Thompson's *The Types of the Folktale* (1961) that appear in Scotland as Migratory Legends include:

AT 300 The dragon slayer (slaying episode only) 30, 154, 256–7, 334, 415–17, 429, 432

AT 325 The sorcerer's apprentice 232–4

AT 326 The youth who wanted to learn fear 317, 320

AT 327 The children and the ogre 396–7

AT 366 The man from the gallows (variant) 32–3, 41–2, 282

AT 470A The offended skull 43, 46, 399–400

AT 503 The gifts of the Little People 110–11

AT 510A Cinderella 238–9

AT 922 The substitute answers the king's questions 111, 114

AT 934A Predestined death 83–4, 274–5

AT 974 The homecoming husband 29–30

AT 990 The lady restored to life 83–4, 315

AT 1170 A man sells his soul to the Devil 106–7, 175–6, 219–20, 231–2, 246–7, 281–2, 338–9

AT 1174 Making a rope of sand 54–5, 150–1, 354

AT 1521M Mak and the sheep 249–51

AT 1640 The brave tailor 160–1

AT 1645 The treasure at home 71–2 (variant), 180–1

AT 1735 The bribed boy sings the wrong song 412

AT 1889C The split dog 72

AT 1920A Contest in lying 72

AT 1960D The great vegetable 72

AT 2412B The man who had no story 105–6

INDEX

Abbey Craig 208
Abbotsford 209, 214
Aberdeen 290–1
   University 291
Aberdeen, Robert Stewart 322
Achadh a' Bheannaich 343
Achinduin 1
Adam, John 156
Adolphus, Gustavus 349
Agnew, Andrew 133, 146, 159
Aikwood Tower 214
Airlie 291, 294
Aiths Rant 390
alchemists 116
Aldie 48–9
Alexander III 84, 249
Allan, John Hay 75, 352
Allanbank 215
Allen, Milner 156
Alloway 170–1
Alva, Lady 95
An t-Òb 455
Anderson, Otto 407
Anderson, Rabbie 379
Angel of Death 297
Angus the Tailor 492
Annandale 121
Anne of Denmark 269
Anstruther or Anster family 69, 98
Anwoth 133–4
Appin Hill 4
Apprentice's Pillar 278–9
Aquhorthies 294
Arbroath 200, 294–5
Arbuthnott 295
Archibald, Malcolm 485

Ardnadrochaid 455, 458
Ardrossan 71
Ardvreck Castle 343, 346
Argyll, Countess of 249
Argyll, Duke of 27, 42, 43
Armstrong, Anne 289
Armstrong, Archie 250
Armstrong, Johnnie 148–50, 218, 250–1
Arran 4–5, 33, 38
Arthur, King 94, 216, 376, 450–1
Arthur's Seat 216–17
artists and architects 156–7, 263
Assipattle and the Mester Stoorworm 415
Athelstaneford 217
Aubrey, John 79, 168, 312, 332, 461, 474
Auchabrick House 124
Auchengruith 124
Auchindarroch 5–6
Auchneight 124–5
Auchriachan 295–6
Auldhame 218
aurora borealis 389, 485

Bail Hill 125
Balcarres 49
Balcomie Castle 49, 54
Balconie 419
Balephuil 458
Balevullin 458–9
Balfour, J. A. 34
Balfour family 397
ballads xi 224–5, 227, 301, 309, 327, 407, 454, 501
Ballater 296–7
Balmachie 297
Balwearie Castle 54–5
Banff 300–1

Banks, Joseph 478
Bannatyne family 176
Bannockburn 57
Banquo 92, 318, 320, 437
banshee 9, 19, 187, 311, 502
Barbour, John 88, 162, 179, 189, 195
Barclay family 330
Baring-Gould, Sabine 263
Barnbougle Castle 217
Barncorkrie fairy 161
Barnhill's Bed 218
Barra 459
Barrapol 458
barren ground 148
Barton, William 231
Bass Rock 218
Baugh 459–60
bean-nigh 469
Bean, Sawney 200–1
Bear's Bait or Ring 394
Beard, Charles 166, 307
Beath, David 84
Beaton, David 341
Beaton's Mill 58
Beattie, George 336
Beauly xi, 418–19
Bede, Cuthbert 4
Bedrule 218–19
beetles 275
beggars 8, 29, 69, 98, 161, 244, 284, 382
Beinn A' Bhric 419
Beinn A' Ghlò 55–6
Beinn Iadain 6–7
Beinn Mhor 460
Bell, Adam 121
Bell, John 142
Bell, Routledge 97
Bell Rock 328
Bellenden, John 108
bells 109 see also church bells
Ben Loyal 346–7
Benderloch 7
Bennachie 301
Bennane Head 200
Bentinck, Charles 356
Beowulf 395
Berneray 460–1
Bessie Bell and Mary Gray 56
Bett, Henry 359

Beveridge, David 77, 82, 89
Bible 33, 80, 112, 114, 124, 133, 140, 147, 162–6, 251,
    255, 291, 342, 383, 415, 441, 464–5, 480, 483
Big Gormal 1
Big Kennedy 440
Big Ploughman 481
Big Smith 482–3
Biggar 171
Bilzy Young 72
Binns, The 219–20
Birsay 403
Bittem, Bessie 73
Black, G. F. 385, 387, 414
Black, Joseph 185
Black Agnes 285
Black Chanter 308
Black Dog's Day 467
Black Doideag 476
Black Donald 7, 494
Black Door, The 6
Black Elf 482
Black Lad MacCrimmon and the Banshee 502
Black Officer of Ballychroar 435
Black Rock Gorge 419, 422–3
Black's Picturesque Tourist of Scotland 56, 58, 68,
    74, 92, 95, 108, 135, 161, 178, 218, 223, 226, 227,
    237, 241, 246, 249, 264, 278, 287, 303, 387, 426,
    450, 454, 470, 471
Blackadder, Jenny 215
Blackett Tower 126
Blackhouse 224
blacksmiths 111, 134, 154, 245, 260, 283, 288, 289,
    338, 369, 479
Blackwaterfoot 33
Bladderum 4
blade-bone (speal-bone) divination 426, 492
Blainslie 230
Blair, John 204
Blair, Robert 106–7
Blind Harry 204
blood stains 249
Bloody Bell 126
Blue Men 400, 485
Blue Stone 65
boars 295, 376
Bodach Glas 19
Boddam 302
Bodesbeck Farm 126–7
body parts 4, 12–13, 28, 117

bodysnatching 85, 244, 298–9, 302

Boe, John A. 160

Boece, Hector 94, 100, 108, 197, 217, 318, 478

Boghall 203

Boghall Farm 56–7

bones 31, 43, 104, 267, 283 *see also* skeleton; skulls

    bonfires 304–5

Bonnie Dundee *see* Graham of Claverhouse, John

Bord, Janet xi, xiii, xv, 44–5, 18, 109–10, 281,

    436, 493

Boreraig 461–2

Borestone 57–8

Borgue 127–8

Bornais 462–3

Borron Point 128

Boswell, James 482

Bovet, Richard 222

Bow-Brig-Sky 220

Bowden 220–1

Bowland 221

Boyfriend's Death 67

Braco, Laird of 300

Bradley, Edward 4

Brahan Seer (Coinneach Odhar) 426, 433, 439,

    448

Bran (Fingal's dog) 8, 11, 38, 429, 467

Brand, John 383, 385, 400, 401, 402, 409

Brave Tailor 160

Breacacha 463–4

Breacan 469

    Prince 496

Brereton, Henry L. 338

Bridge of Awe 7–8

Bridge of Potarch 303

bridges and causeways 139, 354, 356, 477

Brigadoon 170

Brig o' Doon 170

Brig-o'-Stanes 220

Briggs, Katharine ix, 60, 120, 229, 255, 295, 303,

    317, 327, 339, 364, 379, 422, 444

Brims o'Brims 347

Brindister 379

Broadford 464–5

Broch of Houlland 390

brochs 235, 360, 382, 387, 428

Brockaw 222

Brodie, William 157

Brollachan 488, 497

Broon, Tam *see* 'helpin' Tam Broon'

Bromyard, John of 80

Brown, Alexander 458

Brown, Dan 279

Browne, John Hutton 244, 265

brownies 9, 18, 25, 56–7, 60, 78, 79, 80–1, 90, 126,

    140, 147, 159, 177, 180, 191, 220, 229, 287, 310,

    317, 328, 383, 397, 440, 459, 461, 497

Bruan Broch 348–9

Bruce, Robert the x, 19, 33–4, 46, 57, 73, 108, 167,

    192, 246, 256, 260, 264, 311

Brude, King 423, 424, 437

Bruford, Alan 296, 488

Buchan, David 138

Buchan, Peter 235, 239

Buckhaven 58–9

Buckland Glen 129

building legends 133, 176, 180, 255, 256, 307, 323–

    6, 335, 339, 493

Bullock, George 209

Burghead 303

burials 73, 104, 182, 196, 267, 280, 316, 358, 458,

    485

    of hearts 167

Burke, John Bernard 135

Burke, William 244

Burn of Eathie 132

Burnard, Alexander 311

Burness, John 97, 317

Burnett family 311

Burnfoot Pool 274

burning of the clavie 304

Burns, Robert 170, 178, 179, 198–9, 317, 503

Burnside 379, 382

Burrow Head Forts 132

Burton, George 222

Bute 15, 33, 39–40, 46

Caerlaverock ix, 132–3

Cailleach 352–3, 419

    Bhéarra 469

    of Clash Breac 350

cairns 20–1, 31, 39–40, 43, 46, 265, 343, 436, 461

Cairnshee 304–5

Caisteal A Choin Duibh 8–9

cakes 291

Calder, James 348, 354, 362, 366

Caldron Linn 68

calendar 264

Callanish Standing Stones 465–6

Calton Hill 222–3
Calum Clever 22, 27
Calve Island 466
Camden, William 435
Campbell family 19, 23, 26, 30–1, 41, 76, 376
Campbell, Lord Archibald 1, 9, 13–14, 19, 23, 29–31, 34–5, 40, 42–3, 47, 76, 458, 481, 500
Campbell, Sir Colin 29
Campbell, Dugald 40–1
Campbell, Lady Elspeth 23, 27
Campbell, John Francis xi, 14, 127–8, 147, 239, 378, 407, 429, 479, 487–8, 494, 496–7, 501
Campbell, John Gregorson xi, 5–7, 9–12, 18–20, 22, 24, 27–8, 32, 35–7, 39, 43, 55, 63, 67, 77, 83, 90, 111, 133, 190, 192, 353, 363–4, 367, 375, 384, 404, 413, 418, 435–6, 438–9, 441, 448, 450, 455, 463–4, 466–7, 469–70, 473, 480–3, 485, 495, 497, 504
Campbell, Peter 42
Campbell, Rob 347
Campbell, Tam 151
Campdalmore 305–6
Camus, King 335
Camus-a-Ghuirm 1
candles 54, 120, 203, 262, 273
Canmore, Malcolm 97
cannibals 200–1, 294
Canon, James F. 134
Canongate 248
Caol-Reithe 429
Cardenden 59
Cardoness Castle 133–4
Carfin Lourdes Grotto 171, 174
Carlops, The 223
Carlyle, Thomas 145
Carmichael, Alexander 13–14, 25, 440, 458, 460, 486, 489, 493–4, 497, 499
Carnwath 174–5
Carrick 175–6, 206
Carsgoe 349
Carskiey 9
Carterhaugh 223, 226
Cash, C. G. 437
Castle Campbell 68
Castle Duart 501
Castle Knowe 241
Castle Law 59–60
castle of glass 424
Castle Stalker 9, 12

cats 73, 284, 342, 372, 393, 402, 438–9, 476, 501, 504
cattle 5, 6, 18, 22, 232, 284, 305, 341, 360, 446, 455, 459, 466, 470, 486–7
Cauld Lad o'Hilton, The 104
Cauldshiels Loch 226–7
caves and caverns 33–4, 35, 59, 70, 74, 88–9, 108, 110, 130, 163, 178–9, 200, 217, 294, 301, 352, 355, 374, 377, 384, 396, 422, 468–9
 Cave of Gold 502
 Cave of the Goblin 89
 Cave of Raitts 423
 Fingal's 476–9
Cawdor Castle 306
Ceallan 466–7
Challum, Alasdair 77, 450
Chambers, Robert ix, xi, 229, 239, 501
 Book of Days 61, 100, 250
 Domestic Annals of Scotland 158
 Picture of Scotland 68, 70–3, 76, 85, 92–4, 96–8, 116–17, 144, 166, 171, 174–5, 184, 203, 205, 244, 247, 274, 282, 294–5, 319, 328, 435, 441, 451
 Popular Rhymes 32, 100, 126–7, 176–8, 180, 189, 235, 286–7, 329, 334, 431
Chambers, William 131
changelings 28, 125, 132, 290, 411, 473, 479
Changue Forest 175–6
Chanonry Lighthouse 433
Chapel O'Sink 307
Charles, Rev. Mr 327
Charles I 72, 219, 251, 349
Charles II 75, 93, 115, 202, 219, 313
charms 22, 33, 43, 281, 385, 401, 474
Chattan family 308
Cheese Well 265
Cheyne, Reginald 366
Child, F. J. 195
child-stealing see changelings
childbirth 81, 266, 300, 316, 337, 488
children 35, 186–7
 children's customs 190, 246, 255
Chincough Well 44
Christmas 304, 483
churches 102
church bells 77
Cinderella 238, 298, 415
Clach Clais an Tuire 350
Clach-Tholl 13

Clachan 12–13
Clark, Andrew 93
Clarke, George 43
Claunch 134
Clava Cairns 423
Cleish, Lady 266
Cleppie Bells 154
Clochfoldich Farm 60–1
Closeburn Castle 135
clouties 44
Cluny Castle 308
Cnoc na h-Uiseig 348
coats 42–3
cocks 425
Cockburn's Castle 99, 227
Coeffin Castle 13–14
Coilsfield House 197
Coilus, King 196
cold iron 5, 6, 28, 297, 361, 441
Coleheart, Tom 261
Collin Farm 135–7
Colmonell 189
Colonsay 467–8
Colvadale 382
Colvil, Alexander 66
Colzium House 61
Comiston 227–8
Conon House 365, 423–4
Copinsay 383
Cora Linn 176, 207
Coronation Chair 234
Corrichie 308–9
Corrie, John 150
Corryvreckan 468–9, 495
Court of Keeldar's Grave 228
Couthalley Castle 176–7
Coutts, Madge 393
Covenanters 86, 93, 141, 152, 179, 190, 219, 246, 284, 313
Cowhill Tower 137–8
Craig-Aulnaic 310
Craig Phadrig 424
Craigdarroch 138
Craighall 61, 64
Craiginnan 64–5
Craigleith 95
Craignish 8–9, 469
Crail x, 65
Cramond Bridge 228–9

Cranshaws Farm 229–30
Crathes Castle 310–11
Craufurdland Bridge 177
Crawick 138–9
Creag Bheag and Mhór 349–50
Creagan 14–15
Creich 66
Crichton, Abraham 164
Criffel 139
Crockett, Samuel 155, 200
Cromarty 425–6
Cromek, R. H. 124, 126, 132, 137, 139–40, 159, 189, 196, 314
Crotach, Alastair 470
Crowe, C. 215
Crusades 30, 193, 217, 234, 471
Cuddyhall 230
Cullivoe 379, 398
Culloden 308
    Battlefield 426–8
Culross Abbey 65–7, 77
Culzean Castle 178–9
Cumberland, Duke of 426
Cunnigar 264
Cunningham, A. D. 111, 445
Cunningham, Alan 128
Cunningham, William 258
Cunninghame 179–80
cups 219, 312–13, 489
cures 44–5, 90, 108–9, 192, 280, 281, 366, 375, 385, 401, 403, 411, 444, 473, 497
Curry, Walter de 144
curses 13, 54, 189, 270, 321, 340, 359, 362, 463, 484

Dàl Riara 17
Dalbeattie Burn 139
Dalhousie Castle 230
Dalkeith 230–1
Dalmeny 231–2
Dalnacardoch 67
Dalriada 17
Dalry 179–80
Dalrymple, James 241
Dalswinton 140–1
Dalyell, Thomas 86–7 143, 145, 153, 219
Danis Wark 106
Danish 91, 106, 252, 269
Darnley, Lord 249

David I 248, 318
David II 256
Davidson, Thomas 71
dead head 305
Dead-Men's-Holm 197
Dead Men's Rock 216
deafness 90
death, semblance of 84, 315
death lights 150
death omens/prophecies 15–6, 19, 84, 125, 135, 141, 150, 230, 280, 311, 483
Deel 170
Deel Burn 98
deeps of Carsgoe 349
deer 310, 352, 419, 434, 468
Defoe, Daniel 197, 200
Deil's Cauldron 15
Deil's Crale 79
Deil's Mitten 265
Delnabo 311–12
Deloraine 232–4
demons x, 7, 13, 88
Den of the Ghost 89
Den of Pitcarles 295
Denny 67–8
Devil x, 15, 62, 114, 201, 219, 270, 284, 298, 311, 314, 316–17, 325, 338, 435, 503
    appearances of 1, 7, 9, 12–13, 32, 41–2, 65, 72, 77, 79, 85, 96–7, 102, 105, 117, 139, 171, 177, 179, 184, 228, 231, 242, 255, 265, 269, 272, 322, 340, 342, 354, 367–8, 440, 447
    'devil a one' 422
    land set aside for 243
    marks of 41, 354
    pact with 95, 103, 106–7, 142–3, 175, 188, 281, 346, 349, 373–4, 376, 382
Devil's Mill 68
Devorguilla 166
Dhu, Iain 181
Diarmaid's Grave 376
Dick, C. H. 146, 155, 158, 182
Din, Donald 180
Dingwall 449
Dinsdale, Tim 38
Dirk Hatteraick's Cave 130
Dirlot Castle 350–1
Dixon, John 370
Dodags 501
Dog Rock 481

dogs 4, 8, 13, 39, 64–5, 72, 97, 128, 144, 188, 217, 232, 246, 258, 262, 276–8, 312, 333, 339, 422, 439, 446–7, 450, 455, 463, 481, 486, 489, 495–6, 503
Doideagan 501
Dollar 68–9, 93, 104, 114
Dolphinton 180
Domhull Dubh 494
Donaldson, Andrew 194
Donaldson, William 462
Donizetti, Gaetano 242
Donn, Rob (Robert Mackay) 362, 369–70
Doo Wells 45
doppelganger 320
Dornoch Cathedral ix, 351–4
Dornoch Firth 356
Douchtie, Thomas 265
Douglas, George 222, 238, 415, 465
Douglas, James 264
Douglas, Janet 202, 324
Douglas Tragedy, The 224
doves 434
Dowalton Loch 141
Downie 291
dragons 257, 334, 395
Dreamin' Tree Ruin, The 15
dreams 6, 15, 29, 137, 180, 203, 248, 306, 467, 500
    nightmares 369
Dreel Castle 69
Drever, Helen 9
drinking 117–19
drowning 304, 315, 337, 341, 467, 476
Druids 294, 343, 403, 437, 479, 492
Drumelzier 234
    burn 274
Drumlanrig Castle 141, 144
drummer 222
Drummond, James 302
Drummossie Moor 426
Dryden, John 339
Dryfesdale 144
Duffus Castle 312–13
Dugdale, William 181
Dumbarton 70
    Rock 102
Dumbuck Hill 102
Dumyat 71
dun 429
Dun Bhuirg 469

Dun Buidhe 469–70
Dun Ghallain 15–16
Dun Telve 428
Dun Troddan 428
Dunadd 17–18
Dunbar, William 253
Dunblane 72, 96
Dundaff Linn 207
Dundas, Robert 372
Dundee 313–15
Dundee, Bonnie see Graham of Claverhouse,
     John
Dundonald Castle 180–1
Dundreggan 429
Dunfermline 72–4
     Abbey 73
dungeons 54, 76
Dunideen Hill 100
Dunlop, Bessie x, 271, 276
Dunnet Sands 354
Dunollie Castle 18
Dunrossness 384
Dunskey Castle 144
Dunstaffnage Castle 18–20
Dunvegan Castle 470–2
Dunvuilg 469
Durness 363, 374
Dwarfie Stane 384–6
dwarves 347, 385
Dwarwick Head 354

Each Uisge 367
Earlston 234
earth 401, 408
East Yell Parochial School 394
Easter Wemyss 74–5
Ecclefechan 145
Eday 385
Edderton 449
Edgewell Tree 230
Edinburgh Castle 234–5
Edin's Hall Broch 235–7
Edmonston, Biot 382, 384, 392, 393, 430
Edrom 215
Edward I 235, 255, 285
Edward II 255, 260
Edzell 315–16
     churchyard 315–16
eels 90

Eigg 472–3
Eighth Part Measure of a Carle 482
Eildon Hills 100, 237, 240, 260
Eilean Anabaich 473
Eilean Dunibeg 431
Eilean Troddday 473, 476
elf-shot 8, 22, 284, 482, 487
elves 22
Ericstane Hill 145–6
Erne's Knowe
Errack Burn 219–20
Errol 75
Ettrick Water 240
Eyemouth 240–1

Faas/Faws 251
fairies ix, x, 4, 20, 28, 34–5, 56, 78, 85, 90, 95–6,
     112–13, 125, 161, 190–1, 222, 228, 241, 243,
     248, 254, 265, 273, 291, 298, 304, 318, 323,
     332, 333, 337, 348, 354, 356, 359, 360, 382,
     389, 390, 394, 408, 410, 413, 428, 430, 444,
     445, 450, 458, 459, 465, 467, 479, 484, 485,
     486, 503,
     arrows (elf-shot) 8, 22, 482, 487
     borrowing 124, 494
     cups 9, 471, 489
     Fairies Hill/Mound 34, 260, 348, 448
     Fairy Queen 237, 276, 369
     farewell 132
     flag 470–1
     flights with 27, 67, 191, 312, 331–2
     footmark 18
     helpful and grateful 64, 161, 178–9, 218–19,
          279, 469, 482, 488
     mortal held captive 45, 226
     mortal visits fairyland 39, 93, 110, 119, 127,
          147, 451, 504
     request Christianity 464–5
     seeing 83
     stealing children see changelings
     stealing women 6–7, 7, 21–2, 159, 290–1, 297,
          432
     stocks 8, 21, 159, 290, 294, 296–7, 336
     and witches 271
Fairknowe 285
falcons 95
Falkland 75–6
Fall of Connel 352
falling stars 426

Falls of Clyde 176
False Men, The 465
Farnell 316–17
Farnie, Henry 96
Farquhar, Dr 375
Fast Castle 241–2
Fat-lips castle 206
fatal jest 291
Feadan Dubh 308
Fearn 432–3
Fenella 328
Feodail 88
Fergus the Great of Ireland 17
Ferguson, Major 472
Fergusson, Alexander 143
Fergusson, R. Menzies 397, 403, 406, 407
Ferrie's Brass Pan, Da 408
Fetlar 386–7, 389, 392
Fiddes Castle 317, 320
fiddlers 300, 379, 388, 389, 390–1, 413, 451
Finella's Castle 328
Fingal 8, 10–11, 21, 33, 38, 106, 216, 376, 428–9,
    450, 467, 476–9
    Fingal's Cave 476–9
    Fingal's Chair 478
    Fingal's dog *see* Bran
    Fingal's Limpet Hammers 478
    Fingal's Well 439
Finlarig 76–7
Finnieston Quay 181–2
Fir Bhreig 465
Firth of Clyde 182
fish 183–4, 497
Fisher Willie 69
fishermen 58, 96, 128, 189, 206–7, 267, 363, 367,
    382, 398–400, 405, 412–14, 453, 479, 483
Fladda-Chuain 479
flags 57, 217, 470
flax 444
flies 331
Florida (ship) 500
Fluker 386
Flying Dutchman 357
Fodderty 438–9
folklore, definition of ix
fools 18, 111, 114, 221, 250
footprints 17–18, 42, 301, 352, 436
Forbes, Duncan 426
Forres 320

Fort George 156
Fortrose 433–4
Forest, Ettrick 127
Forest of Mar 352
Forss Water 360
fortune-telling 33, 77, 223, 254
Fossoway 77
Foul Ford 259
Foula 387–8
Fraser, Gordon 152
Fraser, James 115, 437–8
Fraser, Simon 462
Frazer, John 472, 474
freemasons 462
Friarton Island 77
Friday 111
fride 498
frogs 337, 476
Fuath 488, 497
Fyvie Castle 321–2

Gabhar 87
Gaick Forest 434
Gairn, Glen 326–7
Galashiels 242–3
Galdenoch Castle 146
Gallow Hill 97
Galloway 124–5, 130–1, 139
gambling 325
Games Loup 182–3
Garbh Shlios 20
Garden, Dr James 312, 331
Garioch 307
Garner, Alan 488
Garrywhin 355–6
Gatehouse of Fleet 147
General Wade's Military Road 435–6
Geoffrey of Monmouth 275
George IV 252
George VI 453
Gervase of Tilbury 424
ghosts 23, 26, 31, 49, 54, 96, 103–4, 118, 124, 129,
    152, 205, 217, 220, 247, 256, 261–2, 272–3, 276,
    284, 298, 310, 325–6, 351, 363, 371, 392–3, 418,
    441, 448, 452, 488–9, 497
    as death omens 19
    body-parts missing 14, 28, 500
    bridegrooms 137–8
    carriages/coaches 134, 141, 143, 297

Dalyell, Tam 219–20
dogs 217, 276–8
dungeons 49, 54, 165
golden arm 32–3
graveyards 28, 164, 184, 282, 286–7, 305
Green Jean 119–20
green ladies 311, 333
grey ladies 267–8
guilty secret 65, 357
headless 129, 167, 483–4
horses 86, 104
John Knox 106
laying 145–7, 273–4
legal cases 221
murders 61, 64, 316–17, 323–4
Old Red-Cap 126
Pearlin Jean 215
pipers 144, 322–3
procession of the dead 259
ships 124, 128
smugglers 59
treasure/goldmine 60, 100, 257–8
white ladies 151–2, 227–8, 333, 433
giants x, 7, 20–1, 35–6, 106, 111, 118–19, 160, 235,
    301, 385–6, 396, 423, 449, 465, 473, 476–7
Giants' Graves 20–1
Gibbon, Lewis Grassic 295
Gicht Castle 322–3
Gill, Walter 291
Gilles, Harry 220, 262
Gilmerton Grange 268
Gilnockie Tower 148–50
Gizzen Briggs 356–7
Glaistigs 5–6, 9, 18–20, 24–5, 35, 43, 440, 455, 464
    Glaistig Stone 5
    Glaistig's young one 43
Glammis Tower 84
Glamis Castle 323–6
Glasgow xii, 156, 183–6
Glasserton Parish 163–4
Glen Errochty 77–8
Glen Fincastle 78–9
Glen Gairn 326–7
Glen Mallie 436
Glen Moriston 436
Glen Nevis 419
Glenbervie 327–8
Glencairn 150
Glendevon 71–2, 79

Glenluce Abbey 150–1
Glenstockdale House 21–2
Glundubh, Nial 471
goats 87, 440
goblins 101
gold 100, 116, 206, 265, 502
Gomme, G. L. 166–7
Goodman's Croft 243
Goomhill 104
Gord 388–9
Gordon, George 309
Gordon, J. F. S. 307
Gordon, Robert 338
Gordon of Strathnaver 366
Gordonstoun 338
Gormal Mor 1
Gormshuil 476
Gormyre 243
Gorrenberry 243–4
Gortan 22
Gould, R. T. 442
Gowdie, Isobel 233
Graham of Claverhouse, John 49, 153, 313–15
Grant family 79, 300, 308, 461
Grant, K. W. 4, 13, 20–2, 36, 352, 419
Grant Stewart, W. 295, 311
Grassmarket 244
graves and graveyards 28, 41, 56, 184, 186, 228,
    282, 284, 358, 485
Gray Hulse, Tristan xiii, xv, 490–1
Green Castle 328
Green Hollow 85
Green Jean 119
Greenbank 389
Greenlaw Moor 244–5
Greenteeth, Jinny or Jenny 186–7
Gregg, John 200–1
Gregor, Walter 321, 326, 340, 365, 444
Grenish Stone Circle 436–7
Grey Dog's Sound 497
grey ladies 267–8
Grey Neighbours see trows
Grey Paw, The xi, 418
Greyfriars Kirk 245–6
Grierson, Robert x, 142–3, 145, 153
Grievehill 185
griffon 295
Grinsell, Leslie 307, 403, 406
Groat, Malcolm 348

Grose, Francis 165, 170, 178, 279
Grot, John 362
Gruagach of Glen Duror 5
Guanora 94–5
Guardian of the Wild 352–3
Guidman of Ballengeich x, 97–9, 228 *see also*
  James IV; James V
Guidman's Croft 243
gulls 382
Gunn family 351
Gunn, David 360
Gypsies and travellers 74, 97, 175, 194, 251, 283,
  298–300, 303

hair 4
  red 299
Halifax, Lord 325
Hall, James 66
Hallidays of Mayfield 142
Hallowe'en 75, 79, 125, 143, 147, 178, 353, 492
Haltadans 289, 392, 410
Hamilton, Lady Jean 195
Hamilton, Judy 16
Hamilton, Sandie 281
Hammar, Gulla 413
hand- or fingerprints x, 354, 419, 422
Handa 358
hanging the monkey 302
Hare, Augustus 215, 259, 280, 325–6
Hare, William 244
hares 37, 72, 169, 214, 262–3, 284, 314, 463
Harg, Alexander or Sandy 159
Haroldswick 392–3
Harte, Jeremy xiii, xv, 390–1
harvest 353
Hascosay 393
Hatfield, Gabrielle xiii, xv–xvi, 252–3
Hattaraik 281–2
hawks 75
hawthorn tree 306
Hay family 75
healing 283–4, 401, 403, 411, 444, 473, 497
Heather Ale 355, 356, 431
'helpin' Tam Broon' 85
Helmsdale 359
Henderland Castle 227
Henderson, Angus 111
Henderson, Brucie 399
Henderson, George 80, 229, 234, 240, 254, 364

Henderson, Hamish 78
Henderson, John 398
Henderson, Lizanne xiii, xvi, 270–1
Henderson, Mary 4
Henderson, T. F. 227, 287
Henderson, William 233, 247, 256–7, 262, 363
Hendrie, William Fyfe 243, 258
Henry VIII 286
Heriot, Isabel 114, 272–3
Hermitage Garden 246–7
Hermitage Water 243–4
Heroes' Hollow 455
Herries, John 267
Herries, Margaret 268
Heselrig 190, 204
Hewison, James King 15, 33, 37, 40
Heywood, Thomas 259
Higgins, Bella 298
Higgins, John 326
High Ardwell 151–2
Hill, H. W. 23
Hill of Durcha 359
Hill o'Many Stanes 359
hill-forts 18, 132, 167, 284, 450
Hillfoot Farm 79, 82
Hobbs, Sandy xiii, xvi, 156–7
Hog, Alexander 304
hogboon 383
hogboy 383
Hogg, James 121, 181
Holinshed, Raphael 232, 234, 249, 318
Holy Trinity Kirk 92
Holydean 247–8
Holyroodhouse 121, 248–9
hoofprints 31, 251, 283, 341, 352, 374
Horn of Leys 310
Horne, Janet 368
horses 86, 93, 104, 251, 260, 314, 316, 333, 337, 387,
  389, 445, 455, 458, 483
Houll 393–4
House, Jack 102
Houstry 360–1
Howie, John 141, 313
Howieson, John 229
Howitt, William 426
Hoy 384
Hugh of the Little Head 484
Hughbo 383
hunchbacks 110

Hungus, King 217
Hunter, Rev. 164
Hunter, Sandie 281
hunting 4, 55, 258, 366, 419, 468

imps 171, 350, 356
Inch Cape Rock 328–9
Ingram, James 382
Innes, Cosmo 307
Innse Orc, Prince of 8
Insulanus, Theophilus 445, 492
Inveraray Castle 23
Inverawe House 23–7
Inverchaolin 46
Inveresragan 27
Invergowrie 329–30
Inverkip 185, 188–9
Inverness 437–8
Inverurie 330
Iomair nam Fear Mora 429
Irving, Washington 226

Jack, John 65
Jackson, Kenneth 492
James II 115, 306
James III 57, 252
James IV x, 74–5, 97–8, 116, 252, 256, 362
James V x, 75, 97–8, 195, 227–8, 235, 250–1, 253, 265, 324
James VI/I 72, 76, 184, 250, 256, 269, 281, 470
Jardine, Alexander 165
jealous craftsman, the 279
Jed Water 222
Jedburgh 249–51
Jenny with the iron teeth 186
Jervise, Andrew 315, 341–2
Joad, C. M. 363
John o' Groats 361–2
Johnson, Captain Charles 200
Johnson, Dr 478
Johnson, Hakki 390
Johny Faa 194
Junraidh, Marie Nic 4

Kaim of Mathers 330–1
Kay family 308
Keats, John 477
Keeldar 228
Keightley, Thomas 79, 80, 90–1, 405, 436, 451

Keil Point 42
Keiths family 351
Kelly Robertson, N. M. 47
Kelpie's Stane 331
kelpies and water-horses ix, 91, 219, 331, 335–7, 341, 351, 356, 363–5, 387, 423, 442, 444, 482, 488, 497
Kelso 251, 265
Keltie's Mends 117
Keltney, Glen 364
Kelvingrove Art Gallery and Museum 156
Kempock Stone 188
Kennedy family 178
Kennedy, Archibald 190
Kenneth I 75
Kenneth II 235
Kenneth III 328
Keppoch family 454
keys, golden 59
Kiel 28
Kilbride 18–20
Kilchoman 479–80
Kilchrenan 28–9
  Castle 29–30
Kildalloig 30
Killiecrankie 313
Kirk, Robert 465
Kirk Yetholm 251, 254
Kilkerran 189–90
Killernie Castle 82–3
Killiecrankie 115
Killin 83
Kilmaronag 30–1
Kilmichael Glassary 31–2
Kilmore 18–20, 31–2
Kilmory 43
Kilneuair ix, 32
Kilpatrick-Fleming 126
Kilvickeon 480–1
king in disguise 99 *see also* Guidman of Ballangeich
King of the Cats 4
King's Cave 33
Kingarth 33
Kinghorn 83–4
Kinnear, George Henderson 302, 317, 327
Kinneston 84–5
Kintail 110, 438
Kintraw 34–5
Kintyre 9, 30, 41–2, 46–7

Kipling, Rudyard 378
Kirk, Robert 112–13
Kirkcaldy 85
Kirkdamdie, Fair of 175
Kirkmaiden 124
Kirkmichael 331
Kirkpatricks of Closeburn 135, 143
Kirkwaugh 152
Knap 35
Knockdolian Castle 189
Knockfarril Vitrified Fort 438–9
Knockin'-stane 393
Knop of Kebister 409
Knox, John 106
Kyle 180–1, 194
Kylerhea 429
Kylesku 362–3

la-bhallan 369
Lady Burn 189
Lady Glen 189–90
lady restored to life 84, 35
Lag Uaine 85
Laggan 439–40
Lailoken 275
Laing, Alexander 60
Lamb's Loch 332
Lament of the Border Widow, The 227
Lamington 206
Lamkin 82
Lamont, Mary 185, 188, 233
Lamont family 46, 455
Lanark 190
land sale 76
Lang, Andrew 103, 106, 113, 135, 154
Langside 287
Langton House 254–5
Lanimer Day 190
Largiebaan 35–6
Largs 190–2
Lasair Gheug 239
Latheron 343, 348
Laurenson, Gibbie 391
Laurenson, William 379
Lavellan 369
Law, Robert 141
lawsuits 221
leaps 115, 223, 303, 429
Lee, The 192, 194

Lees-Milne, James 27
legend, definition of x
    dissemination of x–xi
Leith 255
Leland, John 435
Leslie 331–2
Leven 85–6
Leyden, John 91, 228, 247, 261, 330
Liberton Well 280
Liethin Hall 126
Lightfoot, Anthony 59
lighthouse 329
Lincoln Cathedral 279
Lindsay, Sir James 322, 324
Lindsay, Robert 294
Lindsay family 315
Linga 394–5
Lingo House 86–7
Linlithgow 255–6
Linton 218, 256
Lismore 1, 12–14, 37–8
little washer 469
Littledean, Laird of 220
Littledean Tower 257–8
Livingston 258
Livingstone family 1, 25, 61
Loch an Daimh 87
Loch Assynt 343
Loch Awe x, 36–7
Loch Aweside 40–1
Loch Baile A' Ghobhainn 37–8
Loch Con 88
Loch Dunvegan 461
Loch Ericht 88
Loch Etive 23, 352
Loch Finlaggan 481–2
Loch Fyneside 85
Loch Gelly 104
Loch Glencoul 363
Loch Greran 14–15
Loch Gruinart 482
Loch Katrine 88–9
Loch Leven 89–90, 102
Loch Lomond 85
Loch Meadaidh 363
Loch Meig 441
Loch mo Naire 363, 366
Loch More 366–7
Loch na Mna 482–3

Loch Neldricken 154
Loch Ness 441–4, 490
Loch of Boardhouse 403
Loch Oich 454
Loch Ossian 445
Loch Rannoch 36
Loch Scridain 469
Loch Shin 359, 367, 371
Loch Shurrery 367
Loch Sloy 90
Loch Ussie 439
Loch Venachar 91
Lochaber 38–9, 353, 440–1
Lochan Uaine xii, 332–3
Lochbuie 483–4
Lochmaben 164–6
lochs, lakes and rivers 59, 68, 135, 141, 340, 350,
    367, 424 see also pools
Lochslin 444–5
Lochy Faulds 104
Logan 194
Loireag 460
Lon Cait 467
Longformacus 259–60, 265
Lorn 18, 22, 30–1
Losgaintir 484–5
Loth 368–9
Loth Stone 284
Lothbeg 377
Low, George 402
Lowe, Lilian 38
Lowrie's Den 283
Lucas, Joseph 254
Lucken Hare, The 260–1
Luggie's Knowe 409
lunatics 67, 108, 406
Luncastry 75
Lundin Links Standing Stones 91–2
Luran 39
lying 72
Lyndsay, David 235, 490
Lyon Cup 324
Lynturk 333–4

MacArthur, John 46
MacBain, Alexander 423
Macbeth 92, 97, 232, 269, 318–20, 324, 406, 437,
    452
McCallum family 69

MacCodrum family 404, 451
McCormick, Andrew 131
MacCrimmon family 461, 502
MacCrimmon, Donald Bàn 445
MacCrimmon, John 115
MacCrimmon School of Music 461–2
MacCulloch family 36, 134
MacCulloch, Diarmaid 264
MacCulloch, Godfrey 125, 158
M'Donald, Alexander 488
MacDonald family 287, 308, 454, 481
Macdonald, Allan 462–3
MacDonald, Archibald 475
MacDonald, Donald 488
Macdonald, Ewan 432
Macdonald, Flora 19
MacDonald, James 482
MacDonald, Johnnie 296–7
MacDonald, Neil 459
MacDougall family 18, 19, 30–1, 40
MacDougall, James 5, 502
MacDuff 319, 328
Macduff's Cross 97
MacDuffy family 467
MacEachain, Angus 497
McEwan, Graham 39
MacEwen 146
Mac Gille Chaluim, Iain Garbh 473
MacGregor family 46
MacGregor, Alasdair Alpin 6, 42, 46, 85, 351, 356,
    367, 455, 470, 484
MacGregor, Jeanie 1
Machrie Moor Stone Circle 38
Macinnes, Mary 460
MacKay family 47, 115
Mackay, Aeneas 65
Mackay, Donald 360
Mackay, Donald Duibheal 349, 354, 368, 374,
    375, 469
McKay, John 14
Mackay, Robert (Rob Donn) 362, 369–70
M'Kean, John 338–9
McKelvie, Shalvach 20
Mackenzie, Alexander 221, 433, 438, 448
Mackenzie, D. 363
Mackenzie, George (Bloody) 221, 245–6
Mackenzie, Wully 426
Mackie, Andrew 135–6
Mackie, William 179

MacKinlay, James 42, 108–9, 303, 331, 334, 401
Mackinnon, Malcolm 40
MacKinnon, Nan 488
MacKonochie family 42
Maclean family 484, 500
McLean, Hector 463
MacLean, John 469
MacLean, Lachlan Mor 482
Maclean, Malcolm 493
Macleod, Angus 471, 492
MacLeod, Donald 445, 492
Macleod, Hugh 489
MacLeod, Norman 460, 473
MacLeod's Fairy Banner 470
McLauchlan, Margaret 153
MacMillan, Angus 487
MacMillan family 35, 121, 146
M'Milligan of Dalgarnock 167
MacNab, P. A. 469
MacNab family 76
MacNeill family 9, 492
MacNeill, F. Marian 119
MacNeill, Malcolm 9
McNicol, Patie 114
MacNiven, John 458
MacPhail family 503
MacPhail, Malcolm 343
MacPherson, Captain 434–5
Macpherson, George 16, 181, 465
Macpherson, James 10, 300, 478
Macphie family 467
MacQuarry family 458
Macrae, David 188
MacRitchie, David 141, 424, 431
MacTaggart, John 151
MacVurich family 498
Maelbrigt 370
Maenalrig Mor 440
Maes Howe 383, 395–6
magic 62, 181, 270, 283, 451
magnetic mountain 346
Magnus Muir 92–3
magpies 284
Maiden Castle 93–4
Maiden Well 69
Maiden of Inverawe 24–5
Maitland, William 216
Malcolm II 176, 324, 335
Malcolm III 73

Man, Andrew 271
Manson, W. L. 398, 461, 503
Mar, Earl of 463
Margaret, Queen of Scotland 280
Marischal College 156
markings x, 301, 335–6, 354, 422, 429, 436, 449
Marochetti, Baron 456
marriages 188 see also weddings
Marshall, Billy 131
Martin, Martin 21, 38, 209, 385, 460, 468, 472, 474, 478, 495, 502
Martin's Stone 334
Marwick, Ernest 383
Martyrs' Tomb 152–4
Mary, Queen of Scots 90, 248, 309
Mary King's Close 261
Masoni, Licia xvi, 238–9
masons 82
Mauthe Doog, The 276
Mavor, William 358
Maxton 220, 262–3
Maxwell family 152
Maxwell, George 202
Maxwell, Herbert 164
May Colven 182
May Day 125, 353, 466
May dew 233
Maybole 178–9, 194–6
    Castle 196
Mearnaid Castle 25
Meigle 94–5
Meikle 146
Melgund Castle 335
Melrose Abbey 263–4, 279
Melville, John 247, 327
Melville's Manse 95
Mendelssohn, Felix 478
Menstrie 95
Merlin 95, 216, 234, 274–5
mermaids 69–70, 137, 139, 182, 189, 207, 354, 386–7, 398, 400, 414, 455, 473, 499
Merry Dancers 389, 485
mesmerism 105
meteor 425
mice 401, 466
Mid Calder 264
Mid Clyth 360
Mid Yell 393
Midbrake 396–7

Midsummer 304
midwives 489
Miller, Bessie 406
Miller, Hugh 132, 343, 385, 419, 423, 425, 429, 432, 441, 444, 446–7, 449, 453
millers 247, 357
mills 387, 481
Milnathort 97
Milne, John 341
Minch 485
Minch Moor 265
Mingary 38–9
    Castle 39
Minto 218
Mitchell, James Leslie 295
Mittenfu' Stanes 265
Mittenfull of Stones 265
Mochrum 158–9
Moddey Dhoo 277
Moffat 126
    Ram 157
Moidart, Lord of 467
Moloch, Maggie 78
Moncreiffe Island 77
Moniaive 150
Monk's Grove 77
monkeys 302
Monreith Park 158–9
Monteath, John 72
Montgomerie, Norah 414
Montgomerie, William 372, 414
Moravia, Gilbert de 351
Morison, John 474
Morphie 335–6, 365
Morrison, Peter 466
Morvern 6–7, 28
Moss, Dogden 254
Mote Hill 154
Moubray family 217
moudie-wort 104
Moulach, May 79
Mound of Blessing or Salutation 343
Mowat, Alexander 331–2
Moy Hall 445, 474
mugwort 139, 182
Mull 485–6
Mull of Kintyre 35
Mullack, Meg 79
Munro, Finlay 436

Munro, Henrietta 351, 408
Munster, Countess of 119
Murchison, T. M. 428
murders 100, 129, 174, 220, 248, 278, 283, 286, 316, 322, 324, 327–8, 331, 341, 359, 454, 476
Murder Hole 154–5, 158
Murdostoun 157
Murray family 77
Murray, Patrick 234
Murthly 97
Musselburgh 265–7
Mutiny Stones 265
Myrton Castle 158–9

Na Caplaich 445
names, power of 60
Namur, battle of 251
Napier, Barbara 270
necromancy 33
need-fire 304, 360
Nelson, Mary and John 290
New Abbey 159, 166–7
New Deer 336–7
New Inns 103
New Year 304, 402–3
Newburgh 97, 100
Newhall 223
Newhaven 267
Newtown 267–8
Niall of the Nine Hostages 497
Nicholson, Arthur 398
Nicholson, Daniel 475
Nicholson, Lady 398
Nicholson, John 201
Nicolson, James 401
Nicolson, Johnny 147
Niel, John 244
Nigg 446–7, 453
nigheag 469
Nine Stane Rig 247
Nine Maidens' Well 334
ninth child 386
Nithsdale 167
Noggle 387
Noltland Castle 397
Norrie, Bettie 215
Norrie's Law 100–2
North Berwick 269, 272
North Yell 389, 397–9

Nuckelavee 387
Nunton 486–7
Nygel 387

Odhar, Coinneach *see* Brahan Seer
Ogam 430
Ogilvy, Mrs D. 358
Old Kilpatrick 102
Old King Coil's Tomb 196–8
Old Luce 150–1
Old Red-Cap 126
Oliver, Robbie 222
Ollaberry 399
O'Norrie, Tam 101
O'Noth, Jock 301
O'Shanter, Tam 170
Orkneyinga Saga 370, 396
Orr, John 145, 339
Orsay 487–8
Orwell 102
Ossain 17, 376
Our Lady of Loretto shrine 265
Ousdale 369–70
oxen 393
Oykell Bridge 370

Pabaigh 488–9
Padua, University of 338, 346, 349, 374, 376
Paisley 198–9, 202
Palnackie 160–1
Papa Westray 401
Parson's Sheep 412
Paterson the Pricker 437
peacocks 220
Pearlin Jean 215
Peaston 272–3
Peat Law 273
Pechs 294, 393, 430–1
Pedlar of Swaffham 181
Peebles 273–4
Pends, The 103
Pennant, Thomas 33, 369, 373, 426
Pentland Firth 354
Pentland Hills 219
Percy, Bishop Thomas 224
Peterson, George 388
Pholchrain, Iain 466
Picts 18, 59–60, 74, 78, 94, 197–8, 217, 294, 303–4, 334, 340, 355–6, 423–4, 428, 430–1, 437

pilgrims 44, 164, 174, 265, 281, 286, 363, 436, 479, 490–1
pipes and pipers 13, 65, 93, 98, 115, 144, 151, 171, 184, 232, 308, 322–3, 348, 374–5, 445, 459, 461–2, 481, 502
pirates 144
Pitfirrane 103–4
Pittenweem 108
Pixies 430–1
plague 56, 151–2, 250, 261–2, 330
poaching 370
Poe, Edgar Allan 249–50
point of death 23, 32, 217
Point House Cairn 39–40
Pollok 202–3
Polson, Alexander 374
poltergeists 135, 146, 243
Ponage Pool 336
pools 274, 322, 336, 341, 349–50, 453 *see also* lochs, lakes and rivers
porchwatching 28
Port Appin 13
Portencorkrie Bay 161–2
Porteus 165
Portpatrick 144
Portrigh 47
Pottinger, Captain 472
Powguild 104
Powsail Burn 274
Prentice Window, The 263
Pretty Dancers' Reel 389
prophecies 426, 433, 438, 445, 448, 472 *see also* second sight
Puddlefoot 60

Quarff 400–1
Quarrel Burn 104–5
Queen's Castle 328
Queensbury, Duke of (William) 141

Raasay 489
railways 347
Ramage, Craufurd Tait 135
Ramsay, Allan 150, 195, 223, 230, 240
Ramsay, David 349
Rannoch 67, 111
   Moor 105–6
Rashin-coatie 238–9
rats 340, 466

ravens 88, 143, 236, 316, 358, 434, 440, 448, 476
Reay, Lord 349, 368, 369–70, 375
    Green Tables 368
Red Donald of the fairies 67
Red Etin 235–7
Redcap 247
Reilig Oghrain 489, 492
Reithe 429
Reoch, Elspeth 271
repercussion 372
Rerrick 135–7
    Parish 162
Restalrig Loch x, 276, 281
Rexburghshire 100
Rhys, Sir John 93, 450
ribbons 76
Richard, Frederick 27
riddles 237
Ridge of the Big Men 429
Rigg, James 252
Ring-Croft 136
Ring of Brodgar 402
rings 30, 61, 84, 183–4
Ritchie, David 197
River Shin 371
River Spey 337
Rizzio, David 248–9
robbers 218, 227
Robert III 322
Robertson, George 330
Robertson, James 34
Robertson, Ronald Macdonald 276, 316, 362, 371,
    499
Robertson, Stanley 296, 303
Robertson, William 175, 179, 195, 197, 207
Rockhill 40–1
Rodel 492–3
rope of heather 19–20
ropes of sand 354
Rorie, David 104
Rory Mòr 470
Roslin Castle 276–8
Ross, Anne 45, 353, 454
Ross of Mull 458
Rosslyn Chapel 278–9
Rothesay 33
    Duke of 76
Roud, Steve xiii, xvi, 442–3
Rouen Cathedral 279

Round Square 338–9
Routin' Bridge 162–3
Row, John 266
Roy, Donald 446, 453
Ruabhal 493
Rubers Law Fort 279
Rumbling Bridge 68
Ruthven, Alexander 76

Saddell Castle 41–2
saining 336–7, 394
saints of Scotland 490–1
St Adomnan 490
St Andrew 205, 217
St Andrews 103, 106–7
St Baldred 108, 218, 285, 491
St Boniface's Well 44
St Boswells 279–80
St Brendan's Church 493–4
St Catherine's Well 45, 280–1
St Columba x, 12–13, 18, 28, 42, 366, 423, 425, 437,
    441–2, 479, 489–91, 497
St Conval 491
St Cuthbert 230
St Cyrus 339
St Fillan 218
St Fillan's Cave 107–8
St Fillan's Pool 44, 108–10
St John's wort 485
St Kentigern 275, 284
St Kieran 465–6
St Lucy 281
St Margaret 73, 174, 491
St Medana 281
St Michael's Kirk 447–8
St Michael's Well 331
St Moluag 12–13
St Mungo xii, 183–4, 284, 491
St Ninian's Cave 163–4
St Oran 489
St Patrick 102, 174, 491
St Ronan's Well 45
St Rule 217
St Serf 490
St Torranan 493
St Tredwell 490
    Loch 401
St Triduana 401, 490
    Well 281

St Vigeans 340
Saline 82–3
salmon 371
Sampson, Agnes 271
Samuelston 281
Sanday 415–17
Sandilands, Patrick 264
Sandray 494–5
Sands of Forvie 340
Sandwood Bay 371–2
Sanquhar 164
Sauchieburn 57
Saxby, Jessie 382, 384, 386, 389, 392–3, 402, 410–11, 430
Scarba 495–7
Schiehallion 110–11
School of Scottish Studies xi–xii
Scodaig stone 31
Scone Palace 111, 114
Scot or Scott, Michael 54, 62–3, 71, 82, 84, 139, 143, 145, 148, 150, 171, 196, 214, 237, 264, 354, 451
Scot, Reginald 180, 254, 261
Scota 31, 197, 235
Scott, Mammie 406
Scott, 'Mass' John 273
Scott, Sir Walter xi, 127, 156, 220–1, 226, 229, 232, 244, 257, 280, 283, 325, 406
  Bride of Lammermoor 241
  History of Scotland 24
  Lay of the Last Minstrel 218
  Letters on Demonology and Witchcraft 194, 209, 230, 276, 284
  Minstrelsy of the Scottish Border 158, 214, 219, 224, 240, 243, 246, 256, 268, 273, 275, 287, 290, 489
  Old Mortality 314–15
  Peveril of the Peak 277, 503
  Poetical Works 264
  Talisman, The 192
  Waverley 19, 260
Scrabster 372–4
Scrimgeour, John 83
Scrope, William 377
sea monsters 38–9, 416, 441–4
Seaforth family 433, 448
seals 399, 404, 413
seaweed 470, 499
Seckyban 15

second sight 87, 112, 209, 332, 360, 374, 428, 445, 448, 458–9, 460, 467, 472, 474–5
secret rooms 325
seers see Brahan Seer; second sight
selkies 404–5, 407, 412, 413, 473
Selkirk 282
serpents and snakes 30–1, 36, 154, 375, 416
seventh son 112
shadows 338, 350
Shakespeare, William 4, 75, 80–1, 158, 232, 269, 318–20, 324, 334, 374, 410, 430, 437, 452
Sharp, Archbishop James 92, 103
Sharpe, Charles Kirkpatrick 141, 166, 185, 198, 215, 244, 246, 264, 368
Shaw, Christian 198
Shaw, Duncan 499
Shaw, Lachlan 306
Sheardale Braes 114–15
sheep 279
Shellycoat 240, 243, 255
shepherds 7
Sheriffmuir 463
ships 181–2, 188, 304, 357, 393, 500 see also ghosts, ships
shipwrecks 347, 362, 403, 476
Short-hoggers 287
shrews 369
Sibbald, Robert 106, 369
Sigurd 370
silver shot and bullets 37, 49, 219, 310, 314, 463, 476
Simpkins, John Ewart 58–9, 65, 85, 100
Simpson, Alexander 283
Simpson, David 284
Simpson, Dr 185
Simpson, Eve 267, 304
Simpson, J. W. 156
Simpson, James Young 243, 283
Simpson, Robert 164
simulacra see fairy stock
Sinclair family 359
Sinclair, Alisdair 360
Sinclair, George 66, 184, 202, 231, 242, 256, 261, 272–3, 281, 285–6, 320, 374
skeleton 351, 354 see also bones; skulls
Skene, William Forbes 17
Skinner, William 156
skulls 283, 306, 351
sleeping warrior 260
Sleinanachd 426

sluagh 27, 67, 112, 114, 221, 273, 483, 486, 487
Sleeman, W. H. 378
sleeping hero 216
Slevach Cairn 78
Smailholm Tower 282–3
Small, Andrew 59, 97
Smith, Alexander 333
Smith, Isabel 23, 40
Smith, Kirrsie 384
Smoo Cave 374
smuggling 58, 130–1, 175
sneezing 394
Soldier's Leap 115
Solway Moss 75
Somerville family 176, 257
Sorbie 13
Soulis, Lord 228, 246–7
South Havra 401
South Uist 497
Southend 42
Southey, Robert 329
Soutra Mains 283
speal-bone divination 426, 492
Spedlin's Tower 164–6
Speedy, Anthony 59
Spence, John 411, 413
Spence, Lewis 255, 265, 337, 483, 485
Spens, Dr Harry 58
spiders x, 46
Srontian 43
stag 248
standing stones *see* stones, megaliths and circles
Staoinebrig 497–8
statues 156, 399
Stenlake, Richard 207
Stenness 402
stepmothers 432, 476, 486
Stevenson, Robert Louis 23, 95, 226, 227–8, 246,
    355–6
Stewart family 9, 12, 16, 21
Stewart, Alexander 73
Stewart, Andrew 78
Stewart, Francis 269
Stewart, Geordie 323
Stewart, James 309
Stilligarry 498–9
Stinky Bay xii, 499–500
Stirling 115–16
    Castle 116

Stitt, Robert 139
Stone of Destiny 234–5
Stone of Morphie 335
Stone of Quoybune 403
Stone of Scone 235, 319
Stone of the Little Men 346
stones *see also* cairns
    cures 366
    Dwarfie Stone 385
    fairy arrows 22
    giants' 352–3, 449
    holed 57, 203, 369, 448
    Kelpie's Stone 331
    Knockin' Stone 393
    marks on 31, 283
    megaliths and circles 38, 57, 79, 91, 94, 97, 100,
        188–9, 223, 284, 294, 307, 329, 334, 346,
        350, 359–60, 392, 423, 455, 478
    memorial 426
    of Stenness 402
    plague 330
    stone fire 162
    Stone of Destiny 111
    Stone of Morphie 335
    Weeping Stone 322, 479
    wolves 377
Strachur 42–3
strange visitor, the ix, xi
Strathdon 310
Strathaven 203
Strathglass 25
Strathpeffer 448–9
Strathspey 451
Stream of the Blue Men 485
Stromness 406–7
Struth nan Fear Gorm 485
Stuart, Charles Edward (Bonnie Prince Charlie)
    251, 426, 445
Stuart, Robert 215
students 291
submerged village 88, 141
Sueno's Stone 320
suicides 156
Sule Skerry 407
Summerdale 407
Sunnydale 407
Sutherland, George 347–50, 356–7, 360, 367
Sutor, David 61
Sutor, William 61

sutors 282
Sutors of Cromarty 449–50
Swan of Salen 15–16
swans 135
Sweetheart Abbey 166–7
Swinna Ness 408
Swire, Otta 8–9, 16, 347, 359, 371, 274, 423, 425, 429, 437, 451, 479, 495–6
Swona 408
Symington 206

Tables 460
Tafts 408–9
Tait, E. S. R. 384
Tamlane 223
Tankerness 414–15
tailors xi, 41–2, 96, 160, 232, 351, 418
Tarbert 469
Tarbh Uisge 367
Tarbolton 196
tartans and clans x
Taylor, James W. 58
Tamlane's Well 45
Tealing 334
teetotum 77
Teine-Eiginn 304, 360
Teit, Jan 394–5
Telfair, Alexander 136
Temperley, Alan 160
thistles 252–3
Thom, Alexander 360
Thomas, F. W. L. 17–18
Thomas the Rhymer 59, 75, 84, 205, 216, 234, 237, 250, 254, 260, 275, 296, 301, 329–30, 451, 480
Thompson, Francis 25
Thomson, Edward 95
Thomson, Rev. 342
thong measure 76
Thórhallr Ásgrímsson 396
Thrummy-cap 96–7, 317
Thurso 374–5
Tillicoultry 117
Tingwall 409
Tinto 203, 206
Tir-nan-og 16, 466, 479
toads 48
Tobar a' Chinn 454
Tobar nan Ceann 454

Tobermory 500–2
Tommy's Pot 341
Tomnahurich 450–1
Tongue 375–6
toothache 385
Torphichen 283–4
Torphichen, James Lord 264
Torrylin (Torlin) Cairn 43, 46
Torvean Motte 451–3
Toward Castle 46
Taill Dennison, W. 387, 404, 415
Train, Joseph 315
Traprain Law 284
travellers see Gypsies
treasure 59, 65, 97, 100, 177, 180, 203, 247, 258, 284, 301, 322, 335, 341, 350, 360, 395 see also gold
trees 15, 48, 73, 75, 103–4, 148, 190, 230, 267, 306, 375, 425, 484
Trolld 385
trolls see trows
Trooper's Dubb, The 117
Trotter, Robert de Bruce 15
Trotternish 502–3
Trowie Reel 390, 413
trows ix, 132, 379, 384, 388–91, 393–4, 408, 410–11, 413, 415
Tullibardine 118
Tullibody 119
Tulloch, Tom 397
Tullochgorm family 79, 80
tunnels and passages 13, 65, 144, 335
Turnball, J. 235
Turnberry 206–7
Turnbull, Michael 267
Tuskerbister 412
Tweed 274
Tyninghame 218
Tynron Doon 167

Uaigh Dhiarmaid 376
Uaimh Mhor 423
Ugadale x, 46–7
Uig 465–6
Uisinis, 503–4
Ulva 458
Underwood, Peter 217, 221
Unst 392–3, 408, 412–13
Upper Druimfin 504

urine 469, 472
Urisks 90–1, 310, 436, 488, 497
Urquhart, Thomas 181, 449
Urray 453–4

Vale of Gale 221
Vale of Megget 227
Vallafield 390, 413
vampires 86, 186–7
Vayne Castle 341
Ve Skerries 413
Vedder, David 142, 397
Veltigar 414–15
Virgin Mary 205
Voy, Gilbert 412

Wade, George 434–6
Waldhave 275
Waldron, George 277
Wallace, William x, 73, 190, 203, 204–5, 207–8
Wallace's Cave 207–8
Walls 415
Walsh, William 366
Ward Law 132
washerwoman 469
Wast Side Trows Reel 390
water-beasts 441
water-bulls 36, 226, 367, 455
water-horses see kelpies and water-horses
water-nymphs 460
water-spirits 497
water-woman 352
Watt, Archibald 304, 320, 335, 339
Watt, J. C. 335
Watt, Margaret 348
weavers 7–8, 72, 73, 87, 191, 199, 329, 438, 487
weddings 137, 144, 242, 249, 339, 399
Weeping Stone 322, 479
Weir, Major 284–5
Well of the Heads 454
Wellington, Duke of (statue) 156
wells 36, 44–5, 69, 88–9, 109–10, 171, 174, 265, 280–1, 331, 334, 401, 408, 439
Wemyss, Earl of 96
Wemyss Castle 119–20
West Bow 284–5
Westbrough 415–17
Wester Durie 120
Westray 397

whales 479
Whinnieliggate 167
whisky 355, 362, 373
White Chapel 286
White Sack, The 14–15
Whitehills 341–2
Whitekirk 285–6
Whithorn 132
Whittingehame 286–7
Whuppity Scoorie 190
Whyte, Betsy 81, 105, 298, 337
Wicked Lady of Ardvrock 343
Wigtown 152–4
Wild Merlin 274–5
Wilkie, James 58, 66, 74, 86, 95, 101, 120, 220, 232, 246, 257
Wilkie, Thomas 262, 280
will o' the wisps 22, 59, 65, 120, 240
Willcox Ball and Bridle 444
Williamson, Duncan 133, 298
Williamson, Johnny 127
willow 247, 267
wills 339
Wilson, Annie 278
Wilson, Margaret 153, 242
Wilson, William 138, 185
Winton, Andrew 166
Winwick, Sandy 413
Winyadepla 391
wishes 470, 498
witchcraft and witches x, 4, 16, 48–9, 66–7, 73, 75, 81, 87, 114, 137–9, 151, 167–8, 170–1, 185, 188, 194–6, 214, 220, 223, 230–2, 241–3, 281–5, 308–9, 324, 341–2, 361, 374, 382, 392–3, 407–9, 419, 422, 439–40, 463–4, 473, 476, 501
  Bell o' Brims 347–8
  cats 4, 160, 372–4, 438, 504 see also cats
  counter charms 33
  and Devil 79, 185, 188 see also Devil
  Dunlop, Bessie 276
  gatherings 12, 104–5, 170–1, 179–80, 288–9, 311–12, 503
  hair tether 4, 185, 188, 439–40
  hares 37–8, 262–3, 463–4
  Horne, Janet 368–9
  Macbeth 318–19, 320–1
  magic bridle 288–9
  milk-stealing 19–20, 185, 188, 232–4, 466
  Miller, Bessie 406–7

Paterson the Pricker 437–8
riding in sieve 27–8, 269
rope of heather 19–20
selling wind 406–7
sieve divination 33
Tam o' Shanter 170–1
toads 48–9, 269
trials x, 202, 269, 270–1, 284–5, 368–9, 437–8
Weir, Major 284–5
Witches' Knowe 264
Witches' Stairs 138
Withorn 163–4
Witton 342
wizards x, 9, 338, 409 *see also* Merlin; Scot or
  Scott, Michael
Wizard of Balwearie *see* Scot or Scott, Michael
Wodrow, Robert 103, 107, 153
Wolf Stone, The 377–8

Wolf's Crag 241
wolves 358, 377, 502
Wood, Major James 315
Wood, James Maxwell 124–5, 129–30, 134, 144,
  150–1, 161, 167–8, 194
Woodhouselee 287
worms 385
wraiths 32, 49, 103, 115, 121, 185, 209, 371, 374
Wright, Bessie 271
Wright, David 64
Wyntoun, Andrew de 490

Yarrowford 288–9
Yawkins, Captain 130
Yell 379, 396
Yellow Foot 476
Young, John 303

ILLUSTRATIONS

Black and white illustrations in the text are reproduced by kind permission of:

Alamy: 17 (© Cliff Whittem), 157 (© South West Images Scotland), 416 (© Interfoto), 471 (© Interfoto); The Art Archive: 491 (Bodleian Library Oxford); The Bridgeman Art Library: 145 (Private Collection), 153 (Private Collection), 163 (Private Collection), 253 (Private Collection), 268 (Private Collection), 289 (Private Collection/The Stapleton Collection), 355 (Private Collection), 430 (Private Collection), 452 (British Library, London © British Library Board), 462 (Private Collection); Robert Dawson: 229; Getty Images: 443; Heritage-Images/Imagestate: 29 (© The Print Collector), 34 (© The Print Collector), 70 (© The Print Collector), 84 (© The Print Collector), 89 (© The Print Collector), 199 (© The Print Collector), 337 (© The Print Collector), 427 (© The British Library); Mary Evans Picture Library: 113, 201 (Grosvenor Prints), 324; National Portrait Gallery, London: 98, 143, 205, 434; The Scottish Government: 475 (Crown Copyright); southernnecropolis.com: 187.

Acknowledgements for inset illustrations:

Machrie Moor (© David Robertson/Alamy); Loch Awe (© Skyscan.co.uk); Glenorchy family tree (Scottish National Portrait Gallery, Edinburgh/The Bridgeman Art Library); Wigtown Martyrs' Monument (© South West Images Scotland/Alamy); Dunfermline Abbey (© David Robertson/Alamy); Gilnockie Tower (Taft Museum of Art, Cincinnati, Ohio/ Bequest of Mr and Mrs Charles P. Taft/ The Bridgeman Art Library); Glasgow Lamp Post (© Iain Masterton/Alamy); Culzean Castle (Scotlandsimages.com/© National Trust for Scotland); William Wallace (Smith Art Gallery and Museum, Stirling, Scotland/ The Bridgeman Art Library); Mermaid (© British Library Board. All Rights Reserved/The Bridgeman Art Library); Edinburgh Castle (© Skyscan.co.uk); Bass Rock (Fitzwillian Museum, University of Cambridge/The Bridgeman Art Library); Murder of Rizzio (© Guildhall Art Gallery, City of London/ The Bridgeman Art Library); Bonnie Prince Charlie (© National Portrait Gallery, London); Robert the Bruce (National Library of Scotland, Edinburgh/The Bridgeman Art Library); Crathes Castle (Scotlandsimages.com/© National Trust for Scotland); Highland Shepherd (Private Collection/The Stapleton Collection/The Bridgeman Art Library); Witch (Private Collection/The Stapleton Collection/The Bridgeman Art Library); Macbeth (© The Print Collector/Heritage-Images/Imagestate); Ardveck Castle (© Doug Houghton/Alamy); Smoo Cave (© John Delvin/Alamy); Dwarfie Stane (© orkneypics/Alamy); Ring of Brodgar at Stennes (© David Lyons/Alamy); Well of the Heads (© Fortean Picture Library); Cloutie Well (© Shenval/ Alamy); Robert Burns (Scottish National Portrait Gallery, Edinburgh/The Bridgeman Art Library); Bagpiper (London Library, London/The Bridgeman Art Library).